LUCIFER

A
THEOSOPHICAL MONTHLY

LUCIFER

A
THEOSOPHICAL MONTHLY

H. P. BLAVATSKY

EDITOR

ANNIE BESANT
AND
G. R. S. MEAD

GYAN

Published by

GYAN

Gyan Publishing House
5, Ansari Road
Daryaganj, New Delhi-110002
Phone: 011-47034999, 9811692060
E-mail: books@gyanbooks.com

Distribution Network
gyanbooks.com
India, USA, Canada, UK, Australia

ISBN: 978-93-6780-535-0 (PB)

First Published, 1887

2nd Impression 2024

Printed at: Gyan Press, Delhi.

LUCIFER: A THEOSOPHICAL MONTHLY
Author: H. P. BLAVATSKY

LUCIFER

A

THEOSOPHICAL MONTHLY

FOUNDED BY H. P. BLAVATSKY.

EDITED BY ANNIE BESANT AND G. R. S. MEAD.

MARCH, 1897.

LONDON: Theosophical Publishing Society, 26 Charing Cross, London, S.W.

NEW YORK: Theosophical Publishing Society, 65, Fifth Avenue.

BENARES: Theosophical Publishing Society.

MADRAS: The Proprietors of *The Theosophist*, Adyar.

VOL. XX.—NO. 115. ANNUAL SUBSCRIPTION, 17/6. Price, 1*s*. 6*d*.

VOL. XX. MARCH 15, 1897. No. 115.

LUCIFER.

ON THE WATCH-TOWER.

ON THE TRACK OF THE ATOMS.

WE learn from a recent number of *Nature* (February 25th), that so long ago as 1895, a man of science had an imperfect intuition of that atomic realm which is an open book to occultism, and of which a few details were recently published in our pages. In the number of *Nature* referred to, the reviewer of Mr. Severinus J. Corrigan's *Constitution and Functions of Gases*, says that the author has advanced a dynamical theory "which accounts for some phenomena not explained by any other theory."

The theory of Mr. Corrigan is apparently entirely new, and proceeds on assumptions quite different from those of the ordinary kinetic theory worked out by Maxwell, Clausius and others; its interest is that in some respects it approximates to the occult position.

As to the molecule, "instead of being in continual motion to and fro, it is at rest"; this is absolutely incorrect. But

> The molecule is made up of a larger number of atoms, which revolve in orbits, approximately circular, round the centre of the molecule with enormous velocities.

This is half true, there being as frequently two or more centres.

> The atoms themselves are said to be perfectly elastic, incompressible, spherical [approximately only] solids which are arranged primarily in duads or combinations of two, and the atoms of each duad combination are mutually attracted by a force in each atom, which force, like that of gravity, varies inversely as the square of the distance between the members of the duad.

So far, so good, but there are also triads and tetrads up to heptads.

* * *

THE ATOMIC LIFE OF METALS.

In the February number of *The Nineteenth Century*, Prince Krapotkin, in his article "Recent Science," deals with some new discoveries which are of interest to students of Theosophy; the information as to what may be termed the atomic life of metals is of special interest. The old teaching that the earth is an animal, that is to say, a living creature, is not out of date even for the nineteenth century. For

> It becomes more and more apparent that a solid piece of metal is by no means an inert body; that it also has its inner life; that its molecules are not dead specks of matter, and that they never cease to move about, to change places, to enter into new and varied combinations.

This is supported by facts derived from the behaviour of different metals when mixed to form alloys, and from the phenomena of the "flowing of solids" under pressure, and of the evaporation which takes place from the free surfaces of solid metals. Chorus: "Thus once more we see!" etc.

* * *

Latah.

In Mr. F. A. Swettenham's entertaining little book, *Malay Sketches*, there are some strange stories told of a peculiar nervous derangement prevalent among the Malays, which is known in their vernacular as "latah," and the symptoms of which bear a striking similarity to some of the phenomena which occur with hypnotic subjects and the victims of possession and obsession. Students who are interested in the subject may be referred for further information to the January number of the *Journal of Medical Science*. Dr. W. Gilmore Ellis, the medical superintendent of the Government Asylum, Singapore, in his article, "Latah: A Mental Malady of the Malays," gives a summary of what little has appeared on the subject. Can it be that the strain of Lemurian blood in the Malay race is one of the factors in the explanation of this curious phenomenon which seems to be almost confined to this peculiar race?

* * *

The Basis of Ethics.

There is a tendency in some modern writers on ethics to find the incentive for a moral life in what is called a "purely moral motive"; is not this a begging of the whole question, and a taking of the result of evolution for the cause of evolution in the domain of morals—a vicious circle? In the January number of *The International Journal of Ethics*, Professor Eliza Ritchie, of Wellesley

College, in a paper on "Morality and the Belief in the Supernatural," writes as follows:

> Only very slowly and gradually has the conception of a purely *moral* motive for the moral life dawned on the mind of man; even now it is but very vaguely and hesitatingly recognized, and the reason for good conduct is often sought for everywhere rather than in the intrinsic desirability of such conduct. Extra ethical sanctions, then, have been necessary to form a scaffolding for the building up of that rational morality, which when completed can stand in need of no such extraneous and alien support.

Good for good's sake, morality for the sake of morality, is an appeal to which only those who have the rich experience of many lives behind them can respond to. And as things are at present, such a response is at best but an unintelligent, and therefore an irrational response. What the world wants are reasons which will hasten the evolution of morality, and explain the intuition of ethical truth which the best specimens of the race feel, but for which they can as a rule give no satisfactory reason. Theosophy, by placing ethics on a strictly scientific basis, and explaining the occult nature of man and the laws of the occult world, has so far alone attempted to give an answer to this burning question.

***

MODERN MONARCHISM.

"Unitarianism and Judaism in their Relations to Each Other," is the title of an address given by Mr. C. G. Montefiore to the students of Manchester College, Oxford, at the opening of the present Session.

That a Jew (however "unorthodox") should have been invited to give an address on such an occasion is a remarkable fact, and the address itself is striking in its appreciation of the immense change that has taken place during later years in what is called "liberal thought," this change bringing "reformed or liberal Judaism" into sympathetic relations with modern Unitarianism, and on lines that can hardly fail to interest a student of Theosophy. For instance, "the great doctrine of the Unity of God," having ceased to be a merely "numerical" conception, in its higher metaphorical sense, unites thinkers on both sides. Mr. Montefiore speaks with evident sympathy of the "higher criticism," as applied with the greatest possible freedom to *both* Old *and* New Testaments, and adds:

It is only in a Judaism that is at one with "criticism"—using that word in its widest and fullest sense to include comparative religion as well as biblical interpretation—that modern Unitarianism can feel much interest.

There is throughout a frank recognition of the duty of searching for truth, wherever it can be found, and to whatever conclusions it may lead.

* * *

KIAN YIN.

There is an article in the *Muséon* of last month, by C. de Haarlez, called, "The Most Ancient Psychology Known"—perhaps rather a daring title—on an ancient religious and psychological treatise by the Chinese teacher, Kian Yin. The treatise was written 700 B.C., and is considered to be authentic, with the exception of some easily detected modern interpolations. It contains among many other subjects of interest, a theory of "ideas" very similar to Plato's, though written three hundred years before his time. (Plato, however, did not originate the theory of ideas even in the West, but took it from his predecessors, as he tells us in the *Sophist.*)

Thus, as a complete being must have a real existence, it must have formerly existed ideally in heaven or in the infinite Being. These ideas, however, can not be properly understood, except by seeing the source and end of their life, which is infinite Being.

Among other points of interest, we find stated that the origin of all mental life is in the intelligence, but it is actualized in the heart by will and emotion. The mental power is in consequence spoken of as the heart instead of the mind, and carries a more comprehensive meaning with it, including emotions as well as thoughts.

The two processes in thought must be carefully distinguished, the simple perception of an object and the act of reflection about it. This is, of course, the first proposition laid down in every book on logic; but the ancient philosopher further establishes that this act of reflection does not give reality to the external images thought about, as some schools of philosophy have taught; on the contrary, the objects exist independently, and without them our thoughts could not come into being. We could not think without something to think about.

Another point is that all internal actions of the mind such as thoughts and feelings, are caused by a superhuman power which guides and influences it.

Again, the first great principle may take many forms but it is always essentially the same.

And lastly, the sage and the saint see Universal Being in each and do not observe the individual man, whereas the ordinary man sees a special creation in everything.

These brief excerpts show us that Kian Yin's ideas of twenty-six hundred years ago are not so very unfamiliar to us to-day, and that the preservation and study of such teachings must help to bridge "Oblivion's Sea."

.·.

Why Missionaries Fail in India.

We have so often insisted on the immorality of proselytizing missiondom which barters material comforts and educational benefits for native apostasy, that it is pleasant to read the following outspoken editorial paragraph in the February number of *The Journal of Education*; it shows that the evolution of common sense views among the general public in such matters is not to be despaired of:

> We hear on excellent authority, and the statement has been confirmed over and over again by trustworthy observers, that many a door is closed to the missionaries, where their influence and instruction would be welcomed, simply because they *will* attempt to proselytize. Many a woman has gone out to our Indian Empire as a missionary, there to learn for the first time that there is something noble and beautiful in other religions; and frequently the knowledge has proved disconcerting. Fearing financial results that might accrue to the missions, they leave us uninformed upon a subject in which we need to be told where we stand. Is it not time that our great missionary societies looked this matter frankly in the face and prepared their young missionaries for the fact that their work must be teaching, not proselytizing? By so doing much bitter disappointment would be saved. Nor can we doubt that a distinct understanding that no attempt would be made to proselytize would allow Indian teachers of women to get hold of the Brahman women, the best material for the teachers of the future. Many excellent Christian teachers now renounce proselytizing; women's education in India would greatly benefit if all did so.

.·.

"With Running Foot."

The following is the *Times'* summary of the last presidential address which Mr. William Crookes, F.R.S., delivered to the Society for Psychical Research.

Psychical science was, he said, the embryo of something that might in time dominate the whole world of thought. Human ignorance beset research in this direction with many difficulties, but conscious ignorance was a healthful stimulant if it led to the conviction that one could not possibly lay down beforehand what did not exist in the universe or what was not going on in the world. One of the greatest thorns in the path of the society was the fact that very many people started with certain pre-suppositions depending upon a too hasty assumption that we knew more about the universe than really was known. For instance, among those who believed with him in the survival of man's individuality after death there was an inveterate and widespread illusion that ethereal bodies, if such there were, must correspond to earthly bodies in shape and size. The human body, it was true, was the most perfect thinking and acting machine yet evolved on this earth, but its excellence for its varied purposes depended, of course, upon the conditions by which it was surrounded. Its action was, for instance, entirely governed by the strength of the force of gravitation, which had not apparently varied at all during the ages in which animated thinking beings had existed. Were the force of gravitation to be either doubled or decreased, there would be remarkable changes in the type of humanity to suit the altered state of affairs. Yet popular imagination, taking no heed of this, pre-supposed spiritual beings to be superior to the laws of gravitation, and yet to retain shapes and proportions which gravitation originally determined and only gravitation seemed likely to maintain. His own picture of the constitution of spiritual beings would make them centres of intellect, will, energy, and power, each centre retaining individuality, persistence of self and memory, and each mutually penetrable, while at the same time permeating what we called space. Addressing those who not only took too terrestrial a view, but who even denied the possibility of an unseen world existing at all, Professor Crookes said he would like to point out to them the difference in the apparent laws of the universe which would follow upon a mere variation of size in the observer of them. Following this idea out he imagined, first, a homunculus of microscopic size, and, next, a human being of enormous magnitude, showing by familiar illustrations how the supposed laws of matter and of the universe would appear to such beings to be quite different from those now accepted. Was it not possible, he asked, that we also, by the mere virtue of our size and weight, might fall into misinterpretations of phenomena; and that our boasted knowledge might be simply conditioned by accidental environment and therefore liable to a large and hitherto unsuspected element of subjectivity? Passing thence to the speculation of Professor W. James, of Harvard, which dealt with the possible difference in rapidity of sensation on the part of beings presumably on a larger scale than ourselves, Professor Crookes applied this general conception of the impossibility of predicting what unseen forces might be at work around us specially to telepathy, or thought transference—*i.e.*, the transmission of thought and images directly from one mind to another without the agency of the recognized organs of sense. Was it inconceivable, he said (after making an elaborate calculation as to the vibrations which produce sound and light), that intense thought, concentrated by one person upon another with whom he was in close sympathy, should induce a telepathic chain along which brain waves should go straight to their goal without loss of energy due to distance? Such a speculation was, he admitted, new and strange to science: it was at present strictly provisional, but he was bold enough to make it, and the time might come when it could be submitted to experimental tests. In conclusion Professor Crookes spoke of the work which was being done by the society as likely to form no unworthy preface to a profounder science of man, of Nature, and of "worlds not realized" than we yet had; and said he could see no reason why any man of scientific mind should either shut his eyes to or stand deliberately aloof from it.

Such a pronouncement coming from a man of so world-wide a reputation in the field of science, is a remarkable sign of the times. Indeed, opinion is fast moving with running foot in the right direction, as is evidenced by the favourable leader which the above address called forth from the sapience of one of the *Times'* editorial hierarchy. Mr. Crookes' remarks should encourage the Society for Psychical Research to cease from devoting all its energy to the investigation of the comparative trivialities with which it has become identified, and turn some of its perseverance and intelligence into higher channels. As the *Times'* leader writer correctly remarks:

> Mr. Crookes has little to say of the matters forming the staple of most papers read before the Psychical Society—automatic writings, strange coincidences in dreams, and stories of mysterious communications wafted across continents and oceans to anxious relatives. He is concerned with deeper, wider issues. He offers explanations which, if well founded, make all the fairy tales of telepathy perfectly credible.

What, we wonder, would be the surprise of the leader writer and the members of the S.P.R. if we were to tell them that the presidential address has simply formulated in general terms theories which have for years been worked out in our Theosophical manuals?

* * *

Concerning the Gnosis.

Students of magical papyri and the signs, sigils, symbols, apologies, numbers, and the rest of the paraphernalia which the magical schools of antiquity thought necessary for the good of the soul, are referred to one of the latest finds published by Signor Francesco Rossi in a memoir entitled "Cinque Manuscritti Copti della Biblioteca Nazionale di Torino," which is to be found in vol. xviii. (series ii.) of *Memorie della Reale Academia delle Scienze di Torino.* Mons. Amélineau, the well-known Coptic scholar, has published a notice and translation of one of these MSS. in a small brochure entitled *Le Nouveau Traité Gnostique de Turin* (Paris: Chamuel; 1895). Students interested in getting straight the tangle of the magical names and invocations of the Codex Brucianus and Pistis Sophia MSS. will find a chaos of a like nature in the new Turin fragment.

Lovers of Gnosticism may also be referred to a fairly appreciative article on "The Heretics," by the Rev. W. F. Adeney, Professor of New Testament exegesis, history and criticism, at New College, in the December number of *The New World*, the American Quarterly Review of Religion, Ethics, and Theology. It puts forward a far more enlightened view of the Gnostics than is usual among English theologians.

⁂

Ex Africa semper quid Novi.

It is reported that the workers of the Egyptian Exploration Fund have made a remarkable discovery. Not only have they unearthed a papyrus of the sixth dynasty, but also a copy of the Logia! If this report should prove to be authentic (a telegram is said to have been received at the British Museum to this effect), and the latter MS. prove in very truth to be a collection of the Logia, or Sayings of Jesus, the discovery is simply priceless. The MS. would be incalculably the most precious document of Christendom, and would advance us many steps towards the origins, deciding many points of the greatest obscurity, and giving us a copy of the material on which such men as Papias and Justin worked, and round which the canonical and other Gospels weaved their varied traditions and legends. "From Africa", ran the old saying, "always something new," and its truth is not yet out of date. Many surprises may still be ripening in its womb to be in due time born.

⁂

THE PHÆDO OF PLATO.

(Continued from Vol. XIX p. 462.)

II.

THE doctrine of reminiscence depends, as Socrates points out, upon the doctrine of ideas, and the doctrine of ideas may be regarded as the keystone of Plato's philosophy. If one wished to define briefly what is meant by ideas, it would be difficult, I think, to hit upon a better definition than that which Proclus ascribes to Xenocrates: "Ideas are the exemplary causes of things which perpetually subsist according to nature." They are "exemplary" as being the exemplars or archetypes of all things; the patterns to which, looking within himself, the demiurgic intellect framed the sensible universe. But they are causes, inasmuch as, under their primary aspect of intelligible essences, they contain intellect itself causally; since intellect subsists in the intelligible according to cause, as the intelligible in intellect according to participation. Or perhaps we shall be speaking more accurately with regard to this primary aspect, if we say that Intelligible Idea, rather than ideas, contains intellect causally within itself; because on the intelligible plane all is union, and differentiation is first introduced to the intelligible by intellectual activity. And again, ideas are causes, inasmuch as, under another aspect, we may even say that they are themselves the creative intellect; for intellect, knowing the intelligible, is indeed one with the intelligible which it knows. Lastly, they are the causes of "things which perpetually subsist according to nature." That is to say, there are no ideas of anything mortal and transitory, in so far as it is transitory and mortal. For ideas are eternal being, and whereas everything which exists participates in some measure of being, it participates of ideas; but whereas all sensible things are subject to perpetual change and corruption, they participate also of non-being, which is the negation of all idea.

Ideas, then, are the intelligible realities which underlie, and cause, all phenomenal manifestation. The soul's memory is a stable knowledge of these realities. And, as Socrates says, if we find that these ideas have a prior subsistence, and that all sensible objects are to be referred to them as images to their exemplars; and further, that we possess the knowledge of these ideas within ourselves; then "it is necessary that, as these have a subsistence, so likewise our soul should have subsisted before we were born: but if these are not," he adds, "this discourse will have been undertaken in vain." *

The hearers of Socrates now admit that the pre-existence of the soul appears to them to have been sufficiently demonstrated, but they desire to be further assured of the soul's continuance after its departure from the body. May it not then be dispersed, and thus cease to exist as an individual entity; especially, as Socrates, catching at the words of Simmias, ironically suggests, if one should happen to die during a high wind? This question Socrates regards as being in some measure answered by the former arguments, taken together. For if the soul existed before the body, and if its mortal life, *i.e.*, its conjunction with the body, is produced from death, or separation from body, must it not necessarily exist after death, since its very life here in the body is itself a life after death—a state of conjunction following a state of separation? But to make the matter clearer, he now enters upon his third argument, which deals with the nature of the soul, and the question whether it be liable to dissolution.

We must, in the first place, enquire what kind of nature is that which is capable of being dissolved. Now dissolution is a loosening, so as to cause separation of the constituent parts of anything; and it is therefore evident that only such things as are composite—made up of parts—can be dissolved. But natures which, as Socrates expresses it, "always subsist according to the same," are incomposite. By subsistence according to the same is meant a subsistence at once total and uniform, eternal and incapable of change. Such is the subsistence of all real being, of intellect and of the ideas of which we have spoken. All these are essentially Being, so that any change in their essence would of necessity imply privation of

* Taylor's *Plato*, vol. iv. p. 287.

being; and whereas they are essentially the source of all sensible existence, privation in them would mean privation everywhere, an end to all being, whether true or apparent. Thus, to take an example, the idea of Beauty, the Beautiful Itself, is a simple essence, subsisting always according to the same, and it is the source of all the beauty which we perceive in sensible objects. In other words, the apparently beautiful proceeds from and depends upon the truly, or essentially, beautiful. Now if the idea—the truly beautiful—were susceptible of change, the only change which it, as a simple essence, could possibly receive, would be a total change; a change, namely, into its contrary or from being to non-being; since, not possessing parts, it could not be partially changed. The Beautiful Itself would then cease to subsist; and inasmuch as all sensible beauty depends upon it, this also would come to an end. So that nothing of beauty would in any way exist, if the idea did not always subsist according to the same. This, however, would mean an end to all manifestation, for the beautiful is everywhere present; and so it is with the other ideas, all of which are in each, and each of which is everywhere present, although the measure of its manifestation is limited by the nature of its recipient.

But again, anything which is composite is obviously susceptible of a less complete change than that which can only pass from one contrary to another. For some of its parts may be changed, and not others. Moreover, parts which are put together to form a whole may conceivably be put asunder. It follows, then, that that which subsists according to the same, and with regard to which no change is conceivable short of annihilation, which is itself inconceivable, must be a simple essence, and not composed of parts. Such essences belong to the sphere of intellect and the intelligible.

Intellectual natures being, then, incomposite and incapable of change, and sensible natures, on the other hand, being composite and continually changing, it is necessary that there should be a nature midway between these two, partaking of the characteristics of both, and connecting them. This middle nature is soul. Essentially, as has been already observed, the soul is intellectual, and therefore incomposite and unchanging; it possesses all that it can ever be, perpetually in itself. But the energies of the soul are transitional, and in this respect it partakes of the lower nature,

Plato here roughly distinguishes two species of existing things—the visible and the invisible. I say "roughly," because the division is not perfectly accurate, as we shall presently have occasion to observe, but it is accurate enough for his immediate purpose. All visible natures are subject to ceaseless mutation; the invisible possess perpetual sameness of subsistence; and the soul, being invisible, belongs essentially to the latter species. The soul, then, is an essence possessing sameness of subsistence, and is accordingly incomposite. But composites alone are capable of dissolution; therefore the soul is indissoluble.

Socrates beautifully describes the two-fold activity of the soul. "When," says he, "it employs the body in the speculation of anything, either through sight, or hearing, or some other sense (for to speculate through sense is to speculate through body), then, indeed, it is drawn by the body to things which never subsist according to the same, it wanders and is agitated, and becomes giddy like one intoxicated, through passing into contact with things of this kind. But when it speculates anything, itself subsisting by itself, then it departs to that which is pure, eternal, and immortal, and which possesses a sameness of subsistence; and, as being allied to such a nature, it perpetually becomes united with it, when it subsists alone by itself, and as often as it is lawful for it to obtain such a conjunction; and then, too, it rests from its wanderings, and perpetually subsists similarly according to the same about such natures, as passing into contact with them; and this passion of the soul is denominated prudence" *—*i.e.*, intellectual insight.

Perhaps it will be well to say a word or two upon the expression "passion of the soul," since at first hearing it may seem inconsistent with the teaching of Plotinus, that all incorporeal natures are impassive. There is no real inconsistency, however; only Plato here employs the word "passion" in a somewhat unusual sense. Passion, in the ordinary acceptation of the term, is the impression produced upon anything by an external agent; and it is not, therefore, an affection of the rational soul subsisting by itself, since then the soul is not affected by externals, but sees all things in itself. Plotinus distinguishes in the human soul three principles, of which the first is

* Taylor's *Plato*, vol. iv. pp. 290, 291.

intellect, the second the rational soul, and the third the irrational soul. Now, inasmuch as the soul is a simple essence, these principles do not subsist in it as parts in a whole, but they emanate in succession, the one from the other. Intellect is the source of the soul, and, so to speak, the summit of its essence. From intellect emanates the rational soul, which, as Plato also declares, is the man himself. The rational soul is a certain energy of intellect, manifesting itself in time; and from the rational soul emanates the irrational or animal soul, as a certain energy of the rational soul, manifesting itself in body. The passions, then, are affections of the irrational soul, which, by its conjunction with the body, constitutes the animal.*

They are not affections of the body alone, which of itself is inert and lifeless, but of the body in so far as it is animated by the irrational soul. But the rational soul perceives without passion the passions of the irrational nature; for the latter transmits to the rational soul the impressions which it has itself received through the body, and, inasmuch as the rational soul possesses in itself the forms of all things, the impressions, thus transmitted, affect it no otherwise than by calling into energy the forms which are in it; so that it perceives without passion, since it perceives itself alone, and it employs the body as its instrument by the medium of the irrational soul.

Plato, however, in the passage above quoted, implies by passion simply participation. In this sense Unity may be said to be a passion of Being, since Being subsists by the participation of the One. "Since, therefore, the soul participates of the prudence which subsists in intellect, or, in other words, of intellectual prudence, on this account Plato calls prudence the passion of the soul."† This, however, is not passion in the sense of Plotinus—an impression produced

* Compare Plato's *Timæus*, c. 44: "Of divine natures, indeed, the Demiurgus himself became the author; but he delivered to his offspring, the junior Gods, the fabrication of mortal natures. Hence, these, imitating their father's power, and receiving the immortal principle of the soul, fashioned posterior to this the mortal body, assigned the whole body as a vehicle to the soul, and fabricated in it another mortal species of soul, possessing dire and necessary passions through its union with the body. The first, indeed, of these passions is pleasure, which is the greatest allurement to evil; but the next is pain, which is the exile of good. After these follow boldness and fear, those mad advisers; anger, hard to be appeased; hope, which is easily deceived; together with irrational sense, and desire, the general invader of all things" (Taylor's *Plato*, ii. p. 544).

† Olympiodorus, in Taylor's *Plato*, iv. p. 291, *note*.

by an external agent—for the soul, being intellectual in essence, possesses intellectual prudence in itself.

The soul, then, existing in connection with the body, but being itself intellectual and indissoluble, is naturally adapted to rule the body, which is void of intellect and dissoluble. And the body is to the soul merely as an instrument, by the use of which, in certain stages, it excites and awakens its own latent powers. The virtuous soul, ruling the body, and energizing always in accordance with its true self, departs, when liberated from the body, to "that which is similar to itself, a divine nature," and is freed from the passions which do not indeed affect it essentially, but which are incidental to its connection with the body. On the other hand, the impure soul—the soul, namely, of a man in whom the irrational or animal nature has predominated over the rational; for the rational soul itself is not, strictly speaking, susceptible of impurity, but its proper faculties may remain, as it were, dormant, while its lower power, the irrational soul, is active—such a soul is not released by death from its corporeal bondage, but continues attached to the irrational nature, and to the aerial body which is the immediate vehicle of the latter, until such time as its fate calls it to animate a new terrestrial body. And this is the punishment of its forgetfulness, for, as the philosopher Sallust says: "Universally, the rational soul suffers punishment in conjunction with the irrational soul, the partner of its guilt; and through this that shadowy body derives its subsistence which is beheld about sepulchres, and especially about the tombs of such as have lived an abandoned life." *

There follows, in the *Phædo*, a remarkable paragraph, which taken in connection with passages on the same subject in other Platonic dialogues,† affords us no room to doubt that Plato believed in the possible descent of human souls into the bodies of inferior animals. Such a theory, indeed, would go far to explain much that seems otherwise inexplicable in regard to the apparent inequalities in the lives of brutes, and particularly of such as come into close relations with mankind. It is, of course, impossible that the rational soul should ever become irrational, but it is by no means impossible for it to abnegate, to a great extent, its position of leader, and to

* *On the Gods and the World*, c. 19.

† See especially the *Timæus*, c. 73, and *Republic*, x. 16.

allow the irrational nature, which, after all, emanates from itself, to rule the body almost at its own will. There are men in whom the rational soul is well-nigh dormant; on the other hand, a certain glimmer of rational life, however feeble, is oftentimes discernible in brutes. Porphyry, in the third book of his treatises on *Abstinence from Animal Foods*, has collected many instances and arguments to show that brutes do indubitably possess a certain reason, imperfect indeed, but still reason; and perhaps it may even be said that the irrational nature itself, inasmuch as it emanates from the rational soul, is not without some dim reflection of rationality. The soul assumes such a body as it has fitted itself to occupy; is it not then conceivable that a man who has constantly indulged his lower, and neglected his higher faculties, may come at length to incarnate in a brutal body suitable to the brutal nature which he has developed? What Plato says near the close of his *Timæus*, if it is to be taken literally, means that the entire brute creation was produced from the degeneracy of man. Nor was Plotinus averse to the conclusion that human souls might descend thus far. "If," says he, "there are in the bodies of brutes, as it is said, human souls which have sinned, the human soul, in so far as it is separable from body [*i.e.* rational], does not become the soul of the brute bodies, but being present is yet in a sense not present to them. Their power of sensation belongs in common to the irrational soul [*lit.* image of the soul] and the body; to the body, inasmuch as it is formed by the irrational soul. But those animals into which a human soul has not entered, are generated by an illumination proceeding from the soul of the world."*

By the expression "present and yet not present" is meant that the rational soul which is bound to the body of a brute is for the time unable to dissociate itself from the brutal nature, unable to act by itself, and in accordance with its true character; that the faculties proper to it as a rational soul are for the time in a state of atrophy, and that its energy is merely confined to the supplying of life to its image, the irrational soul, which is inseparable from body. It is thus present to the body, but not actively present.

The souls of those who have completely purified themselves by

* Ennead I. book i. § 11.

philosophy, pass, according to Plato, into the genus of Gods. This statement again may be illustrated by a brief excerpt from Plotinus. "Souls which have body have also to suffer punishment in the body. But such souls as are pure, and attract to themselves nothing of body, have of necessity a subsistence wholly apart from body. If, then, they are nowhere in body (for they have no body), it is there where essence and true being and that which is divine are, namely, in God, that such souls will be; with these and in This. But if thou still inquirest where, thou must needs inquire where these are; and inquiring, search not thou with the eyes, nor as if thou wert inquiring concerning bodies."*

The noble disquisition upon the part of philosophy in setting free the soul with which Socrates concludes this portion of the discourse, scarcely needs comment. Upon one point, however, a few words may be added. Philosophy, he says, when she receives the soul into her protection, finds it strongly "bound and agglutinated to the body, and compelled to speculate things through this, as from a place of confinement: she likewise beholds the dire nature of this confinement, that it arises through desire; so that he who is bound in an eminent degree assists in binding himself." The desire of the soul is twofold: a desire inward and upward, by which it tends towards intellect and a divine life; and a desire outward and downward, by which it tends towards body and a life of sense. Now the rational soul, which, as we said, is the true man, holding a middle position, and containing the reasons of all things in itself, beholds both that which is above and that which is below. It understands by the exercise of its proper faculty, the discursive reason (διάνοια), both intellectual conceptions and sensible forms. In so far as it tends to body, it acts through its lower power, the irrational soul, and reasons about the images which are transmitted to it by this power, and the passions and desires which are related to them. The proper object of the rational soul is intellect and the intelligible, wherein alone true being resides; and looking thither, it comprehends the source and underlying reality of sensible representation, since the higher includes the lower. But when it ceases to look to intellect, it becomes as it were dormant, and reasons by a kind of spurious reasoning, as in a dream; since its object is no longer true

* Ennead IV. book 3, § 24.

being, but the delusions of sense and the irrational nature. Then the irrational nature predominates, and the desire of the soul is diverted from its proper aim, and directed downwards to the things of sense; and this is the bond with which the soul attaches itself to body, whence it is filled with that direst of delusions, "that whatever the body asserts is true."

Socrates having concluded his argument, two further objections are proposed by Simmias and Cebes respectively. To ourselves these objections, and the answers by which they are met, are of peculiar interest, since we may recognize in them a distinct foreshadowing of the views of modern materialism on this subject. The modern hypothesis, that "consciousness is a mere product of molecular action," is substantially the hypothesis of Simmias, expressed in different terms. By Simmias it is stated in words to the following effect: that the soul may be regarded as a certain harmony, resulting from the proper temperament and disposition of the qualities of the body, and analogous to the harmony produced from the strings of a well-tuned lyre. That just as, when the strings of the lyre are broken, the harmony produced from them perishes, although the lyre yet remains; so when the parts of the body are corrupted, the harmony produced from them, namely, the soul, likewise perishes, although the body may continue to exist.

We noticed formerly that Socrates adduced the nature of invisibles, as subsisting always according to the same, and being consequently incapable of dissolution. Here, however, we have an instance of an invisible nature, the harmony proceeding from musical sounds, which is obviously perishable. But by an invisible nature Socrates, I doubt not, intended a nature totally exempt from sensible recognition, taking the sense of sight as a representative of the senses in general. Thus musical harmony is perceived by means of the sense of hearing, and although it is true that the mere sense by itself is cognizant of sounds alone, and not of sounds as harmony, still in this case the harmony is inseparable from the sounds, and consequently from sensible perception. So with the harmony which is perceived by means of the sight and the other senses. But harmony has a triple subsistence. It is firstly an idea belonging to the intelligible world; and this is Harmony Itself. Secondly, it exists in the soul, which participates intelligible harmony; and thirdly, in objects of sensible perception, to which it is communicated by the soul. The sensible harmony, therefore, to which Simmias likens the human soul, is not Harmony Itself, but only a partial expression of harmony; and when it dies, harmony does not perish, but merely ceases to manifest itself through some particular vehicle.

The fallacy which underlies the objection of Simmias is fully exposed by Socrates. In the first place, the objection is inconsistent with assertions which already have been reasoned upon and admitted as true. Thus it was shown that the learning of the soul is reminiscence, and from this it was concluded that the soul must have existed before its conjunction with the body. But if the soul be but a certain harmony resulting from a particular temperament of the parts and qualities of the body, how is it possible that it should have existed before, or separate from, those parts from the temperament of which it is produced? If then the objection is to be sustained, it will be necessary to retract all that was formerly admitted with regard to reminiscence and the pre-existence of the soul. Again, it was allowed that the soul, being of an intellectual and immortal nature, and similar to that which is divine, was naturally adapted to rule the body, which is void of intellect, and mortal. But this is impossible if the soul be a harmony of such a kind, since, in the words of Socrates, "it does not belong to a harmony to be the leader of the materials from which it is composed, but to follow them."

Moreover, the sensible harmony of which Simmias speaks, inasmuch as it is not absolute, but merely participated, harmony, may be more or less harmony; that is, it may participate ideal harmony in a greater or a lesser degree. Whereas the soul, being a simple essence, cannot be more or less soul, nor can one soul be more or less soul than another. The soul, however, may partake both of virtue and of vice, for these belong to its energy, and not to its essence. But even this would be impossible upon the assumption of Simmias, since virtue is the concord of the higher and lower faculties of the soul, and vice the discord thereof. If then, the soul be a harmony, it cannot be discordant with itself, for it would thus be no longer a harmony; and it follows that all souls must be equally virtuous, and incapable of vice. Taylor has an excellent note on this part of the argument, which I transcribe. "As every rational soul is an incorporeal harmony separate from a subject, it does not admit of intensions and remissions; and, therefore, one rational soul is neither more nor less harmony than another, so far as each is *essentially* harmony. One soul, however, may be more similar to intellect, or harmony itself, than another, and so far as it is more similar, will be more harmony in *energy*. Hence virtue may be considered as the concord, and vice as the discord, of the rational and irrational nature; the former being produced from the rational harmonizing the irrational part, in consequence of being a harmony more energetic; and the latter arising from the irrational being unharmonized by the rational part, because in this case the essential harmony of the soul is more dormant than energetic. The reasoning, therefore, of Socrates does not apply to that harmony which is separate, but to that which is inseparable from body."*

The materialistic hypothesis of Simmias is finally disposed of by an argument which is, in fact, an expansion of one of the earlier arguments of Socrates. When we assert that the soul governs the body, we mean that it controls and opposes the passions and desires of the body. But the harmony which is inseparable from a sensible object, follows and obeys the passions of that object; as the harmony which proceeds from a lyre obeys the passions, *i.e.*, the vibrations of the strings, and cannot otherwise exist than in obeying them. It is, however, a matter of common experience that the soul opposes the passions of the body; whence it is evident that it cannot be of the nature of sensible harmony.

W. C. WARD.

(*To be continued.*)

PLATO'S CATEGORIC IMPERATIVE.

WHEN man discovers, or thinks he discovers, that the conditions which regulate his own nature are the laws that rule the whole, he realizes far more surely than before, that the conditions of his own nature are likewise laws, not to be violated without insult to the harmonies of heaven. The categoric imperative "thou shalt" is derived by Plato from the doctrine of man's unity with Nature.—ADAMS.

—THE NUPTIAL NUMBER OF PLATO.

* Taylor's *Plato*, iv. p. 308.

ON SOME REMARKABLE PASSAGES IN THE NEW TESTAMENT.

(*Continued from Vol. XIX. p.* 470.)

BEFORE passing to a remarkable passage in Luke, it will be as well to refer to a singular misapprehension as to the meaning of Isaiah xiv. 12, where it seems generally supposed that the fall of "Lucifer" or Satan is meant. The whole context refutes this; verse 16 shows that a *man* (aīsh) is meant, and that his *former* state is compared to that of Lucifer, the bright morning star, "the bright Son of Dawn" (heīlēl ben sha'har), and contrasted with his subsequent downfall. He was greatest of the great ones of the earth, king, prince or potentate, and so he is compared to Lucifer as "the brightest of created things" (Dante, *Purg.*, xii. 25-27); and it is clear from verse 4 that the king of Babylon there named is meant throughout, and this will some day be the means of fixing the exact date of Isaiah, *viz.*, the downfall of the contemporaneous king of Babylon; *i.e.*, treating the passage in Isaiah not at all as a prophecy, but as a statement of a contemporaneous fact. The whole passage contrasts the former greatness with the utter downfall of the king.

Now Luke x. 17, 18, has generally been referred to this supposed downfall of Lucifer, identified with Satan—and so it does, but not in the theological sense supposed, and it does not refer in any way to the passage in Isaiah.

The true meaning of Luke x. 18, is "I contemplated (ἐθεώρουν, not merely *saw*) Satan (or Lucifer, *i.e.*, the Logos, Λόγος), descending (or falling) like lightning (for its speed) from heaven." And hence what precedes and follows, for τὰ δαιμόνια (spirits) of verse 17, are clearly identified by verse 20, with τὰ πνεύματα; and the English version is altogether erroneous and utterly misleading. It might almost be said to express the exact reverse of what is meant, *i.e.*,

The spirits are subject to you mortals *because* the Logos has descended to earth from heaven.

"The stone which the builders rejected." The passage in Matt. xxi. 42-44, is on the face of it symbolical, and this seems admitted, but the interpretations are very different. Perhaps they are all wrong. One clue is the parable, which just precedes it, of the Lord who sends for the fruit of his vineyard.

The vineyard is of course the world; the labourers or vine-dressers are mankind. When the fruits of the vineyard, or the results of life, are demanded, none are given. Their lives have produced no fruit. (The "wicked servant" in the parable of the "Ten Talents" has the same meaning.) The messengers or servants are the servants of the Good Law, and they are all maltreated, as the teachers of a higher morality have been from time immemorial. The very son, or spirit in man, is slain. The tillers or vine-dressers have not wrought for eternity, but for material pleasure and gain, and rejecting all advice, perish. Then comes the allusion to the corner-stone; had they made *this* the crown of all, it had been well for them, and the building (their life) would have stood fast. For all that, the day comes when it is recognized that the rejected stone, *i.e.*, "the laws of nature" which are everlasting, can alone be safely followed. He who follows them fares well; he who stumbles on them is broken, and he who persists in acting in contravention of them is ground to pieces.

These "laws" may include physical laws, as it is equally true of them. But the highest application is to the eternal moral law, the same now and for ever, the "corner-stone" of all real faith.

The story of Jairus' daughter is remarkable on several grounds. It is found in three Gospels, but not mentioned in John. It is clear no miracle was meant, but only a rapid cure.

1. In Matt. ix. 18, it is said she was "at the point of death," "all but dead"—ἄρτι ἐτελεύτησεν, which can have no other meaning, (though the Vulgate renders "she is just dead"!) "but come and place thy hand upon her and she shall live," *i.e.*, recover. The English version is the worst of all—"is even now dead"!

2. Mark v. 23, in the corresponding passage has the very clear expression ἐσχάτως ἔχει, *i.e.*, "is *in extremis*," "is desperately ill," which

perfectly agrees with the correct translation of the passage in Matt., and is correctly rendered by the Vulgate *in extremis est*, while the Syriac has "is very ill."

3. Luke viii. 42, as clearly expresses the meaning by the imperfect "she was dying," and even the Vulgate has *moriebatur*. But a person supposed to be dying, even by the physicians, does not necessarily die. The Syriac has "was near dying."

In all, Jesus the Therapeute or Healer is made to say, "She is *not dead*, but sleeping" (sleepeth) (Matt. ix. 29; Mark v. 39; Luke viii. 54). So that she was in a death-like swoon, as the Healer saw, "and her spirit returned." But some writer has interpolated (Luke viii. 53), "and they derided him, *knowing* she was dead," thus making Jesus tell a falsehood, rather than give up a pretended miracle.

It is clear:

1. That all writers mean precisely the same.
2. That in all, the meaning is a trance or death-like swoon.
3. That there was no miracle or pretence of one, but a case of healing the sick.
4. That it is *probable* that the whole passage is symbolical or mystical, referring to spiritual death.

It is to be observed that the same Jairus, Ἰάειρος, is neither Greek, Hebrew, nor Syriac, which last has the utterly un-Semitic name Yōrōç.

Some isolated passages in Luke are well worth noticing for their suggestiveness. Luke x. 38-42, Martha and Mary are types respectively of the active and contemplative life, and they correspond to the Leah and Rachel of the O. T., which gives a clue to the interpretation of the legends in Genesis, where we find, singularly enough, a prose poem of a highly imaginative cast in ch. xxiv. and another in ch. xxix.

Dante (*Purg.*, xxvii. 101-8) notices this meaning of the two types—"She (Rachel) rejoices in contemplation, I (Leah) in labour (work)."

Luke xi. 2, in the Lord's Prayer, omits the clause, "Thy will will be done on earth as it is in heaven" (Matt. vi. 10).

The term, ἐπιούσιον (ἄρτον) occurs in both. In Luke (v. 3) the Vulgate renders it *quotidianum*, but in Matt. (rightly) *supersubstan-*

tialem, *i.e.*, mystically. The English version (wrongly) has "daily" in both, which besides restricting the meaning to a lower physical one, has no support from any authority or analogy. Ὀυσία is "essence" (*substantia*), and ἐπιούσιος strictly "supersubstantial," "supernatural" or "superphysical." Mark and John strangely omit the Lord's Prayer altogether, which is the more remarkable because Mark xi. 25, 26, has the passage immediately following, while John xiv. 11-14, differs from the three others.

The "bread" meant is clear from John vi. 32, for it is "the bread which descends from heaven and gives *life* to the world," *i.e.*, the Spirit; and observe, it is said "*this*, Moses did *not* give," *i.e.*, the Jewish teaching was of a lower, terrestrial kind, consisting of ritual, ceremonies, etc., was, in fact, τὸ ἔξωθεν instead of τὸ ἔσωθεν, whereas "the Kingdom of God is *within you*" (Luke xvii. 21), ἐντὸς ὑμῶν.

In Luke xi. 52, γνώσεως corresponds with the Sanskrit gñâna, *i.e.*, spiritual or mystical knowledge, and probably with the "çōwd" (secret or mystical knowledge) of the Rabbins which the priests kept to themselves. The whole Gnosis might be termed the knowledge of initiates.

Luke xii. 16-21. This remarkable parable occurs only in Luke. We may perhaps compare it with Tennyson's "Palace of Art" as relating to the cultivation of physical knowledge only (science without religion), or they may both be illustrations of the Buddhist doctrine of separateness, selfish culture.

Ib., verse 57, explains verses 58, 59, corresponding with the karma of the Buddhists, "the uttermost mite" representing the complete extinction of evil karma.

A number of passages might be selected from the N. T., where the meaning is altogether misunderstood, from a total want of appreciation or ignorance of Eastern thoughts and ideas. *E.g.*, John i. 5, κατέλαβεν does not mean "comprehended" or anything like it, but "eclipsed"; *i.e.*, "the darkness eclipsed it (the light) not," the light overpowered the dense darkness, and thus an impossible and nonsensical phrase is turned into one of the most powerful touches in the whole Gospel. Everyone in a slight degree acquainted with Buddhist texts knows how often the expression "grah" (seize) occurs, of an eclipse of the sun, often as a mythological legend. Of this, κατέλαβεν is the literal version. The Vulgate with its careful rendering of the literal sense of the Greek, has *comprehenderit*, which is capable of both meanings, like the Greek, for its literal sense is "seized on."

In Apoc. xx. 11, ἔφυγεν is "vanished away—flew out of sight," and not merely "fled away," and is exactly equivalent to παρῆλθεν (xxi. 1) "passed away—for ever," except that a more sudden motion is implied in the former; and so "the sea was no more," or "sea there was none." The same is said of time. Both refer no doubt to the close of a great cycle or manvantara.

The mistranslations of Greek words owing to theological predispositions are sometimes of great importance. One instance is δαιμόνιον, τὸ δαιμόνιον. It is strange that this expression, familiar to the times of Socrates and Plato, should be often so mistranslated as to give an entirely erroneous impression. In Luke vii. 33, δαιμόνιον ἔχει is rendered "he hath a devil"! instead of the true rendering "he (John) is inspired," "he hath a divine spirit," as the context shows, and then the contrast intended between verse 33 and verse 34 becomes very forcible; "You took John to be *inspired*, as he neither ate nor drank like ordinary men, but because I do so you call me," etc.; δαιμόνιον in fact expresses an indwelling *divine spirit*, as that of Socrates in Xenophon and Plato.

But the most striking proof that it is so used is found in one of the earliest Fathers, Ignatius, who gives us the genuine words of Jesus: "I am not a spirit (δαιμόνιον) without a body (ἀσώματον)." The Divine Spirit, being one, is always used in the singular. The plural δαιμόνια may be used of obsessing evil spirits, for they may be many. They are "spirits," perhaps good or evil according to their connotation.

Moreover, to translate διάβολος and δαιμόνιον by the same word cannot be justified. The former always means an evil spirit, like the Buddhist Mâra, "the wicked one." The only apparent exceptions as to δαιμόνιον are John viii. 48, 49, and x. 20, 21, where the inspiration is referred to madness, as with the Cassandra of Æschylus, who was inspired, but no one listened to her, and this seems to be shown by the word μαίνεται (verse 20).

We find in the N. T. the strangest mingling of the Jewish religion with an entirely new creed, which had nothing in common with the former, but was an attempt to teach a world-religion in contrast to a mere national or even tribal one.

The number of proper names which are not only not Jewish, but not even Semitic, is very striking.

In Luke vi. 14-16, we find the names, real or reputed, of the so-called Twelve Apostles, few of which seem to be genuinely Jewish, and as to Iskariôtês it is even impossible, for no native Jewish word has five consonants, like ç-k-r-y-t, and in fact no quinque-literals are either Jewish or Syriac. All are borrowed.

One of the most remarkable names is "John," Ιωαννής—in Syriac Yu'hanon. It is clear from Luke i. 61, that this was a *foreign* name, and the passage is plainly intended to account for a supposed Jew having so un-Jewish a name. One may conjecture that it is somehow meant for the Buddhist Ânanda, Buddha's predecessor and afterwards pupil and companion. No Semitic root will give any such form or anything like it.

That "Peter" is an epithet, we find mentioned in many places (Luke vi. 14; John i. 42; Matt. xvi. 18, etc.). In John he is called "Simon, son of Jonā," which seems to mean, "son of the Dove, (Yōnāh)," *i.e.*, Spirit, while σὺ κληθήσῃ Κηφᾶς looks very like an addition, as the following interpretation certainly is.

The number of times that the name "Simon" occurs in the N. T. deserves notice, as it rather seems to designate a *class* than an individual. May it not be the Buddhist (Pâli) "Samana," the Sanskrit "Shramana"—"eremite"? We have besides this "Simon," "Simon the leper," "Simon the Magus," "Simon Zelotês," etc.

The term ζηλωτής is absurdly rendered "zealot," meaning "fanatic." Both Vulgate and Lutheran rightly keep the word "Zelotês." It may be an interpretation of "Simon" itself, *i.e.*, hermit dwelling in the desert. We know that these eremites or dwellers in deserts and rocks existed in Syria ages before Christianity, the Christian era, and long subsequently. They had various technical names, and were of various nationalities.

The Paulician heresy (to say nothing of other sects, as Manichees, Gnostics, etc.) shows the existence of these enthusiasts as late as the eleventh century.

It is at all events worth an enquiry whether they were not really derived from the Hindus, or even actual Buddhist converts.

It is specially noticeable that John "the Baptist" was one of these very eremites. The words in Matt. iii. 4, are conclusive, his food being "locusts and wild honey," nor does this seem noticed as anything astonishing or peculiar to him. He was one of a class.

Luke xv. and xvi. are remarkable as containing the finest and most far-reaching of all the parables of the N. T., yet there is no hint of them in Matt., Mark or John. The χάσμα in xvi. 26, is of course mystical or symbolical, and means perhaps the interval between life and the Buddhist devachan or sukhâvatî, or perhaps the gap or chasm between kâmaloka and devachan. The R.C. suggest it is purgatory, and in one sense this may be true, for purgatory, as its name shows, did not *originally* denote a *place* of torture at all, but only a *state* of purification, and probably meant kâmaloka. Augustin (*De Animâ*, etc., book iv. c. 16) interprets the "bosom of Abraham" as a "remote and secret place of repose," taking, therefore, Abraham as symbolical.

Luke xix. The noble parable of the "Ten Talents" is a deep application of the Buddhist doctrine of karma, and cannot be well understood without it. It is noticeable that the reward is *exactly* proportioned to the desert or merit, which is the very doctrine of karma.

In verse 41 the "city" is the world—as in the Apocalypse, and verse 45, the "shrine" or "temple" is man's own soul or spirit, which should be the home of divine emotion or prayer, but is too often a "den of thieves," the evil passions which take forcible possession of it.

Matt. xxi. 12 is rather more detailed, but substantially the same. Mark xi. agrees, but adds (verse 16) that he (Jesus) would not allow them to carry anything (σκεῦος—which gives its sense in other passages, as Acts xi. 5), through the Temple. In John we find "house of merchandise" (ii. 16) *i.e.*, a mercenary or worldly spirit.

Luke xx. 27. The Sadducees deny a resurrection. But the context shows that they meant resurrection of the body, or that carnal relationships existed in a future state. The answer confirms what they say for this cycle (αἰών), but verse 35 explains the doctrine from a higher point of view, not that the *body* is resurrected, but that it is the spirit which is re-born at the end of the cycle. In the new cycle they are not reborn into this world, but become higher spirits. But this is the lot only of those who are worthy (verses 35, 36). This seems very nearly the doctrine of Buddhism.

Αἰών (æon) ought in perhaps every case to be rendered by "cycle"; and αἰῶνες αἰώνων as the great cycle or manvantara.

Luke xxi. 1-4. The value of an offering does not depend on its worldly estimate, but the spirit in which it is offered. The widow's mite is more than all the offerings of the rich. This is exactly Buddha's doctrine, as well as that of the Bhagavad Gîtâ (ix. 26), where a leaf, a flower, is said to be an acceptable offering to the deity. The "cup of cold water" (Matt. x. 42, and Mark ix. 41) has precisely the same meaning. But such notions are totally alien to Judaism.

Luke xxii. 34 predicts Peter's apostasy. The cock-crow perhaps refers to the awakening of the human spirit from the deep slumber of doubt or denial, and the story which makes Peter deny his Master thrice and tell lies (as ordinarily interpreted) may only refer to a psychical state of mind, and not to actual facts.

F. H. BOWRING.

(*To be concluded.*)

THE OLD SECRET.

Now unto thee, again the secret old of Brahman I will tell, and after death, O Gautama, how is the Self.

Some souls go into wombs, to take a body; into the motionless do others pass, according to their deeds, as is their knowledge.

The Man that wakes when others sleep, dispensing all desires, That truly is pure, That Brahman, That deathless is verily called; in That all worlds are contained: past That truly naught goes at all. This verily is That.

—KAṬHOPANIṢHAD, v. 6-8.

AMONG THE GNOSTICS OF THE FIRST TWO CENTURIES.

(*Continued from Vol. XIX. p.* 489.)

THE SERPENT SYMBOL.

THE serpent symbol played a great part in the mysteries of the ancients, especially in Greece, Egypt and Phœnicia; thence we can trace it back to Syria, Babylonia, and further East to India, where it still survives and receives due explanation. It figured forth the most intimate processes of the generation of the universe and of man, and also of the mystic birth. It was the glyph of the creative power, and in its lowest form was debased into a phallic emblem. Physical procreation and the processes of conception are lower manifestations of the energizing of the great creative will and the evolutionary world-process. But the one is as far removed from the other, as man's body is from the body of the universe, as man's animal desire from the divine will of deity. The mysteries of sex were explained in the Adyta of the ancient temples; and naturally enough the attempt to get back of the great passion of mankind was fraught with the greatest peril. A real knowledge of the mystery led to asceticism; a mere curious prying into the matter led to abuse. Illumination, seership and spiritual knowledge, was the reward of the pure in body and mind; sexual excess and depravity punished the prying of the unfit. This explains one of the most curious phenomena in religious history; the bright and dark sides are almost invariably found together; whenever an attempt is made to shed some light on the mystery of the world and of man, the whole nature is quickened, and if the animal is the stronger, it becomes all the more uncontrolled owing to the quickening. Thus we find that some obscure groups of the Gnostics fell into grave errors, not only of theory but of practice, and that Patristic writers of the subsequent centuries tried by every means to exaggerate this particular into a general charge against "error"; whereas, as a matter of fact, it is in the writings of the Gnostics themselves that we find the greatest condemnation of such abuses.

As man was generated in the womb from a "serpent" and an "egg," so was the universe; but the serpent of the universe was the Great Power, the Mighty Whirlwind, the Vast Vortex, and the egg was the All-Envelope of the World-system, the primordial fire-dust. The serpent was thus the glyph of the Divine Will, the Divine Reason, the Mind of Deity, the Logos. The egg was the Thought, the Conception, the Mother of All. The germinal universe was figured as a circle with a serpent lying diagonally along its field, or twined a certain number of times round it. This serpentine force fashioned the universe, and fashioned man. It created him; and yet he in his turn could use it for creation, if he would only cease from generation. The Caduceus, or rod of Mercury, in the Greek Mysteries, which conducted the soul from life to death, and from death to life, figured forth the serpentine power in man, in its twin modes, and the path whereby it would carry the "man" aloft to the height, if he would but cause the "Waters of the Jordan" to "flow upwards."

The serpent of Genesis, the serpent-rod of Moses, and the uplifting of the brazen serpent in the wilderness, were promptly seized upon by the Gnostics as mythological ideas similar to the myths of the mysteries. To give the reader an insight into their methods of mystical exegesis, which looked to an inner psychological science, we may here append their interpretation of what may be called

The Myth of the Going-forth.

It was common to a number of schools, but Hippolytus ascribes it to an otherwise unknown school called the Peratæ, supposed to mean Transcendentalists, or those who by means of the Gnosis had "passed beyond" or "crossed over." Thus then they explained the Exodus-myth. Egypt is the body; all those who identify themselves with the body, are the ignorant, the Egyptians. To "come forth" out of Egypt, is to leave the body; and to pass through the Red Sea, is to cross over the ocean of generation, the animal and sensual nature, which is hidden within the blood. Yet even then they are not safe; crossing the Red Sea they enter the Desert, the intermediate state of the doubting lower mind. There they are attacked by the "gods of destruction" which Moses called the "serpents of the desert," and which plague those who seek to escape from the "gods of generation." To them Moses, the teacher, shows the true serpent crucified on the cross of matter, and by its means they escape from the Desert and enter the Promised Land, the realm of the spiritual mind, where there is the Heavenly Jordan, the World-Soul. When the Waters of the Jordan flow downwards, then is the generation of men; but when they flow upward, then is the creation of the gods. Jesus was one who had caused the Waters of the Jordan to flow upwards.

Many of the ancient myths had a historico-legendary background, but their use as myths, or religious and mystic romances, had gradually effaced the traces of history. Those instructed in the mysteries were practised in the science of mythology, and thus the learned Gnostics at once perceived the mythological nature of the Exodus and its adaptability to a mystical interpretation. The above instance is a very good example of this method of exegesis; a great deal of such interpretation, however, was exceedingly strained, when not decidedly silly. The religious mind of the times loved to exercise its ingenuity on such interpretations, and the difference between Gnostic exegesis and that of the subsequent orthodox, is that the former tried to discover soul-processes in the myths and parables of scripture, whereas the orthodox regarded a theological and dogmatic interpretation as alone legitimate.

The silliest element which entered into such pious pastimes was the method of word-play or pseudo-philology. In the Upanishads of the Hindus, in the Cratylus of Plato, among the Gnostic and Patristic writers, we find the most fantastic derivations of names, which were put forward in support of theological doctrines, but which were destitute of the most rudimentary philological accuracy. Men, such as Plato, who in many other respects were giants of intellect, were content to resort to such puerile methods. It is, however, pleasant to notice that the nature of the soul and the truths of the spiritual life were the chief interest for such ancient worthies, and not the grubbing up of "roots"; nevertheless, we should be careful when detecting the limitation of such minds in certain directions, to guard against the error of closing our eyes to the limitations of our own modern methods in directions where the ancients have done much good work.

We will now proceed to give a brief sketch of the main outlines of one of the presentations of these Gnostic ideas.

THE "GNOSTICS" OF IRENÆUS.

In the Unutterable Depth were two great Lights, the First Man, or Father, and his Son, the Second Man; and also the Holy Spirit, the First Woman, or Mother of all living. Below this triad was a sluggish mass composed of the four great elements, called Water, Darkness, Abyss and Chaos. The Universal Mother brooded over the Waters; enamoured of her beauty, the First and Second Man produced from her the third Great Light, the Christ; and he, ascending above, formed with the First and Second Man the Holy Church. This was the right-hand birth of the Great Mother. But a Drop of Light fell downwards to the left hand into chaotic matter; this was called Sophia or Wisdom, the World-Mother. The Waters of the Ether were thus set in motion, and formed a body for Sophia (the Light-Æon) *viz.*, the Heaven-sphere. And she, freeing herself, left her body behind, and ascended to the Middle Region below her Mother, who formed the boundary of the Ideal Universe. But her mere contact with the Space-Waters had already generated a son, the chief Creative Power of the Sensible World, who retained some of the Light-fluid; this son was Ialdabaoth, who in his turn produced a son, and he another, until they were seven in all, the great Formative Powers of the Sensible Universe. And they were "fighters," and quarrelled much with their father. And by means of this interplay of forces on matter came forth the "mind," which was "serpent-formed," and "spirit," and "soul," and all things in the world.

And Ialdabaoth was boastful and arrogant, and exclaimed, "I am Father and God, and beyond me is none other." But Sophia hearing this cried out to her son, "Lie not, Ialdabaoth, for above thee is the Father of All, the First Man, and Man the Son of Man." And all the Powers were astonished at the word; but Ialdabaoth, to call off their attention, cried out, "Let us make 'man' after our image." So they made "man," and he lay like a worm on the ground, until they brought him to Ialdabaoth, who breathed into him the "breath of life," that is to say the Light-fluid he had received from Sophia, and so emptied himself of his Light. And "man" receiving it, immediately gave thanks to the First Man and disregarded his fabricators (the Elohîm).

Whereupon Ialdabaoth (Jehovah) was jealous and planned to deprive Adam of the Light-spark by forming "woman." And the six creative powers were enamoured of Eve and by her generated sons, namely, the angels. And so Adam again fell under the power of Ialdaboath and the Elohîm; then Sophia or Wisdom sent the serpent into the Paradise of Ialdabaoth, and Adam and Eve listened to its wise counsels, and so once more "man" was freed from the dominion of the Creative Power, and transgressed the ordinance of ignorance of any power higher than himself imposed by Ialdabaoth. Whereupon Ialdabaoth drove them out of his Paradise, together with them the serpent or "mind"; but Sophia would not permit the Light-spark to descend, and so withdrew it to avoid profanation. And "mind" (the lower mind) the serpent-formed, the first product of Ialdabaoth, brought forth six sons, and these are the "dæmonial" powers which plague man because their father was cast down for their sake.

Now Adam and Eve before the fall had spiritual bodies, like the "angels" born of this Eve; but after their fall, down from the Paradise of Ialdabaoth, their bodies grew more and more dense, and more and more languid, and became "coats of skin," till finally Sophia in compassion restored to them the sweet odour of the Light, and they knew that they carried death about with them. And so a recollection of their former state came back to them, and they were patient, knowing that the body was put on only for a time.

The system then goes on to grapple with the legends of Genesis touching Cain and Noah, etc., and the Old Testament record generally, with moderate success; the main idea being that the prophets were inspired by one or other of the seven Elohîm, but occasionally Sophia had succeeded in impressing them with fragmentary revelations about the First Man and the Christ above.

The rest of the system is devoted to the question of the scheme of regeneration and the interpretation of the Gospel legends. Sophia, or Wisdom, finding no rest in heaven or earth, implored the help of the Great Mother, and she in compassion begged of the

First Man that Christ should be sent to help her. And then Wisdom knowing that her brother and spouse was coming to her aid, announced his coming by John, and by means of the "baptism of repentance" Jesus was made ready to receive him, as in a clean vessel. And so the Christ descended through the seven spheres, likening himself unto the Rulers, and draining them of their power, the Light they had retained all flowing back to him. And first of all the Christ clothed his sister Sophia with the Light-vesture, and they rejoiced together, and this is the mystical "marriage" of the "bridegroom and the bride." Now Jesus, having been born of a "virgin" by the working of God, in other words, after the spiritual "second birth" had been attained by the ascetic Jesus, Christ and Sophia, the one enfolding the other, descended upon him and he became Christ Jesus.

Then it was that he began to do mighty works, to heal and proclaim the Unknown Father, and profess himself openly the Son of the First Man. Whereupon the Powers and especially Ialdabaoth took measures to slay him, and so Jesus, the man, was "crucified" by them, but Christ and Sophia mounted aloft to the Incorruptible Æon. But Christ did not forget the one in whom he had tabernacled, and so sent a power which raised up his body, not indeed his gross physical envelope, but a psychic and spiritual body. And those of his disciples who saw this body, thought he was risen in his physical frame, but to certain of them who were capable of receiving it, he explained the mystery and taught them many other mysteries of the spiritual life. And Jesus now sits at the right hand of his father, Ialdabaoth, and receives the souls who have received those mysteries. And in proportion as he enriches himself with souls, in such measure is Ialdabaoth deprived of power; so that he is no longer able to send back holy souls into the world of reincarnation, but only those of his own substance; and the consummation of all things will be when all the Light shall once more be gathered up and stored in the treasures of the Incorruptible Æon.

Such is the account of this by no means absurd scheme of the Gnosis preserved to us in the barbarous Latin translation of Irenæus' summary. That the original system was far more elaborate we may assume from the now known method of Irenæus to make a very brief summary of the tenets he criticized. The main features of the christological and soteriological part of the system is identical with the main outlines of the system of the Pistis Sophia, and of one of the treatises of the Codex Brucianus. This is a very important point, and indicates that the dates of these treatises need not necessarily be later than the time of the bishop of Lyons, but the further consideration of this important subject is beyond the scope of the present essay. Interesting again is it to remark the influence of the Orphic, Pythagorean and Platonic tradition in the cosmological part, and to observe how both the Hellenic and Jewish myths find a common source in the Chaldæan tradition.

The Gnostics of Hippolytus: Justinus.

Hippolytus devotes the fifth Book of his Refutation to the "Ophites," who, however, all call themselves Gnostics, and not "Ophites," as explained above; he seems to regard them as the most ancient stream of the Gnosis. After treating of three great schools, to which we shall subsequently refer, he specially singles out for notice a certain Justinus, who is mentioned by no other hæresiologist. This account of Hippolytus is all the more important, seeing that the system of Justinus represents one of the oldest forms of the Gnosis of which we have record. This has been disputed by Salmon, but to my mind, his arguments are unconvincing; the fact that the Justinian school makes no reference to the texts of the New Testament collection, in its mystical exegesis, although freely quoting from the Old, should decide the point. One short saying is referred to Jesus, but it is nowhere found in the canonical texts.

The school had a large literature, from which Hippolytus selects a single volume, The Book of Baruch, as giving the most complete form of the system. The members were bound by an oath of secresy not to reveal the tenets of the school, and the form of the oath is given. The cosmogony is based on a Syrian creation-myth, a variant of which is preserved by Herodotus (iv. 8-10), in which Hercules plays the principal part, and a stratum of which is also found in Genesis. The following is the outline of the system.

There are three principles of the Universe: (i) the Good, or all-wise Deity; (ii) the Father, or Spirit, the creative power, called

Elohîm; and (iii) the World-Soul, symbolized as a woman above the middle and a serpent below, called Eden. From Elohîm (a plural used as a collective and presumably a septenary power) and Eden twenty-four cosmic powers or angels come forth, twelve follow the will of the Father-Spirit, and twelve the nature of the Mother-Soul. The lower twelve are the World-Trees of the Garden of Eden. The Trees are divided into four groups, of three each, representing the four Rivers of Eden. The Trees are evidently of the same nature as the cosmic forces which are represented by the Hindus as having their roots or sources above and their branches or streams below. The name Eden means pleasure or Desire.

Thus the whole creation comes into existence, and finally from the animal part of the Mother-Soul are generated animals, and from the human part men. The upper part of Eden is called the "most beautiful earth"; that is to say, Eden is matter, and the body of man is formed of the finest. Man having thus been formed, Eden and Elohîm depute their powers unto him; the World-Soul bestows on him the soul, and the World-Spirit infuses into him the spirit. Thus were men and women constituted.

And all creation was subjected to the four groups of the twelve powers of the World-Soul, according to their cycles, as they move round as if in a circular dance (the precession of the equinoxes); the system having thus intimate points of contact with Chaldæan astrological traditions.

But when the man-stage was reached, the turning-point of the world-process, Elohîm, the Spirit, ascended into the celestial spaces, taking with him his own twelve powers. And in the highest part of the heaven, he beheld the Great Light shining through the gate (? the sun), which led to the Light-world of the Good. And he who had hitherto thought himself Lord of Creation, perceived that there was One above him, and cried aloud: "Open me the gates that I may acknowledge the (true) Lord; for I considered myself to be the Lord." And a voice came forth, saying: "This is the gate of the Lord; through this the righteous enter in." And leaving his angels in the highest part of the heavens, the World-Father entered in and sat down at the right hand of the Good One.

And Elohîm desired to recover by force his spirit which was bound to men, from further degradation; but the Good Deity restrained him, for now that he had ascended to the Light-realm he could work no destruction.

And the Soul (Eden) perceiving herself abandoned by Elohîm, tricked herself out so as to entice him back; but the Spirit would not return to the arms of Mother Nature (now that the middle point of evolution was passed). Thereupon, the spirit that was left behind in man, was plagued by the soul; for the spirit desired to follow its Father into the height, but the soul, incited by the powers of the Mother-Soul, and especially by the first group who rule over sexual passion and excess, gave way to adulteries and even greater vice; and the spirit in man was thereby tormented.

Now the angel, or power of the World-Soul, which especially incited the human soul to such misdeeds, was the third of the first group, called Naas (Heb. Nachash), the serpent, the symbol of animal passion. And Elohîm, seeing this, sent forth the third of his own angels, called Baruch, to succour the spirit in man. And Baruch came and stood in the midst of the Trees (the powers of the World-Soul) and declared unto man that of all the Trees of the Garden of Eden he might eat the fruit, but of the Tree Naas, he might not, for Naas had transgressed the law, and had given rise to adultery and unnatural intercourse.

And Baruch had also appeared to Moses and the prophets through the spirit in man, that the people might be converted to the Good One; but Naas had invariably obscured his precepts through the soul in man. And not only had Baruch taught the prophets of the Hebrews, but also the prophets of the uncircumcised. Thus, for instance, Hercules among the Syrians had been instructed, and his twelve labours were his conflicts with the twelve powers of the World-Soul. Yet Hercules also had finally failed, for after seeming to accomplish his labours, he is vanquished by Omphale, or Venus, who divests him of his power by clothing him with her own robe, the power of Eden below.

Last of all Baruch appeared unto Jesus, a shepherd boy, son of Joseph and Mary, a child of twelve years. And Jesus remained faithful to the teachings of Baruch, in spite of the enticements of Naas. And Naas in wrath caused him to be "crucified," but he, leaving on the "tree" the body of Eden—that is to say the psychic body or soul, and the gross physical body—and committing his spirit to the hands of his Father (Elohîm), ascended to the Good One. And there he beholds "whatever things eye hath not seen and ear hath not heard, and which have not entered into the heart of man"; and bathes in the ocean of life-giving water, no longer in the water below the firmament, the ocean of generation in which the physical and psychic bodies are bathed. This ocean of generation is evidently the same as the Brâhmanical and Buddhistic samsâra, the ocean of rebirth.

Hippolytus tries to make out that Justinus was a very vile person, because he fearlessly pointed out the main obstacle to the spiritual life, and the horrors of animal sensuality; but Justinus evidently preached a doctrine of rigid asceticism, and ascribed the success of Jesus to his triumphant purity.

THE NAASENI OF HIPPOLYTUS.

Prior to the section on Justinus Hippolytus treats of three schools under the names Naaseni, Peratæ, and Sithians or Sethians. All three schools apparently belong to the same cycle, and the first two present features so identical as to make it highly probable that the Naasene work and the two Peratic treatises from which Hippolytus quotes, pertain to the same Gnostic circle.

Although the name Naasene is derived from the Hebrew Nachash, a serpent, Hippolytus does not call the Naasenes Ophites but Gnostics; in fact he reserves the name Ophite for a small body which he classes with the Cainites and Nochaitæ (viii. 20), and considers them of not sufficient importance for mention.

The Naasenes possessed many books, and also regarded as authoritative the following scriptures: The Gospel of Perfection, The Gospel of Eve, The Questions of Mary, Concerning the Offspring of Mary, The Gospel of Philip, The Gospel according to Thomas and The Gospel according to the Egyptians. One of their MSS. had fallen into the hands of Hippolytus. It was a treatise of a mystical, psychological, devotional and exegetical character, rather than a cosmological exposition, and therefore the system is somewhat difficult to make out from Hippolytus' quotations. Its date may be placed somewhere in the second half of the second century, and it is especially valuable as pointing out the identity of the inner teachings of Christianity with the tenets of the mysteries—Phrygian,

Eleusinian, Samothracian, Egyptian, Assyrian, etc. The author of the treatise was not only acquainted with the Old Testament, but also with the Canonical Gospels and several of the Pauline Letters; moreover he was well versed in Greek literature and the mystery-cultus of the Græco-Roman world.

The writer claimed that his tradition was handed down from the apostolic James to a certain Mariamne. This Miriam, or Mary, is somewhat of a puzzle to scholarship; it seems, however, probable that the treatise belonged to the same cycle of tradition as The Greater and Lesser Questions of Mary, The Gospel of Mary, etc., in the frame of which the Pistis Sophia treatise is also set.

The main features of the system are that the cosmos is symbolized as the (Heavenly) Man, male-female, of three natures, spiritual (or intelligible), psychic and material; that these three natures found themselves in perfection in Jesus, who was therefore truly the Son of Man. Mankind is divided into three classes, assemblies or churches: the elect, the called and the bound (or in other words, the spiritual or angelic, the psychic, and the choïc or material), according as one or other of these natures predominates. This reminds us strongly of the three natures (triguṇa) of the Sâṅkhya system in India: light (sattva), passion (rajas), darkness (tamas).

After this brief outline, Hippolytus proceeds to plunge into the mystical exegesis of the writer, and his interpretation of the mysteries, which is mixed up here and there with specimens of the pseudo-philological word-play so dear to the heart of Plato's Cratylus, as remarked above. The system is supposed to underlie all mythologies, Pagan, Jewish and Christian. It is the old teaching of macrocosm and microcosm, and the Self hidden in the heart of all.

The technical character of this exegesis and the nature of our essay compel us to give only a brief summary of the main ideas; but the subject is important enough to demand a special study in itself.

The spirit of man is imprisoned in the soul, his animal nature, and the soul in the body. The nature and evolution of this soul was set forth in the Gospel according to the Egyptians, a work which is unfortunately lost; could it possibly have explained the theriolatry of the Egyptians?

Now the Assyrians (who together with the Egyptians, were regarded by antiquity as the sacred nation *par excellence*), first taught that man was threefold and yet a unity. The soul is the desire principle, and all things have souls, even stones, for they increase and decrease.

Now the real man is male-female devoid of sex; therefore it strives to abandon the animal nature and return to the eternal essence above, where there is neither male nor female but a new creature.

Baptism was not the mere symbolical washing with physical water, but the bathing of the spirit in the "living water above," the eternal world, beyond the ocean of generation and destruction; and the anointing with oil was the introduction of the candidate into unfading bliss, thus becoming a Christ.

The kingdom of heaven is to be sought for within a man; it is the "blessed nature of all things which were, and are, and are still to be," spoken of in the Phrygian mysteries. It is of the nature of the spirit or mind, for as it is written in the Gospel according to Thomas: "He who seeks me shall find me in children from the age of seven years"; and this is the representative of the Logos in man.

Among the Egyptians, Osiris is the Water of Life, the Spirit or Mind, while Isis is "seven-robed nature, surrounded by and robed in seven æthereal mantles," the spheres of ever-changing generation which metamorphoze the ineffable, unimaginable incomprehensible mother substance; while the Mind, the Self, makes all things but remains unchanged, according to the saying: "I become what I will, and I am what I am; wherefore, say I, immovable is the mover of all. For it remains what it is, making all things, and is naught of the things which are." This also is called the Good, hence the saying: "Why callest thou me good? One only is good, my Father in the heavens."

Among the Greeks, Hermes is the Logos. He is the conductor and reconductor (the psychagogue and psychopomp), and originator of souls. They are brought down from the Heavenly Man above into the plasm of clay, the body, and thus made slaves to the demiurge of the world, the fiery or passionate god of creation. Therefore Hermes "holds a rod in his hands, beautiful, golden, wherewith he spell-binds the eyes of men whomsoever he would, and wakes them again from sleep." Therefore the saying: "Wake thou that sleepest, and rise, and Christ shall give thee light." This is the Christ, the Son of the Man, in all who are born; and this was set forth in the Eleusinian rites. This is also Ocean, "the generation of gods and the generation of men," the Great Jordan, as explained in the "Myth of the Going-forth," given above.

The Samothracians also taught the same truth; and in the temple of their mysteries were two statues, representing the Heavenly Man and the regenerate and spiritual man in all things co-essential with that Man. Such an one was the Christ, but his disciples had not yet reached to perfection. Hence the saying: "If ye drink not my blood and eat not my flesh, ye shall by no means enter into the kingdom of the heavens; but even if ye drink of the cup which I drink of, whither I go ye cannot come." And the Gnostic writer adds: "For he knew of what nature each of his disciples was, and that it needs must be that each of them should go to his own nature. For from the twelve tribes he chose twelve disciples, and through them he spake to every tribe. Wherefore (also) neither have all men hearkened to the preaching of the twelve disciples, nor if they hearken, can they receive it."

The mysteries of the Thracians and Phrygians are then referred to, and the same ideas further explained from the Old Testament documents. The vision of Jacob is explained as referring to the descent of spirit into matter, down the ladder of evolution, the Stream of the Logos flowing downward, and then again upward, through the gate of the Lord. Wherefore the saying: "I am the true gate." The Phrygians also called the spirit in man the "dead," because it was buried in the tomb and sepulchre of the body. Wherefore the saying: "Ye are whitened sepulchres, filled within with the bones of the dead,"—"for the living man is not in you." And again: "The dead shall leap forth from the tombs," that is to say, "from their material bodies, regenerated spiritual men, not carnal." For "this is the resurrection which takes place through the gate of the heavens, and they who pass not through it, all remain dead."

Many other interpretations of a similar nature are given, and it is shown that the Lesser Mysteries pertained to "fleshly generation,' whereas the Greater dealt with the new birth. "For this is the gate of heaven, and this is the house of God, where the Good God dwells alone, into which no impure man shall come, no psychic, no fleshly man; but it is kept under watch for the spiritual alone, where they must come, and, casting away their garments, all become bridegrooms made virgins by the Virginal Spirit. For such a man is the virgin with child who conceives and brings forth a son, which is neither psychic, animal, nor fleshly, but a blessed æon of æons."

This is the kingdom of the heavens, the "grain of mustard seed, the indivisible point, which is the primeval spark in the body, and which no man knoweth save only the spiritual."

The school of the Naaseni were all initiated into the Mysteries of the Great Mother, because they found that the whole mystery of rebirth was taught in these rites; they were also rigid ascetics. The name Naaseni was given them because they represented the "Moist Essence" of the universe—without which nothing which exists, "whether immortal or mortal, whether animate or inanimate, could hold together"—by the symbol of a serpent. This is the cosmic Âkâsha of the Upanishads, and the Kuṇḍalinî, or serpentine force in man, which when following an animal impulse is the force of generation, but when applied to spiritual things makes of a man a god. It is the Waters of Great Jordan flowing downwards (the generation of men) and upwards (the generation of gods); the Âkâsha-gangâ or Heavenly Ganges of the Purâṇas.

"He distributes beauty and bloom to all who are, just as the (river) 'proceeding forth out of Eden and dividing itself into four streams.'" In man, they said, Eden is the brain "compressed in surrounding vestures like heavens" and Paradise the man as far as the head only. These four streams are sight, hearing, smell, and taste. The river is the "water above the firmament (of the body)."

Thus, to use another set of symbolic terms, "the spiritual choose for themselves from the living waters of the Euphrates [the subtle world], which flows through the midst of Babylon [the gross world or body], what is fit, passing through the gate of truth, which is Jesus, the blessed," *i.e.*, the "gate of the heavens," or the sun, cosmically; and microcosmically the passing out of the body consciously through the highest centre in the head, which Hindu mystics call the Brahmarandhra. Thus these Gnostics claimed to be the true Christians because they were anointed with the "ineffable chrism," poured out by the serpentine "horn of plenty," another symbol for the spiritual power of enlightenment (Mahâ-buddhi).

We will conclude this brief sketch of these most interesting mystics by quoting one of their hymns. The text is unfortunately so corrupt that parts of it are hopeless, nevertheless sufficient remains to follow the thought. It tells of the World-Mind, the Father, the Chaos, the Cosmic Mother, and the third member of the primordial trinity, the World-Soul. Thence the individual soul, the pilgrim, and its sorrows and rebirth. Finally the descent of the saviour, the first-born of the Great Mind, and the regeneration of all. Back of all is the Ineffable, then comes first the First-born, the Logos:

"Mind was the first, the generative law of all;
Second was Chaos diffused, (child) of the first-born;
Thirdly, the toiling Soul received the law,
Wherefore surrounded with a watery form
It weary grows, subdued by death. . . . .
Now holding sway, it sees the light;
Anon, cast into piteous plight, it weeps.
Whiles, it weeps, it rejoices;
Now wails and is judged:
And now is judged and dies.
And now it cannot pass . . .
Into the labyrinth [of rebirth] it has wandered.
. . . . said: Father!
A searching after evil on the earth
Makes [man] to wander from thy Breath [Spirit].
He seeks to shun the bitter Chaos,
But knows not how to flee.
Wherefore, send me, O Father!
Seals in my hands, I will descend;
Through every æon I will tread my way;
All mysteries I'll reveal,
And show the shapes of gods;
The hidden secrets of the Holy Path
Shall take the name of Gnosis,
And I'll hand them on."

G. R. S. MEAD.

(*To be continued.*)

CATACLYSMS AND EARTHQUAKES.

EVERYTHING, says a familiar proverb, comes to those who wait, even the vindication, at the hands of exoteric science, of information acquired from the great teachers of occultism, however widely this may seem, at first sight, at variance with conventional views. Only within the last few weeks something fresh has come out about earthquakes which has an important bearing on the physical history of this world as interpreted by esoteric teaching and investigation. Almost everything that stands written in encyclopædias and popular textbooks concerning earthquakes is now out of date, and under the highest scientific auspices we are introduced to a view of this subject that begins to be in harmony with Nature's records in reference to the great geographical catastrophes that from time to time have altered the face of the globe.

The modern world is indebted to Japan for having done most up to the present time in the direction of elucidating the mystery of earthquakes. Certainly Japan has been better qualified than any other country to take a leading part in this investigation. It is favoured, if that phrase be admissible, with opportunities for studying earthquakes which no other country enjoys. On an average Japan endures three a day, not always on the scale of that which, in 1891, destroyed 10,000 lives and involved the government in an expenditure of 30 million dollars on repairs, but at all events of one kind or another. Perhaps for scientific purposes the little earthquakes are most useful. When towns are shivering in ruins, and railway viaducts being tied up into knots, the most zealous seismologist may get confused in his observations. But anyhow, taking all sorts together, Japan has plenty of seismological material to work with. The examination of this has become an intellectual fashion in Japan, and a seismograph is as common an article of luxury in a Japanese household, as a mantelpiece clock with us. The government has liberally subsidized the investigation, and a distinguished

English engineer has for some time past occupied what may be called the chair of earthquakes at the Tokio University.

Professor Milne, the engineer in question, has thus become the leading authority on earthquakes, and as such he lectured at the Royal Institution on Friday evening, February 12th. In the hour he had at his disposal he did not survey the various hypotheses that have been put forward from time to time to account for earthquakes, but it may be worth while to glance at these here, for the benefit of readers unfamiliar with the subject. The volcanic theory has perhaps been most in favour. Earthquakes, it has been assumed, have been underground disturbances that have not been near enough to the surface to break out as eruptions, but have nevertheless shaken and dislocated the upper strata. Another notion has been that they were due to the influx of sea water into internal cavities in the crust of the earth. Steam at a high temperature, it was supposed, would be engendered in this way, and an earthquake would ensue on the principle of an explosion in a steam boiler. Yet another theory suggested the reaction of certain chemical ingredients coming into contact in the interior cavities of the earth's crusts. Gases at a high pressure were thus supposed to be developed, and hence the explosive energy displayed. All these conjectures are equally dispelled by the results of the Japanese investigations. Professor Milne did not think it worth while even to notice the steam and chemical theories, but he paid the volcanic theory the compliment of a specific repudiation. We have arrived at the conclusion, he declared, that earthquakes have nothing whatever to do with volcanoes. They are not local phenomena at all, not due to causes engendered in the neighbourhood where they occur, but to great waves or pulsations to which the crust of the earth is constantly subject, the effect of which is not perceived unless some rupture ensues. The huge, slow waves or undulations are described in the new terminology of earthquake science as "bradyseismic" disturbances, and they are going on just as freely and steadily in quiet regions where earthquakes in the ordinary sense of the word are unknown, as in regions like Japan, or the west coast of South America, where they are frequent. But now and then it happens that as the bradyseismic wave encounters some irregular resistance or weakness in the strata it disturbs, something gives way, something cracks, and then a shiver goes through the region where that occurs. Such a shiver may in a few moments destroy property worth millions, and lives by the thousand.

Another influence productive of earthquake disturbance is described by Professor Milne as a "secular crush and flow." Observation has shown how wonderfully responsive the solid earth is to changes of weight pressing upon it. The deposition and evaporation of dew in the evening produces a sensible movement of the ground, sensible that is to say to the new and delicately adjusted seismographs in use for such observations. What then must be the effect of the regular denudation of continents that is always going on, and of the deposition of the mud carried down by rivers on the bottom of the sea? The latest conjecture is that this pressure is sufficient to cause an actual flow of solid rock away from the regions of greatest pressure. We know of course that solid and viscous are merely relative expressions. Treacle is only more viscous than lead, which in the ordinary course of bullet making is now squeezed, cold, out of holes by hydraulic pressure and flows like so much putty. Lead is only more viscous than steel. Ice, it is now suggested, is only more viscous than granite. Every solid substance is viscous in one degree or another. Imagine a thick, evenly spread bed of soft clay; then imagine a weight put down on any part of the surface. One sees at once that the weight would sink into the clay, more or less, and that part of the clay beneath would be squeezed out laterally, heaving up the surface elsewhere. That is just what takes place in connection with the secular flow of the earth's lower strata, and here we get into relations with a second great cause of earthquakes the effect of which, in causing a rupture of the superior strata somewhere, is similar, apparently, to the effect of the bradyseismic wave.

As a matter of fact, earthquakes are most numerous in those parts of the world where the seashore falls very abruptly into deep ocean. That occurs to the eastward of Japan and also on the western side of South America. But one of the most interesting facts now brought to light is that wherever an earthquake takes place, the shock of it is really felt all over the rest of the world. The vibration passes, apparently, through the solid body of the earth. We must leave off talking about the crust of the earth. That phrase is derived from an early hypothesis that has been discredited for a long while—that has been at variance with all the physical teaching permeating theosophical information, and is now clearly untenable in the light of the new seismology. The whole body of the earth is plainly capable of transmitting vibrations of the kind that are transmitted by matter of the utmost rigidity. There is evidence to show that the earthquake waves are communicated from one part of the world to another with definite velocities, and they do not make their way *round* the globe, they pass *through* it, by the most direct line that can be drawn from one point to another. The rate at which the vibrations are transmitted is extraordinarily high, in some instances approaching a speed of twelve kilometres per second, or double the rate at which a wave of compression could pass through steel or glass. Further than this, if this direct line passes only through a shallow segment of the earth, the rate of transmission is less rapid than if it passes through a greater mass. That is to say the most rapid transmission would be straight through, from any given point to its antipodal point. I say "would be" because up to the present time, seismological observations have not been carried out extensively enough to have provided for antipodal stations corresponding to the regions of most frequent disturbance, but the character of all observations that have been made at places widely separated indicate an increasing velocity in direct ratio with the depth through the earth followed by the course of transmission.

The trustworthiness of the inferences already arrived at as regards the rate at which the vibrations travel, is shown by the fact that already it is possible to tell, from observations in England, at what moment an earthquake has taken place in Japan. Professor Milne has a seismological observatory in the Isle of Wight, and already he has been enabled on some occasions to anticipate the announcements of the telegraph in reference to earthquakes in Japan. In August last he announced before any telegraphic news had been received, that such an event had taken place on a certain date, at such and such an hour and minute. When the news came in the ordinary course of things, it turned out that he had been right within an error of one minute only. In another case when the papers announced that a great earthquake had taken place at Kobe, his instruments had given no indications to correspond. He declared the news to be inaccurate, and in due time it turned out to have been without foundation.

The importance of all this as bearing on questions in which theosophical students are interested, has to do with the light it throws on the old standing question of cataclysms. The drift of conventional scientific thinking for some time past has been in the direction of what geologists call uniformity. We do not see cataclysms going on around us at present, but we do see the gradual operation of forces that over very long periods of time may be supposed capable of superinducing the changes of land and water distribution that must assuredly take place. Rain and the rivers are continually washing down the soil of continents to the sea. In this way ocean beds are being filled up and existing land surfaces denuded. Shores in some places are being eaten away by the sea, and in other places slowly raised, so that former beaches are now hoisted half-way up high cliffs. In time it is supposed by the uniformitarians, these gradual processes would suffice to account for the largest changes we like to imagine. They would not account, however, for the violent convulsions of which theosophical teachers speak as having happened in the past, and of which, indeed, advancing theosophical students, beginning to be able to apply their own powers of observation to remote historical investigation, are enabled to speak with much detail. Those of us who comprehend the trustworthiness of investigation of that sort, may have no doubt about the fact, whether modern science yet recognizes it or not, but it is always gratifying to derive from modern science confirmation of theosophic teaching. And while the local theory of earthquakes held the field, no such confirmation was forthcoming in reference to such events in the past as the destruction of Atlantis. Now we begin to perceive along what road the ultimate developments of physical knowledge will converge towards the conclusions of occult investigation. The bradyseismical waves of the new seismology fit in perfectly with a belief, that at long intervals of time, natural convulsions may occur on a very much larger scale than that of any which have been recorded within historic periods. Some of these of course have been fairly big, the Lisbon catastrophe not only killed 60,000 people at the seat of its chief activity, but distributed its influence perceptibly over an area according to Humboldt's calculation four times as great as Europe. As we know now, its influence must really have been felt all over the world, though in distant places too slightly to be measured by instruments then in use. The Calabrian earthquake of 1783 destroyed 40,000 lives. But after all disasters of this magnitude are not commensurable with the least of the great Atlantean catastrophes. According to the Troano MS., translated by Dr. Le Plongeon, sixty *million* people perished in the final Poseidonis convulsion which changed an inhabited territory, measuring over two thousand miles one way by about one thousand two hundred the other, into so much ocean bed. For people to whom the six or seven thousand years of the historic period seem to afford a good basis for generalization, it naturally appears unlikely that if our Lisbon earthquake is the champion convulsion for that period, anything so out of proportion with it should have taken place six or seven thousand years earlier.

The bradyseismic wave system taken in conjunction with the secular flow of rocks, puts a new complexion on all such speculation. Everything we know about vibrations tends to show that in nature these movements are super-imposed one upon another. In electrical phenomena this is certainly the case, and in fact the whole principle of multiplex telegraphy is built upon that idea. Occult investigation into the nature of the ultimate atom points to the same kind of complexity there. In the motion of the planetary bodies we have to recognize similar movements within movements. The diurnal rotation of the earth is super-imposed upon the much slower precessional, or second, rotation. Whatever the great pulsations of the earth's surface may be due to, it is more than imaginable that a larger and slower pulsation passes through it at longer intervals. Earthquakes of the secondary order like those which afflicted Lisbon in the last century are due apparently to a rupture of some rock body giving way to the pressure of one of the relatively minor undulations of the strata below. A pulsation of greater magnitude may easily be supposed to create a superficial disturbance on a different scale altogether, one for which perhaps a long continued operation of the secular rock flow, has prepared the way.

In addressing theosophical readers, a word or two seems desirable here on the question whether such catastrophes as those of the

Atlantean age, should be attributed to causes of uniform regularity or to the intervention of the highest authorities connected with the government of the world, at crises when the depravity of mankind renders the extinction of life on a large scale a necessity of the situation. The destruction of Atlantis has generally been talked of with reference to some such intervention. But everything we learn about the evolution of the race to which we belong, points to the synchronism between the regular progress of natural law and the development of crises in human destiny. The recognition of this synchronism will not interfere with our simultaneous recognition of free will as regards the individual. No one is bound to give way to the temptations of his race or period in evolution, but taking the stupendous numbers concerned into account, it is certain that so many, within a limit of error, will follow the stream, while so many will strike out a path for themselves. In Atlantean ages the course of the stream was in a direction which, at all events for us, would be the direction of evil. Sooner or later it was inevitable that a condition of things should be developed which would require a violent remedy. One need hardly be surprised to find that the remedy under those circumstances was provided for by a geological crisis, towards which the earth's strata had been moving all the while that the Atlantean majority were working out the moral necessity of their own destruction.

A. P. SINNETT.

THE MOST ANCIENT LAWS OF THE GREEKS.

The most ancient law-giver of the Athenians is said to have been Triptolemus, who was also the founder of the Eleusinian Mysteries. Three of his laws were preserved at Eleusis, and ran as follows:

Honour thy parents.

Sacrifice to the gods with the fruits of the earth.

Injure not animals.

THEOSOPHY AND SCIENCE.

(*Concluded from Vol. XIX. p.* 495.)

LET us now see what light materialistic philosophy throws upon morals and religion. Let us see what the doctrine of evolution teaches us in regard to the nature and origin of ethics and morality. I think that we shall find, after we have completed our investigation, that science is unable to account satisfactorily for the moral faculties in man, and that we cannot find in science a sanction for morality or a basis for religion. After all, as Kant said, the ultimate object of all science is to give replies to these three questions:

First. What can I do? Second. What ought I to do? Third. What may I hope for?

Science, then, is not an end in herself, she is only a means to an end. Science is the servant of man, not his master. The service of science consists in placing nature at man's disposal and enabling him to subdue it to his social wants.

I will now show you from one of the greatest lights of modern science, Professor Huxley, that the modern doctrine of evolution fails to account for man's moral nature, or to throw any light upon the origin of man's ethical faculties. Several eminent materialists have tried to elaborate the evolution of ethics without success. Nature casts no light upon this subject. Shortly before Huxley died he read a very remarkable paper before a scientific society in England, entitled "Evolution and Ethics," which created quite a stir in the scientific world at the time. Huxley had always been looked upon as the model scientific materialist by his fellow scientists of the same persuasion, and had acted as their spokesman on all great occasions. When this lecture appeared in the latter part of 1893 it created quite a disturbance among the followers of Huxley, for it was really a confession that scientific materialism had proved a failure. Indeed, the whole lecture may be regarded as an essay showing the relation of ancient eastern philosophies to the modern doctrine of evolution. There you will find the ethics of evolution discussed in the light of the ancient sages and philosophers of India, in such a full and lucid manner, and with such copious references, that you are convinced that Huxley must have been thoroughly acquainted with the literature of Theosophy. Listen to what Huxley writes. He says:

"Modern thought is making a fresh start from the base whence Indian and Greek philosophy set out, and the human mind being very much what it was six and twenty centuries ago, there is no ground for wonder if it presents indications of a tendency to move along the old lines to the same results."

After discussing the attempts of the materialistic evolutionists to account for the moral sentiments by a process of evolution on the principles of natural selection according to cosmic law, he says:

"But, as the immoral sentiments have no less been evolved, there is so far as much natural sanction for the one as for the other. The thief and the murderer follow nature just as much as the philanthropist. Cosmic evolution may teach us how the good and the evil tendencies of man may have come about, but in itself it is incompetent to furnish any better reason why what we call good is preferable to what we call evil than we had before." This is assuredly a confession on the part of Huxley of the inadequacy of science to furnish an ethical standard. Then again he says:

"As I have already urged, the practice of that which is ethically best—what we call goodness or virtue—involves a course of conduct which in all respects is opposed to that which leads to success in the cosmic struggle for existence. In place of ruthless self-assertion it demands self-restraint, in place of thrusting aside or treading down all competitors, it requires that the individual shall not merely respect, but shall help his fellows; its influence is directed not so much to the survival of the fittest, as to the fitting of as many as possible to survive. It repudiates the gladiatorial theory of existence. Let us understand, once for all, that the ethical progress of society depends not on imitating the cosmic process, still less in running away from it, but in combating it.

Laws and moral precepts are directed to the end of curbing the cosmic process and reminding the individual of his duty to the community, to the protection and influence of which he owes, if not existence itself, at least the life of something better than a brutal savage. The pertinacious optimism of our philosophers hid from them the actual state of the case. It prevented them from seeing that cosmic nature is no school of virtue, but the headquarters of the enemy of ethical nature. The logic of facts was necessary to convince them that the cosmos works through the lower nature of man not for righteousness but against it."

Such is the verdict of the great Huxley shortly before his death. What noble words they are! Would that I had the power to sound them throughout the length and breadth of the land. What is the matter with the world to-day? Is it not that it has become saturated with the deadly and degrading doctrines of materialism? Man looks no longer upon fellow-man as a brother, but as an enemy to be crushed in the struggle of life. Those deadly and degrading doctrines have taught men to believe that they are justified in pushing to the wall their weaker brethren, and building their own success upon their downfall. Does not this doctrine saturate the whole of society to-day from top to bottom? As John Morley says: "The souls of men have become void, and into that void have entered the seven devils of secularity." As for me, I am altogether lacking in the breadth of mind necessary to regard such a doctrine with equanimity; I believe that it is dangerous to teach a nation such a doctrine, which can only do one thing, and that is, create hell upon earth. Any doctrine which teaches that morality is but a farce, that duty is but self-interest disguised, and that man must look down to the brutes for an example of proper conduct, must have the most vile and degrading influence. Here we have a confession from science herself, from the mouth of its most advanced advocate, that the materialistic evolutionary theory of morals has proved a failure, and that it is totally inadequate to account for the ethics of morality. This confession tears off the disguise in which this theory has been concealed for half a century. You will notice in this confession that modern science has been compelled to pass beyond the boundaries of materialism; being unable to find the truth within itself, it has been compelled to overleap its own boundaries and to ennunciate the doctrines of Theosophy. What are the teachings of Theosophy in this respect? Theosophy teaches that the path to a higher life lies in the subjection of the lower self to the higher self. This is the path to a higher evolution of human consciousness. It teaches that our lower natures are constantly dragging us downward; they oppose the upward progress. Now we find that this is just exactly the conclusion which Huxley comes to. Listen again to what he says: "The cosmos works through the lower nature of man, not for righteousness but against it." Is not this similar to the esoteric doctrine which Paul preached:

"I find then a law, that, when I would do good, evil is present with me. For I delight in the law of God after the inward man; but I see another law in my members, warring against the law of my mind, and bringing me into captivity to the law of sin which is in my members. O wretched man that I am, who shall deliver me from the body of this death?" You see then that Huxley and St. Paul arrived at the same conclusion by different paths. The one through the theosophical teachings of Jesus, the other through the path of science. Hear Huxley again:

"The practice of that which is ethically best—what we call goodness or virtue—involves a course of conduct which in *all* respects is opposed to that which leads to success in the cosmic struggle for existence. In place of ruthless self-assertion, it demands self-restraint; in place of thrusting aside or treading down all competitors, it requires that the individual shall not merely respect but help his fellows. It repudiates the gladiatorial theory of existence. Let us understand once for all," he says, "that the ethical progress of society depends, not on imitating the cosmic process, still less in running away from it, but in combating it." This also is the conclusion of the philosopher Hegel, who puts it thus:

"Freedom as the ideal of that which is original and natural does not exist as original and natural—rather must it be first sought and won, and that by an incalculable medial discipline of the intellectual and moral powers. The state of nature is therefore predominantly that of injustice and violence, of untamed natural impulses, of inhuman deeds and feelings."

Here then we have Huxley and Hegel preaching pure Theosophy. Theosophy teaches that the higher life of man is a constant warring against his lower nature. Every man contains within himself a higher and a lower self. These two selves are engaged in a perpetual warfare with one another. The lower self is the self of individual desire. It is constantly telling man that he as a rational or self-conscious being, is a law and end to himself. In this is involved the principle that ultimately he can know and obey nothing but himself. As Professor Caird, in discussing the Hegelian philosophy, points out, this doctrine is the denial of all relation of the individual either in thought or action to anything but himself.

In its ultimate analysis, we find that the attempt to realize the lower self as against the higher self is suicidal; it ends in the loss or death of the soul. Now, the life of the higher self depends on the death of the lower. The way to self-realization is through self-sacrifice, through self-renunciation—through self-renunciation of that natural and immediate life of the lower self in which it is opposed to the higher self. Spiritual life is not like natural life—a direct outgoing of energy, which eventually meets death as an external enemy, and in it finds its limits and its end. On the contrary, the life of a spiritual being, as such, is in a true sense a continual dying. Every step in it is won by a break with the lower self—which is opposed to the higher self; for only as the lower self dies can the higher self be developed. For this reason then there is no absolute death for the higher spiritual self. Because it is capable of dying to itself, because, indeed, it cannot live but by some kind of dying to self, it cannot in any final sense die; it takes up death into itself as an element and does not therefore need to fear it as an enemy. This is the language of Jesus Christ himself, and of all the great spiritual teachers of humanity—the language of St. Paul and of St. Augustine, of Thomas à Kempis and Martin Luther. It is the language of the poet Tennyson, who says:

> I hold it true with him who sings,
> To one clear harp in divers tones,
> That men may rise on stepping stones,
> Of their dead selves to higher things.

The great Christian maxim is: "He that saveth his life shall lose it, and he that loseth his life shall save it." St. Paul tells us: "I die daily unto sin." But long before Jesus or St. Paul appeared, this same truth was one of the most important in the ancient philosophy of India. As far back as modern research has been able to investigate, we find that this same doctrine was promulgated by Indian sages and adepts. There is no doubt that the wise men who, as the New Testament tells, came from the east to bow down at the manger of Jesus, knew of this truth, and that in the babe which lay before them, they hoped to see its realization and fulfilment.

There are many other important points in Theosophy which the limits of this article will not allow me to touch upon; such as the law of karma and reincarnation, the astral body, the existence in man of the psychic powers of clairvoyance, clairaudience, psychometry and so on. All of these subjects are of intense interest in the light of recent investigations, and each in itself would form the subject of a special article.

The researches of science are every day proving more and more that there are latent in man psychic powers of which the western world up to the present has never dreamed. These powers are now subjects of investigation by many of the greatest scientists of the age. Such men as Swedenborg, Bruno and Jacob Boehme, are now no longer regarded as crazy dreamers labouring under mental diseases and hallucinations, but as men who saw and experienced wonderful realities beyond the ordinary range of human consciousness. Science, from scoffing at them, has now turned to study them. Scoffing cannot explain. The experiences of these mystics were as real to them as common every-day experiences are to the ordinary individual. The fact that we do not possess these psychic faculties does not warrant us calling others who do possess them fools and lunatics. Science has always been too dogmatic. The Puritans who fled to the new world from political intolerance in the old, themselves fell into the error of religious intolerance in the new world. And so it has been in many cases with science. She emancipates us from one form of dogmatism, and often unconsciously weaves about our necks the chains of another form. Science is by no means entitled to assume the lordly airs she very often puts on. We see on every hand the apotheosis of natural law, as if natural law ever has explained, or can explain anything. After discussing this subject, Jevons in his *Principles of Science*, the greatest work of the kind in the English language, says:

"I fear that I have very imperfectly succeeded in expressing my strong conviction that before a rigorous logical scrutiny, the Reign of Law will prove to be an unverified hypothesis, the uniformity of nature an ambiguous expression."

Nature is too infinitely complicated to be solved by the finite methods of science. All laws and explanations are in a certain sense hypothetical, and mathematicians substitute imaginary objects for the real ones. As Jevons says:

"We speak and calculate about inflexible bars, inextensible lines, heavy points, homogeneous substances, uniform spheres, perfect fluids and gases, and we deduce a great number of beautiful theorems, but all is hypothetical. There is no such thing as an inflexible bar, an inextensible line, nor any one of the other perfect objects of mechanical science; they are to be classed with those mythical existences, the straight line, triangle, etc., about which Euclid reasoned so freely."

Even the great law of gravitation, about which we have heard so much since our childhood, is not absolutely established. Newton himself, who discovered it, admitted that there were motions in the planetary system which he could not reconcile with the law. The greatest mathematicians, such as Euler, Clairaut and D'Alembert did not think the law sufficiently established to account for all the phenomena. They did not feel certain that the force of gravity exactly obeyed the well-known rule. In astronomy, the utmost powers of mathematical analysis have been unable to correctly solve the problem of even three attracting bodies, much less of four, five or six bodies. Now, the universe consists of an infinite number of bodies; how then can mathematical analysis solve it? In all the calculations of science there is always bound to be some factor left out of consideration, and the best solution is only an approximation.

I will now quote you a confession from the greatest scientist of the nineteenth century. I presume that no one will dispute the authority of Lord Kelvin to speak on the subject. As a great scientist, Lord Kelvin is filled with the spirit of true humility, and like Socrates he is wise because he knows his own ignorance. In his address at Glasgow, in June last, on the occasion of the celebration of his jubilee as Professor of Natural Philosophy in the University of Glasgow, he used the following language:

"I might perhaps rightly feel pride in knowing that the University and City of Glasgow have conferred on me the great honour of holding this jubilee. I do feel profoundly grateful, but when I think how infinitely little is all that I have done, I cannot feel pride, I only see the great kindness of my scientific comrades, and of my friends, in crediting me for so much. One word characterizes the most strenuous of the efforts for the advancement of science that I have made during fifty-five years—that word is failure. I know no more of electric and magnetic force, or of the relation between ether, electricity and ponderable matter, or of chemical affinity, than I knew and tried to teach my students of natural philosophy fifty years ago in my first session as Professor."

Here we have the foremost physicist of the age confessing that all his labours of fifty years may be summed up in the one word "failure"; that he knows no more about the deeper questions of science than he did fifty years ago. How different this is from Tyndall, in his famous Belfast address. *He* gave out to the world that he had solved the whole problem; *he* had decided that there was no God in the universe; *he* decided that in matter itself lay the "promise and potency of life." Ah, how the world has changed since that time!

If Lord Kelvin does not know what he is talking about, I would like to know who does? Now, Madam Blavatsky did a great service to the world in breaking many of the idols of science, the idols in the market place which Bacon speaks about. She was a great iconoclast. In her *Isis Unveiled* and the *Secret Doctrine* she exposes many of the weaknesses of science, the absurdity of many of its theories and their self-contradictions, and how that utter anarchy prevails in the scientific world with respect to many of the most important problems of science. Her works have certainly had a most salutary influence on my own mind. I owe to her a debt of gratitude, and I regret I did not become acquainted with them sooner.

I will say one word more in closing. The world to-day is filled with men and women, who, dissatisfied with the old orthodoxy in which they were perhaps reared and nurtured, and tired of the absurdities of its dogmas and traditions, are eagerly looking around for a more rational and ennobling faith. The religious faiths of the world are undergoing a profound transformation. Our conceptions of the universe and man are undergoing a profound transformation. In the opinion of many thinkers, it will end either in the complete extinction of religion or in its transformation. I prefer to believe that it will end in the latter. There is a profound conviction in the minds of our best thinkers to-day that we are now entering upon one of those great critical periods which mark the history of human thought and intellectual advancement. A great religious revolution is now upon us, in which old beliefs are passing away and new ones are being formed in harmony with the new knowledge. The fountains of the deep are breaking out, the old continents of human thought are fast sinking, and the new continents are emerging. The spirit of the age beckons us onward to these new continents. Where then shall we go; to what point shall we migrate? What have the great scientists to offer us? You may well say to them: "You have taken away our religion, what are you going to give us instead?" Alas, they have nothing to offer us! Is it not true, as Matthew Arnold puts it:

> The kings of modern thought are dumb,
> Silent they are though not content,
> And wait to see the future come;
> They have the grief men had of yore,
> But they contend and cry no more.

Man must have religion. He has always called for it; he calls for it still. Can any system of socialism or communism take the place of religion? No; and for this reason. Socialism and communism are simply political solutions of a problem which is far deeper than politics. It involves far higher questions than politics. As has been pointed out: "Communism is the goal towards which society tends, not a path by which that goal may be reached. Neither co-operation, nor watchwords of fraternity, however sincerely translated into action, can pretend to compass the whole problem." For suppose all political questions settled, and everything working harmoniously for the time being. What then? Will all be settled then? Will not the deep and urgent questions of religion and philosophy still demand an answer? Will not the human soul still enquire about its origin and destiny? Will it not cry, Whence came I and whither am I going? These questions then would still be left to the care of the priests and preachers, who cannot agree among themselves, and as every social system is founded on a system of ideas believed in common, as we cannot in social problems isolate the political from the moral, and the moral from the religious, communism would leave society to its anarchy. The present anarchy in politics arises from anarchy in fundamental ideas. The ancient faiths are shattered, and the hearts and minds of men are not yet united on the new faith which is still to come. What the world wants to-day is a system of religion and philosophy which will unite the hearts and souls of men, and which will satisfactorily answer the questions of science,.life and religion, teaching us our relation to the world, to duty and to God.

Deep down in the hearts of men, underneath all social systems, there must first be unity of religious ideas, hopes and aspirations, before there can be political unity. Is there then any philosophy or religion universal enough to do this? Is there any system of truth which will satisfactorily answer all the questions of man's nature? Theosophy makes this claim; it claims to be the universal synthesis of all religions and philosophies. It claims to be the great alembic into which all the great religions and philosophies of the world may be poured, and from which they will emerge purified and purged of their dross and superstition. There are many things in Theosophy which lead me to think that this is its destiny. It is incumbent on every seeker after truth, and upon everyone who would like to be instrumental in promoting that unity tó examine each one for himself that claim.

As for myself, I will say with Lowell:

My soul is not a palace of the past,
Where outworn creeds like Rome's gray senate quake;
The time is ripe and rotten ripe for change;
Then let it come. I have no fear of what
Is called for by the instinct of mankind.
Nor think I that God's will will fall apar
Because we tear a parchment more or less.
Truth is eternal, but her effluence
With endless change is fitted to the hour.
Her mirror is turned forward to reflect
The promise of the future, not the past.

JOHN MACKENZIE.

OUR RELATION TO CHILDREN.

It cannot be denied that from the Theosophic standpoint the subject of our relation to children is an exceedingly important and practical one. Realizing as we must the purpose for which the ego descends into incarnation, and knowing to how great an extent its attainment of that purpose depends upon the training given to its various vehicles during their childhood and growth, we cannot but feel, if we think at all, that a tremendous responsibility attaches to all of us who are in any way connected with children, whether as parents, elder relatives, or teachers. It is well, therefore, that we should consider what hints Theosophy can give us as to the way in which we can best discharge this responsibility.

It may seem presumptuous that a bachelor should venture to offer suggestions to parents upon a subject so especially their own ; so I ought, perhaps, to preface such remarks as I wish to make, by saying that, though I have none of my own, I have always been fond of children, and in very close relation with them through almost the whole of my life—for many years as a Sunday-school and night-school teacher, then as a clergyman, school-manager, and choir trainer, and as head-master of a large boys' school. So that I am at any rate speaking from long, practical experience, and not merely vaguely theorizing.

Before making suggestions, however, I should like to draw attention to the present condition of our relation to children—to boys, at any rate—here in the midst of our European civilization. The practical result of nineteen centuries of ostensibly Christian teaching is that our boys live among us as an alien race, with laws and rules of life of their own entirely different from ours, and with a code of morals of their own, also entirely different from that by which we consider ourselves bound. They regard grown-up people (in the mass) with scarcely-veiled hostility, or at the best with a kind of armed neutrality, and always with deep distrust, as foreigners whose motives are incomprehensible to them, and whose actions are perpetually interfering in the most unwarrantable and apparently malicious manner with their right to enjoy themselves in their own way.

This may sound rather a startling statement to those who have never considered the matter, but any parent who has boys at one of our large schools will appreciate the truth of it; and if he can look back to his own schooldays, and in thought realize once more the feelings and conditions of that period, which most of us have so entirely forgotten, he will recognize, perhaps with a start of surprise, that it is not an inaccurate description of what his own attitude once was.

It is noteworthy that wherever the laws and customs of this race, living among us, yet not of us, differ from ours, they are invariably a reversion to an earlier type, and tend in the direction of primitive savagery—a fact which might be cited in support of the Theosophical theory that in each incarnation, before the ego has acquired control of its vehicles, the earlier stages of our evolution are hurriedly run through once more. The only right recognized among them is the right of the strongest; the boy who rules their little state is not the best boy, nor the cleverest boy, but simply the one who can fight best; and their leadership is usually decided by combat, just as it is to this day among many a savage tribe.

Their code of morals is distinctly their own, and though it cannot be so directly paralleled among primitive races as some of their other customs, it is decidedly on a far lower level than even our own. To oppress and ill-treat the weak, and even to torture them to the utmost limit of endurance, seems to be regarded as a comparatively innocent form of recreation, and it would be only a very severe case indeed which would arouse even a passing manifestation of public opinion against the offender. The theft of money is still, happily, regarded as contemptible, but the theft of fruit or jam is not; nor, indeed, would the stealing of anything eatable be considered criminal. Falsehood of the most outrageous kind is regarded as not only allowable but amusing, when practised upon some too-credulous youngster; if resorted to in order to conceal from an adult the misdeeds of a fellow-criminal it is often looked upon as heroic and noble. But the most heinous crime of all—the very lowest abyss of turpitude—is to call in the intervention of a grown-up person to right even the most flagrant of wrongs; and many a weak and nervous child endures agonies both physically and mentally from the barbarity of bullies without breathing a word of his sufferings either to parent or teacher—so deep is the distrust with which public opinion amongst boys regards the hostile race of adults.

I am in no way blind to the good side of public school life, to the courage and self-reliance which it gives to the strong and hardy lad, and the training in the command of others with which it provides the members of its higher forms. I suppose that England is the only country on earth where the maintenance of order in the small world of school life can be (and is) left practically in the hands of the boys themselves, and there is much in this to be highly commended; but I am at present concerned with the relations between boys as a class and adults as a class, and it can hardly be denied that on the whole these are somewhat strained, the distrust of which I have spoken on the one side being but too frequently met by dislike and entire want of comprehension on the other.

Surely there is something wrong about all this; surely some improvement might be brought about in this unfortunate condition of mutual hostility and mistrust. Of course there are honourable exceptions—there are boys who trust their masters, and masters who trust their boys, and I myself have never found any difficulty in winning the confidence of the juveniles by treating them properly; but in a sadly large number of instances the case is as I have described it.

That it need not be so is shown not only by the exceptions mentioned above, but by the condition of affairs which we find existing in some Oriental lands. I have not yet had the pleasure of visiting the empire of Japan, but I hear from those who have been there and have made some study of this question, that there is no country in the world where children are so well and so sensibly treated—where their relations with their elders are so completely satisfactory. Harshness, it is said, is entirely unknown, yet the children in no way presume upon the gentleness of the older people. In India and Ceylon I have occasionally seen instances of undue severity, but certainly on the whole the relations of children and adults are more rational there than they usually are here.

No doubt this is partly due to the difference of race. The Oriental boy usually has not the irrepressible animal spirits and the intense physical activity of his English representative, nor has he his pronounced aversion to mental exertion. Strange and incomprehensible as it would sound to the ears of a British schoolboy, the Indian child is really eager to learn, and is always willing to do any amount of work out of school-hours in order that he may make more rapid progress. It is no injustice to the average English boy to say that he regards play as the most important part of his life, and that he looks upon lessons as distinctly a bore, to be avoided as far as possible, or perhaps as a kind of game which he has to play against his teacher. If the latter can force him to learn anything, that counts as a score to the side of authority; but if he can anyhow escape without learning a lesson, then he in turn has scored a point. In the East such a boy is the exception and not the rule; the majority of them are really anxious to learn, and co-operate intelligently with their master instead of offering him ceaseless though passive resistance.

Perhaps if I describe a little incident which I have more than once witnessed in Ceylon, it will help my readers to understand how different the position of children really is in an Oriental race. Readers of *The Arabian Nights* will remember how it constantly happens that when some king or great man is sitting in judgment, a casual passer-by—perhaps a porter or a beggar—breaks in and offers *his* opinion on the matter in hand, and is politely listened to, instead of being summarily arrested or ejected for such a breach of the proprieties. Impossible as this seems to us, it was undoubtedly absolutely true to life, and on a smaller scale the same sort of thing occurs to-day. It came in the course of my work to travel about among the villages of Ceylon, trying to induce their residents to appreciate the advantages of education, and to found schools in which their children could be systematically taught their own religion instead of being left either to the haphazard instruction of the monks at the pansalas, or to the proselytizing efforts of the Christian missionaries.

When I arrived at a village I called upon the headman, and asked him to convoke the inhabitants to hear what I had to say; and after the address the chief people of the place usually held a sort of council to decide where and how their school should be built and how they could best set about the work. Such a council was generally held in the verandah of the headman's house or under a great tree close by, with the whole village in attendance around the debaters. More than once on such occasions I have seen a small boy of ten or twelve stand up respectfully before the great people of his little world, and suggest deferentially that if the school were erected in the place proposed it would make it exceedingly inconvenient for such and such children to attend; and in every case the small boy was treated precisely as an adult would have been, the local grandees listening courteously and patiently, and allowing their due weight to the juvenile's arguments. What would happen if in England an agricultural labourer's child publicly offered a suggestion to the county magnates gathered in solemn assembly, one hardly dares to imagine; probably that child's suppression would be summary and unpleasant; but as a matter of fact the situation is absolutely unthinkable under our present conditions.

How, it may be asked, is it proposed that this position of mutual mistrust and misunderstanding should be improved? Well, it is evident that in cases where this breach already exists, it can only be bridged over by unwearying kindness, and by gradual, patient but constant efforts to promote a better understanding by steadily showing unselfish affection and sympathy; in fact, by habitually putting ourselves in the child's place and trying to realize exactly how all these matters appear to him. If we who are adults had not so entirely forgotten our own childish days, we should make far greater allowances for the children of to-day, and should understand and get on with them much better.

This is, however, very emphatically one of the cases in which the old proverb holds good which tells us that prevention is better than cure. If we will but take a little trouble to begin in the right way with our children from the very first, we shall easily be able to avoid the undesirable state of affairs which we have been describing. And this is exactly where Theosophy has many a valuable hint to offer to those who are in earnest in wishing to do their duty by the young ones committed to their charge.

Of course the absolute nature of this duty of parents and teachers towards children must first be recognized. It cannot be too strongly or too repeatedly insisted upon that parentage is an exceedingly heavy responsibility of a religious nature, however lightly and thoughtlessly it may often be undertaken. Those who bring a child into the world make themselves directly responsible to the law of karma for the opportunities of evolution which they ought to give to that ego, and heavy indeed will be their penalty if by their carelessness or selfishness they put hindrances in his path, or fail to render him all the help and guidance which he has a right to expect from them. Yet how often the modern parent entirely ignores this obvious responsibility; how often a child is to him nothing but a cause of fatuous vanity or an object of thoughtless neglect.

Now, if we want to understand our duty towards the child we must first consider how he came to be what he is—that is to say, we must trace him back in thought to his previous incarnation. Fifteen hundred years ago or so your child was perhaps a Roman citizen, perhaps a philosopher of Alexandria, perhaps an early Briton; but whatever may have been his outward circumstances he had a definite disposition of his own—a character containing various more or less developed qualities, some good and some bad. In due course of time that life of his came to an end; but remember that whether that end came slowly by disease or old age, or swiftly by some accident or violence, its advent made no sudden change of any sort in his character. A curious delusion seems to prevail in many quarters that the mere fact of death will at once turn a demon into a saint—that, whatever a man's life may have been, the moment he dies he becomes practically an angel of goodness. No idea could possibly be further from the truth, as those whose work lies in trying to help the departed know full well. The casting off of a man's physical body no more alters his disposition than does the casting off of his overcoat; he is precisely the same man the day after his death as he was the day before, with the same vices and the same virtues.

True, now that he is functioning only on the astral plane he has not the same opportunities of displaying them; but though they may manifest themselves in the kâmalokic life in quite a different manner, they are none the less still there, and the conditions and duration of that life are their result. On that plane he must stay until the energy poured forth by his lower desires and emotions during physical life has worn itself out—until the astral body which he has made for himself disintegrates; for only then can he leave it for the higher and more peaceful realm of Devachan. But though those particular passions are for the time worn out and done with for him, the germs of the qualities in him, which made it possible for them to exist in his nature, are still there. They are latent and ineffective, certainly, because desire of that type requires astral matter for its manifestation; they are what Madame Blavatsky once called "privations of matter," but they are quite ready to come into renewed activity, if stimulated, when the man again finds himself under conditions where they can act.

An analogy may, perhaps, if not pushed too far, be of use in helping us to grasp this idea. If a small bell be made to ring continuously in an air-tight vessel, and the air be then gradually withdrawn, the sound will grow fainter and fainter, until it becomes inaudible. The bell is still ringing as vigorously as ever, yet its vibration is no longer manifest to our ears, because the medium by means of which alone it can produce any effect upon them is absent. Admit the air to the vessel, and immediately you hear the sound of the bell once more, just as before. Similarly there are certain qualities in man's nature which need astral matter for their manifestation, just as sound needs either air or some denser matter for its vehicle; and when, in the process of his withdrawal into himself after what we call death, he leaves the astral plane for the devachanic, those qualities can no longer find expression, and must therefore perforce remain latent. But when, centuries later, on his downward course into reincarnation he re-enters the astral plane, these qualities which have remained latent for so long manifest themselves once more, and become the tendencies of the next personality.

In exactly the same way there are qualities belonging to the lower manas which need for their expression the matter of the rûpa levels of Devachan; and when after his long devachanic period the consciousness of the man withdraws into the true ego upon the arûpa levels these qualities also pass into latency.

But when the ego is about to reincarnate, it has to reverse this process of withdrawal—to pass downward through the very same planes through which it came on its upward journey. When the time of its outflow comes, it puts itself down first on to the rûpa levels of its own plane, and seeks to express itself there as far as is possible in that less perfect and less plastic matter. And in order that it may so express itself and function upon that plane it must clothe itself in the matter of the plane, just as an entity at a spiritualistic séance when it wishes to move physical objects materializes a temporary physical hand with which to do it, or at any rate employs physical forces of some kind to produce its results. It is not at all necessary that such a hand should be materialized sufficiently to be visible to our dull, ordinary sight, but to produce a physical result there must be materialization to a certain extent—as far as etheric matter, at any rate.

Thus the ego aggregates around itself matter of the rûpa planes of Devachan—the matter which will afterwards become its mind-body. But this matter is not selected at random; on the contrary, out of all the varied and inexhaustible store around him he attracts to himself just such a combination as is perfectly fitted to give expression to his latent mental qualities. In exactly the same way, when he makes the further descent on to the astral plane, the matter of that plane which is by natural law attracted to him to serve as his vehicle in that world, is exactly that which will give expression to the kâmic tendencies which were his at the conclusion of his last birth. In point of fact, he resumes his life on each plane just where he left it last time.

Observe that these are not as yet in any way qualities in action: they are simply the germs of qualities, and for the moment their only influence is to secure for themselves a possible field of manifestation by providing suitable matter for their expression in the various vehicles of the man. Whether they develope once more in this life into the same definite tendencies as in the last one, will depend very largely upon the encouragement or otherwise given to them by the surroundings of the child during its early years. Any one of them, good or bad, may be very readily stimulated into activity by encouragement, or on the other hand may be, as it were, starved out for lack of that encouragement. If stimulated, it becomes a more powerful factor in the man's life this time than it was in his previous existence; if starved out, it remains all through the life merely as an unfructified germ, and does not make its appearance in the succeeding incarnation at all.

This, then, is the condition of the child when first he comes under his parents' care. He cannot be said to have as yet a definite mind-body or a definite astral body, but he has around and within him the matter out of which these are to be builded. He possesses tendencies of all sorts, some of them good and some of them evil, and it is in accordance with the development of these tendencies that that building will be regulated. And this development in turn depends almost entirely upon the influences brought to bear upon him from outside during the first few years of his existence.

C. W. LEADBEATER.

(To be continued.)

THE SÂṄKHYA PHILOSOPHY.

(Continued from Vol. XIX. p. 512.)

THE FIVE GROSS ELEMENTS.

THE five gross elements are æther (âkâsha), air, fire, water and earth. There are several different views current in different texts as to the way in which these gross elements are produced from the subtle elements or tanmâtras. The theory which seems to be supported by the older texts is as follows: without in any way entering into combination, but simply impelled by the energy flowing forth from Prakṛiti, the tanmâtra of sound develops from itself the gross element æther or âkâsha; from the combination of the tanmâtras of sound and touch the element air is produced; from the three tanmâtras of sound, touch and sight (colour) fire proceeds; from the above three plus the tanmâtra of taste, we have water; and from the combination of all five tanmâtras earth is produced.

These five gross elements combine with one another to produce the material world (which it must be remembered includes far more than our own physical plane) and work in each of its planes, each supporting the other four by manifesting its own special quality or property. Thus the element earth is the common basis in the bringing forth of all productions, while water moistens and fertilizes, fire (*i.e.*, light and heat) ripens, air dries, and æther provides space for all things, *i.e.*, gives them extension.

Another theory of the way in which the gross elements are produced from the tanmâtras is as follows: each of the gross elements is supposed to consist of sixteen parts, and of these sixteen parts, in the case of æther say, eight consist of the tanmâtra of sound, while the remaining eight consist of two parts contributed by each of the four remaining tanmâtras. Thus using t. s. to denote the tanmâtra of sound; t. t. for that of touch; t. c. for that of sight or colour; t. o. for that of odour or smell; and t. f. for that of taste or flavour; the composition of the five gross elements would be given as follows:

Æther = 8 t. s. + 2 t. t. + 2 t. o. + 2 t. c. + 2 t. f.
Air = 8 t. t. + 2 t. s. + 2 t. o. + 2 t. c. + 2 t. f.
Fire = 8 t. c. + 2 t. t. + 2 t. s. + 2 t. o. + 2 t. f.
Water = 8 t. f. + 2 t. t. + 2 t. s. + 2 t. o. + 2 t. c.
Earth = 8 t. o. + 2 t. t. + 2 t. s. + 2 t. c. + 2 t. f.

This latter theory is the one which is most generally current in India at the present moment, and is naturally, therefore, the one generally alluded to in works written in recent times, when the composition of the grosser elements is mentioned.

We have now completed our more detailed survey of the twenty-four tattvas which constitute the material or Prakṛiti side of the manifested universe according to the Sâṅkhya philosophy; but before leaving this part of the subject, it may be as well to add a few words with regard to a point which has already been alluded to more than once, but has not as yet been specially dealt with. I mean the vâsanâs or "tendencies" which are brought over from birth to birth, and which collectively constitute the roots of character.

The Vâsanâs.

According to the Sâṅkhya theory, every experience or impression leaves behind an indelible imprint in the buddhi, which remains inactive or latent in a germ-like condition until again thrown into activity by the arising of the circumstances and surroundings necessary or favourable for its germination. It is these impressions in the buddhi which constitute memory, instinct, tendency, impulse, capacity, talent, in short, the individual nature and character of the ego, as we have already observed. The following outline of the theory of the vâsanâs is taken from Paul Markus' essay on the Yoga-philosophy of Patanjali; but as the Yoga drew this theory with so much else from the Sâṅkhya system, it forms a fairly accurate presentation of the doctrine as found in the latter.

"Everything that happens leaves a corresponding trace or impress behind in the substance of the buddhi, and this trace remains therein like a seed in a cornfield, or as a latent tendency, that is as an appropriate preparation or predisposition for the future reproduction of the event or action in question. These predispositions (or as Patanjali often calls them, 'intellectual deposits') constitute a very important part of the buddhi, which is literally full of them, so many and various are the tendencies, which in the course of many past births have been stored up therein.

"The life-history of such a vâsanâ is as follows: first it is latent, virtual, a mere potentiality, but yet possessed of the tendency, even the inevitable necessity, of producing its own appropriate effect some time or other, though it has not as yet the ripened energy necessary for doing so. When their time is ripe the appropriate vâsanâs become active, living, and then finally—do not perish but—return to the stillness of the has-been, the eternal rest of the past. Thus these vâsanâs remain a constant possession of the individual, only in differing condition, according as they have, or have not, already produced their appointed effect. First as forces tied and bound, awaiting their freedom, their transformation into living, active forces, which will become decisive factors in the practical conduct of the individual; lying latent thus as unsuspected sleeping impulses which need only to be awakened to be brought into action, to gain potent influence over us. All the capacities indispensable for physical life, the habits and capacities which we bring into the world with us, are the inheritance of former lives; they are impressions, traces, deposits, which in the interim have persisted and retained their latent energy, to manifest their power forcefully and fresh when their hour strikes—like seeds, which for years have been stored away, but at last, when placed under conditions suitable for their germination, unfold themselves and grow as if but just harvested."

Of all the vâsanâs, the most fateful is the "ignorance" (avidyâ-saṁskâra) inborn in every individual, the tendency, that is, to the non-discrimination between spirit and matter, Purusha and

Prakriti. For, in the view of the Sâṅkhya, this is the root of all evil; since it is the cause of desire for earthly enjoyment, and thus the root of merit and demerit (karma), which ever draws man again and again to life in matter and binds him to the wheel of birth and death.

CONCLUSION.

In beginning this series of articles it was my intention to devote the last of them to working out thoroughly the relations between our own Theosophical teachings and the Sâṅkhya view of the universe. But now that the outline of the latter has been pretty fully sketched, it has become only too evident that a great deal more work needs to be done before this intention can be adequately carried out. On the literary side much remains obscure; for nearly all our present knowledge of the Sâṅkhya comes to us through writers whose thought is saturated with Vedântic conceptions, while in modern Indian thought we find much that seems of characteristically Sâṅkhyan origin embodied in the current forms of Vedânta. Indeed, we may almost say that the whole of the Cosmology and Theory of Evolution, as well as much of the Psychology and Eschatology of the Vedânta as now held, and even as contained in the works ascribed to Shankarâchârya, seems to be of distinctly Sâṅkhyan origin, and to have been taken over almost bodily into the Vedântic systems. Hence before such a task as the thorough working out of the relations between the Sâṅkhya, as a distinct system, and the teachings of Theosophy can be undertaken, it is indispensable to determine the real outlines of the original, pure Sâṅkhya. To do this, an immense amount of critical literary work must first be done, not alone upon the texts of the Vedântic and Sâṅkhyan schools, but also upon the Mâyâ and Vaisheṣhika, in order to determine the real source and inter-relation of certain fundamental conceptions. But the time is not yet ripe even to begin upon this work; first because the preparatory task of text publication and editing has really only just begun, and then because our present knowledge of the historical sequence of texts and authors—a most important factor in such a research—is virtually *nil*. When, for instance, we do not know whether the date of Shankarâchârya is the fifth century before, or the ninth century after Christ, and when we are in complete ignorance even of the stratification of the numerous works at present current under his name, it is obvious that several generations of steady scholarly work are indispensable for the mere task of clearing the ground.

But though these considerations preclude all possibility of a systematic attack upon the problem alluded to, it may yet not be without interest for students of Theosophy, who are interested in Hindu philosophic thought, to direct attention to sundry points which emerge from the outline of the Sâṅkhya as sketched in the foregoing pages. And to do so may have the further value of directing Theosophical, or more accurately occult research to some aspects of our own teachings, upon which the comparisons in question seem to throw a suggestive light.

Our first endeavour must necessarily be to find a definite and reliable point of contact between our own Theosophical conceptions of man and nature, and those of the Sâṅkhya, so that we may have a sort of reference datum-line from which we can work backwards and forwards. And it seems to me that we may hope to find this by working out the doctrine of the differentiation of the senses. First, then, from the Theosophical side, we know that our special senses—sight, hearing, etc.—do not properly belong to this physical plane at all but are seated in the astral body, although there they are not nearly so sharply differenced off from one another, and are not so definitely localized as they become when functioning through the physical organism. But it seems to me, on analyzing the facts, that the differentiation of the senses by no means has its *origin* in the astral body. For in the description of the various conditions of devachanic existence, given in Mr. Leadbeater's recent Manual, it is obvious that sense-differentiation persists at any rate throughout all the rûpa levels of that condition. For we read that the greater musicians enjoy a Devachan in which music is the predominant feature, while painters and sculptors bathe in the glories of form and colour, and so on. Now this seems to imply that on those levels there is already a persisting differentiation of the special senses, at least sufficient to give a characteristic mark to the devachanic experiences of the various types of artistic genius. Hence I conclude that, although on the rûpa-devachan levels the senses blend to a very great extent, yet, since they are still distinguishable, we must seek for their common origin, the undifferentiated source whence they proceed, on the arûpa levels, or in other words, in the causal body.

This conclusion appears to be supported by the fact that when consciousness is functioning in the causal body, it does not perceive or learn things through " senses," but takes in the object on which it is focussed within and without, on all sides at once, grasping its complete nature, history, character and essence in a single all-embracing intuition. So that it seems, from what we are told, that when the consciousness is thus functioning in the causal body, it has clearly and definitely transcended anything which could reasonably be spoken of as " special " or differentiated " senses."

Again, we often hear in our literature about the " devachanic sense," though perhaps, " devachanic perception" would be a better term to denote it, since it is described as piercing through illusion and conveying to its possessor an accurate and reliable *understanding* of whatever it is directed to. Hence it seems that besides the special senses, though, as our daily experience shows us, acting in constant conjunction with them, there is another "sense," which not only correlates and combines the impressions received from the senses, but interprets and understands them. And this additional " sense " becomes stronger and more marked in its manifestations as we follow up the senses from their physical manifestations to their source. And this " devachanic sense," though closely resembling, is yet clearly distinguishable from that full intuitive perception which characterizes the functioning of consciousness in the causal body proper.

Turn now to the Sâṅkhya, and it is pretty evident that we have here the exact parallel of the " indriyas " and the " manas " of that philosophy. This is the more striking from the curious fact that the Sâṅkhya so frequently speaks of manas as " one of the indriyas" and that eleven—ten plus one—is the characteristic number of the senses, while at the same time manas is also very closely allied to and associated with the ahaṅkâra, and is so often classed together with the latter and buddhi as the "internal instrument" repeatedly spoken of before.

Now in the Sâṅkhya both manas and the indriyas proceed, though independent of each other, from the ahaṅkâra. And in our Theosophical teachings we have traced the senses to the causal body as their root; while the close resemblance in many points between the special "devachanic sense" and the characteristics of consciousness functioning in the causal body, makes it abundantly clear that the latter is also the source and origin whence proceeds this devachanic sense.

Here are two points upon which further occult investigation is desirable: what is the exact genesis and history of the special senses, and—since on the rûpa levels we undoubtedly have *both* the special senses and the one "devachanic sense" in simultaneous activity—is this devachanic sense simply the characteristic of consciousness when functioning in the mind body as its lowest vehicle, just as full "intuition" is its characteristic in the causal body, or if not, what and whence is this devachanic sense?

To return, however, to our immediate subject. Since the causal body is the source of both the devachanic sense and the special senses in our teaching, and the ahankâra of the Sânkhya is similarly the source of manas and the indriyas, which are clearly identifiable with the devachanic and special senses, it seems certain that the ahankâra of the Sânkhya must be identified with one aspect or facet of our causal body.

Let us check this. The ahankâra of the Sânkhya is defined specifically as the producer of the consciousness "I act," "I feel," "I think," generally, of the consciousness of "I" as a separate entity. In other words, it is the cause of the consciousness of *separateness*. But this again is just what the causal body in man does according to our Theosophical teaching; for it is the true Ego, the real "I am I" in us. But in our teaching the "causal body" seems to be a good deal more than this, and here is another point upon which these comparisons with the Sânkhya seem to suggest a useful line of further investigation; and one or two additional points may be noted as suggestions in this light, as well as tending to strengthen the identification already made.

But the consideration of these must be deferred till next month.

BERTRAM KEIGHTLEY.

(*To be concluded.*)

THEOSOPHICAL ACTIVITIES.

EUROPEAN SECTION.

THE fund started in this Section for the relief of the Indian famine has reached to about £260. Contributions are still coming in, but of course very slowly now.

Mrs. Besant arrived in London late on Sunday, March 7th, having been compelled to come by boat to Plymouth instead of overland from Brindisi. This was owing to the stringent quarantine arrangements at Brindisi, and resulted in the loss of a week, so that it was impossible for Mrs. Besant to catch the boat she had intended to take to America, which left on Saturday afternoon. She left for America by the next boat, after remaining in London a few days.

The twelfth Conference of the North of England Federation of the Theosophical Society was held at Harrogate on Saturday, January 30th, Mrs. Cooper-Oakley presiding. Mrs. Cooper-Oakley spoke on "Occultism in the Eighteenth Century," and during the meetings a discussion on "The Law of Non-resistance" took place.

Mr. Leadbeater conducted two afternoon meetings at Mr. and Mrs. Hope's town house, at which there were excellent attendances, mainly of strangers to Theosophy. Mr. Leadbeater spoke on "States after Death" and "The Heaven-World and its Conditions."

Owing to Mrs. Besant's late arrival, the lecture which she was to have delivered at the Blavatsky Lodge on March 4th had to be abandoned, and Mr. Leadbeater spoke in her place, his subject being the interesting one of "The Âkâshic Records." A new syllabus has been prepared for the Sunday evening lectures, which will be carried on till Easter. This series has been very well attended from the beginning, and the audiences will look forward to their renewal after the usual interval.

A new Branch has just been formed at Rome, of which Mrs. A. C. Lloyd is the President. A considerable number of members joined recently, so that there is every prospect of an active Branch resulting. A journal, *Nova Lux*, has already been obtained as an organ for the Italian members of the Society.

The news from France shows that the activity is increasing rapidly there, Dr. Pascal especially doing good work at Toulon, and M. Courmes, his colleague on *Le Lotus Bleu*, working with his accustomed energy in Paris. The Paris Lodge held its annual meeting in February, and M. Gillard was re-elected President, with M. Renard as Secretary and Mme. Brunnarius as Treasurer.

New Zealand Section.

The following report has been received:

The First Annual Convention of the New Zealand Section which was held in Wellington on January 2nd and 3rd, was a very successful gathering. Delegates attended from Auckland, Waitemata, Wellington, Christchurch and Dunedin, and also from the Branch newly chartered at Wanganui, Pahiatua being represented by proxy. The fact that all the resolutions but one were carried unanimously shows a strong feeling of unity in the deliberations.

The General Secretary reported that in the eight months since the formation of the Section, there had been an increase of twenty-two in the membership, fifteen old members having been taken off the register, while thirty-seven new members had been added, and one new Branch had been chartered at Wanganui, so that the Section, though small, is growing.

The first session of the Convention was held on the afternoon of Saturday, Jan. 2nd, and dealt with the subject of correspondence between members and enquirers. Consideration of some plan for this purpose was left to the Executive, with a proposal to form a sectional lending library; and also with a proposal that the present organ of the Australian Section, *Theosophy in Australasia*, be enlarged and be made the organ also of the New Zealand Section. A committee appointed to go into the last question reported to the effect that it was desirable that some arrangement should be made in the matter, and placed it in the hands of the Executive with a suggestion that the Australian Executive be approached with a view to its being brought up at the Australian Convention held at Easter.

The Chairman, Mr. W. T. Short, Vice-President of the Wellington Branch, in his opening address, referred to the question of the constitution of the Section as being specially important. The whole of the second session, on January 3rd, was devoted to the consideration of this subject. Several changes were made in the provisional constitution, and a few new rules were added, and the new constitution now only awaits the approval of the President-Founder.

There were two meetings held in connection with the Convention,

A social meeting on the Saturday evening added greatly to the success of the proceedings; and at a public meeting on the Sunday evening several short addresses were delivered to a large and interested audience.

Mr. and Mrs. Draffin, who attended at Wellington as the delegates from the Auckland and Waitemata Branches, gave several addresses there, and are now visiting Christchurch and Dunedin, where they also lecture.

The General Secretary, Miss Edger, returned to headquarters after the Convention, and will remain in Auckland until further visits elsewhere are required. She lectured on January 17th on "Theosophy in New Zealand," giving a slight sketch of the history of the Theosophical Society and its growth and extension and showing how the teachings were spreading into all parts of New Zealand and among all classes of people.

American Section.

There is every prospect of this Section having a successful future, as it is slowly but surely recovering from the great blow it sustained two years ago. Undoubtedly its present activity is largely due to the ceaseless work of the Countess Wachtmeister, who has been lecturing in many parts of America, and organizing the Society wherever she has stayed. The Countess has recently visited St. Paul and Minneapolis, where she spent three weeks, giving a series of public lectures, and branch and private meetings, spending the time alternately in the two towns. The lectures were crowded. From there she went to Menomonie and St. Cloud.

The Countess will accompany Mrs. Besant on her tour, and the work she has already done will doubtless greatly assist in increasing the success of Mrs. Besant's lectures. Count Wachtmeister has taken charge of *Mercury* for the time being, and is now in San Francisco. The reports of the various branches are most satisfactory.

Indian Section.

A proposal has been made to form a Federation of the Branches of the Society in the Madras Presidency on somewhat similar lines to the organizations existing in England. A circular has been sent to members of the Indian Section containing suggestions and proposing that a meeting be held at Kumbakonam during the Mahâmagam festival. Regular meetings will probably be arranged, and some scheme adopted which will serve to help in bringing the Branches more in touch with each other.

REVIEWS.

The Threshold Covenant.

By H. Clay Trumbull. [Edinburgh: T. & T. Clark, 1896. Price 6*s.* 6*d.*].

The Myths of the New World.

By Daniel G. Brinton, M.D. [Philadelphia: McKay, 1896. Third Edition. Price 7*s.* 6*d.*]

The Sacred Tree.

By Mrs. J. H. Philpot. [London: Macmillan & Co., 1897. Price 8*s.* 6*d.*].

These three volumes are contributions to the too slowly evolving science of mythology. In *The Threshold Covenant* we have what one might almost call a catalogue of the variations of this covenant and of the places in which traces of it are found. The author endeavours to show that the beginning of all religious rites was the threshold covenant, the view put forward being that the primitive man gained his idea of the Creator from the marriage rite, and that this covenant was founded on and is in reality a representation of the marriage rite. The subject as a whole is rather an unpleasant one, being largely connected with blood and with sexualism, and we are unable to agree with the writer's view that this covenant was the earliest of all religious rites. In discussing the matter the author writes: "It is enough to suggest that the mistake has been too often made of supposing that this 'phallic worship' was a primitive conception of a religious truth, instead of a perversion of the earlier and purer idea which is at the basis of the highest religious conceptions, from the beginning until now," and with this we entirely concur, but it seems to us but a small advance to substitute for a phallic basis, a basis of sexualism. However, the work is a contribution to the science of mythology, a science of which at present only the foundation stones are being laid, and as all the stones in a building have their use, this contribution, calling attention as it does to a new line of research, will no doubt prove of value.

Dr. Trumbull's name is a sufficient guarantee of careful research and scholarly treatment.

Dr. Brinton's *Myths of the New World*, one of the most interesting books we have read for some time, is a treatise on the symbolism and mythology of the Red Race of America. It deals with the beliefs of the various Indian tribes, but of most interest, perhaps, to the Theosophist are those held by the Aztecs and Toltecs, concerning which many interesting details are given, and it is evident that they were possessed of no small amount of occult knowledge. An interesting account is given of the different methods adopted to preserve the records, thus the Peruvians used knotted, twisted and coloured strings called *quipus*, other tribes the *wampum*, composed of bits of wood and shell of equal size but of different colours hung on strings, or parcels of reeds of different lengths, strings of fruit stones, picture writing, etc., and in connection with the latter we are told that the Spanish governor in Mexico destroyed no less than sixteen thousand scrolls, so that very few are left for the benefit of antiquarians.

There is also a very pathetic account of the fall of the race; though the Church of Rome crushed remorselessly the religions of Mexico and Peru, every aboriginal nation, from ocean to ocean, still cherishes the memory of the unfortunate Montezuma. Groaning under the iron rule of the Spaniards, the Peruvians would not believe that the last of the Incas had perished an outcast in the forests of the Cordilleras. When the last generation of the Red Race saw their land fall into the rapacious hands of the Yankees, every morning at earliest dawn they gazed anxiously into the east hoping to see the noble form of Montezuma returning at the head of a conquering army.

"It is but a few years since the Indians on our reservations, in wild despair at the misery and deaths of those dearest to them, broke out in mad appeals, in furious ceremonies, to induce that longed-for saviour and friend to appear. The heartless whites called it a 'ghost dance' and a 'Messiah craze,' and shot the participants in their tracks, hastening the implacable destiny against which the poor wretches had prayed in vain."

But there are so many interesting points, such as the practice of baptism, cremation, the story of creation, the deluge, the ideas of life after death, etc., which it is impossible to touch on here, that we can only advise our readers to read the book for themselves. It is quite refreshing to find an author on these subjects exhibiting such a breadth of view, and so free from the tendency to dogmatize.

In *The Sacred Tree* we have an exposition of that theory which has been not inaptly termed the vegetable origin of the Creator. This book is merely a compilation for the general reader from the standard works on the tree in religion and myth, and as such does not call for criticism at great length. It is well printed and well illustrated, and should prove a useful introduction to those beginning a study of this branch of mythology.

We should, however, like to draw the attention of the student to page 146, where a Puritan, rejoicing in the name of Stubbs, is quoted as having thus denounced the Maypole festival: "And then fall they to banquet and feast, to leape and daunce aboute it, as the Heathen people did at the dedication of their idolles, whereof this is a perfect patterne, or rather the thyng itself."

The pious Puritan is no longer alone in mistaking the perfect pattern for the thing itself, he being followed by a goodly number of mythologists, each of whom starts with the idea that his particular view of the subject, be it mineral, vegetable, animal or solar, is the only one which will really solve the question of primitive religion; finding everywhere customs in some degree similar to those on which his theory is based, he at once assumes them to be identical—a method which we need hardly say is not conducive to the elucidation of truth.

We should scarcely, for example, consider the mythologist of the future justified if, finding the interlaced triangles painted on the remains of a present-day brewer's dray, he assumed that all nineteenth century brewers were Kabalists, and yet a good deal of mythological research is carried out on much the same lines.

Another fetish is the "primitive man" of whom we hear so much; yet where is the primitive man? And without a primitive man, how can we find his primitive religion? Wherever we look, over the various parts of the globe we find traces of civilization after civilization; we also know how remnants of civilized people retain fragments of the religion of their forefathers, how tribes, though isolated, obtain knowledge of various ideas current in other parts of the world, how offshoots from different races still hold, as much distorted traditions, the ideas of the parent stock; how then can we talk of the religion of primitive man? One is inclined to hope that a mythologist will one day arise who will trace out for us the myth of the mythologist—the myth of the primitive man.

The various races of undeveloped men are offshoots of other races, and their religious ideas are distorted remnants of the religions of earlier civilizations. And although it is evident that one key will never solve the whole mystery, still there would seem to be greater promise if enquiry were made from this point of view than by starting with the fixed idea that the mythological primitive man was a monomaniac.

C. H.

THE WASHER OF THE FORD: AND OTHER LEGENDARY MORALITIES.

By Fiona Macleod. [Edinburgh: Patrick Geddes, 1896.]

WE do not think that LUCIFER need offer an apology to its readers for admitting to its pages the notice of a book which would certainly be classed with the literature called "light"; for the volume under consideration is, in its own way, one of the most striking we have read for a long time.

One of the qualifications which we all, as students of Theosophy especially, need to gain, is a real human interest in other peoples and races, in their hopes and aspirations, apart from a merely academic interest, which is a very different thing. There are many in whom this wider and deeper sympathy is more easily awakened by something which stirs the emotions as well as rouses the mind, and to all such we recommend the perusal of *The Washer of the Ford*.

The book is a collection of stories based upon very old legends of the Western Highlands and the Isles, and there is a certain weird beauty about most of them, a beauty wild and rugged as of the heather and the bleak northern hills, and withal an exquisite tenderness. Perhaps the stories showing this rather rare combination most strikingly are those included under the section to which the author has given the name "Legendary Moralities."

Where all are so beautiful it is difficult to select, but the "Fisher of Men" and the "Last Supper" are in particular charmingly written. In both these we have a picture of the solitary figure, Iosa, whom men call Jesus, fishing always in the Shadowy Waters which are the tears of the world, and revealing himself on rare occasions where the conditions are possible and where the need is great. In the latter of these two stories, "The Last Supper," we have the same figure, this time comforting a little child who is lost in the heather. He carries him tenderly to a huntsman's shed, where is prepared the Last Supper, which we are told Iosa eats daily. And then the pure eyes of the child are still further opened, so that he sees the twelve weavers of the web of life. Beside each are three shuttles, and with these they weave wonderful shapes of glorious light and colour, which they send out into the world; all save the dark twelfth, whose shuttles are black, and whose heart is closed to the glory around him. None of it touches him, except the radiant light produced by the Weaver of Hope, and at that even he lifts his head and smiles. He is the dark Weaver of Fear, the Betrayer, and sends out evil shapes into the hearts of men. The dark shadow ever haunts him too, instead of the glory which surrounds the others. The story is no whit less beautiful in that the supper consists of rye-bread, and porridge and milk.

Very beautiful, too, is the account of the "Three Marvels of Hy," of the way in which the holy Saint Colum learns true humility, and gains the love which embraces every living thing, even the flying things of the air and the fish in the sea; and this same idea is carried out later in the Annir-Choille, where the Saint Molios ends his life, having gained also this all-embracing love which extends even to those whom he calls pagans, by performing the ceremony of blessing the seals. In this same story we are introduced to the Hidden People, the luminous green shadows who are the spirits or lives of the trees, the things that we blind mortals call trees being only their outside coverings. We are told that the king who rules these creatures is the god of the green world, who sleeps, while sleeping dreams, and whose dreams are Spring, Summer and Apple-tide.

But to gain an idea of the charm of the book it needs to be read, and read as every book of its kind should be, with all the understanding sympathy of which we are capable. For the highest hopes and aspirations of a people are not evanescent as the foam tossed from the breaking wave; but are far-away echoes of that diviner harmony which sounds unceasingly beyond the shadows that we call life and death, and the measure of whose attainment by any one race, nation or individual is surely wisdom.

S. M. S.

The Ante-Nicene Christian Library.

An additional volume, edited by Allan Menzies, D.D. [Edinburgh: T. & T. Clark, 1897. Price *12s. 6d.*].

Owing to the number of texts of treatises, falling within the Ante-Nicene period, which have been recently discovered, an additional volume has been added to this series, which seemed many years ago to have completed its task. Readers who desire to acquaint themselves with the nature of the recent MSS., apart from commentaries and critical exegesis, will find the volume of service. It includes: The Gospel of Peter; The Diatessaron of Tatian; The Revelation of Peter; The Vision of Paul; The Apocalypse of the Virgin; The Apocalypse of Sedrach; The Testament of Abraham; The Acts of Xantippe and Polyxena; The Narrative of Zosimus; The Epistles of Clement; The

Apology of Aristides; and the Passion of the Scillitan Martyrs. The remaining two-fifths of the volume are taken up with a translation of Origen's Commentaries on John and Matthew. The shape of the work is cumbersome and out of form with the rest of the series, but necessitated by the use of parallel versions in several instances.

The work is carefully done, and the short introductions are invariably written from the standpoint of the Conservative School. The reader, however, who requires a translation simply, cannot do better than turn to this apparently innocent volume which bristles with an armoury of controversial weapons offensive and defensive, according to the taste and fancy of the critic. It is a very theological torpedo-catcher of the latest pattern.

G. R. S. M.

The Mysteries of Magic.

A Digest of the Writings of Éliphas Lévi, with a Biographical and Critical Essay, by A. E. Waite. Second Edition. [London: Kegan Paul, Trench, Trübner and Co.; 10*s*. 6*d*.]

As this work has passed into the second edition, we must suppose that it has a wide circle of readers, and indeed for those interested in the type of occultism of which Éliphas Lévi is the best representative, such a digest of his voluminous writings must be welcome. His wit and his paradoxes render subjects which in other hands might be very dreary, comparatively light and agreeable reading, and here and there the reader meets with an illuminating phrase which may make it worth while to read through long disquisitions on ceremonial magic and descriptions of ceremonies and exorcisms.

The present edition is a revised and enlarged one, and contains between five and six hundred pages, including the biographical and critical essay by Mr. Waite. The latter is a valuable sketch of its interesting subject, and will alone make the book worth obtaining by every student of magical literature.

A. M. G.

The Rosy Cross and other Psychical Tales,

By Mina Sandeman. [The Roxburghe Press, London: 1896. Price 3*s*. 6*d*.]

We have waded through the whole of this book, hoping that we might find therein something to which a word of praise could be given; but the hope was vain. The author appears to have had more than one object in writing these "Psychical Tales," but the most important in her opinion is evidently the spread of "the glorious truth of spiritualism," to use her own expression. Some of the remarks made in this connection are such as tempt one to close the book in disgust, although it is only fair to add that, judging from its general tenour, the word "medium" is used, probably in a somewhat higher sense than that which usually attaches to it. But, even with this reservation, the inevitable conclusion remains—that this collection of stories has nothing in it, so far as we are able to see, which calls for its publication. Some true things are said, and some useful morals enforced, but these are, for the most part, extremely obvious and well-worn, and are, moreover, in no way strikingly expressed. We have searched vainly for one forcible idea or for one original thought.

Beyond this general lack of "edification," the book as a whole is badly written. The sentences are clumsily constructed, there is an almost phenomenal exuberance of adjectives of a somewhat commonplace kind, and on more than one occasion the most elementary rules of grammar are disregarded.

These and other indications lead us to think that the writer may be young, and this perhaps her first excursion into literature. In that case we should be sorry to be over-harsh and discouraging in our criticism; but it is an ancient and familiar saying that "of the making of many books there is no end"—and few, very few are they which are worth reading.

S. M. S.

The History of a Soul.

By Kathleen Behenna. [London: Digby, Long & Co.]

This small volume of poetry treats of the varied incarnations of a human soul from the first as Rameses II. up to the eighth as Philip Bourke Marston.

It seems to be an early attempt at poetry on the part of the authoress, for the verse is not quite all that could be desired, and as far as the incarnations are concerned full advantage has been taken of "poetical license." Nevertheless the book contains some prettily expressed ideas.

C. H.

THEOSOPHICAL

AND

MYSTIC PUBLICATIONS.

Col. Olcott in his "Old Diary Leaves," is still travelling about and making mesmeric cures, meeting as might be expected with a series of curious adventures. "Sun-Worship among the Parsis," is a useful paper on Zoroastrian religion, containing a great deal of information on the subject. "What is a Star?" is one of the most extraordinary articles *The Theosophist* has ever published. It begins with a quotation from a previous article in the same magazine, appropriately entitled "Rhapsody." This is the quotation: "The key-note of the universe is obtained by the law of centre. . . . The truth of the age is the truth of the reigning one" (! !) The quotation is the most lucid part of the article. The remainder may be left to the imagination. The most interesting paper, after that on Zoroastrianism, is an account of spiritualistic phenomena in France, entitled "Mediums and Fire Elementals." Col. Olcott appends some notes to the contribution, which was sent to him by Col. de Rochas. The phenomena include levitation, materialization and those of luminous appearances and of fire.

With *The Thinker* for the New Year comes a calendar, consisting of a card about ten inches in length, humorously described in the advertisement as a "pocket (!) calendar." It contains a portrait of "His Holiness Shri Sringeri Jagad Guru Shri Shankarâchârya." While the portrait is probably not flattering, it indicates a personality sufficiently remarkable to make the readers look forward to his promised contributions to the little Indian journal. Mr. Ramaswami Aiyar contributes a short but interesting paper on "Târaka Light," one of the results of yoga practice. Mrs. Besant's Adyar lectures are reported at considerable length, the report being taken from *The Madras Times*, and some other useful articles are published. *The Journal of the Mahâ Bodhi Society* contains a clear and concise account of Buddhist teaching by D. B. Jayatilaka. The fundamental teachings of Buddhism are put forward in a simple and attractive manner. *The Buddhist* gives a translation from the Jâtakas, a story of an offending Bhikshu. Mr. Leadbeater's "Invisible Helpers" is reprinted, as are several other articles from various sources. In the *Ârya Bâla Bodhini*, there is a sketch of an Indian saint, Tulasi Dâs, to whom, as to some of the early Christian saints, his deity appeared. A report of Mrs. Besant's lecture on "The Value of India to the World" is also given. *The Theosophic Gleaner* opens with a series of predictions under the heading, "The Future of Humanity." A quite surprising list of things to be done away with is given. After a series of reprints the magazine closes with some very technical notes on the Persian calendar. We have also to acknowledge receipt from India of *The Report of the Sixth Annual Convention of the Indian Section*, *The Prasnottara* and *The Sanmârga Bodhini*, and from Ceylon of *Rays of Light*.

Mr. Sinnett's latest contribution to Theosophical literature, *The Beginnings of the Fifth Race*, forming one of the Transactions of the London Lodge, is not inferior in interest to any of his previous work, although it is somewhat meagre in extent. Some twenty pages are hardly sufficient to give a comprehensive account of the fifth race, including the various sub-races forming it, but a very considerable amount of information has been condensed into the pamphlet. Among points of special interest is the description of the work of the Manu and the traditions of his work found in the Hebrew scriptures. It was from the original Semitic Atlantean sub-race that the colony from which the new race was to be formed was taken and thus in a peculiar manner were the early Semites a "chosen people." Fragments of the regulations of the Manu—regulations, it must be remembered, having a specific aim and not suitable for universal laws—still remain in Hebrew literature and the traditional figure of Moses may well have stood, as Mr. Sinnett points out, for the original "lawgiver." The caste system, now so demoralized, is also shown to have had a rational beginning. In fact this scheme throws real light for the first time on this obscure subject.

The Vâhan for March gives a somewhat meagre supply of "Enquirer"; the literary notes and activities being fuller than usual. The "Enquirer" is, however, well up to its general standard of excellence, and the questions are most interesting ones. C. W. L. deals with the astral and devachanic planets of our chain and the influence of gravity, on the origins of a root-race and on the characteristics of root-races. A fairly full description is given of the method by which a new race is differentiated from a previous one and of the work of the Manu in connection with it. B. K. writes on the part which the physical brain plays in the process of abstract thinking, pointing out that the brain does not think or take any part in the process, but that the law of physical evolution is that the evolving essence must strive to express itself through physical matter—in the case of mankind chiefly through the brain.

Le Lotus Bleu for February opens with an appeal reprinted from a spiritualistic periodical, *La Paix Universelle*, for a "congress of humanity" to take place in 1900 at Paris, during the period of the projected Exhibition. The author of the article quoted is stated to be "Amo," a familiar name to the readers of our French review. All our readers who feel an interest in this idea can obtain fuller particulars from the present issue of *Le Lotus Bleu*, and no doubt the following numbers will present the scheme in a more complete form. M. Gillard writes briefly on "Esotericism and Exotericism," tracing the origin of the words and ideas to the school of Pythagoras. Dr. Pascal concludes his useful article on thought-forms and the article by Mme. Blavatsky on "Practical Occultism" is translated. The opening article in *L'Isis Moderne*, deals with the oracles of Greece and the Chaldeans, and gives much interesting information on the subject. M. Bailly contributes a lengthy review of *La Langue Sacrée*, by Emile-Soldi, dealing with magic and symbolism. *L'Hyperchimie* gives the rules and constitution of the "Association Alchimique de France," which presents quite a formidable appearance on paper. Its object is to study the transmutation of metals and kindred subjects, and the members are divided into councillors, honorary members, "membres maitres," who are qualified to teach, and ordinary members.

We have received from Spain a translation in pamphlet form of Mrs. Besant's articles on "Thought Forms" and "Occult Chemistry." The appearance of the pamphlet is most original and attractive, the cover being printed in prismatic colours with reproductions of the oxygen atom and of two thought-forms. The illustrations are also admirably reproduced, being, in fact, indistinguishable from the original drawings. *Sophia* contains two original articles this month, one on Hindu literature and the dates of some of the chief works, and the other on our most familiar friend, the Kali Yuga. The disputes as to the date of the termination of the first 5,000 years are most amusing, and the writer of the article avoids clashing with any received date by investigating the astrological conditions for some two or three years ahead. It is curious to note that most people have preferred to make the period end in 1897, 1898 or even 1900, and to avoid the correct year 1899, which can be obtained by simple addition, counting, of course, the first year of our era as I A. D. and the previous year as I B. C. So there are still two years wherein people may amuse themselves and others by alarming predictions.

The members of the Theosophical Society in Italy have now a journal of their own, or at least a part of a journal. *Nova Lux*, a magazine devoted to occultism and to psychic matters, begins its tenth volume as the Italian journal of the European Section of the Society, and starts well with a translation of Mrs. Besant's lengthy article in *The Nineteenth Century*, which occupies the greater part of the number. The second issue contains Mr. Kingsland on "The Higher Science" and some papers on Martinism and Spiritism. The journal is admirably printed and got up.

Theosophia for February opens with an article by "Afra" on death, dealing with the attitude which should be taken with regard to it by a student of Theosophy. The usual translations are continued, and in addition the excellent answer of A. A. W. in the December *Vâhan* is reproduced.

The Swedish *Teosofisk Tidskrift* begins its seventh year with a few words as to its purpose. Among the contents of the January number is a poem by G. Ljungström on "Reincarnation and Karma," the same writer having a short but interesting article on "The Necessity for the Obscuration of Memory with regard to previous Earth-lives." Mr. Keightley's "Purpose of the Theosophical Society" is translated, and also an article on civilization from an Indian periodical. In the February issue G. H. Liander writes on "Investigation of Religious Conceptions," maintaining Theosophy as the core of all religious beliefs. The same writer contributes a poem, and A. K. writes "A Pyschological Study" dealing with the inner workings of the Scandinavian Section and its recent history. *Theosophia*, which spells its name in precisely the same manner as our Dutch magazine, also comes from Sweden, and contains a number of translations and one or two original articles.

In *Die Uebersinnliche Welt* there is a dispute between Dr. Carl du Prel and Dr. Weinmann respecting a report by the latter of the Psychological Congress held in Munich last year. The dispute is somewhat heated and goes a little beyond the bounds of politeness here and there. It is connected with the adverse attitude of the Congress to the discussion of spiritistic phenomena. This is followed by a paper on the projection of a thought-form and a ghost story. In the *Metaphysische Rundschau* for January a reprint of von Eckartshausen's *Cloud upon the Sanctuary* is begun, and also a somewhat technical article on argon and helium, in which parallels between their discovery and that of the X rays are sought. A curious feature of the second instalment given in the February issue is the arrangement of the atomic weights of the various elements in a magic square having the root number seventeen. Of course most of the numbers are without corresponding elements. It will form an interesting sequel to the famous Mendeléef grouping of the elements if any real relation can be traced between their qualities and their position in a magic square. The opening article of *Lotus Blüthen* is on "Lucifer," which serves as the text for a pious disquisition on "Selbsterkenntnis," "Gotteserkenntnis" and so forth. The present issue is mainly composed of poetry, the old German verses being continued at length and a "Moderne Legende" given at the end. We have also received a report of the German Theosophical Society with a number of communications from various people in the Society and outside, and dealing with the same difficulties that most of the other branches have already had. It is gratifying to notice that the leaders remain firm in their position as members of the Theosophical Society.

In Hungary attention is being turned to psychic and occult matters, as is shown by the publication of a new journal *Sbornik pro Filosofii Mystiku a Okkultismus*. The first number includes translations from Maeterlinck and Papus.

Mercury for February contains a very brief autobiographical note by the Countess Wachtmeister—"How I joined the Theosophical Society." It might have been made more lengthy with advantage, as undoubtedly the Countess could tell many stories which would be of much interest to the readers of *Mercury*. This note is followed by an article on Theosophy and Socialism, a somewhat ill-judged effort. It is surely not wise to write of Socialism in a Theosophical magazine as though it were a necessary consequence of Theosophical teachings. It is likely to prejudice many people whose views are widely different on such matters. Two short stories, one for the "Children's Corner," are given, both of the nature of parables. Some useful questions are answered in the "Forum Department."

In *The Open Court* for February, H. Dharmapâla writes briefly and concisely on the essential features of Buddhism and the doctrines held by all the various sects. This article is in answer to a statement made by another writer as to the divisions in Buddhism. "The Trinity Idea" is an interesting article by the editor, illustrated by some most alarming reproductions of idols and pictures showing Hindu, Buddhist and Christian ideas.

One of the most noticeable contributions to *The Metaphysical Magazine* is "A Psychological Study of Delirium," in the "Department of Psychic Experiences," consisting of a description by a doctor of his own state, the result of using drugs.

Theosophy in Australasia turns its attention to the ever-present Kali Yuga, and states that "a simple addition" of 5000 years to 3102 B.C., makes that cycle end in 1898, the last year beginning next April. This "simple addition" seem to puzzle most people considering the various dates given, and our Australian magazine is no more successful in its calculations than the others. The chief article is on Christmas.

We have also to acknowledge receipt of the following: *Book-Notes*, *The English Mechanic*, *The Literary Digest*, *Modern Astrology*, with an account of the first annual meeting of the Astrological Society, *Light*, *The Agnostic Journal*, *Current Literature*, *Child-Life*, *Theosophy*, *The Irish Theosophist*, *The Pacific Theosophist*, which suddenly appears again after an abrupt departure, *The Theosophical Forum* and *The Mystical World*

A.

Women's Printing Society, Limited, 66, Whitcomb Street, W.C.

VOL. XX. APRIL 15, 1897. NO. 116.

LUCIFER.

ON THE WATCH-TOWER.

THE PLATONIC SOLIDS.

"ΜΗΔΕΙΣ ΑΓΕΩΜΕΤΡΗΤΟΣ ΕΙΣΙΤΩ."

"LET no one who is ignorant of geometry enter"—such was the legend engraved on the portal of the Pythagorean and Platonic school of Grecian antiquity. Why the profane should have been confronted with such an apparently strange warning has never been sufficiently made clear by modern scholarship. That the study of geometry is an admirable mental discipline is acknowledged on all sides, but that there is a really vital side to the mathematical science—a really living interest—has never been seriously advanced by the moderns, who laugh at the "puerile speculations" of Pythagoras with regard to numbers, and look on the mathematical symbolism of Plato as a "joke" of the Athenian sage.

Nevertheless that "God geometrizes" has been made a familiar saying to Theosophical readers, has become more than a suspicion to modern science in some of its departments, and is a known fact of universal application to the small number of really serious Theosophical students. Not without reason was it that the initiated pupils of the Samian sage were called "mathematicians," whose aim was the attainment of that "mathesis" which was the goal of their philosophy, the wisdom whose lovers they declared themselves to be. Nor again did Plato "joke" in his Timæus and Republic and elsewhere, when he laid down the mathematical and geometrical nature of the creation, and based the whole of the scheme of his model state and philosophic utopia on such considerations, as may be seen from Adams' admirable essay on "The Nuptial Number of Plato," lately referred to in our pages.

Nor again were such men as Monoïmus and Valentinus among the Gnostics wild dreamers or puerile thinkers, in founding their systems of the cosmos on such a natural basis. The gnosis of the Gnostics was identical with the mathesis of the Pythagoreans, with the episteme of Plato, and the gñâna of the Vedântin philosophers; and that part of it which dealt with world-formation was the natural geometry of the Great Architect, under the laws of whom every particle of matter and every combination of particles must fall. "Theological arithmetic," as the Alexandrian doctors called it, was the highest application of the mathematical science, and only a huckstering age like our own can have the hardihood to deride an ideal which it has obscured with its vulgar commercialism, and all the concomitants of its "modern side" and "business" education.

It is true that the writings of the ancients have for the most part been destroyed or lost, while such fragments as remain display an ignorance of the material discoveries of our own age—which are indeed perhaps the most admirable of their kind.

But that the genius of to-day should persist in looking at all things merely through the spectacles of its own material discoveries, and be blind to the fact that although the eyes of antiquity gazed at the problem from a different point of view, it was in reality the same problem, and if it would but condescend to put on the spectacles of the past, it would have two points of view of the truth, and therefore an enormously increased power of perception—such a myopic state of affairs is regrettable.

But the self-complacency of to-day and of every present time whose watchword is invariably, "We are the people," ever reckons without its host. Blind to the great fact of rebirth, both of ideas and of men to reformulate them, it looks on its discoveries as entirely novel and owing to its own spontaneous genius. For it, Plato and Pythagoras and the Gnostics, the Theosophists of the past, are dead, and there's an end to them and their fantastic speculations. Platonic solids, indeed! Monads and dyads and triads, and tetractydes, contemplation and ecstasies, and blending of subject and object!—absurd, perfectly absurd! Plato did not invent a steam engine or type writer! True, but Archimedes, for whom even modern mechanism has some respect, invented some engines which are not yet out of date. And what did Archimedes say when he had invented them for his princely patron of Syracuse? He lamented that he had profaned so great a science for such unworthy purposes! That was *his* point of view, although it may be out of date at the latter end of the nineteenth century.

But the ideas which clothed themselves in the garments woven by the genius of ancient Greece, are no longer out of birth, they are coming back again and are once more being re-incarnated, and re-clothed in the vestments woven in the looms of the practical genius of to-day.

Some time ago LUCIFER referred to a book written by the young scientist, Arthur Soria y Mata, entitled *Origen Poliédrico de las Especies*, and published at Madrid in 1894. It was a treatise dealing with the Platonic solids, that is to say, the five regular solids, tetrahedron, cube, octahedron, dodecahedron and icosahedron, as the basis of the origin of species, mineral, vegetable and animal, and contained many luminous ideas of an entirely novel nature so far as orthodox geometry is concerned. The treatise contained many diagrams of the models which had been constructed for Señor Soria by the extraordinary mechanical ability of our colleague Señor Manuel Treviño, the Secretary of the Madrid Lodge. Copies of these models were most kindly sent us by Señor Treviño, and have delighted all who have seen them by the surpassing beauty of their forms and the combinations of the regular polyhedra, some of which have never been previously constructed.

Among a few of our number these models have been carefully studied and a great deal of thought been spent on their genesis from the types which lie behind them in the world of subtle matter, one of the problems, perhaps the most important, which occupied the Pythagorean, Platonic and Gnostic students of such matters. How to express the condition of a state of matter which such thinkers as Hinton have referred to (perhaps erroneously) as the "fourth dimension," is a problem that has at present received no solution, and with it Señor Soria does not deal. It is with the actualities of physical matter that he deals, although the simple polyhedra are of the minutest of the minute ordering of atoms, far beyond the test of any physical organ or instrument.

What then was our delight to receive a few days ago a copy of the French translation of a second treatise by the same indefatigable worker at this absorbing problem, entitled, *Contribución al Origen Poliédrico de la Especies* (Madrid, 1896). (We had already had his first work translated into French owing to the quality of our Spanish at Headquarters not being sufficient to grapple with scientific niceties). The new treatise of Señor Soria, which purports to be only the first part of a larger work, is more than interesting, it is absolutely fascinating to any lover of these studies, and when known will be read by thousands who have previously never heard of such things; for the text is clear, simple and proceeds on purely experimental lines which fall within the observation of the physical senses. The models which Señor Treviño has constructed with such extraordinary patience and ability are made to tell their own tale.

Although Señor Soria is aware of the existence of numerous points of contact between his discoveries and the writings of the ancients, he does not attempt to trespass on a domain which belongs rather to the scholar than the scientist. He confines himself solely to the latter aspect, and in our opinion demonstrates his case fully. He has rediscovered a science of endless possibilities, and the true origin of world-construction and every subordinate species. For the confirmation of this opinion we must, for the present, refer the reader to the book itself. It is of such importance that every effort will be made to have it translated into English, and this is certainly not the last that will be heard of it in the pages of LUCIFER.

The archæological side of the matter will also doubtless be treated in good time, as it enters intimately into the domain of our studies of the great theosophical systems of such giants of intellect as Pythagoras, Plato, Valentinus and Proclus. It is difficult to believe that Señor Soria has not been helped in the same way as those of us who have been studying the same problems; his essays are stuffed from cover to cover with theosophical ideas, and every student of theosophy will readily assimilate every detail of his work. We do not for one moment claim that the details are perfect or final, but we do assert that the main outlines of the theory are those of an infinite science of formative nature, supported by that most convincing of all proofs, ocular demonstration.

The nature of monadic existence, the laws of syzygy, similitude, harmony and perfect equilibrium, of types, and a thousand and one things familiar to students of cosmological science as taught by the ancients, meet us on every page, though, of course, the nomenclature is different.

In the volume before us, the author treats of natural geometry, the geometry of solids, which he thus distinguishes from the abstractions of Euclidean geometry, under the main headings, Polyhedric Geometry, Chemical Geometry, Mineral Geometry or Crystallogenesis, Vegetable Geometry and Animal Geometry; and the Second Part is to deal with such ideas as Rational and Social Geometry, and World-formation.

Señor Soria, in making a distinction between Euclidean and natural geometry, like the rest of the general does not seem to be aware that the Elements which Euclid collected and formulated, in the fashion of his own peculiar genius, were only intended as an *introduction* to the contemplation of the Platonic solids which formed the crown of all geometry. There used to be a legend at school that certain books of Euclid were lost, but this is not so, as Professor De Morgan writes in that most admirable article of his in Smith's Dictionary of Greek and Roman Biography, the best in the three volumes:

> The Elements consist of thirteen books written by Euclid, and two of which it is supposed that Hypsicles is the author. The first four and the sixth are on plane geometry; the fifth is on the theory of proportion, and applies to magnitude in general; the seventh, eighth and ninth, are on arithmetic; the tenth is on the arithmetical characteristics of the divisions of a straight line; the eleventh and twelfth are on the elements of solid geometry; the thirteenth (and also the fourteenth and fifteenth) are on the regular solids, which were so much studied among the Platonists as to bear the name of Platonic, and which, according to Proclus, were the objects on which the Elements were really meant to be written.

And if this is so, as indeed is the case, what can we say of the neglect of subsequent ages which have considered those solids as the most useless part of geometry?

The perfect Platonic, and even the irregular Kepler and Archimedean solids, are left severely alone, just as the admirable Elements of Theology of Proclus, formulated with the exactitude and logical sequence of a Euclid, are neglected by a generation which boasts that it has outgrown Plato.

When his royal patron, Ptolemy, asked Euclid whether he could not make the Elements easier, the sage replied: "There is no royal road to geometry," even a king must go through the necessary discipline. But that referred to the abstract conceptions of the science; as to the solids themselves, Señor Soria has found a way that is almost as simple as a Kindergarten building game.

***

THE PASSING OF J. C. STAPLES.

Last autumn our colleague, Mr. J. C. Staples, the General Secretary of the Australasian Section, came back to England for a brief visit. He had decided to return to the work he loved beyond all else by the boat of January 18th; but January found him confined to his bed, suffering most cruelly from pains in the head and lapses of memory, the cause of his sufferings at first escaping the detection of the most skilful physicians. As time went on, however, it became evident that the trouble arose from a deep-seated tumour, which gradually led to the paralysis of the optic nerve and the total blindness of the patient. The disease drew on, and finally all hopes of restoring the brain to health had to be abandoned. It is, therefore, with gladness that we have to announce that our friend was permitted to abandon his worn-out body on April 1st, and pass on to that rest which he has so well won, and which will be illumined with the ever-present aid of those who know not the name of ingratitude. When he comes again to resume his work on earth, let us hope that he will return to a better age than the unpropitious time in which we are at present labouring.

John C. Staples was a man respected and beloved by all who knew him. We have never heard a disparaging word spoken of our colleague, for he was courtesy and gentleness itself in all his words and deeds. Though his name was not so familiar to the general Society as the names of our most prolific writers, he was nevertheless personally known and highly esteemed by many in this country, and by all in his own Section in Australia.

It seems almost regrettable that when a body has been trained for such admirable theosophical work as our colleague was engaged in, it should have to be given up; but it needs must be that the right has befallen, and so we cannot be permitted to express regret.

Indeed in any case *that* would be foolish. Theosophy has long convinced us of the absolute certainty that "there is no death"—to use a hackneyed phrase. J. C. Staples is not only as much alive as but more alive than we are, as far as his continued consciousness is concerned; he is merely shut off from the murky interludes of the externalities of this unsatisfactory state of affairs called earth-life.

"Poor Staples!" we heard someone remark, thus bringing into his thought an idea totally foreign to theosophical realities. Why indeed lip-believers in Christianity should almost invariably speak of the "dead" as "poor so-and-so" is beyond our comprehension. They clearly do not believe that "poor so-and-so" has been taken to "the arms of Jesus," as the hymn has it; still, on the other hand, they can hardly believe that their departed friend is gone to eternal damnation, for one generally makes an exception to one's own friends. Is it, then, that they think that "so-and-so" is to be commiserated for being deprived of the "joys of life"—meaning life down here? Then, are the joys of heaven inferior to earthly delights?

But all the ideas of the generality, not only in Christian lands, but in every other land of to-day, concerning "death"—(mark the stupid word itself)—are absurd and contradictory; and the hideous funereal trappings and signs of woe in which Christians rejoice are a ghastly affront to the idea of a benign Providence, who is even at the lowest estimate an "all-merciful Father."

Why should we grieve for the "dead"? Surely we ought to rejoice; unless indeed the person has been very evil! Thousands of years ago the ancient Thracians, of whom Herodotus tells us, used to sit round the lifeless bodies of their friends, and rejoice to think them at last free of their prison house. Are we then so far behind the common sense of thousands of years ago?

We should ever remember that in reality we are not sorry for the dead; our grief is not for the dead but *for ourselves*. This *selfish* grief hinders and does not aid the soul of our beloved on its journey to rest between two lives.

Let us have flowers and white horses, and happy music at funerals, and not that eternal black for everything, which would damp the enthusiasm of a martyr, and is an insult to nature.

If the Theosophical Society could but bring about the overthrow of the black fetish of death which the people hug to their bosoms, what a great work would be accomplished!

The Platonists of old—mere Pagans of course—did not refer to death in such an ignorant fashion. They did not say of one of their friends, "Poor A. is dead," or "It is so sad; poor B. breathed his last yesterday"—they recited to each other triumphant declarations of the soul's immortality, and of its real nature, saying "Agathocles is now blessed," "Melita is at length truly happy."

Therefore, too, we say that John C. Staples, not our *late* colleague, but our colleague still, is now happy, nay, even blessed.

* * *

Fair offerings of flowers were sent by the European Section in the name of the whole Society, by the Australian from members of that Section in England, by Mrs. Besant and the Blavatsky Lodge, and by other friends. The General Secretary represented the Society when the body was buried at Brighton on the 6th; Mrs. Parker and Miss Minet, late officers of the Melbourne Branch, represented Australia; and Dr. King, the President, and a number of members of the Brighton Lodge, by whom Mr. Staples was well-known and loved, were also present.

* * *

G. R. S. M.

A Pure Heart penetrateth Heaven and Hell.—THOMAS À KEMPIS.

REINCARNATION.

OUR view of Reincarnation will become clearer and more in congruity with natural order, if we look at it as universal in principle, and then consider the special case of the reincarnation of the human soul. In studying it, this special case is generally wrenched from its place in natural order, and is considered as a dislocated fragment, greatly to its detriment. For all evolution consists of an evolving life, passing from form to form as it evolves, and storing up in itself the experience gained through the forms; the reincarnation of the human soul is not the introduction of a new principle into evolution, but the adaptation of the universal principle to meet the conditions rendered necessary by the individualization of the continuously evolving life.

Mr. Lafcadio Hearn * has put this point well in considering the bearing of the idea of pre-existence on the scientific thought of the West. He says:

> With the acceptance of the doctrine of evolution, old forms of thought crumbled; new ideas everywhere arose to take the place of worn-out dogmas; and we now have the spectacle of a general intellectual movement in directions strangely parallel with Oriental philosophy. The unprecedented rapidity and multiformity of scientific progress during the last fifty years could not have failed to provoke an equally unprecedented intellectual quickening among the non-scientific. That the highest and most complex organisms have been developed from the lowest and simplest; that a single physical basis of life is the substance of the whole living world; that no line of separation can be drawn between the animal and vegetable; that the difference between life and non-life is only a difference of degree, not of kind; that matter is not less incomprehensible than mind, while both are but varying manifestations of one and the same unknown reality—these have already become the commonplaces of the new philosophy. After the first recognition even by theology of physical evolution, it was easy to predict that the recognition of psychical evolution could not be indefinitely delayed; for the barrier erected by old dogma to keep men from looking backward had been broken down. And to-day for the student of scientific psychology the idea of pre-existence passes out of the realm of theory into the

* Mr. Hearn has lost his way in expression, but not, I think, in his inner view, in part of his exposition of the Buddhist statement of this doctrine, and his use of the word "ego" will mislead the reader of his very interesting chapter on this subject if the distinction between the real and the illusory ego is not steadily kept in mind.

realm of fact, proving the Buddhist explanation of the universal mystery quite as plausible as any other. "None but very hasty thinkers," wrote the late Professor Huxley, "will reject it on the ground of inherent absurdity. Like the doctrine of evolution itself, that of transmigration has its roots in the world of reality; and it may claim such support as the great argument from analogy is capable of supplying." (*Evolution and Ethics*, p. 61, ed. 1894). *

Let us consider the Monad of form, Âtma-Buddhi. In this Monad, the outbreathed life of the Logos, lie hidden all the divine powers, but, as the student knows, they are latent, not manifest and functioning. They are to be gradually aroused by external impacts, it being of the very nature of life to vibrate in answer to vibrations that play upon it. As all possibilities of vibrations exist in the Monad, any vibration touching it will arouse its corresponding vibratory power, and in this way one force after another will pass from the latent to the active† state. Herein lies the secret of evolution; the environment acts on the form of the living creature—and all things, be it remembered, live—and this action, transmitted through the enveloping form to the life, the Monad, within it, arouses responsive vibrations which thrill outwards from the Monad through the form, throwing its particles, in turn, into vibration, and re-arranging them into a shape corresponding, or adapted, to the initial impact. This is the action and reaction between the environment and the organism, which have been recognized by all biologists, and which are considered by some as giving a sufficient mechanical explanation of evolution. Their patient and careful observation of these actions and reactions yields, however, no explanation as to why the organism should thus react to stimuli, and the Ancient Wisdom is needed to unveil the secret of evolution, by pointing to the Self in the heart of all forms, the hidden mainspring of all the movements in nature.

Having grasped this fundamental idea of a life containing the possibility of responding to every vibration that can reach it from the external universe, the actual responses being gradually drawn forth by the play upon it of external forces, the next fundamental idea to be grasped is that of the continuity of life and forms. Forms transmit their peculiarities to other forms that proceed from them,

* *Kokoro, Hints and Echoes of Japanese Inner Life.* By Lafcadio Hearn, pp. 237-239 (London, 1896).

† From the static to the kinetic condition, the physicist would say.

these other forms being part of their own substance, separated off to lead an independent existence. By fission, by budding, by extrusion of germs, by development of the offspring within the maternal womb, a physical continuity is preserved, every new form being derived from a preceding form and reproducing its characteristics.* Science groups these facts under the name of the law of heredity, and its observations on the transmission of form are worthy of attention, and are illuminative of the workings of Nature in the phenomenal world. But it must be remembered that it applies only to the building of the physical body, into which enter the materials provided by the parents.

Her more hidden workings, those workings of life without which form could not be, have received no attention, not being susceptible of physical observation, and this gap can only be filled by the teachings of the Ancient Wisdom, given by Those who used superphysical powers of observation, and verifiable gradually by every pupil who studies patiently in Their schools.

There is continuity of life as well as continuity of form, and it is the continuing life—with ever more and more of its latent energies rendered active by the stimuli received through successive forms—which resumes into itself the experiences obtained by its encasings in form; for when the form perishes, the life has the record of those experiences in increased energies aroused by them, and is ready to pour itself into the new forms derived from the old, carrying with it this accumulated store. While it was in the previous form, it played through it, adapting it to express each newly awakened energy; the form hands on these adaptations, inwrought into its substance, to the separated part of itself that we speak of as its offspring, which being of its substance must needs have the peculiarities of that substance; the life pours itself into that offspring with all its awakened powers, and moulds it yet further; and so on and on. Modern science is proving more and more clearly that heredity plays an ever-decreasing part in the evolution of the higher creatures, that mental and moral qualities are not transmitted from parents to offspring, and that the higher the qualities the more patent is this fact; the child of a genius is oft-times a dolt; common-

* The student might wisely familiarize himself with the researches of Weissmann on the continuity of germ-plasm.

place parents give birth to a genius. A continuing substratum there must be in which mental and moral qualities inhere, in order that they may increase, else would Nature, in this most important department of her work, be a creature of erratic uncaused production instead of showing orderly continuity. On this science is dumb, but the Ancient Wisdom teaches that this continuing substratum is the Monad, which is the receptacle of all results, the storehouse in which all experiences are garnered as increasingly active powers.

These two principles firmly grasped—of the Monad with potentialities becoming powers, and of the continuity of life and form—we can proceed to study their working out in detail, and we shall find that they solve many of the perplexing problems of modern science, as well as the yet more heart-searching problems confronted by the philanthropist and the sage.

Let us start by considering the Monad as it is first subjected to the impacts from the formless levels of the mental planes, the very beginning of the evolution of form. Its first faint responsive thrillings draw round it some of the matter of that plane, and we have the gradual evolution of the first elemental kingdom. The great fundamental types of the Monad are seven in number, sometimes imaged as like the seven colours of the solar spectrum, derived from the three primary.* Each of these types has its own colouring of characteristics, and this colouring persists throughout the æonian cycle of its evolution, affecting all the series of living things that are animated by it. Now begins the process of subdivision in each of these types, that will be carried on, subdividing and ever subdividing, until the individual is reached. The currents set up by the commencing outward-going energies of the Monad—to follow one line of evolution will suffice; the other six are like unto it in principle—have but brief form-life, yet whatever experience can be gained through them is represented by an increasedly responsive life in the Monad who is their source and cause; and this responsive life consists of vibrations that are often

* "As above, so below." We instinctively remember the three LOGOI and the seven primæval Sons of the Fire: in Christian symbolism, the Trinity and the "Seven Spirits that are before the throne," or in Zoroastrian, Ahura-mazdâo and the seven Ameshaspentas.

incongruous with each other, a tendency towards separation is set up within the Monad, the harmoniously vibrating forces grouping themselves together for, as it were, concerted action, until various sub-monads, if the epithet may for a moment be allowed, are formed, alike in their main characteristics, but differing in details, like shades of the same colour. These become, by impacts from the lower levels of the mental plane, the Monads of the second elemental kingdom, belonging to the form-region of that plane, and the process continues, the Monad ever adding to its power to respond, each being the inspiring life of countless forms, through which it receives vibrations, and as the forms disintegrate, constantly vivifying new forms; the process of subdivision also continues from the cause already described. Each Monad thus continually incarnates itself in forms, and garners within itself as awakened powers all the results obtained through the forms it animates. We may well regard these Monads as the souls of groups of forms, and as evolution proceeds these forms show more and more attributes, the attributes being the powers of the monadic group-soul manifested through the forms in which it is incarnated. The innumerable sub-monads of this second elemental kingdom presently reach a stage of evolution at which they begin to respond to the vibrations of astral matter, and they begin to act on the astral plane, becoming the Monads of the third elemental kingdom, and repeating in this grosser world all the processes already accomplished on the mental plane. They become more and more numerous as monadic group-souls, showing more and more diversity in detail, the number of forms animated by each becoming less as the specialized characteristics become more and more marked. Meanwhile, it may be said, the everflowing stream of life from the LOGOS supplies new Monads of form on the higher levels, so that the evolution proceeds continuously, and as the more evolved Monads incarnate in the lower worlds their place is taken by the newly emerged Monads in the higher.

By this ever-repeated process of the reincarnation of the Monads, or monadic group-souls, in the astral world, their evolution proceeds, until they are ready to respond to the impacts upon them from physical matter. When we remember that the ultimate atoms of each plane have their sphere-walls composed of the coarsest matter of the plane immediately above it, it is easy to see how the Monads become responsive to the impacts from one plane after another. When, in the first elemental kingdom, the Monad had become accustomed to thrill responsively to the impacts of the matter of that plane, it would soon begin to answer to vibrations received *through the coarsest forms of that matter* from the matter of the plane next below. So, in its coatings of matter that were the forms composed of the coarsest materials of the mental plane, it would become susceptible to vibrations of astral atomic matter; and, when incarnated in forms of the coarsest astral matter, it would similarly become responsive to the impacts of atomic physical ether, the sphere-walls of which are constituted of the grossest astral materials. Thus the Monad may be regarded as reaching the physical plane, and there it begins, or more accurately, all these monadic group-souls begin, to incarnate themselves in filmy physical forms, the etheric doubles of the future dense minerals of the physical world. Into these filmy forms the nature-spirits build the denser physical materials, and thus minerals of all kinds are formed, the most rigid vehicles in which the evolving life encloses itself, and through which the least of its powers can express themselves. Each monadic group-soul has its own mineral expressions, the mineral forms in which it is incarnated, and the specialization has now reached a high degree. These monadic group-souls are sometimes called in their totality the mineral Monad, or the Monad incarnating in the mineral kingdom.

From this time forward the awakened energies of the Monad play a less passive part in evolution. They begin to seek expression actively to some extent when once aroused into functioning, and to exercise a distinctly moulding influence over the forms in which they are imprisoned. As they became too active for their mineral embodiment, the beginnings of the more plastic forms of the vegetable kingdom manifest themselves, the nature-spirits aiding this evolution throughout the physical kingdoms. In the mineral kingdom there had already been shown a tendency towards the definite organization of form, the laying down of certain lines* along which the growth proceeded. This tendency governs henceforth all the building of forms, and is the cause of the exquisite

* The axes of growth, which determine form. They appear definitely in crystals.

symmetry of natural objects, with which every observer is familiar. The monadic group-souls in the vegetable kingdom undergo division and subdivision with increasing rapidity, in consequence of the still greater variety of impacts to which they are subjected, the evolution of families, genera, and species being due to this invisible subdivision. When any genus, with its generic monadic group-soul, is subjected to very varying conditions, *i.e.*, when the forms connected with it receive very different impacts, a fresh tendency to subdivide is set up in the Monad, and various species are evolved, each having its own specific monadic group-soul. When Nature is left to her own working the process is slow, although the nature-spirits do much towards the differentiation of species; but when man has been evolved, and when he begins his artificial systems of cultivation, encouraging the play of one set of forces, warding off another, then this differentiation can be brought about with considerable rapidity, and specific differences are readily evolved. So long as actual division has not taken place in the monadic group-soul, the subjection of the forms to similar influences may again eradicate the separative tendency, but when that division is completed the new species are definitely and firmly established, and are ready to send out offshoots of their own.

In some of the longer-lived members of the vegetable kingdom the element of personality begins to manifest itself, the stability of the organism rendering possible this foreshadowing of individuality. With a tree, living for scores of years, the recurrence of similar conditions causing similar impacts, the seasons ever returning year after year, the consecutive internal motions caused by them, the rising of the sap, the putting forth of leaves, the touches of the wind, of the sunbeams, of the rain—all these outer influences with their rhythmical progression—set up responsive thrillings in the monadic group-soul, and as the sequence impresses itself by continual repetition, the recurrence of one leads to the dim expectation of its oft-repeated successor. Nature evolves no quality suddenly, and these are the first faint adumbrations of what will later be memory and anticipation.

In the vegetable kingdom also appear the foreshadowings of sensation, evolving in its higher members to what the western psychologist would term "massive" sensations of pleasure and discomfort.* It must be remembered that the Monad has drawn round itself materials of the planes through which it has descended, and hence is able to contact impacts from those planes, the strongest and those most nearly allied to the grossest forms of matter being the first to make themselves felt. Sunshine and the chill of its absence at last impress themselves on the monadic consciousness, and its astral coating, thrown into faint vibrations, gives rise to the slight massive kind of sensation spoken of. Rain and drought affecting the mechanical constitution of the form, and its power to convey vibrations to the ensouling Monad—are another of the "pairs of opposites" the play of which arouses the recognition of difference, which is the root alike of all sensation, and later, of all thought. Thus by their repeated plant-reincarnations the monadic group-souls in the vegetable kingdom evolve, until those that ensoul the highest members of the kingdom are ready for the next step.

This step carries them into the animal kingdom, and here they slowly evolve in their physical and astral vehicles a very distinct personality. The animal, being free to move about, subjects itself to a greater variety of conditions than can be experienced by the plant, rooted to a single spot, and this variety, as ever, promotes differentiation. The monadic group-soul, however, which animates a number of wild animals of the same species or sub-species, while it receives a great variety of impacts, since they are for the most part repeated continually and are shared by all the members of the group, differentiates but slowly. These aid in the development of the physical and astral bodies, and through them the monadic group-soul gathers much experience. When the form of a member of the group perishes, the experience gathered through that form is accumulated in the monadic group-soul, and may be said to colour it; the slightly increased life of the monadic group-soul, poured into all the forms which compose its group, shares among all the experience of the perished form, and in this way continually repeated experiences, stored up in the monadic group-soul, appear as instincts, "accumulated hereditary experiences" in the new forms. Countless birds having fallen a prey to hawks, chicks just out of the egg will cower at the approach of one of the hereditary enemies, for the life that is

* The "massive" sensation is one that pervades the organism and is not felt especially in any one part more than in others. It is the antithesis of the "acute."

incarnated in them knows the danger, and the innate instinct is the expression of its knowledge. In this way are formed the wonderful instincts that guard animals from innumerable habitual perils, while a new danger finds them unprepared and only bewilders them.

As animals now come under the influence of man, the monadic group-soul evolves with greatly increased rapidity, and, from causes similar to those which affect plants under domestication, subdivision of the incarnating life is more readily brought about. Personality evolves and becomes more and more strongly marked; in the earlier stages it may almost be said to be compound—a whole flock of wild creatures will act as though moved by a single personality, so completely are the forms dominated by the common soul, and it, in turn, affected by the impulses from the external world. Domesticated animals of the higher types, the elephant, the horse, the cat, the dog, show a more individualized personality—two dogs, for instance, may act very differently under the impact of the same circumstances. The monadic group-soul incarnates in a decreasing number of forms as it gradually approaches the point at which complete individualization will be reached. The desire-body, or kâmic vehicle, becomes considerably developed, and persists for some time after the death of the physical body, leading an independent existence in kâmaloka. At last the decreasing number of forms animated by a monadic group-soul comes down to unity, and it animates a succession of single forms—a condition differing from human reincarnation only by the absence of Manas, with its causal and mental bodies. The mental matter brought down by the monadic group-soul begins to be susceptible to impacts from the mental plane, and the animal is then ready to receive the third great out-pouring of the life of the Logos—the tabernacle is ready for the reception of the human Monad.

The human Monad is, as we have seen, triple in its nature, its three aspects being denominated respectively, the Spirit, the spiritual Soul, and the human Soul, Âtmâ, Buddhi, Manas. Doubtless, in the course of æons of evolution, the upwardly evolving Monad of form might have unfolded Manas by progressive growth, but both in the human race in the past, and in the animals of the present, such has not been the course of Nature. When the house was ready the tenant was sent down; from the higher planes of being the âtmic life descended, veiling itself in Buddhi, as a golden thread, and its third aspect, Manas, showing itself in the higher levels of the formless world of the mental plane, germinal Manas within the form was fructified, and the embryonic causal body was formed by the union. This is the individualization of the spirit, the encasing of it in form, and this spirit encased in the causal body is the soul, the individual, the real man. This is his birth-hour, for though his essence be eternal, unborn and undying, his birth in time as an individual is definite.

Further, this outpoured life reaches the evolving forms not directly but by intermediaries. The human race having attained the point of receptivity, certain great Ones, called Sons of Mind,* cast into men the monadic spark of Âtma-Buddhi-Manas, needed for the formation of the embryonic soul. And some of these great Ones actually incarnated in human forms, in order to become the guides and teachers of the infant humanity. These Sons of Mind had completed Their own intellectual evolution in other worlds, and came to this younger world, our earth, for the purpose of thus aiding in the evolution of the human race. They are, in truth, the spiritual fathers of the bulk of our humanity.

Other intelligences of much lower grade, men who had evolved in preceding cycles in another world, incarnated among the descendants of the race that received its infant souls in the way just described. As this race evolved, the human tabernacles improved, and myriads of souls that were awaiting the opportunity of incarnation, that they might continue their evolution, took birth among its children. These partially evolved souls are also spoken of in the ancient records as Sons of Mind, for they were possessed of mind, although comparatively it was but little developed—child souls we may call them, in distinguishment from the embryonic souls of the bulk of humanity, and the mature souls of these great Teachers. These child souls, by reason of their more evolved intelligencies, formed the leading types of the ancient world, the classes higher in mentality, and therefore in the power of acquiring knowledge, that dominated the masses of less developed men in antiquity. And thus arose, in our world, the enormous differences

* Mânasa-putra is the technical name, being merely the Sanskrit for Sons of Mind.

in mental and moral capacity which separate the most highly evolved from the least evolved races, and which, even within the limits of a single race, separate the lofty philosophic thinker from the well-nigh animal type of the most depraved of his own nation. These differences are but differences of the stage of evolution, of the age of the soul, and they have been found to exist throughout the whole history of humanity on this globe. Go back as far as we may in historic records, and we find lofty intelligence and debased ignorance side by side, and the occult records, carrying us backwards, tell a similar story of the early millennia of humanity. Nor should this distress us, as though some had been unduly favoured and others unduly burdened for the struggle of life. The loftiest soul had its childhood and its infancy, albeit in previous worlds, where other souls were as high above it as others are below it now; the lowest soul shall climb to where our highest are standing, and souls yet unborn shall occupy its present place in evolution. Things seem unjust because we wrench our world out of its place in evolution, and set it apart in isolation, with no forerunners and no successors. It is our ignorance that sees the injustice; the ways of Nature are equal, and she brings to all her children infancy, childhood and manhood. Not hers the fault if our folly demands that all souls shall occupy the same stage of evolution at the same time, and cries "Unjust!" if the demand be not fulfilled.

ANNIE BESANT.

(*To be concluded.*)

THE NATURE OF THE REAL MAN.

Know ye not, and do ye not understand that ye are all angels, all archangels, gods and lords, all rulers, all the great invisibles, all those of the midst, those of every region of them that are on the right, all the great ones of the emanations of the light with all their glory; that ye are all, of yourselves and in yourselves in turn, from one mass and one matter, and one substance; ye are all from the same mixture?

—PISTIS SOPHIA, 247, 248.

THE WISH TO BELIEVE.

It is a fact which theologians may lament, but which is nevertheless beyond question, that even thinking men are for the most part directed in their acceptance of dogma, not so much by the conviction that it is logically proved to them, as by the perception that it rounds out, harmonizes, and completes the view their own experience has already given them; that (to use a common phrase) it answers to their needs, or to speak more correctly, that it does not contradict their prejudices. The old proverb has it, "A man convinced against his will, is of the same opinion still." No one, for example, possessed of a reasonable amount of sympathy and insight, can fail in reading Cardinal Newman's *Apologia pro Vita sua*, to detect the faint, unconfessed undertone of this which runs all through it. He is thoroughly, profoundly convinced that his beloved *via media* is proved impossible—his *head* is entirely Catholic; but, all the same, to the very end of his life, his *heart* cannot help repeating over and over, Ah! if it only *could* have been possible! This, indeed, seems to me the secret of the book's instant success in reconquering for him the respect and sympathy of the English Protestant world; every line of it was evidence for him that his heart had never for a moment been a traitor to his first love, and the popular instinct (which is often more true and more sensitive than the conclusions of the learned) accepted that heart-homage as far more important than any theological differences.

In like manner, when we undertake to set forth the leading ideas of the Wisdom Religion to an ordinary circle of hearers or readers, there is something even more imperative than to express them clearly. We have to show how far they are compatible with the conceptions which already occupy the field, how little we actually deny and how much we explain and raise to a higher level; and thus (as far as possible) to dispose our hearers to give the new learning a favourable hearing—to make them *wish* to believe. Nearly all our audience will be in every case, at least nominally, Christians; and even those who consider themselves too "enlightened" to believe what are ordinarily understood as the doctrines of Christianity, usually set much store on the name, were it only as an additional sweet morsel to roll under the tongue of their self-complacency. So that whilst we may often have to speak sharply and incisively as to the defects of the Christian faith (as I have myself frequently done), to speak rudely and contemptuously of what is, with all its weakness, the very best thing these Christians have in their souls—the one promise of something better to come—is that sort of mistake which is worse than a crime. It is by the religion which they have that we must draw them onwards.

Now the very first question which will rise to their lips will be something in this shape, "Does your doctrine interfere with our faith in Jesus?" and on the answer we give will depend our whole chance of getting a farther hearing at all. We must not be impatient with them; the fact is, that a vague belief in the "love of Jesus" is very nearly all that the present generation of religious Protestants has left to cling to; and its members feel that if *that* be disturbed, they are driven from their last anchorage and swept away into unknown seas to perish. It would be a serious mistake to suppose that the effect of the last half century's advances in history and criticism is limited to the minds of sufficient intelligence to take in their actual results. Down to the most uneducated Ranter or Salvationist there is everywhere a sense of change, if only such a sense as we may imagine an oyster to have of the ebbing tide, a sense that much which used to be certain may very possibly turn out to be mistaken. Even those who most loudly proclaim "the old Gospel," speak so loud, chiefly to drown the growing whisper in their own hearts, that even in religion "the old order changeth, yielding place to new." Some, in this anxiety, strive to keep their position by the authority of a living Church, supposed the actual, inspired keeper of a changeless Faith. Those to whom this is possible will find there a noble ideal which has power to draw out much (though not all) of the best there is in man, and which will very probably fulfil all the needs of their present incarnation. But for most of those around us this is *not* possible; and these instinctively prepare for the coming storm in the sailor's way, by throwing overboard every thing which can possibly be dispensed with, and reducing themselves to what they call "simple faith in Christ." A dear and good Evangelical friend wrote me not long ago, words which express this condition of mind well enough. "I am afraid," she says, "that the reaction may have a depressing effect on your faith in God and the Bible; and you know that, however your faith may have been shaken in the past, the fact still remains that he that believeth shall be saved and he that believeth not shall be condemned. I shall still keep the hope that you may find the peace that comes from a simple trust in a loving Saviour."

There is an—innocence let us politelv call it, against which we are told that even the Gods fight in vain; and I freely confess that in actual fact I evaded the task of making my position as a Theosophist clear to my affectionate correspondent, honestly judging it beyond my power. But suppose we take her as a type of the class I am speaking of, and consider what we have to reply. Her confession of faith would run. "I believe in Jesus Christ the Son of God, who died to save me; I believe that when I die He *will* save me, and take me to Heaven to live with Him for ever. With St. Paul I am *resolved* to know nothing but Christ and Him crucified."

Now this is to her, and to many thousands of her fellows, an entirely satisfactory account of things. It would be absolutely useless, as it would be unpardonably heartless, to try to raise in her mind the difficulties which crowd in ours, to attempt to make her understand the vastness of the ocean she thinks she has got safely packed into her teacup. Teach her you cannot; but could it be possible to put our views of Jesus in such a way that she and they might perceive, if but dimly and uncertainly, that the reason we refuse to pronounce their formula is simply that we think too highly of Him so to limit our reverence? It would be a vast step in advance if we could thus bring the ordinary Christian to understand that we are not "Atheists" and "Unbelievers"; that we are on their side, "rowing in the same boat," though, as in Jerrold's jest, "with vastly different sculls."

Let us make the attempt. We must have a name for her; let us call her (as St. Francis de Sales called his pupil in his *Introduction to the Devout Life*) Philothea. It designates her kind well enough, the souls whose sole anchor in the confusion around them is that they love God to the best of their power, blindly; knowing nothing of Him except that as they think He sent His Son to redeem them. To wish to know more is sinful, we must be content with this "simple Gospel."

But for all that, my dear Philothea, you would like to know a little more. Suppose we start together, Bible in hand, and see if we can get a little further without risking your salvation. I think it is possible. Like you, we believe in a God, Infinite, beyond time and space, in whom "there is no variableness nor shadow of turning," as your Bible says. We believe that in Him (or Her or It, all is one when we speak of the Infinite) were all things before they were manifested by Him; that in Him at this present moment we "live and move and have our being." That from Him proceeded the "Word," of whom you read in the first chapter of St. John's Gospel; and that from this Word (the only manifestation of God possible to us, for "no man hath seen the Father at any time.") you and I and all mankind proceeded. "Without Him was not anything made that was made." So that in this way all of us are the sons of God, as Jesus Himself so often insisted. When the Pharisees attacked Him because, said they, He made Himself the Son of God, He did not reply by saying that He meant this in the sense of an *origin* different from the rest of mankind, but answered, "If the Prophet called *them* Gods to whom the word of God came, how say ye of the Son of Man whom God has sanctified and sent into the world, You blaspheme?"

Philothea. Do you mean to say then, like the Unitarians, that Jesus was a mere man like ourselves? Don't you believe in the Atonement?

Author. My dear friend, we are very far indeed from thinking Jesus Christ was a mere man like ourselves. But are you sure that you quite understand what it is to be a man like ourselves? St. Paul says, you know, "*Now* are we the sons of God, and it doth not yet appear what we shall be."

Ph. Yes; but then *he* was inspired. He was not speaking to such as we are. *We* are not sons of God, our hearts are desperately wicked. Don't you know the text?

A. My dear child, he was inspired; I quite agree, and by virtue of his inspiration he wrote, "*We* are the sons of God." I believe that text, don't you? If you really want to know what the Bible teaches you, you must not pass over the texts which don't fit your views. Let me tell you what St. Paul meant and what *we* mean when we speak of "a man like ourselves." You look at a man, your outer eyes see a body, and from various indications you conclude there is a mind dwelling in it. Your Bible says there is a "soul" in it; you don't see that, but you believe it, and that that soul will be somehow affected for all eternity by what it thinks and does during this mortal life. But how came the soul there, and what is it?

Your Bible tells you of that Word of God that "in Him dwelt all the fulness of the Godhead"; and of ourselves that "of that fulness we have all received." In another figure we are told that "In Him was life, and the life was the light of men. . . . That was the true Light which lighteth every man that cometh into the world." With such passages as these before you, you can hardly object to our statement that this "soul" of ours is really a detached portion of the Life of the Word, a spark from that Flame, a drop from that Ocean. As such, you have this first dignity of man, that he is not the mere "creature of a day," which moralists make him; that wherever and whenever he may have lived before, he has lived from a time which you are accustomed to express (not so very wrongly) as "all eternity"; and that he will live for all eternity to come. Of every human being in existence that is true which is said of the Word, that he came forth from God, that he (the spirit, the higher portion of him), even now dwells with God, and that to God he will return. It is not possible for any one who believes in an eternal Heaven to question this statement.

But we know something more of man than this. There are many steps in the progress whereby the Divine Spark at last comes to manifestation in this physical body. It is not for us to say with St. Paul that to be "absent from the body" is at once to be "present with the Lord." There are many wrappings to be taken off before we come to the higher soul, still more before we reach the Ocean of Life from which that has descended; and death does not at once remove them. Let us ask a question. Why did the soul choose thus to enwrap itself and to undertake this long and often painful path? Why not stay quietly with God when it was there?

Ph. How can you, how *dare* you ask such questions? It is presumption to pry into the secrets of God. He made our souls and our bodies, we have no right to ask why. "Shall not the Judge of all the earth do right?"

A. My dear Philothea, it is just because we are convinced that God must have done what is right, that we do venture to enquire. It is impossible you can *mean* that He is at liberty to do wrong if such be His pleasure, though you often use words which imply that; but at first sight the world around us looks very much as if the Maker *did* enjoy doing wrong. And this idea is so utterly unendurable to us that we cannot acquiesce in it as being the "Will of God." To a Bushman or a Hottentot you may say, "Believe this; you can't understand why!" But we, the educated and intelligent men of the most advanced races on the globe, *can* understand why; and not only can, but *must*. If your "simple faith" cannot answer our questions, so much the worse; we must have a more complicated faith—that is all.

Now if we lay down the general principle that man came forth from God to gain experience—to grow—to become *worth* reuniting with God at the end of his pilgrimage; I do not think you can find any text to the contrary, and I think I could, if we had time, produce a good many which imply it. But this general principle works out in ways which must considerably modify and enlarge your views, and I hope to show that we believe all you do—and a great deal more!

If we look backwards, it means that we were not "made" or "created" at the time of our last birth into the world; but have grown up from very small beginnings in past ages; and farther, that there is nothing unreasonable in supposing that as our present circumstances are (at least to a great extent) the results of our past conduct, so the condition of things in which we found ourselves at birth—the bodily and mental powers we possessed and the circumstances, favourable or otherwise, which have encouraged or limited their use, were also the result of our previous conduct *before* birth. And if you turn to the Gospel you will find in the narrative of the man born blind this very view actually taken by the disciples and acquiesced in by their Lord. "Master," say they, "who did sin, this man or his parents, that he was born blind?" To this question, He replies, not by what would be *to you* the natural answer, that the man could not have sinned before he was born, but by the statement that in this particular case his blindness was not a punishment of sin committed before his birth, by either himself or his parents, but, in truth, a blessing in disguise.

There can be no difficulty raised over the obvious view that in this series of lives some must have made much more progress than others, and indeed that some may have gone back. We need only watch the lives of those around us to see how little progress a life, in most cases, means. On the other hand, some must have gone ahead. Every man or woman of genius, as we say, is a soul which has thus far outstripped the rest, and has attained an advance which the race in general may require millions of years to reach. Such advance is not a "gift" of a capricious Nature or God, but is an indication that, perhaps for many thousands of years, the soul has dedicated itself with iron resolution to that study which now seems to come by Nature.

If, then, my dear Philothea, you have followed me so far; you will be able to see that even regarding Jesus as a mere man (which we do not), we are, as I said at the beginning, very far from regarding him as a man *like ourselves*. To us he is, simply as a man, almost immeasurably above us, and the reverence we can honestly pay him as such is (I venture to say it) something above the best you know how to give to him as God.

Ph. This is all very fine talking; but if he is man he can't be God, and to worship him would be blasphemy. You can't get over *that!*

A. My dear Philothea, it is the very object with which I set out—to help you to get over that! If you will have patience with me whilst I continue my exposition, I will try to show you what we mean by our advance, looking, no longer backward, but forward, from where we stand; and to suggest what the dignity and power of a soul which is a few millions of years before its fellows may be. No explanation can give us a real idea of it, but at least I think I can show you that it far surpasses all *your* ideas of a God. Then add to that the immediate inspiration of the Word Himself; and when I have shown you the Christ in all this power and glory, all being spent for the salvation of the world now and as long as that world lasts, I will venture to ask you whether such a presentation is not something nobler and greater than your claim of reverence merely because of something done to the physical body he dwelt in two thousand years ago.

A. A. WELLS.

(*To be concluded.*)

THE END OF FAUST.

MANY who have read the first part of Goethe's *Faust* with intense enjoyment and felt the world both explained and illumined by it, may have been slightly discouraged when they made an attempt to understand the second part. In fact it may be considered exceedingly doubtful whether more than a very elect few have ever struggled through and arrived at that rich guerdon for lovers of poetry and mysticism—the extreme end of *Faust*. As a rule, with the exception of the well-known line, "Das Ewig-weibliche," the very beautiful verses which compose it are overlooked. They have been set to music by Schumann, and it is impossible to say more than that he has entirely succeeded in his object. The power of sound is here called in to intensify and enlarge the meaning of the words and explain them to us in a way that mere reading in black and white could never do. It is one of the rare instances of "perfect music set to noble words."

The few pages comprising the third part of *Faust*, or end of the second part, for it is not always divided off, will well repay study and consideration. They show that Goethe should be considered as a mystic as well as a philosopher and a poet. As they practically stand quite alone, this last part may be treated for our purpose as a separate poem. It might also be perfectly well considered as an allegory describing the deliverance of the soul from the bonds that hold it, its intense longing for the divine, and the humility and sympathy that arise from temptation, failure and conquest.

It may be helpful to first briefly explain the course of events which have led up to this final scene through the long and perplexing second part.

We find that Faust has lived a long life with many and varied experiences. His last act however is his best; when quite an old man he spends much time and labour in draining and rescuing a considerable piece of waste land. On this he builds houses and founds a colony, thus enabling many people to live happily on a hitherto useless waste. The world is clearly the better for his work. Forgetting the old agreement with Mephistopheles, by virtue of which he holds his privilege of continued life and prosperity, he exclaims, "I now enjoy the happiest moment of my life," and wishes that it may not pass away. But the contract had enacted that, should the moment ever come when he should be happy enough to wish it to remain because it was so perfect, he should then lose all and resign his soul.

Faust, in his dreary pessimism, after a life of disappointment, had been so certain that he never could or would say this, that he had eagerly agreed to such a condition, thinking himself to be thus perfectly sure of eternal life in this world. For many years his opinion of himself was justified as he wandered wearily to and fro, trying every sort of human experience—pleasure, travel, study, and finding all more or less unexciting. Now, however, when he had devoted himself to practical philanthropy and become really interested in his new occupation, he forgot everything in this great happiness and made the fatal exclamation. He immediately falls back dead, and a struggle takes place for the possession of his soul between the powers of good and evil, which terminates in a victory for the former in consequence of his work for the good of others, work which must result in his final salvation, as is later explained.

Here we take up the last part of the drama. It deals with Faust after his death, and opens with a description of a sacred place where woods wave in the air, and where roots and stems of trees cling to the rocks and climb up on them. It is evidently not on earth, but in some higher sphere. It is called a field or garden of holy love or religious devotion, and holy anchorites wander about mixing freely with wild beasts, which here are tame and harmless. A student of Theosophy when just instructed about the supersensual planes is strongly reminded of these verses.

Next we have the three mystical figures, Patres Ecstaticus, Profundus and Seraphicus, who represent the three aspects of devotion—the ecstatic, the deep and silent, and the angelic. Most striking is the passionate cry of the first, Pater Ecstaticus, declaring the longing of the heart for the divine, and his resolve to destroy all that can hinder or intervene between it and its aim and end. He will welcome shattering blows or wounds, burning by fire, anything that can destroy the worthless and temporal, and let the true lasting star of eternal love shine out in him. The music expresses this wonderful struggling through minor keys and accidentals to a full close at the final consummation when the star of the soul shines out.

Pater Profundus then describes how all the mighty power of the woods, the streams and the rocks, does but show the almighty love which forms and nourishes all; the waterfalls, and the lightning that clears the air, are also love's messengers.

The third speaker, Pater Seraphicus, sees a cloud through the pines, which proves to be a choir of the spirits of young children, "lost to their parents but gained to the angels." These are happy in having no trace of earth's troubles, but are at present under limitations, and so cannot rise to higher circles without his help. They must, therefore, become one with him in a mystical union when they will rise spiritually and enable the God within them to shine more clearly and be seen through the veil. This revelation of love and the divine, he explains, is the food of the spirit, which thus can increase and develop in happiness. The line, "Denn das ist der Geister Nahrung," may in some degree recall the passage in Plato's *Phædo:* "But the soul will calm passion and follow reason, and dwell in her (knowledge) beholding the true and the divine, and thence derive nourishment." And again in the *Phædrus:* "Now the divine is beauty, wisdom, goodness, and the like—and by these the soul is nourished and grows apace." We have the same idea here of the soul obtaining the food necessary for its development, by which only it can live and grow.

This scene of the three Fathers forms a kind of prelude, and the real drama of the closing scenes of the history of Faust now begins.

An angel is seen far above bearing Faust's immortal body and singing a song of triumphant rejoicing at its escape from the powers of evil, the reason being:

Wer immer strebend sich bemüht	(Whoever strives untiringly
Den können wir erlösen.	Salvation can obtain.)

In other words, a man can attain liberation by action or deliverance from the bonds of the flesh and from evil by devoted labour for others.

The angels then sing a splendid chorus of victory. This should be heard as well as read, as the triumphant chords of Schumann's music ring long after in the ears and seem to be hardly earthly, but indeed a song of the angels. An interlude in a softer, more pathetic key shows how the child angels scatter roses over the body of Faust.

A new figure now appears, Dr. Marianus. It is uncertain whether this is meant to be Faust translated into a spiritual form or simply another mystical figure. The last supposition seems more probable, as he describes most movingly the attitude of penitent souls who in earthly life found it "so hard to fight and so easy to fall," and who are now here assembled to intercede for and welcome their erring brother. There is no shade of personal feeling or memory of the past, and the speaker is only an abstraction, as indeed are all the characters with the exception of the one "once called Gretchen," who prays to the One without likeness for him "so beloved formerly who is coming back at last."

Der früh Geliebte
Nicht mehr Getrübte
Er kommt zurück.

It is evident that her continued prayers and the force of her love for Faust have helped to bring him where he is.

The chorus of penitents sing of the chains which held them so tightly and which they broke with such difficulty, of the words and looks that so easily deceived, of the feet that so easily slipped, and all unite in intercession for their new brother. There are more songs and prayers of the same description which lead up to the end of the whole poem, where the new day and higher spheres open before the soul who has raised himself out of the mire and won his freedom by working for others.

The final chorus contains the deepest thoughts of the whole poem in a very few words:

Alles Vergängliche	(All that is transitory
Ist nur ein Gleichniss.	As symbol we see,
Das Unzulängliche	The unattainable

Hier wird's Ereigniss.	Possessed will be.
Das Unbeshreibliche	The indescribable
Hier ist es gethan.	Here is done.
Das Ewig-weibliche	The ever-womanly
Zieht uns hinan.	Draws us on.)

The verse is given here in the original, as it is practically untranslatable, though a faint attempt at a literal rendering in English is appended for the benefit of non-German readers. The first idea that all that is visible and earthly, all that passes away, is only a symbol by which we can get some idea of true Reality, is found at the root of all religions and philosophies, though perhaps never more satisfactorily and adequately expressed than in these lines. And the assurance that in the unseen life there is certain proof of the existeuce of what is here unattainable and indescribable, must rouse a responding chord in many hearts. Everyone who has realized something of what the unattainable is, and also the fact that it *is* unattainable in this physical life with our earthly senses, will understand what the hope of fulfilment of their best dreams and aspirations might be. And those who know most about the indescribable, know well that nothing through which we can express ourselves here, whether music or poetry or art, can do more than give an occasional glimpse of the realities that we are sure must exist somewhere.

The last pages of this poem contain many thoughts in a few very beautiful words, written with great power and conciseness. It has been impossible to do more than select a few of the leading ideas for consideration, such as the necessity of destroying the worthless and trivial before the soul can shine out in its full beauty; the universal love that supports and underlies all; the true food of the spirit necessary before it can grow and develop; or the salvation of an erring and selfish man through unselfish work for humanity; also the difficulties of keeping a sure foot and a steady head in the manifold temptations of life; and the tolerance and charity which those who have got through successfully show to those who have failed to do so.

These are only a few of the closely compressed ideas which are crowded in before the completion of the play in that final chorus which rises to such a height and so completely removes us from the phenomenal world; it forms a fitting close to the great drama of *Faust*, which contains so much metaphysics, such beautiful poetry, so many wise and deep thoughts, and touches on such innumerable points of interest.

C. CUST.

ON SOME REMARKABLE PASSAGES IN THE NEW TESTAMENT.

(*Concluded from p.* 27.)

There are several other passages in the N. T. which can only be interpreted properly by Eastern doctrines. Thus the remarkable and ill understood passage in Luke v. 36-39, that no new patch can harmonize with an old garment, and that new wine cannot be put into old bottles, seems common-place, but acquires a lofty spiritual meaning through the celebrated Sanskrit poem, the Bhagavad Gîtâ, where (ii. 22) it is said that as a man changes old garments for new, so he exchanges his old bodies for new ones (reincarnation). Another passage (*ib.* 26) implies that there was a still unsettled question whether the soul is immortal and never dies, or in a sense mortal and constantly revived or reborn—equally implying reincarnation, for the same soul is meant in either case.

Now these passages determine the real meaning of that in Luke, which has nothing to do with what precedes or what follows, but is an isolated parable. Both passages refer to reincarnation and a question whether the old *body* revives with the soul (assumed to be immortal), and they mean that it does *not*, and a reason is given by the allegory, that the old body could not be suited to the new state of the soul. Both assume re-birth, and controvert the docrine of the resurrection of the *body*, that on rebirth the old body is somehow restored to the immortal revived spirit, notwithstanding every atom of it may have passed innumerable times into other bodies, animal, vegetable or mineral, and been appropriated by other spirits as their temporary garb, and might just as well be claimed by them. The new wine cannot be put into the old bottles (the receptacle of the spirit-body); nor can an old garment be patched up by a new addition, for they would not harmonize.

Other isolated passages may be noticed for their suggestion of Eastern ideas being present to the writer's mind. In Acts viii. 9, μάγον should perhaps be read for μέγαν, which would be so easily confounded with it; *i.e.*, instead of the meaningless "that he was some great one," "that he was a kind of magician or sorcerer," explaining what goes before.

In Acts x. 11, we again find the word σκεῦος, which the English version renders a "vessel." It is, however, ***nomen generalissimum***, and means "some *thing*," as in Matt. xii. 29 ("things"), Mark xii. 16 ("anything"), etc. It seems in fact a mystical term, and probably derived from the Gnostics or their predecessors the Stoics, and instead of rendering it as if the animals descended tied up in a linen bag, it might rather be compared with the mystical descent of the "Sangreal," as in Tennyson's:

> And down the long beam stole the Holy Grail.

The whole is a vision in an ecstatic state.

Another very singular word demands notice. In 2 Peter ii. 3, κρῖμα seems not to mean merely "judgment" (κρίσις), but what is called karma, *i.e.*, used in a mystical sense as designating the whole consequences of a life of sin, of which the result is ἀπώλεια—loss (a lost soul). We might render perhaps, "whose old karma is not idle—is not inactive—and the downfall awaiting them no sluggard." It may possibly be an attempt to connect καρμα with a known Greek root, and naturally so, as implying a kind of final sentence or judgment. Κρῖμα is not classical Greek, but occurs in early Stoic writers, as *Polybius*, xxiv., 1-12. (*Cf.* Apoc. xvii. 1.)

In James i. 23, there is a remarkable passage, κατανοοῦντι τὸ πρόσωπον τῆς γενέσεως αυτοῦ ἐν ἐσόπτρῳ, which is absurdly rendered "beholding his natural face in a mirror"! with a still more absurd note, "Greek, the face of his birth," which is unintelligible. It is clear the translators had not the remotest idea of what was meant. Ἐσόπτρον is indeed a "mirror," but what mirror? Why, a magic mirror, and the true meaning is "contemplating" (not "beholding," as it implies a more continuous act than a mere look) the image (features) of his *nativity* in a magic mirror, for he has hardly clearly discerned it when *it* vanishes away (not, as rendered, "*he* departs"!). The vision or shade is gone, vanished. And what is symbolized by this magic mirror? The answer is, that in which the whole universe is depicted and all that has been acted in it, the great world-mirror, which in Sanskrit is called âkâsha—as different from air, and even ether, as air is from a stone.

Just afterwards (*ib.* v. 25), we find the reason for the illustration, where " ὁ παρακυψὰς εἰς " does not mean "he that looketh into," but "he that *stoopeth down* and looketh at his image," etc. So Coleridge, who no doubt took it from the Berlenberg Bible (which is often more correct than Luther's version), "*bückend einschauet.*" Luther's "*durchschauet in*" is taken from the Vulgate, "*perspexerit in,*" but is less accurate.

The law is compared by the Jewish convert to a mystical mirror in which truth is discernible, as shadows in water, faint and yet real representations, suggesting the real object.

Another noticeable passage is Apoc., vii. 17, where we find τὸ ἀνὰ μέσον τοῦ θρόνου. Both English versions have "(the Lamb) which is *in the midst of* the throne"! which in the first place is not Greek or English, and in the second is not sense. The true meaning is the "central figure of the throne"; *i.e.*, the second person of the Trinity, for of course the "Father" is not supposed to be visible to any eye of saint or mystic. (Ἀνάμεσον is really one word, though that is not material.) Luther has "*mitten im Stuhl,*" which would perhaps bear the meaning above given to the expression, and has been absurdly altered to "*in der mitte des Stuhls*" in the modern version as given by Stier u. Theile.

The three most striking and characteristic narratives in the Gospels are: (1) the Judas legend, which deserves an essay to itself, on account of its object and the skill with which it has been constructed and interwoven with the two following; (2) the Last Supper, and (3) the Crucifixion; which, unless wholly symbolical, have no parallel in any other religion, but if symbolical merely and not narratives of actual events, have more than one. Are they related, for instance, to the ancient Greek Mysteries, or the still more ancient ones from which those were derived?

It is impossible to regard the legend of Judas Iscariot as the relation of a historical fact, but it forms a fitting introduction to those that follow.

Judas may perhaps be identified with the Devadatta of the Buddhists. The whole of Matt. xxvii. is full of strange and suspicious passages. Although the Judas story is inserted with consummate skill (xxvi. 14-16, 25; xxvii. 3-10), it is impossible, when the attention is once directed to it, not to suspect that the whole story was got up to save the character of Peter. As to him, it was not doubted that he was a traitor (though not in the viler sense), that he thrice denied his Master. How then could this be got over? Only by the substitution of a scapegoat. Strike out all that relates to Judas—who may possibly be the author of the strange epistle that goes by that name—and the whole is intelligible, as also the doubt and even detestation in which Peter was held by Paul. Clearly Paul did not think Peter held the keys, as he everywhere speaks of Peter as maintaining the *Jewish* traditions, even to the extent of circumcision! But this painful question is dropped by the adherents of Peter in modern times. Nor do we often hear cited, "Begone, *Satan!* for thou (Peter) art my stumbling-block," etc. (Matt. xvi. 23), "for your thoughts are ever bent on (φρονεῖς) not divine but mundane matters."

In ch. xxvii. 22, Bar-abbas is Bar-Abba*a* (Syriac), "Son of the Father," who in Matt. is not exhibited as a criminal, but only as "a noted prisoner"; and the story (which is unintelligible as told) receives some light by supposing that he was a rival Messiah or Christ and had his own followers. Pilate has to judge between the two (verse 17), and obviously inclines to Jesus; the vile mob favour his rival and get him off (verse 21, etc.), though according to *a totally different tradition* Barabbas was a robber in prison for his crimes (Luke xxiii. 19, and Mark xv. 7), where we find ὁ λεγόμενος βαραββᾶς, the so-called "Son of the Father," exactly as we find, Matt. xxvii. 17, 22, τὸν λεγόμενον Χριστὸν, "the so-called Christ," both terms probably implying a denial of an assumed fact. Mark treats Barabbas as leader of a faction and riot, whose *followers* (not himself) had committed murder in the riot.

Pilate seems not to know (verse 17) who Christ was or claimed to be, or which of the two claimants they mean (verse 21), and he names Barabbas first, perhaps as at least known to him by name.

Seeing Jesus a mere man, and falsely supposing he claims to be the Jewish Messiah, the mob deem him guilty of the greatest of crimes as a blasphemer, but as under the Romans their judges had no power of life and death, they prefer to save a criminal to the man they deemed both criminal and blasphemer.

The inimitable pathos of the description of the "Last Supper" and the "Crucifixion" implies writers of considerable power and poetical imagination; and probably the best intellects of the religious of those days (the second century of our era) were employed in depicting these scenes of abiding interest, and connecting them with existing traditions.

Yet they may not be more tenable as actual facts that occurred than the almost equally poetic legend of the Sangreal in the Middle Ages, which might almost be regarded as an accessory legend, and one written quite in the same spirit. Here if anywhere we should find hints taken from the ancient Mysteries.

In the case of the Last Supper, there may be a secret reference to older Mysteries.

The *bread* recalls the name of Demeter (Ceres) and the Eleusinian Mysteries; ἄρτος is in strictness a *loaf* of wheat-bread only.

The *wine*, the Mysteries of Iacchus. That they have a symbolical meaning, few can doubt. Here, too, we may perhaps trace the original reason of the *cup* being refused to the laity by the Roman Catholic Church, it implying a higher initiation. Baptism, as the first initiation, entitles to the former, but not to the latter.

This, indeed, assumes that the rites of Iacchus were more important than those of Demeter, which is contrary to the common opinion. But the correctness of this opinion is very doubtful, as the Eleusinian rites of Demeter and Kore (Proserpine, Persephone) were properly merely local and peculiar to Eleusis, and those of Iacchus certainly Eastern and probably far more extensive, venerable and ancient. That they may have degenerated to orgies and revelling was probable from the nature of the symbol.

The very fact that the Eleusinian Mysteries were divided into Greater and Lesser seems to imply a complete independence of the other Mysteries, while the fact of their being originally local and confined to Eleusis shows that they must have been relatively of less importance, while the Mysteries of Iacchus were derived from Egypt or Asia, and widely celebrated.

But it does not seem that the Eleusinian Mysteries were known at all outside the sphere of Greek influence.

The ancient doctrine of the Mysteries, which is now again attracting attention, seems likely to explain many hitherto unsolved problems. An instance from the O. T. may be the strange story of the intended sacrifice of his son Isaac by Abraham, which perhaps really refers to the son's initiation in the Mysteries, as we are told that on initiation the neophyte passed under the knife of the hierophant, the sacrifice being symbolical and of course not consummated. In Gen. xxii., it is said that Abraham was ordered by the *A*ĕlōhīm to sacrifice his son in the land of Moriyāh. It is very remarkable that in the Samaritan version we have the land of H-z-y-th-h, *i.e.*, the "Vision," for Moriyāh, which seems to show that the latter word is really derived from the root r-a-h (see). Hence the explanation in verse 14, which substitutes the later name of "to-day"—Y'hōwāh—for *A*ĕlōhīm. This is absurdly referred by modern commentators to verse 13, as if it could mean "the Lord will provide," *i.e.*, the substituted *ram*. At the end of verse 14, the Samaritan version is "Y'hōwāh will restore his soul (or him) to life," strangely different from the Hebrew.

The whole legend cannot be taken literally. It might be more rationally interpreted as a vision attributed to the personage called Abraham.

The double name of Abraham and Abram implies two very different and distant periods. Neither is, nor can be, Jewish, the supposed derivations being nonsensical (Ab-ra'ham and Ab-ram). They are certainly symbolical, and probably come from the root b-r-y, analogous to the Sanskrit root bṛih, like Brahma and Brahman—a strange fact, which will no doubt some day receive its explanation.

Again, we find in the Gospels reference to the "mysteries of the kingdom of heaven," to which the Apostles only are admitted (Matt. xiii. 11; Mark iv. 11). And this is the reason given for the parables, or exoteric teaching, as the ordinary teaching suited to the multitude.

We may reasonably conclude that the parables have one and all a symbolical meaning, higher than the mere words convey.

With the saying in Mark iv. 11, the "mysteries of *the kingdom of God*," we must combine what is perhaps the most remarkable of all the sayings attributed to Jesus in any Gospel. "The kingdom of God *is within you!*" (Luke xvii. 21, where the word used is the unmistakable ἐντὸς, not the ambiguous ἐν), so strangely misunderstood by most Christians to this hour. (*Cf.* John iii. 3, which refers to rebirth, ἄνωθεν, from on high.)

It can only refer to the progress of the human soul, the culture of which is the only true civilization, morality and worship.

This World-Religion is taught by the Great Teacher, in direct opposition to the Jewish religion of a mere race.

F. H. BOWRING.

THE PHÆDO OF PLATO.

(*Continued from p.* 19.)

Let us turn now to the objection of Cebes, who, admitting the pre-existence of the soul, and that it is more lasting than the body, suggests that nevertheless, after wearing out many bodies (whether in one earth-life or in several), it may itself ultimately perish. The discourse in which this objection is refuted, and the argument for immortality carried to a triumphant conclusion, is an admirable example of Socratic dialectic. It opens with an enquiry into the cause of generation and corruption. When Socrates was a young man he was "wonderfully desirous of that knowledge which is called a history of nature." In other words, he occupied himself, as our modern men of science occupy themselves, in tracing effects to their so-called natural or material causes; as, for example, the senses to the action of the brain, the faculties of memory and opinion to the senses, and so forth. But, unlike the moderns, he soon discovered that he was on a wrong track. These so-called natural causes are not, properly speaking, causes at all, but rather conditions. For it is important to distinguish clearly between the cause by which a thing exists, and the conditions which make its existence in a certain respect possible. The cause is simple and always the same; the conditions are manifold and various. Thus, to take one of Socrates' own illustrations, the addition of one to one produces two; and again, by a process directly the reverse of this, *viz.*, the halving of one, two are produced; yet the cause of two subsists neither in addition nor in division. These are merely conditions under which it becomes possible for the idea of duality to manifest itself. Or, to take another instance, a picture is said to be beautiful when the forms and colours which constitute it are harmoniously composed and skilfully contrasted. But these sensible forms and colours are not the cause of its beauty. The cause subsists in the idea of beauty, which is participated by the soul of the artist, and by him expressed on his canvas under the material conditions of colour and form. A further illustration given by Socrates shows with great clearness the mistake which is made by those who look not beyond physical reasons for the causes of things. They argue as one who should say that the cause of his (Socrates') sitting there is, that his body contains certain bones and sinews, naturally adapted to assume such a position. But the true cause is in the mind, and not in the body at all. He sits there because he judges it best to do so. It is quite true that without such bones and sinews it would be impossible for him to sit; but the bones and sinews are not the cause of his sitting, but simply the conditions under which the cause is enabled to proceed into effect.

The earlier Greek philosophers, for the most part, occupied themselves with the investigation of the physical causes or conditions of things. Anaxagoras, however, perceived that in order to set in motion the corporeal particles, by the combination and separation of which the sensible world is manifested, there was need of some moving principle, exempt from its participants; since body, of itself, is inert and motionless. This moving principle he denominated intellect (νοῦς), "the rarest and purest of all things," which imparted a revolving motion to the infinite mass of mingled particles, a motion beginning in one point and gradually extending itself to infinity. By this motion the particles were separated, and the order of the universe was evolved. But although Anaxagoras thus established, as the cause of sensible manifestation, a transcendent principle, to which he himself attributes absolute power and absolute knowledge, it is clear from the evidence of both Plato and Aristotle that he did not carry out his own doctrine to its logical conclusion. Aristotle says of him that he "uses intellect as a machine to the fabrication of the world, and when he doubts on what account it necessarily is, he introduces it arbitrarily. But in other things he considers everything else rather than intellect as the cause of generated natures." * This statement is perfectly consistent with the account of Anaxagoras given by Socrates in the dialogue which we are now discussing.

To arrive at the true cause of things we must investigate in what manner it is best for them to subsist; since the First Cause, which is also the Final Cause, is that which is beyond all things best—*viz.*, the Good Itself. By the final cause I mean that for the sake of which everything subsists, that to which all things naturally tend as the supreme object of their desire. This is the Good, and it is identical with the One from which all things primarily proceed; for all good is rooted in union, as all evil in disunion; and thus the first Good is also the first Unity. In the second rank comes the Exemplary Cause, which is, as we said before, the intelligible Idea emanating from the Good. In this abide, in occult union, the ideas, or forms (εἴδη), as they are also called, which are the exemplars or archetypes of all existing things. All these ideas, subsisting occultly in intelligible being, are differentiated and manifested by the third, or efficient, Cause, which is Intellect. Each of these ideas is said to be, in relation to the whole series which participates it, as the One Itself is to the entire universe. "The whole world," says Proclus, "is suspended from the all-perfect monad of ideas, and the parts of the visible universe from monads which are separated from one another." † Now the monad of ideas, the first Idea wherein all ideas are comprehended, is nothing else than Being Itself, the intelligible exemplar of the sensible universe. This is, to the whole world, the cause of such being, or appearance of being, as it possesses, for being is the one idea of which all things without exception participate so far as they are capable. Moreover, all the parts of the universe participate further of the particular ideas which are comprehended in this "all-perfect monad." All ideas are everywhere similarly present, although the measure of their participation depends upon the aptitude of the recipient; not, indeed, upon its essential aptitude, since all things possess the whole in potentiality; but upon its aptitude in energy. Every recipient of forms energizes more fully according to certain forms, and less fully according to certain other

* *Metaphysics*, i. 4 Taylor's translation, p. 13.

† Cited in Taylor's *Plato* iii. p. 13.

forms, and it is therefore said to belong especially to the series proceeding from that idea which its energies chiefly manifest. Thus, every animated body belongs primarily to the series of Animal Itself; and again, some things energize principally according to the form, or idea, of the good,* others according to that of the beautiful, and so forth. The power which discriminates ideas, and calls them into manifestation, is Intellect, the active or efficient cause of the universe.

But it has been already observed, that without contraries there could be no manifestation. In order, therefore, for the manifestation of being it is necessary to introduce its contrary, non-being. We remarked that being was denominated the monad of ideas, as the exemplary cause of all existence. In the sensible world existence is manifested as a circle of generation and corruption. Generation, then, as a passing into being, is referred to being itself as its cause; while the cause of corruption, or the passing out of being, is consequently non-being; and intellect is, as we said, the active cause which produces manifestation. But the energy of intellect is eternal, and, in order for the production of temporal manifestation—*i.e.*, the circle of generation and corruption—there is need of an energy manifesting itself in time. This is the energy of soul, which proceeds from intellect, and translates into the language of time the ideas of eternity. Thus, to recapitulate: beyond intellect and the intelligible, beyond being itself, is the causeless cause of being, which we indicate by the names of the Good and the One. Then, of all that participates of being, the Idea is the cause: as intelligible being, exemplary; as intellect, efficient. In intellect, therefore, the cause of all things primarily subsists, and it subsists secondarily in soul, which is intellectual in its essence, and the vehicle by which the creative intellect acts upon the universe. Soul manifests in time the ideas which it derives from intellect, and is the immediate cause of all that exists and takes place in the sensible world.

Now, with regard to contraries: we have already seen that in generated natures—natures which subsist in becoming—contrary proceeds from contrary. This, of course, does not mean that a certain thing actually becomes the contrary to itself, which is obviously

* A distinction must be made between Good, as an intelligible idea, and *the Good*, which transcends all being.

impossible; but it means that the subject which participates of contraries, from being in the condition represented by one contrary, proceeds into that represented by the other. If we consider, for example, an animal as a subject participating of the contraries heat and cold, we may say that from being cold it becomes hot, or from being hot becomes cold; but we may not say that heat itself becomes cold, or that cold itself becomes heat. Or if we take as an instance the contraries generation and corruption, we say that every thing which is generated becomes corrupted, and that from this corruption a new generation is produced; but we do not say that generation itself, abstracted from the subject of generation, becomes corruption, or that corruption becomes generation. When, therefore, to one contrary another accedes, the former, being incapable of receiving that which accedes, is either destroyed, or, if it be indestructible, withdraws from the subject in which it is manifested. Thus, if cold approach a body which participates of heat, in proportion as the cold accedes, the heat withdraws; since heat itself is incapable of receiving cold. And further, not only is one contrary incapable of receiving its contrary, but if anything, which is not itself a contrary, so subsists as to partake essentially, or as a condition of its very existence, of the nature of some contrary, this thing also can never receive the contrary of that of which it thus participates. For instance, the odd and the even are contraries. But the number three, although not itself the contrary of anything, is what we term an odd number; that is, a number which essentially participates of the idea of odd, and cannot exist without participating it. Not only, then, is the odd itself incapable of receiving the even, but the number three, which is not the odd itself, but which necessarily partakes of the nature of the odd, is likewise incapable of receiving the idea of even.

It was said that soul is the cause of all existence in the sensible world. It is soul, therefore, which imparts form to matter, life and motion to body. Now the productive energy of the soul is twofold; for it produces either by its essence or by will. But it imparts life to the body by its essence, as fire imparts heat; since if the presence of life in the body depended alone upon the will of the soul, that life might at any moment be withdrawn from the body by the mere cessation of the will that it should continue. This, however, is not the case. Wherever soul is present, there of necessity is life; and whenever the soul departs from the body, death of necessity accedes to it. If, therefore, the soul imparts life, not by will, but by its very essence, it is essentially vital; for it cannot impart that which it does not possess. But life is a contrary, and death is the contrary of life. It has been shown already that that which essentially participates of a contrary is incapable of receiving the contrary of that of which it participates. Since the soul, therefore, participates essentially of life, it is incapable of receiving death, and is consequently immortal.

Again, fire imparts heat to body by its essence; that is to say, from the mere fact of fire being present the participation of heat by a body adapted to participate it, follows as a matter of necessity. Heat, therefore, is an essential property of fire, without which fire would not be fire. But since fire is thus incapable of receiving the contrary of heat, if cold approach it, it either departs or perishes. For in a certain sense fire may be said to perish, since this terrestrial fire which we so designate is not a simple essence, not the pure element at all, but a composite, dependent for its existence upon the concurrence of other elements. But since all composites may be dissolved, fire also perishes as fire by dissolution, and the heat which it essentially contains, is not indeed annihilated, but is dissipated into the surrounding atmosphere. Now life is an essential property of the soul, as heat is of fire; and when death approaches, the soul must in like manner either withdraw from the body which it animates, or suffer dissolution. But the soul, being incorporeal, is a simple essence, and cannot be dissolved, since it is not composed of parts. When death, then, arrives, the body perishes, for the life which it contains is not of its own essence; but the soul, being essentially vital and incomposite, is not receptive of death or of dissolution. It does not, therefore, in any wise cease to exist, but withdraws itself, safe and sound, from the perishing body.

W. C. Ward.

(To be continued.)

AMONG THE GNOSTICS OF THE FIRST TWO CENTURIES.

(*Continued from p.* 42.)

THE PERATÆ OF HIPPOLYTUS.

HIPPOLYTUS says that the mysteries symbolized by the serpent are at the root of all Gnosticism, and though the Church father himself has not the ghost of an idea what these mysteries really are, as is amply proved by all his remarks, we agree with him, as we have demonstrated above. He then proceeds to treat of the system of the Peratæ, to whom we have already referred, and whose mysteries (Hippolytus calls them their "blasphemy against Christ") had been kept secret "for many years." We know from other sources that the school was prior to Clement of Alexandria. The system of the Peratæ was based on an analogy with sidereal considerations, and depended on the tradition of the ancient Chaldæan star-cult. In Book iv., Hippolytus had already endeavoured to refute the Chaldæan system of the star-spheres, and though he makes some good points against the vulgar astrology of the time, does not affect the mysterious doctrine of the septenary spheres of which the empirical horoscopists had long lost the secret, and for which they had substituted the physical planets; this theory is adopted by Plato from the Pythagorean tradition in his Timæus. Hippolytus had the Peratic school especially in mind in his attempted refutation of the art of the astrologers and mathematicians, of which however he admits he had no practical knowledge, but space compels us to simply refer the student to the fourth book of his Philosophumena for the outline of astrology which the Church father presents.

According to the Peratic school, the universe was symbolized by a circle enclosing a triangle. The triangle denoted the primal trichotomy into the three worlds, ingenerable, self-generable, and generable. Thus there were for them three aspects of the Logos, or in other words, three Gods, or three Logoi, or three Minds, or three Men. When the world-process had reached the completion of its devolution, the Saviour descended from the ingenerable world or æon; the type of the Saviour is that of a man perfected, "with a threefold nature, and threefold body, and threefold power, having in himself all [species of] concretions and potentialities from the three divisions of the universe"; according to the Pauline phrase: "It pleased Him that in him should dwell all fulness (the plerôma) bodily."

It is from the two higher worlds, the ingenerable and self-generable, that the seeds of all sorts of potentialities are sent down into this generable or formal world.

Hippolytus here breaks off, and after informing us that the founders of the school were a certain Euphrates (whom Origen calls the founder of those Ophites to whom Celsus referred about 150 A.D.) and Celbes, whom he elsewhere calls Acembes and Ademes, proceeds to tell us something more of the Chaldæan art. He then says that he will quote from a number of Peratic treatises to show that their ideas were similar to those of the Chaldæans.

The Saviour has not only a human but a cosmic task to perform, the cosmic task is to separate the good from the bad among the sidereal powers and influences; the same peculiarity of soteriology is brought into prominence in the Pistis Sophia treatise to which we shall refer later on. The "wars in heaven" precede the conflict of good and evil on earth.

The treatise from which Hippolytus proceeds to quote is evidently a Gnostic commentary on an old Chaldæan or Syrian cosmogonic scripture, which the commentator proceeds to explain in Greek mythological terms. The beginning of this mysterious treatise runs as follows:

"I am the voice of awakening from slumber in the æon (world) of night. Henceforth I begin to strip naked the power that proceedeth from Chaos. It is the power of the abyssmal slime, which raiseth up the clay of the imperishable vast moist [principle], the whole might of convulsion, of the colour of water, ever moving, supporting the steady, checking the tottering . . . the faithful steward of the track of the æthers, rejoicing in that which streameth forth from the twelve founts of the Law, the power which taketh its type from the impress of the power of the invisible waters above."

This power is called Thalassa, evidently the Thalatth or World-Mother of the Chaldæans. The twelve sources are also called twelve mouths, or pipes, through which the world-powers pour hissing. It is the power which is surrounded by a dodecagonal pyramid or dodecahedron, a hint which should persuade astrologers to reconsider their signs of the zodiac.

Hippolytus' quotations and summary here become very obscure and require a critical treatment which has not yet been accorded them; we are finally told that the matter is taken from a treatise dealing with the formal or generable world, for it is denominated The Proasteioi up to the Æther; that is to say, the hierarchies of powers as far as the æther, which were probably represented diagramatically by a series of concentric circles, a "proasteion," being the space round a city's walls.

Hippolytus here again points out the correspondence between astrological symbolism and the teaching of this school of Gnosticism; it is, he says, simply astrology allegorized, or rather we should say cosmogony theologized. These Peratics, or Transcendentalists, derive their name from the following considerations.

They believed that nothing which exists by generation can survive destruction, and thus the sphere of generation is also the fate-sphere. He then who knows nothing beyond this is bound to the wheel of fate; but "he who is conversant with the compulsion of generation [saṁsâra], and the paths through which man has entered into the [generable] world" can proceed through and pass beyond (transcend) destruction. This destruction is the "Water" which is the "generation of men," and which is the element in which the hierarchies of generation hold their sway, and have their being. It is called water because it is of that colour, namely, the lower ether.

The treatise from which Hippolytus quotes, again dives into the depths of mythology, and among other things adduces the "Myth of the Going forth," and its mystical interpretation; finally, the Gnostic commentator explains the opening verses of the prologue to the fourth canonical Gospel. Hippolytus, however, is beginning to be baffled by the amazing intricacy of the system, as he tells us, and thus breaks off, and apparently takes up another treatise from which to quote. The new treatise is of an exceedingly mystical character, and seemingly deals with the psychological physiology of the school.

The universe is figured forth as triple; Father, Son and Matter (Hylê), each of endless potentialities. The Son, the fashioning Logos, stands midway between the immovable Father and moving Matter. At one time he is turned to the Father and receives the powers in his disk (face, or "person"), and then turning casts them into Matter which is devoid of form; and thus the Matter is moulded and the formal world is produced.

We here see an attempt to graft a higher teaching of the same nature as the Platonic doctrine of types and ideas on to the primitive symbolism of imperfectly observed natural phenomena. The sun is the Father, the moon is the Son, and the earth is Matter. The moon is figured as a serpent, owing to its serpentine path, and its phases are imagined as the turning of its face towards the sun, and again towards the earth. If this is correct, however, the immobility of the sun and the motion of the earth give us reason to believe that the Chaldæans were better acquainted with astronomy than the followers of the far later Hipparcho-Ptolemæic geocentricism. The Gnostic writer also has a correct theory of magnetic and other influences, which he quaintly sets forth. We can, moreover, distinguish three strata of interpretation: (i.) metaphysical and spiritual—the ideal world, the intermediate, and the visible universe; (ii.) the world of generation—and its sun, moon and earth forces; and (iii.) the analogical psycho-physiological process in man.

The last is thus explained. The brain is the Father, the cerebellum the Son, and the medulla Matter or Hylê. "The cerebellum by an ineffable and inscrutable process, attracts through the pineal gland the spiritual and life-giving essence from the vaulted chamber [? third venticle]. And on receiving this, the cerebellum [also] in an ineffable manner, imparts the 'ideas,' just as the Son does, to Matter; or, in other words, the seeds and the genera of things produced according to the flesh flow along into the spinal marrow." And, adds Hippolytus, the main secrets of the school depend on a knowledge of these correspondences, but it would be impious for him to say anything more on the matter, a scruple which is surprising to find in a Church father.

THE SETHIANS OF HIPPOLYTUS.

Closely connected with the Gnostics above described, are the Sethians to whom Hippolytus next devotes his attention. He speaks of their "innumerable commentaries," and refers his readers especially to a certain treatise, called The Paraphrase of Seth, for a digest of their doctrines. But whether or not Hippolytus quotes from this document himself or from some other treatise or treatises, is not apparent. The title, Paraphrase of Seth, is exceedingly puzzling; it is difficult to say what is the exact meaning of the term "paraphrasis," and the doctrines set forth by Hippolytus have no connection with the Seth legend. Can it possibly be that there is a connection between the name "Seth" and the mysterious "Setheus" of the Codex Brucianus?

The term Sethians, as used by Hippolytus, is not only puzzling on this account, but also because his summary differs entirely from the scraps of information on the system of the Sethites supposed to have been mentioned in his lost Syntagma, and allied to the doctrine of the Nicolaitans by the epitomizers. In the latter fragments the hero Seth was chosen as the type of the good man, the perfect, the prototype of Christ.

The Sethians of whom we are treating, begin with a trinity, Light, Spirit and Darkness, which again, in one respect, reminds us of the Sâṅkhya triguṇa, or triple powers of nature, sattva, rajas, tamas.

The Spirit is not, however, to be thought of as a breath or wind, but as it were a subtle odour spreading everywhere. All three principles then are intermingled the one with the other. And the Darkness strives to retain the Light and the Spirit, and imprison the Light-spark in matter; while the Light and the Spirit, on their side, strive to raise their powers aloft and rescue them from the Darkness.

All genera and species and individuals, nay the heaven and earth itself, are images of "seals"; they are produced according to certain pre-existent types. It was from the first concourse of the three original principles or powers that the first great form was produced, the impression of the great seal, namely, heaven and earth. This is symbolized by the world-egg in the womb of the Universe, and the rest of creation is worked out on the same analogy. The egg is in the waters, which are thrown into waves by the creative power, and it depends on the nature of the waves as to what the various creatures will be. Here we have the whole theory of vibrations and the germ-cell idea in full activity.

Into the bodies thus brought into existence by the waves of the waters (the vehicles of subtle matter), the Light-spark and the fragrance of the Spirit descend, and thus "mind or man" is "moulded into various species."

"And this [Light-spark] is a perfect god, who from the ingenerable Light from above, and from the Spirit, is borne down into the natural man, as into a shrine, by the tide of nature and the motion of the wind [the creative power which causes the waves]. . . . . Thus a minute spark, a divided splinter from above, like the ray of a star, has been mingled in the much compounded waters [bodies of various kinds made of subtle matter] of many (existences). . . . Every thought, then, and solicitude actuating the Light from above is as to how and in what manner mind may be set free from death—the evil and dark body—from the 'father' below, the [generative impulse] wind, which with agitation and tumult raised up the waves, and [finally] produced a perfect mind, his own son, and yet not his own in essence. For he [the mind] was a ray from above, from that perfect Light, overpowered in the dark and fearsome, and bitter, and blood-stained water; he also is a Light-spirit floating on the water."

The generative power is called not only "wind," but also "beast," and "serpent," the latter because of the hissing sound it produces, just like the whirling wind. Now the impure womb, or sphere of generation, can only produce mortal men, but the virgin or pure womb, the sphere of Light, can produce men immortal or gods. It is the descent of the Perfect Man or Logos into the pure man that alone can still the birth-pangs of the carnal man.

This natural and spiritual process is shown forth in the Mysteries; after passing through the Lesser Mysteries, which pertain to the cycle of generation, the candidate is washed or baptized, and putting off the dress of a servant, puts on a heavenly garment, and drinks of the cup of life-giving water. That is to say, he leaves his servile form, the body which is subjected to the necessity of generation and is thus a slave, and ascends in his spiritual body to the state where is the ocean of immortality.

The Sethian school supported their theosophical tenets by analogies drawn from natural philosophy, and by the allegorical interpretation of the Old Testament, but, says Hippolytus, their system is nothing else than the tenets of the Orphic mysteries, which were celebrated in Achæa at Phlium, long before the Eleusinian. No doubt the Sethians based their theories on one or more of the traditions of the mystery-cult, but we need not follow Hippolytus in his selection of only one tradition, and that too in its grossest and most ignorant phase of vulgar phallicism.

The school seems also to have had some affinities with the Hermetic tradition, and used the analogy of natural and "alchemical" processes for the explanation of spiritual matters. For instance, after citing the example of the magnet, one of their books continues: "Thus the Light-ray [human soul] mingled with the water [animal soul], having obtained through discipline and instruction its own proper region, hastens towards the Logos [divine soul] that comes down from above in servile form [body]; and along with the Logos becomes Logos there where the Logos has its being, more speedily than iron [hastens] to the magnet."

THE DOCETÆ OF HIPPOLYTUS.

As previously remarked, the remains of the ancient bed of the stream of the Gnosis which we are endeavouring to survey, are so obscure, that nothing but a most imperfect outline, or rather a series of rough sketches of certain sections that some day further discovery may enable us to throw into the form of a map, can be attempted. Chronological indications are almost entirely wanting, and we can as yet form no idea of the correct sequence of these general Gnostic schools. We must therefore proceed at haphazard somewhat, and will next turn our attention to a school which Hippolytus (Bk. viii.) calls the Docetæ; seeing that their tenets are very similar to those of the three schools of which we have just treated. There is nothing, however, to show why this name is especially selected except the obscure reason that it is derived from the attempt of these Gnostics to theorise on "inaccesible and incomprehensible matter." It may, therefore, be possible that they believed in the doctrine of the non-reality of matter; and that the name Docetæ ("Illusionists") is of similar derivation to the Mâyâ-vâdins of the Hindus. The system of the Gnostic circle bears a strong family likeness to the doctrines of the Basilidian and Valentinian schools, but the doctrine of the non-physical nature of the body of the Christ, which is the general characteristic of ordinary Docetism, is not more prominent with them than with many other schools. The outline of their tenets given by Hippolytus is as follows.

The primal Being is symbolized as the seed of a fig-tree, the mathematical point, which is everywhere smaller than small, yet greater than great, containing in itself infinite potentialities. He is the "refuge of the terror-stricken, the covering of the naked," and much else as allegorically set forth in the Scriptures. The manner of the infinite generation of things is also figured by the fig-tree, for from the seed comes the stem, and then leaves, and then fruit, the fruit in its turn containing seeds, and thence other stems, and so on in infinite manner; so all things come forth.

In this way, even before the sensible world was formed, was there an emanation of a divine or ideal world of three root-æons, each consisting of so many sub-æons, male-female; that is to say worlds, or beings, or planes, of self-generating powers. And this æon-world of light came forth from the one ideal seed or root of the universe, the ingenerable. Then the host of self-generable æons uniting together produce from the one Virgin (ideal cosmic substance), the Only-begotten (generated) one, the Saviour of the universe, the perfect æon; containing in himself all the powers of the ideal world of the æons, equal in power in all things to the original seed of the universe, the ingenerable. Thus was the Saviour of the ideal universe produced, the perfect æon. And thus all in that spiritual world was perfected, all being of the nature of that which transcends intellect, free from all deficiency. Thus was accomplished the eternal and ideal world-process in the spaces of the æons.

Next with regard to the emanation of the ideal world into the sensible universe. The third root-æon, in its turn, made itself threefold, containing in itself all the supernal potentialities. Thus, then, its Light shone down upon the primordial chaotic substance, and the souls of all genera and species of living beings were infused into it. And when the third æon, or Logos, perceived that his ideas and impressions and types (χαρατῆρες)—the souls—were seized upon by the darkness, he separated the light from the darkness, and placed a firmament between, but this was only done after all the infinite species of the third æon had been intercepted in the darkness. And last of all the resemblance of the third æon himself was impressed upon the lower universe, and this resemblance is a "life-giving fire, generated from the light." Now this fire is the creative god which fashions the world as in the Mosaic account. This fabricating deity having no substance of his own, uses the darkness (gross matter) as his substance, out of which he makes bodies, and thus perpetually treats despitefully the eternal attributes of light which are imprisoned in the darkness. Thus until the coming of the Saviour, there was a vast delusion of souls, for these "ideas" are called souls (ψυχαί) because they have been breathed out (ἀποψυγεῖσαι) from the (æons) above. These souls spend their lives in darkness, passing from one to another of the bodies which are under the ward of the creative power or world-fabricator.

In support of this the Gnostic author refers to the saying: "And if ye will receive it, this is Elias that was for to come; he that hath ears to hear, let him hear"; and also to Job ii. 9: "And I am a wanderer changing place after place and house after house." The latter passage is found in the version of the Seventy, but is omitted in the English translation.

It is by means of the Saviour that souls are set free from the circle of rebirth (metensomatosis), and faith is roused in men that their sins should be remitted. Thus, then, the Only-begotten Son gazing upon the soul-tragedy—the "images" of the supernal æons changing perpetually from one body to another of the darkness—willed to descend for their deliverance.

Now the individual æons above were not able to endure the whole fulness of the divine world, *i.e.*, the Son; and had they beheld it they would have been thrown into confusion at its greatness and the glory of its power, and would have feared for their existence. So the Saviour indrew his glory into himself, as it were the vastest of lightning flashes into the minutest of bodies, or as the sudden cessation of light when the eyelids close, and so descended to the heavenly dome; and reaching the star-belt there, again indrew his glory, for even the apparently most minute light-giver of the star-sphere is a sun illuminating all space; and so the Saviour withdrew his glory again and entered into the domain of the third sphere of the third æon. And so he entered even into the darkness; that is to say, was incarnated in a body.

And his baptism was in this wise: he washed himself in the Jordan (the stream of the Logos), and after this purification in the water he became possessed of a spiritual body, a copy or impression of his virgin-made physical body; so that when the world-ruler (the god of generation) condemned his own plasm (the physical body) to death, *i.e.*, the cross, the spiritual body, nourished in the virgin physical body, might strip off the physical body, and nail it to the "tree," and thus the Christ would triumph over the powers and authorities of the world-ruler, and not be found naked, for he would put on his new spiritual body of adeptship instead of another body of flesh. Thus the saying: "Except a man be born of water and of the spirit he cannot enter into the kingdom of the heavens; that which is born of the flesh is flesh."

As to Jesus Christ, the Gnostic writer wisely remarks, that this ideal can be seen from many sides; that each school has its own view, some a low, some a high view; and that this is in the nature of things. Finally none but the real Gnostics, that is those who have passed through similar initiations to Jesus, can understand the mystery face to face.

Monoïmus.

Hippolytus devotes his next section to a certain Monoïmus who is only mentioned by one other hæresiologist, namely Theodoret, in a brief paragraph. Monoïmus was an Arabian and lived somewhere in the latter half of the second century. His system is based on the idea of the Heavenly Man, the universe, and the son of this Man, the perfect man, all other men being but imperfect reflections of the one ideal type. His general ideas attach themselves to the cycle of Gnostic literature of which we are treating, and are elaborated by many mathematical and geometrical considerations from the Pythagorean and Platonic traditions. The theory of numbers and the geometrical composition of the universe from elements which are symbolized by the five Platonic solids—namely, the tetrahedron, cube, octahedron, dodecahedron and icosahedron—are developed. All these geometrical symbols are produced by the monad, which he calls the iota, the yod and the "one horn." It is our old friend the serpentine force, the horn of plenty, the rod of Moses and of Hermes; in other words, it is the atom which is said by seers to be a conical swirl of forces. This monad is in numbers the decad, the perfect number and completion of the first series of numbers, after which the whole process begins again.

Now it was Moses' rod which brought to pass the plagues of Egypt according to the myth. These "plagues" are nothing else but transmutations of the matter of the physical body, *e.g.*, water into blood, etc., all of which is quaintly worked out by the writer.

The whole of this system, indeed, opens up a number of important considerations which would lead us far beyond the scope of the present essay. Monoïmus was undoubtedly a contemporary of the Valentinian school, if not a pupil of Valentinus, and the garbled version of his system as preserved by Hippolytus can be made to yield many important points which will throw light on the "theological arithmetic" of the Gnostic doctors. This may be proved some day to still preserve a seed which may grow into a tree of real mathematical knowledge.

We will conclude our sketch of the tenets of Monoïmus by quoting his opinion on the way to seek for God. In a letter to a certain Theophrastus, he writes: "Cease to seek after God (as without thee), and the universe, and things similar to these, seek Him from out of thyself, and learn who it is, who once and for all appropriateth all in thee unto Himself, and sayeth: 'My god, my mind, my reason, my soul, my body.' And learn whence is sorrow and joy, and love and hate, and waking though one would not, and sleeping though one would not, and getting angry though one would not, and falling in love though one would not. And if thou shouldst closely investigate these things, thou wilt find Him in thyself, one and many, just as the atom; thus finding from thyself a way out of thyself."

(To be continued.)

G. R. S. MEAD.

THE METAPHYSICS OF VEGETARIANISM.

It may be of interest to examine on what grounds Indian thinkers base the *raison d'être* of Vegetarianism. However short this survey may fall of an estimate adequate to the importance of the subject, still it is hoped that an appeal to a profound system of philosophy, which rejects the use of flesh-food, may strengthen the Vegetarian cause.

The starting point of the Vedânta is the self-evident fact that the five senses entirely depend on outside influences. The external objects of sense are the feeders and sustainers of the organs of sense. All sensations, whether agreeable or unpleasant, are conveyed inward to the mind. The mind reflects them, as in a mirror, and throws

the mantle of an alien glow

over the imagery. Sense-objects become changed into the likeness of the mind, and externalized again into thought-forms or language. Sensing, thinking, and naming, are inseparable and interdependent acts of the human mind—the threefold aspect of all knowledge. And just as the restless senses will rush outward for the gratification of their unceasing desires, miserable slaves to this transient world of forms, even so is our much-boasted knowledge itself, necessarily, of a worldly and evanescent character. Therefore, asks the Vedântist, how can man claim immortality as long as he lives in the senses ?

The Vedânta philosophy postulates immortality rather on the ground that, besides sense-impressions and thoughts, there exists an unknown third in man, his true nature, which is latent and subdued while he is under the dominion of the senses, but which becomes manifest in proportion to the degree of restraint he puts on them. After holding back the outward-going energies, man is declared to regain the lost consciousness of his divine portion. This immortal part of man is called Âtman (lit. Self) in Sanskrit terminology. To the question, " How can Âtman be known ? "—the Vedântist has the answer that Âtman cannot be known objectively, because it transcends all knowledge; man knows it by being it. Âtman is the eternal principle in man, free from the weary round of births and deaths. Âtman is said to be independent of external forms, neither attracted by the attractive, nor repelled by the repellent; untouched by joy and sorrow; beyond all actions whether evil or good; serene; self-centred; the inward witness and judge of the historical play in which the outward man is acting his predestined part on the earthly stage. Body and mind, according to the Vedânta, are material vehicles through which Âtman works for outward expression. The fitness of these instruments, that is, physical health and purity of mind, stands in corresponding relationship to the spiritual growth of man. A diseased body and evil passions both cover and stifle the indwelling God, and dim man's knowledge that he is an immortal spirit.

Âtman is made manifest in all flesh. Though invisible, Âtman holds together, nay, calls into existence, the visible universe, for the purpose of revealing its divine nature. It seems many, though, in reality, there can be one Âtman only, eternally struggling for perfect expression in the manifold forms which unceasingly spring into being.

It is here that the Vedântic "Welt-Anschauung" comes in touch with the Vegetarian question. The idea is that he who has fully realized that one and the same Âtman is underlying and sustaining the universe, will, as a matter of course, be brought to identify himself with the whole creation, and gradually lose his individuality, even as a river does which is about to join the open sea. "I am the universe, and I love the universe as my own body." From the consciousness that there is only one force pervading creation, that creation shows variety in degree, but *is* unity in essence, it is but a small step beyond the narrow limits of personal, selfish interest. Once started on the way of unselfishness, human sympathies will grow stronger and wider until they embrace all flesh on earth. Man will even die himself that he may better live in others. The brutes will share in his universal love and compassion, for he will have learnt to see in all created life the manifestation of the same Âtman wherein he lives, and moves, and has his being.

It will now be understood why Vedânta philosophers are

Vegetarians. They reject flesh-food because it can only be obtained by immoral means. Suffering must be caused, and life taken in order to have meat or fish on the dinner table. Infliction of suffering for personal gratification is viewed as an act of selfishness, and selfishness arises out of ignorance. It is the ignorant man who becomes deluded into the mistaken belief that he is a body, whereas the wise man knows that he is a spirit, and that his body is but one expression out of the myriads of "words become flesh" which the same Holy Spirit illumines. When the veil of delusion is once removed from the mind, these foolish ideas of separateness in the universe will vanish, and so will all cruelty, and slaughter of what are seemingly different beings.

Vedântism, in common with the teachings of Christ, looks at human life as a deserved degradation and correction for the fall of man, and at this body of flesh as a temporary prison-house for man to repent this original sin which caused his birth down here, and to accomplish his own redemption. Both religious systems point to the same road of salvation, leading out of this vale of tears, upward, Godward, into perfect freedom—the road of self-denial and brotherly love. But while Vedântism, from very early times, has accepted the animal world into this universal brotherhood, Christianity strangely disregards the rights of the dumb creation.

ERNST HORRWITZ.

ON THE TRACK OF THE MSS.

The Globe of Feb. 12th, in its "Echoes of Science," is responsible for the statement that, "The Negus of Abyssinia has decreed the foundation of a great library in his capital of Addis-Ababa. It will contain all the best manuscripts of Ethiopia. Many of these are said to have been hidden on an island of Lake Zouay, called Debra-Sina, during the Moslem invasion of the sixteenth century, and recovered by Menelik, the present ruler."

OUR RELATION TO CHILDREN.

(*Concluded from p.* 68.)

IT is simply impossible to exaggerate the plasticity of these unformed vehicles. We know that the physical body of a child, if only its training be begun at a sufficiently early age, may be modified to a very considerable extent. An acrobat, for example, will take a boy of five or six years old, whose bones and muscles are not as yet as hardened and firmly set as ours are, and will gradually accustom his limbs and body to take readily and with comfort all sorts of positions which would be absolutely impossible for most of us, even with any amount of training. Yet our own bodies at the same age differed in no essential respect from that boy's, and if they had been put through the same exercises they would have become as supple and elastic as his, though now that they are definitely set no efforts that we could make, however long continued, could give them the same easy flexibility.

Now if the physical body of a child is thus plastic and readily impressible, his astral and mental vehicles are far more so. They thrill in response to every vibration which they encounter, and are eagerly receptive with regard to all influences, whether good or evil, which emanate from those around them. And they resemble the physical body also in this other characteristic—that though in early youth they are so susceptible and so easily moulded, they very soon set and stiffen and acquire definite habits, which when once firmly established can be altered only with great difficulty.

When we realize this we see at once the extreme importance of the surroundings in which a child passes his earliest years, and the heavy responsibility which rests upon every parent to see that the conditions of the child's development are as good as they can be made. The little creature is as clay in our hands, to mould almost as we will; moment by moment the germs of good or evil quality brought over from the last birth are awakening into activity; moment by moment are being built up those vehicles which will condition the whole of his after life; and it rests with us to awaken the germ of good, to starve out the germ of evil. To a far larger extent than is ever realized by even the fondest parents, the child's future is under their control.

Think of all the friends whom you know so well, and try to imagine what splendid specimens of humanity they would be if all their good qualities were enormously intensified, and all the less estimable features absolutely weeded out of their characters. *That* is the result which it is in your power to produce in your child, if you do your full duty by him; such a specimen of humanity you may make him if you will but take the trouble.

But how? you will say; by precept? by education? Yes, truly, much may be done in that way when the time comes; but another and far greater power than that is in your hands—a power which you may begin to wield from the very moment of the child's birth, and even before that; and that is the power of the influence of your own life. To some extent this is recognized, for most civilized people are careful of their words and actions in the presence of a child, and it would be an unusually depraved parent who would allow his children to hear him use violent language, or to see him give way to a fit of passion; but what a man does not realize is that if he wishes to avoid doing the most serious harm to his little ones he must learn to control not only his words and deeds, but also his *thoughts*. It is true that you cannot immediately see the pernicious effect of an evil thought or desire upon the mind of your child, but none the less it is there, and it is more real and more terrible, more insidious and more far-reaching than the harm which is obvious to the physical eye.

If a parent allows himself to cherish feelings of anger or jealousy, of envy or avarice, of selfishness or pride, even though he may never give them outward expression, the vibrations which he thereby causes in his own desire-body are assuredly acting all the while upon the plastic astral body of his child, tuning its vibrations to the same key, awakening into activity any germs of these sins that may have been brought over from his past life, and setting up in him also the same set of evil habits, which when they have once become definitely formed will be exceedingly difficult to correct. And this is exactly what is being done in the case of most of the children whom we see around us.

As it presents itself to a clairvoyant, the aura of a child is very often a most beautiful object—pure and bright in its colour, free as yet from the stains of sensuality and avarice, and from the dull cloud of ill-will and selfishness which so frequently darkens all the life of the adult. In it are to be seen lying latent all the germs and tendencies of which we have spoken—some of them evil, some of them good; and thus the possibilities of the child's future life lie plain before the eye of the watcher. But how sad it is to see the change which almost invariably comes over that lovely child-aura as the years pass on—to note how persistently the evil tendencies are fostered and strengthened by his environment, and how entirely the good ones are neglected! And so incarnation after incarnation is almost wasted, and a life which, with just a little more care and self-restraint on the part of the parents and teachers, might have borne rich fruit of spiritual development, comes practically to nothing, and at its close leaves scarce any harvest to be garnered into the ego of which it has been so very one-sided an expression.

When one watches the criminal carelessness with which those who are responsible for the bringing-up of children allow them to be perpetually surrounded by all kinds of evil and worldly thoughts, one ceases to marvel at the extraordinary slowness of human evolution, and the almost imperceptible progress which is all that the ego has to show for life after life spent in the toil and struggle of this lower world. Yet with so little more trouble so vast an improvement might be introduced! It needs no astral vision to see what a change would come over this weary old world if the majority, or even any large proportion of the next generation, were subjected to the process suggested above—if all their evil qualities were steadily repressed and atrophied for lack of nourishment, while all the good in them was assiduously cultivated and developed to the fullest possible extent. One has only to think what they in turn would do for *their* children to realize that in two or three generations all the conditions of life would be different, and a true golden age would have begun. For the world at large that age may still be distant, but surely we who are members of the Theosophical Society ought each to be doing our best to hasten its advent; and though the influence of our example may not extend very far, it is at least within our power to see that our own children have for their development every advantage which we can give them.

The very greatest care, then, ought to be taken as to the surroundings of children, and people who will persist in thinking coarse and unloving thoughts should at least learn that while they are doing so they are unfit to come near the young, lest they infect them with a contagion more virulent than fever. Much care is needed, for example, in the selection of the nurses to whom children must sometimes be committed; though it is surely obvious that the less they are left in the hands of servants the better. Nurses often develope the strongest affection for their charges, and treat them as though they were of their own flesh and blood, yet this is not invariably the case; and, however that may be, it should be remembered that the servants are almost inevitably less educated and less refined than their mistresses, and that therefore a child who is left too much to their companionship is constantly subjected to the impact of thought which is at least not unlikely to be of a less elevated order than even the average level of that of his parents. So that the mother who wishes her child to grow up into a refined and delicate-minded man should entrust him to the care of others as little as possible, and should above all things take good heed to her own thoughts while watching over him.

Her great and cardinal rule should be to allow herself to harbour no thought and no desire which she would not wish to see reproduced in her son. Nor is this merely negative conquest over herself sufficient, for happily all that has been said about the influence and power of thought is true of good thoughts just as much as of evil ones, and so the parents' duty has a positive as well as a negative side. Not only must they abstain most carefully from fostering, by unworthy or selfish thoughts of their own, any evil tendency which may exist in their child, but it is also their duty to cultivate in themselves strong unselfish affection, pure thoughts, high and noble aspirations, in order that all these may react upon their charge, quicken whatever of good is already latent in him, and create a tendency towards any good quality which is as yet unrepresented in his character.

Nor need they have any fear that such effort on their part will fail in its effect, because they are unable to follow its action for lack of astral vision. To the sight of a trained clairvoyant the whole transaction is obvious; he would distinguish the vibrations set up in the mind-body of the parent by the inception of the thought, would see it radiating forth, and note the sympathetic vibration created by its impingement upon the mind-body of the child; and if he renewed his observations at intervals during some considerable period he would discern the gradual but permanent change produced in that mind-body by the constant repetition of the same stimulus to progress. If the parents themselves possessed the astral sight, it would no doubt be of great assistance to them in showing exactly what were the capabilities of their child, and in what directions he most needed development; but if they have not yet that advantage, there need not therefore be the slightest doubt or question about the result, for that must follow sustained effort with mathematical certainty, whether the process of its working be visible to them or not.

And not only should a parent watch his thoughts, but his moods also. A child is quick to notice and to resent injustice; and if he finds himself scolded at one time for an action which on another occasion caused only amusement, what wonder that his sense of the invariability of nature's laws is outraged! Again, when trouble or sorrow comes upon the parent, as in this world it sometimes must, it is surely his duty to try as far as possible to prevent his load of grief from weighing upon his children as well as upon himself; at least when in their presence he should make a special effort to be cheerful and resigned, lest the dull leaden hue of depression should extend itself from his aura to theirs. Yet again, many a well-meaning parent has an anxious and fussy nature—is always fidgetting about trifles, and worrying his children and himself about matters which are really quite unimportant. If he could but observe clairvoyantly the utter unrest and disquiet which he thus produces in his aura, and could further see how these vibrations introduce quite unnecessary agitation and irritation into the susceptible auras of his children, he would no longer be surprised at their occasional outbursts of petulance or nervous excitability, and would realize that in such a case he is often far more to blame than they. What he should contemplate and set before him as his object is a restful, unruffled spirit—the peace which passeth all understanding—the perfect calm which comes from the confidence that all will at last be well.

It is further obvious that the training of the parents' character which is necessitated by these considerations is in every respect a splendid one, and that in thus helping on the evolution of their children they also benefit themselves to an extent which is absolutely incalculable, for the thoughts which at first have been summoned by conscious effort for the sake of the child will soon become natural and habitual, and will in time form the background of the parents' entire life.

It must not be supposed that these precautions may be relaxed as the child grows older, for though this extraordinary sensitiveness to the influence of his surroundings commences as soon as the ego descends upon the embryo long before birth takes place, it continues in most cases up to about the period of maturity. If such influences as are above suggested have been brought to bear upon him during infancy and childhood, the boy of twelve or fourteen will be far better equipped for the efforts which lie before him than his less fortunate companions with whom no special trouble has been taken. But it must be remembered that he is still far more impressionable than an adult, and the same strong help and guidance upon the mental plane must still be continued in order that the good habits both of thought and of action may not yield before the newer temptations which are likely to assail him.

Although in his earlier years it was naturally chiefly to his parents that he had to look for such assistance, all that has been said of their duties applies equally to anyone who comes into contact with children in any capacity, and most especially to those who undertake the tremendous responsibilities of the teacher. This influence for good or for evil over his pupils is one that cannot readily be measured, and (exactly as before) it depends not only upon what he says or what he does, but even more upon what he thinks. Many a master repeatedly reproves in his boys the exhibition of tendencies for the creation of which he is himself directly responsible; if his thought is selfish or impure, then he will find selfishness and impurity reflected all around him, nor does the evil caused by such a thought end with those whom it immediately affects. The young minds upon which it is reflected take it up and magnify and strengthen it, and thus it reacts upon others in turn and becomes an unholy tradition handed down from one generation of boys to another, and so stamps its peculiar character upon a particular school or a particular class. The epidemic of vice which saps the life-blood of so many of our great schools could never have attained its present terrible dimensions if the thoughts of those who should have guided them had always remained pure and true. But happily a good tradition may be set up almost as easily as a bad one—not quite as easily, because there are always undesirable external influences to be taken into account; but still a teacher who realizes his responsibilities and manages his school upon the principles that have been suggested will very soon find that his self-control and self-devotion has not been fruitless.

I am convinced that there is only one way in which either parent or teacher can really obtain effective influence over a child and draw out all the best that is in him—and that is by winning his love and confidence. It is true that obedience may be extracted and discipline preserved by inspiring fear, but rules enforced by such a method are kept only so long as he who imposes them (or someone representing him) is present, and are invariably broken when there is no fear of detection; the child keeps them because he must, and not because he wishes to do so. But if, on the other hand, his affection has been invoked, his will at once ranges itself upon the side of the rule; he wishes to keep it, because he knows that in breaking it he would cause sorrow to one whom he loves; and if only this feeling be strong enough it will enable him to rise superior to all temptation, and the rule will be binding no matter who may be present or absent. Thus the object is attained not only much more thoroughly, but also much more easily and pleasantly both for teacher and pupil, and all the best side of the child's nature is called into activity, instead of all the worst. Instead of rousing the child's will into sullen and persistent opposition, the teacher arrays it on his own side in the contest against distractions or temptations; and thus results are achieved which could never be approached on the other system.

It is of the utmost importance always to try to understand the child, and to make him feel certain that he has one's friendliness and sympathy. All appearance of harshness must be carefully avoided, and the reason of all instructions given to him should always be fully explained. It must indeed be made clear to him that sometimes sudden emergencies arise in which the older person has no time to explain his instructions, and he should understand that in such a case he should obey even though he may not fully comprehend; but even then the explanation should always be given afterwards. Unwise parents or teachers often make the mistake of habitually exacting obedience without understanding—a most unreasonable demand; indeed, they expect from the child at all times and under all conditions an angelic patience and saintliness which they are very far indeed from possessing themselves. They have not yet realized that harshness towards a child is always not only wicked but absolutely unreasonable and foolish as well, since it can never be the most effective way of obtaining from him what is desired.

It often happens that many of a child's faults are the direct results of the unnatural way in which he is treated. Sensitive and nervous to a degree, he constantly finds himself misunderstood and scolded or ill-treated for offences whose turpitude he does not in the least comprehend; is it wonderful that when the whole atmosphere about him reeks with the deceit and falsehood of his elders, his fears should sometimes drive him into untruthfulness also? Certainly in such a case the karma of the sin will fall most heavily upon those who by their criminal harshness have placed a weak and undeveloped being in a position where it was almost impossible to avoid it. If we expect truth from our children, we must first of all practise it ourselves; we must think truth as well as speak truth and act truth, before we can hope to be strong enough to save them from the sea of falsehood and deceit which surrounds us on every side. But if we treat them as reasonable beings—if we explain fully and patiently what we want from them, and show them that they have nothing to fear from us (for "perfect love casteth out fear")—then we shall find no difficulty about truthfulness.

A curious but not at all uncommon delusion—a relic perhaps of the terrible days when this unhappy country groaned under the ghastly tyranny of Puritanism—is that children can never be good unless they are unhappy, that they must be thwarted at every turn, and never by any chance allowed to have their own way in anything, because when they are enjoying themselves they must necessarily be in a condition of desperate wickedness! Absurd and atrocious as this doctrine is, various modifications of it are still widely prevalent, and it is responsible for a vast amount of cruelty and unnecessary misery wantonly inflicted upon little creatures whose only crime was that they were natural and happy. Undoubtedly nature intended that childhood should be a happy time, and we ought to spare no efforts to make it so, for in that respect as in all others if we thwart nature we do so at our peril.

It will help us much in our dealings with children if we remember that they also are egos, that their small and feeble physical bodies are after all but the accident of the moment, and that in reality we are all about the same age. Our business in training them is to develope only that in their lower nature which will co-operate with the ego—which will make it a better channel for the ego to work through. Long ago, in the golden age of the old Atlantean civilization, the importance of the office of the teacher of children was so fully recognized that none was permitted to hold it except a trained clairvoyant, who could see all the latent qualities and capabilities of his charges, and could therefore work intelligently with each so as to develope what was good in him and to amend what was evil. In the distant future of the sixth race it may be that that will be so once more; but that time is as yet far away, and we have to do our best under less favourable conditions. Yet unselfish affection is a wonderful quickener of the intuition, and those who really love their children will rarely be at a loss to comprehend their needs; and keen and persistent observation will give them, though at the cost of much more trouble, some approach to the clearer insight of their Atlantean predecessors. At any rate it is well worth the trying, for when once we realize our true responsibility in relation to children we shall assuredly think no labour too great which enables us to discharge it better.

A word should be said in conclusion upon the subject of religious training. Many members of our Society, while feeling that their children need something to take the place filled in ordinary education by the religious training, have yet found it almost impossible so to put Theosophy before them as to make it in any way intelligible to them. Some have even permitted their children to go through the ordinary routine of bible lessons, saying that they did not know what else to do, and that though much of the teaching was obviously untrue it could be corrected afterwards. This, however, is a course which is entirely indefensible; no child should ever waste its time in learning what it will have to unlearn afterwards. If the true inner meaning of Christianity could be taught to our children, that indeed were well, because of course that would be pure Theosophy; but unfortunately that is not the form which religious instruction takes in our schools.

Nor is there any real difficulty in putting the grand truths of Theosophy intelligibly before the minds of our children. Certainly it is useless at first to trouble them with rounds and races, with lunar pitris and mânasaputra; but then, however interesting and valuable all this information may be, it is of little importance in the practical regulation of conduct, whereas the great ethical truths upon which the whole system rests can happily be made clear even to the childish understanding. What could be simpler in essence than the three great truths which are given to Sensa in *The Idyll of the White Lotus?*

"The soul of man is immortal, and its future is the future of a thing whose growth and splendour have no limit.

"The principle which gives life dwells in us and without us, is undying and eternally beneficent, is not heard nor seen or smelt, but is perceived by the man who desires perception.

"Each man is his own absolute law-giver, the dispenser of glory or gloom to himself—the decreer of his life, his reward, his punishment.

"These truths, which are as great as is life itself, are as simple as the simplest mind of man. Feed the hungry with them."

We might express these more tersely by saying: "Man is immortal; God is good; as we sow, so shall we reap." But surely none of our children can fail to grasp these simple ideas in their broad outline, though as they grow older they may spend many a year in learning more and more of the immensity of their full meaning. Teach them the grand old formula that "death is the gate of life"—not a terrible fate to be feared, but simply a stage of progress to be welcomed with interest. Teach them to live, not for themselves, but for others—to go through the world as friends and helpers, earnest in loving reverence and care for all living things. A child's sympathies are so easily roused, and his delight in doing something is so great that he responds at once to the idea that he should try to help, and should never harm, all the creatures around him. He should be taught to be observant, that he may see where help is needed, whether by man or by animal, and promptly to supply the want so far as lies in his power.

A child likes to be loved, and he likes to protect, and both these feelings may be utilized in training him to be a friend of all creatures. He will readily learn to admire flowers as they grow, and not wish to pluck them heedlessly, casting them aside a few minutes later to wither on the road side; those which he plucks he will pick carefully, avoiding injury to the plant; he will preserve and tend them, and his way through wood and field will never be traceable by fading blossoms and uprooted plants.

As the parent teaches the child he will also be obliged to set the example in this as in other things, and so the child will thus again civilize his elders as well as improve himself. Birds and butterflies, cats and dogs, all will be his friends, and he will delight in their beauty instead of longing to chase or destroy them. Children thus trained will grow up into men and women recognizing their place in evolution and their work in the world, and each will serve as a fresh centre of humanizing force, gradually changing the direction of human influence on all lower things.

If thus we train our children, if we are thus careful in our relations with them, we shall bear nobly our greatest responsibility, and in so doing we shall help on the grand work of evolution; we shall be doing our duty, not only to our children, but to the human race—not only to their egos, but to those of the many millions yet to come.

C. W. LEADBEATER.

THE SÂṄKHYA PHILOSOPHY.

(*Concluded from p.* 74.)

BEFORE entering upon the comparison which follows, I ought to state that the particular Sâṅkhyan doctrine which is to be discussed here rests primarily upon the Bhagavat Gîtâ, while the form in which I use it is drawn from Shrî Shankarâchârya's Commentary upon that scripture. At the present day in India it would undoubtedly be accepted as orthodox Sâṅkhyan teaching, but as I am unable to adduce any older authorities for it than the Gîtâ and Shankarâchârya's commentary, it is at least open to question as to how far it belongs to the original Sâṅkhya. The statement in the Gîtâ most probably embodies an ancient oral tradition, so that in this respect we are likely to be upon fairly safe ground; but with Shankarâchârya's explanation of it the matter stands otherwise. In the first place, the commentary ascribed to that great teacher seems to me to lack those internal evidences which one expects to find in a genuine work of his, and seems rather to belong to a comparatively late stage in the development of Vedântic thought; secondly, the explanation of the passage in question, though undoubtedly embodying a very ancient tradition, is given as a Vedântic rather than as an explicitly Sâṅkhyan teaching. Still it may well be of true Sâṅkhyan origin, because the Vedânta has so obviously taken over the whole of the Sâṅkhyan teaching on cosmology that this particular point, if Sâṅkhyan originally, would naturally be adopted along with the rest. But the question cannot be decided in the present state of our knowledge, and so I shall treat the teaching in question as orthodox Sâṅkhya for the purposes of this comparison.

The passage in the Gîtâ which is of interest to us occurs in the seventh chapter, shlokas 4 and 5, which run as follows:

"Earth, water, fire, air, space, mind, understanding and egoism, thus is my nature divided eight-fold. But this is a lower (form of my) nature. Know (that there is) another (form of my) nature, and higher than this, which is animate, oh, you of mighty arms! and by which this universe is upheld."

These verses are explained in the commentary ascribed to Shankarâchârya, as meaning that the life informing these various modifications of Prakṛiti is to be distinguished from the mere matter which encases it, though in concrete manifestation the two are so intimately associated that they are commonly taken together under the one name of Prakṛiti and its various modifications.

Turning now to our theosophical teaching, we have learnt, comparatively recently, that there are three distinct outpourings of the Divine Life. Of these, the first, proceeding from the Third Logos, calls into existence the matter of the various planes, and constitutes the life of atoms and molecules of matter. Into the great ocean of matter thus formed, the Second Logos pours forth the second great life-wave, which becomes the evolving monadic essence on plane after plane, building matter into form, and constituting the informing life and consciousness of all forms and creatures; always working in and through the matter called into existence by the first outpouring, ever functioning in conjunction with it in such intimate association, that for practical purposes even close students take them both together and only emphasize the distinction when there is special need for so doing. Finally, it is into the vehicle ultimately evolved by the monadic essence working upwards through matter that there descends the third outpouring, which is the pledge and guarantee of man's true immortality.

It seems that we have here a teaching very closely resembling the Sâṅhkyan doctrine which I have sketched above. There we had the matter and the informing life, both termed Prakṛiti, and both presided over and subservient to the interests of the Purusha, the individual soul, which would thus answer to the ray from the third outpouring of the divine life, which becomes individualized in the causal body of man, which is formed from the upward evolving monadic essence of the second life-wave veiled in the matter of the arûpa levels of the mânasic plane.

If this idea be true, it explains also why, in the Sâṅkhya, all action and its resultant karma is ascribed to Prakṛiti, while Purusha is always asserted to be actionless and ever in itself exempt from suffering, stain or evil.

For we know that the binding effect of karma arises entirely from the self-centered desire which prompts to, or accompanies action. But this self-seeking desire obviously belongs exclusively to the causal body and the lower vehicles of man, and disappears more and more completely when consciousness becomes focussed and seated in the buddhic plane. This is clear from the fact that the dominant characteristic of consciousness when functioning on the buddhic plane is the complete absence of that "sense of separateness," which we all must recognize as the very root and mainspring of all self-seeking and desire to possess or enjoy. Therefore it seems not improbable that we shall be right in associating desire for self with the upward evolving monadic essence which has formed the causal body, and which—in present ordinary humanity—is the highest *active* element in man's constitution. For it is well-known that although the âtmic ray, or third outpouring, does exist within the causal body, yet it plays no active part, exerts no direct control or action upon its vehicles until these have attained a comparatively advanced condition of unfoldment and evolution. Thus for all practical purposes it would seem to be true—in regard to ordinary humanity in its present stage of progress—that all action proceeds from this monadic essence which has formed the causal body, or from the impulsions arising in the still lower vehicles. In other words, it all proceeds from Prakṛiti, and the saying of the Gîtâ becomes intelligible that "all action is Prakṛiti-born." For in ordinary mankind the âtmic ray is as yet quite undeveloped, even its buddhic vehicle is the merest thread, so that even in a man of well-developed intellect all his actions and activities have no higher source than the activity of the monadic essence of the second great outpouring, which forms his causal body.

The reader must here be reminded that these views are put forward as suggestions, as tentative gropings claiming neither authority, weight nor finality other than such as their inherent reasonableness may seem to deserve. For in the present state of our knowledge both of Theosophy and of Hindu philosophical thought, it is a most difficult task to determine with any accuracy the points of contact and the true parallelisms between the two.

For those who are able to perceive and know the truth of things on this and on higher planes by direct, immediate perception, such purely intellectual studies as these will, I am fully conscious, appear uninteresting and of small, if any, value. But I would humbly venture to remind them that even such exalted faculties as they enjoy must, of necessity, be liable to error and imperfection so long as any, even the smallest, trace of the personality remains. For in the language of the Sâṅkhya, until the ahaṅkâra, the individual "I," with its special idiosyncrasies and peculiarities, has become perfectly assimilated to and unified with the Divine Ray which informs it, all that can be seen even on the plane of the ego itself must, it would seem, be tinged and coloured by those special peculiarities and characteristics. This at least is the unanimous burden of Hindu teaching, and it certainly seems both inherently reasonable and entirely consonant with all our experience on this plane, where we members of the Theosophical Society have only too often had to lament in ourselves and in others the purblindness of intellect and of heart which results from prejudice, preconception, national or racial inheritance, and individual idiosyncrasy of mind or feeling.

Recognizing this, and bearing in mind that all free progress in knowledge has been the work of many minds, it may not be unprofitable for us to seek in the works of those who have gone before us for clues and indications by which to check our own observations and theorizings no less than to guide our attention to what might otherwise escape us. Herein, it seems to me, lies the great value for us all of such work as Mr. Mead is doing upon the Gnostic systems, and I should welcome with enthusiasm the appearance among us of workers who would qualify themselves to undertake, in the immensely vaster field of Hindu thought, such work as he is doing in that of the Gnostic schools.

BERTRAM KEIGHTLEY.

THEOSOPHICAL ACTIVITIES.

European Section.

Three new Branches of this Section have been formed in Holland within the past month, at Rotterdam, the Hague and Vlaardingen. These Branches bring the number in Holland to seven, the number required to form an independent Section. Application will shortly be made by these Lodges to the President-Founder so that they may form the Dutch Section, which will be the seventh belonging to the Society. Very close and friendly relations have always existed between the Dutch members and the European Headquarters, but owing to the difficulty of language, the office at Amsterdam has always been the real centre of the Dutch members for local business. The two Sections will of course work together as closely as heretofore, excepting only in purely business matters.

The Blavatsky Lodge lectures have been well attended throughout the past month, this being especially the case with the Sunday evening meetings, which concluded with the one on the Sunday before Easter. The last few meetings dealt with the subjects of hell and its correspondences in real nature, karma, with a series of illustrations drawn from the observations of successive incarnations, yoga, and magic in its various forms. Mr. Leadbeater in this course has condensed an immense amount of information, much of it quite fresh to his hearers, into a very short space of time. Mr. Mead in his lecture on "Theological Geometry" illustrated his somewhat abstruse subject by an excellent series of models of the Platonic solids and their variations.

Australian Section.

The Sydney Branch began a course of meetings with the new year, giving a progressive outline of Theosophical teachings, the course to extend over four months. The quarterly general meeting was held on Jan. 5th, at which Mons. Coulomb, formerly well-known in Theosophical literature under the pseudonym of Amaravella, was present and assisted. Some of the Lodges had a vacation of two or three weeks at Christmas, but have begun their meetings again as usual. The "Dayspring" Branch at Sydney held its annual meeting on Jan. 11th, when the usual business matters were discussed. The President read a short general paper on Theosophy, following which was a discussion.

AMERICAN SECTION.

Mrs. Besant's long and stormy journey of nearly five weeks from India to America was completed on Thursday, March 18th, when she arrived in New York, and was welcomed by Mr. Fullerton, the General Secretary of the American Section.

Even on the landing-place a number of reporters surrounded Mrs. Besant, and a paper, *The Tribune*, received on the way to the hotel, already contained a notice of her arrival. The whole afternoon was occupied in interviews, and the papers next day contained accounts—more or less inaccurate, but on the whole very friendly in character—of what Mrs. Besant had said.

Time flew on Friday and Saturday in receiving people, writing articles and letters, and in making final arrangements for the lecture to be given in Chickering Hall on Sunday evening.

Early on Sunday morning the Countess Wachtmeister arrived from Buffalo and Toronto, where she had been lecturing daily and working with many people in the movement. The Countess is still very exhausted after her arduous labours, which resulted in the formation of thirteen Branches and one centre for study and also in many new members.

The Countess accompanies Mrs. Besant, and thus the tour will be one of double activity

During the absence of Mr. Walters, Count Axel Wachtmeister has been the acting editor of *Mercury*, the American Theosophical journal, and under his careful direction the paper has improved and is largely extending its circulation.

Mrs. Besant's first lecture in Chickering Hall on Sunday was a distinct success; the audience was attracted and interested, and the slides representing sketches of thought-forms and auras showed up well.

On Monday evening, after a busy day spent in seeing enquirers, in correspondence and in arranging the details of the proposed six months' tour through the States, a reception was held in the largest room of the hotel, and for an hour and a half a crowd of attentive listeners proved that the Americans are ready to hear and appreciate Theosophy.

The next two weeks are full of appointments, and Mrs. Besant is now well launched on her American work, with every indication so far that the result will be a great revival of public interest in the Theosophical movement and that groups of students will be formed into Lodges of the Society.

On March 29th we leave for Washington, and the week is to be spent between that place and Philadelphia, the return to New York being in time for the Sunday lecture. On Monday, April 5th, we start for St. Louis, and will go on to Kansas, Topeka, Denver, Colorado, Leadville, Salt Lake City, and Ogden, on the way to Los Angeles.

A. J. W.

Ceylon Letter.

The latest movement organised in Ceylon is entitled the "Ceylon Band of Mercy." It is founded in connection with the Musaeus School and Orphanage and its object is to protect animals from ill-usage. We hope that several branches of the movement will be established.

The buildings in connection with the Musaeus School and Orphanage are practically finished now. The Institution was re-opened in February, and the house is now quite full of pupils.

Through the kindness of Mr. Hack, a competent assistant to Mrs. Higgins has been found in Miss Gweiner, from Adelaide.

The Hope Lodge meets every Sunday regularly. Beside the usual syllabus the reading of the *Growth of the Soul* has been taken up.

Mrs. Pickett, the mother of the late Miss Pickett, has assumed the direction of the Sangamitta Girls' School.

New Zealand Section.

The following report has been received:

The holidays are now quite over, and Branch meetings and classes have begun again.

The Auckland lectures and public meetings of late have been very well attended, there having been a steady growth of public interest during the last six months. Miss Edger's lectures since her return have drawn very large audiences and have been followed by long and interesting discussions. The subjects of the last two were "Practical Theosophy" and "Reincarnation."

There also seems to be a great interest in Theosophy in Christchurch, and the Branch grows steadily. Mrs. Draffin's recent lectures there evoked much interest, all of them being very well attended; one in particular, given in "Our Father's Church" and forming part of the evening service, drawing an audience of about 700.

Mr. and Mrs. Draffin's visit to the Branches has been very successful on the whole, and in conjunction with the General Secretary's recent tour should lead to increased activity everywhere.

We have to announce the final passing from his present body of our colleague John C. Staples, the General Secretary of the Australasian Section. For further details readers are referred to "On the Watch-Tower."

REVIEWS.

The Rational or Scientific Ideal of Morality.

By P. F. Fitzgerald. [London: Swan Sonnenschein; 1897.]

This work is not at all an easy one to review conscientiously. Its title page leads one to expect a systematic, consecutively coherent attempt to formulate the basis of a science of morals, and therefore the reader is unpleasantly affected when on attacking the book itself he finds these qualities absent to an irritating extent. The table of contents is to some degree a help in ascertaining what the author is aiming at; but one is brought up sharply every few pages by finding the thread of argument breaking off suddenly, and what seems a new and quite disconnected line abruptly taken up.

The effect of this is to produce the impression that the author has never fused his work into a whole in the fire of thought, but has contented himself with stringing together the notes, observations and reflections which from time to time he has jotted down, into this semblance of a book. Most assuredly it is not a creation, but a patchwork, and as such very disappointing to every lover of good and thorough work. Still that is not all which must be said in fairness to the author. For the book contains a certain amount of real thought—a rare enough commodity in these days—and here and there luminous and acute remarks. Besides, there is a queer flavour about it which attracts one's interest towards the writer. Think of a quasi-scholastic theologian, transplanted from the atmosphere of Augustine and St. Thomas Aquinas and grafted upon the stock of nineteenth century neural psychology and German philosophy, and one has the two main currents which feed the author's mind. The result is, to say the least, singular and interesting from its very strangeness.

The basis of the whole is a philosophical theism—mediæval theism in the garb of later German philosophy—the validity of which, it is to be presumed, the author believes himself to have established in other works. Mediæval as his theism appears in phrase and tone, yet it is in several points very much up-to-date, if not *fin de siècle*, and no appeal whatsoever is made to revelation as such, though the writer seems to lean towards a vague theory of the divine revealing or unfolding itself through the minds of men, and his scriptures appear to be the works of all great poets and thinkers. His rather laboured paragraphs of philosophico-theological reasoning are interspersed with bright, acute remarks and quotations from many writers, which break in, not unwelcome, on the heaviness of many a page.

With a theistic basis of this kind, the problem of an ethic is not very difficult of solution, and with such broad lines to work upon it is not surprising that the conclusions should in many points coincide with those at which theosophical students have arrived. But it is certainly an original idea to make the doctrine of complemental or counterpartal souls—one male, the other female—a cardinal principle and conspicuous feature of his ethical philosophy. It is perhaps hardly fair to demur, on such a point, to the author's assumption that the soul *per se* is either male or female. But the fact remains that so far as I can discover not the smallest attempt is anywhere made in this work to justify, let alone to prove, this very gigantic assumption. And of course unless the assumption is either proved or granted, the moral theories built upon it are wholly baseless and void. Even thus, however, it may be interesting to see what the author makes out of the assumption he so calmly takes for granted.

To begin with, he holds, though nowhere does he prove, that complemental union is not only necessary for happiness, but for spiritual evolution. His argument in support of this amounts merely to the remark that since every human being is *eo ipso* imperfect and one-sided in development, as well as possessed of definite individual idiosyncrasies, hereditary and other, *therefore* perfection can only be attained through spiritual union with a complemental spirit. But in Heaven's name, why? One can imagine other ways of reaching such perfection, *e.g.*, our own theosophical doctrine of continual reincarnation. This conception and argument turns up again and again throughout the book, but one never seems to get at any sounder reasoning and more satisfactory proof.

To conclude: there is much of interest in this work for the thoughtful and *patient* reader; but judged according to its title page, one must class it as a failure lacking in many most important essentials of lasting, solid work.

B. K.

THE NIGHT OF THE GODS.

By John O'Neill, Vol. II. [London: David Nutt: 1897.]

THE first volume of this work was reviewed in LUCIFER for October, 1893, by Mr. Mead, who dealt so thoroughly with the general purpose and scope of the work as to render it needless to go over the ground again in connection with the second volume. We must, however, thank Mr. Nutt for sending both volumes together at the present time, for the book is an exceeding useful and valuable one for purposes of reference, and contains an immensity of matter most interesting to students of comparative religion. And therefore, while confining this notice mainly to the new volume, we must again draw the attention of all students in our ranks to the claim which the now complete work has for a place on their shelves.

The present volume, while following out the same general lines of thought and research as its predecessor, deals mainly with myths embodying the idea of the wheel, circle or sphere of the heavens. The original feature in Mr. O'Neill's theory of the origin of these myths is that he substitutes for the time-worn solar theory the conception that it was the profound impression made upon the imagination of primitive man by the sublime spectacle of the revolution of the star-bespangled heavens as a whole round the north pole, which become symbolically associated, even if it did not originate, the idea of the wheel, whether in the form of the revolving millstone, the cart-wheel, the fire-wheel, the potter's wheel, etc., or any other symbol or example of rotary motion. This is at any rate an advance on the worn out solar theory of myths; though naturally from the theosophical standpoint it is even ludicrously inadequate for an explanation of the facts. But at any rate it serves as a not inefficient thread upon which Mr. O'Neill can string a large and most interesting collection of facts and instances, of legends and stories, of striking and, alas, very often unsound, etymologies.

In the first chapter we find quite a unique collection of examples grouped under the sub-heads of the praying-wheel, the fire-wheel, the heavens-wheel, the wheel-god, the wheel of fortune, the Egyptian glyph Ra, the wreath, all culminating in the Romaunt of the Rose and the Rose-windows of our Gothic cathedrals.

The second chapter carries on the wheel idea into association with

Buddha's footprints and other sacred imprints of the kind; the connecting idea being that of the God or hero of the heavens circumnambulating the Pole and leaving behind him his footprints as he does so. And so we are led through the three Steps of Vishnu, the three Legs of Manx and Irish legend to the Svastika, the labyrinth, the conch-shell and the Chakra or discus as a weapon. Thence to other allied weapons of various gods is an easy step, and so we find the wheel-theory threatening, like the solar theory, to swallow up the whole of mythology within its octopus grasp. For this same circular motion again is clearly the origin of dancing in religious rites; while the sphere in all its varieties from the winged sphere to the winged scarab only too obviously come into the same category. So at the end of this part, while full of gratitude to the author for the mass of materials which his learning and untiring research has thus focussed into an accessible form, one cannot help wondering whether it ever struck him that a theory which explains too much explains nothing at all. And thus the very ingenuity and vastness of his work raises one's doubts as to the soundness of the substructure upon which he builds. And this feeling only tends to grow after reading—with intense interest, one cannot deny—the remaining chapters dealing with gods, rivers and mountains in myth and explaining any number of them in the same way. But one thing is certain, and that is the great debt which all serious students are under to the author for the immense mass of materials which he has amassed with such ungrudging labour and, with but few exceptions, minute and careful accuracy. An admirable index doubles the value of the work, and we only regret that stern death should have deprived us of one from whose continued labours so much valuable work was to have been expected.

B. K.

THE TATTVA KAUMUDÎ OF VÂCHASPATI MISHRA.

A commentary on the Sâṅkhya-Kârikâ of Îshvara-Kṛiṣhṇa, translated into English by Gangânâtha Jhâ, with the Sanskrit Text appended. [Bombay: 1896.]

BOTH the Sâṅkhya-Kârikâ of Îshvara-Kṛiṣhṇa and the Sâṅkhya system of philosophy which the Kârikâ summarizes, are too well known to need any introduction here. But the Tattva-Kaumudî, or the Moonlight of Truth, as Vâchaspati Mishra calls his commentary on the Kârikâ, though as famous in India as its reputed author, is probably unknown to most people outside the limited circle of Sanskritists. A translation, therefore, of such a work is welcome, and as far as I know this is the first attempt to put the Tattva-Kaumudi into an English form.

Although such books will not have much interest for those students of Theosophy whose object is more to realize truth at first hand than merely to reason upon it, they will, nevertheless, appeal to people who are still mainly concerned with the intellectual aspect and consider, as Mr. Davies, the translator of the Kârikâ, does, such inferential speculations as true philosophy. For the Tattva-Kaumudi, also the Kârikâ, and even the very Sâṅkhya aphorisms attributed to Kapila, as we now have them, are nothing more than inductions and inferences which can never satisfy the student who desires first hand knowledge. They are all entirely different from the original Sâṅkhya, which meant nothing more than "exposition" (Saṅkhyâyate anena iti), or "systematizing" of the *theory*, as opposed to Yoga, which originally meant *practice* or "application," in which sense it has been used even in the Gîtâ, when Shri Kṛishna says: "Yoga is skilfulness in action" (II. 50). This contrast of Sâṅkhya and Yoga, science and art, theory and practice (or application, applying or joining oneself to *activity* and *not* to the Universal Self, for the Upanishads never recognized two Selfs, individual and universal), is noticeable even in the Upanishads. The Sâṅkhya, in fact, originated in an attempt to systematize and put into *scientific* and exact form the teachings of the Upanishads, which in their spiritual enthusiasm disregarded all rules of a scientific language, such as exact definition of terms, the use of the same terms in the same sense throughout, and so on. They are indeed outbursts of poetry. They supplied, no doubt, facts and observations of seers in the transcendental regions, forming thus the basis of a transcendental science, which is what true philosophy is. But their loose terminology and poetical form caused much confusion to those who had no direct knowledge and had only to infer and speculate. To remove this difficulty, to bring down truth from the domain of poetry to the region of exact science, was the purpose of the Sâṅkhya, which, as has been noticed above, meant nothing more than "exposition" or "theorizing." Thus it is that the Sâṅkhya is the oldest of all schools of Hindu philosophy, being, in fact, synonymous with philosophy. But in later times the expositors almost left the transcendental behind, and dragged down the sublime system of thought to the mere speculation, in which form alone we find it to-day under the name of the Sâṅkhya School of philosophy. To remedy this evil appeared the Vedânta as a system which at once combined the transcendental and the rational. The present translation, therefore, representing as it does the later Sâṅkhya, will be of interest chiefly to those who want to know more about the speculative life of the Hindus.

One word, however, regarding the author of the commentary, the Moonlight of Truth. Vâchaspati Mishra had such a remarkable adaptability of mind that he could study and write upon almost any school of philosophy from the standpoint of a strong advocate of that school. Thus he has written on the Vedânta, Sâṅkhya, Yoga, and Nyâya, always as a most orthodox representative of his theme. His intellectual life is an excellent example of the manner in which a man can study all subjects and identify himself with all and yet retain his own individuality. His greatest work is the Bhûmatî, a commentary on the Shârîraka Bhâṣhya of Shri Shaṅkarâchârya.

As regards the present translation, it begins with an introduction giving the main ideas of the technical and speculative Sâṅkhya which will be of use to the beginner, though I am afraid the translation of the technical terms will not give adequate ideas to the reader. This is a very difficult task, as is known to any one who has attempted to translate Sanskrit technical terms into English. The translation also is in many cases rather free, this being probably due to the fact that the language and forms used by a Sanskrit scholiast can hardly be retained in every case. In many instances, however, the translation could be improved. In some cases the omission of a word or two has rendered the meaning imperfect. On page 57, for instance (Kârikâ xviii.), the omission of the phrase "not existing before" (apûrvâbhiḥ), has weakened the strong argument of the original. The translation of the technical term "adhidaivika" by "the supernatural" is more than unpardonable, for a learned Hindu ought to have known that there is no such thing. On the whole, however, the translation will be of service to those who want knowledge more general than critical.

The Sanskrit part is not, of course, meant for English readers. It is prefaced by a short account, or rather a legend, of Vâchaspati Mishra's life.

As regards the get up of the book, I am sorry I cannot say much in its favour. The author is not free from the chronic Hindu malady of mistransliteration of Sanskrit terms, which in this case may be due to the fault of the printer, who, though he may be excused for misprints in the English part of the book, is surely to be blamed for the numerous errors in the Sanskrit text, which, if the author tried to collect all, would swell his list of errata to a far greater bulk. It is a great pity that our Hindu people are so careless in this respect. J. C. C.

The Bible and the East.

By Lt.-Col. C. R. Conder, R.E. [London: William Blackwood and Sons.]

THIS work promises to give its readers in small compass the results of the latest explorations in Palestine, Egypt, and Assyria, and their bearings on the narratives of the Old Testament. Written, as it is, by one so thoroughly competent for the task as Lt.-Col. Conder (for so many years the leader of the Palestine Survey), it cannot fail to be valuable reading. It is written throughout from the standpoint of a devout believer in "the Bible, the whole Bible"—I cannot, however, conclude the quotation, for even in its pages we come on many an admission that "nothing but the Bible" is now out of date. With the cheery, breezy confidence which generally marks the religion of an old military or naval officer, he opens his batteries against the destructive school of criticism, and with a few sharp paragraphs like cannon-balls, finishes off to his own satisfaction the whole German position. On his main contention he is entitled to be heard with respect. He points out, not only that on many points the Egyptian and Assyrian records now first read off by our scholars confirm the Bible narrative, but that the use of the names of places is generally correct; the ancient names of places which did not exist or were otherwise named in Ezra's time, being correctly given in the history which purports to be of the ancient time—a thing we could hardly expect to find in a writer *inventing* it centuries afterwards. Whether however his demonstration goes beyond proof that the severe re-editing, which the sacred books certainly underwent after the captivity, had a foundation of real ancient narrative to work upon, may be fairly questioned. To discuss the matter at full length is a task we may leave to the critics he assails.

The writer would, however, indignantly repudiate what is to us the chief service of his book. He and such as he do a work for the enlightenment of mankind, perhaps at this present time even more useful than if he himself saw clearly the bearings of the new facts he speaks of. We are apt to think that the world's progress depends entirely on those great leaders who stand far ahead and call to us to come on. It might be so were all mankind fully grown, able to see and follow them; in reality the vast mass are children still, and need not an Alpine guide to lead them over glacier and precipice, but a judicious nursemaid to coax them into putting one foot before the other on level ground. These would never open one of our books, but will read with avidity such a work as this, written by one who shares their faith, in defence of the orthodox view of the Bible. Confident in such a leader, they will take unquestioning such statements as these (to quote one or two out of many such):

"In natural science the belief in a slow development of life on the planet and in the great antiquity of man—historically speaking—is now generally accepted. . . . In the study of antiquity the early civilization of Asia has been proved to have been more perfect and more widely spread than scholars were willing once to believe. . . . The first chapter of Genesis no longer stands alone in literature as an ancient story of creation. The brick tablets of Assyria contain more than one ancient poem of creation. . . . The honest student may be forced to give up much that he once believed, to own that tradition among Hebrew writers in time, as in other cases, sometimes overlaid the figures of great heroes with popular legend, and that they speak to us in the tongue of their own age, not in the language of to-day."

It is far better that the suspicions of the orthodox Christian should not be roused by recognizing the logical bearing of this mode of thought upon his faith. His children will be brought up upon it, and will draw the conclusions he fails to see; and in the next generation (a class we could never have *directly* reached) our position will seem a mere matter of course—the world will have taken its single step forwards and be ready for the next.

A. A. W.

The Lute of Apollo.

By Clifford Harrison. [London: A. D. Innes & Co., 1896. Price 5s. net.]

This charmingly arranged little book is an attempt to sketch the lines of an answer to that very deeply-rooted and widely-ramified question—What is Music? And in pointing out the paths which seem to him most nearly to reach the end of his enquiry, the author finds himself very close indeed to the Theosophical view. The student of occultism will be dissatisfied with this essay only on the ground of its incompleteness. Looked at from the vantage ground of Theosophical teaching, it is not that the author has trodden ways diverse, but that he has not pursued his road quite far enough. It should have brought him to the solution of his questions concerning what he calls "preternatural senses," to an explanation of that Pythagorean maxim to which he refers, "Everything is Number and Harmony."

But it may be that this criticism is uncalled for, and that Mr. Clifford Harrison has but remembered how much more important it is to stimulate than to answer enquiry. It seems unlikely that so suggestive a writer would have neglected, in connection with a discourse upon music, to study such side-lights (among others) upon his subject as the law of cycles, the phenomena of clairvoyance touching the identity of colour with sound, and the mantram considered in reference to the laws of vibration.

Deserving of special attention are Mr. Harrison's remarks on the universal appeal of music; his strictures upon the miserably inadequate explanations of it by modern science; his discussion of music in nature, particularly bird-songs; his thoughts on the major and minor, and on the "two polarities," and his defence of the mysteries of number, where he excellently says:

"Before any opinion on the subject can be justly taken there must, at the least, be an acquaintance with the original meaning of numbers: the way they evolve from one another and their significance in other sciences, the meaning of the Monad, opposition, action and return; the resolution of the Ternary into the Quaternary, and back to Unity, not only algebraically but also geometrically, and on other planes; the working and meaning of Theosophical Reduction and Addition; the answering systems in geometry, and the fact that these principles work out in chemistry and all other sciences."

Here are a few sentences worth remembering:

"It is scarcely too fanciful to see in the recognition—intuitive, irrepressible and often unreasonable—which we sometimes give to the beauty of music, even when listening to music of a very poor and trivial character, a proof of the greatness of the force which is at work, and which no limitation or even degradation can make wholly inoperative.

"The mysterious authority and high investiture of music would be more understood and confessed, if we only believed with more than empty phrase, that a great poet is, in the deepest sense of the word, a *seer*. . . .

"The 'poetic' thought or image that will not stand the cold touch of 'scientific' truth, is not worth a moment's consideration, and the sooner it vanishes the better. But a true thought must gain life and force as it faces scrutiny and is handled by 'fact.' . . .

"Everything must surely have its meaning, and one would rather believe that we cannot, in our furthest and most extravagant imaginings, overstate those meanings, than that our feeble and wandering thought can go beyond reality."

Mr. Clifford Harrison has long been known as an exquisite artist in recitation; he shows himself here an artist no less in prose. His style is delicate, lucid, apt.

The *Lute of Apollo* may be commended to every lover of music, and every lover of thought.

L. Ll.

The Bhagavad Gita.

Translated by Annie Besant. [The Theosophical Publishing Society; 1897.]

We have just received a copy of a new and revised edition of Mrs. Besant's translation of the Gîtâ, printed in America by the T.P.S. The whole work has been carefully revised by the translator and one of her Indian colleagues mentioned in the preface. We doubt whether any translator of an old-world theosophical treatise can ever be satisfied with his or her translation. Each time we re-read the original we see some new shade of meaning that has hitherto escaped our notice, and in other respects we believe in Horace's rule to polish and repolish. This our colleagues have done and several passages which remained somewhat obscure in the first edition have started forth from their shadow and become as bright as day. Everyone with the instinct of the true scholar revises, only the stupid or careless rest content with what they have once done.

G. R. S. M.

A bad habit is lessened by abstaining from evil doing; but in order to acquire a good habit, this is not enough; we must practise it actively and steadily.

St. Francis de Sales.

He that works, whatsoever be his work, he bodies forth the forms of Things Unseen.

Carlyle.

But this thing is God,
To be man with thy might,
To grow straight in the strength of thy spirit, and live
Out thy life as the light.

Swinburne.

The Universe is the externalization of the Soul.

Emerson.

THEOSOPHICAL AND MYSTIC PUBLICATIONS.

THE Oriental Series of "Old Diary Leaves" has brought us, in *The Theosophist* for March, down to the end of Colonel Olcott's long tour through India, which he spent in lecturing and making mesmeric cures at every halting place. A picturesque description is given of a lecture delivered in front of the famous Hall of a Thousand Columns. Mrs. Besant contributes a valuable article on "The Education of Hindu Youth," sketching briefly a course of instruction especially adapted to the Indian character and present Indian conditions of life. In "Sun-Worship among the Parsis" the author interprets some of the statements by the use of Indian yoga ideas, comparing the nâdis with the symbolical accounts of the action of the sun on the earth. Under the title "Old Indian Theosophy," I. M. Hora translates into English a series of popular poems from the vernacular. The poems all deal with more or less religious subjects, but of course, in the translation, the original rhythm and sound are lost, so that they can hardly appeal to the reader as the translator tells us they do to those who hear them recited in the original. A note on the alleged second rotation of the earth, General Drayson's theory, is of interest to students of astronomy, but somewhat too technical for the general reader.

The Dawn is the title of a new Indian magazine, the first number of which is before us. The purpose of the journal is to give a picture of Hindu life and religion. Among the articles in the first number are: "A Plea for Karmakanda,' "The Situation in India," and "What the Time needs." *The Thinker* for February is well up to its proper standard, and contains several articles of interest; S. Ramaswami Aiyar in "Body and Mind as Energy," applies modern psychological ideas to the teachings of the Upanishads. We notice in a reprinted interview with the Swâmi Vivekânanda that this gentleman is now "His Holiness Shrî Swâmi." *The Arya Bâla Bodhini*, has an interesting article on "Dev Dharm," and a sketch of the founder of this sect, followed by "Superstition supported by Science," in which the science is somewhat erratic. We have also to acknowledge the receipt from Benares of *The Prashnottara*, from Calcutta of *The Journal of the Mahâ Bodhi Society*, from Bombay of *The Theosophic Gleaner*, and from Ceylon, of *Rays of Light*.

The Vâhan for April appears without the literary notes that have recently formed so important a feature, but, instead, gives its readers an exceptional quantity of "Enquirer." The answers are much longer than usual, and this is by no means a disadvantage, as there is more opportunity for a really satisfactory reply when space is not cramped. C. W. L. contributes an answer to a question respecting the present representatives of the various sub-races of the Atlantean race and gives some interesting particulars. Some of the answers are of an ethical description and one by A. A. W on savage animals is calculated to raise a good deal of dispute, the point of view of the writer not being theosophically "orthodox."

Mercury for March opens with a paper by Mrs. Buffington Davis on "The Mission of Theosophy," followed by one on "Hindu Cycles and the Circle's Ratio," by Mr. Marques. The subject is an extension of a curious fact published in "Notes on Cycles," LUCIFER, August, 1894. In these notes it was pointed out that the addition of the well-known Hindu figures representing an age, a year and a day of Brahmâ gave *pi* to several places of decimals. The present writer makes the addition of other sub-divisions representing hours, minutes, seconds, and so on. This does not appear to make the result much closer to *pi* (3·1415927). We do not quite understand why the *most accurate* value of *pi* should be given in the article as between 3·1415926 and 3·1415942, seeing that there is no question in mathematics as to its true value, which can be obtained to any desired degree of accuracy, short of its absolute value. The subject is however of interest, and possibly the writer of the paper may discover some further properties which will make the curious calculations of the Hindu cycles intelligible.

Theosophy in Australia contains an article on "The Growth of the Soul," really a paper on national karma, showing how "the powers that be" may use great men for the working out of their plans. Copious extracts are given from Colonel Olcott's historical sketch of the Society, and the number concludes with the usual questions and answers and activities.

Le Lotus Bleu begins a translation of Mr. Leadbeater's "Invisible Helpers" this month, and continues that of "Dreams." The issue includes an exceptional amount of original matter, "Anikéta" writing "Karma Carmen," a bright and chatty paper on philosophy and literature, treated in a somewhat flippant manner. The article on "Dreams" is followed by an account of a Yogin, Subhapaty Swâmi, and a paper, "The Decisive Step," by M. Gillard, taking as its text the Swâmi's life. We are afraid that our colleagues are not acquainted with the "Meditation Hall" at Bombay over which the much betitled Swâmi presides. M. Guymiot writes on the broad subject of man, and Dr. Pascal on "Pantheism" and "Theosophical Prayer," the latter article being an answer to a criticism in a Parisian review on *l'A. B. C. de la Théosophie*.

L'Isis Moderne, opens with a translation by M. Burnouf of an Indian story. The articles on the oracles and the Gnostics are continued, and Mme. Brunnarius gives an adaptation of a German paper by P. Braun on the power of thought.

M. Jules Bois contributes an article to *La Revue Hebdomadaire* for Feb. 27th, on the after-death states of man, according to Spiritualism, Catholic and other mystics, and Theosophy. The paper, which is entitled "The Pilgrimage of the Soul" is naturally somewhat scrappy as it goes over so wide a ground, but it presents the different views in a clear and sensible manner. *Le Bulletin de la Presse* for March 10th, gives a list of periodicals devoted to "Neo-Spiritualism," in which it has included some Theosophical magazines. The list is, however, very imperfect and would require a much larger supply of names to make it complete. *La Paix Universelle*, a small fortnightly Spiritist journal, gives a long article on "Spiritism in the Theatre," dealing largely with M. Sardou's recent efforts to bring the subject before the public by the aid of Mme. Sarah Bernhardt. Another Parisian play, however, *Kermaria*, at the Opéra Comique, treats of spiritistic matters, so that there are at the time of writing two plays going on simultaneously in Paris dealing with matters more or less occult. *L'Hyperchimie*, for March, opens with an article on the "Principles of Hermetic Science," consisting largely of quotations from M. Pernéty, illustrating the Hermetic ideas of physics. The journal does not deal solely with alchemy, as commonly understood, but endeavours to discover all kinds of curious connections between apparently detached facts. The concluding paper, on chemistry, points out among other facts that the mean temperature of the blood is also a temperature which plays a prominent part in some physical experiments. Probably, however, most other temperatures would be found to have nearly as many phenomena connected with them.

Sophia for March continues its useful series of translations and also reproduces Mr. Keightley's article on animal reincarnation. The paper on the dates of Indian literature is concluded. *Nova Lux* for March contains the conclusion of the translation of Mr. Kingsland's "Higher Science." In the sketch of the present day movement in the direction of occultism a good deal of information as to various societies and their leaders is given, but the grouping of the bodies is somewhat peculiar.

Lotus Blüthen, for March, reprints a series of short extracts from von Eckhartshausen of ethical and mystical import, and follows this with an article on the teachings of the *Bhagavad Gîtâ*, a new German edition of which is promised. The papers on Karma, which had been discontinued for several months, are now again continued. A little variety in the matter of the articles would be no disadvantage, as the same pious views are repeated at length in each contribution.

Die Zeit, a Vienna weekly journal, publishes in its issue of March 6th, an article from an Indian contributor on "Indian and European Spiritualism." Spiritualism is used, as explained, in an oriental sense and not in the one familiar to us. Theosophy is mentioned in the somewhat scoffing manner usually associated with the degree of knowledge displayed by the writer. When Mrs. Besant's *Reincarnation* is described as a translation of an old Indian book one wonders why the writer should have been tempted to publish his lack of information. We have also to acknowledge the receipt from Vienna of the *Theosophische Rundschau*, in which we are somewhat surprised to note that Mr. Harrison's *Transcendental Universe* has been translated into German by a member of the Theosophical Society. The *Metaphysische Rundschau*, of Berlin, translates Mrs. Besant's "Occult Chemistry" and reproduces the diagrams, the first article is mainly of interest because of the mysterious letters following the pseudonym of the author: "Kama, Censor of the R.O.O.o. S.B.a.S." The paper on argon and helium is concluded.

Theosophia, our Dutch journal, opens with a paper by Afra on a text from the Gospel of John speaking of the love of God for humanity. A translation of the Chinese "Classic of Purity" is also given and some further selections from *The Vâhan*. The *Teosofisk Tidskrift* and *Theosophia* come from Sweden. The former contains articles of general Theosophical interest, and also translates Mrs. Besant's "Culture of the Soul," and Mr. Leadbeater's "Dreams."

We have to acknowledge the receipt from America of *The Metaphysical Magazine*, with one or two psychic stories; *Theosophy*, with an article entitled "A Student's Notes and Guesses," having some ingeniously developed ideas; *Notes and Queries*, containing a smaller allowance of curious facts than usual; *The Theosophical Forum*; *Child-Life*; *The Literary Digest*; *Current Literature*; *Food, Home and Garden*; and *The Pacific Theosophist*. Also the receipt of *Modern Astrology*, with its usual series of astrological articles and notes; *The English Mechanic*; *The Vegetarian*, which is making excellent progress in its contents, a story by Mr. Crockett being included: *To-Morrow*; *Sbornik pro Filosofii*; *Mystiku a Okkultismus*; *Ourselves* and *The Irish Theosophist*.

A.

Women's Printing Society, Limited, 66, Whitcomb Street, W.C.

VOL. XX. MAY 15, 1897. No. 117.

LUCIFER.

ON THE WATCH-TOWER.

"FOR THE WORLD-MAKER IS A GEOMETRICIAN."

Mrs. Besant writes:

Remarkable advances are being made in America in a direction justifying the theosophical teachings about vibrations and the forms they create. Dr. J. Mount Bleyer, a New York specialist in ear and throat diseases, has just invented a method of photographing the forms made by light powders, when they are thrown up from a disk vibrating under the impact of waves of sound. It has long been known that geometrical figures are formed when the powder subsides on the disk, and Mrs. Watts Hughes succeeded in obtaining some remarkable results from musical notes. Dr. Bleyer, however, has ingeniously photographed the forms assumed in the air by the powder, and thus obtains the solid figure of which the geometrical shape on the disk is the projection on the flat. New light is thus thrown on the fundamental mathematicality (if the word may be admitted) of nature, and one begins to see that every plane geometrical figure might be thrown upwards into a solid form, and that may be Euclid, thus treated, would reveal some surprising facts. To return to our doctor, he says:

> One remarkable feature of the experiments is that the sounds have been found to take the form of things familiar. Thus, a sharp, staccato tone gave a picture like a snake coiled as if to strike. Sometimes the reproductions are as if a beautiful flower had been photographed. These will make most interesting pictures when they are magnified and thrown upon a screen.

The reports state that:

> Within a few days the biograph is to be brought into use, when three

hundred continuous pictures will be made of one example, say a bar of "Home. Sweet Home." These pictures can then be thrown on a screen, when the music will be shown in what will appear to be reproductions of marvellously pretty submarine vegetation, intermingled with reefs and spidery forms, orchids and other plants, and tracings in new and strange patterns.

The photographs are taken at the rate of 100 a second.

Professor Blake, of Kansas City, lecturing on electricity, has pointed out that the vibrations of the molecules of the brain must affect the ether and that it is probable that it sets up waves therein. "If it does, that disturbance is going to travel out in a straight line. Suppose it should pass through another brain, the molecules of which should be sympathetically affected, then similar vibrations would be set up and we should have thought-transference." Exactly.

***

THE SANSKRIT PUSTAKONNATI SABHA.

Under the auspices of the Theosophical Society, a "Society for the Preservation of Sanskrit MSS." has been inaugurated at Benares, and we take the following from its first prospectus issued by our colleague Mrs. Besant.

There is no country in the world so rich in its ancient lore as is India, and yet how many Indians care to take notice of this or to move one finger to render assistance to rescue the ancient Books from the ravages of time and from countless other evils. Amidst thousands of difficulties the British Government and the Orientalists have succeeded through the people of India in discovering about 15,000 Sanskrit MSS. within the course of twenty-seven years, at the expense of about Rs. 24000 per year, but the work has been done piecemeal and not continuously. Besides this, the Catalogues of Books, prepared by these, are in many respects imperfect, and do not contain detailed information on important points; in these catalogues, for instance, it is generally difficult to distinguish the names of authors from those of their works; nor can it be known what are the nature and the contents of a particular work, where it is to be found, and what other similar works were written by the same or by different authors. For the last thirteen years, materials of this kind have been collected by a learned and devoted Svâmi, and it is now proposed, working under his direction and guidance, to utilise in the first place the work already done by Government and by the Orientalists in Bibliography and to incorporate it with the mass of materials collected, in order to make a comprehensive Catalogue which shall contain in a clear and lucid form all the above details for the information of enquirers. Afterwards it is intended to take in hand and follow up the search for Sanskrit Manuscripts, to collect them into a place of safety and gradually to do other work, that may be thought necessary for the revival of ancient Sanskrit

Literature. The Association now formed for these beneficent purposes confidently hopes to receive support and help from all literary men in every part of the world, because such an effort is likely to benefit not only India but the whole world of scholarship and literature directly, and through them the rest of the world.

This is an excellent undertaking, and it is needless to say that we wish it every success. As the Svâmi is not only an admirable scholar, but also one who knows the grandeur and nature of the inspiration which underlies all that is best in Sanskrit literature, there is more hope of the plan being carried out to a successful issue than would otherwise be the case.

***

A Living Library.

The Prashnottara for March prints some extracts from private letters concerning a remarkable Paṇḍit of the old type. Paṇḍit Dhanrâj, though scarcely twenty years of age, is said to carry in his memory "a mass of Sanskrit literature equal to about thirty Mahâbhâratas in bulk"!

Paṇḍit Dhanrâj says, from the age of about five upwards he has been doing nothing else than "committing to memory" at an average rate of about 1,000 shlokas every day. His work ceased about a year or so ago; and he is now setting about to digest and assimilate his vast mental meal. He studied at the houses of a race of Paṇḍits in his native village, where the "Paramparâ" has come down and where the books are yet found the very names of which have been long forgotten by and are now unknown to the modern generation of "much-talkers" called Paṇḍits.

An appalling list of standard works committed to memory is given with the number of shlokas which each contains. Thus:

Printed into Royal 8vo volumes of 800 pages each, every page containing 15 shlokas on an average, this total of 63,80,700 shlokas, would form a compact little library of 500 volumes, roughly—nothing surprising, by any means, seeing that 20 times that number of volumes is disgorged annually by the press of England alone.

But what *is* surprising is that Paṇḍit Dhanrâj, while modestly denying that he has the whole by heart, yet admits that he carries in his memory at least a good two-thirds of it, besides another ten lakhs or so in miscellaneous literature, novels and histories (yes, *novels* and *histories*) and Purâṇas and modern works!

Our readers will be pained to hear that this phenomenal young Paṇḍit is now totally blind. It is difficult for ordinary Westerns, whose memories are year by year becoming more atrophied owing to the degenerating environment of mechanism in which we live, to realize that the memory can be made a more accurate instrument for transmitting the technical treatises of religion, philosophy and science, than writing. Even Western Orientalists prefer the oral tradition of the text preserved by the Paṇdits to MS. copies.

In the present instance, an important point to bear in mind is that Paṇdit Dhanrâj has not memorized merely a mass of works which are accessible to everyone.

The MSS. out of which Paṇdit Dhanrâj was taught are unavailable. They are kept away with jealous care from the reach of the inquisitive public. And Paṇdit Dhanrâj, though willing to dictate all he has in his memory, cannot be provided with a writer sufficiently fast to reduce any tolerable portion of his stores into writing. Paṇdit Parmeshri Dâs of Barabanki, Oudh, who has been recently contributing to *The Theosophist* some articles on the older Grammar, etc., with the help of this marvellous Paṇdit, is doing all he can in the matter, but however thankful we may be for what he has done we cannot but feel that it is not enough by far. If some system of shorthand Devanâgarî could be devised by a Theosophical brother sufficiently ingenious, it would be a great help indeed —though we must always be prepared for disappointment even after all these old books have become "Lipi" from "Smriti." Such disappointment is by no means the unfrequent lot of Theosophical students. The first view has often aroused surging hopes of the promised land of grapes and honey; and yet a nearer view has often dissipated the illusion and shown that the first spectacle was a mere mirage only.

.˙.

A Logical Clerk.

A sixpenny pamphlet published by J. Vincent and Son, 18, Little Britain, London, contains in full the "Cause and Purport of the Protest," recently made by the Rev. S. D. Brownjohn against the confirmation of the election of Dr. Temple to the See of Canterbury. Those who noticed at the time the short speech of "protest" (on the ground that Dr. Temple was "a self-confessed believer in the full doctrine of Evolution,") may be interested in knowing that it was made not from the stand-point of a "shocked Evangelical," but from that of a clergyman who renounced his own preferment in the Established Church in 1888, on the ground of the incongruity which he "felt to exist between the teachings of Science and the authorized teaching of the Church," believing his benefice to have been entrusted to him in virtue of his consent to the latter. Since that time, Mr. Brownjohn appears to have made sundry efforts to obtain from the authorities of the Church a frank recognition of this "incongruity," and an assurance of some steps being taken to remove it, but without success; and this Protest is his latest attempt to draw attention to what he considers a dishonest and discreditable "spiritual mockery."

* * *

An Important Find of Jewish MSS.

We take the following from *The Jewish Chronicle* of April 2nd.

After a journey which, if we are not mistaken, will prove a momentous incident in the modern history of Jewish literature, Mr. Schechter has returned to Cambridge. The University library in that city was not hitherto particularly rich in Hebrew MSS., but the treasures which Mr. Schechter has been able to bring back from Egypt and Palestine will probably raise the Cambridge Library to the front rank. Mr. Schechter's enterprise has not been without its dangers and difficulties. But everywhere his fame had preceded him, and with the Chief Rabbi of Cairo, the President of the Jewish congregation, Mr. Joseph Cattaui, and his son, Mr. Elie M. Cattaui, Mr. Schechter found a courteous and helpful welcome. It is, of course, too early to form an estimate of the rarity or the worth of the great mass of MSS. which Mr. Schechter has recovered from the dust and oblivion of ages. But that much of historical and literary importance has been unearthed is certain.

The large store of MSS. which Mr. Schechter has now safely deposited in Cambridge comes, like several fragments previously brought to Europe, from the "Geniza" at Cairo. This "Geniza," or "Secret Place," is a curious institution in Jewish life. Old copies of the Law, old Hebrew books in general, were not retained in use. Hence, we do not possess any Scroll of the Law older than the tenth or eleventh century at the earliest. But such mutilated or worn-out books were not actually destroyed. They were put into the "Geniza" or secret hiding place. Either they were piled into a lumber room of the synagogue, or they were buried in the earth hard by the cemetery. In the Talmud (Menachoth 29b.) we are told: "If a Scroll of the Law has two mistakes per page, it must be corrected; if three mistakes, *it must be hidden*," *i.e.*, deposited in some store-room where its preservation would depend on the condition of atmosphere and climate, as well as on the condition of the congregation. Mostly, of course, the hidden or buried treasure has been hopelessly lost. Decay on the one hand, wilful destruction of enemies on the other, have reduced many a spiritual and literary masterpiece to the elemental dust. But in Egypt the clear and limpid atmosphere has been kinder to the sacred remains entrusted to its care. In the cemetery located on the edge of the desert, where to a European visitor respiration is difficult, the old treasures have been preserved better than had they lain on the bookshelves of a Northern library. The common enemies of books could not invade the dusty Egyptian hiding-places. In Hebron, too, Mr. Schechter was fortunate enough to find some rich deposits of learning. Sometimes such treasures were deliberately placed in these secret recesses, sometimes they were hastily cast there by the victims of a sudden raid, who, expelled from their home, thought that in the graveyard their books might perchance be saved. And now the man has come to rescue them from death, to restore them to their long-lost light of day. Books indeed have their fates. Happy the books that fall into the loving hands of the present reader in Rabbinic to the University of Cambridge.

***

Nirvâṇa in the Original Sâṅkhya.

We take the following from a review in the April number of *The Asiatic Quarterly Review*, on Dr. Dahlmann's recent work, *Nirvâṇa Eine Studie zur Vorgeschichte des Buddhismus*.

After stating the many contradictory views on this subject, the reviewer continues:

The explanation of the complicated problem is sought by Dr. Dahlmann in the hypothesis that the doctrine of Nirvâṇa is a fragment of another and an older system. "Buddhism makes a gallant show by the help of a garment borrowed from a strange wardrobe." Nirvâṇa is a pre-Buddhistic idea, borrowed neither from the classical Vedânta nor from the classical Sâṅkhya, but from an older system, in which Nirvâṇa means Brahma-Nirvâṇa, an entering into the absolute Brahma. This system is to be found in the Mahâbhârata, the great poem which Dr. Dahlmann knows so well. It is impossible to exaggerate the eloquence and wealth of illustration which the author employs in developing this part of his subject. He makes great use of the Bhagavad Gîtâ, a portion of the Mahâbhârata, often published separately, and treated practically as an independent work. Dr. Dahlmann's view is summed up in the following words: "The Sâṅkhya of the epic poems is, in its complete form, simply a knowledge of Brahma. From the plurality of its four and twenty principles is deduced the only spiritual twenty-fifth principle. In the knowledge of the Sâṅkhya is embodied the one only immutable knowledge which rests in Brahma. Sâṅkhya as knowledge simply is identified with Brahma, because in the lucidity of this knowledge is reflected the lucidity of this absolute being. 'The Sâṅkhya is the highest knowledge, the intransient, ever-enduring, infinite, everlasting Brahma.' The 'Sâṅkhya is the embodiment of the bodiless Brahma.' Out of this variously ramifying and much diversified system rises as a crown the science of Brahma, in the idea of Brahma-Nirvâṇa dominating the Brahmanical Philosophy."

The Origins of Christianity.

The latest work on this ever absorbingly interesting subject is the impartial and scholarly contribution of Albert Réville, Professeur au Collège de France, entitled *Jésus de Nazareth, Étude Critique sur les Antécédents de l' Histoire Évangéliques et la vie de Jésus* (2 vols., 8vo., Paris; Fischbacher; 1897). It is to be hoped that this important study will be translated for the benefit of English readers.

* * *

À la Recherche de M. le Diable.

Mr. F. Legge, in the May number of *The Contemporary Review*, devotes his attention to "The Devil in Modern Occultism." He finds his "Devil" in the Astral Light, and "Modern Occultism" in the *salade* of Parisian *études esotériques*. Mr. Legge loses his way among these Neo-everythings galvanized into temporary notice by the Diana Vaughan *blague* of Léo Taxil. The same writer tries to persuade the public that he knows something about "Primitive Religion and Primitive Magic," in a second article in the May number of *The Edinburgh Review*.

* * *

A Jesuit Father on Occultism.

The Weekly Register, of March 13th, publishes a lecture on what Father Clarke calls "Occultism," delivered before the Historical Research Society, the Cardinal Archbishop being in the chair. It is, of course, clever, as we should expect; it is also curious. One or two sentences are worth reproducing. Thus:

> Occultism is an accumulation of the most ancient and rudimentary ideas about man and nature, entertained in the very beginnings of civilisation, and transmitted to us without religious or scientific elaboration. It is distinguished from non-occult or ordinary knowledge by preserving almost without mitigation its original crudeness, in consequence of the method—a method well adapted for keeping intact an ancient tradition—by which it has been handed on. There are three points in it: (1) a method of secret or reserved teaching; (2) a pretension to thaumaturgy or wonder-working; and (3) a view or theory set up to explain the wonder-working and other matters.

As to No. 1, we are told:

> You see its working in the founding of Christianity—in the use of parables. in the choice of twelve Apostles, in the precept not to cast pearls before swine.

in St. Paul's teaching wisdom only among the perfect, and to the rest preaching only Christ crucified (1 Cor. ii. 6). and in his direction to commit the Apostolic teaching to faithful men who should instruct others also.

As to No. 2, Father Clarke would draw our attention to four factors—falsehood, conjuring, drugs, and hypnotism. As to No. 3, which should throw light on 1 and 2, the Rev. Father leaves it severely alone.

But what is most surprising is that the *deus ex machinâ* of Father Clarke's prior tragi-comedies on the subject, and of Roman Catholicism generally—the Devil—is for once given a holiday!

***

MANICHEEISM.

Students of Theosophy who know the importance of Manicheeism as a link between the Gnosticism of the first two centuries and the Gnosticism of the Albigeois and kindred movements, will be glad to learn that a new edition of the tract of Alexander Lycopolitanus has been edited by Brinkmann (*Contra Manichaei Opiniones Disputatio*: Leipzig; Teubner). The most important book on this subject of recent years is Kessler's *Mani, Forschungen über die Manichäische Religion* (Berlin; 1889). The second volume is still waited for with impatience. Professor Montet in the *A. Q. R.* says that "it will conclude the demonstration of the Oriental (not Christian) origin of what is called in the Church 'heresy,' and what has been in fact the Manichæan Religion."

G. R. S. M.

REINCARNATION.

(*Continued from p.* 167.)

We shall best understand the evolution of the soul, if we take it up at the point where we left it, when animal-man was ready to receive, and did receive, the embryonic soul. To avoid a possible misapprehension, it may be well to say that there were not henceforth two Monads in man—the one that had built the human tabernacle, and the one that descended into that tabernacle, and whose lowest aspect was the human soul. To borrow a simile again from H. P. Blavatsky, as two rays of the sun may pass through a hole in a shutter, and mingling together form but one ray though they had been twain, so is it with these rays from the supreme Sun, the divine Lord of our universe. The second ray, as it entered into the human tabernacle, blended with the first, merely adding to it fresh energy and brilliance, and the human Monad, *as a unit*, began its mighty task of unfolding the higher powers in man of that divine Life whence it came.

The embryonic soul, the Thinker, had at the beginning for its embryonic mental body the mind-stuff envelope that the Monad of form had brought with it, but had not yet organized into any possibility of functioning. It was the mere germ of a mental body, attached to a mere germ of a causal body, and for many a life the strong desire-nature had its will with the soul, whirling it along the road of its own passions and appetites, and dashing up against it all the furious waves of its own uncontrolled animality.

Repulsive as this early life of the soul may at first seem to some when looked at from the higher stage that we have now attained, it was a necessary one for the germination of the seeds of mind. Recognition of difference, the perception that one thing is different from another, is a preliminary essential to thinking at all. And in order to awaken this perception in the as yet unthinking soul, strong and violent contrasts had to strike upon it, so as to force their differences upon it—blow after blow of riotous pleasure, blow after blow of crushing pain. The external world hammered on the soul through the desire-nature, till perceptions began to be slowly made, and, after countless repetitions, to be registered. The little gains made in each life were stored up by the Thinker, and thus slow progress was made.

Slow progress, indeed, for scarcely anything was *thought*, and hence scarcely anything was done in the way of organizing the mental body. Not until many perceptions had been registered in it as mental images, was there any material on which mental action, initiated from within, could be based; this would begin when two or more of these mental images were drawn together, and some inference, however elementary, was made from them. That inference was the beginning of reasoning, the germ of all the systems of logic which the intellect of man has since evolved or assimilated. These inferences would at first all be made in the service of the desire-nature, for the increasing of pleasure, the lessening of pain; but each one would increase the activity of the mental body, and would stimulate it into more ready functioning.

It will readily be seen that at this period of his infancy man had no knowledge of good or of evil; right and wrong had for him no existence. The right is that which is in accordance with the divine will, which helps forward the progress of the soul, which tends to the strengthening of the higher nature of man and to the training and subjugation of the lower; the wrong is that which retards evolution, which retains the soul in the lower stages after he has learned the lessons they have to teach, which tends to the mastery of the lower nature over the higher, and assimilates man to the brute he should be outgrowing instead of to the God he should be evolving. Ere man could know what was right he had to learn the existence of law, and this he could learn only by following all that attracted him in the outer world, by grasping at every desirable object, and then by learning from experience, sweet or bitter, whether his delight was in harmony or in conflict with the law. Let us take an obvious example, the taking of pleasant food, and see how infant man might learn therefrom the presence of a natural law. At the first taking, his hunger was appeased, his taste was gratified, and only pleasure resulted from the experience, for his action was in harmony with law. On another occasion, desiring to increase pleasure, he ate overmuch and suffered in consequence, for he transgressed against the law. A confusing experience to the dawning intelligence, how the pleasurable became painful by excess. Over and over again he would be led by desire into excess, and each time he would experience the painful consequences, until at last he learned moderation, *i.e.*, he learned to conform his bodily acts in this respect to physical law; for he found that there were conditions which affected him and which he could not control, and that only by observing them could physical happiness be ensured. Similar experiences flowed in upon him through all the bodily organs, with undeviating regularity; his out-rushing desires brought him pleasure or pain just as they worked with the laws of Nature or against them, and, as experience increased, it began to guide his steps, to influence his choice. It was not as though he had to begin his experience anew with every life, for on each new birth he brought with him mental faculties a little increased, an ever-accumulating store.

I have said that the growth in these early days was very slow, for there was but the dawning of mental action, and when the man left his physical body at death he passed most of his time in Kâmaloka, sleeping through a brief devachanic period of unconscious assimilation of any minute mental experiences, not yet sufficiently developed for the active heavenly life that lay before him after many days. Still, the enduring causal body was there, to be the receptacle of his qualities, and to carry them on for further development into his next life on earth. The part played by the monadic group-soul in the earlier stages of evolution is played in man by the causal body, and it is this continuing entity who, in all cases, makes evolution possible. Without him, the accumulation of mental and moral experiences, shown as faculties, would be as impossible as would be the accumulation of physical experiences, shown as racial and family characteristics, without the continuity of physical plasm. Souls without a past behind them, springing suddenly into existence out of nothing, with marked mental and moral peculiarities, are a conception as monstrous as would be the corresponding conception of babies suddenly appearing from nowhere, unrelated to anybody, but showing marked racial and family types. Neither the man nor his physical vehicle is uncaused, or caused by the direct creative power of the LOGOS; here, as in so many other cases, the invisible things are clearly seen by their analogy with the visible, the visible being, in very truth, nothing more than the images, the reflections, of things unseen. Without a continuity in the physical plasm, there would be no means for the evolution of physical peculiarities; without the continuity of the intelligence, there would be no means for the evolution of mental and moral qualities. In both cases, without continuity, evolution would be stopped at its first stage, and the world would be a chaos of infinite and isolated beginnings instead of a cosmos continually becoming.

We must not omit to notice that in these early days much variety is caused in the type and in the nature of individual progress by the environment which surrounds the individual. Ultimately all the souls have to develope all their powers, but the order in which these powers are developed depends on the circumstances amid which the soul is placed. Climate, the fertility or sterility of nature, the life of the mountain or of the plain, of the inland forest or the ocean-shore—these things and countless others will call into activity one set or another of the awakening mental energies. A life of extreme hardship, of ceaseless struggle with nature, will develope very different powers from those evolved amid the luxuriant plenty of a tropical island; both sets of powers are needed, for the soul is to conquer every region of nature, but striking differences may thus be evolved even in souls of the same age, and one may appear to be more advanced than the other, according as the observer estimates most highly the more "practical" or the more "contemplative" powers of the soul, the active outward-going energies, or the quiet inward-turned musing faculties. The perfected soul possesses all, but the soul in the making must develope them successively, and thus arises another cause of the immense variety found among human beings.

For again, it must be remembered that human evolution is individual. In a group informed by a single monadic group-soul the same instincts will be found in all, for the receptacle of the experiences is that monadic group-soul, and it pours its life into all the forms dependent upon it. But each man has his own physical vehicle and one only at a time, and the receptacle of all experiences is the causal body, which pours its life into its one physical vehicle, and can affect no other physical vehicle, being connected with none other. Hence we find differences separating individual men greater than ever separated closely allied animals, and hence also the evolution of qualities cannot be studied in men in the mass, but only in the continuing individual. The lack of power to make such a study leaves science unable to explain why some men tower above their fellows, intellectual and moral giants, unable to trace the intellectual evolution of a Shankarâchârya or a Pythagoras, the moral evolution of a Buddha or of a Christ.

Let us now consider the factors in reincarnation, as a clear understanding of these is necessary for the explanation of some of the difficulties—such as the alleged loss of memory—which are felt by those unfamiliar with the idea. Man, during his passage through physical death, Kâmaloka and Devachan, loses, one after the other, his various bodies, the physical, the astral and the mental. These are all disintegrated, and their particles remix with the materials of their several planes. The connection of the man with the physical vehicle is entirely broken off and done with; but the astral and mental bodies hand on to the man himself, to the Thinker, the germs of the faculties and qualities resulting from the activities of the earth-life, and these are stored within the causal body, the seeds of his next astral and mental bodies. At this stage then only the man himself is left, the labourer who has brought his harvest home, and has lived upon it till it is all worked up into himself. The dawn of a new life begins, and he must go forth again to his labour until the even.

The new life begins by the vivifying of the mental germs, and they draw upon the materials of the lower mental levels, till a mental body has grown up from them that represents exactly the mental stage of the man, expressing all his mental faculties as organs; the experiences of the past do not exist as mental images in this new body; as mental images they perished when the old mind-body perished, and only their essence, their effects on faculty, remain; they were the food of the mind, the materials which it wove into powers, and in the new body they reappear as powers, they determine its materials, and they form its organs. When the man, the Thinker, has thus clothed himself with a new body for his coming life on the lower mental levels, he proceeds, by vivifying the astral germs, to provide himself with an astral body for his life on the astral plane. This, again, exactly represents his desire-nature, faithfully reproducing the qualities he evolved in the past, as the seed reproduces its parent tree. Thus the man stands, fully equipped for his next incarnation, the only memory of the events of his past being in the causal body, in his own enduring form, the one body that passes on from life to life.

Meanwhile, action external to himself is being taken to provide him with a physical body suitable for the expression of his qualities. In past lives he had made ties with, contracted liabilities towards, other human beings, and some of these will partly determine his place of birth and his family. He has been a source of happiness or of unhappiness to others; this is a factor in determining the conditions of his coming life. His desire-nature is well disciplined or unregulated and riotous; this will be taken into account in the physical heredity of the new body. He has cultivated certain mental powers, such as the artistic; this must be considered, as here again physical heredity is an important factor where delicacy of nervous organization and tactile sensibility are required. And so on, in endless variety. The man may, certainly will, have in him many incongruous characteristics, so that only some can find expression in any one body that could be provided, and a group of his powers suitable for simultaneous expression must be selected. All this is done by certain mighty spiritual Intelligences,* often spoken of as the Lords of Karma, because it is their function to superintend the working out of causes continually set going by thoughts, desires and actions. They hold the threads of destiny which each man has woven, and guide the reincarnating man to the environment determined by his past, unconsciously self-chosen through his past life.

The race, the nation, the family, being thus determined, what may be called the mould of the physical body—suitable for the expression of the man's qualities, and for the working out of the causes he has set going—is given by these great Ones, and the new

* Spoken of by H. P Blavatsky in the *Secret Doctrine*. They are the Lipika, the Keepers of the Karmic Records, and the Mahârâjas, who direct the practical working out of the decrees of the Lipika.

etheric double, a copy of this, is built within the mother's womb by the agency of an elemental, the thought of the karmic Lords being its motive power. The dense body is built into the etheric double molecule by molecule, following it exactly, and here physical heredity has full sway in the materials provided. Further, the thoughts and passions of surrounding people, especially of the continually present father and mother, influence the building elemental in its work, the individuals with whom the incarnating man had formed ties in the past thus affecting the physical conditions growing up for his new life on earth. At a very early stage the new astral body comes into connection with the new etheric double, and exercises considerable influence over its formation, and through it the mental body works upon the nervous organization, preparing it to become a suitable instrument for its own expression in the future. This influence, commenced in ante-natal life—so that when a child is born its brain-formation reveals the extent and balance of its mental and moral qualities—is continued after birth, and this building of brain and nerves, and their correlation to the astral and mental bodies, go on till the seventh year of childhood, at which age the connection between the man and his physical vehicle is complete, and he may be said to work through it henceforth more than upon it. Up to this age, the consciousness of the Thinker is more upon the astral plane than upon the physical, and this is often evidenced by the play of psychic faculties in young children. They see invisible comrades and fairy landscapes, hear voices inaudible to their elders, catch charming and delicate fancies from the astral world. These phenomena generally vanish as the Thinker begins to work effectively through the physical vehicle, and the dreamy child becomes the commonplace boy or girl, oftentimes much to the relief of bewildered parents, ignorant of the cause of their child's "queerness." Most children have at least a touch of this "queerness," but they quickly learn to hide away their fancies and visions from their unsympathetic elders, fearful of blame for "telling stories," or of what the child dreads far more—ridicule. If parents could see their children's brains, vibrating under an inextricable mingling of physical and astral impacts, which the children themselves are quite incapable of separating, and receiving sometimes a thrill—so plastic are they—even from the higher regions, giving a vision of ethereal beauty, of heroic achievement, they would be more patient with, more responsive to, the confused prattlings of the little ones, trying to translate into the difficult medium of unaccustomed words the elusive touches of which they are conscious, and which they try to catch and retain. Reincarnation, believed in and understood, would relieve child-life of its most pathetic aspect, the unaided struggle of the soul to gain control over its new vehicles, and to connect itself fully with its densest body without losing the power to impress the rarer ones in a way that would enable them to convey to the denser their own more subtle vibrations.

ANNIE BESANT.

(To be continued.)

THE IGNORANCE OF LEARNED MEN.

A GOOD deal of light may sometimes be thrown on the value of theosophical teaching, by an examination of non-theosophical essays on some of the subjects to which our own inquiries relate. The helpless way in which even profound thinkers and deeply learned men may stumble about amidst misconceptions, the character of which is fairly obvious to theosophical thinkers, has been illustrated lately by Professor Max Müller's bulky and pretentious volumes entitled *Contributions to the Science of Mythology*. Profound sagacity and erudition are exhibited in the way in which he traces the connection between the mythologies of different races and periods, but over the whole treatise there hovers the shadow of a huge ignorance concerning certain fundamental information relating to human progress with which theosophical teaching has long since furnished the minds of students qualified to appreciate its importance. We still find Professor Max Müller harping on the idea that mythologies represent the "infantia" of the human race. He is eager indeed to maintain that they do not represent a period of "dementia." Taking Greek mythology alone as it stands, this last idea might not unnaturally be suggested. A body of people capable of attributing to gods the infamous and preposterous proceedings of the Olympian deities, might come under the suspicion of being idiots and maniacs, and this to Professor Max Müller, although he does not object to the idea that we may be lineal descendants of some Simian species—would be painful, as suggesting the possibility of atavistic influences operative at a later date. He is rescued from this embarrassment by perceiving that the Olympian deities themselves are originally traceable to others that have simply been invented in the first instance as personifications of natural phenomena, and thus gets comfortably back to the "infantia" doctrine. In a very characteristic passage he wants to know "how these so-called gods came to exist at all, what was the meaning of all the facts and circumstances relating to them? After they had been superseded by the true God was there any substance at all left, any real personality behind their personal adventures?" There is a curious naiveté in this reference to "the true God" in the mouth of a philosopher making such large claims on our respect as the present author. He has built up for us, he explains in a previous passage, the Science of Language, the Science of Thought, the Science of Religion, and now he has given us a treatise on the Science of Mythology in order that there may be no gap in the magnificent array of his expositions; and yet he talks as though a finality had been reached in reference to the conception of the sublime power underlying the universe in connection with the views concerning the "true God" entertained at Oxford in 1897.

We may have advanced, he says, "just as our God has advanced beyond Jehovah, and as Jehovah had advanced beyond the Gentiles, but there must be continuity in all the strata of the thought as there is in the strata of the earth." That continuity he can observe as he looks backward, but it does not seem to have occurred to him that time stretches forward as well, and that without waiting for the slow growth of coming centuries we may some of us, even now, stand in possession of ideas concerning the true government of the universe, as far in advance of those current around us, as these, in their turn, may have been advanced compared with the bewildering confusion of a degraded mythology at the period just preceding the Christian era.

Of course an all important point which Professor Max Müller and all comparative mythologists who work on his methods overlook entirely, is this:—the mythologies of the ancient world were not the invention of the infant races amongst whom they prevailed, but were the distorted reflection in the minds of those races of the symbolical teachings conveyed to them in the beginning by Superior Beings, with an infinitely wider grasp of the truth than it was possible for them to convey at the time to the ill-developed consciousness around them. Mythologies in fact will remain disjointed nonsense until students realize that they are the degenerate offspring of adept teaching, confided to the earlier races. Common-place speculations concerning the beginning of human intelligence, leave out this idea altogether and then blunder about in a confusion that can never be cleared up by any speculation along the lines laid down by Professor Max Müller. We know now that going back far behind the beginning of our own race, the earlier humanity of the later third and fourth, was cared for by teachers already on a far superior level than that of the humanity they had undertaken to bring up; and from our present point of view we can in some measure figure to ourselves the problem they had before their minds when endeavouring to formulate something like a religious system for people as little fitted to comprehend the whole truth within their own grasp, as the modern savage would be to comprehend the idea of spiritual existence divorced from flesh and blood. Pure abstractions of thought would have been of no avail in dealing with such a subject. Symbols of some sort or another were required even to foreshadow, however faintly, the knowledge reserved for a later date, and thus it appears that in the first instance, adept teachers of the fourth, and probably those of the fifth race also, resorted to what has been rather inappropriately called the Solar Myth, with a view of inspiring in the minds of the people around them the first sentiment of adoration of a Sublime Power presiding over human affairs. Nothing can be stupider than the treatment of sun-worship, as though it were a blind invention of simple and ignorant people, impressed with the power and force of meteorological phenomena. If we had to do the work to-day over again, for a race entirely devoid of religious feeling, it is difficult to know how a better appeal could be made to the latent sentiment of adoration, than by one which pointed directly to the incomprehensible splendour of that central power within our universe from which there radiated, day by day the benign influences which could be appreciated year by year as the seasons revolved.

From the point of view of the adept teacher, the sun was, of course, a symbol of that mighty consciousness which we ourselves as yet can only figure in our minds in the vaguest fashion. But it was a dignified and worthy symbol, and looking indeed at the ghastly confusion of thought in which the attempt to anthropomorphise deity has thrown the modern world, one is sometimes tempted to wonder whether in the cyclic evolution of things a time may not come again in which for the purposes of ritualistic observance and external religion, something in the nature of a sun-worship may not be revived. But meanwhile it may be plainly perceived in looking back at the mythologies of the past—and in connection with such a retrospect the philological erudition of writers like Professor Max Müller, may be useful even to students who can appreciate in thought the part played by the Root Manus—that the later mythologies have represented as clearly as the later Christianity of the churches, a degradation of beautiful ideals placed before mankind by superior wisdom in the first instance. This thought, indeed, tends to rob the study of comparative mythology of the interest which its more devoted exponents assign to it. There is nothing really to be learned by an investigation of the changes that have degraded the divine Solar Myth in the course of ages, except the ever recurring lessons associated with human stupidity in all its aspects.

No sooner had the race been left with a truly grand religious conception given them by the Manu, than they proceeded to amalgamate it with ideas really arising in their own infant minds, and in the course of time grotesque presentations of the first truth surrounded it like a weed growth. That which is known at the present day as Vedic mythology or symbology, was thus in truth not the actual beginning of the process of thought modern mythologists are endeavouring to trace out, but was itself a degradation thereof. There is reason indeed to suppose that somewhere there still exists an original version of the Vedas free from any of the corruption which crept into the later traditions, though these are treated by our exoteric scholars as primeval in their nature—just in the same way as the real Institutes of Manu will perhaps some day be recoverable, though the versions handed down to recent generations are no better than clumsy caricatures of the original. But no great interest attaches to the investigation of further corruptions imported into the Aryan mythology—already degraded in ancient India—as it in turn gave rise to the pantheon of the Greeks. When a fuller light is eventually let in on the actual beginnings of mythological religion, then, indeed, the subject will rise into an atmosphere quite unfamiliar to the philological student. Then all educated men of that later period will be enabled to smile as we smile to-day at some of Professor Max Müller's dogmatic assertions, dependent for what he considers their proof on a state of blank ignorance concerning the higher potentialities of the human mind. Mythology he calls in one place a "disease of language," meaning by this phrase that thought and language are identical. He tells us in his *Science of Thought* "that language and thought are inseparable." Such a doctrine is really inseparable from the atheistic conception that human consciousness is a function of the nervous system, a condition of activity in the cortex of the brain. One would think that even a professor of so much religion as is involved in the belief that there is a "true God," and, at any rate, possibly a survival of the soul, would be able to imagine that in reaching the plane of that soul's ultimate consciousness, the true God, in dealing with us, would not be entirely dependent for the transmission of thought, either on the use of English or German, of Sanskrit or Greek, or even of some "tongue" of pure celestial derivation, the grammar of which would have to be acquired on the spiritual plane by disembodied souls before they could exchange ideas with one another. Here is another illustration of the absurd crudity of conception into which the most accomplished of our non-theosophical contemporaries may be betrayed for want of information concerning other planes of nature which our own resources have enabled us to control.

A. P. SINNETT.

THE WISH TO BELIEVE.

(*Concluded from p.* 115.)

Author. We now come, my dear Philothea, to another complication. I am afraid you will think we are losing sight altogether of your "simple gospel"—but try to have patience for a while. I was laying down the principle that we may safely regard the Jesus Christ you love as having been far more than *mere* man, such as are the men around us; as having attained a height which it may take *us* millions of years to reach. But this does not satisfy you; you will say, "Whatever height He may have reached this leaves Him still man and not God. You must call Him God as well as man, or your doctrine is not Christian whatever else it may be." Were I arguing with you for victory, I might simply say, "Call Him God, then, by all means!" and leave you to find out in what sense I was using a word which means far more to us than it does to you. But before I speak of this, I must first ask, "In what sense do *you* use the word?"

You do not mean that the Jesus Christ of the Gospel was the Infinite, Eternal God in whom we both believe. The Infinite cannot be *contained* in a human body. You say that He was, in some mysterious way, God's Son. So far, we are agreed. As St. Paul says, we *all* are sons of God. But when you come to identify this Jesus of Nazareth with One who is spoken of in another place as the "Only Begotten Son of the Father"; to assert that God has no *other* sons; and, still farther, to associate this relationship with the circumstances of His physical birth in Palestine, I must ask you to stop—and think. It is, of course, useless to press upon you the metaphysical difficulties (amounting, indeed, to impossibilities) involved in this view; but there is one thing I can put to you. Do you accept the logical conclusion that His mother, Mary, the daughter of Anna, was Mother of God? You say, "He was conceived of the Holy Ghost"; you cannot make these words signify anything less than that she, a human being like yourself, was God's wife, and mother of His Son.

Philothea. How can you ask such a question? You know perfectly that no enlightened Gospel Christian believes in the Virgin Mary! It is only the benighted Papists who do so—you are insulting me!

A. I quite admit that the story seems more like one of the tales told of the Pagan gods than the proceedings of such a Divine personage as should be the ideal of an English Christian of the nineteenth century. But the gospels—the "inspired word of God" —expressly say so.

Ph. Well, you know, *everything* in the Bible must not be taken literally. If we were to admit that, it would give the Papists such a handle against us. They would say, Why don't you worship her then, as we do?

A. I accept your admission that there are certain passages in your Bible which must be explained away because your doctrine disagrees with them. It is an awkward admission for one who professes to believe in "the Bible, and the Bible only." But we have not time to see how much there is in "Revelation" which is thus, according to the old jest, "unscriptural." There is much more than you think. But there is a more fatal difficulty. If you give up the actual, physical birth of Jesus as the Son of God, you give up the only conceivable basis of your fundamental doctrine, the "Atonement." In the minds of those who worked out this doctrine it had a meaning, and an intelligible one. They held that by the mysterious and quite incomprehensible union of the two natures in Jesus Christ, He was not only God—not only *a* man, but Humanity itself, and far more. They believed that by virtue of the infinite extension (so to speak) which His Godhead gave to His Manhood, His obedience to His Father's Will was something so immeasurable that all the transgressions of finite humanity might actually be lost in it, like a brook in the wide ocean; that His Suffering was an infinite suffering—an actual compensation (presupposing, of course, a God who *could* receive suffering as compensation) for all the suffering which mankind could deserve by any sin. Thus God's justice was actually and not metaphorically satisfied—all that could be due was paid, and far more. Granting the premises, the claim of the defenders of this doctrine could hardly be denied. For noble souls there *is* something noble and soul-inspiring in it; though for the small, mean minds which think only of saving their own souls, whatever becomes of the rest of the world, its influence is not so good. It is *so* easy to set every one about us down as belonging to "the wicked," and comfortably to acquiesce in their damnation. As has been often remarked, the Christians of this day are much better than their creed.

Ph. Well, the "free grace of God" *is* a noble doctrine. If you admire it so much, why don't you accept the salvation it offers you? It is the one thing needful. Everything else is vanity.

A. My dear Philothea, the question we are now upon is why don't *you* and your friends believe it? Don't be indignant. I know you use the *words*, but you have just admitted that you dare not say that you believe in the actual identity of God and Man in Christ Jesus which the doctrine of the Atonement assumes—for fear of the Papists! But unless it be so, there is no meaning in the word Atonement. A mere man might have done anything short of that. But let us get a step further.

As soon as the doctrine was formulated, it was seen that there was at least one serious difficulty. It proved too much; for if salvation were gained in this arithmetical way, not only was there salvation provided for all, but no one could in fact fail to be saved, *quod non erat demonstrandum*. What would become of the Gospel if no one was to be damned? The whole history of what is called Protestant theology from the first years of the Reformation onward is the succession of desperate struggles to reconcile the Atonement with what was always assumed without enquiry as the actual fact, that more than half mankind were to spend Eternity in the torments of Hell. Hence all the hair-splitting wrangles as to the nature of the "Faith" which saved; and as it came to be recognized that a definition was impossible, theologians speedily fell to the doctrine of Predestination—the lowest depth that could be reached by man civilized or savage—that men were to be damned forever simply for God's private enjoyment. It was felt to be horrible; but there was no logical escape; no other reason could be given for the assumed fact; and good, kindly Christian men actually preached this astounding doctrine as the glad tidings of salvation!

But whilst theologians were thus descending from Martin Luther down to Calvin and Jonathan Edwards, men around them were growing upwards into a certain amount of common sense, and a faith in *that* which soon become incompatible with subjection to such theology. Jonathan Edwards' congregation after suffering under him for many years, finally, their patience quite worn to its last thread, unanimously voted him out of his pulpit and resolved that he should never under any circumstances preach for them again; and what they did on a small scale the world about them did for his theology on the larger plane. In the last hundred years no one of the smallest intelligence outside of the professional class of preachers and their personal followers has troubled himself in any way as to what they teach as to man's future. You are shocked at this statement, but you know it is true. As you would say, the world is growing more wicked every year. At all events it is growing more drawn away from your idea of goodness. But you must brace up your nerves for a more serious shock than this. You won't understand what we think of Jesus unless you can take this in. The controversies of which I have spoken were really needless. The majority of humankind (those whom you so airily dismiss as "the wicked") are *not* going to be damned for ever, and the Bible does not say so!

[Ph. emits an inarticulate gasp of horror. Is about to faint, but thinks better of it. The Author is somewhat advanced in years and there is no one else to catch her in his arms. She at last recovers herself enough to speak.]

Ph. But the Bible *does* say so. It says "the lake of fire and brimstone . . . for ever and ever," over and over again. How *can* you deny it? [Sobs.]

A. I don't deny that your English Bible says so. But every scholar knows that the original Greek does not. The original word *aionion* means a long space of time, I grant you; and we do not deny that very possibly many will have to suffer for this long space, but an *endless* time it does *not* mean.

Ph. But if the wicked don't go to Hell for ever and ever (and it would be very nice if one *could* believe it) what about the righteous in Heaven? Is it the same word? You don't—you *can't* mean we are to be turned out of Heaven after a time—sent to Hell, perhaps to take their place? [Indignantly.]

A. Did it never strike you that supposing you were in Heaven with all your friends about you (excepting of course those who had gone to Hell instead; and, perhaps, a few as to whom you might possibly feel that you wished them in Heaven indeed, but would, on the whole, prefer they should inhabit *another* of its "many mansions"), it *might* happen in the course of some thousands of years, that you might get rather tired of them; and that, after some more thousands of years you might be almost glad of Hell for a change? Such enjoyment as you look for in Heaven cannot satisfy a human soul for ever; and I don't think you could find any reason to complain if, after you had enjoyed all the reward you deserved for your goodness and (so to speak) used up Heaven for the time, you were set down once more upon earth to learn a fresh lesson and grow bigger and better still.

Ph. I don't see it. What enjoyment could there be in Heaven if one knew it was to come to an end—sooner or later. It would not *be* Heaven at all! What we want is rest from our troubles, no more anxiety about our future, the "peace of God which passeth all understanding," you know. [More sobs.]

A. My dear child, it is quite true. Most of us have found our lives in one way or another a failure, and our first thought of what we should like in the future is, as you say, to have no more trouble. From the poor old woman whose idea of Heaven was to sit in a pew with her hands before her, and a nice clean white apron on, to the poet's highest vision of light and music and joy, it is all the same; and I would not say a word against it. *As long as that feeling lasts*, there is no fear of your being turned out of your Heaven; you are not yet fully rested—not ready to go. But let me remind you that it was to people on earth that this peace was wished. The soul within you is far too great ever to be permanently standing still, and there is only one way of progress—to live on earth and learn, keeping God's peace in our hearts all the time.

Ph. But we can never grow tired of God! There must always be something new to learn about Him in Heaven. We might get tired of our friends, but never of Him!

A. True again, but you must not think that you can continually learn more of God by merely living in Heaven. Heaven is not a place for *growth*, and to know more of God you must grow bigger;

be large enough to take more of Him in. The highest angel cannot exhaust God, but it needs very little of Him to fill *you* up to your highest capacity. The real truth of the matter is, that the huge space between the Infinite God and man is not a mere empty void, over which the Sons of God have, as it were, to spring to come upon earth and to return to Him—betwixt Him and us "a great gulf fixed," as in the vision of Dives. It is, rather, a vast stairway like the ladder which Jacob saw in his dream; and on every step souls (angels, he called them) ever drawing nearer to the Divinity; some but little above ourselves, others so far beyond that, to us, they are utterly lost in the Eternal Light. And this height is gained by love and service, not by dreaming in Heaven. There are great souls (and the Jesus who lived and died two thousand years ago in Syria is one of them) whose longing to know the secrets of God's love for men, and to help more efficiently their fellow-men to reach the heights they themselves have gained, has won them to refuse Heaven altogether, choosing rather to return to earth time after time, to labour, to suffer and to grow greater, more helpful, more loving still. Think of Him, already bringing to His Syrian incarnation all that beauty of character, that fulness of the Divine fire which the Gospel narratives image, yet so faintly; and then try to imagine His life since; not sitting idle on some throne in Heaven listening to angels' harps and the vanity of human praises; but ever working for us, and with each work accomplished Himself gaining more wisdom and more power. See Him living amongst His children, now in a human body, now out of it; but ever (incarnate or no) from day to day, as in Galilee of old, "increasing in strength and wisdom" and in favour with "God and man." Think of that glorious Path which He is thus treading, as one which has no end, but for ever new life and new power, leading Him on beyond earth and sun and stars, to infinities which no thought of unaided human intellect can conceive. What to Him, now and hereafter, anything done to the poor, frail human body which He inhabited for a few short years in Palestine, in the course of His endless life and labour—cast aside like so many before and since as His work required? Why, then, should it be anything to us, his younger brethren, following on the same Path, though so far behind? It is not that *body*, nor any other, which is His title to our love and reverence; but the great, warm, loving

Heart which as a sun draws our hearts to such as He. Our "salvation" is that we too, in virtue of the Divinity within us, are on the same Path—the steps of the same Heavenly stair, and must sooner or later stand with Him and the great souls His fellows; that we and the souls above and below us, form the links of the "great gold chain which binds this earth fast to the feet of God"; through which flash help, guidance, life, in constant streams from the highest Divinity to the lowest organised being; joining all creatures in one great league of mutual love and help, which shall hold and widen and deepen as the centuries pass, resistlessly sweeping away all sin and sorrow and shame, until we all come, perfected and triumphant, to "enter into the joy of our Lord." I use words which are familiar to you; can you not gather from what I have said how much *more* they mean to us than they do to you? Is not so great a life something more and better than merely "meeting our friends in Heaven"?

Ph. [who has been growing very uneasy for some time] I can't *think* how you can go on talking such heathenish nonsense! Give me the simple trust in a living Saviour! I am sure your heart is not right in the sight of God. . . . Philosophy, falsely so called, as the Bible warns us. . . . [Sniffs indignantly.] And wanting us to worship the Virgin Mary, too! *I* see how it is, you are just a Jesuit in disguise! *We* know your ways—always so plausible, so insinuating! I won't hear another word from you! [Rises from her chair and exit, very red in the face, muttering something of which we only catch, "Tenfold more the child of Hell than themselves!" Door closes with a bang.]

Author [soliloquises]. Well, well; I ought, I suppose, to have known better. That people should be so good, so amiable, so useful, and yet so—impracticable! She must live her life out, and have her Heaven, poor soul! Perhaps some time she may learn, or perhaps not; for it always seems to me that it is from her class will come most of the failures of this present humanity. The one indispensable qualification for passing on is the aspiration to something higher; and to this there is no hindrance (not even vice itself) so complete and hopeless as the conviction which the lower forms of religion in England and America force upon their followers that in "simple faith" they have all they need for all eternity. They do much good, and will have their due reward; but that spent, what seed is there in such lives for anything greater, what is there for the forces of evolution to work upon? It is a pity, I meant well, but all one can say is (like Titus), "I have lost a day."

A. A. WELLS.

AMONG THE GNOSTICS OF THE FIRST TWO CENTURIES.

(*Continued from p.* 142.)

THE SO-CALLED CAINITES.

BEFORE returning to the time of the origins along the only line of tradition of which one or two obscure indications still remain—the Carpocrates-Cerinthus trace—we will briefly refer to the obscure chaos of tendencies classed together under the term Cainite and its variants. Our sources of information are scanty, and if we exclude the mere mention of the name, are confined to Irenæus and Epiphanius; the latter, moreover, copies from Irenæus, and with the exception of his own reflections and lucubrations, has only a scrap or two of fresh information to add.

This circle of tradition is generally classed as "Ophite," and as usual we find that its adherents called themselves simply Gnostics. They were distinguished by the honour they paid to Cain and Judas; which fact, taken by itself, was sufficient to overwhelm them with the execrations of the orthodox, who ascribed the perpetration of every iniquity to them. Thus we find that Epiphanius, who wrote two hundred years after Irenæus, embroiders considerably on the account of the Bishop of Lyons, even where he is in other respects simply copying from his predecessor. We will now proceed to see the reason why these Gnostics entertained an apparently so strange belief.

If the reader will bear in mind the systems of Justinus and of the Sethians, he will be in a better position to comprehend what follows. Is it even possible that the name Justinus (Ἰουστῖνος), which we find nowhere else than in the account of Hippolytus, may be an error for Judas (Ἰούδας)? The main features of the system of these Gnostics, then, was as follows.

The creator of the world was not the God over all; the absolute power from above was stronger than the weaker (ὑστέρα—hystera) power of generation, which was symbolised as the power of the impure world-womb, containing heaven and earth within it—the sensible world. But this sensible world was, as it were, an after-birth (ὕστερα—hystera), compared to the true birth from the virgin spiritual womb, the ideal world of the æons above. Epiphanius has made a great muddle of this part of the system; it is evidently consanguineous with the Valentinian "deficiency" (ὑστέρημα—hysterêma), or abortion, the sensible world, without or external to the ideal fulness or perfection (πλήρωμα—plerôma), or world of the æons.

The inferior power, therefore, was the God of generation, the superior the God of enlightenment and wisdom. The Old Testament idea of God went no further than obedience to the commands of the inferior power. Those who had obeyed its behests were regarded as the worthies of old by the followers of the External Law, who seeing no further, had, in their traditions, vilified all who refused to follow this law, the commands of the inferior power of generation. Thus Abel and Jacob and Lot and Moses were praised by the followers of the law of generation; whereas in reality it was the opponents of these who ought to be praised, as followers of the Higher Law who despised the laws of the powers of generation, and were thus protected by Wisdom and taken to herself, to the æon above. They therefore claimed that Cain and Esau, and the inhabitants of the cities of the plain, and Coran, Dathan and Abiram, were types of those individuals or nations who had followed a higher law.

We can here see very plainly the traces of the same antitheses as those worked out by Justinus; the influence of the psychic powers or angels being traceable along the Abel line of descent, and that of the spiritual powers along the Cain line. This antithetical device, in one form or other, was common enough—as for instance, the later Ebionite antitheses of superior and inferior men (Isaac-Ishmael, Jacob-Esau, Moses-Aaron), or the Marcionite antitheses of the God of freedom and the God of the law, the God of Christ and the Jehovah of the Old Testament—but the school whose tenets we are describing, seem in their contempt for Jehovah, to have pushed their theories to the most extravagant conclusion of any. This is especially brought out in their ideas of New Testament history, which in spite of their strangeness, may nevertheless contain a small trace of the correct tradition of the cause of Jesus' death.

This Gnostic circle had a number of writings, chief amongst which were two small summaries of instruction, one called The Gospel of Judas and the other The Ascent of Paul. To take the latter first: The Ascent of Paul purported to contain the record of the ineffable things which Paul is reported to have heard when he ascended into the third heaven. Whether this was the same as the Apocalypse of Paul referred to by Augustine is uncertain; in any case it is lost. A more orthodox version of one of the documents of the same cycle has come down to us in The Vision of Paul, a translation of which may be read in the last volume of the Ante-Nicene Christian Library (1897). If we can rely on this title, for which Epiphanius alone is responsible, the school of the Cainites is consequently post-Pauline.

But the strangest and, from one point of view, the most interesting development of their theory, was the view they took of Judas. The "Poor Men's" (Ebionite) tradition had consistently handed over Judas to universal execration; there was, however, apparently another tradition, presumably Essene in the first place, which took a different view of the matter. Obscure traces of this seem to be preserved in the unintelligent Irenæus-Epiphanius account of the Cainite doctrines.

This circle of students looked upon Judas as a man far advanced in the discipline of the Gnosis, and one who had a very clear idea of the true God as distinguished from the God of generation; he consequently taught a complete divorcement from the things of the world and thus from the inferior power, which had made the heaven, the world and the flesh. Man was to ascend to the highest region through the crucifixion of the Christ. The Christ was the spirit which came down from above, in order that the stronger power of the spiritual world might be perfected in man; and so Jesus triumphed over the weaker power of generation at the expense of his body, which he handed over to death, one of the manifestations of the God of generation. This was the christological doctrine of the school, and it was apparently, judging from the "he says" of Epiphanius, taken from The Gospel of Judas.

But besides this general mystical teaching, there was also a historical tradition: that Jesus, after becoming the Christ and teaching the higher doctrine, in their opinion fell away and endeavoured to overset the law, and corrupt the holy doctrine, and therefore Judas had him handed over to the authorities. That is to say, those to whom Jesus originally taught the higher doctrine, considered that his too open preaching to the people was a divulging of the mysteries, and so finally brought about his condemnation for blasphemy by the Jewish authorities.

Yet another more mystical tradition, preserved in one of their books, declared that, on the contrary, the Christ had not made a mistake, but that all had been done according to the heavenly wisdom. For the world-rulers knew that if the Christ were betrayed to the cross, that is to say, were incarnated, that the inferior power would be drained out of them and they should ascend to the spiritual æon. Now Judas knew this, and in his great faith, used every means to bring about his betrayal, and in this way the salvation of the world. And thus we have preserved a dim trace of the pseudo-historical tradition of the mystery-drama. These Gnostics consequently praised Judas as being one of the main factors in the scheme of salvation; without him the mystical "salvation of the cross" would not have been consummated, nor the consequent revelation of the realms above.

The Cainite circle, therefore, from their doctrines appear to have been rigid ascetics. But says Epiphanius, embroidering on Irenæus, they were very dreadful people, and, like Carpocrates, taught that a man could not be saved without going through every kind of experience. We will therefore now take a brief glance at the views of the Carpocratians, who in other respects are the next link of our chain.

THE CARPOCRATIANS.

Our main source of information is Irenæus; Tertullian, Hippolytus and Epiphanius simply copy their predecessor. Carpocrates or Carpocras was (according to Eusebius) a Platonic philosopher who taught at Alexandria in the reign of Hadrian (A.D. 117-138); he was also the head of a Gnostic circle, whom the Church fathers call Carpocratians, but who called themselves simply Gnostics. With regard to the charge which Epiphanius brings against them two hundred and fifty years afterwards, it is evidently founded on a complete misunderstanding of the jumbled account of Irenæus, if not of malice prepense; for the Bishop of Lyons distinctly says that he by no means believes that they did the things which he thinks they ought to have done if they had consistently carried out their teachings. As a matter of fact, the whole confusion arises through the incapacity of the latter Church father to understand the elements of the doctrine of rebirth. The main tenets of the school were as follows.

The sensible world was made by the fabricating powers, or builders, far inferior to the ineffable power of the unknown ingenerable Father. Jesus was the son of Joseph and Mary, and was born like all other men; he differed from the rest in that his soul, being strong and pure, *remembered* what it saw in its orbit round (or conversation with) the ineffable Father. This is the Platonic idea of the orderly course of the soul in harmonious circuit round the Spiritual Sun, in the Plain of Truth, when it is in its own nature. In consequence of this reminiscence (which is the source of all wisdom and virtue), the Father clothed him with powers, whereby he might escape from the dominion of the rulers of the world, and passing through all their spheres, and being freed from each, finally ascend to the Father. In like manner all souls of a like nature who put forth similar efforts, shall ascend to the Father. Though the soul of Jesus was brought up in the ordinary Jewish views, he soared above them, and thus by the powers he received from above, he triumphed over human passions.

Believing, then, that all souls which rise above the constraints of the world-building rulers, will receive similar powers and perform like wonders, these Gnostics still further claimed that some of their number had actually attained to the same degree of perfection as Jesus, if not to a higher degree, and were stronger than Peter and Paul, and the other disciples who had attained similar powers.

In fact, they boldly taught that men could reach higher degrees of illumination than Jesus; it is not, however, clear whether they made the usual distinction between Jesus and Christ. These powers were of a magical nature, and the next paragraph of Irenæus puts us strongly in mind of the tenets of the Simonian school. Such ideas seem to have been very prevalent, so much so, that Irenæus complains that outsiders were induced to think that such ideas were the common belief of Christianity.

The next paragraph deals with the doctrine that there is no essential evil in the universe, but that things are bad and good in man's opinion only. Let us, therefore, see how Irenæus arrives at this generalization from his summary of their doctrine of rebirth.

The soul has to pass through every kind of existence and activity in its cycle of rebirth. Irenæus is apparently drawing his information from a MS. which asserted that this could be done in one life; that is to say, apparently, that some souls now existing in the world could pay their karmic debt in one life. For the MS. quotes the saying, "Agree with thine adversary quickly whiles thou art in the way with him, lest at any time thine adversary deliver thee to the judge, and the judge deliver thee to his officer, and thou be cast into prison. Amen, I say unto thee, thou shall not come forth thence till thou hast paid the uttermost farthing." Now, the adversary is the accuser (diabolus), that is to say the karmic record in the man's own nature; the judge is the chief of the world-building powers; the officer is the builder of the new body; the prison is the body. Thus the MS., explains the text; precisely the same exegesis as is given to it in the Pistis Sophia treatise, which explains all in the fullest manner on the lines of reincarnation and karma.

But not so will Irenæus have it. He asserts that the doctrine means that the soul must pass through all experience good and bad, and until every experience has been learned, no one can be set free. That some souls can do all this in one life! That the Carpocratians, therefore, indulged in the most unmentionable crimes because they wished to fill full the tale of all experience good and bad, and so come to an end of the necessity of experience.

Irenæus, however, immediately afterwards adds that he does not believe the Carpocratians actually do such things, although he is forced to deduce such a logical consequence from their books. It is, however, evident that the whole absurd conclusion is entirely due to the stupidity of the Bishop of Lyons, who, owing to his inability to understand the most elementary facts of the doctrine of rebirth, has started with entirely erroneous premises, although the matter was as clear as daylight to a beginner in Gnosticism.

The circle of the Carpocratians is said to have established a branch at Rome, about 150, under a certain Marcellina. They had pictures and statues of many great teachers who were held in honour by their school, such as Pythagoras, Plato, and Aristotle, and also a portrait of Jesus.

It is curious to remark that Celsus, as quoted by Origen (c. 62), in referring to these Marcellians, also mentions the Harpocratians who derived their tenets from Salome. Is it possible that this is the correct form of the name? Harpocrates was the Græcised form of Horus, the mystery-god of the Egyptians, and Salome, we know, was a prominent figure in the lost Gospel according to the Egyptians.

"Epiphanes."

We next pass on to the contradictory and manifestly absurd legends which Patristic writers have woven round the second best known name of the Carpocratian circle. We have already referred to the extraordinary blunder of Epiphanius, who has ascribed a whole system of the Gnosis, which he found in Irenæus assigned simply to a "distinguished teacher" (probably the Valentinian Marcus), to this Epiphanes; the Greek for "distinguished" being also "epiphanes."

This is excusable in a certain measure, seeing that Epiphanius wrote at the end of the fourth century, at least 250 years after the time of the actual Epiphanes, when any means of discrediting a heretic were considered justifiable; but what shall we say of Clement of Alexandria, who is generally fair and who lived in the same century as Epiphanes? His blunder is even more extraordinary. This is his legend. Epiphanes was the son of Carpocrates and Alexandria, a lady of Cephallenia. He died at the early age of seventeen, and was worshipped as a god with the most elaborate and lascivious rites by the Cephallenians, in the great temple of Same, on the day of the new moon.

Such an extraordinary legend could not long escape the penetrating criticism of modern scholarship, and as early as Mosheim the key was found to the mystery. Volkmar has worked this out in detail and shown that the festival at Same was in honour of the moon god, and accompanied with licentious rites. It was called the

Epiphany (τὰ Ἐπιφάνια) in honour of Epiphanes (ὁ Ἐπιφανής), the "newly-appearing one," the new moon. This moon lasted some seventeen days. Thus Clement of Alexandria, deceived by the similarity of the names and also by the story of licentious rites, bequeathed to posterity a scandalous libel. It is almost to be doubted whether any Epiphanes existed! Clement further asserts that among the Carpocratians one of their most circulated books was a treatise On Justice, of which he had seen a copy. He ascribes this to Epiphanes, but it is scarcely possible to believe that a boy of seventeen or less could have composed an abstract dissertation on justice.

We thus come to the conclusion that the Carpocratians, or Harpocratians, were a Gnostic circle in Alexandria at the beginning of the second century, and that some of their ideas were set forth in a book concerning justice, a copy of which had come into the hands of Clement. This Gnostic community was much exercised with the idea of communism as practised by the early Christian circles; being also students of Plato they wished to reduce the idea to the form of a philosophical principle and carry it out to its logical conclusion. The false ideas of *meum* and *tuum* were no longer to exist; private property was the origin of all human miseries and the departure from the happy days of early freedom. There was, therefore, to be community of everything, wives and husbands included; thus carrying out in some fashion that most curious idea of Plato's as set forth in the Republic. We have, however, no reliable evidence that our Gnostics carried these ideas into practice; it is also highly improbable that men of education and refinement, as the Gnostics usually were, who came to such views through the Pythagorean and Platonic discipline, and through the teachings of Jesus (the sine quâ non condition of such ideal communities being that they should consist of "gnostics" and be ruled by "philosophers")—should have turned their meetings into orgies of lasciviousness. Such, however, is the accusation brought against them by Clement. This has already been in part refuted by what has been said above, but it is not improbable that there were communities at Alexandria and elsewhere, calling themselves Christian, who did confuse the Agapæ or Love-feasts of the early times with the orgies and feasts of the ignorant Pagan populace. The Pagans brought such accusations against the Christians indiscriminately and the Christian sects against one another; it is quite credible that such abuses did creep in among the ignorant and vicious.

The Carpocratian school has been sometimes claimed, though I think improperly, as the originator of the so-called Monadic Gnosis. This idea has been worked out with much detail by Neander. The following summary of Salmon's will, however, be sufficient for the general reader from which to form an idea of the theory.

"From one eternal Monad all existence has flowed, and to this it strives to return. But the finite spirits who rule over several portions of the world counteract this universal striving after unity. From them the different popular religions, and in particular the Jewish, have proceeded. Perfection is attained by those souls who, led on by reminiscences of their former conditions soar above all limitation and diversity to the contemplation of the higher unity. They despise the restriction imposed by the mundane spirits; they regard externals as of no importance, and faith and love as the only essentials; meaning by faith, mystical brooding of the mind absorbed in the original unity. In this way they escape the dominion of the finite mundane spirits; their souls are freed from imprisonment in matter, and they obtain a state of perfect repose (corresponding to the Buddhist Nirvâṇa) when they have completely ascended above the world of appearance."

The Cerinthians.

Continuing to pick our way back along this trace towards the times of the origins we next come upon the circle of the Cerinthians (or the Merinthians according to the variant of Epiphanius). They are said to derive their name from a certain Cerinthus, who is placed in "apostolic times," that is to say the latter half of the first century.

Epiphanius has busied himself exceedingly over Cerinthus and cleverly made him a scapegoat for the "pillar-apostles'" antagonism to Paul. Most writers have followed his lead and explained away a number of compromising statements in the Acts and Pauline Letters by this device. Impartial criticism, however, has to reject the lucubrations of the late Epiphanius, and go back to the short account of Irenæus from whom all later writers have copied. Irenæus, who was himself a full century after Cerinthus, has only a brief paragraph on the subject.

Cerinthus is the strongest trace between Ebionism, or the original non-Pauline tradition, and the beginning of the second century. He is supposed to have come into personal contact with John, the supposed writer of the fourth Gospel, but the same story is told of the mythic Ebion, and must therefore be dismissed as destitute of all historical value.

Cerinthus is said to have been trained in the "Egyptian discipline," and to have taught in Asia Minor. The Egyptian discipline is supposed to mean the Philonic school, but this is a mere assumption. In any case the importance of Cerinthus, whom some Gnostics claimed to have been the writer of the Apocalypse orthodoxly ascribed to John, is that his name has preserved one of the earliest forms of Christian tradition. Its cosmogony declared the stupendous excellence of the God over all, beyond the subordinate power, the World-fashioner. Its christology declared that Jesus was son of Joseph and Mary; that at his "baptism" the Christ, the "Father in the form of a dove," descended upon him, and only then did he begin to prophesy and do mighty works, and preach the hitherto unknown Father (unknown to the Jews), the God over all. That the Christ then left him; and then Jesus suffered, and rose again (that is, appeared to his followers after death).

Such is the account of Irenæus, which seems to be straightforward and reliable enough as far as it goes. The scripture of the Cerinthians was not the Hebrew recension of the Sayings ascribed to Matthew, which formed one of the four sources of the present Greek text of the first Synoptic, but a still earlier collection in Hebrew. All other collections and recensions were rejected as utterly apocryphal. The Greek writer of the fourth canonical Gospel is said to have composed his account in opposition to the school of Cerinthus.

The Nicolaitans.

We have now got back to such early times that even the faintest glimmer of historical light fails us; we are now deep in the sombre region of legend and speculation. We will, therefore, plunge no further into the dark depths of the cave of the origins; but once more retrace our steps to the mouth of the cavern, where at least some fitful gleams of daylight struggle through. But before doing so, we must call the reader's attention to a just discernable shadow of early Gnosticism, the circle of the Nicolaitans. These Gnostics are of especial interest to the orthodox, because the writer of the Apocalypse has twice gone out of his way to tell us that he hates their doings. Encouraged by this phrase, Irenæus includes the Nicolaitans in the writer's condemnation of some of the members of the church of Pergamus, who apparently "ate things sacrificed to idols and committed fornication." Subsequent hæresiologists, in their turn encouraged by Irenæus, added further embellishments, until finally Epiphanius makes Nicolaus the father of every enormity he had collected or invented against the Gnostics.

And then with all this "evidence" of his iniquity, Epiphanius rhetorically proceeds to address the shade of the unfortunate Gnostic: "What, then, am I to say to thee, O Nicolaus?" For ourselves we are surprised that so inventive a genius as the Bishop of Salamis should have drawn breath even to put so rhetorical a question.

Tradition claims Nicolaus as an ascetic, and relates an exaggerated instance of his freedom from passion. Even granted that he taught that the eating of sacrificial viands was not a deadly sin, there seems no reason why we to-day should follow these Church fathers in their bigotry-begotten condemnation of everything but their own grey view of the Christ's doctrine.

CERDO.

Let us now return to the historical twilight of the second century, and turn our attention to the great Basilidian and Valentinian developments. But before doing so, it will be convenient to give a brief sketch of the great and contemporaneous Marcionite movement which at one time threatened to absorb the whole of Christendom. The method of this school was the direct prototype of the method of modern criticism. Its conclusions, however, were far more sweeping; for it not only rejected the Old Testament entirely, but also the whole of the documents of the "in order that it might be fulfilled" school of Gospel compilation.

The predecessor of Marcion is said to have been a certain Cerdo, of Syrian extraction, who flourished at Rome about 135 A.D. But the fame of Marcion so eclipsed the name of his preceptor, that

Patristic writers frequently confuse not only their teachings but even the men themselves. It is interesting to note that though Cerdo's relationship with the Church of Rome was unsettled, no distinct sentence of excommunication is recorded against him; it, therefore, would appear that the idea of a rigid canon of orthodoxy was not yet developed even in the exclusive mind of the Roman presbytery. It was no doubt the success of Marcion which precipitated the formulation of the idea of the canon in the mind of the Roman church, the pioneer of subsequent orthodoxy.

MARCION.

Marcion was a rich shipowner of Sinope, the chief port of Pontus, on the southern shore of the Black Sea; he was also a bishop and the son of a bishop. His chief activity at Rome may be placed somewhere between the years 150 and 160. At first he was in communion with the church at Rome, and contributed handsomely to its funds; as, however, the presbyters could not explain his difficulties and refused to face the important questions he set before them, he is said to have threatened to make a schism in the church; and apparently was finally excommunicated. But as a matter of fact the origin of Marcionism is entirely wrapped in obscurity, and we know nothing of a reliable nature of the lives of either Cerdo or Marcion.

The Church writers at the end of the second century, who are our best authorities, cannot tell the story of the beginning of the movement with any certainty. For all we know, Marcion may have developed his theories long before he came to Rome, and may have based them on information he gleaned and opinions he heard in his long voyages. This much we know, that the views of Marcion spread rapidly over the "whole world," to use the usual Patristic phrase for the Græco-Roman dominions; and as late as the fifth century we hear of Theodoret converting more than a thousand Marcionites. In Italy, Egypt, Palestine, Arabia, Syria, Asia Minor and Persia, Marcionite churches sprang up, splendidly organized, with their own bishops and the rest of the ecclesiastical discipline, with a cult and service of the same nature as those of what subsequently became the Catholic Church. Orthodoxy had not declared for any party as yet, and the Marcionite view had then as good a chance as any other of becoming the universal one. What then was the secret of Marcion's success? As already pointed out, it was the same as that of the success of modern criticism as applied to the problem of the Old Testament.

Marcion's view was in some respects even more moderate than the judgment of some of our modern thinkers; he was willing to admit that the Jehovah of the Old Testament was just. With great acumen he arranged the sayings and doings ascribed to Jehovah by the writers, and compilers, and editors of the heterogeneous books of the Old Testament collection, in parallel columns, so to say, with the sayings and teachings of Christ, in a series of antitheses which brought out in startling fashion the fact, that though the best of the former might be ascribed to the idea of a Just God, they were foreign to the ideal of the Good God preached by the Christ. We know how in these latter days the best minds in the Church have rejected the horrible sayings and doings ascribed to God in some of the Old Testament documents, and we thus see how Marcion at once voiced a protest which must have already declared itself in the hearts of thousands of the more enlightened of the Christian name.

As for the New Testament, in Marcion's time, the idea of a canon was only just being thought of. Marcion, too, had an idea of a canon, but it was the antipodes of the views which afterwards became the basis of the orthodox canon.

The Christ had preached a universal doctrine, a new revelation of the Good God, the Father over all. They who tried to graft this on to Judaism, the imperfect creed of one small nation, were in grievous error, and had totally misunderstood the teaching of the Christ. The Christ was not the Messiah promised to the Jews. That Messiah was to be an earthly king, was intended for the Jews alone, and had not yet come. Therefore the pseudo-historical "in order that it might be fulfilled" school had adulterated and garbled the original Sayings of the Lord, the universal glad tidings, by the unintelligent and erroneous glosses they had woven into their collections of the teachings. It was the most terrific indictment of the cycle of New Testament legend that had ever been formulated. Men were tired of all the contradictions and obscurities of the innumerable, mutually destructive variants of the traditions of the historical

Jesus. No man could say what was the truth now that "history" had been so altered to suit the new Messiah-theory of the Jewish converts.

As to actual history, then, Marcion started with Paul; he was the first who had really understood the mission of the Christ, and had rescued the teaching from the obscurantism of Jewish sectarianism. Of the manifold versions of the Gospels, he would have the Pauline alone. He rejected every other recension, including those ascribed to Matthew, Mark and John. The Gospel according to Luke, the follower of Paul, he also rejected; at any rate in its subsequent orthodox form. This he regarded as a recension to suit the views of the Judaising party. His Gospel was the Pauline collection of Sayings. Of course the Patristic writers say that Marcion mutiliated Luke's version; but it is almost impossible to believe that, if he did this, so keen a critic as Marcion should have retained certain verses which made against his strong anti-Judaistic views. The Marcionites, on the contrary, contended that their Gospel was written by Paul from the direct tradition, and that Luke had nothing to do with it.

So many orthodox writers wrote against Marcion after his death, that it is possible to reconstruct almost the whole of his Gospel. It begins with the public preaching of the Christ at Capernaum; it is shorter than the present Luke document, and some writers of great ability have held that it was the original of Luke's version. As for the rest of the documents included in the present collection of the New Testament, Marcion would have nothing to do with any of them, except ten of the Letters of Paul, parts of which he also rejected as interpolations by the reconciliators of the Petro-Pauline controversy. These ten Letters were called The Apostle.

The longest criticism of Marcion's views is to be found in Tertullian's invective Against Marcion, written in 207 and the following years. This has always been regarded by the orthodox as a most brilliant piece of work; but by the light of the conclusions arrived at by the industry of the modern criticism, and also to ordinary common sense, it appears but a sorry piece of angry rhetoric. Tertullian tries to show that Marcion taught two Gods, the Just and the Good. Marcion, however, taught that the *idea* of the Jews about God, as set forth in the Old Testament, was inferior and antagonistic to the ideal of the Good God revealed by the Christ. This he set forth in the usual Gnostic fashion. But we can hardly expect a dispassionate treatment of a grave problem which has only in the last few years reached a satisfactory solution in Christendom, from the fanatic Tertullian, whose temper may be gleaned from his angry address to the Marcionites: "Now then, ye dogs, whom the apostle puts outside, and who yelp at the God of truth, let us come to your various questions. These are the bones of contention, which ye are perpetually gnawing!"

(*To be continued.*)

G. R. S. MEAD.

THE SAGE AND THE THREE YOUNG MEN.

A SAGA BY A. KNÖS.

IN the once-upon-a-time there lived an old man who was very wise. His reputation as a sage was known everywhere, and many sought his presence in order that they might gain help and wisdom. One day there came to him three youths. They were all in that golden age of hope and expectancy, full of the joy and vigour of life, when the soul is burning with the desire for activity, before disappointment has occurred to cool the zeal and ardour of youth and whilst the ideal still shines out in unclouded beauty. They seemed most eager to get information from the old man so that afterwards they might be able to benefit others by their knowledge. The first asked:

"Good father, of thy wisdom I pray thee to give me something by which I may be of service to my fellow creatures. I am filled with an intense desire to be of use in the world, and certain it is that thou better than any one else can teach me that which is necessary thereto."

The sage answered:

"I read thy eagerness in thine eyes. But dost thou possess patience and perseverance? The path of knowledge is steep, and at times most wearisome."

"I will do anything, if thou wilt but grant my wish."

"What then, is thy choice? Mark well, though. Thy decision once made, thou must rest satisfied. It cannot be undone, nor canst thou choose again."

"I am well aware that such is the demand made of those who seek to draw the pure water of knowledge from thy fount of wisdom. Well then, my choice is already made. As I journeyed here I saw on the road an afflicted and wretched man, who with much pain and difficulty was trying to creep along. The sight of him set me thinking that it would be a glorious thing to be able to help the suffering and heal the sick. In this way many would be helped to happiness and well-being. Therefore, I pray thee, teach me the remedies for all sickness and disease, and then I shall be eternally grateful, and all mankind will bless thee."

"It is not enough to know the remedies, in the first place thou must learn to know the diseases themselves. For in every case it is necessary to be able to recognise what disease it is that must be cured. To be able to understand this thou must know each separate organ of the body, with its object and functions. Then a knowledge is required of the composition and effects of the various remedies, and to acquire this thou must know the foundations upon which a number of natural laws rest, as well as how these laws further evolve with completely accurate results."

"Is there so much? Is it not enough to know the special remedy for each disease?"

"There are many diseases and many remedies. If thou dost not learn to distinguish each separately, then there would be the risk of committing mistakes, and thy imperfect knowledge would thus become more of a curse than a blessing to those whom thou wouldst aid."

"And how long will it take me then to acquire the amount of information which thou considerest necessary?"

"That dependeth on thy perseverance. But, however industrious thou mayest be, many years must elapse before thou canst gain sufficient experience."

"So long? I have never thought that. I wish to help my fellow creatures much sooner, almost directly. So long I cannot wait. During that time so many would die unhelped. No, there must be a quicker way. I will search for it. So farewell, father."

And he went away.

Then the second youth came forward and said:

"Thou wilt not be rid of me so easily, O sage. I am burning with desire for another kind of knowledge. It does not concern the things of the body, nor does it pertain to this earth alone. My eager longing is aroused by the boundless firmament, and my soul seeks for the wisdom which comprehends cosmic space. I know that this space is full of worlds, which follow courses determined by mysteriously working forces. Teach me, then, O sage, thou who hast knowledge of all things, the laws of these forces. It ought to be a glorious task, with cognizance of these laws, to be able to calculate the course of those onward circling worlds, and moreover ascertain their relation to one another, as well as to reveal those secrets which might give clearer information respecting our own earth. It is a knowledge of the great world which I aspire to, and this gained I will afterwards proceed to investigate the lesser world. According to my belief this is the only lofty path. And when I have once succeeded in increasing my own knowledge, I will go forth and give mankind the benefit thereof, and this ought surely to become a help to enlightenment and happiness."

"Understandest thou that for such knowledge much preparatory study is needed?"

"I see it, and am prepared for it. Prepared to sacrifice years of my life to this study, in order to be able in my turn to instruct others."

"And knowest thou that for the sake of this thy studies must be extended not only to the natural sciences in general, but especially to the mathematical. Thou knowest the whole chain through which these last mentioned run, and how thou must go along this chain, link by link, proof after proof, in order to finally reach thy goal. Art thou prepared for the work all this demands?"

"I am aware of it, and with all diligence I am ready to devote myself seriously to it."

"And thou dost resign thyself to this work not merely that thou mayst increase thy learning, but, as I understand, that thou mayst be able in due time to instruct others? Is this the aim thou hast set before thee?"

"Yes, that is my aim, and it seems to me both grand and worth striving after."

"And dost thou believe then that the multitude will afterwards follow thee upon this laborious path to wisdom, with the same amount of earnestness and endurance which thou thyself hast given?"

"Most certainly! Can there be any subject of research wider and grander than this? It must surely interest all!"

"So thou mayest think. But the subject will appear in a very different light to those who by the sweat of their brow must work to gain their daily bread. The laws of the cosmos will be all the same to them. The interest of the multitude thou couldst never hope to awake. They could not earn their bread by such learning, nor would it influence their hard, every-day existence. Comparatively few would be interested in thy teaching, and out of these only an infinitesimally small number would have courage and patience to tread the hard and troublesome path upon which thou art now prepared to take the first step. Still more! Thou mayest believe me, for well I know the world and its people; and I moreover declare that this knowledge thou art dreaming of will never accomplish the great work thou thinkest possible, neither is it calculated to make mankind, in a true sense, happier. In order to do this something more than wisdom and learning is required—even if these could comprehend all things beneath the heavens."

The youth seemed deeply distressed. The words of the old man had shattered his illusions. The aim which seemed so magnificent, and which had dazzled his eyes with its radiant glitter, now sank down dim and faded, and no longer appeared worth striving for. Sad and heavy of heart, he went his way.

The third youth alone remained, and he was thoughtful and serious.

"And what is the aim and the work that thou art meditating for the sake of others?"

"The words which thou hast spoken to my companions, wise father, have only served to strengthen my idea of what is, and ought to be, the highest aim of all, and most worth striving for. If I am to help others I must give them that which will be of real use to them. To heal the sick and to comfort the sorrowing are beautiful things, to inspire mankind with a desire for wisdom is a splendid thought, but most glorious of all, to my thinking, would be to teach people to lead lives of *truth* and *goodness*."

"Grand and noble is thy thought. But dost thou not look for something in return for thy work in the service of truth?"

"Nothing more than the gratitude of my fellow-beings."

"Thou wilt not even get that."

"Nevertheless, I will work for them; I will not even ask for gratitude. Teach me, O wise father, the profound mysteries of truth, and it shall be my delight to proclaim them, and to suffer for them if it should be necessary."

"Art thou then for thy own part prepared to receive them?"

"In truth, yes! O sage, thou couldst not possibly find a pupil with a more earnest desire for knowledge."

"That is not sufficient. Thy thirst for knowledge must find its development through constant and untiring labour, and this alone can guide thee in the direction of truth. However much wisdom may be possessed by another, it can but help thee a little. If thou wouldst become a defender of truth and a helper of humanity it is requisite that thou must thyself search for the pearl of truth. Without this, thy work amongst mankind will be fruitless and no one can have this precious pearl who has not himself discovered it. Only very rarely wilt thou receive any direction on the path of research, and it will not carry thee far. Through the darkness of doubt, and over the quagmire of the passions must thou pass on thy way. Cast from thee all pleasure, forget thyself, leave all hope behind, and lead a life of self-sacrifice alone, for others' sake. If eventually the pearl of truth thou findest, then thou must promise never to use it for thy own advantage, and finally thou must be prepared to suffer all things for the truth. If thy heart fails thee, and thou canst not be certain that thy strength and courage will suffice to carry thee through all this, then is it wiser to forego the search for the pearl."

"Good father, thy words terrify me. Thou makest me fearful and hesitating, for almost impossible would it be to say now that I should be certain to overcome all these difficulties which must beset my path. Thou seest my uncertainty. Oh! counsel and direct me what I ought to do."

"Bide thy time, and for the present labour to gather strength sufficient to go on and take the great step towards which thy mind is turned, and which has aroused thy ardour."

"Must I then think only of myself? I journeyed hither in the hope that I might learn that which could be of special use to others. Canst thou not give me some small portion of the knowledge which is truth, so that whilst working at my own development, I may at the same time be able to point others to the path?"

"I have already told thee that truth must be found by thyself alone. In proportion as thou findest it, thou mayst endeavour to share it with others. Thy desire is to reform mankind through the preaching of truth. Remember then, that every reformer must first reform himself, if he is desirous that people may listen to his words. His life and actions must be in strict harmony with his teaching. Still one thing more thou must bear well in mind: thy fellow-beings will not be benefited by merely *listening*, nor by ever so much *learning* about the good and the true; for only when they know and understand to do what is right, will they become better."

The young man was silent, sunk in meditation on the words of the sage. He had imagined that with calm delight he would be able to satisfy his thirst for knowledge from the sage's fount of wisdom.

But that which he had been told, was so surprisingly new.

He went his way deep in thought.

(*Translated from the Swedish by* MRS. HAIG.)

THE PHÆDO OF PLATO.

(*Continued from p.* 131.)

III.

WE have now arrived at the conclusion of the great series of arguments by which Socrates endeavours to awaken in the minds of his companions a conviction corresponding to his own in respect to the immortality of the soul. Another consideration, to which he briefly adverts, may be offered as an additional, and perhaps unanswerable, argument to all those who admit an over-ruling Providence, or believe that a law of justice lies at the foundation of the universe. For if to all men death bring the same end, and if the soul perish together with the body, the good are surely placed at a great disadvantage as compared with the wicked, whom death absolves from the retribution due to their sins. Nor can we lessen the force of such a reflection by insisting upon the supposed triviality of human affairs; for if we once assume that the law of justice may fail in any, the most trifling particular, we have no sure ground for our faith that it holds good in the most important concerns.

The remainder of Socrates' discourse deals largely with the soul's life in the afterworld. When the soul arrives at Hades (the unseen place) it is said to possess nothing but discipline and education. To Hades the souls are conducted by their guardian dæmons. There they are judged, and receive their proper allotments; and thence, "after many and long periods of time," they are by other dæmons conducted back to the earth, that they may again incarnate. Now in the *Republic*, Plato describes the soul's journey beneath the earth—*i.e.*, the interval between two incarnations—as a journey of a thousand years. Here in the *Phædo*, however, he speaks of "many and long periods of time." But the former expression is not to be taken literally; by the thousand years is meant not a measure of time, but a measure of perfection.

The Pythagoreans denominated the number ten the perfect number, as the basis of their decimal system of calculation, and as including the forms of all numbers in itself, as the soul contains in herself the forms of all things. In an ancient Pythagorean fragment, attributed to Philolaus, it is written, "We must contemplate the works and the essence of number according to the power which is in the decad; for the power of the decad is great and all-perfect and all-working, a principle and guide and ordainer of divine and celestial and human life." The decad is therefore assimilated to the monad, in which all number causally abides. As, moreover, the duad, being the number of contraries, is the symbol of progression or manifestation, Plato, in the *Republic*, assumes the *second* power of ten (10 × 10), or the period of 100 years, as the sum of a single earth-life, or manifestation of the soul in body. And as the triad is the number of conversion or return, he takes the *third* power of ten (10 × 10 × 10), or the period of one thousand years, as the measure of the interval which brings the soul back to generation. The multiplication of the number of years in an earth-life by ten, to produce the period of the interval, has reference also to the multiplicative nature of both good and evil Karma; as a single action, a single thought, is multiplied in its consequences. And lastly, as the solid figure of the cube is properly adapted to a terrestrial condition, so the cubic figure 1000 (10 × 10 × 10) is chosen as that of the period which concludes with the return of the soul to earth. By the thousand years, therefore, Plato means not a definite measure of time, but the period in which the soul assimilates the experiences of its past life, and prepares for a new incarnation; and this period must be longer or shorter according to the nature of its experiences.

The belief in dæmons, as the guardians and leaders of souls, is an important and most interesting feature of the Hellenic religion, upon which, however, I can here offer but a few observations. It is a fundamental doctrine of Platonic philosophy, that all things, from highest Being to lowest materiality, which is the mere shadow of being, are bound together in a perfectly-ordered gradation; that there is no break in the continuity, that which is first on every plane being closely assimilated to that which is last on the plane immediately above it. Hence it follows that between the eternal Gods and mortal men there are various grades of intelligent beings, some of whom are more nearly allied to the divine, and others to the mortal nature; and all these middle powers are comprehended under the general term of dæmons. It is, indeed, a widely comprehensive appellation, for we find it sometimes applied to the departed souls of virtuous men, sometimes also to beings of a far lower order, and, in general, to almost every kind of intelligent, or semi-intelligent entity, which is not bound to an earthly body. But most of these were called dæmons only by analogy; the true, or essential, dæmons are those which hold a middle position between the Gods and mortal natures, connecting both, and constituting the medium whereby the providential energies of divinity are transmitted to mortals, and the aspirations of mortals are carried upward to the Gods. The dæmonic nature is, therefore, essentially connective, and it is for this reason that Diotima, in the *Banquet*, calls Love a dæmon, as being a power connective of the lover and the beloved.

Now the Gods are indeed One, if we consider them according to their deific characteristic, the unity which transcends being; but they are many, considered according to their relation to inferior natures. Under every mundane deity, or God who rules within the universe, is arranged an attendant throng of dæmons, in order, as Taylor expresses it, "that the divinity may be connected with man, and that the progression of things may form an entire whole, suspended, like the golden chain of Homer, from the summit of Olympus." * The highest order of dæmons consists of those who immediately conjoin to the divine nature such souls as are completely purified, and whose essence and energy are in perfect accord. These dæmons are sometimes called Gods, not as being Gods essentially, bnt from their proximity to deity; as Plato, on the other hand, occasionally gives the appellations of dæmons to the Gods themselves, regarded under certain relations. To this highest order the dæmons of Socrates and Plotinus are said to have belonged; but although every rational soul, being in its essence intellectual and divine, has such a divine dæmon as its essential guardian, souls which have not yet attained liberation are under the especial guardianship of dæmons of a less exalted rank—those, namely, whose office it is to watch over the descent and ascent of souls. It is to dæmons of this order that Plato alludes in the *Phædo*, as conducting the soul to judgment and leading it again in due time to the earth. But since the soul is self-motive, it may follow its dæmon either willingly or reluctantly and with difficulty; only in the long run it is compelled to follow, for, rebel as we may against the guidance, we are never left without a guide, and the dæmon is the medium of divine justice, from which there is no escape. When, finally, the soul returns again to incarnate upon the earth, a new dæmon is allotted to it in accordance with the new life for which it has fitted itself.

There are dæmons of yet lower orders, intermediaries between the Gods and all the productions of nature, but with these we need not at present concern ourselves. It is important, however, to remember that all dæmonic natures, lower as well as higher, are necessary links of the great chain which binds together all the planes of existence. "He who denies the dæmons," says Plutarch, "denies providence and breaks the chain that unites the world with the throne of God." The Christian notion of guardian angels, and the

* Taylor's *Plato*, vol. i. p 16, *note*.

invocation of saints, must be regarded as relics of the ancient faith in dæmons.

The account which Socrates gives of the earth, of its fair abodes on high, and of the subterranean rivers, is in great part avowedly a fable; but it is a fable with an inner meaning of profound truth. Indeed, Socrates himself seems to hint as much when he says that to affirm that these things are exactly as he has described them, is not the part of a wise man, but that it is right, nevertheless, to believe that something of the kind takes place. By these words, it appears to me, he intimates as clearly as possible that we must look beneath the surface to discover the true significance of the fable. He tells us, in the first place, that the earth is of a spherical figure, and situated in the middle of the heavens. That Plato imagined this planet which we call earth to occupy a central and stationary position in the heavens, is I think, scarcely to be doubted; it is possible, though by no means certain, that he knew of the earth's revolution upon its axis. In Plutarch's *Life of Numa*, however, we find the following interesting passage which bears upon this question. "The earth they (the Pythagoreans) suppose not to be without motion, nor situated in the centre of the world, but to make its revolution round the sphere of fire, being neither one of the most valuable nor principal parts of the great machine. Plato, too, in his old age, is reported to have been of the same opinion, assigning the earth a different situation from the centre, and leaving that, as the place of honour, to a nobler element." Now on the surface this passage might seem to point to the conclusion that Plato in his old age, was acquainted with the doctrine of the earth's revolution about the sun, but, as a matter of fact, it will not support any such inference. For by the central fire the Pythagoreans understood not the visible sun at all, but a life-giving principle, irradiating all things from the centre, and about which the sun itself revolved, with the other heavenly bodies. In any case, if we are to take what is said in the *Phædo* and *Timæus* in a literal sense, we can hardly doubt that, when these dialogues were written, Plato was convinced that the earth occupied in the heavens a central and stationary position.

After all, this is perhaps a point of minor importance. Let us take Plato's theory in a more mystical sense, and try if we can arrive at some more satisfactory conclusion. The universe was represented under the figure of a sphere, not because it was supposed to terminate in a circumference, equidistant so many miles from the centre, but rather for the following reasons. The circle is a figure without beginning or end, subsisting always uniformly about its centre, and returning upon itself. It is thus, in the first place, an apt emblem of the intelligible world, or eternal Being. For its having neither beginning nor end denotes eternity, its uniformity with relation to its centre denotes immutability, and its unvarying sameness of progression, returning continually upon itself, denotes a nature which is all-perfect and self-sufficient. In the second place the circle, or sphere, is a fit emblem of the material universe, since this is generated by the creative intellect as an image of the intelligible world; and as the latter is eternal, perfect in itself, and a whole comprehensive of all true being, so the material universe is perpetual, perfect in itself, and a whole comprehensive of all sensible natures. And furthermore, every total nature within the universe—every nature, that is, which comprises in itself all that is necessary to its existence, is likewise said to be constituted in the figure of a sphere. Of such natures are the spheres of earth and the other planets. And this is true physically, no less than symbolically; since even the universe may be regarded physically as an infinite sphere, of which the centre is everywhere and the circumference nowhere.

Now as all the planes correspond with one another, it follows that the four elements of which the sensible universe is constituted must subsist, in an appropriate manner, upon every plane; upon the material plane, corporeally; intellectually, upon the intellectual. Earth, therefore, which is here solid and, of itself, motionless, represents, on the plane of intellect, the solidity and stability which are there; and when it is said to occupy a central and stationary position in the universe, we may understand by this that the universe is established upon a solid and stable foundation. There is, moreover, another method of explaining the assertion that earth is at the centre of the universe. For as earth is the heaviest and grossest of the elements, it may be taken to symbolize the lowest and grossest plane of material existence, and hence the central position is justly assigned to it, since the centre is the lowest point within the sphere, as being the most remote from the circumference. But by the circumference of the universe is signified the least material of its planes, and that which is most closely allied to an immaterial and intellectual nature.*

The true earth, according to Socrates, is prodigiously great, and it is "of a pure nature, and situated in the pure heavens, in which the stars are contained, and which most of those who are accustomed to speak about such particulars denominate æther." But within the earth there are many hollow places, of various forms and magnitudes, into which the dregs of this pure earth continually flow; and such are the places which we now inhabit, imagining, by reason of our blindness, that we dwell upon the upper parts of the earth. That we may understand this portion of this discourse, some information will be requisite concerning the vehicles of the soul, and in the investigation of this subject we shall derive the greatest assistance from the *Timæus* of Plato, and especially from the Commentary of Proclus upon that dialogue.

Soul is the vital and motive power through which the creative intellect imparts life and motion to the world. No atom of the universe is devoid of soul, and every corporeal nature is its vehicle. The universe itself is a divine animal, proceeding from intelligible Animal, and comprising within itself the physical manifestation of every form of life which subsists in the Ideal World. As an animal, therefore, it possesses an intellect in energy, derived from the supermundane Intellect, a rational soul, an irrational nature, and certain bodies, the vehicles of the soul in space. These vehicles are three, of which the first is formed of the æther, or celestial fire, and is termed the ætherial body; the second is formed of the pure elements, and is called the aerial body; while the third, or terrestrial body, consists of what may be dominated the dregs of the elements, of elements, namely, impure and commingled, as we know them on this, the lowest plane of material manifestation.

But the universe is also divine, and a God, inasmuch as it is an all-perfect whole, and contains in itself totally all the mundane progressions of deity. And in a lesser degree, every total nature subsisting within the universe, such as Earth and the other heavenly bodies, is likewise a God and a divine animal, possessing a soul and the vehicles of soul. The universe itself, then, and the divine wholes

* Thus, according to Plato in the *Timæus*, the demiurgus "fabricated *within* soul the whole of the corporeal nature."

which it contains, are the mundane Gods, the divinities who give completion to the sensible world, and from their divine nature are suspended all inferior natures, *viz.*, soul and the three vehicles thereof, inasmuch as the power and providence of deity extend through all things without exception. Partial souls, such as ours, which descend into the lowest material plane, possess also these three vehicles, but whereas our energies are limited by the nature of the vehicle in which we are acting, it is otherwise with the Gods, whose energies are eternal and unrestrained, and whose vehicles are merely a means of manifestation on different planes. To dæmonic souls, holding a middle position, the ætherial and aerial vehicles are alone ascribed, since neither are their powers total and extending to all things, like those of the Gods, nor do they descend into a life grossly material, such as ours.

But it is necessary to investigate more particularly the nature of these vehicles. The highest, or ætherial, body is fabricated by the demiurgic Intellect, and is connote with the mundane existence of the soul. That is to say, as soon as the rational soul proceeds from its source in intellect, and receives its allotment in the universe of space and time, it employs this ætherial body as its vehicle. This vehicle is spherical in form, and is distinguished as "simple and immaterial," being formed of the celestial fire, or æther, which is not the burning fire of earth, but a simple, unburning, vivific radiance, containing in itself causally, but not corporeally, the powers of the other elements. Of this fire the heavens are constituted, as the first vehicle of the universal soul, and of the same fire the ætherial vehicle of every rational soul within the universe is perpetually generated. As being *perpetually* generated, it is immortal, since although, being generated, it may be said to consist of parts, its parts are homogeneous, and therefore not mutually destructive; only it subsists by a continuous influx and efflux of celestial fire. And it is immaterial as compared with the lower and grosser vehicles of the soul; since, being on the highest plane of corporeal existence, it is assimilated as closely as possible to that which is immaterial, and participates of the vital and self-motive characteristics of the soul itself. And as the summit or source of the irrational nature subsists perpetually in the rational soul, so the summits of the senses subsist unitedly, as one impassive sense, in the ætherial vehicle. Now, according to

Proclus, the primary characteristic of fire is not heat, but visibility. Not that this celestial fire is of itself visible to our terrestrial organs of sight, which require an admixture of the earthly element; but it is essentially visible, and to a higher sense than ours. As fire is the source of light, so is earth of darkness, and pure light is invisible to us without its contrary; for which reason we perceive the light of the stars, which have an earthly body, but not that of the interstellar spaces, where earth subsists only causally, and not corporeally. The celestial fire is, then, a kind of link between the purely immaterial light of intellect, and that light which is apparent to our material senses. It is thus a fit vehicle for the rational soul, which, using it, lives a celestial life, assimilated to the life of the Gods.

But since the rational soul possesses in itself the summit of the irrational nature, it may descend in order to develope that nature, which, becoming developed, requires also an appropriate vehicle. Divine and total natures, indeed, develope their lower vehicles without descending, as by a certain illumination proceeding from their essence; but partial souls descend for that purpose, although they are still conjoined to the Gods by their guardian dæmons. The descent, therefore, is from the sphere of perpetually generated life into the sphere of mortality, the region of generation and corruption. In this gradual descent the irrational nature is gradually unfolded, and it clothes itself by degrees in a body formed from the pure elements, which is denominated the aerial or spiritual body (τὸ πνευματικὸν σῶμα). This vehicle is said to be fashioned by the junior or mundane Gods, who weave together the mortal and immortal natures; since that which proceeds from the demiurgus himself is of necessity but one remove from intellectual wholeness, and as intellect is eternal, that which emanates directly from it is immortal. But the irrational nature is mortal, except in so far as it has a causal subsistence within the rational soul; and in like manner its vehicle is mortal, except as regards its causal subsistence in the celestial fire; since it is in time dissolved, and restored to the elements from which it was congregated. The aerial vehicle is distinguished as "simple and material." It is simple, as being constituted of pure elements, and as not possessing separate organs of sense, but having the senses united as one passive sense in every part of it. And it is called material, because it contains all the elements materially, and not according to their immaterial powers alone. Lastly, it is called "aerial" because the element of air predominates in its constitution, and this is more particularly the case with the highest and purest of aerial vehicles, since in their descent they become heavier by degrees through the increase of the moist or watery element. "For souls," says Proclus, "in descending, receive from the elements different vehicles, aerial, aquatic and terrestrial, and thus at last enter into this gross bulk. For how, without a medium, could they proceed into this body from immaterial spirits? Hence before they come into this body they possess the irrational life, and its vehicle, which is prepared from the simple elements, and from these they become invested with *tumult* [*i.e.*, a nature subject to generation and corruption], which is so called as being foreign to the connate [ætherial] vehicle of souls, and as composed of all-various vestments, and causing souls to become heavy. . . . And as the lapse is from that which is incorporeal into body, and a life with body, according to which the soul lives in conjunction with its celestial vehicle; so from this, the descent is into a genesiurgic body, according to which the soul is in generation, and from this into a terrestrial body, according to which it lives with the testaceous body [*i.e.*, our present earthly body]. Hence, before it is surrounded with this last body it is invested with a body which connects it with all generation. And on this account, it then leaves this [aerial] body when it leaves generation. But if this be the case, it then received it when it came into generation. Hence prior to this last [terrestrial] body it received that [aerial] vehicle, and retains the latter after the dissolution of the former. It lives therefore in this [aerial] vehicle through the whole of the genesiurgic period." *

In its lowest descent the soul assumes this terrestrial body, which is also formed from the elements, not now pure, but composite and confused, as being distant in the furthest degree from their intelligible cause. This body is, therefore distinguished as "composite and material," and the element of earth predominates in it. It must not, however, be supposed that the soul, on assuming one of these vehicles, abandons that in which it has previously energized. A soul functioning upon the terrestrial plane possesses its three vehicles

* *Commentary on the Timæus.* Taylor's translation, vol. ii., pp. 416, 417.

simultaneously, although its energies are usually limited by the lowest vehicle with which it is invested. But without the higher vehicles as media, it would be impossible for it to communicate with the terrestrial body. The first vehicle, therefore, is attached to the soul throughout the whole of its mundane existence; the second, so long as it is conservant with generation and corruption; and the third, during the period of a single earth-life, after which it dwells in its aerial body until fate calls it to a new incarnation.

W. C. WARD.

(*To be concluded.*)

PLANTS, INSECTS AND BIRDS.

INTRODUCTORY REMARKS.

WHEN looking at landscapes of those countries where the great nations of ancient times once flourished, nothing strikes the thoughtful observer more than the desolate aspect which generally they now present. Ruins of the most magnificent buildings are found in the midst of deserts, which surely could not have existed when the buildings were planned and raised. The student of nature is further impressed by the scantiness of arboreal or even scrubby vegetation. The travelling naturalist regrets the scarcity of birds; and from this a deficiency of insect life, except of a few usually troublesome species, can be safely inferred, while the soil itself is stated to be usually of the poorest description, with the exception of some well-watered or irrigated areas. Yet ancient history abounds in references to luxurious vegetation. Whence the change since? What is or was the cause?

The reasons usually assigned are so vague and unsatisfactory that one is forced to raise the question whether sterility as now prevailing has not been artificially produced through the treatment accorded to nature, and the methods employed by civilized man himself; and if so, what were the laws of nature which, by their contravention or infraction, were capable of bringing about the dire results? The agencies through which they acted must have been such, that the great mass of the people considered them as unimportant or inexhaustible, on account of their humble aspect or their abundance, or even as interfering with their pursuits in some way or another, else they would surely have taken notice of them and not have been guilty of national suicide.

Having studied Australian nature for nearly half a century, especially that of the southern province, which is favoured only with a moderate and more or less irregular rainfall, and which therefore resembles the climate of the ancient countries alluded to; and having observed the original luxuriance of its native vegetation with the extraordinary productiveness of the soil when first brought under cultivation, while nature still teemed with lower life—I am the more deeply impressed with the contrast the same localities present now Their aspect is more or less that of deserts in bareness of soil and landscape, in scarcity of bird and insect life, except for a limited number of injurious creatures, while productivity has been decreasing year by year for the last twenty years. Here we know that the change is due to man's deliberate and inconsiderate actions; that deserts have been and are being created through the pursuits and prejudices of the people, where nature before their advent had slowly and laboriously succeeded in establishing almost a paradise. All this change is brought about unintentionally and unconsciously through ignorance of the laws of nature.

With the conscious or unintentional suppression of a part of the prevailing organic life, be it plants, insects (under this conventional term I include all lower life more or less similar in function, such as worms, etc.), or birds, together with reptiles, small mammals, etc., changes are inevitably brought about which cause the gradual, though it may be undesired, disappearance of other forms of life, till finally—in decades, centuries or thousands of years—nothing may be left but the bare soil or the barren rock. Inversely, the poorest country, if it only contain a few spots of sufficient size and fertility for the sustenance of a frugal people, can be gradually converted into a more or less prolific one in time by the steady application of simple natural laws. There is, however, this difference, that it requires a much longer time and much higher intelligence to make than to destroy a paradise.

Generally we find that the fertility of the soil remains unchanged for long periods, only in those countries where either the carbonaceous alluvium is of great depth, and kept permanently moist by irrigation, heavy rainfalls, or winter snows, or else in those inhabited only by savage races, who, as a rule, do not much interfere with the economy of nature, while, on the contrary, it is more or less speedily reduced, and finally exhausted, in such tracts where the soil is thin, and the climate hot and dry, and when civilized nations enter on the scene, and encourage excessive trade in raw products, and waste of food materials by their conversion into luxuries or mere conveniences, at a constantly augmenting rate.

Fundamental Definitions.

The vegetable kingdom culminates in trees and forests as the most constructive agents, the animal kingdom in mammals and man as the most destructive. They converge downwards in the Protista, *i.e.*, organic beings which combine the functions of both plants and animals, terminating in mere animated specks of protoplasm. All these beings, from the lowest to the highest, require something daily for their preservation, and that something we call food. It is almost as varied as the organisms themselves, and is all, directly or indirectly, derived from the soil.

What is food? How does it get into the soil?

Food consists of substances capable of replacing the waste of body substance resulting from the exercise of vital functions, and of furnishing material for growth and reproduction. It must, therefore, contain all the elements, in due proportion, of which the respective bodies are built up.

Independently of respiration, the components of all organic bodies, and therefore of food, may be ranged under four general headings: Carbon; Nitrogen; Soluble mineral substances; Water. The original source of the first two is practically the atmosphere; of the last two the soil, as derived from the rocks, which alone cannot support higher plant life.

The proof is furnished by the following simple experiments.

If we subject good rich soil to a temperature of about red heat (as is done on a rather large scale in primitive charcoal burning), or to the fierce rays of the summer sun for a lengthened period, every trace of both carbon and nitrogen disappears, and on such soil no higher plants can grow, because without nitrogen vegetation cannot advance beyond a certain stage. Similarly, if we take the soil like *débris* (crushed rock) from wells or mines, or even the earthy subsoil from a moderate depth, where few or no roots, worms or insects have penetrated, and therefore neither carbon nor nitrogen can be present, we find that scarcely anything will grow on it for years, no matter how well watered it may be. Mineral substances and water cannot support plant life alone, notwithstanding sunshine and rain in due proportion.

How did and does the carbon and nitrogen get into the naturally sterile soil?

Through the interaction of plants (even the most objectionable weeds!), and low animal life (microbes, worms, insects, etc.), by arresting and conserving solar energy, utilizing it for the production of carbonaceous and nitrogenous tissues and compounds with the minerals and water of the soil, and in perfect accord with physical laws of nature.

THE ACTION AND FUNCTION OF PLANTS.

From the sun emanates energy in the form of light, heat, electricity, magnetism, etc., which is intercepted by the earth. For our present object the first two alone concern us as relating especially to what takes place at and near the surface.

The sun's light striking the bare ground is partly converted into heat, elevating its temperature, partly reflected into space. The heat thus gained by the earth by day, is, however, again lost entirely by night, and nothing is saved. When, however, light falls upon the green leaves of plants or their substitutes, the case is very different. In conjunction with their inherent vital energy (or life) it enables them to split up the carbonic acid of the atmosphere into solid carbon and gaseous oxygen, retaining the former and rejecting the latter. The process is usually classed as respiration, but is really of the opposite character to that in animals, for by the latter heat is set free (by combustion), while by the former it is absorbed.

By the action of the plants sunlight is annihilated as such and the energy becomes latent or potential in carbon and its combinations with the terrestrial minerals and water. Thus we have solar energy stored or saved, instead of uselessly dissipated again. Its exact equivalent is again reproduced by the re-union of carbon with oxygen in combustion, no matter whether this take place in brief time in the form of light or fire, or as "low heat" and imperceptibly during extended periods in the form of gradual decay.

But the carbon is not obtained as a chemical deposit, nor as a quasi-mechanical admixture. Atom for atom it is instantly combined *within the leaves* with the constituents of the ascending "sap," consisting of the minerals required, nitrogen (in combination) and water, and thus formed into fluid plant substance. This ascending sap, the "blood" of the plants, has been collected in the soil by the tips of the roots, and is raised through the vital energy of the protoplasm of the living cells to the foliage for the sole purpose of becoming carbonized, while a portion of the water is utilized to reduce the temperature through evaporation, cooling the leaves and the adjoining air. The carbonized sap is then returned in a descending stream of molecules to every part, down to the remotest tips of the root hairs, supplying them in due proportion with the food they need.

Thus the solar energy gathered by the leaves is distributed, and a portion securely deposited below the surface of the ground, each molecule of which contains all the constituents of plant food in due proportion, and secured by the carbon against any rapid dispersion.

When vegetable tissue is slowly deprived of water (and in time nitrogen) through natural decay (slow combustion), it forms mould or humus, which gradually becomes less in course of time. If the same process is rapidly performed through fire, pressure or chemical action, charcoal is the result. The molecular structure of the latter must be a highly complex one, but I have not met with any evidence that it has been exhaustively studied by chemists, it being usually treated in text books as impure (that is, mechanically mixed with other matter) carbon, instead of as a compound body. Through this singular oversight the disastrous error of agriculturists generally has arisen that the ashes, *i.e.*, dead mineral matter, are the essential and the carbon the non-essential factor of fertility, overlooking the fact that the latter is the immediate and sole expression of solar energy. It appears to be self-evident, that in the charcoal, as well as in the mould molecule, every component of plant substance (except nitrogen and water) must be present in the exact proportion required as food for the part it was derived from, and that these are held together quite securely by the carbon even in the most miscroscopical particles. The food atoms are thus effectively secured against dispersion by solar heat, chemical and mechanical agencies, etc., but readily available for use, when these are made subservient to vital energy at the tips of the root-hairs. By the presence of such prepared food substances the higher plants are saved the labour of reaching for each of the atoms separately and can utilize the energy saved in greater luxuriance of development. From this standpoint it is plainly seen, that all complete burning of plants must exhaust the fertility of the soil quite as much as their more or less complete removal, and that the growth even of weeds does not exhaust, but enriches the land; and also that periodical deprivation of all, or the greater part of the limbs or foliage of shrubs or trees, falsely called "pruning" is exceedingly irrational and injurious, and wholly due to prejudice and ignorance of natural laws.

There is no other physical agency in nature than that of plants, known thus to conserve and store solar energy for the support of organic life. Everything human depends also upon its sustained action in one form or another. For the perfect manifestation, however, the greatest possible variety of forms is necessary in order to provide for all changes of conditions and to meet all dangers and risks of failure. The limited number of plants directly useful to man is incapable of doing this, hence the gradual decadence of fertility and prosperity in all countries where other plant life is sacrificed for their exclusive production, is an inevitable result.

THE FUNCTIONS OF INSECTS, ETC.

Thus far extends the exclusive share of plant-action in the creation of fertility, but besides carbon, mineral matter and water, (the conservation of the last in the soil is also largely due to the influence of vegetation), plants require nitrogen for the protoplasmic cell contents and the formation of fruits and seeds, *i.e.*, vitality and reproduction. We have seen, however, that this element is neither an abundant, nor constant ingredient of our rocks, or the soils resulting from them. Moreover, its quantity is so unstable that a very moderate exposure to air or solar heat suffices to dissipate it completely, and within a comparatively short time. Yet in a state of natural growth there is always enough to meet the necessities of a constant drain, and sufficient for all the innumerable host of living beings which imperatively require it. The plants themselves possess no organs to get the nitrogen directly from the air, but they, like the higher animals, attain it second-hand as food through the roots. How does it get into the soil in such enormous quantities as are daily required for exuberant plant and animal life? How and by what agencies or agents is the—at any time—limited stock replenished, and even slowly and gradually augmented? The reply is: only through the vital action of low animal life in the soil.

Until 1891 it was held that rocks and stones in the ground broke up and decayed through chemical and aërial agencies alone, but Winogradsky discovered in that year (Dr. F. Ludwig, *Niedere Cryptomen*, 1892) that the effect was largely due to microbes, the so-called Nitro-bacteria, the lowest known manifestation of life. It is they which attack the surfaces of rocks, etc., containing potash and iron, dissociating the atoms, producing nitrites, and laying the foundation of all fertility. The only conditions necessary are moderate moisture and temperature. Cold, at and below the freezing point, renders them only torpid, heat and drought kill them. Their initial action is subsequently enormously augmented by that of worms, insects, etc., which distribute the nitrogen throughout the upper layers, and fix it more or less in carbonaceous combinations, thus furnishing higher plants, mosses, lichens, ferns, herbs, grasses, etc., in succession with the required pabulum.

Insects perform other most important functious besides that of nitrifying—*i.e.*, fertilizing or manuring the soil, wherein they are aided by all animals, large or small—namely (1) bringing about cross-fertilization, that is, the carrying of the pollen of one individual plant to the stigma of another, by means of which a large proportion of plants (including our fruit trees) are alone enabled to produce perfect seeds, and (2) the general control of plant-life in respect of number of seedlings, flowers and seeds permitted to reach perfection. Without the first service, performed by specially adapted kinds and forms for each other, many of the most useful plants, fruits, and beautiful and showy flowers must soon die out. In the function of plant-control all insects and much of other low life, such as fungi, etc., are concerned (*a*) in reducing largely the number of germs by living on them so that they may not choke themselves and all become incapable of reproduction; (*b*) by reducing the too exuberant foliage so as to permit sufficient light to reach all the remaining leaves, yet allow enough for the work of conserving sun-force and to digest the food sent up from below; and (*c*) finally to reduce sickly, dead and decaying matter as quickly as possible into inoffensive and nutritious mould for other plants to re-absorb, re-digest, and re-form into living tissues.

By these services, which man can only imperfectly emulate, the despised worms and insects surely earn abundantly the food and shelter offered by the plants, for without them plant existence and plant improvement would be impossible, according to the known laws of nature. Wherever the balance of nature has become established in the course of ages, no single plant species could increase unduly so as to threaten the extinction of the weaker ones, except for a very limited period, as the increased food-supply, and in increasing ratio, would foster the more rapid increase of the ordained destroyers, and cause them to overtake that of the plant at some time or another. Then abundance would be speedily succeeded by scarcity, resulting in the starvation of the majority of those special insects. After a few mutations the whole would again revert to the former state by the free increase of the survivors. These usually representing the strongest and fittest individuals under prevailing conditions, would cause a forward step in development.

THE FUNCTION OF BIRDS, ETC.

As, however, insects and low organisms in general are possessed of enormous powers of reproduction, there would be naturally a constant fluctuation between extremes of abundance and scarcity, constantly threatening extermination of one or the other species. To avoid this a further control becomes necessary to produce comparative stability, or at least to restrict the changes within narrow limits, and to ensure that steady and gradual progress in richness and variety which is only found in regions scarcely invaded by "civilized" man. That control is chiefly exercised by the birds, but materially aided by predatory insects, reptiles and small mammals.

Some birds feed almost exclusively upon insects, each species being more or less restricted to a narrow range by the idiosyncrasies of taste, digestibility, habit, etc., others live partly upon insects and partly upon a vegetable diet, a third set is chiefly dependent for its food upon plants, but all the same aids them either against over-production (exhaustion), or securing for them a denser growth of foliage by pruning (like the parrots), while the fourth category, the predatory birds, controls the increase of the others, and by feeding upon the less intelligent, the less well adapted, and the sick and weakly ones, secures a gradual advance to greater perfection of the whole.

Here it must be noted that the reproductory power of birds, reptiles and mammals is incomparably less than that of worms, insects, etc., in general. For while the females of the latter produce from several scores to thousands of eggs each, birds rarely attain to ten, while reptiles as rarely reach a hundred or more per year. It is, therefore, usually very easy to control or exterminate the birds, but impossible to do so in the case of insects, except at enormous loss or expense. Whenever any species of insects appears in injurious numbers, like scales, aphides, locusts, etc, it is an infallible proof that their special control—birds—has been unduly reduced.

Effect of Mammals and Man.

In countries inhabited by civilized people, notably Europeans, the larger animals and man aid very little in the constructive or conservative operations of nature. They rather represent a destructive agency, an ever present and unavoidable danger for all, unless, as in the case of the mammals, controlled by the predatory members, or, of man, restrained by self-control, resulting from reason and moral sentiment, and manifested both in regard to reproduction, and to the protection of all lower life—both vegetable and animal—from the wantoness and avarice of the unthinking and ignorant. Upon that his own prosperity and existence depends either directly or indirectly. In a state of nature, or with uncivilized races, the case is different; the mutual advantages are here normal, or, at least, the destructive tendency very much less. The habitual neglect of the study of the relations between nature and man, and the considerations due to lower life, is a distinctive and very prominent characteristic of modern civilized nations, and therefore the exhaustion of the stores of nature, and the decay and disappearance of the offenders in a not very remote future are apparently inevitable.

CONCLUSION.

The following *résumé* presents the ideas I have attempted to press upon the reader in the preceding pages.

1. All terrestrial life depends upon the conservation and storage of the solar energy. Mineral soil is sterile in itself.

2. Plants, especially the larger and more enduring, are the exclusive agents for this, the solar energy being rendered latent in the form of carbon (carbonaceous tissues and compounds, charcoal, mould, coal). Green foliage denotes conservation, bare ground dissipation of solar energy.

3. The nitrogen required by plants is obtained from the atmosphere through protozoic and other lower and higher animal life, but especially by worms, insects, etc.

4. Without a constant and abundant supply of carbonaceous and nitrogenous substances, the fertility becomes sooner or later exhausted, mineral soil itself being sterile.

5. Insects, etc., control plant life, and assist otherwise most effectively in sustaining it.

6. Birds, reptiles, and small mammals control chiefly the insect world, and secondarily, the plants, while also greatly assisting in the distribution and protection of the latter.

7. The larger mammals, and especially civilized man, tend constantly to disturb the balance of nature, the latter most injuriously, even endangering thereby his own future prosperity and existence, besides those of all other life.

J. G. O. TEPPER, F.L.S.

AN OLD ARAB VIEW OF DEATH.

WE have received the following interesting communication from our valued contributor, Mr. W. F. Kirby.

"Mr. Mead's remarks in the last 'On the Watch-Tower,' on the Passing of J. C. Staples, remind me of the conclusion of a story in *The Thousand and One Nights*, ''Abd-Allah of the Land, and 'Abd-Allah of the Sea,' in which a fisherman entangles a merman in his net, with whom he arranges to exchange terrestrial for marine commodities, and whom he afterwards visits in his submarine abode.

Theosophists must be constantly disgusted with the ridiculous phrase, 'poor So-and So.' referred to by Mr. Mead, and they may be interested to learn the view taken by the Sea-people of life and death. The story is one of those which belong to the latter part of *The Thousand and One Nights*, which was not translated by Galland, and it is therefore not to be found in the ordinary editions. I quote the passage from Vol. I. of Lane's translation."

He then returned with him to his city, and producing to him a purse, he said to him, "Take this as a deposit, and convey it to the tomb of the Prophet, may God bless and save him." And he took it, not knowing what was in it.

Then 'Abd-Allah of the Sea went forth with him, to conduct him to the land; and he saw on his way, people engaged in singing and festivity, and a table of fish spread; and the people were eating and singing, and in a state of great rejoicing. So he said to 'Abd-Allah of the Sea, "Wherefore are these people in a state of great rejoicing? Is a wedding being celebrated among them?" And he of the Sea answered, "There is no wedding being celebrated among them, but a person among them is dead." 'Abd-Allah of the Land therefore said to him, "Do ye, when a person dieth among you, rejoice for him, and sing and eat?" His companion answered, "Yes. And ye, O people of the land," he added, "what do ye?" 'Abd Allah of the Land answered, "When a person among us dieth, we mourn for him and weep, and the women slap their faces, and rend the bosoms of their garments in grief for him who is dead." And upon this 'Abd-Allah of the Sea stared at 'Abd-Allah of the Land and said, "Give me the deposit." So he gave it to him. Then 'Abd-Allah of the Sea took him forth to the land, and said to him, "I have broken off my companionship with thee, and my friendship for thee, and after this day thou shalt not see me, nor will I see thee." "Wherefore," said 'Abd-Allah of the Land, "are these words?" 'Abd-Allah of the Sea said, "Are ye not, O people of the Land, a deposit of God?" "Yes," answered he of the Land. And the other rejoined, "Then how is it that it is not agreeable to you that God should take his deposit, but on the contrary ye weep for it? And how should I give thee the deposit for the Prophet (may God bless and save him!) seeing that ye, when the new-born child cometh to you rejoice in it, though God (whose name be exalted!) putteth into it the soul as a deposit? Then, when he taketh that soul, how is it that it grieveth you, and ye weep and mourn? Such being the case, we have no need of your companionship." He then left him, and went back to the sea.

THEOSOPHICAL ACTIVITIES.

AMERICAN SECTION.

ON the evening of March 26th, Mrs. Besant spoke at Brooklyn, in the Hall of the Y.M.C.A., on "Suffering and Evil: their Causes and their Cure." The audience was a very sympathetic one, and a number of those interested were received by Mrs. Besant and the Countess Wachtmeister the next evening in the parlour of the same fine building, when a Branch was formed.

The good results of the lectures in New York, Brooklyn and Newark, were apparent when, on Sunday morning, March 28th, a number of people met in the Jefferson Hotel and formed a new Lodge. Mrs. Besant then addressed the new members of the Brooklyn and New York Lodges, and said that all Lodges to successfully perform their duty as centres of Theosophical studies and points of contact with the outer world, must extend to each individual member a perfect freedom of thought; the one bond of union being the belief in Brotherhood.

Chickering Hall, on the evening of the same day, again contained an attentive audience, the subject of the lecture was "Materialism undermined by Science."

On Monday Mrs. Besant and the Countess went to Washington, where they were received by members of the Society and were the guests of Mrs. Johnston, who held a well-attended reception in her large and commodious rooms, about 200 people being presented to Mrs. Besant. At the close of this ceremony Mrs. Besant was asked to speak and delivered a short address on Theosophy. The next day the lecture hall was crowded and all were interested in the pictures of Thought Forms which were thrown upon the screen. Mrs. Besant received each afternoon, and intelligent and searching questions were put to her.

The next day, when Mrs. Besant left for Philadelphia, the Countess formed the members into the Washington Lodge, and on Saturday she addressed a meeting at the house of Mrs. Lockwood, who had invited a large number of friends.

On Sunday the Countess lectured to a crowded audience at the People's Church in the morning, and gave another lecture in the Society Temple in the evening.

In Philadelphia the hospitable home of Dr. Emma Brooke had

already welcomed one of the party. A large number of interested visitors gathered there in the afternoon to talk Theosophy with Mrs. Besant, and after she had given her lecture in the New Century Club before a full house, universal regret was expressed that she could not devote more than one day to this promising field of Theosophic labour. Two meetings were held the following day and a Lodge was formed here ere Mrs. Besant and Miss Willson left. It was touching to find one or two old and personal friends of Madame Blavatsky coming forward to tell of the help that she had given them, and to express their pleasure that her work was being carried on.

The return to New York was on Saturday, April 3rd. The third meeting of the New York and Brooklyn Branches was held on Sunday morning. To assist the future studies of the members Mrs. Besant explained some of the workings of the three great waves of evolution and their action on the different planes. In the afternoon she spoke before a crowded assembly, in the large hall of the Brooklyn Philosophical Society, on the proofs of the existence of the soul. The adverse remarks of some materialistic speakers at the conclusion of her address drew forth an answer in Mrs. Besant's well-known style, in which she gently cut the ground from under her critics' feet and showed that the latest discoveries of science were strengthening the Theosophical position.

A lecture to a good audience in Chickering Hall concluded a very busy day. The following afternoon the Countess joined us as we passed through Philadelphia on our way to St. Louis and the West.

The lime-light pictures of Thought Forms and of the Human Aura thrown on to the screen to illustrate the lectures on these difficult subjects, much impressed the audiences with the reality of the investigations, and proved very useful.

In New York we had heard of floods along the valley of the Mississippi, and as we advanced towards St. Louis, which is built at the junction of the Missouri and the "Father of Waters," more and more flooded ground, and traces of recent heavy rains, could be observed from the railway. The papers had been full of the panic caused by the rising of the river and from this and other causes we had received a telegram that no lecture could be given at St. Louis. We passed on to Kansas City, where two lectures were given by Mrs. Besant in the Academy of Music. Both were very badly attended and little interest in Theosophy was shown, although the papers on the whole gave good reports.

Mrs. Besant and the Countess received each afternoon at the

Midland Hotel, and when we left a small group of people had been gathered who would meet and form a Lodge in order to study together.

At a little before 10 o'clock on Monday morning we left Kansas City and went on to Topeka, where we arrived soon after noon. We were told that we were the first members of the Society who had visited this pleasant little place, and the interest in Theosophy was shown by the numerous visitors who came to the National Hotel to see Mrs. Besant and the Countess. In the evening the Library Hall was half filled with a superior audience to whom Mrs. Besant spoke on "Theosophy and its Teachings." The morning of the next day was spent in receiving the numerous inquirers, and, before we left, Topeka had a Lodge with twelve members, and showed promising signs of future active work and study.

We are now at La Junta waiting for the train to take us on to Denver.

On the evening of Mrs. Besant's arrival at Denver City, the large reception-room of the hotel was quite filled with people, who flocked to welcome her, and to express their interest in Theosophy.

Each afternoon from 3 to 5 o'clock, when Mrs. Besant and the Countess received, the crowd of enquirers increased, until at last they overflowed into the hall. Three lectures were given in Denver and were pretty well attended—especially the one on the Aura and Thought-Forms, with lime-light illustrations.

Here quite a strong Lodge of thirty-two members was formed, and one of them volunteered to obtain a room for use as a Theosophical Reading-room and centre for enquiry.

The formation of a Lodge much strengthens the work of old members who have become isolated, and who have remained true to the parent Society, often in the face of much trouble and difficulty.

From Denver we went on Monday morning, April 19th, to Colorado Springs. Here, in spite of the natural beauty of the place, all at first seemed cold in regard to Theosophy. But soon an old member or two called, and the first lecture on Theosophy and its teachings produced the usual result, one after another enquirers appeared, and on Wednesday morning a group of eleven people met and formed themselves into a Lodge.

Once more the train was "boarded," and we climbed across the Rocky Mountains, with all their grand and varied scenery; and after a night in the train, descended through the desert on to the well-watered snow mountain encircled plain, on which stands Salt Lake City.

From many causes this place seemed unlikely soil for Theosophic ideas to take root, and the audiences were small, but once more we found enough people sufficiently interested to form a Lodge for study. This was also the case in Ogden, where after two splendid lectures by Mrs. Besant, setting forth in plain language the nature of man and his high possibilities, a group of people were forming themselves into a Lodge when we left. Thus we leave behind an unbroken chain of Lodges in all the towns visited by Mrs. Besant and the Countess, if we perhaps except Newark, New York, in which the centre had, however, incorporated itself with the New York Lodge.

A. J. W.

European Section.

It was announced last month that an application would be made to the President-Founder by the Dutch Branches to be formed into the Dutch Section of the Society. This application has now been made and the new Section will shortly be constituted. Just before this action was taken another Branch was formed, to be known as the Amsterdam Lodge, in which a number of the oldest members were enrolled. The congratulations of the European Section are due to its younger companion.

The Executive Committee has decided that the Convention of this Section shall be held on Saturday and Sunday, July 10th and 11th, and it is announced that the meetings will take place in the Banqueting Hall and French Drawing-room at St. James's Hall.

Mrs. Hooper visited the Glasgow Centre in April and gave two public lectures on April 18th, the one in the evening attracting a good and attentive audience. On the next day a reception was held, and also a meeting of the Centre at which several enquirers were present.

Mrs. Cooper-Oakley left for Italy shortly before Easter, and is expected back in London towards the end of May. She has visited the Rome Lodge, and stayed some time in that city, holding private and Branch meetings, and visiting various members and others interested in Theosophy. Other parts of Italy have also been included in the tour of which a fuller report will be given on Mrs. Cooper-Oakley's return.

Mr. Mead will be present at the Convention of the Scandinavian Section, to be held at the end of May, and will act as the delegate of the European Section. He will spend some time in Sweden, visiting members and lecturing occasionally.

Australian Section.

The most important news we have to announce is the formation of the first Branch of our Society in the new colony of Western Australia.

From time to time our branches on this eastern coast of Australia have had to regret the departure of some active worker to the west coast. Mingled with this regret has always been the hope that in the new country some fresh work might be done.

The new Branch, which is located at Perth, the capital of Westralia, starts with fourteen members, some of whom are well-known for their work in the Theosophical Society.

The other branches of this Section keep steadily working along the lines which have been found most suitable, holding weekly Sunday night lectures, debating classes, and conversaziones. The libraries and book depôts also report well-sustained activity and inquiry.

Our Sectional magazine, which up to the present has occupied much the position of a poor despised relation, only to be criticized and condemned, will begin its third year enlarged and greatly improved.

We should like to make it known, that, as the main object of our paper *Theosophy in Australasia*, is to assist in spreading Theosophic ideas throughout the Australasian colonies, and to present them in such a manner as will be likely to interest the average colonial, we shall be thankful for any literary contributions written with the above object in view.

H. A. W

New Zealand Section.

Miss Edger's lectures continue to be well attended and are always interesting.

Mrs. Richmond, President of the Christchurch Branch, has been spending a week or two in Auckland this month, and lectured at the Auckland Branch rooms on Sunday, March 14th, on "The Message of Theosophy," dealing largely with the power of thought, and the consequent necessity for thought control. There was a large audience, and the lecture was followed by questions and discussion. Mrs. Richmond lectures in Wanganni and Palmerston North on her way back to Christchurch.

There is increased activity in connection with the Christchurch Branch. One of the members, Mr. McCombs, has been lecturing in the suburbs, and also at Kaiapoi and Rangiora. Enough interest has been aroused to make it a fairly successful attempt, and to encourage Mr. McCombs to continue his efforts in the districts named.

Mr. Sinclair of the Melbourne Branch has been visiting Dunedin during the month, and on March 15th gave an interesting account of the work and methods of the Australian Section.

CEYLON LETTER.

Col. Olcott arrived at Colombo during the latter part of March. He is engaged in preparing the thirty-third edition of the Buddhist Catechism for the press. The Colonel expects to return to Adyar about the end of April.

Meetings of the Hope Lodge are regularly held at the Musæus School every Sunday afternoon. The members are now engaged in reading *The Growth of the Soul.*

Our stock of books in the Library has considerably increased and the members make good use of them.

The Musæus School and Orphanage close on April 8th for a short holiday and Mrs. Higgins and her staff, accompanied by the children, go to the seaside. The work of this Institution is increasing rapidly and Mrs. Higgins is almost daily receiving new applicants for admission.

The King of Siam is expected here in a few days *en route* to London, and the Buddhist Community is making preparations to welcome him.

S. P.

REVIEWS.

OUTLINE OF A PHILOSOPHY OF RELIGION.

Esquisse d'une Philosophie de la Religion d'après la Psychologie et l'Histoire, par Auguste Sabatier. [Paris: 1897.]

THE history of French Protestantism is a curious one. Introduced by the nobles, who found it a convenient political weapon in their struggle with the growing power of the Crown, it took no permanent root excepting in the belt of country across the southern part of France which had already produced the Albigenses and so many more heretics, as Catholics would call them. We are apt to forget how comparatively short a time this country has been, even nominally, French. Known in the Middle Ages by a general name which expressed an actual difference of language, the Langue d'Oc, the distinction still remains. Everyone who has passed that way, and seen anything more than the railway stations and the big hotels, has had it forced upon him, that in a large portion of Southern France the people do not speak French—of Paris, as Chaucer justly distinguishes—at all; just as in North Italy, the mountainous part of Piedmont, the people neither speak nor understand what we call Italian. This difference of speech marks a profound difference of character. I do not myself think the distinction is one so much of race as of climate. It marks a kind of temperate zone, between the colder countries, where the struggle for mere life withdraws the mind from the supernatural altogether, and the warm South where man needs only so much religion as will make him happy in the sun. To walk up and down the streets of Marseille to-day and look at the people you meet, is enough to make you understand the fulness of life and fire which marks off the Marseillais from the colder blooded Parisian, as it did a century ago in the Revolution. And during the great uprising of life and intelligence—the dawn of modern civilisation—which characterised the eleventh and twelfth centuries, this "temperate zone" was the centre of it, for good and for evil. From some part of it came most of the great minds who then ruled the intellectual world; upon it were fought out the great struggles between Faith and Reason, with hard words and harder blows, and the modern world remains to this day very nearly what these struggles left it. Both sides put the whole of their hot hearts into the flight; for many years the Albigenses of Toulouse defied the whole armed power Rome could bring against them; and at a later time the French Protestant pillaged and burnt and murdered, with as full conviction as his Catholic opponent that he was doing the Lord's work. For long it was almost a matter of chance which should finally prevail. In France, as in England, the heavy hand of the King finally crushed out all opposition. When Henri Quatre "exchanged Paris for a Mass," he settled the course of events, and as in England the Protestant Crown and the Protestant law steadily drove the old religion into the far corners of the land, so in France the desperate defences of such places as La Rochelle and Montauban could only delay the end. But between the rival fighters the physical as well as the intellectual life of the poor humanity for which they fought was fairly trampled out; and when the opening of the sea routes destroyed the brisk trade which had in earlier times made South and Central France the business centres for all Europe, the darkness settled down upon what had been for centuries the real focus of civilisation.

We are so accustomed to think of a Frenchman as being always in extremes—atheist or devotee—that to many of my readers the idea of the actual existence of French Protestants will have a quaint flavour almost of absurdity. But France is a much wider country than England, and its central government of much later date than the English; so that we should not be astonished to find that whilst the English Crown, which had been the actual *de facto* as well as *de jure* ruler of all England since William the Conqueror, was able very nearly to stamp out the religion of the people when it changed its own, in France the utmost efforts of the most absolute of kings failed to Catholicise the Protestant districts. Montauban and the district round it is still, like the very similarly situated Canton Vaud in Switzerland, a Protestant country. There has never been much sympathy between English Protestants, who were actually called into existence by the Government, and the French, who have always been oppressed by it: and even the modern Dissenters know little of their French brethren.

There is therefore considerable interest in a work like the present, which gives us from unimpeachable authority and with great literary power, the religious position of a body which may be fairly taken as representative of what Protestantism comes to when worked out by intelligent and learned men free from the influences which have made English religion the curious mixture it is. The Professor states his intentions thus:

This volume comprises three portions, which are related to each other as the three stories of a single edifice. The first treats of religion and of its origin; the second, of Christianity and its essence; the third, of Dogma, and its nature.

Perhaps by an English reader his view will be more easily grasped if we do not follow his exposition in this order. Into his polemic against the Catholic Church, we need not enter at all. His position is that its organisation and the definiteness of its creed, render it almost, if not quite, impossible for it to adapt itself to the ever-changing conclusions of history and criticism, as *his* Protestantism can—"which nobody can deny." I underline the word "his," for in this very first statement he entirely separates himself from the large majority of English and American Protestants, and ranges himself rather with those who are here called Unitarians. English Dissent has always found it difficult to avoid this, and our French professor makes no effort to do so. He himself permits no dogma to stand in his way. His chapters on Miracle and Inspiration and on the religious development of humanity are admirable, and to any one who accepts the usual assumption that this development has proceeded from a primitive savagery (an assumption we Theosophists are at one with more ordinary Christians in denying), entirely convincing. His chapter on the history of the

Hebrew Race I should like to quote in extenso. In speaking of the Creation, the Garden of Eden, etc., he says, "What modern Christian is there who, at this time of day, takes these stories literally? Who is there who does not venture to see in them a large share of poetry, of allegory, of legend, of the infantine language of an age of ignorance?" It is not, therefore, true to maintain that religion requires us to believe in them as actual facts. (Why *therefore*, M. Sabatier?) . . . The Pentateuch appears to us now as an edifice of composite nature, upon which generations of builders, using the most diverse materials, have continued to labour for more than ten centuries . . . it is not the point of departure but the termination and result of the evolution of Hebraism. The Hebrew history is similarly transformed. You may think, says he, that at least in the Temple of Solomon the worship of the One God, spiritual and universal, was duly carried out. How many objects of astonishment, of scandal, should we not have found on entering it; and what a difference between the historical reality and the picture so lovingly drawn by the contemporaries of Esdras and Nehemiah, the latest editors of the books of Kings and Chronicles! The magnificent prayer put into the mouth of Solomon on the day of dedication, is but a pious fraud. This celebrated sanctuary of Jahveh at Jerusalem was precisely similar, both within and without, to those which were then being raised at Byblos, at Tyre and Sidon. The local god had the first place, but he was not alone there; the gods of the neighbouring tribes were worshipped alongside of him. The editors to whom we owe the Bible in its present shape are puzzled at this open polytheism, and can only explain it by the influence exercised upon the king by his heathen wives. Not in the least; Solomon was as eclectic in his belief as in his manners and morals, and all his people were like him. Jahveh has only become a jealous and exclusive God since he was made by the preaching of the Prophets the only and universal God.

So far so good; but when you have thus reduced the Jews in all respects to the level of the tribes around them, two questions at once arise. First, how came these Jews to *think* themselves a chosen and select race, and to act accordingly with such vigour and consistency down to the present time? Those who have kept themselves up with the latest Theosophic teaching will know *our* answer—that there had been a time, many thousands of years before, when the Jews *were* a chosen people, but that they had failed to answer the purpose of their choice; and will also have learned to recognise scattered here and there in the Law, some of the precepts which were then given them to enable them to become what they *should* have been, the founders of the new race of mankind. But for Christians such as M. Sabatier, there is only one resource, to trot out once more the venerable stalking horse or bogey, the Prophets. He is exceedingly, painfully candid about these also; likens them to the Indian medicine men and the Mongolian Shamans, and remorselessly brings up the awkward fact that the great Samuel himself was a regular fortune-teller, and did not disdain to receive a fee of about sixpence of our money for finding lost goods and the like. But this point is best discussed in answer to the second and more important question, How does our author manage still to keep up the old illusion that the history of religion can be confined to that of the Jews? He has elaborately sawn through the branch on which he is sitting; for if the Jews were not in possession of any *exclusive* revelation, no more are the Christians. You may exalt the Prophets to any level you please, exaggerate the extent of their insight and the loftiness of their imagination, as every Christian writer, even M. Sabatier, does most outrageously, but you cannot make them the founders of a new religion. No one can fail, in reading his book, to recognise that in claiming *any* kind of supremacy for the religion (such as it was) of the Jews and the Christians who grew out of them, he is drawing a line differently placed indeed from the Catholic one, but equally imaginary from the point of view of the psychology and history he claims to follow completely. The place where his religion holds him from the full light is best shown in a passage in the preface, when he is dealing with the objection that his view destroys the nature of Sin, as something (in his own words) essentially condemnable. The passage is difficult to translate because of the different meaning of the word "conscience," in the two languages. We English have two words, "consciousness," which is used without any *moral* application at all, and "conscience" which always connotes something we are morally bound to follow. We make a sharp distinction between these, but not only has the French tongue only one word for the two, but the French mind does not seem to make the distinction either. When our author speaks of what is the evidence of his "conscience" it seems needful to warn the reader that neither our English "conscience" nor "consciousness" precisely renders his meaning. He lays down this testimony as including three points. 1. Sin is in the *will* only. 2. This sin arises, however, from a nature *determined* partly by its organic constitution and partly by heredity. So that, as he says "I recognise in myself and in all humanity a *fatality* which subjects me to sin." 3. He continues, "The third affirmation of my conscience is more wonderful and not less certain: this fatality of sin, instead of lightening or destroying my responsibility, increases it . . . so that the sentence of condemnation bears at once upon the act and upon its author, and affirms to me, not only that my sin is evil, because it is the transgression of the law; but that I myself am a sinner, and as such liable to punishment. . . . It is this apparent contradiction alone which renders the moral life serious, repentance possible and the regeneration of the heart—the new birth, necessary according to the doctrine of Jesus Christ." So then, all the new science leaves us at last where St. Paul leaves us—"If it had not been for the Law I had not known sin," and to all enquiry "why then the Law?" M. Sabatier has nothing but the old response, "Our imperfect knowledge of God and the ways of Eternal Providence must always end with an act of prostration, of adoration, and of confidence." Surely the Catholic may fairly ask, "Why *should* I take all this trouble to keep up with the new science if this is all you get from it?" and our author will find it difficult to answer.

So much for theory. One word before we leave this work so beautiful and valuable, in spite of its limitations as to practice. What of Christianity is left to be the consolation of souls in trouble? There is a very beautiful treatment of the impossibility of destroying the religious aspiration in man by any argument, and of the still greater need which is felt the higher the education and culture of the race is raised, of something which shall raise man above all this and restore the failing springs of human action "all sicklied o'er," as they now are "with the pale cast of thought." Then we come to his definition. "The essence of religion," he says, "is an intercourse, a conscious and intentional relationship, into which the soul in distress enters with the mysterious Power on which it feels that it and its destiny depend. This intercourse with God is realised by Prayer. Prayer—this is religion in action—the only real religion. . . Where this interior prayer is wanting there is no religion; on the contrary, wherever this prayer rises and stirs in the soul, even in the absence of all form or doctrine whatever, religion is living."

So then, the last word of Christianity, as of science, is that nothing can be known. Pure Bhakti-yoga; *blind* devotion to a mysterious Power, a Will whose intentions are unknown, before which we are to prostrate ourselves in the dark! Did the most confirmed pessimist ever say anything carrying more complete despair than our author in his declaration, "Prayer springing from our state of misery and oppression *delivers us from it.*" *That* is all the deliverance we are to hope for from the Gospel! Why, surely, it is better with the Salvationist to believe ourselves "saved" by Faith, for we cannot test that until our death, but the other we *know* to be a lie.

No—so far the Catholic is right, we must have knowledge; and this is not to be found by modern psychology and history, we must first have the key given us. Is it not sorrowful to see the world now, as it was two thousand years ago, "perishing for lack of knowledge," yet refusing to open its eyes to see? All these puzzles which the learning and good will of such men as our author cannot solve *have* their key, if they would look round to find it; but century after century men go on, driving themselves to desperation with imaginary sinfulness and vain fears of the impossible anger of God, encouraging themselves with equally vain hopes of an eternity of useless bliss; the world, all the time, waiting and longing for the new Buddha who shall preach to all men the lesson they will not hear from us, that it is from themselves they suffer and that they are in no wise bound to that Sisyphus wheel under which they are crushed.

M. Sabatier's work marks a great advance towards us, though old prejudices still keep him from full liberation, and we hope to see it before long translated into English. It is a book which must do much good.

A. A. W.

BHÂGAVATA PURÂṆA.

A prose English Translation of Shrîmadbhâgavatam. [Edited and Published by Manmatha Nath Dutt, M.A., M.R.A.S., Rector, Keshub Academy. Calcutta: 1896.]

All lovers of Hindu thought and literature must be grateful to Mr. Dutt for thus rendering accessible to the student unfamiliar with Sanskrit, a work which has been often mentioned by European writers, but seldom studied at first hand, owing to the fact that Burnouf's rendering in French, the only one in a European language, has long been out of print, and is practically inaccessible owing to its high price. But our gratitude to Mr. Dutt would have been vastly enhanced if he had obtained the services of some one with a really thorough knowledge of English in the revision of the text of this translation. Unfortunately he has not done so, and the consequence is that the English reader keeps constantly finding his teeth set on edge by passages in which the English is ridiculously faulty, and often quite unreadable.

The correction of the proofs too has been lamentably neglected and every page is disfigured by misprints, which are anything but a credit to all concerned. It must be confessed also that the frequent and erratic substitution of the Bengâlî "B" for the Sanskrit "V" jars unpleasantly upon the reader, while the transliteration of Sanskrit proper names is done absolutely without rule or method in a manner to make even the most patient scholar blaspheme. Again there is only the pretence of an Introduction, not even enough to be of the least assistance to an ordinary reader, an omission greatly to be regretted, for every student is surely entitled to know the methods and principles which a translator has tried to follow, the text he has used, and various other matters. Hence one cannot but regret that Mr. Dutt has not seen fit to comply with this laudable custom, and has thus greatly detracted from the usefulness of his work to close students, as well as to the general reader.

But notwithstanding these deficiencies, every lover of Hindu thought is greatly his debtor, and considering the size of the book, with the very moderate price at which it is sold, one cannot but lose sight of the defects in the translator's work in consideration of the service which he has rendered to us.

Still, before passing on to consider the matter of the Purâṇa itself, one cannot but express a fervent hope that in years to come a real spirit of accurate and careful scholarship will gradually grow up in India among those who engage in this most important and noble task of rendering the treasures of Sanskrit literature accessible to the vast world which speaks the English tongue. Such a spirit will lead them to do their work in a thorough, careful and scholarly manner; to be exact in their renderings, careful even in the minutiæ of transliteration and proof-reading, above all strenuous to ensure the correctness and elegance of the English version which they introduce to the world. For surely it is a shame and a reproach to the sons of India that her treasures of thought and literature should be brought before the world disfigured by a garb of bad English and careless proof-reading.

It is somewhat late in the day to "review" a book which certainly was in existence several hundred years ago at least. Indeed this question of date, even the approximate period, when it was thrown into its present shape, is one of the most difficult and most important questions which arise in connection with the study of any one of these Purâṇas.

For the present, at any rate, the question is wholely insoluble, and even the materials for its preliminary consideration are not yet available in English.

The orthodox canon counts eighteen great Purâṇas, but as the various lists of these given in different works differ, at least apparently, among themselves, the number may be decidedly larger. Of these, two only, the Vishṇu Purâṇa and the Bhâgavata Purâṇa, are accessible in translation; the former is an admirable and scholarly version by Wilson and Fitzedward Hall, the latter in Burnouf's French version, and in that now under consideration.

In form all Purâṇas take the shape of narratives; long stories into which other stories are woven, and others again not infrequently into these, and so on. But they play and have played a most important part in the religious life of the Hindu people, for with the two great epics, the Râmâyana and the Mahâbhârata, which are also classed as Purâṇas they contain practically the religious teaching, the moral, ethical, spiritual, social ideals and norms of the great mass of the population. Everyone in India, even quite among the lower classes, however uneducated he may be, is more or less acquainted with the Purâṇas—not as literary works of course, but through hearing stories and tales drawn from them recited and expounded again and again at every festivity, every marriage, every village fair.

The Vedas, including the Upanishads and the great systematic philosophies, were exclusively the property of the "twice-born" castes, the Brâhman, Vaishya and Kshattriya, and these it must be remembered form only a relatively small section of the entire people of India; and even among them, especially in older times when stricter ideas prevailed, very many never qualified themselves for receiving instruction in these loftier teachings, which even now demand for their useful study an intellectual acumen and power of thought far above the average.

It is the Purâṇas then which for the vast majority of Hindus form their scriptures, the text books of duty, the ideals of life, the living religion which entered into, formed and still moulds so much even of their daily and hourly life. They are, therefore, of great importance to the student of comparative religion, and even more so to one who desires to understand the evolution of the human race, and the way in which religion has helped its progress. But a word of caution may not be amiss to a student taking up the study of the Purâṇas, especially if he be familiar with the terse, direct and exceedingly condensed methods followed in so much of the more specially philosophical literature. We must not regard a Purâṇa as in any sense a treatise, a systematic work, following a definite plan and proceeding by regular, logically connected and successive steps. That it is not, and was never meant to be. Whatever may be the truth as to the genesis of the Purâṇas, the whole of this class of Sanskrit works bears quite unmistakably the imprint of a root-idea, totally different as to form from that which stands out in the Vaidic and scholastic parts of the literature. This idea is the old and ever living one of imparting instruction by story, tale, allegory and concrete instance. This is the dominant feature of all the Paurâṇic literature, which may thus be described, from one aspect not inaccurately, as a collection of stories and illustrations, strung together by a sort of plot, often of the slenderest description, and generally destitute of any very clearly discernable design or scheme running all through the work, which is therefore often lacking in a consecutive and coherent development from beginning to end. This does not apply, however, in its full force to the two great Indian epics already mentioned, though the many long interludes and episodes which break the narrative in both cases, delay the unfolding of the main plot to an extent which according to Western canons of art would be held tedious and inartistic. But it does apply very largely to the Puraṇas proper, as a brief analysis of the Bhâgavata Purâṇa will clearly show.

The main thread—for it scarcely constitutes a plot—of this work is briefly as follows:

After King Yudhiṣhṭhira, the eldest of the five Pâṇḍava brothers, had conquered in the Great War, he ruled his kingdom in peace for some time. Then, learning of the departure from earth of Shrî Kriṣhṇa, he perceived that the Kali or Dark Age was come upon the world, and therefore handed over the kingdom to his son Parikshit and accompanied by his brothers set off on the Great Journey to Heaven as related in the Mahâbhârata.

The Bhâgavata Purâṇa opens with a summary of this state of things, and then goes on to relate how King Parikshit was cursed by the son of a Brâhmaṇa, whom he had wantonly insulted, to die by the bite of a serpent. Learning that his death was to ensue on the seventh day, the king in turn handed over the sovereignty to his son and betook himself to the bank of the sacred Ganges, and summoning about him all the most learned and spiritually wise men in his kingdom, from this assembly he asked for teaching as to what a man on the brink of death ought to do. As he was asking this, the great sage Shuka, son of Vyâsa, of whom it is said that his whole consciousness was so perfectly identified with that of the Deity that he was utterly unconscious of even the slightest sense of difference or separateness between himself and the whole universe, came into the assembly. To him the king addressed his questions, and the Purâṇa is a relation of what passed between them, concluding with the departure of the sage and the destruction of the king's body by the bite of the King of the Serpents.

This is really the conclusion of the whole; but in its present form the Purâṇa goes on with a sort of short appendix of a number of verses which seem to point to some re-arrangement of the matter, as this addition rather spoils the dramatic character of the conclusion.

Such then is the general thread upon which the Purâṇa hangs, the whole account as it now stands being supposed to be narrated by Suta —in whose mouth the Mahâbhârata is also put—to Shaunaka and a gathering of sages in the Naimiṣha forest, the land of the "Winkless Divinity."

The first Book is introductory and the second consists mainly of a description of the universe supposed to be related by Brahmâ, the Creator, and the Ṛishi Nârada, and of the relation of the divine soul and the human soul to the body.

The third Book gives an account of a conversation between Vidhura, one of the opponents of the Pâṇḍavas, and the sage Maitreya, in which the latter gives an account of the various principles which compose the universe, another account of the creation, the raising of the earth from the waters of space by Vishnu in the Boar Avatâra, the stories of some of the great Asuras, the Manu (Svâyam-bhuva?) and his offspring, concluding with the discourse of the sage Kapila to his mother upon Bhakti, the Sâṅkhya philosophy, Yoga and the means of obtaining liberation.

The fourth Book continues Maitreya's discourse, giving more details of the Manu's descendants, the story of Dakṣha's sacrifice, the story of Dhruva, that of the evil king Vena and the raising up of Pṛithu to rule the world with justice. Its concluding chapters give various genealogies, the story of the Prachetas, the allegory of Puranjara and Nârada's instruction upon the soul and liberation by which Puranjara obtains true knowledge.

In Book five we go back again to King Parikshit and the sage Shuka, and find the latter, in reply to the king's questions, giving accounts of Prîyavrata, Bharata, the seeming fool, and concluding with a description of Jambudvîpa, Mount Meru, the other Dvîpas, the course of the wheel of time. These chapters contain a curious miscellany of astronomical and geographical information, including a description of Naraka and the subterranean regions.

Book six opens with the curious story of how Ajamîḷha, a sinful Brâhman, escapes the emissaries of Yama who came to lead him to punishment, unintentionally pronouncing at the moment of death one of the names of Viṣhṇu, which happened to be that of a beloved son on whom his affections were centred and of whom he was in reality thinking in that last moment. This leads to a long discourse, in which Yama explains the Vaiṣhṇava religion—the Bhâgavata is a Vaiṣhnâva Purâṇa—to his discomfited emissaries. We then return to Dakṣha and his efforts to obtain progeny, and to various stories of the battles and wars waged with varying fortunes between the Devas and the Asuras, ending with the birth of the Maruts.

The story of Prahlâda and his unshakable devotion to Viṣhṇu occupies the seventh Book, in the course of which the duties of men in general, of the various castes of women, and those of ascetics are described at some length, concluding with a chapter upon the duties of householders in general in special relation to place and time, and upon the characteristics of final liberation.

This concludes the first volume of the translation, which contains seven out of the twelve Books which make up this Purâṇa.

The second volume opens with Book VIII., in which is given a description of the Manus Svâyambhuva, Svârochisa, Authami and Tâmasa, the great Churning of the Ocean of Space by the Devas and Asuras, having Mount Mandâra as their churning rod and the serpent Ananta as their rope. More conflicts between the Devas and Asuras follow, and the book concludes with an account of the Dwarf and Fish Avatâras of Viṣhṇu.

In the ninth Book we have a number of different matters treated of, beginning with another account of a Manu, the stories of Harishchandra, of King Sâgara's sacrifice, the descent of the Ganges from heaven, the birth of Râma, his slaying of Râvaṇa, his return to Ayodhya, and his descendants. Then we go back rather suddenly to the birth of Buddha—not Gautama Buddha—but the son of Soma or the Moon, and then down to earth again to take up the story of Parashurâma's destruction of the Kshattriyas. Next follows the story of Puru, an account of his descendants, of Bharata and his descendants, the Pâṇḍavas, with various other genealogies bringing us down to the birth of Shrî Kṛiṣhṇa, which had only been briefly mentioned before.

The tenth Book is far the longest of all. It consists of an account of Shrî Kṛiṣhṇa's birth and life, interspersed with numerous anecdotes and stories, with but little which is definitely religious or philosophical teaching, in form at least. The subject is continued in the eleventh Book, but here there is much more formal teaching. It is indeed practically an outline of the Vaiṣhṇava religion, which fills the whole Book, excepting the concluding chapter, which relates the destruction of the Yadu race and the departure of Shri Kṛiṣhṇa from earth.

The twelfth Book gives lists of future dynasties that will rule the earth, describes the peculiar features of the Kali Yuga, gives the duration of the various Yugas and Pralayas, their description and so on. King Parikshit dies, the Purâṇa comes to its natural conclusion. But as already stated there follows a sort of Appendix, describing the special characteristics of Purâṇas in general, the story of the sage Mârkaṇḍeya, a description of the Viraṭ or Universal Form of Vishṇu, a statement of the principles of eternal virtue, and a summary of the whole work. The concluding shlokas give a list of the eighteen great Purâṇas and the number of shlokas contained in each.

B. K.

THE BEAUTIFUL.

"PLOTINUS, in the eight book of the fifth 'Ennead,' after speaking of the beauty that is 'intelligible'—*i.e.*. divine, concludes thus: 'As regards ourselves, we are beautiful when we belong to ourselves, and ugly when we lower ourselves to our inferior nature. Also are we beautiful when we know ourselves, and ugly when we have no such knowledge.' Bear it in mind, however, that here we are on the mountains, where not to know oneself means far more than mere ignorance of what takes place within us at moments of jealousy or love, fear or envy, happiness or unhappiness. Here not to know oneself means to be unconscious of all the divine that throbs in man. As we wander from the gods within us so does ugliness enwrap us; as we discover them, so do we become more beautiful. But it is only by revealing the divine that is in us that we may discover the divine in others."

MAETERLINCK, *The Treasure of the Humble.*

THEOSOPHICAL AND MYSTIC PUBLICATIONS.

COLONEL OLCOTT in the April *Theosophist*, begins the second Oriental series of his "Old Diary Leaves" and opens with an amusing dissertation on the cooking abilities of a military officer to whose house Madame Blavatsky and he were invited. This is followed by the correspondence relating to the government prejudices connected with the Society and the suspicions entertained by officials, the correspondence resulting in a satisfactory settlement. K. Narayansami Aiyer writes on "The Manifestations of Shiva and his Spouse" of which manifestations there are five, illustrating, according to the writer, the development of an ego from the first stage to that of a Jîvanmûkta. An account of Eusapia's *séances* at Choisy-Ivrac is contributed by Col. de Rochas, with illustrations of the room in which the *séance* took place. Col. Olcott gives a list of coming calamities that may be expected, according to several more or less inspired seers, at the conclusion of this cycle, or century, it is not very clear which. We may wait with patience for the horrors, for have we not already passed through several to be calamitous years? An interesting paper by Mr. F. W. Thurston, is on "Hints for developing Mental Power" suggesting that some of the Indian lodges of the Society should start practices similar to those he has been conducting in England, indirectly connected with the Society for Psychical Research. It is questionable whether such a course would be really beneficial.

The Dawn, a recently started Indian magazine of which we have the second issue before us, opens with a statement of its objects and a table of transliterations, followed by a paper on the Vedânta Sutras. Much Sanskrit is scattered over the pages, which are of course more suitable for Indian than for European readers. The number concludes with a lecture by Dr. Turnbull on the future of Hinduism. *The Buddhist*, which has disappeared in its old form, reappears as the supplement to the *Sandaresa*, a Cingalese journal. An amusing note reproduces the complaint of a church missionary, who finds that the Buddhists themselves are now emulating the Christian churches by founding Buddhist schools and even—"to parallel our Christmas"—celebrating Buddha's birthday. We have to acknowledge the receipt of *The Thinker; The Theosophic Gleaner; The Wealth of India*, dealing entirely with the material side of affairs; *The Journal of the Mahâ Bodhi Society*, with notes on the Wesak Festival of the birth of the Buddha, to be held on May 15th, at the time of full moon; and *Rays of Light*.

The Vâhan promises to be well supplied with correspondence for a short time at least. In this issue there is a letter on a reply in a former issue dealing with karma in the animal kingdom, followed by a lengthy note by C. W. L., protesting, amongst other things, against the idea that suffering is necessary to spiritual progress. In the "Enquirer" a most interesting set of questions is dealt with, A. P. S.

writing on soul-consciousness and the loss of the soul, and B. K. on the cause of insanity, C. W. L. also contributing a long answer on the influence of the moon on vegetation. The serious part is lightened by a puzzle from an alleged "mathematical contributor" as a reply to a question respecting a statement that "a straight line prolonged indefinitely will end in a circle." The mathematical readers may exercise their brains and knowledge over a solution of the strange formula, but probably the plain man will jump at the proper answer without the use of the calculus or any other formidable system.

One of the most interesting articles that *Mercury* has published is the opening one in its April issue, on "The Eye the Mirror of the Body." It is headed "Occult Correspondences." Some students, we are afraid, have, after painful experience, come to the conclusion that most "occult correspondences" are among the deepest delusions of the great mâyâ, but we have some particulars here which should be capable of ready proof, though their bearing on Theosophy may not be very obvious. The information is taken from a medical book published in 1890, and written in German, an English translation of which is in preparation. The alleged discovery is that every part of the body is directly connected to a corresponding part of the eye, so that the latter can be mapped out into definite areas each representing a portion of the body. An injury, by disease or accident, to the body, or any nervous disturbance, will, it is said, be at once impressed on the corresponding point of the eye, in a visible manner. The map given is as complete as a phrenological bust or chart of the "bumps," but the very completeness is apt to arouse some suspicion as to the basis of the system. However, that is a matter for experts, and we may hope to hear more of the subject. This is followed by a short but excellent paper on the Vedas by a "Brahmachârin" and one on "The Theosophy of Tennyson"

The Mercury Press has just issued a small pamphlet comprising an article by Mr. Fullerton on "Joining the Theosophical Society," and "How the Divine Nature reveals itself through Physical Nature" by Count Wachtmeister.

We are glad to notice that the next issue of *Theosophy in Australasia* will appear in a new and improved form. It has hitherto been somewhat meagre in proportions and not very attractive in appearance, but served well enough the purpose for which it was started, that of giving news to the members of the Society. It is now hoped that its influence may be extended. The chief article in the present issue is on "The Soul," in which some evidences of its existence are given.

In "Under the Bodhi Tree," of our French journal, *Le Lotus Bleu*, Luxâme meditates on the problems of life, and supplies ethical pabulum to his readers. H. de Castro contributes some notes on recent discoveries in Babylon, and Dr. Pascal concludes his useful article on Pantheism.

The fresh translations in *Sophia* are "Letters to a Catholic Priest" by Dr. Wells and "The Baron's House," the ghost story by Mrs. Hooper, published in LUCIFER last year. John Friar writes or invents an account of a curious dream or nightmare of a symbolical description.

Our Dutch *Theosophia* opens with a little sermonette on "Will and Idea" by Afra, founded on a text from *The Theosophy of the Upanishads*. The translation of the *Bhagavad Gîtâ* concludes in this number. A new Dutch book dealing with Theosophy has just been published entitled *First Acquaintance with Theosophy*. The form of the book is conversational, a number of characters taking part. The chapter-headings are as follows: "First Reports," "A Little Information," "The Theosophical Society," "Reincarnation," "Discourses on the Foregoing" and "Theosophical Contemplation of Life." The book is of course intended chiefly for beginners and we hope that it may be widely circulated.

Nova Lux, for April, contains the first part of an article by Decio Calvari on "The Ego and its Vehicles." The present instalment is mainly a study of *The Secret Doctrine*, with illustrative quotations from some of the Upanishads, and deals with the subject from a philosophical point of view. Two Italian pamphlets have just been published, one containing translations of "In the Shadow of the Gods," by Thos. Williams, and the other "Ignorance and Science" by Amo, one of our French writers. The first paper has evoked a criticism from a Roman Catholic priest which is printed in the second pamphlet referred to, followed by an answer by Mrs. Besant. The critical letter contains little real matter, the main objection being that the ideas contained in the article criticised led towards Pantheism One or two interesting quotations from Catholic writers are given, showing that some of the views, such as "thoughts are real things," were admitted by them. Mrs. Besant does not criticise in her reply but gives a general sketch of some of the Theosophical concepts of spirit and matter, and of Deity. The get-up of the pamphlets is admirable and we hope that some of the more instructive Theosophical literature will be translated and appear in as attractive a form.

Borderland for April, is especially interesting, and not the least attractive portion is that occupied by the communications of Julia. This time they are on what is familiarly known to Theosophists as Yoga, a vague term used to cover a multitude of things, but in this case the Yoga is fairly definite. Instructions are given as to the method of producing or forming a living image of any person desired, making objective any shape. The instructions are excellent, and though they contain nothing that can be fresh to any intelligent student of Theosophy they are clear and well expressed. The possible dangers are, however, but slightly considered, but Mr. Leadbeater, in a letter to Mr. Stead, who forwarded him a proof of the communication, briefly points them out. The dangers are sufficiently obvious to anyone acquainted with the class of people who will inevitably form a large part of the experimenters. The addresses of Dr. Lodge to the spiritualists and of Mr. Crookes to the Society for Psychical Research, are reproduced and Mr. Crookes forms the "Borderlander" for the quarter. Among other interesting matter may be mentioned Miss X. on "Fairies or Spooks ?," "Hauntings of To-day," "The Prayer Telephone," and an account of modern Indian Magic.

In *The Coming Day* there is an article on Theosophy, taking up Mrs. Besant's fourteen "proofs of Reincarnation" given in her manual. The proofs are criticised in a very unfavourable manner and the eccentricities of two prominent writers in the earlier days of the Society are utilized to give point to the criticism.

We have also to acknowledge the receipt of *Book-Notes*, *Light*, *The Agnostic Journal*, *The Metaphysical Magazine*, with the usual array of articles on philosophical and mystical subjects ; *Cæsar Virgin and the Virgin's Son*, from the United States, a queer pamphlet or sermon by Nathaniel + S : : I : :. a formidable array of signs which sufficiently indicate the quality of the production ; *The Sphinx*, a very heavy number ; *Theosophische Rundschau* ; *The Grail*, or *Isis* in a new and not much improved form ; *Sbornik pro Filosofii Mystiku a Occultismus* ; *Ourselves* ; *Modern Astrology*, with most of the articles continued ; *Theosophy*, *The Theosophical Forum*, *The Vegetarian*, *The Second Coming*, a "Manifesto of the Christian Symbolists" ; *Current Literature* ; *The Literary Digest* ; *Food, Home and Garden* ; *The Mystical World* ; *The Vegetarian Review* ; *The Irish Theosophist* ; *L'Hyperchimie* ; a catalogue of second-hand books from Messrs. Sotheran & Co., and the Report of the First Annual Convention of the New Zealand Section of the Theosophical Society.

A.

Women's Printing Society, Limited, 66, Whitcomb Street, W.C.

VOL. XX. JUNE 15, 1897. NO. 118.

LUCIFER.

REINCARNATION.

(*Continued from p.* 192.)

THE ascending stages of consciousness through which the Thinker passes as he reincarnates during his long cycle of lives in the three lower worlds, are clearly marked out, and the obvious necessity for many lives in which to experience them, if he is to evolve at all, may carry to the more thoughtful minds the clearest conviction of the truth of reincarnation.

The first of the stages is that in which all the experiences are sensational, the only contribution made by the mind consisting of the recognition that contact with some objects is followed by a sensation of pleasure, while contact with others is followed by a sensation of pain. These objects form mental pictures, and the pictures soon begin to act as a stimulus to seek the objects associated with pleasure, when those objects are not present, the germs of memory and of mental initiative thus making their appearance. This first rough division of the external world is followed by the more complex idea of the bearing of quantity on pleasure and pain, already referred to.

At this stage of evolution memory is very short-lived, or, in other words, mental images are very transitory. The idea of forecasting the future from the past, even to the most rudimentary extent, has not dawned on the infant Thinker, and his actions are guided from outside, by the impacts that reach him from the external world, or at furthest by the promptings of his appetites and passions, craving gratification. He will throw away anything for an immediate satisfaction, however necessary the thing may be for his future well-being; the need of the moment overpowers every other consideration. Numerous examples of human souls in this embryonic condition can be found in books of travel, and the necessity for many lives will be impressed on the mind of anyone who studies the mental condition of the least-evolved savages, and compares it with the mental condition of even average humanity among ourselves.

Needless to say that the moral capacity is no more evolved than the mental; the idea of good and evil has not yet been conceived. Nor is it possible to convey to the quite undeveloped mind even an elementary notion of either good or bad. Good and pleasant are to it interchangeable terms, as in the well-known case of the Australian savage mentioned by Charles Darwin. Pressed by hunger, the man speared the nearest living creature that could serve as food, and this happened to be his wife; a European remonstrated with him on the wickedness of his deed, but failed to make any impression; for from the reproach that to eat his wife was very bad, he only deduced the inference that the stranger thought she had proved nasty or indigestible, and he put him right by smiling peacefully as he patted himself after his meal, and declaring in a satisfied way, "She is very good." Measure in thought the moral distance between that man and S. Francis of Assisi, and it will be seen that there must either be evolution of souls as there is evolution of bodies, or else in the realm of the soul there must be constant miracle, dislocated creations.

There are two paths along either of which man may gradually emerge from this embryonic mental condition. He may be directly ruled and controlled by men far more evolved than himself, or he may be left to grow slowly unaided. The latter case would imply the passage of uncounted millennia, for without example and without discipline, left to the changing impacts of external objects, and to friction with other men as undeveloped as himself, the inner energies could be but very slowly aroused. As a matter of fact, man has evolved by the road of direct precept and example and of enforced discipline. We have already seen that when the bulk of average humanity received the spark which brought the Thinker into being, there were some of the greater Sons of Mind who incarnated as Teachers, and that there was also a long succession of lesser

Sons of Mind, at various stages of evolution, who came into incarnation as the crest wave of the advancing tide of humanity. These ruled the less evolved, under the beneficent sway of the great Teachers, and the compelled obedience to elementary rules of right living—very elementary at first, in truth—much hastened the development of mental and moral faculties in the embryonic souls. Apart from all other records the gigantic remains of civilizations that have long since disappeared—evidencing great engineering skill, and intellectual conceptions far beyond anything possible to the mass of the then infant humanity—suffice to prove that there were present on earth men with minds that were capable of greatly planning and greatly executing.

Let us continue the early stage of the evolution of consciousness. Sensation was wholly lord of the mind, and the earliest mental efforts were stimulated by desire. This led the man, slowly and clumsily, to forecast, to plan. He began to recognize a definite association of certain mental images, and, when one appeared, to expect the appearance of the other that had invariably followed in its wake. He began to draw inferences, and even to initiate action on the faith of these inferences—a great advance. And he began also to hesitate now and again to follow the vehement promptings of desire, when he found, over and over again, that the gratification demanded was associated in his mind with the subsequent happening of suffering. This action was much quickened by the pressure upon him of verbally-expressed laws; he was forbidden to seize certain gratifications, and was told that suffering would follow disobedience. When he had seized the delight-giving object and found the suffering follow upon the pleasure, the fulfilled declaration made a far stronger impression on his mind than would have been made by the unexpected—and therefore to him fortuitous—happening of the same thing unforetold. Thus conflict continually arose between memory and desire, and the mind grew more active by the conflict, and was stirred into livelier functioning. The conflict, in fact, marked the transition to the second great stage.

Here began to show itself the germ of will. Desire and will guide a man's actions, and will has even been defined as the desire which emerges triumphant from the contest of desires. But this is a crude and superficial view, explaining nothing. Desire is the outgoing energy of the Thinker, determined in its direction by the attraction of external objects. Will is the out-going energy of the Thinker, determined in its direction by the conclusions drawn by the reason from past experiences, or by the direct intuition of the Thinker himself. Otherwise put: desire is guided from without, will from within. At the beginning of man's evolution, desire has complete sovereignty, and hurries him hither and thither; in the middle of his evolution, desire and will are in continual conflict, and victory lies sometimes with the one, sometimes with the other; at the end of his evolution desire has died, and will rules with unopposed, unchallenged sway. Until the Thinker is sufficiently developed to see directly, will is guided by him through the reason; and as the reason can only draw its conclusions from its stock of mental images—its experience—and that stock is limited, the will constantly commands mistaken actions. The suffering which flows from these mistaken actions increases the stock of mental images, and thus gives the reason an increased store from which to draw its conclusions. Thus progress is made and wisdom is born.

Desire often mixes itself up with will, so that what appears to be determined from within is really largely prompted by the cravings of the lower nature for objects which afford it gratification. Instead of an open conflict between the two, the lower subtly insinuates itself into the current of the higher and turns its course aside. Defeated in the open field, the desires of the personality thus conspire against their conqueror, and often win by guile what they failed to win by force. During the whole of this second great stage, in which the faculties of the lower mind are in full course of evolution, conflict is the normal condition, conflict between the rule of sensations and the rule of reason.

The problem to be solved in humanity is the putting an end to conflict while preserving the freedom of the will; to determine the will inevitably to the best, while yet leaving that best as a matter of choice. The best is to be chosen, but by a self-initiated volition, that shall come with all the certainty of a fore-ordained necessity. The certainty of a compelling law is to be obtained from countless wills, each one left free to determine its own course. The solution of that problem is simple when it is known, though the contradiction looks irreconcilable when first presented. Let man be left free to choose his own actions, but let every action bring about an inevitable result; let him run loose amid all objects of desire and seize whatever he will, but let him have all the results of his choice, be they delightful or grievous. Presently, he will freely reject the objects whose possession ultimately causes him pain; he will no longer desire them, when he has experienced to the full that their possession ends in sorrow. Let him struggle to hold the pleasure and avoid the pain; he will none the less be ground between the stones of law, and the lesson will be repeated any number of times found necessary; reincarnation offers as many lives as are needed by the most sluggish learner. Slowly desire for an object that brings suffering in its train will die, and when the thing offers itself in all its attractive glamour it will be rejected, not by compulsion but by free choice. It is no longer desirable, it has lost its power. Thus with thing after thing; choice more and more runs in harmony with law. "There are many roads of error; the road of truth is one;" when all the paths of error have been trodden, when all have been found to end in suffering, the choice to walk in the way of truth is unswerving, because based on knowledge. The lower kingdoms work harmoniously, compelled by law; man's kingdom is a chaos of conflicting wills, fighting against, rebelling against, law; presently there evolves from it a nobler unity, a harmonious choice of voluntary obedience—an obedience that, being voluntary, based on knowledge, and on memory of the results of disobedience, is stable and can be drawn aside by no temptation. Ignorant, inexperienced, man would always have been in danger of falling; as a God, knowing good and evil by experience, his choice of the good is raised for ever beyond possibility of change.

Will in the domain of morality is generally entitled conscience, and it is subject to the same difficulties in this domain as in its other activities. So long as actions are in question which have been done over and over again, of which the consequences are familiar either to the reason or to the Thinker himself, the conscience speaks quickly and firmly. But when unfamiliar problems arise, as to the working out of which experience is silent, conscience cannot speak with certainty; it has but a hesitating answer from the reason, which can draw only a doubtful inference, and the Thinker cannot speak, if his experience does not include the circumstances that have now arisen. Hence conscience often decides wrongly; that is, the will, failing clear direction from either the reason or the intuition, guides action amiss. Nor can we leave out of consideration the influences which play upon the mind from without, from the thought-forms of others, of friends, of the family, of the community, of the nation. These all surround and penetrate the mind with their own atmosphere, distorting the appearance of everything, and throwing all things out of proportion. Thus influenced, the reason often does not even judge calmly from its own experience, but draws false conclusions as it studies its materials through a distorting medium.

The evolution of moral faculties is very largely stimulated by the affections, animal and selfish as these are during the infancy of the Thinker. The laws of morality are laid down by the enlightened reason, discerning the laws by which Nature moves, and bringing human conduct into consonance with the divine Will. But the impulse to obey these laws, when no outer force compels, has its root in love, in that hidden divinity in man which seeks to pour itself out, to give itself to others. Morality begins in the infant Thinker when he is first moved by love to wife, to child, to friend, to do some action that serves the loved one without any thought of gain to himself thereby. It is the first conquest over the lower nature, the complete subjugation of which is the achievement of moral perfection. Hence the importance of never killing out, or striving to weaken, the affections, as is done in many of the lower kinds of occultism. However impure and gross the affections may be, they offer possibilities of moral evolution from which the cold-hearted and self-isolated have shut themselves out. It is an easier task to purify than to create love, and this is why "the sinners" have been said by great Teachers to be nearer the kingdom of heaven than the Pharisees and scribes.

The third great stage of consciousness sees the development of the higher intellectual powers; the mind no longer dwells entirely on mental images obtained from sensations, no longer reasons on purely concrete objects, nor is concerned with the attributes which differentiate one from another. The Thinker, having learned to discriminate clearly between objects by dwelling upon their unlikenesses, now begins to group them together by some attribute which appears in a number of objects otherwise dissimilar, and makes a link between them. He draws out, abstracts, this common attribute, and sets all objects that possess it apart from the rest which are without it; and in this way he evolves the power of recognizing identity amid diversity, a step towards the much later recognition of the One underlying the many. He thus classifies all that is around him, developing the synthetic faculty, and learning to construct as well as to analyze. Presently he takes another step, and conceives of the common property as an idea, apart from all the objects in which it appears, and thus constructs a higher kind of mental image than the image of a concrete object—the image of an idea that has no phenomenal existence in the worlds of form, but which exists on the higher levels of the mental plane, and affords material on which the Thinker himself can work. The lower mind reaches the abstract idea by reason, and in thus doing accomplishes its loftiest flight, touching the threshold of the formless world, and dimly seeing that which lies beyond. The Thinker sees these ideas, and lives among them habitually, and when the power of abstract reasoning is developed and exercised, the Thinker is becoming effective in his own world, and is beginning his life of active functioning in his own sphere. Such men care little for the life of the senses, care little for external observation, or for mental application to images of external objects; their powers are indrawn, and no longer rush outwards in the search for satisfaction. They dwell calmly within themselves, engrossed with the problems of philosophy, with the deeper aspects of life and thought, seeking to understand causes rather than troubling themselves with effects, and approaching nearer and nearer to the recognition of the One that underlies all the diversities of external Nature.

In the fourth stage of consciousness that One is seen, and with the transcending of the barriers set up by the intellect, the consciousness spreads out to embrace the world, seeing all things in itself and as parts of itself, and seeing itself as a ray of the LOGOS, and therefore as one with Him. Where is then the Thinker? He has become Consciousness, and while the spiritual soul can at will use any of his lower vehicles, he is no longer limited to their use, nor needs them for his full and conscious life. Then is compulsory reincarnation over, and the man has destroyed death—has verily achieved immortality. Then has he become "a pillar in the temple of my God, and shall go out no more."

To complete this part of our study we need to understand the successive quickenings of the vehicles of consciousness, the bringing them one by one into activity as the harmonious instruments of the human soul.

We have seen that from the very beginning of his separate life, the Thinker has possessed coatings of mental, astral, etheric and dense physical matter. These form the media by which his life vibrates outwards, the bridge of consciousness, as we may call it, along which all impulses from the Thinker may reach the dense physical body, all impacts from the outer world may reach him. But this general use of the successive bodies as parts of a connected whole is a very different thing from the quickening of each in turn to serve as a distinct vehicle of consciousness, independently of those below it, and it is this quickening of the vehicles that we have now to consider.

The lowest vehicle, the dense physical body, is the first one to be brought into harmonious working order; the brain and the nervous system have to be elaborated and to be rendered delicately responsive to every thrill which is within their gamut of vibratory power. In the early stages, while the physical dense body is composed of the grosser kinds of matter, this gamut is extremely limited, and the physical organ of mind can respond only to the slowest vibrations sent down. It answers far more promptly, as is natural, to the impacts from the external world caused by objects similar in materials to itself. Its quickening as a vehicle of consciousness consists in its being made responsive to the vibrations that are initiated within, and the rapidity of this quickening depends on the co-operation of the lower nature with the higher, its loyal subordination of itself in the service of its inner ruler. When, after many, many life-periods, it dawns upon the lower nature that it exists for the sake of the soul, that all its value depends on the help which it can bring to the soul, that it can win immortality only by merging itself in the soul—then its evolution proceeds with giant strides. Before this, the evolution has been unconscious; at first, the gratification of the lower nature was the object of life, and while this was a necessary preliminary for calling out the energies of the Thinker, it did nothing directly to render the body a vehicle of consciousness; the direct working upon it begins when the life of the man establishes its centre in the mental body, and when thought begins to dominate sensation. The exercise of the mental powers works on the brain and the nervous system, and the coarser materials are gradually expelled to make room for the finer, which can vibrate in unison with the thought vibrations sent to them. The brain becomes finer in constitution, and increases by ever more complicated convolutions the amount of surface available for the coating of nervous matter adapted to respond to thought vibrations. The nervous system becomes more delicately balanced, more sensitive, more alive to every thrill of mental activity. And when the recognition of its function as an instrument of the soul, spoken of above, has come, then active co-operation in performing this function sets in. The personality begins deliberately to discipline itself, and to set the permanent interests of the immortal individual above its own transient gratifications. It yields up the time that might be spent in the pursuit of lower pleasures to the evolution of mental powers; day by day time is set apart for serious study; the brain is gladly surrendered to receive impacts from within instead of from without, is trained to answer to consecutive thinking, and is taught to refrain from throwing up its own useless disjointed images, made by past impressions. It is taught to remain at rest when it is not wanted by its master—to answer, not to initiate vibrations.* Further, some discretion and discrimination will be used as to the food-stuffs which supply physical materials to the brain. The use of the coarser kinds, such as animal flesh and blood and alcohol, will be discontinued, and pure food will build up a pure body. Gradually the lower vibrations will find no materials capable of responding to them, and the physical body will thus become more and more entirely a vehicle of consciousness, delicately responsive to all the thrills of thought, and keenly sensitive to the vibrations sent outwards by the Thinker. The etheric double so closely follows the constitution of the dense body that it is not necessary to study separately its purification and quickening; it does not normally serve as a separate

* One of the signs that this is being accomplished is the cessation of the confused jumble of fragmentary images which are set up during sleep by the independent activity of the physical brains. When the brain is coming under control this kind of dream is very seldom experienced.

vehicle of consciousness, but works synchronously with its dense partner, and when separated from it either by accident or by death, it responds very feebly to the vibrations initiated within. Its function in truth is not to serve as a vehicle of mental consciousness, but as a vehicle of Prâna, of specialized life-force, and its dislocation from the denser particles to which it conveys the life-currents is therefore disturbing and mischievous.

The astral body is the second vehicle of consciousness to be vivified. When it is thoroughly organized, the consciousness which has hitherto worked within it, imprisoned by it, when in sleep it has left the physical body and is drifting about in the astral world, begins not only to receive the impressions through it of astral objects that form the so-called dream-consciousness, but also to perceive astral objects by its senses—that is, it begins to relate the impressions received to the objects which give rise to those impressions. These perceptions are at first confused, just as are the perceptions at first made by the mind through a new physical baby-body, and they have to be corrected by experience in the one case as in the other. The Thinker has gradually to discover the new powers which he can use through this subtler vehicle, and by which he can control the astral elements, and defend himself against astral dangers. He is not left alone to face this new world unaided, but is taught and helped—and, until he can guard himself, protected—by those who are more experienced than he is in the ways of the astral world. Gradually the new vehicle of consciousness comes completely under his control, and life on the astral plane is as natural and as familiar as life on the physical.

ANNIE BESANT.

(*To be concluded.*)

AMONG THE GNOSTICS OF THE FIRST TWO CENTURIES.

(*Continued from p.* 218.)

MARCION (*continued*).

ENOUGH has now been said to give the reader a general idea of the Marcionite position, a very strong one it must be admitted, both because of its simplicity and also because it formulated the protest of long slumbering discontent. It is, however, difficult to formulate anything like a clear system of cosmogony or christology from the onslaughts of the best known hæresiologists on Marcionite doctrines. It has even been doubted whether Marcion should be classed as a Gnostic, but this point is set at rest by the work of Eznik (Eznig or Esnig), an Armenian bishop, who flourished about 450 A.D. In his treatise, The Destruction of False Doctrines, he devotes the fourth and last book to the Marcionites, who seem to have been even at that late date a most flourishing body. Although it is doubted whether the ideas there described are precisely the same as the original system of Marcion, it is evident that the Marcionite tradition was of a distinctly Gnostic tendency, and that Marcion owed more to his predecessors in Gnosticism than was usually supposed prior to the first translation of Eznik's treatise (into French) in 1833.

It will be sufficient here to shorten Salmon's summary of this curious Marcionite myth, calling the reader's attention to the similarity of parts of its structure to the system of Justinus.

There were three Heavens; in the highest was the Good God; in the intermediate the God of the Law; in the lowest, his Angels. Beneath lay Hyle or root-matter. The world was the joint product of the God of the Law and Hyle. The Creative Power perceiving that the world was very good, desired to make man to inhabit it. So Hyle gave him his body and the Creative Power the breath of life, his spirit. And Adam and Eve lived in innocence in Paradise, and did not beget children. And the God of the Law desired to take Adam from Hyle and make him serve him alone. So taking him aside, he said, "Adam, I am God and beside me there is no other; if thou worshippest any other God thou shalt die the death." And Adam on hearing of death was afraid, and withdrew himself from Hyle. Now Hyle had been wont to serve Adam; but when she found that he withdrew from her, in revenge she filled the world with idolatry so that men ceased to adore the Lord of Creation. Then was the Creator wrath, and as men died he cast them into Hell, from Adam onwards.

But at length the Good God looked down from Heaven and saw the miseries which man suffered through Hyle and the Creator. And he took compassion on them and sent them down his Son to deliver them saying: "Go down, take on thee the form of a servant [? a body], and make thyself like the sons of the Law. Heal their wounds, give sight to their blind, bring their dead to life, perform without reward the greatest miracles of healing: then will the God of the Law be jealous and instigate his servants to crucify thee. Then go down to Hell [Hades, Kâmaloka], which will open her mouth to receive thee, supposing thee to be one of the dead. Then liberate the captives thou shalt find there, and bring them up to me."

And thus the souls were freed from Hell and carried up to the Father. Whereupon the God of the Law was enraged, and rent his clothes and tore the curtain of his palace, and darkened the sun and veiled the world in darkness. Then the Christ descended a second time, but now in the glory of his divinity, to plead with the God of the Law. And the God of the Law was compelled to acknowledge that he had done wrong in thinking that there was no higher power than himself. And the Christ said unto him: "I have a controversy with thee, but I will take no other judge between us but thy own law. Is it not written in thy law that whoso killeth another shall himself be killed; that whoso sheddeth innocent blood shall have his own blood shed? Let me, then, kill thee and shed thy blood, for I am innocent and thou hast shed my blood."

And then he went on to recount the benefits he had bestowed on the children of the Creator, and how he had in return been crucified.

And the God of the Law could find no defence, and confessed and said, "I was ignorant, I thought thee but a man, and did not know thee to be a god, take the revenge that is thy due."

And the Christ thereupon left him and betook himself to Paul and revealed the path of truth.

The Marcionites were the most rigid of ascetics, abstaining from marriage, flesh and wine, the latter being excluded from their Eucharist. They also rejoiced beyond all other sects in the number of their martyrs. The Marcionites have also given us the most ancient dated Christian inscription. It was discovered over the doorway of a house in a Syrian village and formerly marked the site of a Marcionite meeting-house or church, which curiously enough was called a synagogue. The date is Oct. 1, A.D. 318, and the most remarkable point about it is that the church was dedicated to "The Lord and Saviour Jesus, the Good,"—Chrêstos not Christos. In early times there seems to have been much confusion between the two titles. Christos is the Greek for the Hebrew Messiah, Anointed, and was the title used by those who believed that Jesus was the Jewish Messiah. This was denied, not only by the Marcionites, but also by many of their Gnostic predecessors and successors. The title Chrêstos was used of one perfected, the holy one, the saint; no doubt in later days the orthodox who subsequently had the sole editing of the texts in pure ignorance changed Chrêstos into Christos wherever it occurred, so that instead of finding the promise of perfection in the religious history of all the nations, they limited it to the Jewish tradition alone, and struck a fatal blow to the universalism of history and doctrine.

There was naturally a number of sub-schools of the Marcion school, and in its ranks were a number of distinguished teachers, of whom, however, we have only space to refer to Apelles.

APELLES.

We owe our most reliable information on this Gnostic to a certain Rhodon, who opposed his views some time in the reign of Commodus (180-193 A.D.); an excerpt from this lost "refutation" has fortunately been preserved for us by Eusebius. At this time Apelles was a very old man and refused the controversy, saying that all sincere believers would ultimately be saved, whatever their theology might be, a most enlightened doctrine and worthy of the best in Gnosticism. As Hort says, "the picture which Rhodon unwittingly furnishes of his [Apelles'] old age is pleasant to look upon. We see a man unwearied in the pursuit of truth, diffident and tolerant, resting in beliefs which he could not reconcile [?], but studious to maintain the moral character of theology."

Apelles seems to have taken up a less exclusive position than Marcion, though his book of Reasonings, directed against the Mosaic theology, seems to have been drastic enough, and he is further said by Eusebius to have written a "multitude of books" of the same nature. He was, however, especially taken to task for his belief in the clairvoyant faculty of a certain Philumene whom he came across in his old age. Her visions were recorded in a book called The Manifestations, by which Apelles set great store. Strangely enough the man who pours on his head the greatest abuse for this, accompanied with the usual charges of immorality, is Tertullian who, in his own treatise On the Soul, following out his own Montanist convictions, confesses his full belief in the prophetical power of a certain voyante of his own congregation, in a most entertaining and naïve fashion! Rhodon, on the contrary, who knew Apelles personally at Alexandria, says that the old gentleman thought himself protected from such slanderous insinuations, by his age and well-known character.

Philumene seems to have enjoyed certain psychic faculties, and also to have been a "medium" for physical phenomena. She belonged to the class of holy women or "virgins," who were numerous enough in the early Church, though it is exceedingly doubtful whether any of them were trained, except perhaps in the most advanced Gnostic circles.

There is an entertaining account of Philumene in a curious fragment of an anonymous author, which was printed in the early editions of Augustine's work On Heresies, in the section devoted to the Severians. The following is Hort's rendering of the passage:

"He [Apelles] moreover used to say that a certain girl named Philumene was divinely inspired to predict future events. He used to refer to her his dreams, and the perturbations (aestus) of his mind, and to forewarn himself secretly by her divinations or presages." [Here some words appear to be missing.] "The same phantom (phantasmate), he said, shewed itself to the same Philumene in the form of a boy. This seeming boy sometimes declared himself to be Christ, sometimes Paul. By questioning this phantom she used to supply the answers which she pronounced to her hearers (ea respondere quae . . . diceret). He added that she was accustomed to perform some wonders, of which the following was the chief: she used to make a large loaf enter a glass vase (ampullam) with a very small mouth, and to take it out (levare) uninjured with the tips of her fingers; and was content with that food alone, as if it had been given her from above (divinitus)."

All of which is very monkish, and very spiritualistic, and quite in keeping with the records of phenomenalism.

We should, however, remember that this account is not from the side of the Gnostics, but from an unfriendly source. We shall perhaps never know whether Apelles had a knowledge of the sources of the phenomena he witnessed, or like the vast majority of that time, as indeed of all times, ignorantly assumed that the fact of psychic powers proved the truth of theological doctrines.

THE BASILIDIAN SYSTEM.

Let us now return to the earlier years of the second century and devote our attention to Basilides and his followers ("them of Basilides") who elaborated perhaps the most abstruse and consistent system of the Gnosis, the outlines of which are plainly recoverable from the garbled fragments which Patristic polemics have left us.

Of the life of this great doctor of the Gnosis we know nothing beyond the fact that he taught at Alexandria. His date is entirely conjectural; he is, however, generally supposed to have been immediately prior to Valentinus. If, therefore, we say that he flourished somewhere about B.C. 130-140, it should be understood that a margin of ten years or so either way has to be allowed for. Of his nationality again we know nothing. But whether he was Greek, or Egyptian, or Syrian, he was steeped in Hellenic culture, and learned in the wisdom of the Egyptians. He was also well versed in the Hebrew scriptures as set forth in the Greek version of the Seventy. The Gospel teachings were his delight, and he wrote no less than twenty-four books of commentaries on them, although he does not appear to have used the subsequently canonical versions. He also quotes from several of the Pauline Letters.

Of the writings of Basilides the most important was the commentary already referred to; it was the first commentary on the Gospels written by a Christian philosopher, and in this, as in all other departments of theology, the Gnostics led the way. Basilides is further said to have written a Gospel himself, and to have claimed to be the disciple of a certain Glaucias who was an "interpreter of Peter." There is also mention of certain Traditions of Matthias, as held in great honour by their school. These purported to be teachings given to Matthias in secret by Jesus after the "resurrection." It is therefore to be supposed that the Gospel of Basilides was not a new historical setting of the Sayings of the Lord, but an exposition of that "knowledge of supermundane things," which was the definition he gave to the Gospel. In other words, Basilides wrote a commentary on the Sayings of the Lord, which were in general circulation in many different collections and recensions, with or without the so-called various historical settings, and also his own elaboration of certain inner instructions which had been handed down by a secret tradition. Whether or not this inner Gospel formed part of the twenty-four books of his Exegetica is doubtful; most critics, however, are in favour of this view. In any case, it is to be supposed that his commentary aimed at explaining the public Sayings and Parables by the light of this secret Gospel.

Basilides is also said to have written certain Odes, but of these no fragment has reached us.

Our main sources of information are three in number and consist of the very fragmentary quotations (i) of Hippolytus in his later work, The Philosophumena, (ii) of Clement of Alexandria in his Miscellanies, and (iii) presumably in the first place (either of the lost Syntagma of Justin or) of the lost work of Agrippa Castor, who is said by Eusebius to have written a refutation of the views of Basilides in the reign of Hadrian (c. 133 A.D.), and whose very unsatisfactory and inaccurate data were copied by Irenæus, and the epitomators of the earlier, smaller, and now lost work of Hippolytus.

Turning to the great work of Hippolytus we come upon the most valuable information extant for the reconstruction of this most highly metaphysical system. The Church father had evidently before him a treatise of Basilides, but whether it was the Exegetica or not, is by no means clear; what is certain, however, is that it set forth the real Gospel, or "knowledge of supermundane things," as Basilides understood it, and we can only regret that we have not the original text of the Gnostic doctor himself before us instead of a most faulty copy of the text of the Church father's refutation, whose method is of the most provoking. Hippolytus muddles up his own glosses and criticisms with mutilated quotations, imperfectly summarizes important passages which treat of conceptions requiring the greatest subtlety and nicety of language, and in other respects does scant justice to a thinker whose faith in Christianity was so great, that so far from confining it to the narrow limits of a dogmatic theology, as the poor opinion of their faith forced the Patristic writers to do, he would have it that the Gospel was also a universal philosophy explanatory of the whole world-drama.

Let us then raise our thoughts to those sublime heights to which the genius of Basilides soared so many centuries ago, when faith in the universal possibilities of the Glad Tidings was really living. And first we must rise to that stupendous intuition of Deity which transcends even Being, and which to the narrow minds of earth seems pure nothingness, instead of being that which beggars all fulness. Beyond time, beyond space, beyond consciousness, beyond Being itself—

"There was when naught was; nay, even that 'naught' was not aught of things that are [even in the world of reality]. But nakedly, conjecture and mental quibbling apart, there was absolutely not even the One [the ruler of the world of reality]. And when I use the term 'was,' I do not mean to say that it was [that is to say, in any state of being]; but merely to give some suggestion of what I wish to indicate, I use the expression 'there was absolutely naught.' For that 'naught' is not simply the so-called ineffable; it is beyond that. For that which is *really* ineffable is not named ineffable, but is superior to every name that is used.

"The names [we use] are not sufficient even for the [manifested] universe [which is outside the world of real being], so diversified is it; they fall short."

Much less, then, he continues to argue, can we find appropriate names for the beings of the world of reality and their operations, and far more impossible, therefore, is it to give names to That which transcends even reality. Thus we see that Basilides soared beyond even the ideal world of Plato, and ascended to the untranscendable intuition of the Orient—the That which cannot be named, to be worshipped in silence alone.

We next come to the inception of the germ of universality in this state beyond being, a discrete stage, so to speak, beyond the unmanifested or noumenal world even.

Hippolytus summarizes this condition of non-being which transcends all being as follows, from the original treatise.

"Naught was, neither matter, nor substance, nor voidness of substance, nor simplicity, nor impossibility of composition, nor inconceptibility, nor imperceptibility, neither man, nor angel, nor god, in fine neither anything at all for which man has ever found a name, nor any operation which falls within the range either of his perception or conception. Such, or rather far more removed from the power of man's comprehension, was the state of non-being, when [if we can speak of 'when' in a state beyond time and space] the Deity beyond being, without thinking, or feeling, or determining, or choosing, or being compelled, or desiring, willed to create universality.

"When I use the term 'will,'" writes Basilides, "I do so merely to suggest the idea of an operation transcending all volition, thought or sensible action. And this universality also was not [our] dimensional and differentiable universe which subsequently came into existence and was separated [from other universes], but the Seed of all universes."

This is evidently the same concept as the mûlaprakṛiti of Indian philosophy, and the most admirable statement of the dogma of the creation out of nothing which has been put forward by any Christian philosopher.

"This universal Seed contained everything in itself, potentially, in some such fashion as the grain of mustard seed contains the whole simultaneously in the minutest point, roots, stem, branches, leaves, and the innumerable germs that come from the seeds of the plant, and which in their turn produce still other and other plants in manifold series.

"Thus the Divinity beyond being created universality beyond being from elements beyond being, positing and causing to subsist a single something"—which poverty of language compels us to call a

Seed, but which was really the potentiality of potentialities, seeing that it was "containing in itself the entire all-seed-potency of the universe." From such a "Seed," which is everywhere and nowhere, and which treasures in its bosom everything that was or is or is to be, all things must come into manifestation in their "proper natures and cycles" and times at the will of the Deity beyond all. How this is brought about is by no means clear. Basilides seems to have had some idea of a "supplementary development" (κατὰ προσθήκην αὐξανόμενα) which, however, is beyond definition; one thing is clear, that he entirely repudiated every idea of emanation, projection or pullulation (προβολή).

"For of what sort of emanation is there need, or of what sort of matter must we make supposition, in order that God should make the universe, like as a spider weaves its webs [from itself], or mortal man takes brass or timber or other matter out of which to make something? But 'He spake and it was,' and this is what is the meaning of the saying of Moses, 'Let there be light, and there was light.' Whence then was the light? From naught. For it is not written whence, but only from the voice of the Speaker of the word. And He who spake the word, was not, and that which was, was not. For the Seed of the universe, the word that was spoken, 'Let there be light,' was from the state beyond being. And this was what was spoken in the Gospels, 'It was the true light which lighteth every man that cometh into the world.' Man both deriveth his 'principles' from that Seed and is also enlightened by it." This primordial Light and Life is the source of all things.

The next stage deals with the outcome, first fruits, highest product, or sublimest consummation, of universal potentiality, which Basilides calls the Sonship.

"In the absolute Seed there was a triple Sonship, in every way consubstantial with the God beyond being, coming into being from the state beyond being. Of this triply divided Sonship, one aspect was the subtlest of the subtle, one less subtle, and one still stood in need of purification. The subtlest nature of the Sonship instantly and immediately, together with the depositing of the Seed of universality by the God beyond being, burst forth, rose aloft, and hastened from below upward, 'like wing or thought,' as Homer sings, and was with Him beyond being [πρὸς τὸν οὐκ ὄντα—'with,' the very same word as the mysterious preposition in the Prologue of the fourth canonical Gospel.] For every nature striveth after Him because of His transcendency of all beauty and loveliness, but some in one way and others in another.

"The less subtle nature of the Sonship, on the other hand, still remained within the universal Seed, for though it would imitate the higher and ascend, it could not, seeing that it fell short of the degree of subtlety of the first Sonship which had ascended through it [the second], and so it remained behind. The less subtle Sonship, accordingly had to find for itself as it were wings on which to soar, ... and these wings are the Holy Spirit." . . .

Just as a bird cannot fly without wings, and the wings cannot soar without the bird, so the second Sonship and the Holy Spirit are complementary the one to the other, and confer mutual benefits on one another.

We here see that Basilides is dealing with the second aspect of the Logos, the positive-negative state; we also perceive the anticipation of the ground of the great controversies which subsequently arose hundreds of years later, such as the Arian, and the "Filioque." But if we enquire whence was the Holy Spirit, Basilides will tell us, from the universal Seed, from which all things came forth under the will of Deity.

"The second Sonship, then, borne aloft by the Spirit, as by a wing, bears aloft the wing, that is the Spirit; but on drawing nigh to the first Sonship and the God beyond being, who createth from the state beyond being, it could no longer keep the Spirit with it, for it [the Spirit] was not of the same substance with it, nor had it a nature like unto that of the Sonship. But just as a pure and dry atmosphere is unnatural and harmful to fish, so to the Holy Spirit was that state of the Sonship together with the God beyond being—that state more ineffable than every ineffable and transcending every name.

"The Sonship, therefore, left it [the Spirit] behind near that Blessed Space which can neither be conceived of nor characterized by any word, yet not entirely deserted nor yet divorced from the Sonship. But even as the sweetest smelling unguent poured into a vessel, though the vessel be emptied of it with the greatest possible care, nevertheless some scent of the unguent still remains and is left behind; the vessel retains the scent of the unguent, though it no longer holds the unguent itself; in such a way has the Holy Spirit remained emptied and divorced from the Sonship, yet at the same time retaining in itself as it were the power of the unguent, the savour of the Sonship. And this is the saying, 'Like the unguent on the head which ran down unto Aaron's beard'—the savour of the Holy Spirit permeating from above and below even as far as the formlessness [crude matter] and our state of existence, whence the [remaining] Sonship received its first impulse to ascend, borne aloft as it were on the wings of an eagle. For all things hasten from below upward, from worse to better, nor is anything in the better condition so bereft of intelligence as to plunge downward. But as yet this third Sonship still remains in the great conglomeration of the seed-mixture, conferring and receiving benefits," in a manner that will receive subsequent explanation.

The Holy Spirit, which in reality permeates everything, but phenomenally separates the sensible universe from the noumenal, constitutes what Basilides terms the Limitary Spirit, midway between things cosmic and supercosmic. This Firmament is far beyond the visible heaven whose locus is the moon's track.

"After this, from the universal Seed and conglomeration of seed-mixture there burst forth and came into existence the Great Ruler, the head of the sensible universe, a beauty and magnitude and potency that nought can destroy." This is the demiurge; but let no mortal think that he can comprehend so great a being, "for he is more ineffable than ineffables, more potent than potencies, wiser than the wise, superior to every excellence that one can name.

"Coming into existence he raised himself aloft, and soared upward, and was borne above in all his entirety as far as the Great Firmament. There he remained because he thought there was none above him, and so he became the most potent power of the universe," save only the third Sonship which yet remained in the seed-mixture. His limit, therefore, was his own ignorance of the supercosmic spaces, although his wisdom was the greatest of all in the cosmic realms.

"Thus thinking himself lord, and ruler, and a wise master-builder, he betook himself to the creation of the creatures of the universe."

This is the supercelestial or ætherial creation, which is beyond the moon; our still lower world and its "atmosphere" terminating at the visible heaven, or lower firmament, its periphery, marked by the moon. Beyond lay the ætherial realms which apparently no mortal eye has seen, but only the reflection of their inhabitants, the stars, in the surface of the sublunary waters of space.

The ætherial creation of the Great Ruler proceeds on the theory of similarity and analogy.

"First of all the Great Ruler, thinking it not right that he should be alone, made for himself, and brought into existence from the universal Seed, a Son far better and wiser than himself. For all this had been predetermined by the God beyond being when he deposited the universal Seed.

"And the Great Ruler on beholding his Son was struck with wonder and love and amazement at his marvellously great beauty, and he caused him to sit at his right hand." And this space where is the throne of the Great Ruler they called the Ogdoad. "And the Great Demiurgos, the Wise one, fabricated the whole ætherial creation with his own hand; but it was his Son, who was wiser still, who infused energy into him and suggested to him ideas."

That is to say, that the Great Ruler made the creatures of the ætherial spaces, and these evolved souls, or rather were ensouled. And thus it is that the son is, as it were, greater than the father, and sits on his right hand, or above him; the right hand in Gnostic symbolism signifying a higher condition. They mutually confer benefits also, one giving the body and the other the mind or soul. All ætherial spaces then, as far as the moon, are provided for and managed by the son or soul of the Great Ruler, the consummation or perfection of his evolution or creation.

"Next, there arose a second Ruler from the universal Seed, far inferior to the first, but greater than all below him, except the Sonship which still remained in the Seed." This was the Ruler of the sublunary spaces, from the moon to the earth. This Ruler is called effable, because men can speak of him with understanding, and the space over which he rules is named the Hebdomad. And the second Ruler also "brought forth a Son far greater than himself from the universal Seed, in like manner to the first," and the lower creation was ordered in the same manner as the higher.

As to the earth, the conglomeration of the seed-mixture is still in our own stage or space, and the things that come to pass in this state of existence "come to pass according to nature, as having been primarily uttered by Him who hath planned the fitting time and form and manner of utterance of the things that were to be uttered. Of things here on the earth, then, there is no special chief or manager or creator, for sufficient for them is that plan which the God beyond being laid down when he deposited the universal Seed."

That is to say, that the earth-stage is the moment between the past and future, the turning-point of all choice, the field of new karma; here all things verily are in the hand of God alone, in the highest sense. Thus does Basilides avoid the difficulties both of fate and free-will absolute.

G. R. S. MEAD.

To be continued.)

THE WORLD'S FAIRY LORE.

THOSE who have not turned their attention to the beliefs of the peasantry, and to the nursery tales told to the children of gentle and simple alike, are probably little aware of the most salient facts concerning them. That there are such things as folk-lore tales, they know. Their knowledge stops there.

A minority of people know that there are at least forty-two variants of the child's story of "Cinderella." Those who are vaguely aware of the wide diffusion of fairy legend, have never regarded these tales as being proper subjects for serious study and grave dispute.

Nevertheless, the members of the English Folk-lore Society devote considerable attention to these legends; and the folk-lore literature is both wide and erudite.

Mr. E. S. Hartland, in his *Science of Fairy Tales*, demonstrates what careful criticism and comparison will do towards the elucidation of the myth.

G. W. Cox in his *Mythology of the Aryan Nations*, and Professor A. D. Gubernatis in his exhaustive works on kindred subjects, see in nearly all these tales the personification of the powers of nature by a savage people.

These authorities hold that primitive man, noting natural phenomena of varied kinds, wove romances concerning them, and translated these every-day occurrences, through the medium of his own consciousness, into the fairy tale.

It would be presumptuous in me to dispute with such authorities. I would only point out one or two possible clues to the underlying meaning of the myths. In doing this I would use the light of such teaching as we, as students of theosophic philosophy, have received and understood.

Let us consider,

1. The universal diffusion of these tales.

2. Are some of the touches in the stories compatible with the traits pointed out by Mr. Hartland as characteristic of the savage?

3. What are the characteristics of the undeveloped person, as regards fancy and imagination?

4. What points in these tales are to be attributed directly to half-forgotten and distorted occult teaching concerning the laws of nature?

We find these tales in England, Wales, Scotland and Ireland, in France, Germany, Russia, Spain, Portugal, Denmark, Finland, Iceland, Greece, Austria and Poland. We find them also among the gypsies. Variants of the same stories are found in Lapland, Swabia, Bulgaria and Lithuania—they are in the Rabbinical books, in the Arthurian legends, in New Zealand, Australia, and North and South America; among the Maoris, the Esquimaux, and in the West Indies. The Bretons have their variants. The Chinese and Japanese are among the band. All over India and Africa are found such stories. The tales of the Punjaub present most interesting features. They are in Persia. They are in Pomerania, Sweden, Norway, Switzerland, Italy and Transylvania. They were told in Ancient Rome. They were told by Gervase of Tilbury in the thirteenth century.

One of these tales is repeated, with very little variation, in modern Cornwall, namely the story of "Cherry of Zennor" a tale which carries a very sound moral lesson.

These legends often inculcate a useful moral. One of the exceptions is very curious. I refer to the tale of *The Clever Thief*. This story is told by Heredotus, under the title of *Rhampsinitus*. It is traced to Egypt by Professor Maspero (*Contes Populaires de l'Egypte ancienne*), who states the name to be a Greek form of Ram-sio-si-nit, or Ramses, the son of Nit. The story also appears in Cyprus, in India, in Tibet, and in Ireland, under the title of *The Shifty Lord*. The tale is given in Mr. Ralston's translation of A. von Schiefner's volume of *Tibetan Folk Tales from the Bkah Hgyur*.

The author of *The Mythology of Aryan Nations* gives an interesting explanation of this story. Only, in my humble judgment, the conclusion at which he arrives raises a fresh difficulty. By reason of its comparative subtlety of thought, it seems to be an unlikely key with which to unlock the wisdom of a savage.

Always assuming, as do these commentators, that the extremely primitive man was responsible for the primal thought enshrined in the tales, it becomes necessary to make that thought excessively simple. If the savage was responsible only for the form and the auxiliary thought, the local colouring and scenic effects, then the matter becomes very different.

The following is a quotation from the *Mythology of Aryan Nations:* "There is scarcely an important feature in it (*i.e.*, modern fairy mythology) which has not its parallel in the so-called classical mythology of Greece and Rome." Mr. Baring Gould remarks, in his book on *Were-wolves:* "When a form of superstition is prevalent everywhere, and in all ages, it must rest upon a foundation of fact." This seems to be reasonable. For the observable laws of nature, which hold good in all lands, would surely give rise to a consonance of legend. Only, where shall we find these competent observers to set forth the germ-truth, to be dressed and re-dressed by the tale-tellers of all ages?

Shall we seek such an one among simple semi-savages, hunting, eating, drinking, sleeping, and living a rudimentary life of the senses alone? How shall we explain the universality of legend?

When a tale is incorporated with the very genius of a people, it is rarely imparted from without. Its germ is sown in infant days. It grows with the growth of the nation. It is distorted as social life and human nature are distorted and warped by pressure from without, and pressure from within. It takes local colouring from their customs. Like a ray of light shining through tinted glass, it takes the hue of their thoughts.

The customs of the various nations have not been borne round the world by travellers, to be grafted in all lands. It is surprising to note how the varied English counties and French departments keep their distinctive customs, dishes and patois. Why should mere romances be so carried about the world in days when locomotion was slow and difficult?

Then as to the evolution of the myth. In days when there was no printing press, the tale-teller was yet in request. Mr. Hartland's view calls up a picture of the savage community gathered round the camp fire in the primeval forest. From such a group steps forth the romancist—the novelist in embryo—the man endowed with a livelier fancy than his fellows, with a picture-making trick at least, if not with the desire of diving down amid the motives and emotions of his fellow savages, and showing them the why and wherefore of their deeds.

Perhaps this picture is not an utterly untrue one. Mr. Hartland bids us observe that in these savage stories the animals are endowed with human motives and emotions; that the primitive tale-teller was quite unaware of the gulf dividing the animal from the human kingdoms. His beasts and birds, his gnomes and elves, have like passions with himself. Says Mr. Baring Gould: "Our forefathers failed to detect the line of demarcation between instinct and reason." Perhaps it would not be too much to say that their sons have not yet learnt to draw the said line very accurately.

All these experienced critics ascribe the myth to the bewilderment caused by meteorological phenomena, and to the fact that the savage endows all things with the same emotions as those experienced by himself. The belief in metempsychosis is also ascribed by Mr. Baring Gould to the latter cause.

Now I do not presume to say that these distinguished students of folk-lore are wrong. But let us see whether we can discover any points in the undeveloped person, and in these tales, which formed the theory of the one having been solely responsible for the other. I will take my second and my third points together.

What are the imaginative qualities of the exceedingly undeveloped person? To this I answer—either very slight or altogether nil. Anyone who has observed such people must have been struck by their lack of imagination. They may be exceedingly receptive. Impress them with an imaginary terror, and those with any sensitiveness of the nervous system will readily believe, and be greatly alarmed. Animals are often receptive of such impressions. Let any rider suffer him or herself to be frightened, and see how readily that impression will communicate itself to the horse. It is not necessary to shrink back, nor to manifest terror, in order to tell a savage animal that it is feared. But neither the animal nor the savage are capable of the play of imagination, much less of the subtle allegorical thought that lies at the back of these myths. They are coloured by the impressions and stamped with the customs of those who have handed them down through the centuries. But they were adapted by more developed minds for the charming and impressing of an infant race.

Take the innumerable tales of celestial brides. Sometimes the story is of a celestial bridegroom. All these tales have their masculine and feminine variants; but the germ idea is the same. The Swan maiden myth is in all lands. It is in Persia, Sweden, Transylvania, Russia, Pomerania, Syria, Burmah, the Celebes Islands, India and Wales. It is found among the Samoyeds and the Passamaquoddies. The tales vary, the myth is the same. In almost all these stories the number seven plays a part; as, for example, there are seven islands to which the bride is caught away.

In every case the bridegroom wins his bride—usually her garment makes a magnetic link whereby he holds her—and is parted from her. Usually this parting comes about through his mother. In Guiana the Swan maiden bride bears her husband above the skies. He, desiring to see his mother, is banished thence. He is finally borne back again, and is there slain by a young warrior, *like himself*, which is his son. In some variants the bride is occasionally metamorphosed into a serpent. At such times the bridegroom is forbidden to enter her presence. In other versions he is forbidden to gaze upon her when she is unclothed. Generally it is the mother who persuades her son to break this taboo. In yet another version, the heavenly bride instructs her earthly bridegroom to tend the child of their union. It is his dislike of this task which causes her to take the child, and leave him.

Mr. Hartland comments upon this, saying that in savage tribes the mother is the owner of the child. Paternal rights are not recognized, nor paternal duties enforced, any more than they are in the animal kingdom, for in the majority of cases the father does not care for the young. We have an indication of this state of affairs in the bridegroom's scorn at being requested to care for his child.

But there is no indication that the celestial bride's request was unreasonable. Moreover, if this be so, and the savage only recorded what he saw—which, if he alone created the tale, is most probable—why do we find this singular and often malicious part played by the mother?

The natural tendency of the savage is to materialize and anthropomorphize all that he sees. The present day European savage ascribes his own motives to every person with whom he comes into contact. He does not spiritualize nor allegorize. He crudely notes the more obvious parts of those things which he sees. The savage mother would not invariably act in opposition to the interests of her child. Mr. Hartland says that the savage imputes his own motives, his own sensations, to the beasts. It may be so; but whence then come touches to which the savage is a stranger? When the rudimentary human creature hears the thunder, he believes his deity to be shouting in anger, as he himself shouts. He dowers his god with hatred, favouritism, rage; he manifests his own passion by shouts or blows; so his god does the like. But that is not imagination, it is the lack of such a faculty. Whence then this conception of the mother as the temptress? Whence this motive of the bride, caught up above the skies, as to some enchanted island, and won again by the bridegroom after struggles in which water plays an almost invariable part, and in which the fighting of monsters coming forth from the sea is often a feature? Lastly, what is the meaning of that variant in which we have the scorn of the child, and the final slaying of the husband by the young warrior above the skies?

Let us view this story in the light of theosophic teaching.

It becomes the Cupid and Psyche myth, save that the bride is celestial, and the bridegroom earthly. Let this bride stand for Divine Wisdom, or for spiritual âtmic force. The earthly bridegroom is the personality, and the "mother" stands for matter—Kâma, the temptress, sometimes blindly, sometimes wilfully malignant, according to the amount of will and mentality put into the action.

She urges her son to break the taboo with regard to his celestial bride—in other words, tò profane the Divine Wisdom for unworthy ends, and from selfish motives. She it is who parts the bride and bridegroom. The seas and wilderness traversed by the bridegroom may well stand for the astral plane, which he must conquer ere he regains his bride.

Now, as to the child. What is indeed the result of the union of spirit and matter—of heaven and earth? Is it not the permanent individuality, the forming of the causal body of man? Is it not the part of the earthly personality to "tend" this "child"? Is not scorn of that task the cause of the parting of the personality from the presence of the spiritual "Bride"? And when the difficulties are surmounted, would not this "child" who is "like the father," finally "slay" him "above the skies"? In other words, the personality would be merged in the glorified individuality, the finally perfected fruit of the union between heaven and earth.

But if we should accept this theory, what becomes of the primitive instincts of savage man? For a savage could not invent this allegory; it argues knowledge.

Mr. Hartland reckons among savage beliefs the following:

"That man consists of body and spirit." "That the spirit leaves the body in sleep." "That the universe swarms with beings embodied and disembodied"—a savage belief which I have heard seriously canvassed by no less a scientist than Professor Oliver Lodge. "That everything in the world has a spirit."

Now I venture to say that these beliefs are not natural to an unassisted savage. It is notorious that the undeveloped gain almost all their impressions from without, and are in the main materialistic. None of these authorities would be prepared to admit that a rudimentary race might pass through a psychic stage on the downward arc of evolution. The savage, as we know him, is materialistic. But if the savage tribe be the remnant of a simple race, now dying out, and once directly instructed by those who knew the workings of nature's laws, then it is easy to see how these deep conceptions sprang into existence, and were handed down, couched in a romantic form, and now greatly distorted.

In the *Mythologies of the Aryan Nations* it is stated that all these legends are solar myths and allegories of the forces of nature. As, for example, that in the curious story of the *Master Thief*, the thief is the air. If this be true, then the man who gave that myth was not a savage, not a crude thinker, though he gave it in a form suitable for such persons.

With all diffidence I would put forward my own theory on the point, which is that he was an Egyptian of great knowledge of the workings of Nature's laws, for the allegory is most ingenious and beautifully worked out. Professor Maspero, in pointing out the Egyptian origin, combats the objections of commentators by asserting (*a*) that temples in Egypt did possess hiding-places as described; (*b*) that Egyptians could wear beards if it pleased them; (*c*) that the soldiers who guarded the corpse would belong to a Lybian-tribe called Mation, and would be bearded.

Again, in Cox's *Mythology of the Aryan Nations*, it is stated that Grimm's tale of "The Nix of the Mill Pond" is a myth of the gradual lengthening of the days after the winter Solstice; and that the Priapas Myth (Priapas, son of Dionysos, Adonis, Hermes or Pan and Aphrodite, or the Maid Chianê) denotes simply the relations of the water with the wind or sun. But again, grant that this be true; such a tale is not the work of a savage.

"It is difficult," says Mr. Baring Gould, "to unlearn all that we know respecting meteorological phenomena."

I question whether the originator of the world's nursery tales had much to *un*learn respecting the forces of nature. It is this knowledge behind the tales which gives them their charm and their influence over the minds of many. There is something there for which one may dive down. Their quaint sweetness, and the insight they give into the thought and customs of the people, are minor attractions.

I remember well when I was but eight years old coming across a fanciful tale in which the author had seen fit to include two words from that sacred sentence of the East *Om mani padme hûm*. I can recall most distinctly the inexplicable fascination those words had for me. I felt their power and meaning, and now I know that it must have been because of that meaning that they stirred me as the rest of the tale did not, charming though it was.

And so, in a lesser degree, with these fairy myths. Behind them lies a meaning; and the thought of those who knew that meaning yet cleaves to them and gives them life. And so, distorted, mingled with much folly, they live through the centuries.

They are still full of interest for the student; especially such tales as treat of the exterior soul, with its wrappings, and the distinctive characteristics of the Indian tales. These subjects, and the methods whereby local custom and racial influences have coloured them, I hope to take up upon some future occasion.

IVY HOOPER.

THE PHÆDO OF PLATO.

(*Continued from p.* 233.)

THESE three vehicles are appropriated in the first place to the mundane soul, whose body is the entire universe. In this connection they are all perpetual, as subsisting continually and without diminution according to their totality in the universe, although with constant generation and corruption of parts. Further, they are ascribed to every total nature, which subsists as a world within the world; and here also they subsist perpetually in relation to the wholeness of the nature from which they are suspended. Of such a nature is the planet which we now inhabit. And as the mundane elements in their totality constitute the three vehicles of the universal soul, so all the elements within the terrestrial sphere constitute those of the earth-soul. Under every total soul subsisting as a part of the universe, is arranged a multitude of partial souls, whose vehicles are formed from the elements which in their entirety form the vehicles of that total soul. Now, with respect to ourselves, seeing that this planet is in itself a kind of lesser universe, comprising parts corresponding to all the parts of the cosmos, it is perhaps unnecessary to separate our mundane existence from that of the planet. In this case, we must regard the ætherial or luciform vehicle of our planet as being, to us, the "kindred star" to which Plato alludes in the *Timæus*, and in which our souls energize in their ætherial vehicles. The aerial body of the earth-planet will then correspond to the upper earth of the *Phædo*, which is situated "at the summit of the air," *i.e.*, beyond the sphere of our gross elements; and here also we shall dwell in our aerial vehicles, just as in our terrestrial bodies we inhabit the gross body of the earth. For that he does not intend the ætherial vehicle by the upper earth, is perhaps to be inferred from his mention of the elements which are there, and from the fact that its inhabitants are not represented as immortal, although far longer lived than we.*

It is right, however, to interpret our text also in a wider sense. For by the many hollow places, into which the dregs of the pure earth continually flow, Plato clearly intimates the lowest plane of material existence, and by the upper earth the higher regions of the aerial plane, the state of souls who are purified from the grosser stains of earth, although not yet liberated from the irrational and mortal nature. His description of this upper earth, with its trees and minerals, and wondrous colours, and the excellent temperament of its seasons, indicates its correspondence on a higher plane with the earth which we inhabit; since these correspondences exist upon every plane, according to the Hermetic saying, "That which is below is as that which is above, and that above as that below, that the marvel of one thing may be accomplished." The statement that this pure earth, surveyed from above, appears like a ball covered with twelve skins, contains, according to Proclus,† an allusion to the figure of the dodecahedron. It will be remembered that in the *Timæus* the four material elements are said to be generated from triangles. The regular dodecahedron is a solid figure bounded by twelve equal and regular pentagons, and is, of all solid figures containing angles, the nearest in resemblance to a sphere. But the sphere is a symbol of intellectual wholeness. and the dodecahedron, therefore, as applied to the earth, is an emblem at once of its intellectual source and its material condition.

"This [upper] earth too," says Socrates, "contains many other animals and men, some of whom inhabit its middle parts; others dwell about the air, as we do about the sea; and others reside in islands which the air flows round, and which are situated not far from the continent." By these various abodes we are to understand the various degrees of materiality existing in the aerial plane, since there, as here, lives vary in degrees of purity, the highest approaching more nearly to the celestial state, the lowest to the terrestrial. And

* He says also, that "what air is to us, that æther is to the inhabitants of this pure earth," implying thereby that as our present vehicles are not aerial, neither are theirs ætherial. Proclus moreover observes: "that he (Plato) also knew another man, *viz.*, the soul which uses the middle [or aerial] vehicle, is evident from the *Phædo*, where he says that men dwell on the summit of the earth, who live for a much longer time than the men who are here." (*On the Timæus*, vol. ii. p. 426.)

† *On the Timæus*, vol. ii. p. 290.

when he speaks of the beautiful colours with which this upper earth is adorned, so combined that "one particular various form of the earth continually presents itself to the view;" and again, of the pure stones and metals and other things which are there, "diffused everywhere throughout the earth;" he seems to indicate the nature of the senses on the aerial plane, which are not separate as with us, but united in one common sense, diffused through every part of the vehicle.

But the highest form of life on the aerial plane is perhaps intimated by a residence in "islands which the air flows round," and these islands are the same with the Islands of the Blessed, mentioned by Plato in the *Gorgias*. For it is there said that "the man who has passed through life in a just and holy manner, when he dies, departing to the Islands of the Blessed, shall dwell in all felicity, removed from evil."* Furthermore, these islands are identical with the Elysian Fields, and it will be interesting to compare Virgil's description of Elysium with Plato's of the upper earth:

"So, all being done, the Goddess' gift well paid in manner meet,
They come into a joyous land, and greensward fair and sweet
Amid the happiness of groves, the blessèd dwelling-place.
Therein a more abundant heaven clothes all the meadows' face
With purple light, and their own sun and their own stars they
have."†

So also Plato asserts of the dwellers upon the upper earth, that "the sun and moon and stars are seen by them such as they really are, and in every other respect their felicity is of a correspondent nature." But the expression "such as they really are" must be taken relatively, since he is not here speaking of intelligible essences, and refers to the purity of their manifestation on this plane; as Virgil's "solemque suum, sua sidera, nôrunt" implies that upon every plane the manifestation is peculiar and appropriate thereto.

Again, these inhabitants of the upper earth "have groves and temples of the Gods, in which the Gods dwell in reality; and likewise oracles and divinations, and sensible perceptions of the Gods, and such-like associations with them." We may assume in the first

* Taylor's *Plato*, vol. iv. p. 450.

† *Æneid*, Book vi. William Morris's translation.

place from these statements that souls which have risen to the aerial plane perceive more clearly than those which are still plunged in the mire of gross matter the divine nature which is present in everything. But by a sensible perception of the Gods is meant, of course, a sensible perception of the vehicles which they employ, since these only are cognizable by sense. In the *Timæus* Plato divides the mundane deities into two orders—"such as visibly revolve, and such as become visible when they please." The former are the Gods of the starry spheres and of the planets, of whom we have already spoken. The latter are the sublunary Gods, who proceed, as powers of the supermundane deities, into the universe, and preside over all that is subject to the law of generation and corruption; for the term "sublunary" must here be referred rather to a state than to a place, since the moon is regarded as the cause of generation and corruption, and the monad of the sublunary Gods. But by the Gods to whom he assigns a location in groves and temples, and sensible communications with mortals, I think it probable that Plato signifies dæmons who energize in aerial as well as in ætherial vehicles. "For every mundane God," says Proclus, "is the leader of a certain dæmonic order, to which he proximately imparts his power; *viz.*, if he is a demiurgic God, he imparts a demiurgic power; if immutable, an undefiled power; if telesiurgic, a perfective power. And about each of the divinities there is an innumerable multitude of dæmons, which are dignified with the same appellations as their leading Gods. Hence they rejoice when they are called by the names of Zeus, Apollo, Hermes, etc., as expressing the idiom or peculiarity of their proper deities. And from these mortal natures also participate of divine influxions."*

So much, then, for the upper parts of the earth. But there is more yet to be said about the lower parts, the cavities into which flow the dregs of earth, and one of which we now inhabit. For whereas it is said that of these cavities some are deeper and others less deep than this place of our abode, by these are signified states of the soul more or less profoundly plunged in the darkness of matter and the material life. And whereas they are said to be connected by rivers flowing underground, by this is denoted the material condition common to them all; since, as earth is a symbol

* Taylor's *Plato*, vol. i. p. 18 *note*.

of the material nature, and water of generation, the subterranean rivers clearly symbolize the nature of generation on the lowest material plane. By the rivers of fire is perhaps intimated a passional and violent nature, and by those of mud a nature more grossly sensual and bestial. And by the continual oscillation upwards and downwards is meant the unstable and fluctuating character of material life.

The gulf into which the rivers discharge themselves is denominated Tartarus, and is described as a mighty chasm, perforated through the whole earth. By this is signified the lowest depth of the material condition, the very bottomless pit; for, in the words of Proclus, "to matter there is neither bound, nor bottom, nor a seat, as being infinite, unstable and indefinite."* Into this chasm the rivers flow, and from thence they flow again upwards; for this is the centre or lowest point of the universe, whence the progression is again upwards towards the circumference. And it is bottomless also for this reason, that the bottom of Tartarus, could it be supposed to exist, would be absolute evil, which is equivalent to absolute nothingness; for evil, in so far as it has an existence, exists only by a certain participation of good. The air which accompanies the rivers in their course denotes the irrational nature, and its vehicle, the aerial body, by which the soul descends into terrestrial life. By the longer and shorter courses of the rivers about the earth we may perhaps understand the varying periods of our incarnations; and lastly, the places of their influx into Tartarus are deeper than those of their efflux, inasmuch as the soul which descends is in a worse condition than the ascending soul, though the ascent be from the pit itself.

That the rivers are many and various accords with the manifold variety of material life, but the four great rivers which are distinguished by name sum up in themselves the powers of all the rest. For these rivers correspond with the four elements, which have again their correspondences as elements on every plane of existence. The first river is Ocean, which encompasses the whole earth; and this corresponds with the element of water, and symbolizes a life conversant with generation and corruption. But the second river which flows in a contrary direction to the first, is called Acheron, the

* *On the Timæus*, vol. i. p. 324.

River of Woe; it corresponds with the element of air, and is a symbol of death, which separates the aerial body from its earthly shell. The third is Pyriphlegethon, the River of Flaming Fire, and it symbolizes in Tartarus the passion which burns and consumes, being as it were, a kind of inverted reflection of its higher correspondences, the celestial fire which is life, and the supercelestial which is love.* Cocytus, the River of Wailing, is the fourth and last of the Tartarean streams, and the place whereinto its waters are discharged is denominated Styx, the Abhorred. Cocytus corresponds with the element of earth, and signifies the lowest depth of all, a nature sunk in the very mire of sense, too gross and sluggish for the flames of Phlegethon, which is therefore said to run in a contrary course. By the dark-blue colour of Styx is denoted the darkness of matter, and it is interesting in connection with our interpretation to note that in the Greek the word is used to signify extreme cold. So, too, in Dante's "Inferno," the name of Cocytus is given to the frozen lake which forms the ninth and lowest circle of Hell.

The Acherusian marsh, into which the waters of Acheron flow, is the place (*i.e.*, state) of purgation, where souls which have passed a middle kind of life, neither excellently good nor eminently bad, dwell after death in their aerial vehicles; "till being purified, and having suffered punishment for any injuries they may have committed, they are enlarged; and each receives the reward of his beneficence, according to his deserts." This state of purgation is symbolized by a marsh, because souls departing from their earthly bodies are still for the most part clogged and weighted by the moisture of the lower life, and need a process of purgation before they are fitted to ascend to the pure regions of the upper earth. But more sinful souls are cast into Tartarus, and rising again from thence, are purged in the floods of Pyriphlegethon and Cocytus, until they, too, are received into the Acherusian marsh and "find an end to their maladies." As to Plato's assertion that souls incurably evil are *never* discharged from Tartarus, and the similar statement which occurs in the Gorgias, it is best to believe, with Olympiodorus, that he does not intend an eternity of punishment, but a state

* Elementaris [ignis] urit, cœlestis vivificat, supercœlestis amat.—*Pico della Mirandola.*

enduring throughout an entire mundane period, *i.e.*, a period of which the beginning and end are marked by the conjunction of the revolutions of the seven planets with the inerratic sphere. But souls which have lived "most excellently with respect to piety," are restored to the abodes of the upper earth, whence they descend to this terrestrial plane; since the ascent is made by the same media as the descent. "And among these," says Socrates, "those who are sufficiently purified by philosophy shall live without bodies through the whole of the succeeding time, and shall arrive at habitations yet more beautiful than these, which it is neither easy to describe, nor is the present time sufficient for such an undertaking."

It is possible that by these habitations yet more beautiful, where the soul abides without body, Plato intimates the celestial and ætherial state of which we have spoken; since the aerial vehicle may be regarded as the first body, accurately speaking, of the soul—*i.e.*, its first material vehicle; and, indeed, in one passage of his Commentary on the *Timæus*, Proclus himself thus defines it. This ætherial state is the highest mundane condition of the soul, which is then "co-arranged with the mundane powers of its God," and rules the world in conjunction with deity. But there is a yet higher state, when the soul is reunited with its intellectual source. Taylor has here the following note: "Those who have lived a holy and guiltless life, without philosophy, will after death dwell on the summit of the earth; and their bodies will consequently consist of the most attenuated air. Those who have philosophized politically, says Olympiodorus, will live in the heavens with luciform [*i.e.*, ætherial] bodies. And those that are perfectly purified will be restored to the supermundane place, without bodies." We may add that as the planes of being interpenetrate each other, so also do the states which they represent; that in so far as the soul philosophizes politically, it is necessarily connected with mundane concerns, and that the perfection of this state is attained when the soul's connection with the world has become, like that of the Gods, wholly guardian and providential. It is in this respect said to dwell in its ætherial vehicle. But in so far as the soul philosophizes cathartically, it elevates itself above the nature of body; and in so far as it philosophizes theoretically and paradigmatically it is raised into the region of pure intellect, and to intelligible essence.

There is a passage in Virgil's *Æneid* (vi. 735-751) respecting the life after death, which may be profitably compared in detail with this portion of the *Phædo*. I translate, therefore, as closely as possible.

"But even when with the last light life has departed from them, not yet does all evil, nor all the plagues of body, totally forsake the unhappy souls; and many evils, long engrained, must needs grow and adhere within them in wondrous ways. Therefore are they plagued with punishments, and pay the penalties of their former sins. Some are exposed, suspended, to the empty winds; of others the stain of guilt is washed away beneath a mighty flood, or burned out with fire. We suffer each his own Manes [*i.e.*, Karma]: thence are we sent through wide Elysium, and few in number we possess the joyful fields; until the long course of time, when the cycle is accomplished, has removed the engrained ill, and left the unmixed ætherial sense, and the flame of pure air. All these souls, when for a thousand years they have turned the wheel of time, a God calls forth in a great company to the river Lethe; that, nought remembering, they may revisit the vaulted world above [*i.e.*, this earth], and may become again desirous of returning into bodies."

My task is now ended, for the remaining portion of the *Phædo* needs no comment. I will say only that the manner of Socrates' death is an argument for immortality at least as powerful as any of those which preceded it. For, as Mr. Rolleston excellently observes: 'Unless the soul is in some sense immortal, Socrates and all martyrs who have preceded and followed him were the victims of a miserable delusion. Man has been cheated by the deepest instincts of his heart, and it is a fundamental belief with Plato that the universe does not cheat."* In the last words of the philosopher his faith shines clearly forth. "Crito," he said, "we owe a cock to Æsculapius. Discharge this debt, therefore, for me, and do not neglect it." To Æsculapius the Healer it was the ancient wont to sacrifice a cock upon recovery from sickness; and thus to Socrates, consistent to the end, death presented itself no otherwise than as a happy recovery from the malady of earthly life.

W. C. WARD.

* *Selections from Plato*, Introduction, p. xxii.

A LINK IN THE CHAIN.

OUR teacher Madame Blavatsky used often to say that more than one attempt had been made by the Great White Lodge in times past to spread the truths in Their keeping among the nations of the West, but that none of these attempts had achieved any great measure of success, and hence that the present effort, taking the form of our own Theosophical movement, had been forced as it were to begin afresh, starting from zero. Now although various students in our ranks have pointed with more or less convincing force to the many similarities, points of contact, nay even to actual identities discoverable between our own Theosophical teachings and those of earlier mystics here in Europe, none of us, so far as I am aware, had succeeded in definitely proving any direct and traceable line of connection, on the physical plane, between the West and East, any definite mystic organization in the East along these lines. But in the course of some literary researches concerning the famous Cagliostro upon which she is engaged, Mrs. Cooper-Oakley has had the good fortune to come across a curious little book which seems to supply at least one link in the chain, and to show that this direct connection may be actually traceable—at least in the second half of last century—with far more clearness and certainty than any of us had suspected. At her request I have undertaken the task of writing a short article for LUCIFER giving some account of the book in question, and calling attention to what at present seem the most salient points in it which bear upon the question before us.

It must be premised that towards the close of last century, say from 1770 to the outbreak of the French Revolution and even later, there is abundant evidence to show the existence of a great, almost feverish activity among the various Masonic, quasi-Masonic, Rosicrucian and other secret organizations with which the continent, especially Germany, Austria, Italy and France, was then honeycombed. All sorts and kinds of such societies sprang up, mushroom-like, on every side, and naturally enough, as the public interest in such matters was almost at fever heat, quantities of "revelations," "exposures" and controversial literature of all kinds poured forth from the press. The Jesuits seem to have taken an active hand in the game,—or at all events were credited with so doing—and as these various organizations did not escape from coming into mutual conflict, one of the very commonest accusations which each side hurled at the other was that of "Jesuitism," of being secretly influenced, guided and controlled by the ubiquitous Jesuits to the end of distorting and destroying Freemasonry, Rosicrucianism, or whatever it might be. And along with this charge of being "Jesuits in disguise" went naturally enough that of bad citizenship, of holding principles and teaching doctrines incompatible with decent conduct as the members of a civilized state, and especially antagonistic to the principles of Christianity—as then understood.

The booklet with which we are here concerned belongs more or less to this class of polemical literature, as its title, which runs as follows, shows: "Abfertigung an den ungenannten Verfasser der verbreiteten sogenannten: Authentische Nachricht von den Ritter- und Brüder-Eingeweihten aus Asien; von Hans Heinrich, Freiherrn von Ecker und Eckhoffen." * I have given the title-page at length in its somewhat cumbrous old German because it is almost impossible to convey in English any idea of its flavour. In substance it may be best rendered in rather slangy English thus: "A settler for the anonymous author of the so-called, widely circulated, pamphlet: Authentic information concerning the Initiated Knights and Brothers from Asia, etc."

In his preface the Freiherr explains that as his name and address are given in the pamphlet in question, and he is directly and personally challenged by name, he feels it impossible to pass it by with the contemptuous silence it deserves, and therefore once and for all he will answer the challenge, after which neither he nor his associates will deign to take any further notice of anonymous attacks. He then proceeds to reprint his anonymous antagonist's pamphlet in full—it contains some twenty small octavo pages of preface and general matter *plus* thirty-two pages of lengthy extracts from what

* Hamburg. Auf Kosten des Verfassers, 1788.

purport to be the statutes and instructions of the "Brothers from Asia," with notes and comments by the anonymous writer. These are followed by the Freiherr's reply, which extends to about sixty pages. In this reply the Freiherr states that he is a member of the order in question, gives an account of how he came to join it, and, what is most important for our purpose, admits that the statutes and instructions as printed in his adversary's pamphlet are on the whole authentic and correct, though erroneous on some points; while he asserts also that the extracts are deliberately chosen and arranged in a wrong manner, so as to place the order in question in as false a light as possible. This, however, is of small importance for our immediate purpose, as it is some of the points in the statutes which the Freiherr admits without question which seem to have an interest for us as members of the Theosophical Society. It must, however, be borne in mind that this organization rested upon a specific masonic basis, and required the degree of Master-mason as a prior qualification for its membership. The term "Brother," therefore, used in its statutes most probably means "Brother Mason."

Its first articles run thus:

"1. Every Brother, of whatsoever religion, social status or system, is admissible to the order, provided only he be a noble-thinking, right-living and true man of honour. This chiefly because the welfare and happiness of men, which is the only object of our system, cannot be dependent upon the religion in which a man is born, nor the social position in which he is brought up.

"2. Every such Brother must be duly legitimated as Knight and Master-mason in some regular, ordinary Melchisedec or St. John's Lodge of Freemasons.

"3. By the name Melchisedec Lodge we mean such Masonic Lodges as admit to membership Jews, Turks, Persians, Armenians, Copts, and so on, of whom there are many in Italy, Holland, England, Portugal and Spain. For the order is designed for the whole of Europe for the great cause of Unity. The St. John's Lodges, as is known, consist only of Christians."

There seems to be a curious identity between the keynote struck in these basic statutes and that which has so long been the essential basis of our own movement. Granting that this "Order of the Brothers from Asia" was restricted to Freemasons, yet universality, unlimited by race, religion or station, is so emphatically the keynote struck that we can hardly wonder at the indignant astonishment which the anonymous attacker displays in a footnote to these articles, where he points out that the first, fundamental law of every regular, working Lodge of Freemasons of all kinds is that *only* Christians can be admitted to membership. To this in his reply the Freiherr retorts that there *are*, as a matter of fact, Masonic Lodges in all the countries named, as well as Lodges in Europe, notably in Spain, which do admit to their membership non-Christians of all kinds, and he reminds his opponent of the sentence which he himself quotes elsewhere from the Book of Constitutions of English Masonry, which runs: "But since Masonry is to be found among all peoples, even those of other religions, etc." In addition the Freiherr gives several names of well-known Jews who, remaining non-Christians, have been admitted to membership in regular Masonic Lodges.

These points to us of interest, like some of those which will follow, as helping establish an identity of origin between the impulse which worked in and through this order of the "Brothers from Asia," and that which inspires our own Society. For it by no means follows that because an order calls itself the "Brothers from Asia," it is therefore connected with the Great Lodge; although when once an identity of teaching, of spirit and purpose, of keynote, has been established by other evidence, then the name itself becomes of real significance. So we will pass on to some other points bearing upon this question.

With regard to the knowledge in the possession of the order the statutes say:

"(6). In respect to the knowledge in its possession, the order has only the following declaration to make.

"(*a*). That the order possesses no other secrets than the true moral and physical explanations of the hieroglyphics of the most venerable order of Knights and Brother Freemasons, because the order as such is concerned with no other truths than these. (*b*). That the order itself is nothing more than a brotherly union of all honourable and separated children of men, who are striving with one accord to achieve the perfecting of man in his natural condition and the discovery of all healing things and natural secrets, towards the attaining whereof the order will also impart instruction to each man gratis, according to his individual nature."

When we remember, as Madame Blavatsky so often said, and as any Mason can verify for himself, that the symbols and hieroglyphics of Freemasonry, *fully* understood, contain the whole of the Secret Doctrine and our modern Theosophy in the form of glyph and symbol, it seems clear that the teaching to be imparted in this order was identical with what we now study as the Wisdom Religion or Theosophy, and that the programme outlined in clause (*b*) was nothing less than what we should call the preparation for the Path, for even the alchemists considered the perfecting of man as the *Magnum Opus*, the crown of Occult teaching and knowledge. That this is the correct view of the meaning of the clause is proved by the Freiherr's explanations in reply to a footnote upon it by his opponent, in which the latter tries to make out that what is meant is the making of gold. This the Freiherr indignantly repudiates, alluding to a secret initiation which is *not* miraculous, but giving no more detailed explanation. Still a careful consideration of all that he says in reply to his opponent about the order, the demands which it makes upon its members, the teaching which it gives, especially the constant insistence upon the ethical and moral side of development, show an identity of purpose, spirit and teaching between our own theosophical movement and this last-century order, so strong as to convince me that the two movements owe their inception and inspiration to one and the same source.

It will therefore be of interest to us to piece together one or two other points in relation to this order of the "Brothers from Asia," which can be gathered from the Freiherr's reply.

In the first place he tells us that the Asiatic Brothers do exist, that he himself has the honour of belonging to them, and that they possess the full and final explanations of all and each of the symbols and hieroglyphics in the three grades of regular Freemasonry. But, he says, the Asiatic Brothers are not Rosicrucians, nor would the Rosicrucians recognize them as a branch of their society.

He further remarks that the symbols in Masonry have also a physical meaning, and that those who know this meaning are among the greatest and most learned searchers into nature's secrets. Why then do not they publish their knowledge to the world?

Just, he replies, because they *are* secrets—a not very enlightening reply.

In relation to Masonry he lays stress upon the point that, whatever people in general may think, the fact remains that there *are* secrets in and concerning good—ethical good—which Masonry teaches, though not perhaps in all their fulness.

Regarding the history of the Asiatic Brothers, the Freiherr gives some particulars which are not without interest, as it may lead perhaps to the discovery of further and fuller sources of information. He first points out that the truths and teachings which are veiled under the symbols of Freemasonry must be older than these symbols, and hence, since it is precisely these truths themselves which the Asiatic Brothers have in their keeping, this knowledge must be older than Freemasonry itself, although, as in the case of the latter, its custodians have not always formed a definite and outwardly organized body such as the present order of the Asiatic Brothers. But, he says, even that order dates back to the earliest antiquity in the East, whence, as he points out, Freemasonry itself came originally. He then goes on to say that he has himself seen documentary evidence proving that in A.D. 1510, 1638, 1752, and 1755, definite attempts were made to organize a branch of the order in Europe, and he mentions several names in connection with these efforts, *e.g.*, Odorat the Scot, Hans Wühren of Hall on the Inn and others. These attempts to transplant the Eastern Wisdom and its teachings into Europe were unsuccessful, one at least of them being abandoned for a curious reason. It had been proposed to form a sort of inner school in Freemasonry with classes and divisions, to give people definite teaching and instruction before they actually entered the Asiatic Order, in return for certain definite payments or instruction fees. But this proposal, which came from the European side, was rejected by the Asiatic Brothers on account of the money payments it involved, as among them no such payments were customary or even permissible. And then the Freiherr continues in a passage which seems worth translating textually:

"Such a transplanting of this most ancient knowledge of the East into European soil was naturally bound to involve all the greater difficulties the more the progress made in other branches of science and the differing character of the periods and nationalities concerned, had to be taken into account. Still, it seemed to us unpardonable, in view of the various catastrophes to which Masonry had been exposed in Europe, and in view of the crises in which it was actually involved, not to admit at least some worthy men in our hemisphere to a share in these true and complete explanations of Masonry. Whoever is at all acquainted with the many efforts made by Freemasons to attain this goal, will regard this matter with quite other eyes than the rest of the public, and therefore cannot blame this purely unselfish wish of ours."

And later on he gives us to understand that the mother-order in Asia consists of *seven* Lodges—a curious coincidence, at the least —while in conclusion I cannot do better than quote textually what he describes as the main and chief content of its laws:

"Art. 7. The chief content of all laws is, however: Honesty, brotherly love, loyalty, pity and compassion towards all in need, silence, self-denial, obedience, humility and modesty, prudence and watchfulness over heart and life, forgiveness of enemies, in short, the highest possible perfecting of oneself in one's station and calling, whether as ruler or subject, master or servant, alien or citizen in the state, father or husband, brother or son, friend, companion or neighbour; in short, every brother of our order shall honour God, the King, and the State, shall be a true friend of his brethren, a benefactor of humanity, a noble-minded seeker after truth—in one word, an honourable man in the fullest sense of the term."

If we compare this declaration with Madame Blavatsky's famous definition of the true Theosophy, the identity of spirit and inspiration is more than striking, and leaves little room for doubt that in this curious little book Mrs. Cooper-Oakley has discovered one of the links which go to form the great chain that unites the direct action of the Great Lodge upon the world in centuries that are passed, with the present movement in which we have the privilege of sharing.

BERTRAM KEIGHTLEY.

THE ÂKÂSHIC RECORDS.

ALTHOUGH it is well-known in Theosophical circles what is meant when we speak of âkâshic records, the word is in truth somewhat of a misnomer, for though the records are undoubtedly read from the âkâsha, yet it is not to it that they really belong. Still worse is the alternative title, "records of the astral light," which has sometimes been employed, for these records lie far beyond the astral plane, and all that can be obtained on it are only broken glimpses of a kind of double reflection of them, as will presently be explained.

Like so many others of our Theosophical terms, the word âkâsha has been very loosely used. In some of our earlier books it was considered as synonymous with astral light, and in others employed to signify any kind of invisible matter, from mûlaprakṛiti down to the physical ether. In later books its use has been restricted to the matter of the devachanic plane, and it is in that sense that the records may be spoken of as âkâshic, for although they are not originally made on that plane any more than on the astral, yet it is there that we first come definitely into contact with them and find it possible to do reliable work with them.

This subject of the âkâshic records is by no means an easy one to deal with, for it is one of that numerous class which requires for its perfect comprehension faculties of a far higher order than any which humanity has yet evolved. The real solution of its problems lies on planes far beyond any that we can possibly know at present, and any view that we take of it must necessarily be of the most imperfect character, since we cannot but look at it from below instead of from above. The idea which we form of it must therefore be only partial, yet it need not mislead us unless we allow ourselves to think of the tiny fragment which is all that we can see as though it were the perfect whole. If we are careful that such conceptions as we may form shall be accurate as far as they go, we shall have nothing to unlearn, though much to add, when in the course of our further progress we gradually acquire the higher wisdom. Be it understood then at the commencement that a thorough grasp of our subject is an impossibility at the present stage of our evolution, and that many points will arise as to which no exact explanation is yet obtainable, though it may often be possible to suggest analogies and to indicate the lines along which an explanation must lie.

Let us then try to carry back our thoughts to the beginning of this solar system to which we belong. We are all familiar with the ordinary astronomical theory of its origin—that which is commonly called the nebular hypothesis—according to which it first came into existence as a gigantic glowing nebula, of a diameter far exceeding that of the orbit of even the outermost of the planets, and then, as in the course of countless ages that enormous sphere gradually cooled and contracted, the system as we know it was formed. Occult science accepts that theory, in its broad outline, as correctly representing the purely physical side of the evolution of our system, but it would add that if we confine our attention to this physical side only we shall have a very incomplete and incoherent idea of what really happened. It would postulate, to begin with, that the exalted Being who undertakes the formation of a system (whom we sometimes call the Logos of the system) first of all forms in His mind a complete conception of the whole of it with all its successive chains. By the very act of forming that conception He calls the whole into simultaneous objective existence on the plane of His thought—a plane of course far above all those of which we know anything—from which the various globes descend when required into whatever state of further objectivity may be respectively destined for them. Unless we constantly bear in mind this fact of the real existence of the whole system from the very beginning on a higher plane, we shall be perpetually misunderstanding the physical evolution which we see taking place down here.

But occultism has more than this to teach us on the subject. It tells us not only that all this wonderful system to which we belong is called into existence by the Logos, both on lower and on higher planes, but also that its relation to Him is closer even than that, for it is absolutely a part of Him—a partial expression of Him upon the physical plane—and that the movement and energy of the whole system is *His* energy, and is all carried on within the limits of His aura. Stupendous as this conception is, it will yet not be wholly unthinkable to those of us who have made any study of the subject of the aura.

We are familiar with the idea that as a person progresses on the upward path his causal body, which is the determining limit of his aura, distinctly increases in size as well as in luminosity and purity of colour. Many of us know from experience that the aura of a pupil who has already made considerable advance on the Path is very much larger than that of one who is but just setting his foot upon its first step, while in the case of an Adept the proportional increase is far greater still. We read in quite exoteric Oriental scriptures of the immense extension of the aura of the Buddha; I think that three miles is mentioned on one occasion as its limit, but whatever the exact measurement may be, it is obvious that we have here another record of this fact of the extremely rapid growth of the causal body as man passes on his upward way. There can be little doubt that the rate of this growth would itself increase in geometrical progression, so that it need not surprise us to hear of an Adept on a still higher level whose aura is capable of including the entire world at once; and from this we may gradually lead our minds up to the conception that there is a Being so exalted as to comprehend within Himself the whole of our solar system. And we should remember that, enormous as this seems to us, it is but as the tiniest drop in the vast ocean of space.

So of the Logos, who has in Him all the capacities and qualities with which we can possibly endow the highest God we can imagine, it is literally true, as was said of old, that "of him and through him, and to him are all things," and "in him we live and move and have our being."

Now if this be so, it is clear that whatever happens within our system happens absolutely within the consciousness of its Logos, and so we at once see that the true record must be His memory; and furthermore, it is obvious that on whatever plane that wondrous memory exists, it cannot but be far above anything that we know, and consequently whatever records we may find ourselves able to read must be only a reflection of that great dominant fact, mirrored in the denser media of the lower planes.

On the astral plane it is at once evident that this is so—that what we are dealing with is only a reflection of a reflection, and an exceedingly imperfect one, for such records as can be reached there are fragmentary in the extreme, and often seriously distorted. We know how universally water is used as a symbol of the astral light, and in this particular case it is a remarkably apt one. From the surface of still water we may get a clear reflection of the surrounding objects, just as from a mirror; but at the best it is only a reflection—a representation in two dimensions of three-dimensional objects, and therefore differing in all its qualities, except colour, from that which it represents; and in addition to this, it is always reversed. But let the surface of the water be ruffled by the wind, and what do we find then? A reflection still, certainly, but so broken up and distorted as to be quite useless or even misleading as a guide to the shape and real appearance of the objects reflected. Here and there for a moment we might happen to get a clear reflection of some minute part of the scene—of a single leaf from a tree, for example; but it would need long labour and considerable knowledge of natural laws to build up anything like a true conception of the object reflected by putting together even a large number of such isolated fragments of an image of it.

Now in the astral plane we can never have anything approaching to what we have imaged as a still surface, but on the contrary we have always to deal with one in rapid and bewildering motion; judge, therefore, how little we can depend upon getting a clear and definite reflection. Thus a clairvoyant who possesses the faculty of astral sight only can never rely upon any picture of the past that comes before him as being accurate and perfect; here and there some part of it *may* be so, but he has no means of knowing which it is. If he is under the care of a competent teacher he may, by long and careful training, be shown how to distinguish between reliable and unreliable impressions, and to construct from the broken reflections some kind of image of the object reflected; but usually long before he has mastered those difficulties he will have developed the devachanic sight which renders such labour unnecessary.

On the devachanic plane conditions are very different. There the record is full and accurate, and it would be impossible to make any mistake in the reading. That is to say, if three clairvoyants possessing the powers of the devachanic plane agreed to examine a certain record there, what would be presented to their vision would be absolutely the same reflection in each case, and each would acquire a correct impression from it in reading it. It does not however follow that when they all compared notes later on the physical plane their reports would agree exactly. It is well known that if three people who witness an occurrence down here on the physical plane set to work to describe it afterwards, their accounts will differ considerably, for each will have noticed especially those items which most appealed to him, and will insensibly have made them the prominent features of the event, sometimes ignoring other points which were in reality much more important.

Now in the case of an observation on the devachanic plane this personal equation would not appreciably affect the impressions received, for since each would thoroughly grasp the entire subject it would be impossible for him to see its parts out of due proportion; but, except in the case of carefully trained and experienced persons, this factor does come into play in transferring the impressions to the lower planes. It is in the nature of things impossible that any account given down here of a devachanic vision or experience can be complete, since nine-tenths of what is seen and felt there could not be expressed by physical words at all; and since all expression must therefore be partial there is obviously some possibility of selection as to the part expressed. It is for this reason that in all our Theosophical investigations of recent years so much stress has been laid upon the constant checking and verifying of clairvoyant testimony, nothing which rests upon the vision of one person only having been allowed to appear in our later books.

But even when the possibility of error from this factor of personal equation has been reduced to a minimum by a careful system of counterchecking, there still remains the very serious difficulty which is inherent in the operation of bringing down impressions from a higher plane to a lower one. This is something analogous to the difficulty experienced by a painter in his endeavour to reproduce a three-dimensional landscape on a flat surface—that is, practically in two dimensions. Just as the artist needs long and careful training of eye and hand before he can produce a satisfactory representation of nature, so does the clairvoyant need long and careful training before he can describe accurately on a lower plane what he sees on a higher one; and the probability of getting an exact description from an untrained person is about equal to that of getting a perfectly-finished landscape from one who has never learnt how to draw.

It must be remembered, too, that the most perfect picture is in reality infinitely far from being a reproduction of the scene which it represents, for hardly a single line or angle in it can ever be the same as those in the object copied. It is simply a very ingenious attempt to make upon one only of our five senses, by means of lines and colours on a flat surface, an impression similar to that which would have been made if we had actually had before us the scene depicted. Except by a suggestion dependent entirely on our own previous experience, it can convey to us nothing of the roar of the sea, of the scent of the flowers, of the taste of the fruit, or of the softness or hardness of the surface drawn.

Of exactly similar nature, though greater in degree, are the difficulties experienced by a clairvoyant in his attempt to describe upon the physical plane what he has seen upon the astral; and they are furthermore greatly enhanced by the fact that, instead of having merely to recall to the minds of his hearers conceptions with which they are already familiar, as the artist does when he paints men or animals, fields or trees, he has to endeavour by the very imperfect means at his disposal to suggest to them conceptions which in most cases are absolutely new to them. Small wonder then that, however vivid and striking his descriptions may seem to his audience, he himself should constantly be impressed with their total inadequacy, and should feel that his best efforts have entirely failed to convey any idea of what he really sees. And we must remember that in the case of the report given down here of a record read on the devachanic plane, this difficult operation of transference from the higher to the lower has taken place not once but twice, since the memory has been brought through the intervening astral plane. Even in a case where the investigator has the advantage of having developed his devachanic faculties so that he has the use of them while awake in the physical body, he is still hampered by the absolute incapacity of physical language to express what he sees.

Try for a moment to realize what is called the fourth dimension.

It is easy enough to think of our own three dimensions—to image in our minds the length, breadth and height of any object; and we see that each of these three dimensions is expressed by a line at right angles to both of the others. The idea of the fourth dimension is that it might be possible to draw a fourth line at right angles to all three of those already existing. Now the ordinary mind cannot grasp this idea in the least, though some few who have made a special study of the subject have gradually come to be able to realize one or two very simple four-dimensional figures. Still, no words that they can use on this plane can bring any image of these figures before the minds of others, and if any reader who has not specially trained himself along that line will make the effort to visualize such a shape he will find it quite impossible. Now to express such a form clearly in physical words would be, in effect, to describe accurately a single object on the astral plane; but in examining the records on the devachanic plane we should have to face the additional difficulties of a fifth dimension! So that the impossibility of fully explaining these records will be obvious to even the most superficial observation.

We have spoken of the records as the memory of the Logos, yet they are very much more than a memory in any ordinary sense of the word. Hopeless as it may be to imagine how these images appear from His point of view, we yet know that as we rise higher and higher we must be drawing nearer to the true memory—must be seeing more nearly as He sees; so that great interest attaches to the experience of the clairvoyant with reference to these records when he stands upon the buddhic plane—the highest which his consciousness can reach until he attains the level of the Arhats. Here time and space no longer limit him; he no longer needs, as in the devachanic plane, to pass a series of events in review, for past, present and future are all alike simultaneously present to him, meaningless as that sounds down here. Indeed, infinitely below the consciousness of the Logos as even that exalted plane is, it is yet abundantly clear from what we see there that to Him the record must be far more than what we call a memory, for all that has happened in the past and all that will happen in the future *is happening now* before His eyes just as are the events of what we call the present time. Utterly incredible, wildly incomprehensible, of course, to our limited understanding; yet absolutely true for all that.

Naturally we could not expect to understand at our present stage of knowledge how so marvellous a result is produced, and to attempt an explanation would only be to involve ourselves in a mist of words from which we should gain no real information. Yet a line of thought recurs to my mind which perhaps suggests the direction in which it is possible that that explanation may lie: and whatever helps us to realize that so astounding a statement may after all not be wholly impossible will be of assistance in broadening our minds.

Some thirty years ago I remember reading a very curious little book called, I think, *The Stars and the Earth*, the object of which was to endeavour to show how it was scientifically possible that to the mind of God the past and the present might be absolutely simultaneous. Its arguments struck me at the time as decidedly ingenious, and I will proceed to summarize them, as I think they will be found somewhat suggestive in connection with the subject which we have been considering.

When we see anything, whether it be the book which we hold in our hands or a star millions of miles away, we do so by means of a vibration in the ether, commonly called a ray of light, which passes from the object seen to our eyes. Now the speed with which this vibration passes is so great—about 186,000 miles in a second—that when we are considering any object in our own world we may regard it as practically instantaneous. When, however, we come to deal with interplanetary distances we have to take the speed of light into consideration, for an appreciable period is occupied in traversing these vast spaces. For example, it takes eight minutes and a quarter for light to travel to us from the sun, so that when we look at the solar orb we see it by means of a ray of light which left it more than eight minutes ago. From this follows a very curious result. The ray of light by which we see the sun can obviously report to us only the state of affairs which existed in that luminary when it started on its journey, and would not be in the least affected by anything that happened there after it left; so that we really see the sun not as he *is*, but as he was eight minutes ago. That is to say that if anything important took place in the sun—

the formation of a new sun-spot, for instance—an astronomer who was watching the orb through his telescope at the time would be quite unaware of the incident while it was happening, since the ray of light bearing the news would not reach him until more than eight minutes later.

The difference is more striking when we consider the fixed stars, because in their case the distances are so enormously greater. The pole star, for example, is so far off that light, travelling at the inconceivable speed above mentioned, takes a little more than fifty years to reach our eyes ; and from that follows the strange but inevitable inference that we see the pole star not as and where it is at this moment, but as and where it was fifty years ago. Nay, if to-morrow some cosmic catastrophe were to shatter the pole star into fragments, we should still see it peacefully shining in the sky all the rest of our lives ; our children would grow up to middle age and gather their children about them in turn before the news of that tremendous accident reached any human eye. In the same way there are other stars so far distant that light takes thousands of years to travel from them to us, and with reference to their condition our information is therefore thousands of years behind time.

Now carry the argument a step farther. Suppose that we were able to place a man at the distance of 186,000 miles from the earth, and yet to endow him with the wonderful faculty of being able from that distance to see what was happening here as clearly as though he were still close beside us. It is evident that a man so placed would see everything a second after the time when it really happened, and so at the present moment he would be seeing what happened a second ago. Double the distance, and he would be two seconds behind time, and so on ; remove him to the distance of the sun (still allowing him to preserve the same mysterious power of sight) and he would look down and watch you doing not what you *are* doing now, but what you *were* doing eight minutes and a quarter ago. Carry him away to the pole star, and he would see passing before his eyes the events of fifty years ago ; he would be watching the childish gambols of those who at the very same moment were really middle-aged men. Marvellous as this may sound, it is literally and scientifically true, and cannot be denied.

My little book went on to argue logically enough that God,

being almighty, must possess the wonderful power of sight which we have been postulating for our observer; and further, that being omnipresent, He must be at each of the stations which we mentioned, and also at every intermediate point, not successively but simultaneously. Granting these premises, the inevitable deduction follows that everything which has ever happened from the very beginning of the world *must* be at this very moment taking place before the eye of God—not a mere memory of it, but the actual occurrence itself being now under His observation.

All this is materialistic enough, and on the plane of purely physical science, and we may therefore be assured that it is *not* the way in which the memory of the Logos acts; yet, as I have said before, it is not without its use, since it gives us a glimpse of some possibilities which otherwise might not occur to us. But even if in a dim sort of way we feel ourselves able to grasp the idea that the whole of the past may be simultaneously and actively present in a sufficiently exalted consciousness, we are confronted by a far greater difficulty when we endeavour to realize how all the future may also be comprehended in that consciousness. If we could believe in the Mohammedan doctrine of kismet, or the Calvinistic theory of predestination, the conception would be easy enough, but knowing as we do that there is no truth in either of these we must look round for some more acceptable hypothesis.

There may still be some people who deny the possibility of prevision, but such denial simply shows their ignorance of the evidence on the subject. The large number of authenticated cases leaves no room for doubt as to the fact, but many of them are of such a nature as to render a reasonable explanation by no means easy to find. It is evident that the ego possesses a certain amount of previsional faculty, and if the events foreseen were always of great importance one might suppose that an extraordinary stimulus had enabled him for that occasion only to make a clear impression upon his lower personality of what he saw. No doubt that is the explanation of many of the cases in which death or grave disaster is foreseen, but there are a large number of instances on record to which it does not seem to apply, since the events foretold are frequently exceedingly trivial and unimportant.

A well-known story of second-sight in Scotland will illustrate what I mean. A man who had no belief in the occult was forewarned by a highland seer of the approaching death of a neighbour. The prophecy was given with considerable wealth of detail, including a full description of the funeral, with the names of the four pall-bearers and others who would be present. The auditor seems to have laughed at the whole story and promptly forgotten it, but the death of his neighbour at the time foretold recalled the warning to his mind, and he determined to falsify part of the prediction at any rate by being one of the pall-bearers himself. He succeeded in getting matters arranged as he wished, but just as the funeral was about to start he was called away from his post by some small matter which detained him only a minute or two. As he came hurrying back he saw with surprise that the procession had started without him, and that the prediction had been exactly fulfilled, for the four pall-bearers were those who had been indicated in the vision.

Now here is a very trifling matter, which could have been of no possible importance to anybody, definitely foreseen months beforehand; and although a man makes a determined effort to alter the arrangement indicated he fails entirely to affect it in the least. Certainly this looks very much like predestination, even down to the smallest detail, and it is only when we examine this question from higher planes that we are able to see our way to escape that theory. Of course, as I said before about another branch of the subject, a full explanation eludes us as yet, and obviously must do so until our knowledge is infinitely greater than it is now; the most that we can hope to do now is to indicate the line along which an explanation may be found.

There is no doubt whatever that, just as what is happening now is the result of causes set in motion in the past, so what will happen in the future will be the result of causes already in operation. Even down here we can calculate that if certain actions are performed certain results will follow, but our reckoning is constantly liable to be disturbed by the interference of factors which we have not been able to take into account. But if we raise our consciousness to the devachanic plane we can see very much farther into the results of our actions. We can trace, for example, the effect of a casual word, not only upon the person to whom it was addressed, but through him on many others as it is passed on in widening circles, until it seems to have affected the whole country; and one glimpse of such a vision is far more efficient than any number of moral precepts in impressing upon us the necessity of extreme circumspection in thought, word and deed. Not only can we from that plane see thus fully the result of every action, but we can also see where and in what way the results of other actions apparently quite unconnected with it will interfere with and modify it. In fact, it may be said that the results of all causes at present in action are clearly visible—that the future as it would be if no entirely new causes should arise lies open before our gaze.

New causes of course do arise, because man's will is free; but in the case of all ordinary people the use which they will make of their freedom can be calculated beforehand with considerable accuracy. The average man has so little real will that he is very much the creature of circumstances; his previous karma places him amid certain surroundings, and their influence upon him is so very much the most important factor in his life-story that his future course may be predicted with almost mathematical certainty. With the developed man the case is different; for him also the main events of life are arranged by his past karma, but the way in which he will allow them to affect him, the methods by which he will deal with them and perhaps triumph over them—these are all his own, and they cannot be foreseen on the devachanic plane except as probabilities.

Looking down on man's life in this way from above, it seems as though his free will could be exercised only at certain crises in his career. He arrives at a point in his life where there are obviously two or three alternative courses open before him; he is absolutely free to choose which of them he pleases, and although some one who knew his nature thoroughly well might feel almost certain what his choice would be, such knowledge on his friend's part is in no sense a compelling force. But when he *has* chosen, he has to go through with it and take the consequences; having entered upon a particular path he may, in many cases, be forced to go on for a very long way before he has any opportunity to turn aside. His position is somewhat like that of the driver of a train; when he comes to a junction he may have the points set either this way or that, and so can pass on to whichever line he pleases, but when he *has* passed on to one of them he is compelled to run on along the line which he has selected until he reaches another set of points, where again an opportunity of choice is offered to him.

Now in looking down from the devachanic plane these points of new departure would be clearly visible, and all the results of each choice would lie open before us, certain to be worked out even to the smallest detail. The only point which would remain uncertain would be the all-important one as to which choice the man would make. We should, in fact, have not one but several futures mapped out before our eyes, without necessarily being able to determine which of them would materialize itself into accomplished fact. In most instances we should see so strong a probability that we should not hesitate to come to a decision, but the case which I have described is certainly theoretically possible. Still, even this much knowledge would enable us to do with safety a good deal of prediction; and it is not difficult for us to imagine that a far higher power than ours might always be able to foresee which way every choice would go, and consequently to prophesy with absolute certainty.

On the buddhic plane, however, no such elaborate process of conscious calculation seems to be necessary, for, as I said before, in some manner which down here is totally inexplicable, the past, the present, and the future, appear there all to be existing simultaneously. One can only accept this apparent fact, and suppose that its cause lies in a faculty of the plane which would be quite incomprehensible to our physical brains. At any rate, the evidence undoubtedly shows that, whether from the calm certainty of this plane, or the rapid reasoning of the one below it, occasional pictures of futurity are reflected even into astral levels, and are sometimes observed and recorded more or less correctly, just as are the pictures of the past.

C. W. LEADBEATER.

(To be continued.)

A GLIMPSE INTO KÂMA-LOKA.

FROM A STORY IN PLUTARCH.

[THE following story is taken from the Morals of Plutarch, and will be found in Chap. xxii. of the Treatise "On those who are punished by the Deity late." A certain Thespesius of Soli, a town on the sea-coast of Cilicia, in Asia Minor, apparently died from the effects of a severe fall, and was buried. After three days, however, he recovered consciousness and escaped from his tomb. After this unpleasant experience, Thespesius became an entirely changed person; from being a man of very shady character indeed, he became an example of virtue. The following is the account which he gave to his intimate friends of the extraordinary experiences he passed through while out of the body. The translation is Shilleto's.]

He told his friends that when his soul left the body the change he first underwent was as if he were a pilot thrown violently into the sea out of a ship. Then raising himself up a little, he thought he recovered the power of breathing again altogether, and looked round him in every direction, as if one eye of the soul was open, but saw none of the things he had ever seen before, but stars enormous in size and at immense distance from one another, sending forth a wonderful and intense brightness of colour, so that the soul was borne along and moved about everywhere quickly and easily, like a ship in fair weather. But omitting most of the sights he saw, he said that the souls of the dead mounted into the air, which yielded to them and formed fiery bubbles, and then, when each bubble quickly broke they assumed human forms, light in weight, but with different kinds of motion, for some leapt about with wonderful agility and darted straight upwards, while others like spindles flitted round all together in a circle, some in an upward direction, some in a downward, with mixed and confused motion, hardly stopping at all, or only after a very long time. As to most of these, he was ignorant who they were, but he saw two or three that he knew, and tried to approach them and talk with them, but they would not listen to him, and did not seem to be in their right minds, but out of their senses and distraught, avoiding every sight and touch, and at first they turned round and round alone, but afterwards meeting many other souls whirling round and in the same condition as themselves, they moved about promiscuously with no particular object in view, and uttered inarticulate sounds like yells mixed with wailing and terror.

Other souls in the upper part of the air seemed joyful, and frequently approached one another in a friendly way, and avoided those troubled souls, and seemed to mark their displeasure by keeping themselves to themselves, and their joy and delight by extension and expansion. At last he said he saw the soul of a relation whom he thought he knew but was not quite sure, as he died when he was a boy, which came up to him and said to him, "Welcome, Thespesius." And he wondering and saying that his name was not Thespesius, but Aridenus, the soul replied, "That was your old name, but henceforth it will be Thespesius. For assuredly you are not dead, but by the will of the gods are come here with your intellect, for the rest of your soul you have left in the body like an anchor; and as a proof of what I say, both now and hereafter notice that the souls of the dead have no shadow and do not move their eyelids." Thespesius, on hearing these words, pulled himself somewhat more together again, and began to use his reason, and looking more closely he noticed that an indistinct and shadow-like line was suspended over him, while the others shone all around and were transparent, but were not all alike, for some were like full moon at its brightest, throwing out one smooth, even and continuous colour; others had spots or bright marks here and there, while others were quite variegated and strange to sight with black spots like snakes, while others again had thin scratches. Then the kinsman of Thespesius (for there is nothing to prevent our calling the soul by the name of the person) pointed out everything, and told him that Adrastea, the daughter of Necessity and Zeus, was placed in the highest position to punish all crimes, and no criminal was either so great or so small as to be able to escape her either by fraud or violence. But as there were three kinds of punishment, each had its own officer and administering functionary.

"For speedy vengeance undertakes the punishment of those that are to be corrected at once in the body and through their bodies, and she mildly passes by many offences that only need expiation; but if the cure of vice demands further pains, then the deity hands over such criminals after death to Justice, and those whom Justice rejects as altogether incurable, Erinnys (the third and fiercest of Adrastea's officers) pursues as they are fleeing and wandering about in various directions, and with pitiless severity utterly undoes them all, and thrusts them down to a place not to be seen or spoken about.

"And, of all these punishments, that which is administered in this life of vengeance is most like those in use among the barbarians. For as among the Persians they pluck off and scourge the garments and tiaras of those that are to be punished, while the offenders weep and beg them to cease, so most punishments by fine or bodily chastisement have no sharp touch, nor do they reach vice itself, but are only for show and sentiment. And whoever goes from this world to that incorrigible and impure, Justice takes him aside, naked as he is in soul, and unable to veil or hide or conceal his villainy, but descried all round and in all points by everybody, and shows him first to his good parents, if such they were, to let them see what a wretch he is, and how unworthy of his ancestors; but if they were wicked too, seeing them punished and himself being seen by them, he is chastised for a long time till he is purged of each of his bad propensities by sufferings and pains which as much exceed in magnitude and intensity all sufferings in the flesh as what is real is more vivid than a dream.

"Observe also," he continued, "the different and various colours of the souls. That dark, dirty brown colour is the pigment of illiberality and covetousness, and the blood-red the sign of cruelty and savageness, aud when the blue is there, sensuality and love of pleasure are not easily eradicated, and that violet and livid colour marks malice and envy, like the dark liquid ejected by the cuttle fish. For as, during life, vice produces these colours by the soul being acted upon by passions and reacting upon the body, so here it is the end of purification and correction when they are toned down, and the soul becomes altogether bright and one colour.

"And some of these souls, by being again and again corrected, recover their proper disposition and condition, while others again by their violent ignorance and excessive love of pleasure are carried into the bodies of animals; for one, by weakness of reasoning power and slowness of contemplation, is impelled by the practical element in him to generation, while another, lacking an instrument to satisfy his licentiousness, desires to gratify his passions immediately, and to get that gratification through the medium of the body, for here there is no real fruition, but only an imperfect shadow and dream of incomplete pleasure."

After he had said this, Thespesius' kinsman hurried him at great speed through immense space, as it seemed to him, though he travelled as easily and straight as if he were carried on the wings of the sun's rays. At last he came to an extensive and bottomless abyss, where his strength left him, as he found was the case with the other souls there; for keeping together and making swoops, like birds, they flitted all round the abyss, but did not venture to pass over it. To internal view it resembled the caverns of Bacchus, being beautiful throughout with trees and green foliage and flowers of all kinds, and it breathed a soft and gentle air, laden with scents marvellously pleasant, and producing the effect that wine does on those who are topers; for the souls were elevated by its fragrance, and gay and blithe with one another, and the whole spot was full of mirth and laughter, and such songs as emanate from gaiety and enjoyment.

And Thespesius' kinsman told him that this was the way Dionysus went up to heaven by, and by which he afterwards took Semele, and it was called the place of oblivion. But he would not let Thespesius stay there, much as he wished, but forcibly dragged him away, instructing and telling him that the intellect was melted and moistened by pleasure, and that the irrational and corporeal element being watered and made flesh stirs up the memory of the body, from which comes yearning and strange desire for generation, so called from being an inclination to the earth, when the soul is weighed down with moisture. Next Thespesius travelled as far in another direction, and seemed to see a great crater into which several rivers emptied themselves, one whiter than the foam of the sea or shore, another like the purple of the rainbow, and others of various hues, whose brightness was apparent at some distance, but when he got nearer the air became thinner and the colours grew dim, and the crater lost all its gay colours but white. And he saw three genii sitting together in a triangular position, mixing the rivers together in certain proportions. Then the guide of Thespesius' soul told him that Orpheus got as far as here, when he came in quest of the soul of his wife, and from not exactly remembering what he had seen spread a false report among mankind that the oracle at Delphi was common to Apollo and Night, though Apollo had no communion with Night: but this, pursued the guide, is an oracle common to Night and the Moon, that utters forth its oracular knowledge in no particular part of the world, nor has it any particular seat, but wanders about everywhere in men's dreams and visions. Hence, as you see, dreams receive and disseminate a mixture of simple truth with deceit and error. But the oracle of Apollo you do not know, nor can you see it, for the earthiness of the soul does not suffer it to soar upwards, but keeps it down in dependence on the body. And taking him nearer, his guide tried to show him the light from the tripod, which, as he said, shone as far as Parnassus through the bosom of Themis, but though he desired to see it he could not for its brightness, but as he passed by he heard the shrill voice of a woman speaking in verse several things, among others, he thought, telling the time of his death.

That, said the genius, was the voice of the Sibyl, who sang about the future as she was being borne about in the orb of the moon. Though desirous then to hear more, he was conveyed into another direction by the violent motion of the moon, as if he had been in the eddies of a whirlpool, so that he heard very little more, only a prophecy about Mount Vesuvius and that Dicæarchia [Puteoli] would be destroyed by fire, and a short piece about the Emperor then reigning [Vespasian] that "though he was good he would lose his empire through sickness."

After this Thespesius and his guide turned to see those that were undergoing punishment. And at first they saw only distressing and pitiable sights, but after that Thespesius, little expecting it, found himself among his friends and acquaintances and kinsfolk who were being punished, and undergoing dreadful sufferings and hideous and bitter tortures, and who wept and wailed to him.

And at last he descried his father coming up out of a certain gulf covered with marks and scars, stretching out his hands, and not allowed to keep silence, but compelled by those that presided over his torture to confess that he had been an accursed wretch and poisoned some strangers that had gold, and during his life-time had escaped the detection of everybody, but had been found out here, and his guilt brought home to him, for which he had already suffered much and was being dragged on to suffer more.

So great was his consternation and fear that he did not dare to intercede or beg for his father's release, but wishing to turn and flee he could no longer see his gentle and kind guide, but he was thrust forward by some persons horrible to look at, as if some dire necessity compelled him to go through with the business; and he saw that the shades of those that had been notorious criminals and punished in their life-time were not so severely tortured here or like the others, but had an incomplete though toilsome punishment for their irrational passions.

Whereas those who, under the mask and show of virtue, had lived all their lives in undetected vice, were forced by their torturers with labour and pain to turn their souls inside out, unnaturally wriggling and writhing about, like the sea-scolopendras who, when they have swallowed the crook, turn themselves inside out; but some of them their torturers flayed and crimped so as to show their various inward vices, which were only skinned over, which were deep in their soul, the principal part of man. And he said he saw other souls, like snakes, two or three or even more twined together, devouring one another in malignity and malevolence for what they had suffered or done in life.

He said also that there were several lakes running parallel, one of boiling gold, another most cold of lead, another hard of iron, and several demons were standing by like smiths, who lowered down and drew up by turns, with instruments, the souls of those whose criminality lay in insatiable cupidity.

For when they were red-hot and transparent through their bath in the lake of gold, the demons thrust them into the lake of lead and dipped them in that; and when they had got congealed in it and hard as hail, they dipped them into the lake of iron, and there they became wonderfully black, and broken and crushed by the hardness of the iron, and changed their appearance, and after that they were dipped again in the lake of gold, after suffering, he said, dreadful agony in all these changes of torment. But he said those souls that when they seemed to have escaped justice were arrested again, suffered most piteously of all, and these were those whose crimes had been visited on their children or descendants. For whenever one of these latter happened to come up he fell into a rage and cried out, and showed the marks of what he had suffered, and upbraided and pursued the soul of the parent, who wished to fly and hide himself, but could not. For quickly did the ministers of torture pursue them and hurry them back again to justice, wailing all the while on account of their fore-knowledge of what their punishment would be.

Last of all he saw the souls of those that were to come into the world a second time, forcibly moulded and transformed into various kinds of animals by artificers appointed for the very purpose, with instruments and blows, who broke off all the limbs of some and only wrenched off some of others, and polished others down, or annihilated them altogether, to fit them for other habits and modes of life.

Among them he saw the soul of Nero tortured in other ways, and pierced with red-hot nails.

And the artificers having taken it in hand and converted it into the semblance of a Pindaric viper, which gets its way to life by gnawing through its mother's womb, a great light, he said, suddenly shone, and a voice came out of the light, ordering them to change it into something milder, so they devised of it the animal that croaks about lakes and marshes; for he had been punished sufficiently for his crimes, and now deserved some favour at the hands of the gods, for he had freed Greece, the noblest nation of his subjects and the best-beloved of the gods.

So much did Thespesius behold, but as he intended to return a horrible dread came upon him. For a woman, marvellous in appearance and size, took hold of him and said to him, "Come here, that you may the better remember everything you have seen." And she was about to strike him with a red-hot iron pin, such as the encaustic painters use, when another woman prevented her, and he was suddenly sucked up, as through a pipe, by a strange and violent wind, lit upon his own body, and woke up and found that he was close to his tomb.

AUTHORITY.

"It is false that equality is a natural law. Nature has made nothing equal. Its sovereign law is subordination and dependence." —VAUSENARQUES.

Thus wrote a mystic philosopher of the last century. His conclusion is worth our attention and study, both from the point of view of the individual and as students of doctrines which are, to a large extent, based upon the authority of teachers. I propose briefly to discuss the question of the reality of authority as a law of the universe, to indicate its working in human life and social organization, and suggest the value of its due recognition as an aid to individual development.

That law or authority governs the universe is a proposition that hardly any thoughtful man disputes. There may be difference as to terms, one speaking of the Law of God, another of the Laws of Nature, but on the fact that law exists there is no disagreement. The recognition of this truth—very dimly, of course—must have been coeval with the dawning of human self-consciousness. Infant humanity coming into collision with it on the very first out-going after sensation, learnt the reality and inexorable character of natural law, just as on the microcosmic scale, the human infant repeats in every incarnation the experience of the race. Up to the point of the development of self-consciousness the One Life moves in unconscious obedience to the law, manifesting in the elemental, mineral, vegetable and animal kingdoms ever in accordance with the pressure of the evolutionary force behind it; moving downwards towards richest diversity of form, and anon upwards towards harmony of vibration. But at the awakening point of our evolution there comes consciousness of the existence of authority—that is, the something outside of ourselves with which we more or less frequently come into collision. This is the eating of the fruit of the Tree of Knowledge of good and evil, and acts of disobedience—not necessarily wilful disobedience—bring us into conflict with universal law and so make us aware of its existence. If we had been always in harmony with it we should not recognize it as authority but as our own will, and since we profess to believe that the whole purpose of our being here is to achieve *conscious* union with the Divine, and as we know that the less cannot include the greater but the greater must include the less, we must realize eventually, whether we do now or not, that we have consciously to bring our wills into harmony with the supreme will, so that, retaining the lesson—individuality—which disobedience has taught us, we may achieve perfection—harmony—which conscious obedience has to bestow.

It is important in any discussion of the subject to recognize the universality of law at the outset. We exist by virtue of it, we cannot escape from it. It governs our coming hither and our going hence independent of our conscious will. A man cannot even fling himself suddenly out of the universe and say, "I will cease to be;" only by untold ages of Titanic force and fury can he dash himself to pieces by repeated collisions with the on-rolling car of evolution. The law alters not, and only by making ourselves vibrate in harmony with it can we ever achieve. It is, therefore, useless to argue, as some have done, that the *idea* of authority is repulsive to us, or that "revolt against authority is the one thing common to every step in human progress." In such a statement there is mental confusion between the idea of authority *per se* and its degradation or abuse in specific cases, between the light and dark aspects, the good and evil in the world. Such writers fail to see how utterly and entirely we are bound by the bonds of authority in our daily thought. For how few of us is it possible to verify the statements we habitually accept on the authority of others. Our system of education is to a large extent the imposition upon many minds of statements more or less unverifiable by those who are expected to give them credence; and our social system, our daily lives, are regulated largely in accordance with statements made on "authority." We meet frequently with the phrase, "independent or original thinker!" There is no such anomaly in Nature. We are all bound together by indissoluble chains, more closely on the mind plane than on the physical. A thinker is dependent on the thoughts of all who have gone before him, on all who have recorded the *facts* on which his thinking is based, on the spirit of the age, and perhaps, above all, on the waves of spiritual light which flood the higher planes of mind, and of these grand harmonies he may nobly have fitted himself to be the transmitter to his day and generation.

We cannot but see in much that passes current for the "heaven-born instinct of freedom" and love of liberty, something which often degenerates into insolent disregard of all authority but self-will, and is near akin to a fatal tendency to constitute oneself an authority for other people. Possibly we are all too apt to repeat in pride "Behold I know," and to forget to preface our statements with the humbler "Thus have I heard," but an instinctive dislike to authority because it *is* authority, without regard to condition or circumstance, seems to indicate simply a degree of remoteness from harmony with the universal Divine Law; and that, I take it, is the first thing to overcome in beginning the path of liberation. The need for humility has been taught by the Masters of Wisdom, "Except ye become as little children ye shall not enter into the kingdom of heaven"; "Be humble, if thou would'st attain to wisdom. Be humbler still when wisdom thou hast mastered." If we at all realize that the rung we occupy on the ladder of evolution is still very low down, and that if there are millions of entities below us to whom we seem perchance as gods, so there are myriads above us to whom we are as gnats or worms, we gain a more level-headed idea of our true position. And if, still further, we can realize that within the limits of the human kingdom itself there are many grades and stages of development, we may haply clear our minds of much cant about liberty, equality, and fraternity. It is too often the case that:

> Envy wears the mask of love, and, laughing sober fact to scorn,
> Cries to weakest and to strongest, "Ye are equals, equal born."
> Equal born? O yes, if yonder hill be level with the flat,
> Charm us, orator, till the lion look no larger than the cat.

Surely it is but a little soul that can conceive of none greater than itself, can realize no more kingly being to whom it owes allegiance. Carlyle, in his *Heroes and Hero-worship*, has in his own trenchant way given expression to this truth.

"And now, sure enough, the cry is everywhere for Liberty and Equality, Independence and so forth; instead of *kings*, Ballot-boxes and Electoral Suffrages; it seems made out that any Hero-sovereign, or loyal obedience of men to a man, in things temporal or things spiritual, has passed away for ever from the world. I should despair of the world altogether, if so. One of my deepest convictions is that it is not so. Without sovereigns, true sovereigns, temporal and spiritual, I see nothing possible but an anarchy, the hatefulest of things. . . . Hero-worship never dies nor can die. Loyalty and sovereignty are everlasting in the world; and there is this in them, that they are grounded not on garnitures and semblances, but on realities and sincerities. All this of Liberty and Equality, Electoral Suffrages, Independence and so forth, we will take, therefore, to be temporary phenomenon, by no means a final one."

Now, if it be admitted that the scheme of evolution is a graded scheme, wherein it is the right and duty of the higher to guide, direct, control, and help the lower from top to bottom of the evolutionary scale, then the sooner we realize this practically in our lives the more rapidly and perfectly we shall fit ourselves into our niche of the universe, and be prepared to ascend to the next degree. As it is, we commonly assume the rights of governance over the less developed creatures, be they men or animals, and disregard our obligations to those above us, forgetting that before we can govern wisely we must learn how to obey, and that an effective army is composed, not of captains and commanders alone, but of disciplined rank and file. "We cannot all be Masters." I venture to think that it is because of this neglect of true discipline that we manage our share of the governing so badly. We give our brethren in the animal world every reason to regard us as devils, rather than gods, and our civilized (?) treatment of what we term "native" races will not bear reflection. In the general "muddlement" towards which we have gradually drifted down the ages, as we have moved further and further away from the divinely organized social life in which the infancy of our race was passed, the functions of the Brâhman and the Kshattriya have come to be exercised by the Sudra and the outcast, and the results are such as would naturally follow when authority is assumed by egos whose experience is limited to the lower standards of the world's great school. Revolt and anarchy are but the natural outcome; "sad enough embroilments for us all," says Carlyle, but we "must welcome them as the penalty of sins that are past, the pledge of inestimable benefits that are coming."

It is precisely this confusion of functions that has led to the innumerable instances of the abuse of authority with which history and daily experience furnish us, and is thus responsible for the narrow and mistaken, though not unnatural, view which so many liberty-loving people have taken of authority in itself.

> There's naught so vile that on the earth doth live,
> But to the earth some special good doth give;
> Nor aught so good, but strain'd from that fair use,
> Revolts from true birth, stumbling on abuse.

I hold that to our own shortcoming are due the ever-recurring examples of misapplied authority—to our want of discipline, our lack of knowledge how to obey. Did we more fully recognize our own particular function and sphere we should grasp the idea that we are a section of a double-linked chain, whereof the one side is service, the other authority; and if we are for ever overstraining the side of authority on the link below us, and hanging back from the side of service on the link above, we bid fair to weaken our own section of the chain and throw the whole out of gear.

It may be contended that in practice abuse of authority creeps in on both sides, a too great complaisance or credulity on the one hand, an overweening self-assertiveness on the other. Both in reality have their roots in ignorance—lack of experience—and since the *sincerity* with which the belief is held, or the self-appointed mission fulfilled, is after all the real measure of the soul's possibility of progress, it may be questioned whether the evils as between individuals are so great as we in our short-sighted way of judging are apt to infer. Where the reverence is given to the *man* because he is sincerely believed to be a greater than oneself, and not to the holder of an office, there the soul is not cramped by its idol, poor though that idol be in other eyes. Doubt, insincerity, are the real death-knells of worship.

When we consider the abuse of authority, where communities are affected, civil and religious history alike point to it as setting back the clock of human progress, and show that revolt from *such* authority has been the natural and legitimate swing of the pendulum, but none the less it has to be admitted that all great movements for the uplifting of humanity have begun in authority. Whose authority? That of the great teacher or teachers who established them. It could not be otherwise. They depended for their initiation upon him who taught—taught as one having authority and not as the scribes—because he was the one who *knew*, and without whom the movement would not have been. "Knowledge," says the copybook maxim, "is power." It certainly confers authority of a very real kind, and though, in the case of the teacher, there may be no compulsion to accept either the teaching or the authority, to accept the first is virtually an acceptance of the second, and the fact plays an important part in all great movements. Important in early stages because strength and cohesion are gained, important also because of a possible danger to be guarded against in later stages of all purely human societies, namely that of deferring in all affairs to what one may call the authority of the specialist. In other words, conferring upon the man whose knowledge in one or two departments is superb the authority or prestige due to the greater being whose knowledge is superb in all. Still later, creeps in the greater evil of deferring to the authority not of knowledge but of office merely, and then "lest one good custom should corrupt the world" the old order changeth and revolt brings forth a new order of progression. But ever, we must remember, under the guidance or command of a *new* teacher or commander, a leading spirit whose authority, beginning in love and free will, may or may not eventually become the source of another despotism.

Mr. Herbert Spencer, in his latest volume of Synthetic Philosophy, says that "ancient forms of dissent habitually stand for the authority of the Past over the Present," a statement which the history of religion appears amply to justify. They have arisen in the effort of some one or more thinkers to reinstate the purer teachings of the past, which we may well believe have been ever fundamentally the same, drawn from the one source of spiritual light and knowledge which is common to all sections of the human race, but "with revelations fitted to their growth and shape of mind."

It is in the very nature of humanity in the mass to need leaders and guides, just as it is in the nature of sheep; but the leaders, to be worthy of honour, must themselves serve and follow. What? The law whose authority is supreme, the law embodied in intelligences higher than their own, to whom they in turn owe conscious, or even perhaps unconscious allegiance, and by whom they are in turn directed and helped. So, if we would be distinguished from the mass, the way is open; not by raising the standard of revolt against all authority, but by learning to know the law, and working with and within the law, the law itself places us on the high platform we desire. "Whosoever of you will be the chiefest, shall be servant of all."

Before leaving this general aspect of the question, it may be well to allude to one form of authority which can hardly be left untouched—the authority of organization. We are all bound by it who live in communities; born and nurtured in it, we realize comparatively seldom how complete and binding it is, and even when not of the most ideal kind we submit to it, as to the rest of our environment, and "render unto Cæsar the things that are Cæsar's". Whether our particular "Cæsar" be a monarchy, an oligarchy, or "the will of the people," matters not, it is authority as affecting the individual. Within the big authority of the common-weal we build up the lesser authority of the municipality, and not content with that we are always voluntarily combining ourselves into leagues, guilds, associations, societies and the like, for the furtherance of definite objects. These voluntary combinations are invariably guided by some definite conceptions formulated in rules and bye-laws which have authority for the individual because they are the outcome of the sense or will of the majority, and the individual takes the obligation of them upon himself. Singularly enough, it is perhaps this particular form of authority which gives most occasion for strife, and apparently, in exact ratio to the non-necessity there is for him to submit to it and remain within the organization which imposes objectionable conditions, is the vigour of a man's determination to upset the authority to which he is opposed. This tendency, which is constantly recognizable in all sorts of organized bodies, is of course merely an illustration of what was stated earlier in this paper, that the instinct of revolt was near akin to a fatal inclination to constitute oneself an authority for others.

EDITH WARD.

(*To be continued.*)

THEOSOPHICAL ACTIVITIES.

European Section.

Mrs. Cooper-Oakley, who has recently visited Italy, found a promising centre of work in the new Rome Lodge. The Rome Lodge is fortunate in having Signor Calvari for its secretary. The work that he has done has been quite invaluable for Theosophy in Rome. At present the members are devoting their energies to translating the most important works into Italian. Mrs. Cooper-Oakley was at the library every day from five to seven, in order to meet those members who were desirous of studying seriously. Mrs. Lloyd has proved a most devoted and untiring Librarian and President, combining the two duties with unfailing energy and good-will.

The Rome Lodge is fortunate also in having two old members of the society in the Conte and Contessa Frenfanelli-Cibo, whose assistance and sympathy have been of much service to Mrs. Lloyd. After working with the members in Rome, Mrs. Oakley went to Florence, and there in conjunction with Mr. and Mrs. Hope, whose guest she was, a meeting was held to which the Spiritualists in Florence were invited. This meeting proved very successful. On leaving Florence *en route* for Nice, Mrs. Oakley stopped a few hours at Genoa to see some members there.

At Nice, Mrs. Cooper-Oakley found a group of fifteen students under the guidance of Mrs. Terrell. A new lodge will shortly be formed there. Accompanied by Mrs. Terrell and Mons. de Castro, Mrs. Cooper-Oakley went to Toulon to see Dr. Pascal. At Toulon three days were spent full of work, interviews and meetings, with a flying visit to Marseilles. Mrs. Cooper-Oakley then went to Paris, where again interviews and meetings filled every hour that was available. She lectured at the Ananta Lodge on "The Book of Life," and left for London on May 19th.

The Thirteenth Conference of the North of England Federation was held at Harrogate on May 8th, Mr. Keightley taking the chair. After the usual general business, Mr. Keightley spoke on "Individuality and Unity," and in the evening Miss Shaw read a paper on "The Use and Abuse of Prayer."

Mr. Keightley visited most of the Northern Branches of the Section, lecturing at Liverpool, Manchester, Middlesborough, Harrogate, Leeds, Hull, Bradford, Sheffield and Nottingham.

The Scandinavian Section.

The General Secretary of the European Section has been spending a fortnight in Sweden, working chiefly at Göteborg and Stockholm. A public lecture has been delivered in both cities, and a number of meetings, receptions and interviews have been held. The greatest interest was manifested. Mr. Mead chose as the subject of his lecture "The Theosophy of the First Two Centuries," and our members in Scandinavia seemed never to be tired of hearing of this remarkable period of the origins of the great religion of the West. Mr. Mead will also stop at Copenhagen on his return journey to London at the request of the members there, with whom he spent a couple of hours on his way to Sweden. The Convention of the Scandinavian Section was held at Stockholm on May 29th and 30th, and the European Section was represented by its General Secretary, who received a most hearty welcome, and was entrusted with the presentation of the greetings of the Scandinavian Section to the forthcoming Convention of his own Section to be held in London on July 10th and 11th.

Australasian Section.

The third Annual Convention met at Sydney on Good Friday, April 16th.

Mr. Peall, President of the Sydney Branch, was elected to the chair, and delegates from Melbourne, Adelaide and Brisbane were present, besides proxies for South Yarra, Hobart and Maryborough Branches.

It was with sincere regret that the chairman had to announce to the Convention the death of our universally respected and beloved General Secretary, Mr. J. C. Staples, and the representatives of all Branches testified to the debt of gratitude they owed to him for the help, sympathy, and guidance which he had ever freely given them.

It was decided to appoint an Honorary Acting General Secretary until a successor could be found to fill the vacancy; and as Mr. T. H. Martyn, who has been Acting General Secretary for the past eight months, is leaving very shortly for England, Mr. J. Scott was elected to that office, with Mr. H. A. Wilson as Assistant Secretary.

Miss Edger, General Secretary of the New Zealand Section, has generously volunteered to help in any way this Convention should see fit, and it was decided that she be asked to give a lecturing tour throughout the branches in Australia as early as possible.

Much discussion took place as to the best methods of increasing the usefulness of the Section.

Systems of correspondence between members, Lecture Bureaux, Colporteurs, and a Sectional Lending Library, were suggested, and it was decided to do as much on these lines as funds would admit.

The formal business of the Convention being concluded, the chairman gave his closing address, congratulating the members and delegates on the progress the Section had made during the year, and upon the harmonious and successful Convention which had been held.

The meeting then became an informal one, and discussed several points of disagreement in some of the later manuals and Theosophical publications, much good being done by the interchange of thought.

On Saturday evening, April 17th, the members of the Sydney Branch gave a Conversazione, so that their members might have a chance to meet and to become acquainted with the visiting delegates.

On Sunday evening Mr. H. W. Hunt from Melbourne, Mr. N. A. Knox from Adelaide, and Mr. T. H. Martyn of Sydney, delivered addresses on "Invisible Helpers," "Masters of Wisdom," and "The Theosophical Movement," to a large and attentive audience, thus bringing the Third Annual Convention to a fitting conclusion.

H. A. W.

New Zealand Section.

The General Secretary left Auckland on April 3rd on an extended lecturing tour, the first place visited being Gisborne.

The increased activity in Christchurch still continues.

As showing a growth of interest in Theosophy, the Secretary of the Dunedin Branch reports that one of the members there has been invited to read a paper on the subject to a Literary Institute.

An address on the "Septenary Universe" was given in Dunedin on the 8th inst, by Mr. A. W. Mavrais.

Mrs. Draffin lectured in Auckland on Sunday, 11th inst. on "Invisible Helpers," and will take the same subject in her next lecture.

American Section: Mrs. Besant's Tour.

On Monday afternoon, April 26th, we left Ogden, one of the largest towns in Utah, and speeding round the head of the Salt Lake, across the desert and over the Sierra Nevada mountains, right down the length of California, we arrived on Wednesday evening at San Diego, beautifully situated on its land-locked bay, not far from the frontiers of Mexico. Here we rejoined the Countess, who had gone on direct from

Salt Lake City to join Count Axel Wachtmeister, her son. In the evening the drawing-room of the hotel was filled two or three times in succession by the crowds of people who flocked to see Mrs. Besant. Amongst them were a few old members, and it was pleasant to see them expand into a wider understanding of the aims and objects of the organization to which we belong, as they listened, during the three days we were in San Diego, to the lucid and convincing lectures given by Mrs. Besant. They were also present at the daily conversations, where they had an opportunity of asking some of the questions which had puzzled them, and they finally united with the new members to form a Lodge. One old member, especially, was very glad to have an opportunity of coming into closer touch with others, after several years of outward isolation on her husband's ranche at San Louis Rey.

Mrs. Besant lectured twice in the pretty little theatre at San Diego, and thanks to Count Axel's care and business capacity all the arrangements were well carried out. An afternoon lecture on "Theosophy and its Teachings" enabled many to hear Mrs. Besant who could not attend in the evening.

Several members of the Los Angeles Lodge met us at the station, and we were driven to the pleasant home of Mrs. Freeman, who was hospitality itself during our stay. In the evening a reception was given by the Harmony Lodge, and the two or three hundred people who attended were presented to Mrs. Besant and the Countess. Some good music by friends, and short speeches by Mrs. Besant and the Countess, filled up a pleasant evening.

The six days spent in Los Angeles were utilized for daily Lodge meetings, four public lectures, conversations and meetings at the Headquarters of the Society, and private interviews—besides a visit to Pasadena, and a lecture and afternoon talk there.

Last night, Friday, May 7th, we left our many kind members in Los Angeles, and wishing them success in their work, took the train for San Francisco. From there our proposed route goes through Portland, Tacoma, Seattle and Olympia to Spokane, where we expect to arrive on June 3rd.

A. J. W.

THE PRESIDENT-FOUNDER IN CEYLON.

The President-Founder spent the whole of April at Colombo in active service for the Buddhists. Within an hour of his landing they had him in the chair at a school meeting at the Society's Ânanda College and up to our latest dates he had been working early and late with his staunch colleagues. He has gone over and revised the *Buddhist Catechism* (33rd edition) with the High Priest Sumangala, who has renewed his original certificate of approval of the first edition. The work now contains nearly two hundred more questions and answers than hitherto, and the matter is grouped in five parts, *viz.*, the life of Buddha; the Dharma or Doctrine; the Sangha; the History of Buddhism; and its scientific aspect. It is now a really comprehensive epitome. The work will shortly appear.

Colonel Olcott did a great deal of hard work in helping the Sinhalese to organize a fitting reception of the King of Siam, who stopped at Colombo on his way to the Queen's Jubilee celebration. The reception was arranged in good style, with a beautiful decorated pavilion near the jetty.

Being the last reigning Buddhist sovereign, the King had a peculiarly cordial welcome from the Sinhalese. In the pavilion His Majesty shook hands with Colonel Olcott, and warmly expressed his pleasure in meeting one who had been long known to him for his services to Buddhism.

The Colonel and the Prince Prisdon Choonsai of Siam, who recently put on the yellow robes, have perfected a scheme for the unification of the Buddhists of Siam, Ceylon and Burma under one Sangha, and hope to get the Siamese King to consent to its adoption.

On April 23rd, Colonel Olcott met at Colombo, by appointment, some Russian noblemen who wished to consult him about Buddhism. They then proceeded on their way to China and Mongolia.

Ceylon Letter.

At a meeting of the Trustees of the Musæus School held on the 11th ult., with Colonel Olcott in the chair, it was resolved to raise a Sustentation Fund by a Committee consisting of the Trustees. Dr. Peebles, of San Diego, U.S.A., has promised a hundred dollars in aid of the proposed school building, and Colonel Olcott fifty dollars for the same object. Prince Hespère Outkhoksmy of St. Petersburg, who was *en route* to China, visited the Musæus School with Colonel Olcott. He was much pleased.

The Hope Lodge holds its meetings regularly on Sunday afternoons. The members are reading *The Growth of the Soul*.

S. P.

REVIEWS.

THE ACTS OF JOHN.

Texts and Studies, Vol. V., No. 1.: Apocrypha Anecdota II., by M. R. James, Litt.D. [Cambridge University Press: 1897. Price 7*s*. 6*d*. net.]

The new volume of that most valuable series Texts and Studies, among much of minor importance, contains a long fragment of the Acts of John, most of which has never been previously published. About a fourth of it is preserved in the Acts of the Second Council of Nice (A.D. 787), and is known; but the rest is quite new. It has been rescued from a fourteenth century MS. preserved in Vienna, which consists of a transcription of a collection of sermons, lives of saints and other edifying tales. The original of these Acts of John is early. Seeing that Clement of Alexandria quotes from them, we must assign the third quarter of the second century to them as the *terminus ad quem*. We have therefore before us an early document, our interest in which is further increased by the fact of its Gnostic nature. Nearly the whole of the fragment consists of a monologue put into the mouth of "John," in which he preserves for us a most remarkable tradition of the occult life of Jesus. The whole setting of the christology is docetic, and the fragment is thus a most valuable addition to our knowledge on this interesting point of Gnostic tradition. As readers of LUCIFER are now sufficiently familiar with the general tendencies of docetism, it is unnecessary to explain this cycle of ideas further. It is sufficient to point out that docetism was the rank growth of the legends of certain occult powers ascribed to the "perfect man," which were woven into the many christological and soteriological theories of the Gnostic philosophers; and also, as I believe, of a veritable historical fact, which has been obscured out of all recognition by the many pseudo-historical narrations of the origins. After his death Jesus, the Christ, did return and teach his followers among the "Essenes," and this was the part-origin of the protean Gnostic tradition of an inner instruction. He returned in the only way he could return, namely in a "psychic" or "spiritual" body; this body could be made visible at will, could even be made sensible to touch, but it was, compared to the ordinary physical body, an "illusionary" body—hence the term docetic. But just as the external tradition of the Poor Men in time finally exalted Jesus from the lowly position of a prophet into the power and glory of the Godhead itself, so the internal tradition extended the original docetic notion to every department of the huge soteriological structure raised by Gnostic genius. The Acts of John pertain to the latter cycle of tendencies, and "John" is the personification of one of the lines of tradition of the protean docetism which took its origin in an occult fact, and of those marvellous teachings of initiation which became subsequently historicised, and which "John" sums up in the words, "I held firmly this one thing in myself, that the Lord contrived all things symbolically and by a dispensation toward men, for their conversion and salvation."

That Jesus during his ministry was possessed of occult powers of a high order is easy of belief to any student of occultism. That he could appear to others in a mâyâvi rûpa and change its appearance at will, is quite possible of credit. But that the tradition of these and other such happenings should have been handed down without exaggeration and fantastic embellishment would have been contrary to human experience in such matters. Thus, then, we are told that at the calling of James and John, first of all James saw Jesus as a child, while John saw him first as a man "fair and comely and of a cheerful countenance"; afterwards he saw him as one "having a head rather bald, but a thick and flowing beard," while James asserted that he appeared "as a youth whose beard was newly come."

Moreover another peculiarity which John remarked was that his eyes never closed. Strangely enough this is one of the signs of a "god" given in the Hindu scriptures. Many changes of appearance did John remark, sometimes as of "a man small and uncomely, and then again as one reaching to heaven"—a fact quite credible when related of a pupil in sympathetic contact with the powerful aura of an adept teacher. But stranger still, when John lay upon his breast "sometimes it was felt of me to be smooth and tender, and sometimes hard, like stones." Moreover, when Jesus was in prayer and contemplation there was seen in him "such a light as it is not possible for a man that useth corruptible speech to tell what it was like."

The following naïve story will perhaps bring a smile to the face of the orthodox, but will give the student of occultism the proof that the legend is not based entirely on the imagination, but pertains to the domain of occult fact, if the many similar legends current in India concerning the touch of yogins when in certain states of ecstasis are at all to be credited.

"Again in like manner he leadeth us three up into the mountain, saying 'Come ye to me.' And we again went: and we beheld him at a distance praying. Now therefore I, because he loved me, drew nigh unto him softly as though he should not see, and stood looking upon his hinder parts. And I beheld him that he was not in any wise clad with garments, but was seen of us naked thereof, and not in any wise as a man: and his feet whiter than any snow, so that the ground there was lighted up by his feet: and his head reaching unto the heaven; so that I was afraid and cried out, and he turned and appeared as a man of small stature, and took hold of my beard and pulled it and said unto me 'John, be not unbelieving, and not a busy body.' And I said unto him, 'But what have I done, Lord?' And I tell you, brethren, I suffered great pain in that place where he took hold upon my beard for thirty days." On this occasion also it was noticed that someone was speaking to Jesus while he was in the state of illumination, and this phenomenon was subsequently repeated in the presence of John, as recorded in the following naïve narrative.

"Again, once when all of us his disciples were sleeping in one house at Gennesaret, I alone, having wrapped myself up, watched from under my garment what he did, and first I heard him say, 'John, go thou to sleep,' and thereupon I feigned to be asleep; and I saw another like unto him come down, whom also I heard saying unto my Lord, 'Jesus, do they whom thou hast chosen still not believe in thee?' And my Lord said unto Him, 'Thou sayest well: for they are men.'"

Here is the direct tradition of a fact which led to the subsequent great doctrinal distinction between Jesus and Christ in Gnostic christology. The Christ was the higher teaching power; Jesus was the man through whom He taught during the time of the ministry.

Interesting again is the simple story that when Jesus and his disciples were each given a loaf by some well-to-do householder, Jesus would bless his loaf and divide it among them, and each was well satisfied with his portion, and thus "our own loaves were saved whole"—an incident credible enough to any student of occultism, and supplying a basis on which the gorgeous oriental imagination could easily in time construct the legends of the feeding of the five thousand, etc.

Next follows the hymn which was sung before he was taken by "the lawless Jews." The disciples hold one another's hands so as to make a ring round Jesus, who stands in the midst, and to each line he sings, they intone in chorus the sacred word "Amen." It is evidently some echo of the mysteries and the ceremony is that of a sacred dance. The whole is exceedingly mystical, as may be seen from the following excerpts.

. . . . .

"Grace is dancing. I would pipe: dance, all of you. Amen.
I would mourn; lament, all of you. Amen.
One Ogdoad is singing praise with us. Amen.
The twelfth number is dancing above. Amen.
Also the Whole, that can dance. Amen.
He that danceth not, knoweth not what is being done. Amen.

. . . . .

I would be united and I would unite. Amen.
I have no house and I have houses. Amen.
I have no place and I have places. Amen.
I have no temple and I have temples. Amen.
I am a lamp to thee who beholdest me. Amen.
I am a mirror to thee who perceivest me. Amen.
I am a door to thee who knockest at me. Amen.
I am a way to thee, a wayfarer.
Now respond thou to my dancing.
See thyself in me who speak: and when thou hast seen what I do, keep silence about my mysteries.

. . . . .

Thou hast me for a bed, rest upon me.
Who am I? Thou shalt know when I go away.
What I am now seen to be, that am I not: but what I am thou shalt see when thou comest.

. . . . .

I would keep time with holy souls."

The hymn begins and ends with the following doxology, to which the disciples "going about in a ring" answer back "Amen."

"Glory to Thee, Father. Amen.
Glory to Thee, Word: Glory to thee, Grace. Amen.
Glory to Thee, Spirit: Glory to Thee, Holy One: Glory to thy glory. Amen.
We praise Thee, O Father: we give thanks to Thee, O Light, wherein dwelleth not darkness. Amen."

Now at the time of the execution of Jesus, the Lord appeared unto John who had fled into the Mount of Olives.

"Our Lord stood in the midst of the cave and lighted it up and said, 'John, unto the multitude down below in Jerusalem I am being crucified, and pierced with lances and reeds, and gall and vinegar is given me to drink: but unto thee I am speaking, and hearken thou to what I say. I put it into thy heart to come up into this mountain, that thou mightest hear matters needful for a disciple to learn from his teacher, and from a man to learn from his God.'"

Then follows a most interesting vision and interpretation of the Cross, which receives its further explanation in the cycle of ideas prevalent in the Valentinian circle of Gnosticism, which will be brought before the readers of LUCIFER in two or three months' time.

The Gnostic writer of the Acts of John does not labour under the disadvantage of the Valentinians, however; we have not to recover the battered fragments of his thought from the Church fathers; our author can speak for himself, in his own fashion. Would to heaven bigotry had not silenced so many sweet voices of the past!

"And the Lord having thus spoken, he showed me a cross of light set up, and about the cross a great multitude: and therein was one form and one likeness: and in the cross another multitude, not having one form. And the Lord himself I beheld above the cross, not having any shape, but only a voice: and a voice not such as was familiar to us, but a sweet (*or* peculiar) and kind voice and one truly of God, saying unto me: 'John, it is needful that one should hear these things from me: for I have need of one that will hear. This cross of light is sometimes called the Word by me for your sake, sometimes Mind, sometimes Jesus, sometimes Christ, sometimes a Door, sometimes a Way, sometimes Bread, sometimes Seed, sometimes Resurrection, sometimes Son, sometimes Father, sometimes Spirit, sometimes Life, sometimes Truth, sometimes Faith, sometimes Grace. Now these things it is called as toward men: but as to what it is in truth, as conceived of in itself and as spoken of to you—it is the marking off of all things, and the uplifting and foundation of those things that are fixed and were unsettled, and the joining together of wisdom. And whereas it is wisdom fitly compacted together, there are on the right and on the left of it, powers, principalities, dominations and dæmons, operations, threats, wrath, devils (*or* slanderings), Satan, and the Lower Root, from which the nature of the things that come into being proceeded.'"

The last sentence requires fresh translation; Dr. James has lost his way among the Gnostic nomenclature.

"This, then, is the Cross which fixed all things apart by a word, and marked off the things from birth and below it, and then compacted all into one: but this is not the cross of wood which thou wilt see when thou goest down hence, neither am I he that is upon the cross, whom now thou seest not, but only hearest a voice. I was reckoned to be what I was not, not being what I was unto many others: but they will call me something else, which is vile and not worthy of me. As therefore the place of rest is neither seen nor spoken of, much more shall I, the Lord of that place, be neither seen nor spoken of.

"Now the multitude of one aspect that is about the Cross is the lower nature: and those whom thou seest in the Cross, even if they have not one form, it is because not yet hath every member of Him that came down been comprehended. But when the upper nature shall be taken up, and the race which is repairing to me, in obedience to my voice, then that which now hears me not shall become as thou art; and shall no longer be what it now is, but above them, as I am now. For so long as thou callest not thyself mine, I am not that which I am. But if hearing thou hearkenest unto me, then shall thou be as I am, and I shall be what I was, when I have thee as I am with myself. For from this thou art. Care not therefore for the many, and them that are outside the mystery despise: for know thou that I am wholly with the Father, and the Father with me.

"Nothing therefore of the things which they will say of me have I suffered: nay, that suffering also which I showed unto you and unto the rest in the dance, I will that it be called a mystery. For what thou seest, that did I show thee: but what I am, that I alone know, and none else. Let me therefore keep that which is mine own, and that which is thine behold thou through me, and behold me in truth that I am, not what I said, but what thou art able to know, because thou art akin thereto. Thou hearest that I suffered, yet I suffered not: that I suffered not, yet did I suffer: that I was pierced, yet was I not smitten; hanged, and I was not hanged; that blood flowed from me, yet it flowed not; and, in a word, those things that they say of me I had not, and the things that they say not, those I suffered. Now what they are I will signify unto thee, for I know that thou wilt understand. Perceive thou therefore in me the praising (*perh.* slaying) of a Word, the piercing of a Word, the blood of a Word, the wound of a Word, the hanging of a Word, the passion of a Word, the nailing of a Word, the death of a Word. And thus speak I, separating off the manhood. Think thou therefore in the first place of the Word, then shalt thou perceive the Lord, and in the third place the Man, and what he hath suffered.'

"When he had spoken unto me these things, and others which I know not how to say as he would have me, he was taken up, no one of the multitudes having beheld him. And when I went down I laughed them all to scorn, inasmuch as he had told me the things which they said concerning him: and I held firmly this one thing in myself, that the Lord combined all things symbolically and by a dispensation towards men, for their conversion and their salvation."

All students of Gnosticism will naturally regard the Acts of John as a most precious fragment of the Gnosis, and even the orthodox will see in it many beauties which they cannot but admire in spite of what they are forecondemned to call its "heretical" setting.

We hope to return to a consideration of this most profoundly interesting fragment later on, and to furnish the reader with a translation and explanatory notes when the series of sketches, "Among the Gnostics," appears in book form.

G. R. S. M.

The Religions of India.

By E. W. Hopkins, Ph.D.Leipsic. [Boston: 1895.]

In *The Religions of India* we have one more instance of the impossibility of a Western mind grasping the inner significance of Eastern faiths without the key furnished by the Esoteric Philosophy. In this volume we have a careful and scholarly *résumé* of the shells of the religions of India. The author is acquainted only with the most exoteric teaching. He devotes no little attention to the climatic and social influences which he holds to be responsible for the Ṛig Veda. He traces the development of the Vedic hymns, and follows the ramifications of the varied tenets with considerable care, and occasionally with some sympathy. The Atharva Veda is commented upon, and our author then proceeds to review Brâhmanism, the Upanishads, Jainism, Buddhism, the Purâṇas, etc.

On concluding the perusal of this careful work the reader is seized with a sense of barrenness, and a realization of the real fruitlessness of an analysis that entirely misses the living spirit of these great faiths.

Dr. Hopkins strangely enough professes to approach the Hindu religions from within, and admits India to be the "land of religions," *par excellence*. He states, however, that only a few centuries are sufficient to account for the development of Hindu literature, yet marvels that two or three thousand years B.C. it "should be possible to produce such finished work." He holds the belief that the Vedic hymns were the work of primitive poets, worshipping natural phenomena, and supremely ignorant of Nature's laws. He is sympathetic towards the sublime teachings of the Upanishads, but fails to comprehend the spirit of Buddhism when he states Buddha to have been an atheist and pronounces Nirvâṇa to be annihilation. How the learned author reconciles the absolute annihilation theory with the statement that Nirvâṇa is attainable during life it is hard to say.

In reviewing the teaching of the Bhagavad Gîtâ, Dr. Hopkins denies the influence of Christian teachings. He does not believe that the doctrine of the Hindu Trimurti is borrowed from the Christian conception, and in other respects he writes without religious bias.

I. H.

THEOSOPHICAL AND MYSTIC PUBLICATIONS.

COLONEL OLCOTT'S now familiar stories of mesmeric cures come to an end in the May portion of "Old Diary Leaves," he having received instructions to suspend his healing operations. As he had treated eight thousand patients within twelve months it was evidently time to stop. The Colonel tells the story of a yogi who had achieved certain physiological powers and could do the feats of Hatha Yoga, but who knew so little of the higher training that he asked the Colonel to teach him how to concentrate the mind. The report from Colonel de Rochas of Eusapia's *séances* at Choisy-Yvrac concludes with this number. The phenomena are for the most part of the familiar materialization and object-moving kind. N. F. Bilimoria writes on "The Plague and its Causes." After mentioning the ordinary physical causes, astrology is brought to bear on the subject and some admirable examples of prophesying after the event are given. This paper is followed by some letters and a note by Colonel Olcott on the discovery of Kusinâra, where it is said that the body of the Buddha was cremated. The particulars given are as yet somewhat meagre.

The Journal of the Mahâ Bodhi Society contains the story of the temptation of Buddha by Mâra, a story that will always remain one of the finest in Buddhist tradition. Following this is "The Buddhist View of Relics," with a letter from a prominent priest and quotations from the "Questions of King Milinda." The subject is due to the gift of an alleged relic of Buddha to Dr. Paul Carus, in recognition of his services to the religion. *The Theosophic Gleaner* opens with the paper on Zoroastrianism entitled "Gaiyomard and Zarathushtra." The curious legend is expounded according to the system of *The Secret Doctrine*, the evolution of the races of mankind serving as the key to the allegory. In the *Ârya Bâla Bodhini* the story of Nachiketas is told in a manner suited for youthful readers, and for the encouragement of the same the life of one of the Indian sages is given. An interesting account of Colonel Olcott's free school for Pariah children is given, Lord Havelock having visited the school and received the report. *Rays of Light* contains a letter from Mrs. Mona Caird on some possible dangerous consequences of the Prince of Wales's Hospital scheme.

The Vâhan for June is not a specially entertaining number, the "Enquirer" having been reduced to very small dimensions, owing chiefly to the insertion of three long letters. The writers were aroused by an answer of A.A.W. in a recent issue on the sufferings of animals, and the letters contain vigorous protests against the views expounded therein. The short "Enquirer" is made up by two answers of C. W. L. on the question of astral help given by children, and one by P. S. on the duty of "non-receiving." The first one contains a short note by "Cyril," the child to whom the question mainly refers.

Mercury opens with an article by Mrs. Besant on the work of the Theosophical Society. She distinguishes the nature of the work which should be undertaken by a Theosophist from that which is the part of an ordinary religionist or a social reformer. The importance of self-training and of ordinary education is also emphasized. The incidents of the growth of Christianity and the overcoming of the few cultured by the many ignorant, are given as indications of dangers which may possibly menace the spread of Theosophy. The now too-familiar "close of the cycle" forms the subject, not only for the other article of the number but also for an answer in "the Forum Department." The paper contributes a good deal of information, mainly astrological. On two or three different occasions in the years 1897 to 1899 there are to be five and six planets in one sign, which would appear to portend horrors. According to Hindu astrology, we are told five planets in one sign means the destruction of all towns, and six of all kingdoms. We have the promise of some very exciting times. There is an amusing letter from Mr. Fullerton on the duties of a General Secretary, which throws a side-light on the responsibilities and the delights of office.

Theosophy in Australasia appears in its new garb, and the improvement is most noticeable. It now gives place to three articles besides the usual notes and activities. The first paper is on "Some Ancient Conceptions of Hell." The story of Theseus and the labyrinth is told as an illustration of the idea of hell. Miss Edger writes on "Unity," and L. E. Harcus on the Darwinian theory and the Theosophical view of evolution.

Le Lotus Bleu opens with a translation of Mr. Keightley's article on "The Desire-Body" from LUCIFER, followed by the continuation of Mr. Leadbeater's "Invisible Helpers." Another paper on cycles, this time by Mons. Courmes, helps to fill our French magazine. Luxâme's papers "Under the Bodhi Tree" come to an end this month, life and the means of emancipation from rebirth forming the subject of the discourse.

Sophia begins with memorial articles, the first on Madame Blavatsky, the sixth anniversary of her death giving rise to the article. The second is on Señor Montolíu, the devoted Spanish Theosophist who founded the Spanish review and was largely instrumental in obtaining a hold for Theosophy in Spain. The body of the journal is made up of well-chosen translations. Along with this issue appears the first section of a Spanish translation of *The Story of Atlantis*, which will appear with the maps.

Nova Lux continues with the article by Signor Calvari on "The Ego and its Vehicles," the physical body being dealt with, and the processes by which it may be purified. Following the Theosophical article is a paper on "Idealism and Materialism" by a gentleman having an elaborate mystical title, and a letter from a Martinist writer.

Afra in the Dutch *Theosophia* writes on "Consciousness," explaining the different states and stages. The other original paper is one of some length on "Magnetism" dealing with the discoveries of Mesmer and the more recent investigations into the subject.

The *Teosofisk Tidskrift* continues Mr. Leadbeater's paper on dreams and concludes one by Mrs. Besant, a number of original contributions completing the issue. *Theosophia* also arrives from Sweden.

The German magazines, *Metaphysische Rundschau* and *Lotusblüthen* are somewhat dull reading, the subjects chosen being for the most part of a very heavy order.

La Nuovissima Antologia Italiana contains two articles on Spiritualism, one of which originates in a criticism of Eusapia, the now famous medium. The other is a lengthy continued paper dealing with phenomena and their explanation, written from an independent point of view.

La Irradiacion, the Spanish spiritualistic journal, opens with a letter on dreams and presentiments from a Russian contributor, and is filled for the most part with general notes and ethical reflections. Dr. Simms' work on physiognomy is now being published in Spanish by the journal.

Reformador, a Portuguese fortnightly magazine, published in Rio de Janeiro, is devoted mainly to spiritism and psychic matters and contains numerous translated and original articles. Allen Kardec is, of course, the master followed. Spiritism, excepting the English and American branches, has done much to spread the ideas of reincarnation and karma taught by that writer.

Yet another "end of the cycle" publication! This time it is a production of the Lake Harris school, one of the funniest pamphlets that have appeared for a long time. It is called *The Impending World Crisis*, and consists largely of extracts from letters by Lake Harris and other specially privileged initiates of his school. The crisis appears to be coming by way of the "Fire-Breath," which is beginning to manifest through the body of the prophet in several very eccentric manners. The gem of the communication is an account of how "father" (Lake Harris) lost the skin of his "arch-natural body." This was removed "excepting in three places, one at the neck, one at the solar plexus, one at the back of the neck; the skin was pulled off, as I pull off my jersey"! The appearance of "father" under these circumstances must have been interesting if the operation was visible to mere ordinary mortals. This, however, was probably not the case. But even this production is almost surpassed by some pamphlets issued by "The Order of the Temple." It appears that God the Father (not merely the Son of orthodox Christianity) has now incarnated, and as a woman! The author pathetically says: "Surely common-sense might assist Men's Faith on this point." With all the eccentricities, however, there is a welcome lack in these pamphlets of the vulgarity so commonly associated with pseudo-mysticism, and some of the ideas are likely enough to be useful to those whose thoughts run in such peculiar channels.

We have to acknowledge the receipt of *Notes and Queries*; *The Metaphysical Magazine*; *The Vegetarian*; *Light*; *The Agnostic Journal*; *Current Literature*; *The Literary Digest*; *The New Unity*, a semi-religious Chicago paper, with a series of articles by Mr. George F. Wright, a well-known Theosophist in Chicago; *Theosophy*; *The Pacific Theosophist*; *The Mystical World*; *The Irish Theosophist*; *The Theosophical Forum*; *The English Mechanic*.

A.

Women's Printing Society, Limited, 66, Whitcomb Street, W.C.

VOL. XX. JULY 15, 1897. NO. 119.

LUCIFER.

ON THE WATCH-TOWER.

"THE SECRET DOCTRINE." VOLUME III.

IN 1888 the first edition of Volumes I. and II. of H. P. Blavatsky's greatest work, *The Secret Doctrine*, was placed in the hands of the public. In 1893 the third and revised edition of these volumes was issued, and completed in 1895 by an exhaustive Index. The revised edition was a work of much labour, and every effort was made by the editors to verify every quotation they could and correct the many errors of form of the earlier issues. The errors of substance the editors had no right to amend. One of the substantial misconceptions that H. P. B. laboured under was that she had in hand a sufficient mass of MS. to make two additional volumes. This was not actually the case. No doubt had she lived she would have carried out her promise, for her custom was to write at least half of the work she was engaged upon as it was going through the press—a costly and disorderly custom; nevertheless such was her way, and only too glad should we all have been had she thus carried out her usual programme.

As it is, sufficient matter for only one volume has been left behind, and the contents of this part are not exactly on the lines she promised her readers. Nevertheless, Volume III. is a bulky tome, and among other things contains a number of valuable hints, embodied in "Some Papers on the Bearing of Occult Philosophy on Life," which fill the concluding pages (433-594) of the volume. These papers were originally circulated privately among a large body of students, from among whom it was hoped that some would gradually be fitted for further instruction of a more intimate nature. The papers having now served their purpose are made public, and thus exhaust all the literary remains of H. P. B.

It is somewhat a novel experience for the present writer, who has edited, in one form or another, almost all that H. P. B. has written in English, with the exception of *Isis Unveiled*, to find himself turning over the leaves of Volume III. of *The Secret Doctrine* as one of the general public, for with the exception of pp. 433-594 he has seen no word of it before. But other work has prevented his sharing in the labour of editing the MS., and the burden has fallen on the shoulders of Mrs. Besant.

What, then, is the first impression of one who has minutely studied every turn and twist of H. P. B.'s phraseology and literary methods, and read everything she has written on theosophical subjects?

We cannot disguise the fact that the first feeling is one of disappointment. The spirit of the stanzas and commentaries, which for the theosophist make the two first volumes stand out a head and shoulders beyond all other theosophical literature, is entirely absent. The pages are eagerly scanned for the discovery of a new gold-mine of the nature of stanza or commentary, but with the exception of one or two paragraphs none is to be found. In fact, until we come to p. 359 and "The Mystery of Buddha," the sections on which fill pp. 359-432, we find but *disjecta membra*—sections, the majority of which were evidently excluded from Volumes I. and II. because of their inferiority to the rest of the work. The editor was bound to publish these, but we entirely share her private opinion, that it would have been better to have printed them as separate articles in LUCIFER, than to have included them as part of *The Secret Doctrine*. One thing is almost certain, that had Mme. Blavatsky lived these sections in their present form would not have formed part of her great work. They represent her in her least important capacity.

All educated students of H. P. B.'s writings have to make a great distinction between what she wrote from her own first-hand knowledge, or from hints she gleaned from the numerous friends with whom she was in psychic contact, and set down as she understood them, or what she had actually impressed on her mind by her living teachers (for instance the stanzas and commentaries), and what she compiled from such books as were in her possession, as being in her opinion confirmatory of the great science she knew to be true. The first 358 pages of Volume III. fall mostly within the latter category. It is all her own unaided work, and the task for which she was least fitted. This is of course patent to all really educated readers, though it may still surprise some who, unable to form any opinion of their own on matters of science and scholarship, have laboured under the erroneous impression that H. P. B. was a most learned writer in the usual sense of the term. This was not so. She had no scientific or literary training of any kind whatever. That she had the ability—a rare and extraordinary ability—which would have enabled her to shine most brilliantly in science or letters, had she trained herself in either, is indubitable. But as a matter of fact she was entirely destitute of that training. In her books she deals with the most abstruse mathematical problems; in actual life she counted on her fingers. In her books she deals with all kinds of languages; in actual life she knew, when I knew her, only Russian, French, and English, all of which she wrote most fluently and with a rare literary force, but none of which she wrote grammatically. She has herself told me that her articles to the *Russi Vyestnik*, which were the originals of her brilliant sketches *From the Caves and Jungles of Hindostan*, and made her famous throughout the length and breadth of Russia as "Raddha Bai," nearly drove the editor Katkoff into an early grave because of her contempt for the *convenances* of literary Russian.

Why, then, in spite of this want of training, did she deal at such length with the work not only of the scientist and scholar, but of the specialist? Simply because she could find no one else to do the task. Her work could brook no delay, and better to do something, though very imperfectly, than to do nothing. H. P. B. was essentially a pioneer; she went to work with an axe and lusty muscles, she left the plane and sandpaper of the specialist for those who came after her. She set up finger-posts, and left a "blaze" through the jungles for the emigrants who followed in her footsteps to the unknown land.

She, who was so courageous for theosophy, was timid as to herself. Not content to let the stanzas and commentaries, and what she wrote of her own knowledge, stand alone and on their own merits, she needs must try to substantiate them by evidence drawn from ordinary scientific and literary sources. She did not know that in the future students would read *The Secret Doctrine* solely for the stanzas and herself, and not because of her controversial and explanatory appendices; that they would welcome with joy, as the sight of an oasis in the desert, her own views without admixture of De Mirville, Ralston Skinner, Kenealy, and the *tutti quanti* (as she would say) of unscholarly and unreliable *dilettanti*, with whom she interlards her pages.

It is strange to observe how frequently when her contention is right, she seems to have chosen, with fatal accuracy, the very worst author to support her view. Books of past generations, which have been entirely discredited by more accurate modern research and scholarship, were just the supports which she singled out, and this in spite of the fact that the *more recent discoveries frequently confirmed her view far more strongly* than the fantastic and chaotic views of slipshod writers whom she, and she alone, had disinterred from deserved oblivion.

Who, for instance, ever heard of De Mirville until unkind fate placed his six volumes in the hands of Mme. Blavatsky? Not that her treatment of him, however, is without its humorous side. Here we have a French writer of fifty years ago reviving the corpse of the old Patristic theory of "plagiarism by anticipation," and producing a mass of "learned" (certainly not scholarly) evidence that the Devil anticipated the whole of the ceremonies and doctrines of Roman Catholic Christendom thousands of centuries before the time of Christ, in all lands and climes. Of course no sane person to-day believes so preposterous an imbecility. H. P. B., taking advantage of this, with great good-humour uses the whole of De Mirville's researches to establish the diametrically opposite position, namely, that Roman Catholic Christendom has copied from the whole of Paganism, and not only copied, but copied badly. Poor De Mirville; *requiescat in pace.* But there will be "much talk" if his spook should come across H. P. B. on the astral.

Such being the facts with regard to this side of H. P. Blavatsky's literary work, we find, as we should expect, many errors of detail and many fantastic mistakes, which every trained student can immediately detect. This is regrettable, for it strongly prejudices every scientist and scholar against a writer whose value lies in quite a different direction. The theosophist, however, will understand this, and he alone will be benefited by the information which H. P. B. really possessed. In this connection it is interesting to observe how H. P. B. threw back to the literary habits of antiquity. This is shown not so much in her revised and re-edited works as in her early writings, such as *Isis Unveiled* and her unedited MSS. Antiquity dispensed almost entirely with quotation marks and references. H. P. B., being innocent of any literary training in her present birth, threw back to the literary habits of her past. Hence many tears for her modern editors, and much searching for quotations and references.

We therefore appreciate deeply the labour which has been expended on editing the present volume, for we know only too well the long toil of verification necessitated by Volumes I. and II. How Mrs. Besant in her too busy life has found time for the task of supervision and general editing is a marvel. For some of the proof-reading she had, owing to her many absences from London, to be dependent on others, and on the whole Volume III. is not so carefully done as Volumes I. and II. A glance at the Index of the first volumes would have saved the proof-readers from passing over some errors. The most regrettable errors, however, are the mistakes in Greek words. The editor was under the impression that the reader who had the Hebrew in charge was also responsible for the Greek, and only at a late date discovered that her colleague was not a double-barrelled paṇḍit, and that he repudiated any responsibility for the accuracy of words in the Hellenic language. The Hebrew also seems to have been maltreated occasionally after leaving his hands. The Sanskrit transliteration is also sometimes inconsistent; as for the Tibetan and other more obscure tongues we cannot pronounce an opinion. Of course such matters are of no consequence to the general reader, but they are a considerable scandal, or stumbling-block, to the very people who would be most useful to the Society if we could but win their adhesion. The printing also is not quite so good as that of the first two volumes. On the other hand the price is small for a book of this nature, being but 15*s.* net., to be obtained of course at the T. P. S., 26,

Charing Cross, S.W. Simultaneously with the English edition, an American edition has been published at Chicago.

But enough of explanation and criticism. It goes without saying that every student will complete his set of the volumes of *The Secret Doctrine*. With page 359 we come to a more definite subject and the interesting speculations as to the Buddha. Here we bid good-bye to De Mirville and company, and meet with H. P. B. in another vein. She here treats us to a series of veiled hints, some of which seem to be most valuable. Too few students are aware how most of real worth in her work is hidden away in a note or parenthesis. When we further come to page 433, we are made a present of a number of notes which many have already found of great value. Not, however, that anything is worked out in detail. That was no part of H. P. B.'s task. She was a comet, not a planet, and her orbit was erratic. But she was a bright luminary for all that.

In conclusion we may take the opportunity of saying something in general as to H. P. B., who more than anyone else inaugurated the present great theosophical movement. This is all the more necessary seeing that at one time there was danger in the Society of promulgating a very erroneous notion of her task and character. And let me preface this by saying that I yield to no one in my love for my old teacher, or in my gratitude to her for setting my feet once more on the path that leads to the Gods. But I am no worshipper of persons, and as yet I have not found my ideal on earth. I love her, but I am not blind to her manifold imperfections. I love her for her greatness and not for her littlenesses. If I had found her perfect, I needs must have worshipped her. But no one is perfect but God alone. H. P. B. was far from perfection, but she was and is in many ways great.

By the light then of what is said above—and to that much could be added—how is it possible to make a scripture out of *The Secret Doctrine?* And yet we have seen a tendency in this direction in the Society! Like the *ipse dixit* of the mediæval schoolmen, we have heard appeal made to *The Secret Doctrine* as the arbiter of discussions; and even to this day, in the *devia et longinqua loca* of the theosophical movement, such an unhealthy frame of mind is occasionally revealed. "But *The Secret Doctrine* says" so-and-so is the sacramental formula. Curiously enough the same people are ready enough to appreciate the arguments which dispose of the absurd dogma of plenary inspiration of the *Bible*, and are prepared to treat it as a human document in the fullest sense of the words! Now the arguments which apply to the one subject equally apply to the other; I say equally, I should say far more fully. The *Bible* is surrounded by the glamour of centuries, *The Secret Doctrine* is of yesterday, of to-day. It is only necessary to state the position to recognize the absurdity of it. From the volumes called *The Secret Doctrine* you can quote diametrically contradictory passages, just as you can in the *Bible* or in any large collection of writings dealing with similar subjects. Again, we do not know what *the* "Secret Doctrine" *is*; H. P. B. has only laboured to show that there is *a* "*Secret* Doctrine."

Who more than she has dinned into our ears the wise advice that we should hold to the "spirit" and not to the "letter" of any doctrine? How consumedly she would have laughed to find herself in the minds of some erected into a sort of prophet of a new faith! How graphic would have been her characterization of such stupidity! "My theosophical geese"!!

Now one of the things she was naturally compelled to do in her task of initiating the movement was to form a link with the past—that is to say, to put the present movement in karmic relation with past movements of a similar nature. Just as a man at a birth takes on a body which is the expression of his old karmic tendencies, his virtues *and his vices*, so the present public theosophic movement had to have a body formed for it which represented the virtues and the vices of all past public movements of such a nature. H. P. B. played the function of the "builder" who fashioned this karmic body, her writings are the first mould of its bones, and sinews, and brain.

But just as a man, if he is to progress, must eliminate the vicious tendencies of his nature and cultivate the virtuous, so must the theosophical movement choose the best in H. P. B.'s writings and let the worst go. In more general terms, we must study the past only for experience and to glean the best we can from that past; we must sift out error and absurdity and ignorance and childishness, and above all we must start *fresh causes* in our new body which shall make for righteousness, and clear thought, and sweet reason.

We must not slavishly copy the past, unless we wish to lose our present incarnation and make it of no effect.

H. P. B. speaks with unqualified enthusiasm of many things in the past which were not unqualified blessings. No doubt she was thoroughly in earnest, but in that she acted as the karmic builder of the embryonic body of the Theosophical Society, into which she had to collect as many elements as that karma demanded, Kabalists, Rosicrucians, Alchemists, Astrologers, Vedântins, Buddhists, Zoroastrians, Hellenists, Stoics, Gnostics, Ceremonialists, Devotees, Sceptics, Hermetists, Phenomenalists, Charlatans, Tricksters, Adventurers, all and divers. Such being the elements, the "tañhic elements" of the Society, how will the Ego of our movement purify them? The future alone will show; meanwhile it is open for each one of us to work consciously with that Ego or to be absorbed in the unconscious host of "tañhic elements."

Of one thing we are assured, namely, that we cannot "put new wine into old bottles." If the "new wine" of real initiation is to be poured into any of us, it will only be when we have evolved in ourselves a new vessel to contain it. To fashion ourselves in the old moulds of the movements of the past is retrogression, not progression, at least so it seems to me. And though I love some of that past as much as most people, and have worked hard to bring back some of it to the memory of my fellow students, and shall continue to do so, it is only my playing in my turn the part of a minor "building elemental" and weaving into the body some more subtle matter with the old karmic tendencies. This must be done; but the vehicle of the "new man" must be made of still purer material, and this we should never for one instant forget.

It is now for two years that the Theosophical Society has felt the benefit of its recent purification, and every student in it knows that it is healthier and stronger and more conscious than it has ever been before. And this being so, it is natural that Volume III. of *The Secret Doctrine* should be read with greater intelligence than Volumes I. and II., and that its publication should have led to the remarks which have been made by a lover of H. P. B. and your obedient servant,

G. R. S. M.

REINCARNATION.

(*Concluded from p.* 274.)

THE third vehicle of consciousness, the mental body, is rarely, if ever, vivified for independent action without the direct instruction of a teacher, and its functioning belongs to the life of the disciple at the present stage of human evolution. It is re-arranged for separate functioning on the mental plane, and here again experience and training are needed ere it comes fully under its owner's control. A fact—common to all these three vehicles of consciousness, but more apt to mislead perhaps in the subtler than in the denser, because it is generally forgotten in their case while it is so obvious that it is remembered in the denser—is that they are subject to evolution, and that with their higher evolution their powers to receive and to respond to vibrations increase. How many more shades of a colour are seen by a trained eye than by an untrained. How many overtones are heard by a trained ear, where the untrained hears only the single fundamental note. As the physical senses grow more keen, the world becomes fuller and fuller, and where the peasant is only conscious of his furrow and his plough, the cultured mind is conscious of hedgerow flower and quivering aspen, of rapturous melody down-dropping from the skylark and the whirring of tiny wings through the adjoining wood, of the scudding of rabbits under the curled fronds of the bracken, and the squirrels playing with each other through the branches of the beeches, of all the gracious movements of wild things, of all the fragrant odours of field and woodland, of all the changing glories of the cloud-flecked sky, and of all the chasing lights and shadows on the hills. Both the peasant and the cultured have eyes, both have brains, but of what differing powers of observation, of what differing powers to receive impressions. Thus also in other worlds. As the astral and mental bodies begin to function as separate vehicles of consciousness they are in, as it were, the peasant stage of receptivity, and only fragments of the astral and mental worlds, with their strange and elusive phenomena, make their way into consciousness; but they evolve rapidly, embracing more and more, and conveying to consciousness a more and more accurate reflection of its environment. Here, as everywhere else, we have to remember that our knowledge is not the limit of Nature's powers, and that in the astral and mental worlds, as in the physical, we are still children, picking up a few shells cast up by the waves, while the treasures hid in the ocean are still unexplored.

The quickening of the causal body as a vehicle of consciousness follows in due course the quickening of the mental body, and opens up to man a yet more marvellous state of consciousness, stretching backwards into an illimitable past, onwards into the reaches of the future. Then the Thinker not only possesses the memory of his own past and can trace his growth through the long succession of his incarnate and excarnate lives, but he can also roam at will through the storied past of the earth, and learn the weighty lessons of world-experience, studying the hidden laws which guide evolution and the deep secrets of life hidden in the bosom of Nature. In that lofty vehicle of consciousness he can reach the veiled Isis, and lift a corner of her down-dropped veil; for there he can face her eyes without being blinded by her lightning glances, and he can see in the radiance that flows from her the causes of the world's sorrow and its ending, with heart pitiful and compassionate but no longer wrung with helpless pain. Strength and calm and wisdom come to those who are using the causal body as a vehicle of consciousness, and who behold with opened eyes the glory of the Good Law.

When the buddhic body is quickened as a vehicle of consciousness, the man enters into the bliss of non-separateness, and knows in full and vivid realization his unity with all that is. As the predominant element of consciousness in the causal body is knowledge, and ultimately wisdom, so the predominant element of consciousness in the buddhic body is bliss and love. The serenity of wisdom chiefly marks the one, while tenderest compassion streams forth inexhaustibly from the other; when to these is added the Godlike and unruffled strength that marks the functioning of Âtmâ, then humanity is crowned with divinity, and the God-man is manifest in all the plenitude of his power, of his wisdom, of his love.

The handing down to the lower vehicles of such part of the consciousness belonging to the higher as they are able to receive, does not immediately follow on the successive quickening of the vehicles. In this matter individuals differ very widely, according to their circumstances and their work, for this quickening of the vehicles above the physical rarely occurs till probationary discipleship is reached, and then the duties to be discharged depend on the needs of the time. The disciple, and even the aspirant for discipleship, is taught to hold all his powers entirely for the service of the world, and the sharing of the lower consciousness in the knowledge of the higher is for the most part determined by the needs of the work in which the disciple is engaged. It is necessary that the disciple should have the full use of his vehicles of consciousness on the higher planes, as much of his work can only be accomplished in them ; but the conveying of a knowledge of that work to the physical vehicle, which is no way concerned in it, is a matter of no importance, and the conveyance or non-conveyance is generally determined by the effect that the one course or the other would have on the efficiency of his work on the physical plane. The strain on the physical body when the higher consciousness compels it to vibrate responsively is very great, at the present stage of evolution, and unless the external circumstances are very favourable, this strain is apt to cause nervous disturbance, hyper-sensitiveness with its attendant evils. Hence most of those who are in full possession of the quickened higher vehicles of consciousness, and whose most important work is done out of the body, remain apart from the busy haunts of men, if they desire to throw down into the physical consciousness the knowledge they use on the higher planes, thus preserving the sensitive physical vehicle from the rough usage and clamour of ordinary life.

The main preparations to be made for receiving in the physical vehicle the vibrations of the higher consciousness are : its purification from grosser materials by pure food and pure life ; the entire subjugation of the passions, and the cultivation of an even, balanced temper and mind, unaffected by the turmoil and vicissitudes of external life; the habit of quiet meditation on lofty topics, turning the mind away from the objects of the senses, and from the mental images arising from them, and fixing it on higher things; the cessation of hurry, especially of that restless, excitable hurry of the mind, which keeps the brain continually at work and flying from one subject to another; the genuine love for the things of the higher world, that makes them more attractive than the objects of the lower, so that the mind rests contentedly in their companionship, as in that of a well-loved friend. In fact, the preparations are much the same as those necessary for the conscious separation of "soul" from "body," and those were elsewhere stated by me as follows: the student

"Must begin by practising extreme temperance in all things, cultivating an equable and serene state of mind; his life must be clean and his thoughts pure, his body held in strict subjection to the soul, and his mind trained to occupy itself with noble and lofty themes; he must habitually practise compassion, sympathy, helpfulness to others, with indifference to troubles and pleasures affecting himself, and he must cultivate courage, steadfastness and devotion. In fact, he must live the religion and ethics that other people for the most part only talk. Having by persevering practice learned to control his mind to some extent, so that he is able to keep it fixed on one line of thought for some little time, he must begin its more rigid training by a daily practice of concentration on some difficult or abstract subject, or on some lofty object of devotion; this concentration means the firm fixing of the mind on one single point, without wandering, and without yielding to any distractions caused by external objects, by the activity of the senses, or by that of the mind itself. It must be braced up to an unswerving steadiness and fixity, until gradually it will learn so to withdraw its attention from the outer world and from the body that the senses will remain quiet and still while the mind is intensely alive, with all its energies drawn inwards to be launched at a single point of thought, the highest to which it can attain. When it is able to hold itself thus with comparative ease, it is ready for a further step, and by a strong but calm effort of the will it can throw itself beyond the highest thought it can reach *while working in the physical brain*, and in that effort will rise to and unite itself with the higher consciousness and find itself free of the body. When this is done there is no sense of sleep or dream nor any loss of consciousness; the man finds himself outside his body, but as though he had merely slipped off a weighty encumbrance, not as though he had lost any part of himself; he is not really 'disembodied,' but has risen out of his gross body 'in a body of light,' which obeys his slightest thought and serves as a beautiful and perfect instrument for carrying out his will. In this he is free of the subtle worlds, but will need to train his faculties long and carefully for reliable work under the new conditions.

"Freedom from the body may be obtained in other ways: by the rapt intensity of devotion or by special methods that may be imparted by a great teacher to his disciple. Whatever the way, the end is the same—the setting free of the soul in full consciousness, able to examine its new surroundings in regions beyond the treading of the man of flesh. At will it can return to the body and re-enter it, and under these circumstances it can impress on the brain-mind, and thus retain while in the body, the memory of the experiences it has undergone." *

Those who have grasped the main ideas sketched in the foregoing pages, will feel that these ideas are in themselves the strongest proof that reincarnation is a fact in nature. It is necessary, in order that the vast evolution implied in the phrase, "the evolution of the Soul," may be accomplished. The only alternative—putting aside for the moment the materialistic idea that the Soul is only the aggregate of the vibrations of a particular kind of physical matter—is that each Soul is a new creation, made when a babe is born, and stamped with virtuous or with vicious tendencies, endowed with ability or with stupidity, by the arbitrary whim of the creative power. As the Mahommedan would say, his fate is hung round its neck at birth, for a man's fate depends on his character and his surroundings, and a newly-created soul flung into the world must be doomed to happiness or misery according to the circumstances environing him and the character stamped upon him. Predestination in its most offensive form is the alternative of reincarnation. Instead of looking on men as slowly evolving, so that the brutal savage of to-day will in time evolve the noblest qualities of saint and hero, and thus seeing in the world a wisely planned and wisely directed process of growth, we shall be obliged to see in it a chaos of most unjustly treated sentient beings, awarded happiness or misery, knowledge or ignorance, virtue or vice, wealth or poverty, genius or idiocy, by an arbitrary external will, unguided by either justice or mercy—a veritable pandemonium, irrational and unmeaning. And this chaos is supposed to be the higher part of a cosmos, in the lower regions of which are manifested all the orderly and beautiful workings of a law that ever evolves higher and more complex forms from the lower and the simpler, that obviously "makes for righteousness," for harmony and for beauty.

If it be admitted that the Soul of the savage is destined to live and to evolve, and that he is not doomed for eternity to his present infant state, but that his evolution will take place after death and in other worlds, then the principle of Soul-evolution is conceded, and the question of the place of evolution alone remains. Were all Souls

* "Conditions of Life after Death." *Nineteenth Century*, November, 1896.

on earth at the same stage of evolution, much might be said for the contention that further worlds are needed for the evolution of Souls beyond the infant stage. But we have around us Souls that are far advanced, and that were born with noble mental and moral qualities. By parity of reasoning, we must suppose them to have been evolved in other worlds ere their one birth in this, and we cannot but wonder why an earth that offers varied conditions fit for little-developed and also for advanced Souls, should only be paid one flying visit by Souls at every stage of development, all the rest of their evolution being carried on in worlds similar to this, equally able to afford all the conditions needed to evolve the Souls at different stages of evolution, as we find them to be when they are born here. The Ancient Wisdom teaches, indeed, that the Soul progresses through many worlds, but it also teaches that he is born in each of these worlds over and over again, until he has completed the evolution possible in that world. The worlds themselves, according to its teaching, form an evolutionary chain, and each plays its own part as a field for certain stages of evolution. Our own world offers a field suitable for the evolution of the mineral, vegetable, animal and human kingdoms, and therefore collective or individual re-incarnation goes on upon it in all these kingdoms. Truly, further evolution lies before us in other worlds, but in the divine order they are not open to us until we have learned and mastered the lessons our own world has to teach.

There are many lines of thought that lead us to the same goal of re-incarnation, as we study the world around us. The immense differences that separate man from man have been already noticed as implying an evolutionary past behind each Soul; and attention has been drawn to these as differentiating the individual re-incarnation of men—all of whom belong to a single species—from the re-incarnation of monadic group-souls in the lower kingdoms. The comparatively small differences that separate the physical bodies of men, all being externally recognizable as men, should be contrasted with the immense differences that separate the lowest savage and the noblest human type in mental and moral capacities. Savages are often splendid in physical development and with large cranial contents, but how different their mind from that of a philosopher or of a saint.

If high mental and moral qualities are regarded as the accumulated results of civilized living, then we are confronted by the fact that the ablest men of the present are overtopped by the intellectual giants of the past, and that none of our own day reaches the moral attitude of some historical saints. Further, we have to consider that genius has neither parent nor child, that it appears suddenly and not as the apex of a gradually improving family, and is itself generally sterile, or if a child be born to it, it is a child of the body, not of the mind. Still more significantly, a musical genius is for the most part born in a musical family, because that form of genius needs for its manifestation a nervous organization of a peculiar kind, and nervous organization falls under the law of heredity. But how often in such a family its object seems over when it has provided a body for a genius, and it then flickers out and vanishes in a few generations into the obscurity of average humanity. When are the descendants of Bach, of Beethoven, of Mozart, of Mendelssohn, equal to their sires? Truly genius does not descend from father to son, like the family physical types of the Stuart and the Bourbon.

On what ground, save that of reincarnation, can the "infant prodigy" be accounted for? Take as an instance the case of the child who became Dr. Young, the discoverer of the undulatory theory of light, a man whose greatness is scarcely yet sufficiently widely recognized. As a child of two he could read "with considerable fluency," and before he was four he had read through the Bible twice; at seven he began arithmetic, and mastered Walkingham's *Tutor's Assistant* before he had reached the middle of it under his tutor, and a few years later we find him mastering while at school, Latin, Greek, Hebrew, mathematics, book-keeping, French, Italian, turning and telescope-making, and delighting in Oriental literature. At fourteen he was to be placed under private tuition with a boy a year and a half younger, but the tutor first engaged failing to arrive, Young taught the other boy.* Sir William Rowan Hamilton showed power even more precocious. He began to learn Hebrew when he was barely three, and "at the age of seven, he was pronounced by one of the Fellows of Trinity College, Dublin, to have shown a greater knowledge of the language than many candi-

* *Life of Dr. Thomas Young*, by G. Peacock, D.D.

dates for a fellowship. At the age of thirteen he had acquired considerable knowledge of at least thirteen languages. Among these, besides the classical and the modern European languages, were included Persian, Arabic, Sanscrit, Hindustani, and even Malay. . . . He wrote, at the age of fourteen, a complimentary letter to the Persian Ambassador, who happened to visit Dublin; and the latter said he had not thought there was a man in Britain who could have written such a document in the Persian language." A relative of his says: "I remember him a little boy of six, when he would answer a difficult mathematical question, and run off gaily to his little cart. At twelve he engaged Colburn, the American 'calculating boy,' who was then being exhibited as a curiosity in Dublin, and he had not always the worst of the encounter." When he was eighteen, Dr. Brinkley (Royal Astronomer of Ireland) said of him in 1823, "This young man, I do not say *will be*, but *is*, the first mathematician of his age." "At college his career was perhaps unexampled. Amongst a number of competitors of more than ordinary merit, he was first in every subject, and at every examination."*

Let the thoughtful student compare these boys with a semi-idiot, or even with an average lad, note how, starting with these advantages, they become leaders of thought, and then ask himself whether such Souls have no past behind them.

Family likenesses are generally explained as being due to the "law of heredity;" but differences in mental and moral character are continually found within a family circle, and these are left unexplained. Reincarnation explains the likenesses by the fact that a Soul in taking birth is directed to a family which provides by its physical heredity a body suitable to express his characteristics; and it explains the unlikenesses by attaching the mental and moral character to the individual himself, while showing that ties set up in the past have led him to take birth in connection with some other individual of that family. A "matter of significance in connection with twins is that during infancy they will often be indistinguishable from each other, even to the keen eye of mother and of nurse. Whereas, later in life, when Manas has been working on his physical encasement, he will have so modified it that the physical likeness lessens, and

* *North British Review*, September, 1866.

the differences of character stamp themselves on the mobile features."* Physical likeness with mental and moral unlikeness seems to imply the meeting of two different lines of causation.

The striking dissimilarity found to exist between people of about equal intellectual power in assimilating particular kinds of knowledge is another "pointer" to reincarnation. A truth is recognized at once by one, while the other fails to grasp it even after long and careful observation. Yet the very opposite may be the case when another truth is presented to them, and it may be seen by the second and missed by the first. "Two students are attracted to Theosophy and begin to study it; at a year's end one is familiar with its main conceptions and can apply them, while the other is struggling in a maze. To the one each principle seemed familiar on presentation; to the other new, unintelligible, strange. The believer in reincarnation understands that the teaching is old to the one and new to the other; one learns quickly *because he remembers*, he is but recovering past knowledge; the other learns slowly because his experience has not included these truths of nature, and he is acquiring them toilfully for the first time."† So also ordinary intuition is "merely recognition of a fact familiar in a past life, though met with for the first time in the present,"‡ another sign of the road along which the individual has travelled in the past.

The main difficulty with many people in the reception of the doctrine of reincarnation is their own absence of memory of their past. Yet they are every day familiar with the fact that they have forgotten very much even of their lives in their present bodies, and that the early years of childhood are blurred, and those of infancy a blank. They must also know that events of the past which have entirely slipped out of their normal consciousness are yet hidden away in dark caves of memory, and can be brought out again vividly in some form of disease or under the influence of mesmerism. A dying man has been known to speak a language heard only in infancy, and unknown to him during a long life; in delirium, events long forgotten have presented themselves vividly to the consciousness. Nothing is really forgotten; but much is

* *Reincarnation*, by Annie Besant, p. 64.

† *Ibid.*, p. 67.

‡ *Ibid.*, p. 67.

hidden out of sight of the limited vision of our waking consciousness, the most limited form of our consciousness although the only consciousness recognized by the vast majority. Just as the memory of some of the present life is indrawn beyond the reach of this waking consciousness, and only makes itself known again when the brain is hypersensitive, and thus able to respond to vibrations that usually beat against it unheeded, so is the memory of the past lives stored up out of reach of the physical consciousness. It is all with the Thinker, who alone persists from life to life; he has the whole book of memory within his reach, for he is the only "I" that has passed through all the experiences recorded therein. Moreover, he can impress his own memories of the past on his physical vehicle, as soon as it has been sufficiently purified to answer to his swift and subtle vibrations, and then the man of flesh can share his knowledge of the storied past. The difficulty of memory does not lie in forgetfulness, for the lower vehicle, the physical body, has never passed through the previous lives of its owner; it lies in the absorption of the present body in its present environment, in its coarse irresponsiveness to the delicate thrills in which alone the soul can speak. Those who would remember the past must not have their interests centered in the present, and they must purify and refine the body till it is able to receive impressions from the subtler spheres.

Memory of their own past lives, however, is possessed by a considerable number of people, who have achieved the necessary sensitiveness of the physical organism, and to these, of course, reincarnation is no longer a theory, but has become a matter of personal knowledge. They have learned how much richer life becomes when memories of past lives pour into it, when the friends of this brief day are found to be the friends of the long-ago, and old remembrances strengthen the ties of the fleeting present. Life gains security and dignity when it is seen with a long vista behind it, and when the loves of old reappear in the loves of to-day. Death fades into its proper place as a mere incident in life, a change from one scene to another, like a journey that separates bodies but cannot sunder friend from friend. The links of the present are found to be part of a golden chain that stretches backwards, and the future can be faced with a glad security in the thought that these links will endure through days to come, and form part of that unbroken chain.

Now and then we find children who have brought over a memory of their immediate past, for the most part when they have died in childhood and are reborn almost immediately. In the West such cases are rarer than in the East, because in the West the first words of such a child would be met with disbelief, and he would quickly lose faith in his own memories. In the East, where belief in re-incarnation is almost universal, the child's remembrances are listened to, and where the opportunity serves they have been verified.

There is another consideration with respect to memory that will repay consideration. The memory of past *events* remains, as we have seen, with the Thinker only, but the results of those events embodied in *faculties* are at the service of the lower man. If the whole of these past events were thrown down into the physical brain, a vast mass of experiences in no classified order, without arrangement, the man could not be guided by the outcome of the past, nor utilize it for present help. Compelled to make a choice between two lines of action, he would have to pick, out of the unarranged facts of his past, events similar in character, trace out their results, and after long and weary study arrive at some conclusion—a conclusion very likely to be vitiated by the overlooking of some important factor, and reached long after the need for decision had passed. All the events, trivial and important, of some hundreds of lives, would form a rather unwieldly and chaotic mass for reference in an emergency that demanded a swift decision. The far more effective plan of Nature leaves to the Thinker the memory of the events, provides a long period of excarnate existence for the mental body, during which all the events are tabulated and compared and their results are classified; and then these results are embodied as faculties, and these faculties form the next mental body of the Thinker. In this way, the enlarged and improved faculties are available for immediate use, and the results of the past being in them, a decision can be come to in accordance with those results, and without any delay. The clear quick insight and prompt judgment are nothing else than the outcome of past experience moulded into an effective form for use; they are surely more useful instruments than would be a mass of unassimilated experiences, out of which the relevant ones would have to be selected and compared, and from which inferences would have to be drawn, on each separate occasion on which a choice arises.

From all these lines of thought, however, the mind turns back to rest on the fundamental necessity for re-incarnation if life is to be made intelligible, and if injustice and cruelty are not to mock the helplessness of man. With re-incarnation man is a dignified, immortal being, evolving towards a divinely glorious end; without it, he is a tossing straw on the stream of chance circumstances, irresponsible for his character, for his actions, for his destiny. With it, he may look forward with fearless hope, however low in the scale of evolution he may be to-day, for he is on the ladder to divinity, and the climbing to its summit is only a question of time; without it, he has no reasonable ground of assurance as to progress in the future, nor indeed any reasonable ground of assurance in a future at all; why should a creature without a past look forward to a future? he may be a mere bubble on the ocean of time. Flung into the world from non-entity, with qualities, good or evil, attached to him without reason or desert, why should he strive to make the best of them? Will not his future, if he have one, be as isolated, as uncaused, as unrelated as his present? In dropping re-incarnation from its beliefs, the modern world has deprived God of His justice and has bereft man of his security; he may be "lucky" or "unlucky," but the strength and dignity conferred by reliance on a changeless law are rent away from him, and he is left tossing helplessly on an unnavigable ocean of life.

ANNIE BESANT.

AMONG THE GNOSTICS OF THE FIRST TWO CENTURIES.

(*Continued from p.* 287.)

The Basilidian System (*continued*).

We next come to the soteriology of Basilides, the redemption and restoration of all things.

"When then the supercosmic planes and the whole universe [ætherial, sublunary and terrestrial] were completed, and there was no deficiency," that is to say, when the evolutionary stream of creative energy began to return on itself, "there still remained behind in the universal Seed the third Sonship, which bestows and receives benefits.

"But it needs must be that this Sonship also should be manifested, and restored to its place above, there beyond the highest Firmament, the Limitary Spirit of cosmos, with the most subtle Sonship, and the second which followed the example of its fellow, and the God beyond being, even as it was written, 'And the creation itself groaneth together and travaileth together, waiting for the manifestation of the sons of God'"—the third Sonship.

The sons of God are the divine sparks, the real spiritual men within, who have been left behind here in the seed-mixture, or bodies, "to order and inform and correct and perfect our souls, which have a natural tendency downwards to remain in this state of existence."

Before the Gospel was preached, and the Gnosis came, the Great Ruler of the Ogdoad was considered to be the only God, nevertheless no name was given to him, because he was ineffable.

The inspiration of Moses came from the Hebdomad only, as may be seen from the words, "I am the God of Abraham, Isaac and Jacob, but the name of God I did not make known unto them." This God to whom Moses and the Prophets gave names was of the Hebdomad, which is effable, and their inspiration came from this source. But the Gospel was that mystery which was ever unknown not only to the nations, but also to them of the Hebdomad and the Ogdoad, and even to their Rulers.

"When, therefore, the time had come," says the Gnostic doctor, "for the revelation of the children of God (who are ourselves), for whom the whole creation groaneth and travaileth in expectation, the Gospel, [the Glad Tidings, the Gnosis,] came into the universe, and passed through every principality, and authority, and lordship, and every title that man can use. It 'came' of very truth, not that anything 'came *down*' from above, or that the blessed Sonship 'departed from' that blessed God beyond being who transcends all thought. Nay, but just as the vapour of naphtha can catch fire from a flame a great way off from the naphtha, so do the powers of men's spirit pass from below from the formlessness of the conglomeration up to the Sonship.

"The Son of the Great Ruler of the Ogdoad, as it were, catching fire, lays hold of and seizes on the ideas from the blessed Sonship beyond the Limitary Spirit. For the power of the Sonship which is in the midst of the Holy Spirit, in the limit space, shares the flowing and rushing thoughts of the [supreme] Sonship with the Son of the Great Ruler.

"Thus the Gospel first came from the Sonship through the Son that sits by the Great Ruler to that Ruler, and the Ruler learned that he was not the God over all, but a generable deity, and that above him was set the Treasure of the ineffable and unnameable That beyond being and of the Sonship. And he repented and feared on understanding in what ignorance he had been. This is the meaning of the words, 'The fear of the Lord is the beginning of wisdom.' For he began to grow wise through the instruction of the Christ sitting by him, learning what is That beyond being, what the Sonship, what the Holy Spirit, what the apparatus of the universe, what the manner of its restoration. This is the 'wisdom, declared in a mystery,' concerning which Scripture uses the words, 'Not in words taught of human wisdom, but in those taught of the Spirit.'

"The Great Ruler, then, being instructed and taught and made afraid, confessed the sin which he had done in boasting himself. This is the saying, 'I have recognized my sin, and I know my transgression, and I will confess it for the eternity.'

"After the instruction of the Great Ruler, the whole space of the Ogdoad was instructed and taught, and the mystery became known to the powers above the heavens.

"Then was it that the Gospel should come to the Hebdomad, that its Ruler might be instructed and evangelized in like manner. Thereupon the Son of the Great Ruler lit up in the Son of the Ruler of the lower space, the light which he himself had had kindled in him from above from the Sonship; and thus the Son of the Ruler of the Hebdomad was illumined, and preached the Gospel to the Ruler, who in his turn, like as the Great Ruler before him, feared and confessed [his sin]. And then all things in the sublunary spaces were enlightened and had the Gospel preached unto them.

"Therefore the time was ripe for the illumination of the formlessness of our own world, and for the mystery to be revealed to the Sonship which had been left behind in the formlessness, as it were to one born out of due time [an abortion]—'the mystery which was not known unto former generations,' as it is written, 'By revelation was the mystery made known unto me,' and 'I heard unspeakable words, which it is not lawful for man to utter.'

"Thus, from the Hebdomad, the Light—which had already come down from above from the Ogdoad unto the Son of the Hebdomad—descended upon Jesus, son of Mary, and he was illumined, being caught on fire in harmony with the Light that streamed into him. This is the meaning of the saying, 'A Holy Spirit shall come upon thee'—that is to say, that which came from the Sonship through the Limitary Spirit to the Ogdoad and Hebdomad down as far as Mary [the body]—and 'a power of the Highest shall overshadow thee'—that is to say, the divine creative power which cometh from the [ætherial] heights above through the Demiurgos, which power belongeth to the Son."

The text of Hippolytus is here exceedingly involved, and he evidently did not seize the thought of Basilides. The "Son" apparently means the soul. The power belongs to the soul and not to Mary—the body—the divine creative power making of man a god, whereas the body can only exercise the power of physical procreation. Moreover, Jesus seems to stand for a type of every member of the Sonship, every son of God.

"For the world shall hold together and not be dissolved until the whole Sonship—which has been left behind to benefit the souls in the state of formlessness, and to receive benefits, by evolving forms for them [the spirit requiring a psychic vehicle for conscious contact with this plane]—shall follow after and imitate Jesus, and hasten upward and come forth purified. [For by purification] it becometh most subtle, so that it is able to speed aloft through its own power, even as the first Sonship; for it hath all its power naturally consubsistent with the Light which shone down from above.

"When, then, the whole Sonship shall have ascended, and passed beyond the Great Limit, the Spirit, then shall the whole creation become the object of the Great Mercy; for it groaneth until now and suffereth pain and awaiteth the manifestation of the sons of God, namely that all the men of the Sonship may ascend beyond it [the creation]. And when this shall be effected, God will bring upon the whole universe the Great Ignorance [mahâ-pralaya], in order that all things may remain in their natural condition, and nothing long for anything which is contrary to its nature.

"Thus all the souls of this state of existence, whose nature is to remain immortal in this state of existence alone, remain without knowledge of anything different from or better than this state; nor shall there be any rumour or knowledge of things superior in higher states, in order that the lower souls may not suffer pain by striving after impossible objects, just as though it were fish longing to feed on the mountains with sheep, for such a desire would end in their destruction. All things are indestructible if they remain in their proper condition, but subject to destruction if they desire to overleap and transgress their natural limits.

"Thus the Ruler of the Hebdomad shall have no knowledge of the things above him, for the Great Ignorance shall take hold of him also, so that sorrow and pain and lamentation may go from him. He shall desire naught of things impossible for him to attain and thus shall suffer no grief.

"And in like manner the Great Ignorance shall seize upon the Great Ruler of the Ogdoad as well and all the [ætherial] creations which are subject to him in similar fashion, so that nothing may long after anything contrary to nature and thus suffer pain.

"And thus shall be the restoration of all things which have had their foundations laid down according to nature in the Seed of the universe in the beginning, and which will all be restored [to their original nature] in their appointed cycles.

"And that everything has its proper cycle and time, the Saviour is sufficient witness in the saying, 'My hour hath not yet come,' and also the Magi in their observation of his star. For he also was foreordained in the Seed to be subject to the nativity of the stars and the return of the time periods to their starting places."

Now the Saviour, according to the Basilidian school, was the perfected spiritual "man," within the psychic and animal man or soul. And when a man reaches this stage of perfection, the Sonship in him leaves the soul behind here, "the soul being no longer mortal but remaining in its natural state [that is to say, having become immortal], just as the first Sonship [left behind] the Holy Spirit, the Great Limit, in its proper space or region"; for it is only then (on reaching perfection), that the real "man" is "clothed with a proper [and really immortal] soul."

Every part of the creation goes up a stage, and the whole scheme of salvation is effected by the separating from their state of conglomeration the various principles into their proper states; and Jesus was the first-fruits, or great exemplar, of this process.

"Thus his physical part down here—which belongs to formless matter—alone suffered, and was restored to the formless state. His psychic vesture or vehicle—which belongs to the Hebdomad—arose and was restored to the Hebdomad. That vehicle in him which was of the nature of the height of the Great Ruler he raised aloft, and it remained with the Great Ruler. Moreover he raised still higher that which was of the nature of the Great Limit, and it remained in the Limitary Spirit. And it was thus through him that the third Sonship was purified, the Sonship left behind in the state of mixture [or impurity] for the purpose of helping and being helped, and it passed upwards through all of these purified principles unto the blessed Sonship above."

The main idea at the back of this system is the separating forth, classification or restoration, of the various elements or principles confused in the original world-seed, or universal plasm, into their proper natures, by a process of purification which brought unto men the Gnosis or perfection of consciousness. Man was the crown of the world-process, and the perfected man, the Christ, the Saviour, was the crown of manhood, and therefore the manifestation of Deity, the Sonship.

So far Hippolytus, who undoubtedly gives us the outline of the true Basilidian system. It was only in 1851 that the Philosophumena were published to the world, after the discovery of the MS. in one of the Libraries on Mount Athos in 1842; prior to this nothing but the short and garbled sketches of Irenæus and the Epitomators was known of the great Gnostic's sublime speculations. The Philosophumena account has revolutionized all prior views, and changed the whole enquiry, so that the misrepresentations of Irenæus, or those of his prior authority, are now referred to as "the spurious Basilidian system." To this we shall refer later on. Meantime let us turn to Clement of Alexandria, who deals purely with the ethical side of the Basilidian Gnosis, and therefore does not touch the "metaphysical" part, using the term "metaphysical" in the Aristotelian sense, namely, of things beyond the Hebdomad, the things of the Hebdomad or sublunary space, being called "physics" or in the domain of physis or nature.

As to marriage, Basilides and his son Isidorus taught that it was natural but not necessary, and seem to have taken a moderate ground between the compulsory asceticism of some schools and the glorification of procreation by the Jews, who taught that "he who is without a wife is no man."

As to the apparently undeserved sufferings of martyrs, Basilides, basing himself on the doctrines of reincarnation and karma, writes as follows in Book xxiii. of his Exegetica:

"I say that all those who fall into these so-called tribulations are people who, only after transgressing in other matters without being discovered, are brought to this good end [martyrdom] by the kindness of providence, so that the offences they are charged with being quite different from those they have committed without discovery, they do not suffer as criminals for proved offences, reviled as adulterers or murderers, but suffer merely for being Christians; which fact is so consoling to them that they do not even appear to suffer,

And even though it should happen that one comes to suffer without previously committing any outward transgression—a very rare case—he will not suffer at all through any plot of any [evil] power, but in exactly the same way as the babe who apparently has done no ill.

"For just as the babe, although it has done no wrong previously, or practically committed any sin, and yet has the capacity of sin in it [from its former lives], when it suffers, is advantaged and reaps many benefits which otherwise are difficult to gain; in just the selfsame way is it with the perfectly virtuous man also who has never sinned in deed, for he has still the tendency to sin in him; he has not committed actual sin [in this life], because he has not as yet been placed in the necessary [karmic] circumstances. In the case even of such a man we should not be right in supposing entire freedom from sin. For just as it is the will to commit adultery which constitutes the adulterer, even though he does not find the opportunity of actually committing adultery, and the will to commit murder constitutes the murderer, although he may not be actually able to effect his purpose; for just this reason, if I see such a 'sinless' man suffering [the pains of martyrdom], even if he has actually *done* no sin, I shall say that he is evil in so far as he has still the *will* to transgress. For I will say anything rather than that providence is evil."

Moreover, even if the example of Jesus were to be flung in his face by those who preferred miracle to law, the sturdy defender of the Gnosis says that he should answer, "If you permit, I will say, He has not sinned; but was like a babe suffering." And if he were pressed even more closely, he would say, "The man you name is man, but God [alone] is righteous; for 'no one is pure from pollution,'" as Job said.

Men suffer, says Basilides, from their deeds in former lives; the "elect" soul suffers "honourably" through martyrdom, but souls of another nature by other appropriate punishments. The "elect" soul is evidently one that will suffer for an ideal, in other words, it is possessed of faith, which is the "assent of the soul to any of the things which do not excite sensation"; such a soul, then, "discovers doctrines without demonstration by an intellective apprehension."

The vulgar superstition of transmigration, the passing of a human soul into the body of an animal—so often confused by the uninstructed with the doctrine of reincarnation, which denies such a possibility—received a rational explanation at the hand of the Basilidian school. It arose from a consideration of the animal nature in man, the animal soul, or body of desire, the ground in which the passions inhere; the doctrine being thus summarized by Clement.

"The Basilidians are accustomed to give the name of appendages [or accretions] to the passions. These essences, they say, have a certain substantial existence and are attached to the rational soul, owing to a certain turmoil and primitive confusion."

The word translated essences is literally "spirits"; curiously enough the whole animal soul is called the "counterfeit spirit" in the Pistis Sophia treatise, and in the Timæus of Plato the same idea is called "turmoil" as may be seen from the commentary of Proclus. The primitive confusion is of course the chaotic conglomeration of the universal seed-mixture, and the differentiation of the "elemental essence" of some modern writers on Theosophy.

"Onto this nucleus other bastard and alien natures of the essence grow, such as those of the wolf, ape, lion, goat, etc. And when the peculiar qualities of such natures appear round the soul, they cause the desires of the soul to become like to the special natures of those animals, for they imitate the actions of those whose characteristics they bear. And not only do human souls thus intimately associate themselves with the impulses and impressions of irrational animals, but they even imitate the movements and beauties of plants, because they likewise bear the characteristics of plants appended to them. Nay, there are also certain characteristics [of minerals] shown by habits, such as the hardness of adamant."

But we are not to suppose that man is composed of several souls, and that it is proper for man to yield to his animal nature, and seek excuse for his misdeeds by saying that the foreign elements attached to him have compelled him to sin; far from it, the choice is his, the responsibility is his, the rational soul's. Thus in his book, On an Appended Soul, Isidorus, son of Basilides, writes:

"Were I to persuade anyone that the real soul is not a unit, but that the passions of the wicked are occasioned by the compulsion of the appended natures, no common excuse then would the worthless of mankind have for saying, 'I was compelled, I was carried away, I did it without wishing to do so, I acted unwillingly,' whereas it was the man himself who led his desire towards evil, and refused to battle with the constraints of the appendages. Our duty is to show ourselves rulers over the inferior creation within us, gaining the mastery by means of our rational principle."

In other words, the man is the same man, no matter in what body or vesture he may be; the vestures are not the man.

One of the greatest festivals of the school was the celebration of the Baptism of Jesus on the fifteenth day of the Egyptian month Tobe or Tybi. "They of Basilides," says Clement, "celebrate his Baptism by a preliminary night service of readings; and they say that 'the fifteenth year of Tiberius Cæsar' means the fifteenth day of the month Tybi." It was then that the Father "in the likeness of a dove"—which they explained as meaning the Minister or Holy Spirit—came upon him.

It is evident, therefore, that the Basilidians did not accept the accounts of the canonical gospels literally, as Hippolytus claims; on the contrary, they explained such incidents as pseudo-historical legends of initiation, the process of which is magnificently worked out in the Pistis Sophia treatise, to which I must refer the reader for further information.

We learn from Agrippa Castor, as preserved by Eusebius, that Basilides imposed a silence of five years on his disciples, as was the custom in the Pythagorean school, and that he and his school set great store by the writings of a certain Barcabbas and Barcoph, and by other books of Orientals. Scholars are of opinion that Barcabbas and Barcoph, and their variants, point to the cycle of Zoroastrian literature which is now lost, but which was in great favour among many Gnostic communities. It must have been that among the learned Jews and Essenes, after the return from Babylonia, and also among the theosophically-minded of the time, the traditions of the Magi and of the great Iranian faith were an important part of eclectic and syncretistic religion. The Avesta literature which has come down to us, is a very late recovery from memory of a very small portion of the great library of Persepolis destroyed by the "accursed Alexander," as Pârsî tradition has it.

Such then, is all that can be deduced of the real Basilidian system from the writings of Hippolytus and Clemens Alexandrinus, who respectively selected only such points as they thought themselves capable of refuting, that is to say, such features of the system as they considered most erroneous. To the student of comparative religion it is evident that both Church fathers misunderstood the tenets they quoted, seeing that even such hostilely selected passages easily fall into the general scheme of universal theosophy, once they are taken out of the setting of Patristic refutation, and allowed to stand on their own merits. It is therefore a matter of deep regret that the writings of the school have been lost or destroyed; they would doubtless have thrown much light not only on Christian theosophy but also on the obscure history of the origins.

It now remains for us to refer briefly to the spurious Basilidian system. The following points are taken from Irenæus and the epitomators, and are another proof of the unreliability of Irenæus, the sheet-anchor of orthodox heresiology. The series of writers and copyists to which we refer, had evidently no first hand information of the teaching of Basilides, and merely retailed whatever fantastic notions popular rumour and hearsay attributed to the school.

The main features of the confection thus brewed are as follows. The God of the Basilidians, they said, was a certain Abraxas or Abrasax, who was the ruler of their first heaven, of which heavens there were no less than 365. This power was so denominated because the sum of the numerical values of the Greek letters in the name Abrasax came to 365, the number of days in the year.

We learn, however, from Hippolytus (II) that this part of the system had to do with a far lower stage of creation than the God beyond all. It is not, however, clear whether Abrasax is to be identified with the Great Ruler of the Ogdoad or the Ruler of the Hebdomad, and the region of the "proasteioi up to the æther." In any case the 365 "heavens" pertained to the astrological and genetical considerations of Egyptian and Chaldæan occult science, and represented from one point of view the 365 "aspects" of the heavenly bodies (during the year) as reflected on the surface of the earth's "atmosphere" or envelope, which extended as far as the moon.

Now it is curious to notice that in the Pistis Sophia treatise, the mysteries of embryology are consummated by a hierarchy of elemental powers, or builders, 365 in number, who follow the dictates of the karmic law, and fashion the new body in accordance with past deeds. The whole is set forth in great detail, and also the astrological scheme of the one ruler of the four, which in their turn each rule over ninety, and so on, making in all 365 powers.

Not till Schwartze translated this treatise from the Coptic, in 1853, was any certain light thrown on the Abrasax idea, and this just two years after Miller in 1851 published his edition of The Philosophumena, and thus supplied the material for proving that the hitherto universal opinion that the Abrasax was the Basilidian name for the God over all, was a gross error based on the ignorance or misrepresentation of Irenæus and company. The elemental forces which fashion the body are the lowest servants of the karmic law; the God over all is the supreme ruler of an endless galaxy of rulers, gods, archangels, authorities, and powers, all of them superior to the 365.

In fact the mysteries of the unseen world were so intricate in detail, that even those who devoted their lives to them with unwearied constancy could scarcely understand some of the lower processes, although the general idea was simple enough; and thus Basilides imposed a silence of five years on his disciples, and declared that "only one out of 1,000, and two out of 10,000" could really receive the Gnosis, which was the consummation of many lives of effort. Curiously enough this very phrase is also found in the Pistis Sophia treatise.

The term Abrasax is well known to students of Gnosticism because of the number of gems on which it is found and which are attributed to the followers of Basilides; in addition to the great continental scholars who have treated the matter, in this country King has devoted much of his treatise to the subject. The best and latest authorities, however, are of opinion "that there is no tangible evidence for attributing any known gems to Basilidianism or any other form of Gnosticism."

In fact, in the Abrasax matter, as in all other things, Gnosticism followed its natural tendency of going "one better," to use a colloquialism, on every form of belief or even superstition. Doubtless the ignorant populace had long before believed in Abrasax as the great power which governed birth and everyday affairs, according to astrological notions; talismans, invocations, and the rest of the apparatus which the vulgar mind ever clamours for in some form or other, were all inscribed with this potent "name of power." Back of the superstition, however, there lay certain occult facts, of the real nature of which, of course, the vulgar astrologers and talisman makers were naturally ignorant; the real facts, however, seem to have been known to the doctors of the Gnosis, and they accordingly found the proper place for them in their universal systems. Thus Abrasax, the great God of the ignorant populace, was placed among the lower hierarchies of the Gnosis, among the building powers of the physical body.

As to the rest of the "spurious system," there is nothing of interest to record; we cannot, however, omit the silliest tale told against the Basilidians, which was as follows: they are said to have believed that at the crucifixion Jesus changed bodies with Simon of Cyrene, and then when his substitute hung in agony, stood and mocked at those he had tricked!—with which cock and bull story we may come out of the Irenæic "store-house of Gnosticism" for a breathing space.

Of the history of the school we know nothing beyond the fact that Epiphanius, at the end of the fourth century, still met with students of the Basilidian Gnosis in the nomes west of the Delta from Memphis to the sea. It seems most probable, however, that the school was gradually amalgamated with the general stream of Gnosticism of the latter half of the second century and the great Valentinian movement of which we have next to treat.

G. R. S. MEAD.

(To be continued.)

THE ORDER OF THINGS.

It has been, and remains, a standing puzzle to the Christian apologists how the first presentation of the new religion—to their minds so immeasurably superior to the old in morality—a revelation, as they believe, for the first time made to the world of the *goodness* of God, was received by the ancient world with a shock of most unmistakable horror and disgust. Of the *fact* there can be no doubt. As soon as the Christians came to be distinguished from the Jews (themselves perhaps the sect most unpopular in Rome—*their* history repeats itself in all ages!) it was universally understood that the difference lay in a still deeper and more unspeakable depravity; and the popular imagination exhausted itself in wondering what secret horror was the object of their diabolical worship. How came this about?

Was it, as is usually said, that the immorality of the Pagan world was roused against the purity of the new religion? This is, at first sight, a plausible explanation; and Cardinal Newman in his classical tale *Callista* has worked it out with vast power and learning. But it is not true; the Roman world was *not* given over to vice and dissipation. The accounts which Tacitus gives of the extravagances of the Emperors and the young nobles about them, no more furnish a complete picture of Roman society than the cases which come now and then before the divorce and police courts in relation to the morals of *our* young nobles, do of our modern English life. The main characteristic of the Roman world was precisely that of our own Anglo-Saxon race—an intense *respectability*; inclined in the one case as in the other, to run into actual cant and hypocrisy, rather than open, shameless vice.

Had there been nothing more than *this* in Christianity the *bourgeois* of ancient Rome would have received it as the corresponding society of modern London or New York does now—would have welcomed it—professed it, occasionally burnt other people for not doing the same; and for the rest, have gone on their own way regardless, as ever, of its precepts and views of life. But the evident satisfaction with which the moral and religious society of Rome received Nero's brilliant idea of illuminating his gardens with blazing Christians as a due and fitting sacrifice to the Proprieties (with a big P) means much more than that.

For one thing, of course, it means the indignation of respectability in all ages against anyone who presumes to have any other standard of value than its own. Whether that new standard is in itself higher or lower does not matter; it is an insult always deeply felt and energetically resented. The Roman Christian who would not swear by the genius of the Emperor—a mere, harmless legal form as the bystanders considered it, was simply a forerunner of the Elizabethan Catholic who would not take the sacrament in his parish church, of the Friend who would not remove his hat to the justice nor swear to speak the truth.

Only a week or two ago there was in one of our daily papers an amusing example of the same feeling, as strong as ever. It seems that amongst the multitudinous sects in England there is a Peculiar People who think it wrong to vote at a Schoolboard Election, and it was simply comical to read how evidently the leader-writer would have enjoyed having them hauled before the justices and bullied and beaten, as they certainly would have been but a couple of hundred years ago.

This, then, is something; but it is not enough. Was it that Christianity was a *secret* society, one which kept its doctrines to itself and allowed no one to enter its meetings but the professed? This, to a Roman, *was* a serious accusation, and one which could not be denied. For the Roman, like his re-incarnation, the Anglo-Saxon, looked at religious matters mainly from the police point of view. For the gods he cared very little; for their orderly and regular worship, under an "established" priesthood, whose "convocations" could be properly kept in order by the civil power, he cared very much. Similarly, he was liable occasionally to lose his head in a panic, when confronted with faiths and practices he did not understand. Many thousands of mostly innocent victims were slaughtered as Initiates of unlawful mysteries, as witches, as poisoners, long before the Roman world became Christian. Nay, the very persecutions under which the Christians suffered were simply such outbreaks of nervous terror; as were the cruelties against the Jews in Spain and the witch-burnings in Germany, England and America in later times. Men did these things in the Middle Ages, not because they were Christians, but because they were of the great Roman family, great in its powers—great, vast, and terrible even in its panic terror.

But even this is not enough to explain the universal outcry against the Christians, in every place and time, that they were *hostes humani generis—enemies to the human race.* Preposterous as it seems to a modern Christian, whose ideas of society and of life have been formed by nearly 2000 years of the Christian tradition, this was the first and last impression the new faith made on the world around it, the honest, even if mistaken, judgment of the leaders of thought—the prejudice of the crowds who yelled tumultuously "Christians for the lions" in the amphitheatres, the "common form" of the indictment of a Christian before the magistrates. *Hostes humani generis*—what *could* it mean?

It meant the instinctive recognition of a new and utterly unpardonable crime, a crime which has darkened the western world until now; which renews itself in many a plausible shape even amongst those who regard themselves (and rightly), as the most enlightened of their time, a stain in the air we breathe and through which we see the world around us, from which the wisest of us can hardly completely free ourselves; in a word, Disloyalty to the Order of Things!

I have spoken of it before in these pages as a declaration of *want* of Faith in Man—the peculiar characteristic of the three *exclusive* religions which have plagued mankind, the Jewish, the Christian, and the Mohammedan; the true origin of the torrents of human blood which these three religions (and these *only*), have shed, and the desolation which has followed their path. But the wider statement has the advantage of linking itself to a still broader view which may be worth the consideration of a good many even amongst ourselves.

The ante-christian world, however low fallen from its earlier height of knowledge, had never quite lost the tradition of its continuous evolution upwards. No more than we, would its philosophers and sages have claimed that "all that is, is right;" *that* was left for the wooden, mechanical "philosophy" of the eighteenth century Anno Domini. But at least when confronted with the crude pessimism of the new Christian faith, declarations that "the whole world lieth in wickedness," "the imagination of man's heart is only evil continually," and so forth, it felt itself outraged, indignant; and not without reason. And when men came to them insisting that the noblest of their ancestors, with all the public and domestic virtues which had gained them renown and love (we must not forget that reverence for the ancestors was in truth the *real* Roman religion, not any worship of God, their own or any other) were burning in an everlasting hell for want of believing in a "Saviour," who was not even born till hundreds of years after their time—can you much wonder that men who believed this and who tried to press it upon them as a Gospel, a glad tidings! seemed to them a new and unheard of degradation of mankind, and that they reached out instinctively to sword and faggot to rid the world of them.

Look down the history of the Church, and what do we see? Common-sense, the natural and uneradicable love of man for his fellowman, growing time after time too strong for dogma—Popes and Bishops speaking and acting as if the wisdom of this world were *not* "all foolishness with God"—religion entering into a *modus vivendi* with the movements of a world it could not control and had not the heart to denounce; and then a "Reformation" to reprobate such "corruptions" and reaffirm the original sin. What is the actual state of things about us at the present time but a tacit confession of religious people that this process is a failure—that the world is in reality far better and wiser than their doctrines can allow or explain—that it moves on its way quite regardless of all said against it; and that the only thing to be done is to live accordingly—to adapt ourselves to it as we do to the law of gravitation and leave our formal dogmatic religion to do the same as best it can. It is a sort of "slack water," between tides; and our mission as Theosophists is to take advantage of this. The essence of *our* gospel is a justification of this very position; a formal declaration that the world does *not* lie in wickedness, and that true and right religion actually *demands* that men shall openly and with a good conscience place themselves in full sympathy with its movement, knowing that it *can* end in nothing but God.

But we ourselves have mostly come to our present position through Christianity, and the habit of abusing the world—the feeling that religion requires of us the hopeless attempt to turn back its course instead of aiding it—is hard to get rid of, even when our intellect has learned wisdom. And the new view is not altogether easy to make our own. Frequently we perceive that the world is in fact moving *downwards*, not upwards; and it needs courage as well as faith to sit steady and not pull at the reins. The great claim of Christianity is that after the fall of the Roman Empire the Church succeeded in holding back some part of the world from the lowest depth; and that was good. But now, as the world is again on the downward arc of the spiral, we who know must not forget that downward and upward are *both* onward, and the downward arc moves forward the faster for the very rapidity of the fall. The Golden Age with its Divine Rulers and its wise laws was good; but thousands upon thousands of years passed and left humanity much as it found them—happy but not moving on; and the traces of it left on earth now are simply wide regions where the people to this day are absolutely incapable of corporate life and of self-defence—children still. In this Iron Age of ours men suffer, beasts suffer; "the whole creation groaneth and travaileth"; but out of all this comes life and growth. A single life now means more progress for the true Self than many lives in what we foolishly call better times. It was good that children should be nursed as children; now we are men, and have to be developed to our full growth by toil and labour and hardship.

Does this mean that we are to be careless of suffering? Not so. Our own growth is only possible as we do our best to remove hindrances out of the way of our fellows. If we can plan a new society on new lines in which the struggle for life which now ruins so many, body and soul, may be replaced by a holy and joyous labour for the life of others, good; if we can do anything to bring such a society into actual existence—good also. If we, feeling our limited possibilities, prefer to concentrate our efforts on some smaller relief of the world-suffering, or some improvement in our social habits or our diet, good again—provided only we keep our loyalty to Nature. We are told that we must set ourselves in harmony with, work along with, Nature; our difficulty is to understand that this Nature is not Nature as we think it should be improved, but the actual order of things in which we find ourselves. It is true that there is a teaching that certain developments of the present Nature are not in accordance with the primitive plan on which the world was originally framed, but we must not suppose that it is left to *us* to set things straight. It is our faith and our happiness to know that the Powers who guided the evolution of the early world guide it still, and have made the needful adaptations for the new course. Unless we thus keep ourselves in harmony with the actual movement of the world we risk what befel the Church in later times—to miss the turn of the spiral and find too late that our habit of hanging back has been trying to keep the world from *rising*, and that we are left behind.

Another thing in which we are apt to miss the full *comfort* of our new faith is the enormous relief to the horror with which the Christian faith invests the world around us, contained in the knowledge of the renewal of our earth-lives. As long as this one life was *all*, and "after death the (final) judgment," there was excuse—nay, reason—for hysterics over the suffering of the world. As I think it is O. W. Holmes says, there are religions such that it is discreditable to their members if they *don't* go mad over them. But now that we know that the end of a life, to man or beast, is not the blind huddling-up of everything to a chance conclusion which popular theology teaches, but a passage to a state of happiness in which every suffering undergone is shaped into new power and hope for the new life; we can look calmly, though often sorrowfully, on the world about us, and see in what goes on not the mad and aimless blow of a blinded Titan, but the measured, calculated hammer-strokes of the Powers who know fully, completely, what to make of us, and how best to do their work. What we chiefly have to avoid is the sad catastrophe of one known and reverenced by many of us who, loving "not wisely but too well" one single small portion of the universe, rashly set herself in its defence across the order of things, and was crushed like a gnat under the great wheels. The Powers have no need of us—even the wisest and best of us; and They will see that no suffering in this world fails of its appointed help and service to the soul which has needed it. Let us take for ourselves the assurance given to an English Mystic of six hundred years ago by her "Father in Heaven"—"I *can* make all things well; and I *will* make all things well; and thou shalt see with thine own eyes that every manner of thing shall be well."

A. A. WELLS.

AUTHORITY.

(*Concluded from p.* 337.)

IT is not going too far to say that many organizations lose much of their effectiveness as agents, because of the want of discipline resulting from too popular a method of control. The tie that binds a number of people together (*i.e.*, the aim) may be of the widest, but if it is worth while to organize at all, it is worth while to organize *well;* and if an organization is to be effective, "discipline," as Sergeant Bagnet used to say, "must be maintained," or there will be no cohesion. This is entirely irrespective of aim or motive, purely from the point of view of effectiveness *as a body*, and the effectiveness of a body depends not alone upon the healthy working of all the parts, but upon the due control of the brain over the whole system. Otherwise the spasmodic desire of one limb to travel in an opposite direction to the others might lead to disastrous results. So that here again we see that control or authority is the price to be paid for power of achievement, and perhaps there is no better illustration of the working of this law than we find in the history of the Society of Jesus.

We may now turn to the question of authority as it affects individual evolution. If we grant that authority exists universally, that the only way to escape it is to become one with it—the Divine Will; that this is our aim; that to put our aim into practice we must begin by endeavouring to discover what *is* the Divine Will; that we cannot learn this all at once because we are so far off from the Divine that its nature must filter down to ours through the hierarchies of entities on stages of "the great world's altar stairs" above our own; that within our own stage there are many grades and through these from highest to lowest must come the divine light which is to make us wise unto salvation—then surely there can be no degradation, no sycophancy, in receiving with gratitude to the light-bringer the light which we thus obtain, even though it be said to come "on authority."

There is a very right and proper attitude of independence of judgment (not to be confounded with "cocksureness" and conceit) which is nevertheless humble; and there is a humility (not to be confounded with servility) which is nevertheless firm and confident. A man may be thoroughly self-governed and yet be immeasurably helped by a teacher whom he recognizes as standing on a higher platform than himself, one to whom he looks as an ideal—a standard in ethics and wisdom—one whose regard is, before everything, a stimulus to the best that is in him, and of whom the very thought is sufficient to make him refrain from deceit or meanness of any degree. In short, one in whom he recognizes "the true king, or able man, who *has* a divine right over him" and whose command he is prepared to obey. The necessity for such an ideal seems to have been inculcated by the Stoics, and it has been urged that the influence of their teaching was largely instrumental in building up round the very slight framework of the historic Jesus, the glories of the Ideal Man—the Type—and this has meant much indeed to Western civilization. On this necessity for an ideal the words of Seneca are worth quoting. "We should," he says, "choose out some good man, and keep him ever before our eyes that we may live as in his sight and do all things as if he were looking on. . . . Let the soul have some one to reverence; by whose authority he may hallow even his innocent nature. O happy he who corrects not only appearances, but also thoughts! Happy he who can so revere some one, as to compose and order himself in accordance with his memory. He who can so revere another, will quickly be himself an object of reverence. . . . . If you see a man unterrified by dangers, untouched by desires, happy in adversity, calm in the midst of storms, looking down upon men from higher ground, from a level among the gods, do you not feel veneration for him? Will you not say, This thing is too great and lofty to be believed like to this little body in which it is? A divine power has descended thither; an excellent soul under government, that passes over all things as if too small, smiling at all that we fear and desire, is stirred by heavenly power. So great a thing cannot stand without the aid of deity. For the most part it is yonder whence it came down. Even as the rays of the sun touch the earth, but are there whence they are sent; so a great and sacred soul, for this end sent down that we might more nearly apprehend divine things, converses with us indeed, but cleaves of its origin." A theosophic conception, surely.

It may be urged that there are difficulties which human experience meets in this connection. For large numbers of mankind an ideal conception is not enough, there must be a living embodiment of the virtues as an aid to their spiritual growth. Where are these rarely embodied ideals to be found? I would suggest that as man is in such innumerable stages of growth and development, he naturally makes innumerable varieties of ideals, and the ideals of some of us may well be found among historic or living characters. Even in what we call friendship—if it is the real thing and not acquaintanceship or mere passion—this stimulating and corrective function is present. In the sight of our best friend we would wish to be at our highest level—to be worthy the love we have received—and the desire ever acts as the spring of worthier actions. George Eliot has put this truth in the words: "There are some natures in which, if they love us, we are conscious of having a sort of baptism and consecration; they bind us over to rectitude and purity by their pure belief about us; and our sins become the worst kind of sacrilege, which tears down the invisible altar of trust."

But there is the further difficulty that these human ideals or idols have sometimes feet of clay. There are those who have gone through life setting up idol after idol and worshipping thereat, only to be as often overwhelmed in the ruins of their fall. Albeit, I hold that if the worship be *sincere* it is not entirely in vain, for it is the attitude of sincere love and devotion, even if misplaced, that is the real stimulating force in the soul. The shocks and disappointments are but the necessary painful experiences by which the growing ego assimilates the lessons of life.

Granting that some are fortunate enough to find a living man or woman whose influence is ever towards the highest, who draws out that which is instinctively felt to be the best we know—is the attitude of obedience misplaced? I say attitude of obedience advisedly, for it seems to me that given such a relationship—of teacher and pupil, helper and devotee—it would not be a case for the issuing of orders and commands, but rather the mind of the lesser being ever in process of turning to respond to the vibrations of the greater soul, the impulse of the latter would find answer in the former, in thought and action according to the degree of his ability and devotion. In readiness of response would be the measure of the pupil's fitness or progress. "There is no act more moral between men than that of rule and obedience. Woe unto him that claims obedience when it is not due; woe unto him that refuses it when it is!" is Carlyle's answer to the question, and Ruskin in the following quaint passages enforces the attitude of obedience.

"It has been a prevalent notion in the minds of well-disposed persons, that if they acted according to their own conscience, they must, therefore, be doing right. But they assume, in feeling or asserting this, either that there is no law of God, or that it cannot be known, but only felt or conjectured.

"'I must do what *I* think right.' How often is this sentence uttered and acted on, bravely, nobly, innocently; but always, because of its egotism, erringly. You must not do what *you* think right, but, whether you or anybody think or don't think it, what *is* right.

"'I must act according to the dictates of my conscience.' By no means, my conscientious friend, unless you are quite sure that yours is not the conscience of an ass.

"'I am doing my best, what can man do more?' You might be doing much less, and yet much better: perhaps you are doing your best in producing, or doing, an eternally bad thing.

"All these sayings, and the convictions they express, are wise only in the mouths of wise men; they are deadly, and all the deadlier because bearing an image and superscription of virtue, in the mouths and minds of fools.

"'But there is every gradation, surely, between wisdom and folly?' No. The fool, whatever his wit, is the man who doesn't know his master, who has said in his heart, There is no God, no Law. The wise man knows his master. Less or more wise, he perceives lower or higher masters; but always some creature larger than himself, some law holier than his own. A law to be sought, learned, loved, obeyed; but in order to its discovery, the obedience must be begun first, to the best one knows. Obey *something*, and you will have a chance some day of finding out what is best to obey. But if you begin by obeying nothing, you will end by obeying Beelzebub and all his seven invited friends."

I have quoted at some length because this extract raises the question of conscience in a way which is provocative of discussion. It cannot be too clearly stated that what we call our conscience is the best guide we have got, and that we are not called upon to commit its keeping to another; although it may, after all, be only what Ruskin calls the "conscience of an ass"; but what is needful, and what I think Ruskin means to enforce, is the necessity for making a real endeavour to find out what *is* the law, and not allowing the prejudices of our personality to masquerade as the divine light within. Such endeavour will be best promoted by a true humility. Nor must it be forgotten that those to whom we feel we could readily render obedience, on whose wisdom or teaching we can implicitly rely, are those with whom we have brought ourselves into harmony, possibly in past lives. Responsive to their vibrations we feel them as our own. Their words and acts call forth in us approval because they are in harmony with, but octaves higher than, our own. "Freely we serve because we freely love," and in the case of a teacher or helper, "perfect love casteth out fear"—doubt. Where there is love—harmony—there is no doubt of the teacher, but ever illumination as the result of the teaching. No degradation in obedience, but pleasure in the rendering of service.

It may be that some never find such a helper in the flesh. Well for them if their strength is such that they can stand outside the bond at once human and divine, without developing a crustacean armour of self-righteousness; let them not despise others whose help and teaching come through human lips, for, be it remembered, the helper must not be too far off, nor the teaching too high, otherwise the help is not felt nor the teaching assimilated. The light may be there, but too blinding for our eyes to sense, "for all *we* have power to see is a straight staff bent in a pool." Strong meat is not for babes, and the more effective help must often be rendered to us by those nearer our own level, just as we see the Salvation Army more successful as a reforming agency to a certain class than many more refined methods, because the ideal it presents is not beyond the conception of those to whom it appeals, whereas it may happen that effort from a higher level, so to speak, fails utterly because the moral sense of those who are to be helped is absolutely incapable of realising the standpoint of the would-be helper.

There is one other point for consideration which, in the case of teaching, may from time to time arise, namely, the conflict of authorities. Many not unwilling to accept authority in itself, are yet puzzled to decide between authorities making conflicting claims. This may and does occur in all departments of human knowledge, and the unfortunate laity, lacking the information of the specialist, take refuge for the most part in blank indifference, or swing with blind impartiality from side to side. But in matters theological this does not apply, for, unhappily, rival authorities have herein the vigorous support of numbers, and the bitterness of religious warfare is painful evidence of our distance from the goal of the race. In its more individual aspect, this question is really settled on the authority of the law of affinity, to which reference has already been made; for in the long run, the authority we accept will be the one with which we have brought ourselves most into harmony, the authority whose appeal or teaching causes responsive vibrations in our own souls. This inner standard will alone enable us to distinguish the true from the false guide as far as we are concerned, but, being based on past experience, our standard is not necessarily the standard for others, and the remembrance of this working of the law might do much to modify the rigor of sectarian differences. This recognition of one's own helper or teacher can only be a spontaneous thing, one cannot conceive of it being ever associated with fluctuation between two opinions, or decided with painful doubt and uncertainty. The following lines seem to express the truth in this matter:

> Thou shalt know him when he comes,
> Not by any din of drums,
> Nor the vantage of his airs;
> Neither by his crown,

Nor his gown,
Nor by anything he wears:
He shall only well-known be
By the holy harmony
That his coming makes in thee!

For a teacher, coming with such credentials, reverence, gratitude, devotion are the rightful meed; obedience to such authority the natural outcome. For the rest, we may find with Aristotle, that "virtue lies in a first medium between two extremes." Not the blind subservience to the authority of priest, person or party, is asked of any of us, nor yet the hedgehog-like attitude bristling with suspicion of tyranny and priest-craft at every point, but a due and reasonable recognition of the fact that we are here as part of a vast and complicated mechanism, in which it falls to each to fill a different sphere; in which some play more commanding parts than others, not by favour, but by merit, by law. A system in which some who have learnt to obey through service, now serve by ruling; they who have been faithful over a few things are made rulers over many; whereas others are still in the ranks of the Shûdras. By such due recognition and the determination to fill worthily the niche assigned by karma, shall those whom the builders rejected as not yet ready, become later the headstones of the corner.

EDITH WARD.

ERRATUM.

Page 331, line 3. For "Vausenarques" read "Vauvenargues."

THE GEOMETRY OF NATURE.

In the April number of Lucifer, Mr. Mead wrote on a recently published work by a Spanish author, Señor Soria y Mata, in which some remarkable discoveries were said to have been disclosed. Some months ago the first book of the author, *Origen Poliédrico de las Especies*, appeared, and was noticed in this journal. This contained only the beginning of a system which has been since elaborated and is now more fully displayed in two small volumes entitled, *Contribución al Origen Poliédrico de las Especies.* The first volume has already been translated into French, and it is hoped that ere long it will also appear in an English form; the second is as yet only obtainable in Spanish.

The purpose set before himself by the author is indeed a huge one, nothing less than to find a general law underlying all nature, whether in the physical realm, or in the mental, or spiritual. The scheme is, in truth, the old formula "as above, so below," *in excelsis*, that mysterious and much-abused occult axiom having at last a real meaning attached to it, providing the discoveries *are* discoveries and not the product of an ingenious imagination. Roughly put, the main theory of Señor Soria is that the basis of nature is geometric law, and the essence of this geometric law is to be found in the five regular solids, the tetrahedron, the cube, the octahedron, the dodecahedron and the icosahedron. These, with the sphere, are the only regular solids which can possibly exist in space (three dimensional, of course), that is, they are the only solid bodies of which all the points are at the same distance from the centre, and the faces of the same size and shape.

The development of this idea is really most ingenious. The laws of chemical combination, of crystal-formation, of vegetable and animal growth, of mental processes, and even of social organizations, are drawn upon to illustrate the theory—not, it must be confessed, with unvarying success.

Fundamentally, the whole of physical nature is regarded as built of these regular polyhedra, or solids. They are very small, much smaller than the chemical atoms, these being groups, perhaps of a complicated description, of the primary forms. Throughout all the complications, however, the same laws of combination hold.

The first pamphlet published by Señor Soria, while it does not give quite the same views as his more recent works, is remarkable chiefly for a scheme of geometrical development in which all the regular solids are built from the tetrahedron as a unit. It seems scarcely credible that such a simple fact as that of the tetrahedron being the basis of regular solids should have remained undiscovered, but I am unable to find any trace of it. Very little indeed is known as to the formation of solids, this branch of geometry having apparently been almost disregarded.

Whether or not our Spanish investigator has been the first to search out the strange relationship between the Platonic or regular solids, the relation is one not generally known, even to masters of modern mathematics, and is of singular interest to all who pay heed to the old ideas of mystical geometry. The philosophical Greeks, and by tradition Pythagoras especially, regarded the regular solids as the groundwork of nature. How much or how little they knew of that nature we may not be able to say, but it is worthy of note that long before any light had come from modern methods of research, the idea of a regular mathematical order in the universe existed. Now we know how true this idea is. We have in chemistry alone a vast range of examples of the fundamental fact, and there can be no doubt but that in the future chemical science will use not only ordinary mathematics, but also the long disregarded geometry of solid bodies, to investigate the relations which exist between the atoms of the various groups.

To make the subject at all clear diagrams are necessary. Those accompanying this article are rough drawings showing the method of building up the bodies from the primary figure. Fig. 1 is a cube, the most familiar of all solid figures. On joining the four points, *a*, *b*, *c*, *d*, the four-sided figure shown by chain lines is obtained. This is a tetrahedron, or four-sided body with all the sides and edges equal. Joining up the other four points in the same way we obviously obtain a precisely similar figure crossing the first symmetri-

FIG. 1

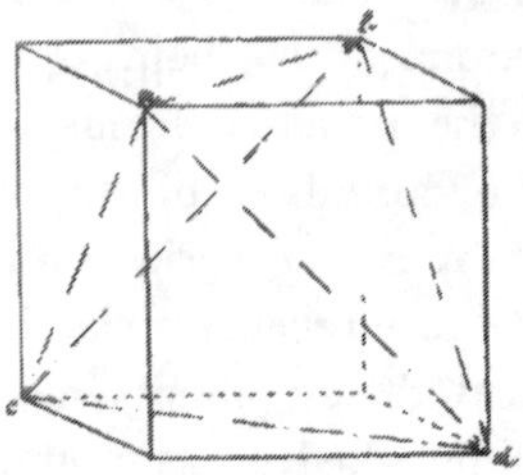

FIG. 2

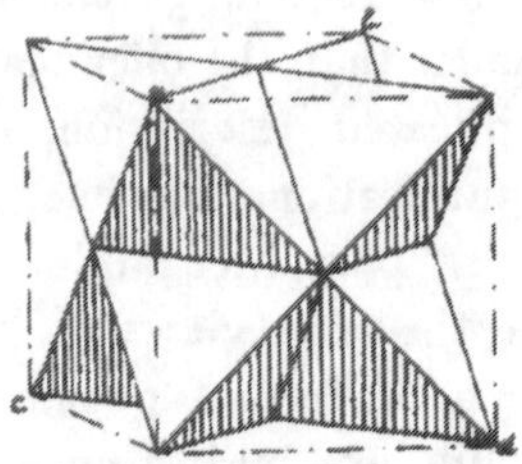

cally. The result is shown in Fig. 2, where two intersecting tetrahedra are drawn, and the enclosing cube is indicated in chain lines. As the edges of each figure are diagonals of the sides of the cube, they cross at the central point of each side. Joining these six points we have the octahedron, or regular eight-sided figure. This is not quite so familiar as the cube, but is like two pyramids placed with their bases against each other. Thus both the cube and the octahedron are formed by the symmetrical crossing of two tetrahedra.

Fig. 3 shows the dodecahedron. On joining the points *a'*, *b'*, *c'*, *d'*, at equal distances from each other, a tetrahedron is formed, as shown in chain lines. Starting at each of the five points in the

FIG. 3

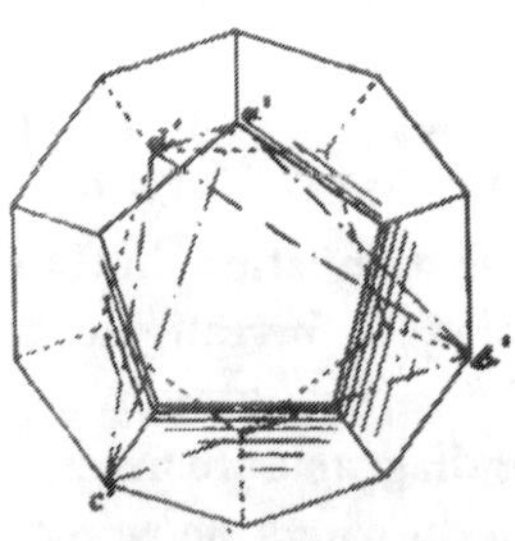

FIG. 4

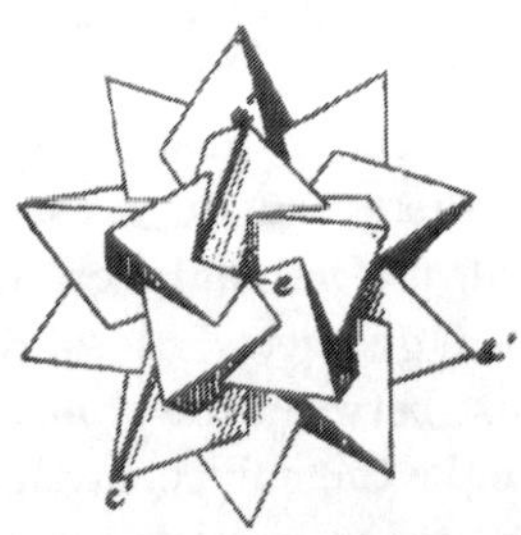

central pentagon we have evidently a series of five tetrahedra. All these are symmetrical, that is, intersect each other at regular intervals. The result is shown in Fig. 4, where the points *a'*, *b'*, *c'*, show the relation between this figure and Fig. 3. Each point in the latter can in a similar manner be traced in Fig. 4, so that it is obvious that the twenty points of the five intersecting tetrahedra correspond exactly to the twenty equidistant points of the dodecahedron.

As we have seen in the case of the cube that the octahedron is formed from it by joining the central points of its six sides (an octahedron having eight sides and six points) so there is a figure having a similar relation to the dodecahedron. This is the icosahedron, a regular figure with twenty sides and twelve points, each side forming an equilateral triangle. This icosahedron, or twenty-sided figure, is formed by joining the twelve inner points of the five tetrahedra, or the points at which they intersect. Only one of these, *e*, is visible, at the centre of Fig. 4.

We have thus a series of regular solids, all of which are related to the one type—the tetrahedron.

The order is. (*a*) Tetrahedron. (*b*) Two tetrahedra intersecting; cube, formed by joining the outer points of tetrahedra; octahedron, the result of joining the inner points, or points of intersection. (*c*) Five tetrahedra intersecting; dodecahedron, formed by joining the outer points; icosahedron, produced from the inner points.

We have here seven figures in three groups, a curious example of the "mystic" number. In fact a fresh field of symbolism seems to be opened, and it may be that in some such scheme we shall find the key to many of the so-called "occult" numbers, which have played an important part in mystical systems.

Before leaving this branch of the subject it may be of interest to give a further development of Señor Soria's discovery, a development that the ingenious Spaniard does not appear to have noticed. Figs. 5 and 6 show us a somewhat unfamiliar figure and its analysis.

FIG. 5

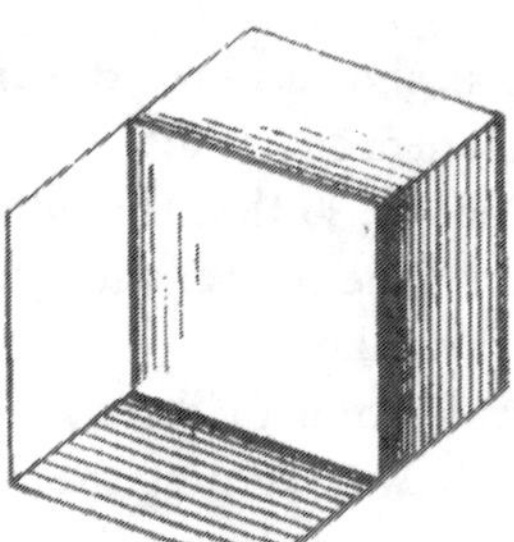

FIG. 6

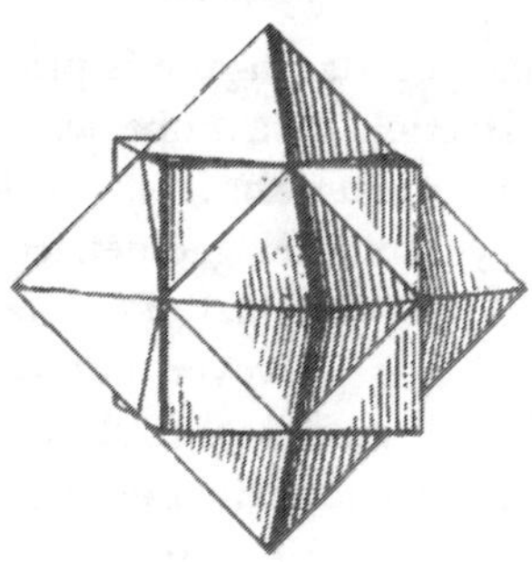

This figure is known as the rhombic dodecahedron, so-called because each face, instead of being a pentagon, as in the case of the regular dodecahedron (Fig. 3), is a rhomb, or surface enclosed by four equal lines not at right angles to each other. This figure possesses a peculiar interest as it is the one which would be formed by each one of a series of equal spheres packed together and touching each other, and then compressed equally, or expanded equally, to form cells. All space could be filled by a series of such cells without an aperture or crack, the sides of one meeting the sides of the adjacent ones. As can be easily seen, one sphere or ball can be surrounded by twelve equal spheres, all of which touch the next ones, and if any number of equal spheres be placed in a box each one of the inside ones will be surrounded and touched by twelve others. Again we meet numbers (twelve and thirteen) playing an important part in mystical tradition.

I have said that space could be completely filled by such figures, but if we accept occult observations of the nature of the ether, space actually *is* so filled. Such observations, some of which appeared in Mrs. Besant's article, "Occult Chemistry," in a previous issue of LUCIFER, show that the highest form of ether (interplanetary) is of cellular structure. This is produced by the arrangement of atoms, all of which are at equal distances from their surrounding ones. Each atom is the centre for a stream of energy, this stream meeting the opposing streams from adjacent atoms and having to return upon itself. Each atom is thus the centre of a vortex, the sides or walls of which are of the form of a dodecahedron or rather rhombic dodecahedron. To such a structure is probably due the elasticity of the ether which allows it to transmit waves of light and electricity.

This peculiar figure is produced, as shown in the drawings, by the intersection of a cube and an octahedron. Both of these are built from the tetrahedron, as shown above, so that the latter is the basis for yet another geometrical solid. The edge of the octahedron is equal to the diagonal of one face of the cube.

All this is, however, but the introduction to the main theme. Señor Soria's purpose is to show that the laws governing the formation of these solids and their combinations are the true laws of the universe, underlying all things from the atom to the solar system, and from the first dim glimmering of sensation to the thoughts and designs of the creative mind.

One of the fundamental conceptions is the law of combination, giving rise to new forms. In the cases already described we have the combination of two tetrahedra, giving rise to the cube and the octahedron, and five tetrahedra to the dodecahedron and icosahedron. Of these two resulting figures, one is regarded as positive or masculine, and the other as negative or feminine. The cube and dodecahedron, resulting from the joining of the external points, are masculine, and the octahedron and icosahedron, formed by joining the internal points, are feminine. It may be noted that in the so-called male figures the points predominate over the surfaces, while the reverse is the case in the female or negative ones.

This triple grouping is one of the chief points of the scheme, endless illustrations being given in all directions.

Señor Soria in his second work, *Contribución al Origen Poliédrico de las Especies*, begins with the ultimate atom, many stages behind anything that comes under the observation of science. This atom is regarded as the result of force (used apparently in the Spencerian sense as an equivalent for the "Unknowable"!) welling up from a mathematical point, expanding and returning again upon itself. Each atom is thus an oscillation or vibration. It is not a permanent thing, but one gives birth, so to speak, to its successor. An atom has itself but a momentary existence, but as it is followed at once by another, there is no break in the apparent continuity. The energy of motion thus inherent in the atom becomes transformed by the various combinations into our known forces of light, heat, and so forth. This atom is also rotating, and is regarded as having poles. In its formation we have two elements, force and matter, the combination of which brings forth the atom as the third in this trinity.

The next combination is that of one atom with another. These atoms are represented as at each end of a line, placed so that one end is positive and the other negative, this combination bringing a new form into play. Two of these lines or groups then combine in such a way that they are placed perfectly symmetrically, and a fresh geometrical form is the result. This is the tetrahedron; for if we place two of such pairs of atoms so that they are equi-distant or symmetrical, it is obvious that we must obtain the tetrahedron. Two points of this will be positive and two negative.

Our progress has been, up to the present, from the first two unknowables, force and matter, to the point of junction, or the atom; from the atom to the line or union of two, and from the line to the tetrahedron.

The fourth form, that of the octahedron, is obtained by three lines or pairs, giving the six points of that figure. A new kind of polarity appears here. It will be seen on drawing the figure that one side will have all its three corners composed of positive poles or atoms, one of negative, and the others partly of positive and partly of negative poles.

The other regular figures are produced in a corresponding manner, the underlying conception being that of balance or symmetry, the pairs of atoms, having + and – poles, being grouped so as to balance themselves, and thus to attain stability. The result is, that they will by their inherent forces arrange themselves into the shapes of the regular solids; not, of course, actually solids, but shapes in three dimensions, at each corner or point of which is an atom or centre of force, linked to the other atoms in the group.

The method by which polarity is maintained is of interest, as in the different forms there are always (excepting in the case of the tetrahedron) positive sides and negative sides, and others intermediate. Assuming some kind of polar attraction, it is easy to trace the building of geometrical forms by the union of one with another.

It will be seen that no attempt—beyond the peculiar theory of the vanishing atom—is made to enlighten us as to the real nature of the atom or the forces employed. The scheme does not touch such fundamental points as the modern vortex-ring and like hypotheses. It deals with the arrangement or plan, and not with the actual concrete things. It tells us nothing, for instance, of the cause of the atoms' attraction, or the mechanism by which such attraction (or repulsion) is brought about. What it gives us is a possible system, worked out on mathematical and geometrical lines, in which the forces work—a system, according to the enthusiastic originator, of universal application.

As far as we have gone, we have arrived at the differentiation from the primordial atoms (regarded as all of similar nature) into groups constituting the five regular solid figures. This, as already said, is the result of the balancing of the forces, the double polarized atoms arranging themselves in a symmetrical manner.

The next development is most ingenious. The regular solid figures are regarded as possessing regularity of the first class, but we have an infinite number of classes of regularity. The second class or order is produced when we place a number of the regular solids around a central one of the same kind, the faces of course lying together. For example, on each of the six faces of a cube another cube can be placed. The figure so produced is called by Señor Soria an octahedron of the second class, the six points of the octahedron being represented by the outer surfaces of the six surrounding cubes. On placing eight octahedra around a central one a cube of the second class is produced. Similarly thirteen dodecahedra give a icosahedron of the second order and twenty-one icosahedra (a central one on each side of which an external one is placed) a dodecahedron. There is no need to stop here, for these figures again will reproduce themselves in more complicated forms.

Señor Soria enunciates a law of the reproduction of forms which is of great interest. He shows how the geometrically regular figures can be made to reproduce themselves infinitely. But immediately we introduce irregularity such power is destroyed. This we can easily see by drawing a pentagon or hexagon and continuing the sides to form a star. These form the points of a second pentagon or hexagon and so on. But if the sides are not of equal length the inequalities are magnified at each operation until the projected lines diverge instead of coming to a point, and no further geometrical figure is possible. For infinite reproduction, that is, for continuance of life, there must be perfect harmony or symmetry. This is found in the regular solids and in no other forms. Hence these must be the material basis of nature.

Continuing the series of combinations on the lines laid down, and by interpenetrating one form with another, we arrive at the atoms and molecules of the chemist, and here Señor Soria claims to have discovered the general laws governing the combinations of the elements. This is one of the most interesting parts of the subject, but its elucidation would take up too much space for this article. I hope to devote a short paper especially to this branch of the subject in a subsequent issue. Briefly, however, the system is but a continuation of the laws of combination already given, in which the geometrical bodies (formed by an ultimate atom at each point, linked by some unknown force of attraction to the others) arrange themselves around each other symmetrically.

How many stages from the primary five solids we have to go before we reach the chemical atom we are not told. Probably many, as the atom of the chemist is a most complicated body and may contain many thousands of those ultimate five forms. The first combination of the five regular bodies, one with the other, in every possible symmetrical manner, produces what may be called the meta-elements, of which there must be twenty-six. The combinations of these again produce an enormously greater number of more complicated forms, all, however, having lines of symmetry. The number of chemical elements possible might thus be calculated, if we knew the degree of complexity. This we do not know, but we can easily prove that the weights of the elements follow generally a certain law, which has been variously set forth, but which is commonly known as the Mendeléef grouping of the elements. It is known that when these are arranged in order of their weight, those bodies whose weights are multiples or integral parts of each other have properties in common. All this fits into the geometrical scheme of combination, as do the combinations of atoms to form molecnles. The various acids, salts and bases can all be represented by forms built out of the primary figures.

In the formation of crystals we have the most obvious illustration of the geometry of nature. Each crystal has definite angles formed by its faces, which angles never vary, whatever may be the sizes of the surfaces. If the basis of forms be the geometrical bodies claimed by Señor Soria, it is obvious that their combinations must form geometrically regular bodies, the angles of which will depend on the nature of the substance—or, according to the theory, on the geometrical structure of the atoms and molecules forming it.

So far the inorganic world. Can the same laws be applied to the organic? An attempt is made so to apply them. By placing one body—cube, octahedron, or the like—on another, a chain or line is formed. Not a line according to Euclid, but a line of real bodies, the only kind of line that can, if this theory be true, exist in nature. Previously in combining the bodies we had a central one around which the others were placed, and so we could imagine lines or chains radiating from this point. This is regarded as the arrangement of the atoms in inorganic nature. But if we start now with the line and group other lines around it, we get quite different figures. By grouping dodecahedra and icosahedra together we can obtain curves, and some illustrations are given in the works referred to showing how cylinders, cones and spirals can be produced. These are the fundamental forms of the vegetable kingdom. One of the predominant features of vegetable life is the formation of stems and leaves around axes, producing spirals and various curves. These are considered as due to the fundamental law governing vegetable life—the grouping of the geometrical bodies around lines of symmetry. A practically infinite number of forms is thus possible, far greater complexity being obtained than in the mineral kingdom.

And now we have another step to take. By arranging these bodies around a line we can form a plane, or rather an infinite number of planes can be constructed differing in constitution. Such planes can serve as the basis of further development, and by arranging the bodies around a plane of symmetry we have the origin of animal forms. Still further extensions carry us to the human form, then to the social constitution, to astronomy and to metaphysics, these five geometrical forms being the root of all.

In the later developments one cannot resist the feeling that there is something fantastic in the scheme. It is too great for its foundation. The effort to include all things in nature, physical or spiritual, over-reaches itself. An astonishing amount of ingenuity is displayed in the working out of details, but at least in the scheme as applied to social matters and to the laws of thought and metaphysics I feel sure that the writer will see reason to modify his views, whether or not he retain his fundamental ideas.

I have not attempted to do more than mention this wider region, partly because of the lack of space, and also because of the difficulty of rendering the subject intelligible.

Briefly summarizing the main conceptions and avoiding details, we may give the following bald scheme :

The universe is built through the application of geometrical laws, applying to all forms of life. The matter is built of ultimate atoms grouped into geometric forms. These forms are essentially the five regular solids, which are all combinations of the tetrahedron, this being the basic figure. By combining these primary figures in every possible symmetrical manner we arrive at a gradual evolution of form giving us chemical elements and combinations, crystalline bodies, plant, animal and human forms and so on, up to the universe itself. Symmetry and regularity are found everywhere, and are essential to life and reproduction.

The further developments of the subject (for certainly Señor Soria will not stand still in the matter) will be looked for with interest by all who have come into contact with the fascinating speculations, and we may hope to hear more ere long.

A. M. GLASS.

THE ÂKÂSHIC RECORDS.

(*Concluded from p.* 323.)

BUT, it may be asked, how is it possible, amid this bewildering confusion of records of the past and previsions of the future, to find any particular picture when it is wanted? As a matter of fact, the untrained clairvoyant usually cannot do so without some special link to put him *en rapport* with the subject required. Psychometry is an instance in point, and it is quite probable that our ordinary memory is really only another presentment of the same idea. It seems as though there were a sort of magnetic attachment or affinity between any particle of matter and the record which contains its history—an affinity which enables it to act as a kind of conductor between that record and the faculties of anyone who can read it.

For example, I once brought from Stonehenge a tiny fragment of stone, not larger than a pin's head, and on putting this into an envelope and handing it to a psychometer who had no idea what it was, she at once began to describe that wonderful ruin and the desolate country surrounding it, and then went on to picture vividly what were evidently scenes from its early history, showing that that infinitesimal fragment had been sufficient to put her into communication with the records connected with the spot from which it came. The scenes through which we pass in the course of our life seem to act in the same manner upon the cells of our brain as did the history of Stonehenge upon that particle of stone; they establish a connection with those cells by means of which our mind is put *en rapport* with that particular portion of the records, and so we "remember" what we have seen.

Even a trained clairvoyant needs some link to enable him to find the record of an event of which he has no previous knowledge. If, for example, he wished to observe the landing of Julius Cæsar on the shores of England, there are several ways in which he might approach the subject. If he happened to have visited the scene of the occurrence, the simplest way would probably be to call up the image of that spot, and then run back through its records until he reached the period desired. If he had not seen the place, he might run back in time to the date of the event, and then search the Channel for a fleet of Roman galleys; or he might examine the records of Roman life at about that period, where he would have no difficulty in identifying so prominent a figure as Cæsar, or in tracing him when found through all his Gallic wars until he set his foot upon British land.

People often enquire as to the aspect of these records—whether they appear near or far away from the eye, whether the figures in them are large or small, whether the pictures follow one another as in a panorama or melt into one another like dissolving views, and so on. One can only reply that their appearance varies to a certain extent according to the conditions under which they are seen. Upon the astral plane the reflection is most often a simple picture, though occasionally the figures seen would be endowed with motion; in this latter case, instead of a mere snapshot a rather longer and more perfect reflection has taken place.

On the devachanic plane they have two widely different aspects. When the visitor to that plane is not thinking specially of them in any way, the records simply form a background to whatever is going on, just as the reflections in a pier-glass at the end of a room might form a background to the life of the people in it. It must always be borne in mind that under these conditions they are really merely reflections from the ceaseless activity of a great Consciousness upon a far higher plane, and have very much the appearance of an endless succession of the recently-invented *cinematographe*, or living photographs. They do not melt into one another like dissolving views, nor do a series of ordinary pictures follow one another; but the action of the reflected figures constantly goes on, as though one were watching the actors on a distant stage.

But if the investigator turn his attention specially to any one scene, or wishes to call it up before him, an extraordinary change at once takes place, for this is the plane of thought, and to think of anything is to bring it instantaneously before you. For example, if a man wills to see the record of that event to which we before referred—the landing of Julius Cæsar— he finds himself in a moment not looking at any picture, but standing on the shore among the legionaries, with the whole scene being enacted around him, precisely in every respect as he would have seen it if he had stood there in the flesh on that autumn morning in the year 55 B.C. Since what he sees is but a reflection, the actors are of course entirely unconscious of him, nor can any effort of his change the course of their action in the smallest degree, except only that he can control the rate at which the drama shall pass before him—can have the events of a whole year rehearsed before his eyes in a single hour, or can at any moment stop the movement altogether, and hold any particular scene in view as a picture as long as he chooses.

In truth he observes not only what he would have seen if he had been there at the time in the flesh, but much more. He hears and understands all that the people say, and he is conscious of all their thoughts and motives; and one of the most interesting of the many possibilities which open up before one who has learnt to read the records is the study of the thought of ages long past—the thought of the cave-men and the lake-dwellers as well as that which ruled the mighty civilizations of Atlantis, of Egypt or Chaldæa. How the vistas of the past open up before such a student —not only the story of all the vast achievements of man, but also of the processes of nature, of the strange chaotic life of earlier rounds—we can indicate only slightly here; but the reader will readily realize that in these directions an almost limitless field lies waiting for the patient investigator.

In one especial case an even closer sympathy with the past is possible to the reader of the records. If in the course of his enquiries he has to look upon some scene in which he himself has in a former birth taken part, he may deal with it in two ways; he can either regard it in the usual manner as a spectator (though always, be it remembered, as a spectator whose insight and sympathy are perfect) or he may once more identify himself with that long-dead personality of his—may throw himself back for the time into that life of long ago, and absolutely experience over again the thoughts and the emotions, the pleasures and the pains of a prehistoric past. No wilder and more vivid adventures can be conceived than some of those through which he thus may pass; yet through it all he must never lose hold of the consciousness of his own individuality—must retain the power to return at will to his present personality.

The accurate reading of the records, whether of one's own past lives or those of others, must not, however, be thought of as an achievement possible to anyone without careful previous training. As has been already remarked, though occasional reflections may be had upon the astral plane, the power to use the devachanic sense is necessary before any reliable reading can be done. Indeed, to minimize the possibility of error, that sense ought to be fully at the command of the investigator while awake in the physical body; and to acquire that faculty needs years of ceaseless labour and rigid self-discipline. Many people seem to expect that as soon as they have signed their application and joined the Theosophical Society they will at once remember at least three or four of their past births; indeed, some of them promptly begin to imagine recollections. At the present moment there are, I think, four people who are all quite certain that in their last incarnation they were Mary Queen of Scots (why Mary Queen of Scots should be so frequently selected is not very clear, considering the character which history assigns to her, but she certainly is), two who were Cleopatra (another not very desirable progenitor, surely), and several who were Julius Cæsar! Of course such extravagant claims simply bring discredit upon those who are so foolish as to make them; but unfortunately some of that discredit is liable to be reflected, however unjustly, upon the Society to which they belong, so that a man who feels seething within him the conviction that he was Homer or Shakespeare would do well to pause and apply common-sense tests on the physical plane before publishing the news to the world.

It is quite true that some people have had glimpses of scenes from their past lives in dreams, but naturally these are usually fragmentary and unreliable. I had myself in earlier life an experience of this nature. Among my dreams I found that one was constantly recurring—a dream of a house with a portico overlooking a beautiful bay, not far from a hill on the top of which rose a graceful building. I knew that house perfectly, and was as familiar with the position of its rooms and the view from its door as I was with those of my home in this present life. In those days I knew nothing about reincarnation, so that it seemed to me simply a curious coincidence that this dream should repeat itself so often; and it was not until some time after I had joined the Society that, when one who knew was showing me some pictures of my last incarnation, I discovered that this persistent dream had been in reality a partial recollection, and that the house which I knew so well was the one in which I was born more than two thousand years ago.

But although there are several cases on record in which some well-remembered scene has thus come through from one life to another, a considerable development of occult faculty is necessary before an investigator can definitely trace a line of incarnations, whether they be his own or another man's. This will be obvious if we remember the conditions of the problem which has to be worked out. To follow a person from this life to the one preceding it, it is necessary first of all to trace his present life backwards to his birth and then to follow up in reverse order the stages by which the ego descended into incarnation. This will obviously take us back eventually to the condition of the ego upon its own plane—the arûpa level of Devachan; so it will be seen that to perform this task effectually the investigator must be able to use the sense corresponding to that exalted level while awake in his physical body—in other words, his consciousness must be centred in the reincarnating ego itself and no longer in the lower personality. In that case, the memory of the ego being aroused, his own past incarnations will be spread out before him like an open book, and he would be able, if he wished, to examine the conditions of another ego upon that level and trace him backwards through the devachanic and astral lives which led up to it, until he came to the last physical death of that ego, and through it to his previous life. There is no other way but this in which the chain of lives can be followed through with absolute certainty; and consequently we may at once put aside as conscious or unconscious impostors those people who advertise that they are able to trace out anyone's past incarnations for so many shillings a head. Needless to say, the true occultist does not advertise, and never under any circumstances accepts money for any exhibition of his powers.

Assuredly the student who wishes to acquire the power of following up a line of incarnations can do so only by learning from a qualified teacher how the work is to be done. There have been those who persistently asserted that it was only necessary for a man to feel good and devotional and "brotherly," and all the wisdom of the ages would immediately flow in upon him; but a little common-sense will at once expose the absurdity of such a position. However good a child may be, if he wants to know the multiplication table he must set to work and learn it; and the case is precisely similar with the capacity to use spiritual faculties. The faculties themselves will no doubt manifest as the man evolves, but he can learn how to use them reliably and to the best advantage only by steady hard work and persevering effort.

Take the case of those who wish to help others while on the astral plane during sleep; it is obvious that the more knowledge they possess here, the more valuable will their services be on that higher plane. For example, the knowledge of languages would be useful to them, for though on the devachanic plane men can communicate directly by thought transference, whatever their languages may be, on the astral plane this is not so, and a thought must be definitely formulated in words before it is comprehensible. If, therefore, you wish to help a man on that plane, you must have some language in common by means of which you can communicate with him, and consequently the more languages you know the more widely useful you will be. In fact there is perhaps no kind of knowledge for which a use cannot be found in the work of the occultist.

It would be well for all students to bear in mind that occultism is the apotheosis of common-sense, that every vision which comes to them is not necessarily a picture from the âkâshic records, nor every experience a revelation from on high. It is better far to err on the side of healthy scepticism than of over-credulity; and it is an admirable rule never to hunt about for an occult explanation of anything when a plain and obvious physical one is available. Our duty is to endeavour to keep our balance always, and never to lose our self-control, but to take a reasonable, common-sense view of whatever may happen to us; so shall we be better Theosophists, wiser occultists, and more useful helpers than we have ever been before.

C. W. LEADBEATER.

DELIVERANCE.

SEEKING for some one supreme condition wherein may be found the happiness and the rest that are denied us in this Saṁsâra, we are told that Nirvâṇa is. We joyfully receive this news of solace and forthwith begin to feel a foretaste of that Bliss Unspeakable in the Peace of Faith, when lo! another comes and speaks of a Paranirvâṇa, beyond that Nirvâṇa wherein we had begun to think our final haven of rest from turmoil would be found. Then a third passes by speaking of Mahâparanirvâṇa that is far higher still, and throws us back amazed into the old whirl of doubts and fears. Mukti, deliverance's self, is similarly broken into pieces and classified in many ways—Salokya, Saṁîpya, Sarûpya, Sayugya; or Jîvan-mukti, Videha-mukti, etc.; till in that deliverance we find no whit of freedom from the old questionings. Whence this confusion as to the meaning of a single word, and why?

. . . . .

A world-period, any and every world-period, between Pralaya and Pralaya, call it a Manvantara if you like, or better still, take a whole Kalpa (with its ready-made division into Purvârdha and Parârdha) is divided into two equal halves, one the semi-circle of the Pravṛitti-mârga, the downward arc, of the fall into matter, the other the semi-circle of the Nivṛitti-mârga, the upward arc, of the return from matter to the "original state." At that turning-point where the one ends and the other begins, every Jîva comes in sight of Mukti, and so in one sense may be said to attain Mukti.

. . . . .

Every Jîva, I say. Doubt thou not, O timid Soul! that in thy blessed humbleness of spirit thinkest thou art not fit for that last goal of all, but that thou, too, shalt surely reach it; aye, and none other shall attain it sooner. For art not thou, too, one with the Supreme? A Self amidst all Selfs? A part of the one Whole? Nay, even the Whole itself? And how, then, can a Self that is none other than the Highest Self be lost and perish? Thou thinkest thou hast sinned! But so have all thy brothers in their time. For did not even He who grew to be the blessed Buddha say, when thorns once pierced those holy feet that wandered bare over the earth, bringing soft peace to all who needed it, and they who were with him doubted and questioned him why one so sinless and so holy should still suffer pain, did He not say, how in some long-past life his brother died and left his infant son and all his wealth into his trustful keeping; how he broke the trust, and how for avarice of that wretched gold he stabbed his little nephew in the night, and how he had to expiate that sin in many later lives, and how it was only the blood drops of the last thorn-prick which had washed away the last remaining Shesha of that sin? So fear thou not, but take heart from that example! *Because* thou art a Self like all thy brother Selfs, so thou, and all, must pass through all experiences of ever-varied pain and pleasure, which make the essence of all, the experience of all. Thy present doubt itself is but one of such moods.

. . . . .

How could the Omnipotent be omnipotent if It possessed not the power to render Itself wholly helpless? How could the Omniscient be omniscient if It knew not the means to become the most ignorant of the ignorant? How could the Eternal be Master of All Time if It could not become limited in time? As the Upanis̤hads say:

"It moveth and It moveth not; 'Tis far and yet 'Tis near;
All It pervades and yet It is outside of All and aught."

O Self! Thou art the very home of all gross contradictions,

wherein they all are reconciled, wherein they lose themselves, each in its opposite!

. . . . . .

When all the permutations of all the possible experiences of a world-period are completed, what is the difference between the various permutations except of insignificant time and space? What is the difference between abcd, adbc, acbd, adcb, etc.? And still more so where a=-b, and c=-d, good balancing evil, pleasure pain (for all experiences whatsoever are absolutely nothing else than different *forms* of pleasure *or* pain, and all life whatsoever, so-called lowest or so-called highest, nothing else than a ceaseless series of such different forms)? Every Jîva is but such a permutation of experiences, and the *particular order* of the permutation is the Sûtrâtman, the Kâraṇa Sharîra, the Individuality, of the Jîva!

. . . . . .

Thus it is that the Upanishad says that all the Jîvas of a Brahmâṇḍa attain deliverance together with the Brahmâ of that world, this Mukti meaning the true Mukti of a Pralaya.

But truly that is not the Mukti which every professing Mumukshu looks for! To most, such Pralaya-mukti presents a very desolate and gloomy picture of "do-nothingness," whereas what these want is the very reverse—ability to fly in air, to dive through earth, fire and water, to turn all metals into gold, to pry into the secrets of sun, moon and stars while sitting comfortably here on the earth; to them psychic powers, the Siddhis of Yoga-shâstra, mean Mukti. To a few who have realized that psychic powers are no more and mean no more than our ordinary present physical and mental powers, though Mukti may not mean such "spirituality" as mere psychic powers denote, it still means but an undefined, glorious, mystic haze of blissful and altruistic emotion (vaguely approaching to the Maitrî, Karuṇâ, etc., of the same Yoga-shâstra).

Neither of these classes has yet experienced the true Vairâgya, the cessation of Râga (Vâsanâ, Trishṇâ), the Passion-Force that is the form assumed by the "Necessity of Manifestation" for driving the Jîva down the arc of Pravṛitti (as the Vairâgya-force is the form assumed by it on the opposite arc); neither has quite passed the turning-point where begins the Path of Nivṛitti; though the latter is perhaps very close to it, in any case much nearer to it than the former.

The Jîva that has passed through the true Vairâgya, in whom the outward-driving Force of Passion is exhausted, longs for the "do-nothingness" of Pralaya as ardently as the over-worked labourer longs for the rest and the peace of night after his day's heavy task-work. . .

. . . . .

"The Self-born pierced the senses outwards, and so the Jîva seeth only the things outside and not the Âtman within. Some satiated one, longing for immortality, turned his eyes inwards and beheld the Supreme Self." (Upanishads.)

. . . . .

"If thou hast access at the Monarch's gate,
Neglect thou not the Monarch for the gift.
Against the Way 'twould be if devotee
Wished aught of God but God Himself alone." (Sâdi.)

. . . . .

"Who from the world did turn his face away
Was lost not, but found his lost Self again." (Sâdi.)

. . . . .

But the work of repayment of the debts incurred, of the renunciation of the world's goods acquired, takes just as long as the incurring of the debts and the acquisition of the goods. The two arcs are equal. The sun can take no less a period to ascend from the nadir to the zenith than it has taken to descend from the zenith to the nadir. And even as throughout the process, from the starting-point to the turning-point, the Jîva may appropriately be called Baddha (bound), so throughout the return, from the turning-point up to the starting-point back again, it is entitled to be, in a certain sense, called Mukta (free). It is possible to say that throughout this period it is Jîvanmukta, and therefore, in Pralaya, Videhamukta, although this is scarcely the sense in which the two words are ordinarily used, the ordinary use implying that a Jîvanmukta is still attached to a living, physical human organism and Sthûla Sharîra, while a Videhamukta has become dissociated therefrom, though he may have got an Upâdhi of subtler matter instead. But the stages from the turning-point upwards to the starting-point are numberless, and each stage may be called a special sort of Mukti or Nirvâṇa if it be found necessary to do so for any special reason; and hence have arisen the many classes and sorts of Mukti, the later stages, attained by the advanced Jîvas, being called the states of the Amarâḥ, the Immortal Gods. But what this immortality is, is explained by the books themselves.

"Existence up to the Mahâpralaya of the elements is known as immortality." (Purâṇas.)

. . . . .

The tree has been cut down, the huge Ashvattha that has its branches on the earth, its roots in the sky; its ultimate death is certain, yet its limbs are full of sap, and before they dry up and the whole vast framework crumbles and perishes, periods as long must lapse as were spent in the building up of the whole, and there may even be new sprouts, though short-lived, from the dying branches.

How are these periods to be spent?

"Surely none may rest even a moment absolutely actionless. . . . The journey of thy Upâdhi, too, could not be accomplished without action." (Gîtâ.)

The world-plan has already laid down the law. The life will pass through subtler and subtler matter, through psychic conditions as now called, the conditions of the Gods, till the very end in the nothing that is everything. And thus it comes about that much shall be given to them that want not, while from those that want may be taken away perhaps even what they have.

. . . . .

To such Viraktas, who would sit down on their cars, casting aside the bow Gâṇḍiva, saying they will move no more, is the teaching of the Bhagavad Gîtâ well addressed. After Virâga follows necessarily the Sight of the Truth, the One Supreme Self that slays not nor is slain, and after the sight thereof follows the journey thereunto, which is nothing else than the exhaustion of remaining past Karma, the repayment of old debts, the manful doing of the duty of the moment, and the quiet waiting for and experiencing the gradual thinning of the veils of matter.

. . . . .

The place of Yoga, in chronological order, is after the Vedânta, not before.

Knowledge begins the Path; knowledge lights it throughout; knowledge ends it. Karma Yoga accompanies the traveller on the way, and amuses him and helps to pass his time. Bhakti, the spirit of self-surrender and self-sacrifice to *all*, not to one particular fellow-creature, or if to one fellow-creature then to him only as embodiment of still greater self-sacrifice for all if possible, and therefore entitled to the name of teacher, guides the Upâdhi onwards.

Beware, O man! thou fix not thy faith too deeply on any particular Upâdhi for the sake of that Upâdhi only.

. . . . .

"Thy will be done, O Lord! not mine," the Bhâkta cries. O noble-hearted one! who layest out that noble heart of thine in utmost sacrifice before thy idol and passest into ecstasy and bliss! Would that thy cry were true! Would that that ecstasy and bliss lasted for evermore! Alas! the cry is not true. That ecstasy is not the peace thou shalt search for again. That idol of thine—monstrous as the ravening tigress that rended the self-proferred flesh of the future Buddha, if it selfishly accept thy sacrifice; or beneficent and self-sacrificing in turn as the mother that accepts a service of affection from her child, if it have the spirit to reward thy homage befittingly—that idol must in any case, as *other* than thee, render thee back full measure of the loan advanced by thee, though thou ask not, if it make thee do *its* will and *not* thine own. The true cry is the cry that sayeth: "Thy will and mine are but the same."

The calm that cometh when the Self perceives its oneness with all other Selfs hiding behind the tiniest atoms of so-called dead matter; when it sees clearly that these outward veils, though they be gross or subtle, are all but mere illusion, and that naught abideth but the Self alone; when all the multifarious movement of the world is seen to be but one vast sacrifice unto that Self, that calm, that peace and goodwill unto all is true Devotion.

. . . . .

As the various stages on the upward Path make the different kinds of Mukti, so Nirvâṇa, Paranirvâṇa, Mahâparanirvâṇa, etc., have their explanation as representing the culminating stages at the end of gradually greater and greater world-cycles. Thus if the final condition at the later end of the upward arc of the circle of a Manvantara is to be called Nirvâṇa, the corresponding condition at the end of a Mahâmanvantara may be called Paranirvâṇa, that at the end of a Kalpa, Mahâparanirvâṇa, and so on through unending circles. For there is no absolutely final dissolution of any individuality, but it will lie dormant through the Great Sleep and rise again with renewed Desire for work and activity, to return again to sleep, and so on, endlessly.

. . . . .

How should that *begun* not *end?* And yet how also should anything ever partaking of Sat, of existence, ever cease to be? The result of the two laws is the feigning, the illusion, of both conditions, the Anâdi-pravâha, the beginningless and endless flow of Mâyâ, the ever-becoming. The Supreme includes, or excludes, both Bandha and Moksha, Kalpa and Pralaya, whence Shankara sang:

"(The) I desire(th) not Moksha, nor yet the wealth of the world."

GOVINDA DÂSA.

ECKHARTSHAUSEN'S CATECHISM.

Translated from the German by MADAME DE STEIGER.

PREFACE.

I HAVE endeavoured in the translation of the following curious "Catechism" to keep the archaic simplicity of style intact. The first translation made by a friend, has been carefully revised by me with the original German work, so that though I have tried to put it into at least readable English in the obscurest passages, I have faithfully kept a necessary literalness, lest in altering a word, the sense appearing to me deficient, I might really obscure the author's own meaning, for it most evidently requires a key; and whether there *are* any readers who *really* understand the drift of this strangely interesting and most suggestive "Catechism" I do not know, but I should be sincerely glad to understand more myself, seeing that it evidently refers to the Higher Alchemy or the true spiritual work of regeneration.

This "Catechism" is a separate work included in the three volumes before me. The publisher dates his preface from Munich, September 1st, 1818, and his part of the work appears to consist in publishing two essays. The first is entitled the "Magic of Nature, a Free Translation of Egyptian MSS. from the Coptic with a Supplement of Magical Symbols deciphered from these MSS." The second is the "Catechism" now translated. The publisher states that there may be doubts respecting the authenticity of these works, in view of their posthumous appearance, but he adds, those readers who are well acquainted with Eckartshausen's style in his other works will recognize this and the flow of his ideas to their entire satisfaction. He adds, moreover, that the MSS., with title pages in the hand of Eckartshausen, are recognized by his former copyist, still living (1818).

With regard to the "Catechism" I cannot help thinking it might never have been intended for publication, that it may refer to a society for mystic association and research of a very high and spiritual nature. However, as no manual secrets seem to be revealed, there possibly was no harm in the publisher printing the MS. or in my offering this translation to LUCIFER.

The greater part of the same volume before me is occupied by a work (not posthumous) of Eckartshausen's, entitled "The Arithmetic of Nature, or a Key to the Hieroglyphs of Nature," printed at Leipzig, 1794. The second volume is "An Explanation of Magic from Experimental Knowledge of the Hidden Philosophy and Secret Science of Nature," printed at Munich, 1788. The third volume is much smaller, and entitled, "Mystic Nights or the Key to the Secrets of the Miraculous," published at Munich, 1791. Leutner is the publisher of all but the posthumous works. Those bear the name of Lindauer. "The Arithmetic of Nature," brought out at Leipzig, is "commissioned by Herrn G. E. Beer."

Whether any or all of these works are translated into English I cannot ascertain.

I. DE S.

CATECHISM OF THE HIGHER CHEMISTRY FOR THE PROOF OF THE ANALOGY BETWEEN THE TRUTHS OF NATURE AND THOSE OF FAITH: BY ONE WHO IS A DEVOTED STUDENT OF RELIGION AND NATURE: WHOSE AGE IS FIFTEEN: TO THOSE RECEPTIVE OF LIGHT CONCERNING MAGICAL STUDIES: HELIOPOLIS.

Question. Who art thou?

Answer. I am a human being, who knows the Light and follows it.

Q. What constitutes such a person?

A. He is one who, after he perceives the Light, is illuminated by it, and follows implicitly, clearly and intelligently, what the old real Light-Community always knew and practised, were it inscribed, or not, in the Light-Book.

Q. By what mark is the follower of Light recognised?

A. By this, that he knows the Cross-Sign of nature, the great symbol of the science of analysis, of the separation of the clean from the unclean, and of the perfect from the imperfect, that he avoids all impure works and errors, which the true teachers of the real Light-Community unanimously reject.

Q. How is the follower of Light distinguished?

A. He is distinguished by the great sign of the cross of nature †, that is by the sign of the science of analysis he speaks and performs all in the name or the qualities of Fire, Light, and Spirit, by which he brings all to its conclusion and completion.

Q. How many of the principles of the real Light-Community is it necessary for each follower of Light to know?

A. There are five; the first is the true conviction and belief in or dependence on the Light.

The second contains the seven means to attain the Light.

The third, the ten commandments of Light.

The fourth, the knowledge of the creative power as the active, and of the pure form as the passive.

The fifth is the knowledge of the analysis of Light.

FIRST PRINCIPLE.

DEPENDENCE ON LIGHT.

Q. What is the first principle of the real Light doctrine?

A. The dependence on and knowledge of Light; for without

this dependence and knowledge it is impossible to obtain strength, to accomplish and effect anything.

Q. In what should each son of Light believe, and on what should he depend?

A. All that the men of Light have taught and written in the twelve articles of the Light-Community.

Q. Which are the twelve articles of the real Light-Community?

A. 1st. I depend on and believe in a creative Fire-force, out of which originated heaven and earth, or the "extensum" and "concretum," the volatile and the fixed.

2nd. And in one Light, produced by this Fire-force, the ruler of the world, or the omnipotent force in nature.

3rd. This pure Light, which proceeds from the Fire, is received from the purest Spirit, and demitted into the purest form.

4th. But it must suffer in the kingdom of the impure; it must be divided, put to death, and buried in the earth.

5th. Then the Light descends into the inmost part of matter, and after three epochs, that is, after three unions of three spiritual forces with three purified forms, it rises again as living.

6th. It rises to the highest perfection as a glorious Light-force of the omnipotent Fire.

7th. And after the attainment of this highest perfection, it is capable of making all the dead living, and the imperfect perfect.

8th. I believe in and recognize the Light-spirit, which proceeds from fire and warmth.

9th. I believe in the holy, universal, real Light-Community, the Communion and Union of the followers of Light.

10th. The annulling of sickness and misery.

11th. The renewing of our being.

12th. And the extreme happiness of life.

Q. In what consists the main tenor of those twelve articles?

A. It consists in this, that a follower of Light obeys the laws of Light, which he knows through his reason, and practises by his will, namely, that universal force is one in substance and in essence, and that at the same time it is threefold in its development, namely, the Fire-force as the creative, the Light-force as the connective, and the Spirit-force proceeding out of Fire and Light, as the formative force of all things.

This final force brings all to perfection, and by pre-arranged means to their true completion.

Second Principle.

The Seven Means of Help to Obtain the Light.

Q. What is the second principle of the doctrine of the true Light-Community?

A. There are seven means of help to obtain the Light, which the Community holds most venerable and holy.

Q. What is such a means of help?

A. It is a visible baptismal operation, by which an invisible force effects inner perfection.

Q. How many are there of these means of union?

A. Seven, and they stand in analogy with the seven sacraments

1. Baptism, by water and light.
2. Confirmation of matter, according to water and light.
3. Purification.
4. Reception of Light from above in essence and substance.
5. Consecration, perfecting of the process.
6. Heavenly chrism.
7. The union of Fire and Light into a perfect body.

Q. What is Light baptism?

A. It is that first most necessary means of union, by which matter is purified by water and by the Word, operating in water, and is again placed in the Light-being as a new and perfect body.

Q. What is confirmation?

A. Light confirmation is a means of union, by which the above prepared matter is strengthened by the Light chrism and by the Spirit, which is therein, and is made further capable of perfection.

Q. What is the third means of union?

A. It is that, by which Light and Fire receive their being in the ceremonial form of the principles of bread and wine, when a Priest of nature knows how to change these principles on the altar.

Q. What is the fourth means of union?

A. It is the means of union by which the Priest of nature, who is a receiver of Light, purifies the matter, which is susceptible of Light, and even takes away all the effects of imperfection.

Q. What is the fifth?

A. It is that means of union by which the pure Light-force is raised in the form of chrism to the perfection of healing forces.

Q. What is the sixth?

A. The sixth is that by which matter is consecrated through seven operating forces, and made receptive of Light.

Q. What is the seventh?

A. It is the perfect union of Light with Fire by a medium, which proceeds out of Light and Fire, thereby effecting the union of perfect parts.

THIRD PRINCIPLE.

THE TEN LIGHT COMMANDMENTS.

Q. What is the third principle of the Light-Community?

A. The ten Light commandments, of which it is written: If you wish to accomplish anything, bring it to pass by fulfilling the commandments of the law.

Q. Which are the ten Light commandments?

A. The following:

1. There is but one Substance.

2. The properties of this Substance must be used in order.

3. In six operations, matter completed its day's work, since three forces produce three essences, and rest in the seventh force, as in the fulfilment of their workings, and this seventh force shall be holy to thee as the Sabbath of Light.

4. Light and Fire, as passive and active, are sacred to thee; for Fire is the male and Light is the female—Father and Mother of all things.

5. Light must not be robbed of its living power, in case the matter, which is to be raised up, die.

6. Confuse not the order of thy work. Everything has its time and rotation. Let it be thy duty to unite the scattered forces.

7. Neither draw their properties away from Light and Fire, it is wise to let both work fully. To each should be left its property.

8. Mistake not a false appearance for true, neither take anything impure and foreign, which is not capable of receiving Light, so that thy skill may not lead thee falsely.

9. The Spirit, proceeding from Light and Fire, desires nothing which is not united with others, neither anything separate.

10. This Spirit longs for no matter strange and dissimilar to it.

Q. In what consists the main tenor of this Light law?

A. In this, that Light shall entirely penetrate thy body or matter, so Fire through Light becomes one, and the Spirit, proceeding from Light and Fire, entirely animates thy body. This is the first law.

The second is like unto it, namely: In this manner shalt thou treat the matter upon which thou workest and all such that thou wilt bring to perfection.

On these two leading conditions the whole knowledge of the science of Light depends, and all those which are subject to it.

Q. What are the commandments of the working Light-Community?

A. There are five.

First: Keep holy the resting-point in thy work, for Light has its sabbath, and the worker must observe it.

Secondly: On these Light holidays consecrate the matter to the holy sacrifices; separate by Light-water the pure from the impure, the active from the passive.

Thirdly: Abstain in thy work from everything that is against the law of Light, in the forces and their operations, as well as in the forms and essences of things; these are the four divisions of the Light school.

Fourthly: At least once in the year, try to talk with a wise friend about the progress which thou makest, and make known to him what hinders thee, that thou mayest have support on thy way, which leadeth thee to perfection.

Fifthly: At these seasons, which thy reason appoints for thee, avoid opening thy heart too freely to another, as well as also closing it too hastily.

Q. Why should the commands of the Light-Community, the true knowers of nature, be kept?

A. For this reason, that the Light-laws, or Light-conditions, require that man shall not obey that only which is requisite for the attainment of the aim within nature, but that also is required which is without as well, for the fourth Light commandment presupposes this requisite, and he who listens not to the Light-Community and honours not their good laws and statutes, shall be considered an infidel and a materialist, who knoweth not the laws of the Spirit.

(*To be concluded.*)

THEOSOPHICAL ACTIVITIES.

AMERICAN SECTION: MRS. BESANT'S TOUR.

May 25th.—On White Lotus Day we reached San Francisco, and were met in Oakland and escorted across the bay by Mr. Walters, the earnest and energetic Editor of *Mercury*, as well as by Mr. J. C. Chaṭṭopâdhyâya, who is doing such good work by his classes and lectures on Theosophy and Eastern Philosophy. We were most hospitably received in the house of one of our members, and a celebration of White Lotus Day and a reception took place in the evening; over 300 people were present.

In San Francisco, amongst other people, we had the pleasure of meeting Mr. Marques, whose observations on the human aura have lately been brought to the notice of the public.

Mrs. Besant's time was much taken up by the usual routine, with the addition of as many Branch meetings and talks to members as could be crowded into a limited time. On one day *five* meetings were addressed by Mrs. Besant, for by some misapprehension a public announcement had been made of a lecture which had been refused from want of time, and yet she would not disappoint those who might come, for it is difficult for her to draw the line when it seems that good can be done.

From this centre visits were made by Mrs. Besant and the Countess Wachtmeister to Alameda, Oakland and Stamford University, and lectures were given in each place, with the result that many new members joined the Society.

Then we passed on to San José, Santa Cruz, with its earnest group of members, and to Sacramento, and at each place lectures and talks helped the people to a fuller comprehension of the realities of the inner life.

At midnight on Friday, May 21st, we left Sacramento by the beautiful Mount Shasta route, and on Sunday morning found ourselves in Portland, Oregon, and some of our members on the station platform to greet us with the same warm welcome and kindness that have been shown everywhere.

A halt of two days for two public lectures was made there, and then we came on to Tacoma, on Pugit Sound, where last night Mrs.

Besant's lecture was attended by the more thoughtful people of the town.

June 4th.—Pugit Sound with its fir and cedar clothed hills, guarded by isolated snow-capped peaks, is left behind us. We visited three towns upon its shores. At Tacoma, where two members of the Society met us in rather a hopeless state of mind about the prospects of Theosophy in their town, we only remained one full day, a very short time to start things when little work has already been done, but even in that time the town showed its readiness to respond, for Mrs. Besant's lecture was attended by the most thoughtful people in the place, and a group gathered round her on the night before she left.

We passed on to Olympia early on Friday morning, and a very quiet day was spent in this little tidal town, whose life ebbs and flows with the coming of the judges to the court-house.

The Countess knew one or two of the people who had been interested in Theosophy, but all was very quiet, and Olympia only began to rouse up after Mrs. Besant's evening lecture. Amongst others the Governor of the State attended, and was afterwards presented. Much regret was expressed that we could not remain, but we had already arranged to take the 6.30 boat next morning.

In beautifully situated and pure-aired Seattle we found a strong Branch of the Society, and much hopeful work progressing. This is one of the many Branches which owe their origin to the tireless energy of the Countess Wachtmeister. It was only started last summer, but already has its lecture room and library, and over fifty members. Its President, Mr. Barnes, is a capable and devoted worker, and the Seattle Lodge promises to be a strong centre.

Mrs. Besant gave three lectures in the Theatre to a full and deeply appreciative audience. "Theosophy and its Teachings," "Man, the Maker of his Destiny," and "Thought Forms, a Glimpse of the Unseen Universe." This last lecture was with the illustrations of the human aura and thought-forms, which, as I have before mentioned, do such good service in making the subject comprehensible. The five days spent in Seattle passed swiftly, and much good work was done by Mrs. Besant in interviews and meetings for the members and the public at the Society's rooms, and by the Countess who, wherever we go, is engaged in her whole-hearted endeavours to create and foster interest in the Society.

Two members came over from Tacoma for the lectures and returned when we left, with a better understanding of the real strength of the Theosophical Society and of the important work that it has to do.

One of the ideas mooted by Mrs. Besant here was that of a Federation of all the Lodges in the State of Washington, on the plan of the Northern Federation in England, for the purpose of the interchange of Theosophic thoughts and help in the work generally. This would mean a meeting each six months in one or other of the towns, and would tend to foster outside interest and to promote a closer tie amongst our members by personal intercourse.

On leaving Chicago after the Convention, it is proposed to visit the following towns, though the exact dates cannot yet be given. Streator, Clinton (Iowa), Minneapolis, St. Paul, St. Cloud, Menomonia, Milwaukee, Detroit, Windsor, Toledo, Sandusky, Cleveland, Buffalo, Hamilton, and Toronto.

June 19th.—From the Sound we went direct to Ellensburg, a small town interested chiefly in dairy farming. We were met by Mr. Ross, one of our members, who had gladly undertaken the supervision of proceedings in the hope that his fellow townspeople might be sufficiently interested to form a branch. On Friday evening, June 4th, Mrs. Besant lectured to a small audience in the Opera House and again the next afternoon. Here the people were remarkable for their unpunctuality, and at the time the lecture was advertized to begin *two* people only had arrived. This did not look promising, but Mr. Ross was quite cheerful, and explained that it was the custom of the place to be late for everything. It certainly proved to be so, not only here, but at other towns also, whose inhabitants have evidently been spoilt by past lecturers. At last they came, and Mrs. Besant spoke clearly and eloquently upon the power of man over his own future, and the work of the Theosophical Society, and twice during our short stay held her usual reception for inquirers. When we left by the night train some new members had joined, and enough were expected to come in to form a branch there very shortly.

On we went then to Spokane, a mining centre of importance, again to be met and driven to the Hotel by members of the Society, who were glad to have Mrs. Besant and the Countess amongst them. The usual routine was followed, and Spokane distinguished itself by flocking in such crowds to the first lecture that some hundreds had to be turned away.

Butte, in Montana, came next, a desert of hills—honeycombed by mines of copper, silver, iron and gold. We arrived there on Wednesday, June 9th, and the next day Mrs. Besant gave a splendid practical lecture to a good-sized audience, amongst whom were many miners. It created a very good impression in the town, as could be seen by the tone of the notices in the local papers, and some people joined the Society on our return from Anaconda, where Mrs. Besant spent one night, lectured, and formed a promising group for study.

From Butte it was only three hours to Helena, the last of our mining towns; we arrived there at 1 o'clock on Sunday, and found it quite a new field in regard to the Theosophical Society, though a number of its inhabitants were more or less interested in various "occult" studies. Thanks to the kindness of Mr. Brown, the Unitarian minister, who gave up a lecture in a course he was in the midst of, and advertized Mrs. Besant's instead, we had a good audience at each of the two lectures, and there is now a group of people who are interested and intend to study with the view of ultimately forming a branch.

On Tuesday, June 15th, after a night in the train, we found ourselves in Sheridan, Wyoming, near the home of Buffalo Bill and many of his "Wild West" riders. Here we encountered quite a distinct type of men from the miners amongst whom we had been lately working, and it was a cheering sign that the young Branch had already thirty members.

Mrs. Besant held several talks at Coffeen's Hall and gave two fairly attended lectures in the Opera House. Three new people joined the Lodge and we hope that some of the scattered ranchers carried back to their homes ideas to work into their daily lives.

A. J. W.

The report of the General Secretary, Mr. Fullerton, is most satisfactory. Nineteen Branches have been formed since the last Convention, the number of active Branches, deducting two which have disbanded, being now thirty-two. The membership has increased to about two and a half times its number in the past year, 405 new members having been admitted and forty-four restored. The work of the Countess Wachtmeister has been largely instrumental in this increased activity and Mrs. Besant's lectures have had remarkable results in strengthening the Section. The financial report is also very satisfactory, showing a good surplus after all expenses have been paid. There is every sign of the Section flourishing and recovering rapidly from the injury it received.

European Section.

A valuable gift has been made to the Library of the Section by an anonymous donor. It consists of *Texte und Untersuchungen der Altchristlichen Literatur*, edited by von Gebhardt and Harnack, a large collection of texts and studies of early Christian works, the most complete undertaking of its kind that has yet appeared.

At Nice a new Branch has just been formed, with Mrs. Terrell as President. Several members have recently joined in order to make up the necessary number, but most of them have been attending for some time at the meetings held by Mrs. Terrell. There is every reason to hope for a good future for the Branch.

The South-Western Federation of Branches of the Section held meetings at Bournemouth on July 3rd and 4th. A good number of members attended. The special feature was an open-air meeting in the New Forest, to which the members drove or rode on bicycles. Mr. Leadbeater presided and lectured on "Life on the Astral Plane."

The Blavatsky Lodge held its business meeting on July 3rd, and elected delegates for the Convention.

Australasian Section.

The activities of this Section pursue the even tenor of their way. We have hopes that one or more branches will shortly be established in various centres in Western Australia, and our membership slowly but steadily increases.

Miss Edger, M.A., General Secretary of the New Zealand Section, generously volunteered to help us and to give three months of her time lecturing to and visiting our various Branches.

Arriving in Sydney, May 12th, she delivered three public lectures in the Hall of the Sydney Branch to crowded and appreciative audiences, also a public lecture in the room of the Dayspring Branch, besides holding meetings for enquirers and for members.

On May 25th she leaves for Brisbane, Maryborough and Bundaberg, and will spend about six weeks working with these Branches. Then coming southwards she will visit Melbourne, Adelaide, and Hobart, finishing in the latter city about the middle of August.

H. A. W.

New Zealand Section.

The General Secretary left New Zealand on May 8th for a lecturing tour in Australia, and will probably be away for three months.

The loss sustained by the Australian Section in the death of Mr. Staples is also keenly felt in New Zealand. The Branches and individual members alike testify to the love and esteem which were felt for him throughout the Section.

Active public work is carried on in Auckland, Wellington, Christchurch and Dunedin; there is a good deal of general public interest, and the meetings and lectures are fairly well attended, and membership increases.

The number of "unattached" members has been increasing lately. They are most numerous in the neighbourhood of Auckland, but are pretty well scattered over the Colony.

REVIEWS.

Some Thoughts on the Textual Criticism of the New Testament.

By George Salmon, D.D. [London: Murray, 1897. Price 3*s.* 6*d.*]

Everything that comes from Dr. Salmon's pen must be received with respect by the student, and the few "Thoughts" which he has so modestly put forward on the chaotic subject of the "Textual Criticism of the New Testament," show that he has a thorough grasp of the difficult problem he discusses. The essay before us presupposes some familiarity of the reader with the subject, but only such as may be expected from a well informed layman.

The problem discussed is as follows:

The Authorised Version of the N. T., was made from the "received text," which had "taken its origin in a haphazard way from the edition hastily scrambled together by Erasmus." This text is innocent of the most elementary critical treatment, the most unreliable and untrustworthy of guides.

When the so-called Revised Version was attempted, the first requisite was to settle on a text which should stand the canon of the most elementary criticism. In the college of revisers there were two men who had made a speciality of textual criticism, and the rest of the revisers were afraid to oppose their opinion to the judgment of this pair of noted specialists. The consequence was that the text from which the Revised Version was made, was practically the text of West cott and Hort, and in the last analysis of Hort alone.

Hort's one idea, the prime clause of his textual creed, was the plenary inspiration of Codex B.

The opponents of the W. H. text were headed by the learned and boisterous tongued Burgon. His theory was that the "received text" had been specially looked after by the Holy Ghost. No matter what corruptions had crept into the older texts, the "textus receptus" was directly inspired of set purpose by the Holy Ghost, to upset the rascality of the mutilators and falsificators of the original texts.

The reader should remember that we are not dealing with the views of mediæval divines, but of men who were with us but a year or two ago.

Burgon is to-day represented by Miller, while Westcott and Hort are represented by their many pupils, that is to say, by the main body of the theologians of the Established Church. The W. H. text is regarded with as much reverence by them as the "textus receptus" was regarded by Burgon.

It is evident to the outside student, who has no interests to serve, that both positions are not only untenable, but so stupendously silly, that he can only suppose that much learning has made our theologians mad.

Dr. Salmon wisely declares that the whole matter must be re-opened; he rudely arouses the younger men from their slumbers on the soft couch of the W. H. text. True, he does it all so modestly, and so timorously, scarce daring as it were to breathe a word against the great idol, that one does not at first see the full effect of his criticism; but the blow is struck and the whole propped fabric is once more on the totter.

G. R. S. M.

Religion of the Ancient Egyptians.

By A. Wiedemann, Ph. D. [London: Grevel & Co., 1897. Price 12*s*. 6*d*.]

The success attending the translation of his short essay on *The Ancient Egyptian Doctrine of the Immortality of the Soul* (1895), has induced Professor Wiedemann to venture the translation of one of his larger works, *Religion of the Ancient Egyptians*. Those who have read the learned Professor's clear and scholarly exposition of the present state of Egyptological knowledge as to the doctrine which formed the subject of his shorter work, will know that they are not to expect any surprises or startling theories, but simply the striking of an average opinion, and the most stringent endeavour to keep to the texts and monuments. This expectation is fulfilled on every page of Wiedemann's new work, which is thus of enormous value to the lay student who desires to know the exact state in which modern Egyptological research stands.

The main impression left with us is that Egyptologists are still in the twilight when not in the dark; they are puzzled immensely if not entirely baffled by ninety-nine things out of a hundred. Moreover the vast majority of important texts have not yet been translated.

The Egyptian religion is apparently a specimen of the maddest syncretism which has ever existed on the face of the earth. The Egyptian mind was so fanatically conservative, that it could dispense with not even the meanest rags of its past; the sublimest views are found alongside of pure fetishism. So it appears. Add to this the fact that in official Egyptology, any hypothesis may be entertained except the absurd assumption that there can be such a thing in reality as the unseen world, and you have the frame of mind of orthodoxly scientific Egyptological research, especially of the German mould!

On these lines Professor Wiedemann has done most admirably: his book is the most useful which has appeared on the subject, and will serve as an excellent introduction to the vast subject of ancient Egyptian religion, not only because of its moderate views, but also because of the excellent bibliographical notes which will supply the student with a guide for further exploration. *Religion of the Ancient Egyptians* is a splendid drag on the enthusiasm of the mystic who would find in Egypt the pansophy of the ages; it will teach him "so far canst thou go and no farther," if he would base himself on really acquired facts, and not plunge into a wild whirlpool of speculation.

But as there is a middle ground for Professor Wiedemann among his scientific colleagues, so there is a middle ground for the theosophical student among the mystics. Scores of times after Wiedemann has questioned the texts and stated the acquired facts, he is ludicrously at sea for an explanation, which immediately occurs to a mind furnished with the most elementary theosophical information. On the other hand, the careful theosophical student will in no case seek to alter the facts merely to accommodate some vague mystical theory. He knows that though his general point of view must be the view to which real science in the long run will approximate, in details he must carefully weigh evidence and take an infinity of pains before he can be satisfied with even the most overwhelmingly convincing solution of any difficulty.

It is a matter of profound regret that so few members of the Theosophical Society have entered the field of Egyptological research; the work to be done in this direction is endless, the crop of theosophical knowledge to be reaped inexhaustible. "The Theosophy of the Egyptians" could form the title of a series of volumes of the greatest value to modern theosophical research, and form a link in that great chain of theosophical tradition of which a few of the links are being reforged by two or three of our members. Who will attempt it?

G. R. S. M.

THE TREASURE OF THE HUMBLE.

By Maurice Maeterlinck, translated by Alfred Sutro. [London: George Allen, 1897. Price 5*s*. net.]

IN this volume we have a series of mystical and philosophical essays which will prove of much interest to those who have hitherto only known M. Maeterlinck as a dramatist. He is here devoting himself to analyzing the ideas of life which he has previously illustrated in his plays; strongly imbued with the doctrines of Neo-Platonism, these essays bear the impression of the thought of that period and the dominant note running through all of them is that which insists on the importance of the supra-sensuous world, that which "lies well beyond the domain of thought." In taking this line M. Maeterlinck sets himself in direct opposition to most of the current thought and literature of the day which tend more to the exposition of the realistic side of life. These essays will furnish many useful thoughts and suggestions to those who feel that the deepest and best emotions of their lives do not deal with the concrete so much as with the abstract, "the veiled life of the soul." It seems as if at times M. Maeterlinck grasps intuitively the theosophical conception of the true man, "the thinker," who stands behind all thought and is beyond intellect; indeed there are many points of sympathy which students of theosophy will at once perceive.

In the essay on "The Awakening of the Soul," M. Maeterlinck points out that in various periods of the world's history there have been spiritual epochs, during which "the soul . . . seemed to rise to the very surface of humanity," and he cites India and Egypt as especially showing the traces of such epochs. Since then there have been periods when the intellect has reigned supreme but the soul has slept. To-day, however, "it is clearly making a mighty effort. Its manifestations are everywhere." After showing how in every department of life old barriers are being broken down, and orthodoxy is being assailed on all sides, he goes on, "I feel that a more pressing offer of spiritual freedom has rarely been made to mankind," spiritual phenomena are manifesting themselves more widely than ever before, and are being universally studied, showing "that the human soul is a plant of matchless unity whose branches, when the hour is come, all burst into blossom together." It is the realization of this unity, though still only half comprehended, that draws men closer to each other, and heralds the time when "souls will know of each without the intermediary of the senses."

Many more passages might be quoted but space only permits the special mention of "The Star," "The Deeper Life," and "The Inner Beauty," as the essays of peculiar interest. L. M. C.

Four Great Religions.

Four Lectures delivered on the Twenty-first Anniversary of the Theosophical Society, at Adyar, Madras, by Annie Besant. [London. T.P.S.: 1897. Price 2*s.* net.]

Most interesting and most useful are the four lectures which our prolific colleague has added to the literature of the Theosophical Society. The great religions of which Mrs. Besant treats are Hinduism. Zoroastrianism, Buddhism and Christianity. Without surprise we read that it was with feelings of dismay that our greatest speaker stood on the platform to deal with these four mighty and complex themes in the short time allotted to her. How was she to treat the enormous wealth of material which lay before her? Libraries could not exhaust even one of her subjects; what hope then was there that she could make four such stupendous themes intelligible in four short hours? The solution of this difficult problem was only to be found in the theosophic method, the method of synthesis, of eliminating non-essentials. In brief, Mrs. Besant has made a "symphony" of these four great faiths, has pointed to their common origin and common truths, and most worthily contributed to the carrying out of the second object of our Society.

The principles underlying the treatment of her subjects are stated by Mrs. Besant in her preface to have been as follows: (1) each religion is looked at in the light of occult knowledge, both as regards its history and its teachings; (2) each religion is treated as coming from one great Brotherhood, which is the steward and guardian of spiritual knowledge; (3) an attempt is made to distinguish the essential from the non-essential in each religion; and to treat chiefly the former. Moreover Mrs. Besant tells us: "I have striven to sketch each religion in its best, its purest, and most occult form, and each as though I belonged to it and were preaching it as my own."

This is the really theosophic method, to believe in the best in each of the great religions with all the ardour of an exclusive religionist, to write and speak of the essential truths of each with deepest sympathy and a full heart, to do this honestly and not merely academically—this is the method which shall revolutionize the study of comparative religion and make it the grandest and most helpful work that any one can engage in.

As Professor Max Müller justly says, the study of "comparative religion," is a misnomer, it should be called the study of "comparative theology." This remark is profoundly true, but not in the sense that our veteran orientalist intends it.

He is finding fault with the term "comparative religion" on philological grounds. He avers that we cannot use such a term as "comparative religion," and can only speak legitimately of "comparative theology." He is right, for so far all our scholars have paid attention to "comparative theology" alone, with "comparative religion" they have had nothing to do, seeing that they none of them *believe* in all the great religions of which they treat. Some of them may believe in Christianity, some of them may be philosophically drawn to the main tenets of the Vedânta or Buddhism, but none can say I believe with all my heart and soul in all the great truths which the great religions teach. They are mostly critics trying to insist on differences, making their reputations by the number of differences they can discover, shrinking from synthesis as from the pest, and contemptuously referring to it as "syncretism." It is just here that the theosophical student takes his stand. Our second object bids us encourage the study of "comparative religion," and not "comparative theology," and this Mrs. Besant has most worthily done in her present work.

It should of course be remembered that the lectures were addressed to an almost exclusively Hindu audience, and that Mrs. Besant was compelled to continually bear this in mind in many of her explanations. If, however, we may venture to particularize, we would say that our Pârsî members owe most to our colleague for her admirable exposition of Zoroastrianism. The magnificent description of the first Zoroaster bringing down the sacred fire from heaven is perhaps the finest passage in the book.

The attempt to reconcile Hinduism and Buddhism is admirable, but we doubt whether the Buddhist will consider it so admirable as the Hindu. Fundamentally the doctrines are the same indubitably for the student of comparative religion, and the Buddha was an Hindu in his body, but caste and the Vedas, as such, are hard to find in the tradition. The lecture devoted to Christianity is, as we should expect, entirely Catholic, in the original and true sense of the term; we would, however, point out with regard to the doctrine of reincarnation, that it cannot be *orthodoxly* established, and that its evidences—overwhelming evidences—must be found in the Gnostic Schools alone and their interpretation of the Sayings. With the exception of Synesius, no Father of the Church accepted the doctrine, though some few believed in the doctrine of pre-existence. The passage quoted from Tertullian's *Apology* is most remarkable, it is true, and apparently confirmatory of reincarnation, but we should recollect the numerous other passages in which the Church Father inveighs most bitterly against the tenet, and then we shall be inclined to believe that the Bishop of Carthage is elaborating a mystical doctrine—of a somewhat materialistic nature, as we might expect from his Montanist tendencies—of the "resurrection of the body."

As a student of comparative religion, however, we would refrain from further theological criticism, and have only referred to the point to show that our deep appreciation of our colleague's labours is not prompted by mere indiscriminate endorsement of every statement to be found in her lectures. We have read the book with the greatest interest and pleasure, and warmly recommend it, not only to students but also to all who wish to inbibe the spirit which ensouls the four great religions which have been so admirably treated in the volume before us.

As with all books printed in India, there are a number of misprints, the worst of which is "historical" for "heretical" on page 133. Mrs. Besant, however, is to be congratulated that the printer's devils of all sorts have not made more, for the name of the errors of the said devils is legion in that ancient land.

G. R. S. M.

THEOSOPHICAL AND MYSTIC PUBLICATIONS.

COL. OLCOTT fills his "Old Diary Leaves" for June with accounts of phenomena and occult matters in general. Damodar is the chief figure in the story just now, and his interior development and relations with his teacher are freely described. At this time the letters and messages appear to have been in full swing, and several were, according to the Colonel's account, evidently quite free of Madame Blavatsky's influence, as she was distant several days' journey. A visit of the Master to the Colonel in his tent is told in an interesting manner. The sketch is followed by a Theosophical disquisition on character and its formation, translated from the Swedish by Mrs. Haig. "The Plague and its Causes" deals with the causes with what may appear to many to be unnecessary fulness, as not only have we the physical, astrological and karmic reasons for the plague, but also the religious, the astral and the auric, and the plague considered as a sign of the close of the first 5,000 years of Kali Yuga! Truly the trouble had a multiplicity of causes. "The Union of Three Buddhist Nations" is an intimation of what may prove a most important movement. This movement has been begun by Prince Prisdan Choomsai of Siam and Colonel Olcott, and its purpose is to unite the Buddhists of Siam, Burmah and Ceylon. A petition has been laid before the King of Siam, and the result of the efforts will be awaited with interest by all friends of Buddhism. K. Narayansami Iyer contributes a "White Lotus Day" appreciation of Madame Blavatsky, and Mr. Marques an account of the occult correspondences of the days of the week. The concluding papers are on Mlle. Couédon, the prophetess, and on the symbology of astrology.

A new edition of Mrs. Besant's *Seven Principles* has just appeared. This manual is now in its fifteenth thousand, and with the present edition it has been extensively revised according to the later and more complete information available. It is now properly "up-to-date," and those possessing it in the original form should obtain the new one, as the improvements and emendations are many and important.

The Vâhan for July is noticeable for a very lengthy answer by C. W. L., probably the longest that has yet appeared in "The Enquirer." The subject of the question is the three Logoi, and in the reply we are taken into the loftiest regions of the universe, regions not often described with the detail now afforded us. The whole paper is of remarkable interest, in spite of the fact that it deals with matters entirely beyond human intelligence. A. P. S. and A. A. W. continue (and we hope, conclude) the correspondence aroused by the latter. A. A. W., as usual, forms delightful reading, whether we agree with his views or not. A. P. S on beef and claret is also likely to stagger "the orthodox."

Mercury begins its June number with a paper having the title "The Royal Road," by which is meant the "Path" of occultism, and continues with articles on vegetarianism and politics. The latter paper endeavours to show the influence that Theosophical ideas should have in expanding political views. The "Forum Department" discusses the question as to whether the astral body of a person cut off prematurely continues to exist and grow until the karmic hour of death.

Theosophy in Australasia contains an excellent portrait of the late and much-regretted General Secretary of the Australian Section, Mr. J. C. Staples. The body of the journal is made up of the report of the third Annual Convention of the Australian Section. The section devoted to questions and answers is excellently conducted and the replies are interesting.

Along with *Le Lotus Bleu* each month comes a section of the French translation of *The Secret Doctrine*, and this laborious undertaking has now reached the commentary on the sixth stanza Our French workers are to be congratulated on the energy and devotion they are displaying in such work. Amo contributes a very short ethical discourse entitled "Towards the Light," and following this is a good article on Bhakti Yoga. Mons. Courmes writes on the terrible fire in Paris, and attributes it to our old friend, the end of the cycle. Some interesting questions are answered in the department devoted to that purpose.

Sophia consists entirely of valuable translations, including Dr. Wells' "Letters to a Catholic Priest," Mr. Keightley's "Sânkhya Philosophy," and a historical sketch of the Jews from the French.

Nova Lux continues Signor Calvari's article on man and his vehicles and publishes various papers and notes on mystical subjects, Martinism especially. *Theosophia* from Holland opens with "A Fable" by Afra, and contains articles on "Magnetism" and "Teachers," besides one or two translations.

From Germany come the *Metaphysische Rundschau* and *Lotusblüthen*, the latter opening with a new article on Paracelsus, purposing to give an account of his life and teachings. A lecture by Hermann Krecke, "Our Daily Bread," has also been published in pamphlet form in Berlin.

The *Prashnottara* contains a somewhat amusing though not very intelligible note on the pandit, to whom some attention was paid recently in LUCIFER. "The Last of the Old-world Pandit?" is the heading of the note, and it appears that but little can be expected from him. The freedom with which doubts of the good faith of the learned gentleman are expressed, and the criticism of what little he has done, form entertaining reading. The "Questions and Answers" is occupied by a discussion of the relations of Buddhism to the Upanişhads. The *Ârya Bâla Bodhinî*, is filled with chatty notes and short papers, generally well adapted for their purpose. The May number contains a short parable about a stone-cutter whose desires were all gratified until by experience he discovered their futility. *The Theosophic Gleaner* opens with a paper on "The Doctrine of Reincarnation in the West," quoting from various authors. The other articles are reprinted, and brief notes on current topics end the number. *The Dawn*, the new Indian religious magazine, contains some excellent but rather technical articles. All show a care in their preparation that might well be imitated by other publications of a similar nature. The May issue contains papers on Hindu philosophy, "Reality and Appearances," and the situation in India. *The Journal of the Mahâ Bodhi Society*, is more interesting than usual, containing an account of a great Buddhist traveller, the Cingalese address to the King of Siam, and "The Mythology of Buddhism." *The Buddhist* is filled with the difficulties arising out of the visit to Ceylon of the King of Siam. The King wished to touch the sacred tooth of Buddha kept by the priests as a relic, and his request was refused by some officious guardian. As many others, including Europeans, had touched it before, His Majesty was not unreasonably indignant at the affront. The plentiful apologies of the other officials it is hoped will smooth matters a little. We have also to acknowledge the receipt from India of *The Thinker* and *The Sanmârga Bodhinî*.

The Metaphysical Magazine appears in a new form as *Intelligence*. Considering the nature and size of the journal, its present price, 10 cents (or 5*d*.), is astonishingly cheap and we hope it may continue prosperously in the same form. The articles are of the kind characteristic of it, among them being "Man and Nature," "Modern Astrology," and "The Bhagavad Gîtâ," by C. Johnston. *The Open Court* has always been one of the best publications of its kind, and the number now before us is well up to the proper standard. An excellent portrait of Schiller is given, accompanying an article on "Schiller as a Prophet," by the editor, Dr. Paul Carus. He points out that even after many of Schiller's works appeared, the very things described in the poems took place. "The Lion and the Ass" is a delightful old fable of Martin Luther, translated from the German. The most interesting paper is an illustrated one, also by the editor, on the Inquisition.

We have also to acknowledge the receipt of a number of pamphlets from "The Order of the Temple"; *Rays of Light*; *Light*; *The Agnostic Journal*; *Modern Astrology*; *The Vegetarian*; *The Vegetarian Review*; *Theosophy*; *The Theosophical Forum*; *A Plan of Moral Instruction*; *The Mystical World*, filled with astonishing "Thought Awakeners," by Jos. M. Wade, and equally amazing poetry by William Sharpe, M.D.; *Reformador*, from Rio de Janeiro; *The English Mechanic*; *The Zoophilist*, an anti-vivisectionist publication; *The Literary Digest*; *Food, Home and Garden*; *Star Lore*, in the March issue of which is a horoscope of Mr. Barnato, with a warning to avoid dangerous places in spring and winter—an apparent approach to a true prophecy.

A.

Women's Printing Society, Limited, 66. Whitcomb Street, W.C.

VOL. XX. AUGUST 15, 1897. No. 120.

LUCIFER.

AMONG THE GNOSTICS OF THE FIRST TWO CENTURIES.

(*Continued from p.* 384.)

THE VALENTINIAN MOVEMENT.

BACK of the whole Valentinian movement stands the commanding and mysterious figure of Valentinus himself, universally acknowledged to have been the greatest of the Gnostics. His learning and eloquence are admitted even by his bitterest opponents to have been of a most extraordinary nature, and no word has ever been breathed against his moral character. And yet when we come to analyze the chaos of "information" which Patristic writers have left us on the subject of so-called Valentinianism, we find the mysterious character of the great master of the Gnosis ever receding before our respectful curiosity; he who has been made to give his name to the modelling of the whole structure still remains the "great unknown" of Gnosticism. We know nothing of him as a man, nothing of him as a writer except the few mutilated scraps which hæresiological odium has vouchsafed to us.

(I am of course leaving entirely aside the vexed question of the authorship of the Pistis Sophia treatise, which is still *sub judice*. My own opinion is that we owe the original draft of it to Valentinus, but the reasons which have led me to this conclusion must be reserved for the commentary on that treatise, which I am preparing.)

And yet, in spite of this appalling ignorance of the man and his teachings, the so-called Valentinian Gnosis is the *pièce de résistance* of nearly every hæresiological treatise. We shall, therefore, have to trespass on the patience of the reader for a short space while we set up a few finger-posts in the maze of Valentinianism as seen through the eyes of its Patristic opponents.

With the exception of the few fragments to which we have referred, all that has been written by the Fathers refers to the teachings of "them of Valentinus," and even then it is but very rarely that we have an unmutilated quotation from any written work of theirs; for the most part it all consists of fragments torn from their contexts or mere hearsay. Now the followers of Valentinus were no slavish disciples who could do nothing else but repeat parrot-like the "words of the master"; the *ipse dixit* spirit was far from their independent genius. Each of them thought out the details of the scheme of universal philosophy in his own fashion. True that by this time the presentation of the Gnosis, from being of a most diverse nature, had become more settled in its main features, and doubtless Valentinus had initiated this synthesizing tendency; nevertheless it was still free and independent in innumerable details of a very far-reaching character, and its adherents were imbued with that spirit of research, discovery, and adaptation which ever marks a period of spiritual and intellectual life.

Thus we understand the complaint of Irenæus, who laments that he never could find two Valentinians who agreed together. And if this be so, what good is there in any writer talking of the Valentinian System? We know next to nothing of the system of Valentinus himself; as to his followers, each introduced new modifications, which we can no longer follow in the unintelligent representations of the Church fathers, who make them flatly contradict not only one another, but also themselves.

From The Philosophumena, published in 1851, we first heard of an Eastern and Western (Anatolic and Italic) division of the school of Valentinus, thus explaining the title superscribed on the Extracts from Theodotus appended to the Miscellanies of Clement of Alexandria in one MS. A great deal has been made of this; the meagre differences of doctrine of the Anatolic and Italic schools of Valentinianism indicated by Hippolytus (II.) have been seized upon by criticism and had their backs broken by the weight of argument which has been piled upon them. But when Lipsius demonstrates that the Extracts from Theodotus, which claim in their superscription to belong to the Eastern school, are, following the indications of Hippolytus, half Eastern and half Western, the ordinary student has to hold his head tightly on to his body and abandon all hope of light from the division of Valentinianism into Anatolic and Italic schools, in the present state of our ignorance, unless indeed we simply assume that they were originally mere geographical designations to which in later times a doctrinal signification was unsuccessfully attempted to be given.

Although we have no sure indication of the date of Valentinus himself, it may be assumed to extend from A.D. 100 to A.D. 180, as will be seen later on.

Of the other leaders of the movement, the earliest with whose names we are acquainted are Secundus and Marcus. Now Marcus himself had a large following as early as 150; his followers were not called Valentinians but Marcosians, or Marcians, and what we know of his system differs enormously from those of the rest of "them of Valentinus." Marcus is sometimes supposed to have been a contemporary of Irenæus, but this is only on the supposition that Irenæus, in using the second person in his hortatory and admonitory passages, is addressing a living person and not employing the "thou" as a mere rhetorical effect, as Tertullian with Marcion.

Next we come to Ptolemæus many years later, who again is supposed to have been a contemporary of Irenæus somewhere about A.D. 180.

Irenæus had certainly no personal knowledge of Ptolemæus, and dealt for the most part with his followers, who are said to have differed greatly from their teacher.

Later still is Heracleon, whom Clement (c. 193) calls the most distinguished of the disciples of Valentinus. Both Heracleon and Ptolemæus, however, are known not so much for the exposition of a system as for the exegetical treatment of scripture from the standpoint of the Gnosis of their time.

Still later, and as late as, say, about 220, Axionicus and Bardesanes flourished, the former of whom taught at Antioch, and the latter still further east. They are, therefore, called heads of the Anatolic or Oriental school.

Theodotus, from whom the Excerpts appended to Clement's Miscellanies were taken, was of course far earlier in date, but of him we know nothing. We also hear of a certain Theotimus and Alexander, who are earlier than 220.

In brief, the influence of Valentinus spread far and wide, from Egypt eastwards to Syria, Asia Minor and Mesopotamia, and westwards to Rome, Gaul, and even Spain.

A review of the teachings ascribed to these doctors of the Gnosis will bring our task to a close as far as the indirect sources of Gnosticism for the first two centuries are concerned. But the point we would here insist upon is, that we are face to face with a great movement and not a single system. The older forms of the Gnosis, many of which were exceedingly antagonistic to Judaism, were being modified and toned down. On the one hand, such tendencies found a rational outcome in the great Marcionite movement which cut Christianity entirely apart from Judaism; on the other a basis of reconciliation was sought by the more moderate and mystical views of the movement inaugurated by Valentinus, which found room for every view in its all-embracing universalism, and explained away contradictions by an inner secret teaching which was claimed to have come from the Saviour himself.

The main outline of the Gnosis is presumably to be most clearly seen to-day in the system of Basilides, but those infinite spaces which either Basilides himself left unfilled, or Hippolytus (II.) has omitted to mention in his quotations, were afterwards peopled with an infinitude of creations and creatures by the genius of the Gnostics, who could brook no deficiency in the exposition of their universal science. Into this outline, or one closely resembling it, they fitted the various aspects of the ancient Gnosis and the postulates of the old religions and philosophies, adopting these world-old ideas and adapting them by the light of the new revelation, retaining sometimes the old names, more frequently inventing new ones.

This synthesizing of the Gnosis was owing to the initiative of the genius of Valentinus. His technical works are said to have been most abstruse and difficult of comprehension, as well they might be from the nature of the task he attempted. What has become of these writings? No Church father seems to have been acquainted with a single one of his technical treatises; at best we have only a few ethical fragments from letters and homilies. But what of his own followers, whom Church fathers and critics make responsible for a certain Valentinian system of a most chaotic nature? Were they in possession of MSS. of Valentinus; or did they depend on general notions derived from his lectures? Did Valentinus work out a consistent scheme of the Gnosis; or did he set forth several alternatives, owing to the difficulty of the matter, and the innumerable points of view from which it could be envisaged? If the Pistis Sophia document and the other two Codices can be made to throw any light on the matter, it will be a precious acquisition to our knowledge of this most important epoch; if not, we must be content to remain in the dark until some fresh document is discovered.

Meantime we must confine our attention to the certain traces of Valentinus and the general movement; but before doing so, we must briefly review our authorities among the Fathers.

In this review I shall mostly follow Lipsius, who is not only one of the latest authorities on the subject (Art. in S. and W.'s Dict. of Christ. Biog., 1887), but who long ago inaugurated the admirable critical investigations into our Gnostic sources of information by his analysis of the Panarion of Epiphanius.

Tertullian informs us that prior to himself no less than four orthodox champions had undertaken the refutation of the Valentinians, namely Justin Martyr, Miltiades, Irenæus and the Montanist Proculus. With the exception of the five books of Irenæus, the rest of these controversial writings are lost.

Irenæus wrote his treatise somewhere about A.D. 180-185. He devotes most of his first book to the Valentinians exclusively, and isolated notices are found in the remaining four books.

Irenæus claims to have come across certain Memoranda of the Valentinians and had conversations with some of their number. But these Notes belonged only to the followers of Ptolemæus, and only one short fragment is ascribed to a writing of Ptolemæus himself. The personal conversations were also held with followers of the same teacher, presumably in the Rhone districts, not exactly a fertile soil in which to implant the abstruse tenets of the Gnosis, we should think, in spite of the martyrs of Lyons.

In dealing with Marcus, Irenæus derived his information for the most part from the same unreliable oral communications, but also seems to have been in possession of a Memoir of a Marcosian; Marcus himself living and working far away in Asia Minor years before.

In chapter xi. Irenæus professes to give the teaching of Valentinus himself; but here he is simply copying from the work of a prior refutator. Lipsius also points out that Irenæus drew some of his opening statements from the same source as Clement in the Excerpts from Theodotus.

From all of which it follows that we are face to face with a most provoking patch-work, and that the system of Valentinus himself is not to be found in the Refutation of the Bishop of Lyons.

Our next source of information is to be found in the Excerpts from the otherwise unknown Theodotus, which are supposed by Lipsius to have probably formed part of the first book of Clement's lost work, The Outlines. These excerpts "have been dislocated and their original coherence broken up" in so violent a manner, and so interspersed with "counter-observations and independent discussions" by Clement himself, that it is exceedingly difficult to form a judgment upon them. When, moreover, Lipsius assigns part of these extracts to the Oriental and part to the Occidental school, he practically bids us erase the superscription which has always been associated with them—namely, Extracts from the (Books) of Theodotus and the so-called Anatolic School. In any case, we are again face to face with another patch-work.

Hippolytus (I.), in his lost Syntagma, recoverable from the epitomators Pseudotertullian, Philaster, and Epiphanius, seems to have combined the first seven chapters of Irenæus with some other account, and the chaos is still further confused.

Hippolytus (II.), in that most precious of all hæresiological documents, The Philosophumena, gives an entirely independent account, in fact the most uniform and synoptical representation of any phase of the Gnosis of the Valentinian cycle that has reached us through the Fathers.

Tertullian simply copies from Irenæus, and so also for the most part does Epiphanius. The latter, however, has preserved the famous Letter of Ptolemæus to Flora, and also a list of "barbarous names" for the æons not found elsewhere. Theodoret of course simply copies Irenæus and Epiphanius.

So many, and of such a nature, then, are our indirect sources of information for an understanding of the Valentinian movement; a sorry troop of blind guides it must be confessed, where everything requires the greatest care and discrimination. Let us now return to Valentinus himself and endeavour to patch together from the miserable fragments that remain some wretched silhouette of a character that was universally acknowledged to have been the greatest among the Gnostics.

VALENTINUS.

As to his biography, we know next to nothing. Valentinus was an Egyptian, educated at Alexandria in all that Egypt and Greece had to teach him. The mysterious lore of ancient Khem, the "mathesis" of Pythagoras, the wisdom of Plato, all helped to fashion his character. But the greatest inspiration of all he found in the last outpouring from the same source from which the wisdom of every true philosopher comes—the stream of Christianity that was swirling along at full tide. But what kind of Christianity did Valentinus encounter at Alexandria? There was no Catechetical School when he was a boy. Pantænus and Clement were not as yet. There were the Oracles, the Sayings of the Lord, and many contradictory traditions; a Pauline community also, doubtless founded by some missionary from Asia Minor; and numerous legends of the mysterious Gnosis which Jesus had secretly taught to those who could comprehend. Valentinus doubtless also came under the influence of Basilides, though he is said to have stated that a certain Theodas, an "apostolic man," that is to say one of those who came from Judæa after the destruction of Jerusalem in A.D. 70, was his witness to the direct tradition of the Gnosis. Nothing is known of this Theodas or Theudas, and Ussher has even assumed that it was a contraction for Theodotus, a conjecture in which he has been followed by Zahn. This theory would thus make the Theodotus of the Excerpts in Clement an older authority than Valentinus himself, which would still further complicate the Eastern and Western school question, and, in fact, change the whole problem of Valentinian origins. All we can say here is that the view is not entirely improbable, and would clear the ground on certain important points.

In addition there were at Alexandria, in the great library, all those various sources of information, and, in the intellectual and religious atmosphere of the place, all those synthetical and theosophical tendencies which make for the formulation of a universal system of religion. And this we know was the task that Valentinus set before him as his goal. He determined to synthesize the Gnosis, every phase of which was already a synthesis. But in so doing, Valentinus did not propose to attack or abandon the Christian faith, or to estrange the popular evolution of Christianity which has since been called the Catholic Church. He most probably remained a catholic Christian to the end of his life. It is true that we read of his excommunication in Tertullian, coupled with the favourite accusation brought against prominent heretics, that he apostasized from the Church because his candidature for the episcopal office was rejected. Tertullian imagined that this took place at Rome; but, even if so, did Rome speak in the name of the Catholic Church in those early days? Would Alexandria, the philosophic, recognize the ruling of disciplinarian Rome? Or did Rome excommunicate Valentinus after his death, a favourite way with her in after times of finishing a controversy? Or is not Tertullian romancing here as is not infrequently the case? Epiphanius distinctly states that Valentinus was regarded as orthodox as long as he was at Rome, and Tertullian himself also, in another place, adds fifteen years of orthodoxy on to the date of his leaving Rome!

Valentinus seems to have passed the greater part of his life in Egypt; he was, however, if one can trust our authorities, for some considerable time at Rome, somewhere between 138 and 160. One authority also says that he was at Cyprus.

The date of his death is absolutely unknown; critics mostly reckon it about 161, but in order to arrive at this conclusion they reject the distinct statement of Tertullian that Valentinus was still an orthodox member of the Catholic Church up to the time of Eleutherus (c. 175), and the equally distinct statement of Origen, that he was personally acquainted with Valentinus. This would set back Origen's own date of birth and advance the date of Valentinus' death, but as both are problematical, we have nothing to fear from the putting back of the one and the putting forward of the other ten years or so.

On the whole I am inclined to assign the date of Valentinus to the first eighty years of the second century. In further support of this length of days I would invite the reader to reflect on the extraordinary fact that though the name of Valentinus is in the mouth of everyone of the time, and though his fame entirely eclipses that of every other name of that most important Gnostic cycle, the words and deeds of the great coryphæus of Gnosticism are almost entirely without record, and, stranger than all, he is regarded at any rate for the major part of his life as orthodox. This strange fact requires explanation, and I would venture to suggest that the explanation is to be found to a great extent in the extraordinary reserve and secresy of the man. He was an enigma not only to the generality but even to those who regarded him as a teacher.

The Gnosis in his hands is trying to forestall orthodoxy, to embrace everything, even the most dogmatic formulation of the traditions of the Master. The great popular movement and its incomprehensibilities were recognized by Valentinus as an integral part of the mighty out-pouring; he laboured to weave all together, external and internal, into one piece, devoted his life to the task, and doubtless only at his death perceived that for that age he was attempting the impossible. None but the very few could ever appreciate the ideal of the man, much less understand it.

None of his technical treatises were ever published; his letters and homilies alone were circulated.

After leaving Rome he is practically lost to the sight of the Western hæresiologists. Where he went, what he did, and how long he lived after that, is almost entirely conjectural. But if it ever be shown to be true that such documents as the Pistis Sophia are specimens of the workshop to which he belonged, we can at least conjecturally answer that he went back to Alexandria, where he finished his life in that retirement which such abstruse literary labours required.

Of his writings, besides the fact that they were numerous and his technical treatises exceedingly difficult and abstruse, we know very little. He composed numerous Letters and Homilies and Psalms. We are also told that he composed a Gospel, but this is supposed to be a false assumption—false, that is to say, if by Gospel is meant a Gospel containing the Sayings of the Lord. But may not Gospel here be used in the Basilidian sense of an exposition of the Gnosis, or knowledge of the things beyond the phenomenal world?

Tertullian also tells us that Valentinus composed a treatise entitled Sophia, or Wisdom. Some critics have asserted that the words of Tertullian do not refer to a book but to the Wisdom which Valentinus claimed to teach; but if this were so the antithesis which Tertullian makes between the Wisdom of Valentinus and the Wisdom of Solomon would lose all its point. The Wisdom of Solomon is a book, the Wisdom of Valentinus should also be a book; if it were intended to mean simply the Gnosis which Valentinus taught, then its proper antithesis would have been the Wisdom of God and not of Solomon.

We now have to treat of the few miserable fragments of the works of this prolific writer which have come down to us in the writings of the Church fathers. The latest collection of them is by Hilgenfeld (1884), whose "emendations" however, we shall not always follow. The fragments consist of a few scraps of letters and homilies preserved by Clement of Alexandria, and two pieces in The Philosophumena, the narrative of a vision and the scrap of a psalm.

The Fragments of the Writings of Valentinus which are still Preserved to Us.

I. *From an Epistle: Concerning the Creation of the First Race of Mankind.*

"And just as terror of that creature [lit. plasm] seized hold of the angels [the fabricative powers], when it gave voice to things greater than had been used in its fashioning, owing to the presence in it of Him [the Logos] who unseen to them [the powers] had bestowed on it the seed of the supernal essence [the ego] and who spake of realities face to face; in like manner also among the races of humanity, the works of men become a terror to them who make them—such as statues and images, and all things which [men's] hands fashion to bear the name of God. For Adam being fashioned to bear the name of the [Heavenly] Man [the Logos], spread abroad the terror of that pre-existing Man, for in very truth he had His being in him. And they [the powers] were struck with terror and [in their terror] speedily marred the work [of their hands]."

Here we have the Gnostic myth of the genesis of man which is already familiar to us in the general tradition of the Gnosis.

The plasm or primitive form of man, which could neither stand nor walk—the embryonic sphere of Plato's Timæus—is evolved by the powers of nature, as the crown of evolution; into it Deity breathes the mind, and man is immediately raised above the rest of the creation and its powers. Nevertheless his body is still feeble, and the nature-powers, in fear of the mind within—the "name" of the Heavenly Man—war on him, and only by slow degrees does the mind of man learn to overcome them.

The Heavenly Man is the perfect type of all humanities, and the "name" is no name but that mysterious something which decides the nature and class and being of every creature. Man alone as yet has the divine "name" or nature alive within him.

The "prehistoric" world with which Egypt was in direct traditional contact, made much of this "name"; statues and talismans and amulets, if made in a certain manner, were supposed to be a nearer approach to the perfect type either of manhood or of nature organism, and on these fabrications of men's hands the "name" of this or that supernal power was thought to be bestowed by "Him who speaks face to face." Here we have a hint of the explanation given of "idol-worship" by the initiated priests of antiquity, and this idea was thus woven into the scheme of universal Gnosis by Valentinus.

II. *From an Epistle: On the Pure in Heart.*

"One [alone] is Good, whose free utterance is His manifestation through His son [the Sonship of Basilides]; it is by Him alone that the heart can become pure, [and that too only] when every evil essence has been expelled out of it. Now its purity is prevented by the many essences which take up their abode in it, for each of them accomplishes its own deeds, outraging it in divers fashions with unseemly lusts. As far as I can see, the heart seems to receive somewhat the same treatment as an inn [or caravanserai], which has holes and gaps made in its walls, and is frequently filled with dung, men living filthily in it and taking no care of the place as being someone else's property. Thus it is with the heart so long as it has no care taken of it, ever unclean and the abode of many demons [elemental essences]. But when the Alone Good Father hath regard unto it, it is sanctified and shineth with light; and he who possesseth such a heart is so blessed that 'he shall see God'."

Here we have the very same doctrine as that enunciated by

Basilides and Isidorus with regard to the "appendages" of the soul, as indeed is pointed out by Clement. The doctrine was an exceedingly ancient one in Egypt. In the Book of the Dead we read that the "heart" is a distinct personality within the man (the "purusha in the æther of the heart" of the Upanishads); and not only this but the formula referred to and its explanatory texts teach us that "it is not the heart that sins but only its fleshly envelope" (Cf. Wiedemann's Relig. of the Ancient Egyptians, p. 287; 1897). Isidorus, as we have already seen, guarded against making the "appendages" the scapegoat, and fixed the responsibility on the "heart" proper, the "ancestral heart"—"guardian of my fleshes"—the reincarnating entity. It is, however, quite true that the passions are connected with the blood, and so with the "fleshly envelope," or physical heart, in which the real "heart" is said to be enshrined.

III. *From the Epistle to Agathopus: Concerning one of the Powers attained to by the Perfect Man.*

The "free utterance," or perfect expression, of the Alone Good can only be manifested by the man made perfect. Such a man was Jesus. Thus we find Valentinus writing to Agathopus as follows:

"It was by his unremitting self-denial in all things that Jesus attained to [lit. gained by working] godship; he ate and drank in a peculiar manner, without any waste. The power of continence was so great in him, that his food did not decay in him, for he himself was without decay."

It is said that the physical body can be gradually accustomed to less and less nutriment, and innumerable cases are on record in the East of holy ascetics who have been able to support life on incredibly small quantities of food. The "power" described above by Valentinus is one of the siddhis mentioned in every treatise on yoga in India, and in the Upanishads we read that "very little waste" is one of the first signs of "success in yoga." We are also told that in the highest stages, after the particles of the body have been entirely refined and made to obey the higher will of the ascetic, that a body of a still higher grade of matter can be substituted, and apparently it is some such ideas as these and other similar notions that lay back of the doctrine of docetism which was an integral part of the Gnosis. Clement himself also shared like views, as also did some other Fathers.

IV. *From a Homily: Ye are the Sons of God.*

"From the very beginning have ye been immortal and children of life—such life as the æons enjoy; yet would ye have death shared up among you, to spend and lavish it, so that death might die in you and by your hands, for inasmuch as ye dissolve the world and are not dissolved yourselves, ye are lords of all creation and destruction."

Here we have the burden of the teaching in one of the treatises of the Codex Brucianus—to crucify the world and not let the world crucify us—and of the Pistis Sophia treatise, "Know ye not that ye are all gods and lords?" The Self within the heart, the seed of the divine, the pneumatic light-spark, the dweller in light, the inner man, was the eternal pilgrim incarnated in matter; those who had this alive and conscious within them, were the spiritual or pneumatic. To such Valentinus is speaking.

V. *A few sentences preserved in the controversial matter of Clement following the above quotation, and probably taken from a writing of Valentinus.*

The "elect race," the third Sonship of Basilides, has incarnated here for the abolition of "death," the domain of the Ruler of the phenomenal world, the saṁsâra of the Buddhist and Indian philosophers, the realm of the "ever-becoming" of Plato. This Ruler is the God of the Old Testament. "No man shall see the face of God and live." This is the face of death, but there is also a face of life, concerning which Valentinus writes:

"As far removed as is the [dead image] from the living face, so far is the [phenomenal] world removed from the living æon [the noumenal]. What then is the cause of the image? The majesty of the [living] face, [or person,] which exhibits the type [of the universe] to the painter, and in order that it [the universe] may be honoured by its name [—the name or real being of the majesty of the godhead]. For it is not the authentic [or absolute] nature which is found in the form; it is the name which completes the deficiency in the confection. The invisible nature of deity cooperates so as to induce faith in that which has been fashioned."

Here we have the same idea as in Fragment I., and presumably it was taken from the same Letter. The "painter" is of course the user of the creative forces of the phenomenal world, who copies from the types or ideas in the noumenal world of reality. He whom the Jews called God and Father, was said by Valentinus to be the "image and prophet of the true God," the word prophet meaning one who speaks for and interprets. The "image" is the work of Sophia or Wisdom, who is the "painter" who transfers the types from the noumenal spaces on to the canvas of the phenomenal world, and the "true God" or the "God of truth" is the creator of the noumenal world, which contains the types of all things. He is the god of life, the "image" is the god of death.

"All things that come forth from a pair [or syzygy] are fulnesses (plerômata), but all which proceed from a single [æon] are images."

This will be explained later on; it refers to the "fall" of Sophia from the æon-world, whereby the phenomenal universe came into existence.

The remarks of Clement which immediately follow are almost unintelligible; they deal with the coming of the "excellent" spirit, the infusion of the light-spirit into man.

VI. *From the Epistle on the Community of Friends: Concerning the People of the Beloved.*

"Many of these things which are written in the public volumes are found written in the Church of God. For those teachings which are common are the words which proceed from the heart, the law written in the heart. This is the people of the Beloved who are loved by and love him."

Clement assumes that Valentinus means by "public volumes," the Jewish writings and the books of the philosophers.

The "public volumes," however, for Valentinus included not only the works of the philosophers and the scriptures of the Jews, but also the scriptures of all other religions, and also the Christian documents in general circulation. He merely asserts that the only "common" or general truths, are those pertaining to the community of Friends, or Saints, who form the Church of God, the People of the Beloved. These truths come from the heart; he protests against the narrow view that can find truth in only one set of scriptures; and declares it is in all scriptures and philosophies, if one looks to the spirit and not the letter.

VII. *A very doubtful fragment from Eulogius of Alexandria writing at the end of the sixth century.*

If this fragment can be accepted as genuine, we learn that the early Christians, whom Valentinus calls "the Galileans of the time of Christ," believed in the doctrine of two natures, whereas the Valentinians asserted that there was but one. This is quite credible, following on the lines of argument of Isidorus concerning the unit consciousness of the soul and its responsibility, and the teaching of Valentinus that Jesus "worked out" his own divinity.

VIII. *The Myth which Valentinus made.*

Hippolytus (II.) inserts the following scrap of information in the midst of the lengthy description of the system of Marcus, which he copied from Irenæus.

"Valentinus says that he once saw a child that had only just been born, and that he proceeded to question it to find out who it was. And the babe replied and said it was the Logos." To this, says Hippolytus, Valentinus subjoined a "tragic myth," which formed the basis of his teaching. Have we here an incident from the prologue to one of Valentinus' treatises; and is the "tragic myth" Valentinus' modification of the great Sophia-mythus which was the *deus ex machinâ* of the whole of his cosmogony?

IX. *From a Psalm: The Chain of Being.*

Finally from the same source, The Philosophumena, we recover the following lines; it is probable that Hippolytus took them from the same treatise from which he derived the above information, and that the Psalm endeavoured to explain why the new-born babe was the Logos, why "this" is "That," as the Upanishads have it, and all is one.

"All things depending in spirit I see;
All things supported in spirit I view;
Flesh from soul depending;
Soul by air supported;
Air from æther hanging—
Fruits borne of the deep—
Babe borne of the womb."

Whether or not this exceedingly mystical psalm was taken in

the sense we have suggested above is merely problematical. Such mystic utterances could of course be interpreted from both the microcosmic and macrocosmic standpoints; and Hippolytus gives us what he asserts to be a Valentinian interpretation from the latter point of view.

The "flesh" is the Hyle (the Hebdomad of Basilides); the "soul" is that of the Demiurge (the material force of the ætheric spaces, the Ogdoad of Basilides); the Demiurge hangs from the Spirit, which from one point of view is the Great Limit or Boundary, separating the Plerôma, or world of reality, from the Kenôma or phenomenal universe, and from another is Sophia or Wisdom, in the Kingdom of the Midst. Thus the Demiurge hangs from Sophia; Sophia from the Great Boundary or Horos (a further differentiation of the Basilidian simple idea of the Great Firmament); Horos from the Plerôma, the Blessed Treasure of the æons; and this world of ideas, or Living Æon, from the Abyss or Great Depth, the Father, the God beyond being.

This is the Valentinian chain of being, the subordinate details of which are so abstruse and so complicated, that no one has hitherto been able to make any consistent scheme out of their chaotic and contradictory representations in the writings of the Fathers.

In the MS. of The Philosophumena, the above fragment is prefixed by the disconnected word "Harvest." Hilgenfeld accordingly speaks of Valentinus "hymning the Great Harvest," which is a very grandiose conception, but an idea difficult to connect with the lines quoted.

G. R. S. MEAD.

(*To be continued.*)

THE CADET'S STORY.

THE story which I am about to relate is one of my earliest recollections, for I heard it many years ago from a very old man. Though at the time of which I write he had passed by several years that limit of fourscore winters which is scripturally announced as the extreme period of human existence, he was erect and soldierly still, and displayed not only a perfect retention of all his faculties, but a degree of both mental and physical vigour very unusual at so advanced an age—as may be inferred from the fact that he was in the habit of riding out daily until within three weeks of his death, which occurred at the age of ninety-two. It will not, therefore, be open to the sceptic to dismiss my tale as distorted by the dreamy semi-recollection of dotage; nor, on the other hand, can he ignore it as exaggerated by the childish fancy of the listener; for I depend not on my own memory, but on a carefully written account of the affair (dated in the year of its occurrence) found among the old man's papers after his death. It is fair to add that, though it was not until some twenty years later that I had an opportunity of perusing this paper, I found it to agree in every particular with my own vivid recollection of the story. That written account I reproduce almost literally, supplying from my memory only some few details of the conversations, and of course altering the names of all the actors.

I remember that the old man used to tell us that some author (he had forgotten the name) called upon one of the friends who shared this experience with him, and begged to be allowed to take down his deposition to the facts of the case, and I have since found that the story is recorded in Mrs. Crowe's *Night Side of Nature*, but in a very brief form, omitting some of the phenomena now related. I believe, however, that it will be new to the majority of our readers, and if there should be any to whom it is an old acquaint-ance, they will at any rate have the additional confirmation of an account from an entirely separate source. What follows, then, is the old man's tale.

When I was a youngster I entered as a cadet into the service of the Honourable East India Company, and set sail from Plymouth one fine morning in the good ship *Somerset*, with several other young fellows who were eastward bound on the same errand as myself. Those were stirring times, and many a vision of glory to be won on the battle-field floated before our youthful eyes. A merry company we were, for they were good fellows all—gay, light-hearted, and careless; and so with story, jest, and song we did our best to make the long hours of that tedious voyage pass as rapidly as we could.

One among my comrades had a peculiar attraction for me, perhaps because he alone of all the party seemed to have occasional fits of sadness—spells of serious thought, as it were, during which he withdrew into himself, and almost repelled the advances of his companions. He was a young Highlander named Cameron, handsome, dark, and tall; a well-read man, but one who shrank from displaying his knowledge; a man, one felt instinctively, somewhat out of the ordinary run; a man perhaps with a history.

As I said, he had a peculiar attraction for me, and though he was reserved at first, we ultimately became firm friends; and in his more melancholy moods, when he avoided the society of others, he yet seemed to find a sort of passive pleasure in mine. At such times he would say but little, but would sit for an hour gazing steadily at the horizon, with a strange far-away look in his deep, earnest eyes. So would a man look (I often thought) whom some terrible sorrow or some ghastly experience had marked off for ever from the rest of his kind. But I asked no questions; I waited patiently till the time should come when our ripening friendship would reveal the secret.

One thing more I observed, that whenever the conversation turned, as it did several times during the voyage, upon what is commonly called the supernatural (a subject upon which most of us were derisively sceptical) my friend not only expressed no opinion whatever, but invariably withdrew himself from the party or contrived to change the subject. No one else, however, appeared to notice this, and of course I said nothing about it.

Well, in due course we arrived at Madras, and, after staying there about a fortnight, five of us, including my friend Cameron and myself, received orders to join our regiment at an up-country station. Our party was under the charge of a certain Major Rivers, whom, during the short time we had known him at Madras, we had all learnt to like very much. He was a small, spare man, with short-sighted grey eyes and a peculiarly pleasant smile; a man of extreme punctuality in trifles, but frank, kindly, and genial; a thorough soldier and a thorough sportsman—indeed his devotion to sport had left its mark upon him in the shape of a very perceptible limp, the result of an accident in the hunting field.

A considerable part of our journey had to be performed by water, so a kind of barge was put into requisition for us, and we started at daybreak one morning. It soon grew insufferably hot, and as the country was flat, and our progress extremely slow, you will not be surprised to hear that we found the time hang somewhat heavily upon our hands. Sometimes we got out and walked a few yards to stretch our legs, but the heat of the sun soon drove us under our awning again, and by the evening of the second day we were in a state of *ennui* bordering on desperation, when the Major suddenly said with a smile:

"Gentlemen, I have a proposal to make."

"Hear, hear," we all shouted; "anything to vary this detestable monotony."

"My idea," said the Major, "is this. You see that little hill over there to the right? Well, I know this part of the country thoroughly, and I know that the river passes just on the other side of that hill. Now though it is, as you see, only a few miles off in a straight line, it is at least four times that distance by water in consequence of the windings of the river. We are now about to stop for the night, and I thought that if we left the boat here to-morrow morning, arranging to meet it again in the evening at the base of that hill, we might relieve the tedium of the journey by a little shooting in those jungles, where I know from experience there is good sport to be had."

Of course we hailed the suggestion with acclamation, and at an early hour the next morning we took our guns and leapt ashore, accompanied by a large dog which belonged to one of the party—a fine, intelligent animal, and a general favourite. The Major had created some amusement by appearing in an enormous pair of top-boots, many sizes too large for him; but when someone suggested that he seemed more prepared for fishing than shooting, he only laughed good-naturedly and said that before the day was over we might perhaps wish that we had been as well protected as he was.

In sooth he was right, for we found the ground for some distance decidedly marshy, and in many places, to obtain a footing at all, we had to spring from bush to bush and stone to stone in a way that, encumbered as we were with our guns, soon made us most unpleasantly warm. At last our difficulties culminated in a muddy stream or ditch about twelve feet broad.

"Rather a long jump for a man with a heavy gun!" I said.

"Oh," replied the Major," I think we can manage it; at any rate I am going to try, and if I get over with my game leg it ought to be easy enough for you young fellows."

He took a short run and sprang, just clearing the ditch; but unluckily the slimy edge of the bank gave way under his feet, and he slipped back into the water. In a moment the rest of us took the leap, all getting safely across, and rushed to his assistance. He was quite unhurt, and, thanks to the enormous top-boots, not even wet; but his gun was choked with mud, and required a thorough cleaning. He threw himself down with a laugh under the nearest tree, and began fanning himself with his hat, saying: "You will have to go on without me for a while."

We protested against leaving him, objecting that we did not know the country, and offered to stop and help him; but this he refused to permit. "No, no," he said, "you must push on and see what you can find; I shall follow in half-an-hour or so; we cannot miss one another, and at the worst there is always the hill as a landmark, so you have only to climb a tree and you will get the direction at once; but in any case do not fail to meet at the boat at five o'clock."

Somewhat reluctantly we obeyed, and plunged into the jungle, leaving him still lying fanning himself under the tree. We had walked on for about an hour without much success, and were just beginning to wonder when the Major would join us, when Cameron, who happened to be next to me, stopped suddenly, turned pale as death, and pointing straight before him cried in accents of horror:

"See! see! merciful heaven, look there!"

"Where? what? what is it?" we all shouted confusedly, as we rushed up to him and looked round in expectation of encountering a tiger—a cobra—we hardly knew what, but assuredly something terrible, since it had been sufficient to cause such evident emotion in our usually self-contained comrade. But neither tiger nor cobra was visible—nothing but Cameron, pointing with ghastly haggard face and starting eyeballs at something we could not see.

"Cameron! Cameron!" cried I, seizing his arm, "for heaven's sake, speak! what is the matter?"

Scarcely were the words out of my mouth when a low, but very peculiar sound struck on my ear, and Cameron, dropping his pointing hand, said in a hoarse strained voice, "There! you heard it? Thank God it's over!" and fell to the ground insensible. There was a momentary confusion while we unfastened his collar, and I dashed in his face some water which I fortunately had in my flask, while another tried to pour brandy between his clenched teeth; and under cover of it I whispered to the man next me (one of our greatest sceptics, by the way), "Beauchamp, did *you* hear anything?"

"Why, yes," he replied, "a curious sound, very; a sort of crash or rattle far away in the distance, yet very distinct; if the thing were not utterly impossible I could have sworn it was the rattle of musketry."

"Just my impression," murmured I; "but hush! he is recovering."

In a minute or two he was able to speak feebly, and began to thank us and apologize for giving trouble; and soon he sat up, leaning against a tree, and in a firm, though still low voice said:

"My dear friends, I feel I owe you an explanation of my extraordinary behaviour. It is an explanation that I would fain avoid giving; but it must come some time, and so may as well be given now. You may perhaps have noticed that when during the voyage you all joined in scoffing at dreams, portents and visions, I invariably avoided giving any opinion on the subject. I did so because, while I had no desire to court ridicule or provoke discussion, I was unable to agree with you, knowing only too well from my own dread experience that the world which men agree to call that of the supernatural is just as real as—nay, perhaps even far more so than—this world we see about us. In other words, I, like many of my countrymen, am cursed with the gift of second-sight—that awful faculty which foretells in vision calamities that are shortly to occur.

"Such a vision I had just now, and its exceptional horror moved me as you have seen. I saw before me a corpse—not that of one who has died a peaceful, natural death, but that of the victim of some terrible accident; a ghastly, shapeless mass, with a face swollen, crushed, unrecognizable. I saw this dreadful object placed in a coffin, and the funeral service performed over it; I saw the burial-ground, I saw the clergyman; and though I had never seen either before, I can picture both perfectly in my mind's eye now; I saw you, myself, Beauchamp, all of us and many more, standing round as mourners; I saw the soldiers raise their muskets after the service was over; I heard the volley they fired—and then I knew no more."

As he spoke of that volley of musketry I glanced across with a shudder at Beauchamp, and the look of stony horror on that handsome sceptic's face was one not to be forgotten. The spell of the vision was upon us all, and no one liked to be the first to speak; and for a long minute, or perhaps two minutes, there was a silence which could be felt—that silence of tropical noon which is so far deeper than that of midnight.

And then—it was broken. Broken, not by any of the ordinary sounds of the forest, but by one which under the circumstances startled us far more than the growl of the tiger or the hiss of the serpent would have done—the deep solemn "clang!" of a great church bell.

"Good God, what is that?" cried Beauchamp, thoroughly unnerved, as we all sprang to our feet, while the dog threw up his head and howled.

"It's the bell tolling for that funeral of Cameron's," said Granville, the wit of our party, trying to smile with a very white face; but I doubt if ever a joke fell flatter, for we were in no mood for laughter. While we still stood awe-stricken, gazing at one another, again the unmistakable sonorous "clang!" rang out in our ears—not borne by the wind and mellowed by distance, but in the very midst of us, close over our heads—so close that we felt the ground vibrate in response to its stroke.

"Let us leave this accursed spot!" cried I, seizing Cameron's arm. Beauchamp caught him by the other, and between us we half supported, half dragged him along. The others followed; but we had not gone ten yards before that hollow knell sounded once more in our midst, adding wings to our speed; and again the dog howled dismally.

For a mile or more we hurried along in silence, until we came upon a beautiful grassy dell through which meandered a clear silvery streamlet. On its edge we threw ourselves down to rest; indeed Cameron, not yet thoroughly recovered, seemed incapable of going further. After a long draught of the cool water we became more composed, and began seriously to review our late remarkable experience.

As to Cameron's vision, after witnessing his intense and painful agitation it was impossible to doubt that it was sufficiently real to *him*, and the phenomenon being a purely subjective one there was little more to be said. More difficult to deal with was the faint, distant, yet surprisingly distinct sound of a volley of musketry which Beauchamp and I had both heard. Granville and Johnson, who had heard nothing, declared that the sound had existed only in our heated imagination, excited as we naturally were by Cameron's strange condition; and, when reminded of its singular agreement with the termination of his vision, attributed that fact to mere coincidence.

Neither Beauchamp nor I were at all satisfied with this; *we* had heard the sound, and we knew that this theory was not the true explanation; but as we were entirely unable to suggest a more rational one, it was useless to argue. But then that weird church bell! No one dreamt of suggesting imagination in that case; we had all alike heard it; all had felt the vibration of the earth which it caused; all agreed exactly in the description of its sound, and in locating it in the very midst of us.

"Still," said Granville, "of course there *must* be some means of accounting for it naturally; even if there were such things as spirits it would be absurd to suppose them capable of producing a noise such as that; and I have read of cases in which some unusual description of echo has been found capable of reproducing a sound with startling fidelity even at an almost incredible distance."

"An echo!" replied Cameron, scornfully; "there is not a church bell of any sort within fifty miles of us—not such an one as that, probably, in the whole of India, for it sounded like the Great Bell of Moscow."

"Yes, that sound had certainly not travelled fifty miles," remarked Beauchamp reflectively; "you have heard, I suppose, of the *campanero* of South America?"

We had all read of this lovely bird and its wonderful bell-like note, but we had no reason to believe that any such creature existed in India; besides, we all agreed that no specimen of the feathered tribe was ever hatched which could have produced that tremendous metallic clang.

"I wish the Major had been with us," said Granville; "he knows the country, and perhaps he might be able to suggest something. Ha! I have it! I see the explanation of the mystery! How absurd of us not to have thought of it before! Of course the Major, who stayed behind, has been playing some trick upon us, and is now having a good laugh somewhere or other at the recollection of our foolish fright!"

"A bright idea! that must be it!" exclaimed Beauchamp and Johnson together.

"But stay," interposed I, "*how* could he have done it? He can hardly have been carrying a bell weighing two or three tons or so in his coat-pocket."

"Oh, no doubt he found some method or other," answered Granville; "for example, I have heard that a properly prepared bar of iron will when struck give out a very fair imitation of a bell sound."

"Perhaps so, but then properly prepared bars of iron are not usually to be found lying about in an Indian jungle, and he certainly brought nothing with him from the boat."

"Well, possibly, the barrel of his gun might be made—" but here a general smile checked the speaker, and Cameron quietly remarked:

"No, Granville, I don't think that will quite answer as an

explanation; besides, how do you account for the sound coming from a point close above our heads?"

"Much may be done by skilful management of ventriloquism," replied Granville.

"Ventriloquism! my dear fellow, can you seriously suppose that such a sound as that ever proceeded from any human throat?"

"Well," answered Granville, "I cannot say; but until you can find me a better, I cling to my hypothesis that the Major is responsible for our fright in some way or other."

To this Beauchamp and Johnson somewhat hesitatingly agreed. Cameron smiled sadly and shook his head, but said no more; as for myself, I knew not what to think, for my scepticism was considerably shaken by the strange events of the morning.

We lay there by that pleasant stream for some hours, each ransacking his memory in turn for some half-forgotten story of the supernatural, of goblin, ghost, or fairy, told perhaps by some old nurse in happy childish days. The only tale that dwells in my recollection is a short one told by Cameron in answer to a question as to his first experience of the faculty of second sight.

"The first experience I well remember," he said; "I was a little lad of six or seven, and one evening when my father and I were out walking together, we stood to watch the fishermen who lived in the little village attached to our house push off their boats and start for their night's work. Among them were two fine lads—Alec and Donald—who were particular favourites of mine, and used frequently to bring strange fish for 'the little laird' (as they called me) to see: and once I had even been out in their boat. So I waved my hand to them as they set sail, and then we continued our ramble, ascending the cliffs so that we could watch the boats as they stood far out to sea.

"We were nearly at home again when, coming round an angle of the grey old castle wall, I was much surprised to see Alec and Donald leaning against it. I was about to speak to them when the sudden tightening of my father's grasp upon my hand caused me to look up in his face, and the stern, set expression that I saw there diverted my attention for the moment from the lads, though I noticed that they did not give us the customary salute—in fact, did not seem to see us at all.

"'Father,' I asked, 'what can Alec and Donald be doing there?'

"He looked down on me with deep compassion, and said, 'And did ye see them too? Eh! my lad, my lad!' and after that he took no notice of my questions, and spoke no more till we reached home. He retired to his room, while I ran down to the beach to see why my young friends' boat had returned; but to my astonishment there was no boat there, and an old woman, who had been sitting spinning at her door close by the whole time, assured me that there certainly had been none since the whole fleet set sail together two hours before.

"I was puzzled, but still I never doubted but that somehow my friends had been there in real flesh and blood; even the great storm which woke me in the night suggested nothing, and it was only when in the early morning I saw men reverently bearing two bodies into the house where Alec and Donald had lived, that I had any idea of the true nature of what I had seen."

Thus time passed on, till the declining rays of the sun warned us that we must think of returning to the boat. We had not far to go, for the hill at whose foot we were to meet was full in sight, and we had only to pass through a wood which skirted its base. By this time we had somewhat recovered our normal tone, and were laughing and chatting gaily, wondering where we should find the Major, and thinking what an incredible story we had to tell him.

Beauchamp, who was leading, had just called out, "Here is the end of the wood at last!" when his dog, which had been roaming about in advance, came flying back and cowered down among us with every sign of excessive fear. We had no time to wonder at this unusual behaviour before again in our midst sounded that solemn sonorous "clang!" just as before, and again the trembling dog threw up his head and howled.

"Ha!" exclaimed Cameron, quickly turning upon Granville, "echo? ventriloquism? an iron bar? a musket barrel? which hypothesis do you prefer now?"

And as his voice ceased the dread unearthly knell again crashed forth. With one consent we sprang towards the open ground at the end of the wood, but before we could reach it the spectral bell rang in our very ears—almost in our very brains, as it seemed—

once more, amid the frantic howls of the dog. We rushed out in great disorder into the broad meadow sloping down to the river, and it was with an unutterable sense of relief that we saw our boat, already moored, waiting to receive us, and the Major some distance in front of us limping hastily towards it.

"Major! Major!" we shouted; but he did not turn his head, sharp though his ears were generally; he only hurried on towards the boat, so we all started in pursuit, running as hard as we could. To our surprise the dog, instead of accompanying us, uttered one final dismal yell and dashed back into the haunted wood; but no one thought of following him—our attention was fixed on the Major. Fast as we ran we were unable to overtake him, and we were still some fifty yards from the boat when he hurried across the plank that the boatmen had just put down as a gangway. He went down the stairs, still in the same hurried manner, and we rushed after him, but to our intense surprise were unable to find him anywhere. The door of his cabin stood wide open, but it was empty; and though we searched the whole barge, not a trace of him could we find.

"Well," cried Granville, "this is the strangest trick of all."

Cameron and I exchanged glances, but Granville, not observing us, rushed on deck and demanded of the head boatman where the Major was.

"Sahib," replied the man, "I have not seen him since he left with you this morning."

"Why, what do you mean?" roared Granville; "he came on board this barge not a minute before we did, and I saw you put down a plank for him to cross with your own hands!"

"Sir," answered the man, exhibiting the greatest astonishment, "you are certainly mistaken; you were yourself the first person to come on board, and I laid down the plank because I saw you coming: as for the Major Sahib, I have not set eyes upon him since morning."

We could do nothing but stare at one another in blank amazement, not unmingled with awe; and I heard Cameron mutter as if to himself, "He *is* dead, then, as I feared, and the vision was for him after all."

"There is something very strange about all this," said Beauchamp, "something which I cannot at all understand; but one thing is clear—we must at once go back to the place where we left the Major this morning, and search for him. Some accident may have happened."

We explained to the head boatman where we had parted from the Major, and found that he at once shared our worst fears. "That is a very dangerous place, Sahib," he said; "there was once a village there, and there are two or three deep wells whose mouths are entirely overgrown by bushes and weeds; and the Major Sahib being so short-sighted would be very likely to fall into one of them."

This intelligence naturally increased our apprehensions tenfold, and we lost no time in setting off, taking with us three of the boatmen and a coil of stout rope. As may be imagined, it was not without a shudder that we plunged again into the wood where we had heard those mysterious sounds which we had now so much reason to fear might have been in some inexplicable way intended as warnings to us of a calamity impending, or perhaps even then taking place.

But the conversation turned chiefly on the latest marvel—the appearance and disappearance of what we could hardly help calling the Major's ghost. We carefully compared notes, and ascertained beyond a doubt that all five of us had clearly seen him; we had all observed his hurried manner, we had all noticed that though still wearing the top-boots, he had no hat upon his head and was no longer carrying his gun; we had all seen him descend the stairs on board the boat, and of course we were all perfectly certain that it would have been impossible for him, if a man in the flesh, to escape us unobserved.

Sceptics though some of us had been as to supernatural visitations, I think none of us now ventured to hope that we should find him alive; and perhaps it is no discredit to our prowess as soldiers to confess that we kept very close together as we retraced our steps through those woods, and that we spoke chiefly in whispers, except when at intervals we stopped, let off our pieces, and all shouted together, so that if the Major were lying disabled anywhere in the neighbourhood he would be aware of our approach.

However, we met with nothing unusual on our way, and found

without difficulty the place where we had crossed the ditch, and the tree under which we had left the Major. From this spot the boatmen easily tracked his footsteps for a few hundred yards, till one of them, running forward, picked up the hat and gun of the missing man—"the very articles," whispered Cameron to me, "which he had not when we saw him just now."

We now felt certain that some terrible accident had occurred—probably close to the very spot where we stood; and sure enough the natives pointed out to us only a few yards off the concealed mouth of one of those old wells of which they had warned us. Alas! at its edge there were the unmistakable marks of slipping feet; and from the blackness of the depth into which we looked, we could hardly doubt that our poor friend must have been fatally injured, even if not at once killed, by the fall.

The sun was already setting, and night comes on so rapidly in the tropics that we had but little time to lose; so, as no answer came to our shouts, we hastily passed our rope round the branch of a tree which hung over the mouth of the well, and by its means one of the boatmen descended. Soon from an immense depth a shout came up; the man had reached the bottom, and had discovered a body, but was unable to tell u whether it was the Major's or not. We directed him to attach it to the rope, and with fast beating hearts drew it to the surface of the earth.

Never shall I forget the ghastly sight that met our eyes in the rapidly-fading light; the corpse was indeed the Major's, but it was only by the clothes and the top-boots that we could identify it; scarcely anything of human shape was left in it, and the face was swollen and crushed past all recognition, as Cameron had seen it in his vision: and, horrible to relate, entangled in the rope which had been so hurriedly tied round it was also the mangled, but yet warm and palpitating body of Beauchamp's dog, which had rushed so madly into the jungle but an hour before! Sick with horror, we twined together a rude litter of branches, laid the Major's remains upon it with averted eyes, and bore it silently back to our boat.

So ends my sad story, and few will wonder that a permanent effect was produced upon the life of each one of its witnesses. Since then I have borne my part in many a battle-field, and faced death in its most dreadful forms calmly enough (for familiarity breeds contempt); but yet there are times when that unearthly bell, that spectral figure, that awful corpse rise once more before my mind, and a great horror falls upon me, and I dread to be alone.

One more fact I ought to mention to make my tale complete. When, on the following evening, we arrived at our destination, and our melancholy deposition had been taken down by the proper authorities, Cameron and I went out for a quiet walk, to endeavour with the assistance of the soothing influence of nature to shake off something of the gloom which paralyzed our spirits. Suddenly he clutched my arm, and, pointing through some rude railings, said in a trembling voice, "Yes, there it is! that is the burial-ground I saw yesterday." And when later on we were introduced to the chaplain of the post, I noticed, though my friends did not, the irrepressible shudder with which Cameron took his hand, and I knew that he had recognized the clergyman of his vision.

As to explanations, I have none to offer. I know the story is incredible, but I also know that it is true. The Indian boatmen told us that according to local tradition the site of the abandoned village had for a long time borne an extremely bad reputation. It was said that the gods, in anger at the sorceries of its inhabitants, had exterminated them by means of a plague, and that the demons invoked by those men of old still haunted the spot, and in their thirst for blood lured men and beasts to their destruction by every means in their power. Such enquiry as we were able to make confirmed the report that the village had been abandoned in consequence of an outbreak of some plague which almost depopulated it; but we can hardly admit the rest of the native theory, convenient though it would be as accounting for much that is otherwise inexplicable.

Such is the old man's story. As for its occult rationale, I presume Cameron's vision to have been a pure case of second-sight, and if so the fact that the two men who were evidently nearest to him (certainly one—probably both—actually touching him) participated in it to the limited extent of hearing the concluding volley, while the others who were not so close did not, would show that the intensity with which the vision impressed itself upon the seer occasioned vibrations in his mind-body which were communicated to those of the persons in contact with him, as in ordinary thought-transference.

The bell-sounds seem to have been an exceedingly powerful manifestation—probably produced by the Major in the attempt to apprise his friends of the accident which had befallen him.

It is possible that, finding himself unable to speak to them, it may have occurred to him that the tolling of a bell, as commonly associated with the idea of death, would be likely to suggest to them what had happened; but it is more probable that the immense effort of will, called forth by the intensity of his desire to communicate with them in some way, acted blindly in the first instance upon the elemental essence in causing that wonderful sound, which he then repeated again and again because it was the only physical effect that he found himself able to produce.

From what we hear of his extreme punctuality, it is probable that the idea of reaching the boat at the time arranged would have been prominent in his mind immediately before death, and that prominent idea would account for the apparition; while the fact that the officers all saw it, and the boatmen did not, might be attributed to the intense excitement under which the former were labouring, in addition to the fact that they, as constant companions, would be much more *en rapport* with the deceased.

The dog, as often happens, realized the character of the appearance sooner than the men did; but perhaps the most extraordinary point of the whole story is the discovery of its body along with the Major's—a point which distinctly suggests that there may be more in the native theory than the narrator was willing to admit. The only alternative hypothesis which occurs to me is that in an additional attempt to turn the attention of his friends in the right direction, the Major's will-power may have drawn the dog back to the scene of the accident, though he could not draw the men, and that being unable to check itself in its headlong rush, it met with its death as he had done; but I offer this only as a conjecture.

C. W. LEADBEATER.

THE DESIRE FOR PSYCHIC EXPERIENCES.

One of the most common questions addressed to the older members of the Society by those who have come to take a sufficiently serious interest in Theosophy to desire to apply it in their lives is in substance as follows: How shall I develope my astral senses? The answer given will naturally largely depend upon the knowledge and experience of the person addressed, but broadly speaking it will probably run along one or other of two divergent lines. If the answer is given by an old and experienced student, who has really assimilated theosophical teachings and grasped the true relation of human growth and progress to the possession of such more extended faculties and their wider responsibilities, it will be broadly as follows: Devote yourself to the accomplishment of your own higher evolution; make the perfecting and unfolding of your nature into the full ideal of human perfection in Wisdom, Power and Love, the *one* object of your life. In short, set yourself to qualify for entry upon and ultimately for the treading of those stages of more rapid evolution which are called the "Steps of the Path," and in due course of time, when you are fitted and ready to use them, you will find yourself in possession of all these higher faculties and powers.

On the other hand, if the answer is given by one less thoroughly attuned to Theosophy, more especially if by one whose mind has become entangled in some of the semi- or pseudo-occult arts and practices which figure so largely in the modern non-theosophic literature of psychism in its many and varied forms, then very likely that answer will contain elaborate recommendations as to crystal gazing, self-hypnotization, staring at a spot, breathing practices, *et hoc genus omne*, which are said to be conducive to the artificial stimulation of psychic vision.

Both answers will generally leave the inquirer discontented. If he gets a reply of the second kind, he will perhaps set himself with great ardour to carry out the practices recommended, only to find in ninety-nine cases out of a hundred at the end of a few months that the only results he has obtained are physical disturbance of his health, and an occasional flash of coloured light or black spots before his eyes, which are probably due to indigestion. At best he may get a few sporadic glimpses of etheric or lower astral conditions, but he soon finds that he is no nearer to seeing at will than he was, and that he is totally unable to make any practical use of these incoherent and spasmodic manifestations of psychic sensitiveness.

But let us leave this case on one side, since fortunately it is well-nigh certain that the majority of our older members at least are too well read in theosophic literature to give such an answer at all. Taking up then the lines of the first answer suggested above, it still remains true that in many cases such a reply arouses a feeling of dissatisfaction, more especially when after two or three years of really strenuous effort the aspirant begins to realize by experience the magnitude and difficulty of the task he has undertaken. And it seems worth while to consider the situation in some detail with reference to the various attitudes of mind in which such efforts may be approached, so that we may see how far this feeling of discontent has any reasonable foundation and whether the demand (which very often arises from it) for more direct and "practical" instruction in the development of the higher senses is one that can rightly or rationally be addressed to the leaders and teachers in our movement.

Consider first the most favourable case. A man has thoroughly convinced himself *intellectually* of the truth of reincarnation, karma, and the other fundamental teachings of Theosophy. He feels much the same certainty of conviction in these matters as he does with regard to the heliocentric system, the law of gravitation, etc., and probably upon much the same grounds, namely, that they afford the best and most satisfactory explanation of the known facts. In the course of his studies he finds that the ideal constantly held before his eyes is that of helping on the evolution of his fellow-men in every possible way. Work for others, thought for others, the sacrifice of self for the sake of others, the gaining of knowledge, of power, the acquisition of faculties, all are to be striven after for the one purpose of fitting oneself for the work of helping others. And then he finds in books like *The Astral Plane*, in articles such as

"Invisible Helpers," descriptions of the far wider and more efficient usefulness to which man attains when he learns to function and work on these higher planes. Thus just in proportion as the sincerity and earnestness of his desire to help, to live out the theosophic ideal, grows stronger, so does his longing for these wider capacities of usefulness increase and intensify. And so when year follows year of unrelaxing effort, and yet the door into the higher world still seems to remain closed against him, it is not unnatural that he should feel some dissatisfaction. Now just at this point there often exists a misunderstanding, the clearing away of which sometimes removes the whole trouble.

It is not the case that the power of functioning and working for others on the astral plane is in any degree dependent upon or affected by the fact of whether or not one remembers or knows anything about it down here in the waking consciousness. A man may well be leading a very active and most useful life in the astral world during all the hours that his body lies asleep, and yet not have the very smallest knowledge or recollection thereof upon awakening. Nor does this in the least diminish his usefulness or capacity upon the astral plane; though it is the case that upon the *physical* plane he might sometimes be able to act more effectively and wisely if he did bring back the recollection of his nightly work. But even this drawback is in reality of much less importance than it seems, because such a man's speech and action will be very largely guided from the higher plane, even though he may remain physically unconscious of that guidance, and unaware of the circumstances and facts the knowledge of which is actually directing his inner self in what it makes the waking personality say and do.

Now, the very moment anyone has made himself fit to be a helper and worker on the astral plane, and is likewise really inspired and dominated by the unselfish desire to be of use—just so soon as that is the case he will be awakened and taught to work there, whether or not he remembers it in his waking state. Now as soon as this is realized, it is seen that each one of us is utilized for the work to be done to the full extent of our *fitness* and that our knowing and recollecting that other life down here, however great a satisfaction it might be to ourselves, has very little bearing upon the work itself. And this being so, if our desire is truly the pure and unselfish wish to give help in the great work, then we have no good reason for discontent because we have not "astral vision" in the sense of the knowledge and perception of astral things down here.

But many know all this and are still discontented; why? Because they are *not* animated purely by the unselfish desire to help; but their sincere and honest desire to do so is mingled with other motives, such as the craving for new sensations and experiences, an almost sub-conscious lurking doubt and uncertainty, while it may be even that still lower elements enter all unknown to them, such as the wish to stand out from among their fellows, the desire of power, or even curiosity pure and simple. It is because there is so much of the selfish and the personal sub-consciously present in us that the Path is so hard and long-drawn out; for only under the pressure of disappointed expectation, of long waiting, of apparently fruitless endeavour and sacrifice, does our real deep-down nature become revealed and brought before ourselves for conquest and purification. Thus it is only by long-continued and patient effort that slowly our real motives and actuating impulses become known to us, submitted to searching analysis, and finally cleansed from the taint of selfishness. And he who believes himself to be really and truly drawn into the stream by the one right motive, the desire to help, soon learns to be thankful for the slowness with which extended powers come to him, for he learns to realize his own unfitness for such far-reaching responsibility.

Such then, it seems to me, is the reply one would make to the ideal aspirant—to one in whom the inner conviction was strong and vivid, to whom the sublime ideal of the Masters appealed as the only goal worth striving towards, to whom the fitting himself for the Path seemed the one thing worth living for. And such an one will surely see and feel its reasonableness, so that though restlessness and discontent may still often arise within him, he will yet be able to realize that they spring from his own imperfections and weaknesses, and so utilize them as pointers indicating the directions along which he must strive towards the uplifting and strengthening of his own nature. Indeed, such an aspirant to-day is far better off than were those of ten or fifteen years ago; for he now has older students to put before him explanations of his difficulties and advice as to how to meet them, while in those old days each had to find out for himself, and learn the "why" of many a painful experience, many a delay, many a disappointment, by slow and patient study and analysis of himself, sustained only by the strength of an inward conviction which had to uphold him and give him courage amid apparent contradictions, blunders, half hints, will-o'-the-wisp illuminations, and all sorts of uncertainties and incoherences.

But such ideal aspirants to Theosophy are naturally few and far between, seeing that so intense a conviction as this implies the work and the building of one or more previous lives directed to these studies and efforts. However, practically much the same reply must be given to the ordinary student of Theosophy who has definitely accepted its teachings and who therefore, professedly at least, admits the doctrine that power and faculty should only be desired as means to help others, and that the greater Teachers cannot be expected to put knowledge, and the power which knowledge gives, into the hands of any who have not proved their fitness as well as their capacity to use it well, by entirely conquering and purifying their lower natures. If he has not the intensity of conviction and deep earnestness needed to make his whole life an effort thus to fit himself, he cannot logically or reasonably complain that he is not taught how to do things for which he is unfit, nor given lessons in the work of the astral plane before he has learnt to deal intelligently and wisely with that of the physical.

But there is another class of people among those attracted by theosophical teachings who take up an altogether different position, and about whom a word must also be said. I mean especially those of a scientific and logical turn of mind, who have become more or less sceptical about all religious matters as ordinarily understood, who are uncertain whether or not man has a soul which survives the death of the body, but who are yet quite free from the dogmatic attitude on these points which characterizes the negations of the materialist quite as often as the assertions of the churchman. To such minds as these the teachings of Theosophy appeal mainly in virtue of the claim that they are actually verifiable and experimentally ascertainable by living men who have become specialists in such studies. Admitting freely that the great teachings of reincarnation and karma are by far the most logical and coherent theories in the field, and that viewed as hypotheses they give by far the best and most adequate explanation of the facts of evolution and human life, as well as render intelligible a very large number of rare and curious or abnormal but constantly recurrent phenomena, these people find themselves still uncertain at heart. Intellectually they admit these doctrines to be satisfying and in the highest degree probable, but they are unable to pass from the mental attitude which regards them as highly probable and most reasonable hypotheses to a sense of conviction that they are actual facts in nature. And taking up as their text the statement that some of these most important teachings have been and daily are being verified by members of our Society, they want to know how this is done, and then as soon as they realize that such verification is only possible by at least carrying through recollection from the astral plane into the full waking consciousness, they at once turn upon us with the old question, How is this conscious memory of the astral to be developed? And when they find that the only advice they get is that given above, and that they are almost certain to spend years, if not lives in the undertaking ere they can expect to verify the teachings for themselves, they often feel dissatisfied and disappointed, whether they give expression to what they feel or not. Let us see what can be said from their point of view.

You claim, they may justly urge, that the teachings of Theosophy are verified and verifiable facts in nature, ascertainable and demonstrable according to the canons of scientific research. True, the Theosophist will answer, but since these facts belong to regions of nature not coming within the range of the physical senses, other powers of perception must be employed for their investigation; and there is ample evidence on quite ordinary lines that such powers and faculties do exist in us, though generally in a latent condition. But—the objector may continue—even granting all this, your statements as to facts no less than your explanations of them differ very materially from the records of other observers and investigators who have also given proof—more or less adequate—that they too are in possession of these wider faculties. And though your position is that your teachings as to the main facts rest upon a basis of experiment and observation resulting from the labours of untold generations of specially trained workers, yet this claim of yours has not yet been proved to my satisfaction; and hence to me the only satisfactory proof still remains my own direct experience and verification of at least the main facts of your teaching, such as the survival of the soul, its *post-mortem* history, its rebirth on earth, and especially the fact of the existence of such a school of workers and investigators as you speak of. Now you practically demand of me to shape and mould my whole life upon faith in the theories you propound, not merely for a few years but very probably for life, without even any very strong hope that before I die I shall be able to get the verification I seek. How then does your position differ from that of the religionist who says: "Live the life and ye shall know of the doctrine whether it be true?" For that is exactly what each of these other schools, who differ from you more or less radically, say of their own claims and statements.

In answer to an argument of this kind, the Theosophist may reply by pointing out that a sound, scientific conviction as to the existence and survival of the soul as a fact in nature may be reached by an adequate study of the evidence and the arguments in the case, apart altogether from personal verification. This conviction being once reached, the probability on purely evidential grounds of reincarnation becomes so great as practically to amount to certainty. And when once a real conviction on these fundamental issues is formed, it will no longer seem so unreasonable to demand that a whole life or more should be devoted to the reaching of that higher development which enables one to know at first hand the superphysical worlds. And it may be politely pointed out in addition that the study of every science demands years of work and patience, and that of all sciences this is obviously the greatest and most practically important.

It might also be explained that strictly speaking we Theosophists do not "demand" anything at all, neither belief in our teachings nor that people shall live according to any special *régime*. What we really do—or rather aim to do, since all human nature is imperfect and we make many mistakes—what we aim to do, then, is to put the facts as we know them, and the teachings as we have received them, as clearly and plainly as we can before people, leaving them to accept or reject what is offered according as it appeals to them or not. And though we undoubtedly are anxious that people should realize these facts and laws of life, for their benefit, not ours, and though we feel confident in the general correctness of our knowledge as far as it goes, yet we do not ask people to *believe* our teaching, for mere "belief" is of small value. What we do desire is that people shall see and feel the truth of these things for themselves, by the awakening of the inner sense or perception of truth as truth, which gives the only living and forceful conviction. This is very different, or so it seems to me, from *demanding* that people shall believe, or that they shall follow some special mode of life, under pain of hell fire, damnation, or some other threat.

Perhaps it will be urged that, since some writers and lecturers amongst us often speak of "knowing" at first hand, and assure us that what they say they have themselves seen and experienced, this amounts to a "claim" to be believed. There may be some force in the argument when used about a question not of fact, but of logic, law, generalization or principle. But it does not apply in the general way in which it is here sought to be used. For as regards matters of fact—the survival and *post-mortem* states of the soul, re-birth, etc., in relation to which the phrase is almost exclusively used —it is a mere statement that the speaker has personally observed such and such a thing; a statement exactly parallel to those which every scientist is continually making. It is thus no "claim" at all, even by implication, and the utmost that can be said is that there is a tacit claim to *bonâ fides* made by the speaker. But that we all make, all our lives through, and the Theosophist has quite as much right to assert and maintain his own *bonâ fides* and truthfulness as has anybody else.

One might, too, reiterate what has been said often enough, and point out very emphatically that we Theosophists don't ask people for anything. We don't ask them for money, nor social considera-tion, nor anything else. It is we who give, who offer freely and fully the best we have, the fruits of years of hard work and effort, to all who care to profit by them. It is no benefit to any of us when people join the Theosophical Society or read our books and magazines. We should one and all be only too pleased to remain quiet, and neither draw the notice of the world nor endeavour to call attention in any special direction. Of all men the real Theo-sophist most keenly desires retirement and silence, not noise and publicity. But recognizing as our basic principle the fact of human solidarity and unity, we cannot shirk the duty which has fallen to us of trying to help all who are seeking for light to the best of our power, and hence the teachings of Theosophy must be put forward as plainly and as widely as possible, thereby bringing into publicity more than one who suffers not a little thereby. It is thus not unnatural that they should object to the assertion that they make "claims," and are therefore bound to prove this and that, to provide a short cut by which the doubtful or sceptical may "satisfy" themselves without undergoing the laborious self-discipline which others have had to go through.

Still it is not very likely that our questioner will be satisfied, and the only thing one can then say is this: From the Theosophical standpoint the road that has been pointed out is the only one along which these wider faculties can be developed wisely and safely. There are other methods, but the results obtained by their use are unsatisfactory; unsatisfactory first in point of accuracy and reliability in the results, as well as because great dangers to both mind and body attend their use; secondly, because the faculties when so acquired are not permanent, but end with the present body, and in most cases cause deterioration rather than real progress to the permanent individuality. Hence we must entirely decline to have anything to do with them, still less to put anyone in the way of discovering and applying them. Our questioner will probably remain discontented; but if he is *really* in earnest and follows even the mere study of these subjects with any earnestness, he will almost certainly come to feel and appreciate the rightness of the position taken up in the course of quite a moderate time.

Now let us leave for a moment anything like a logical or thought-out position and consider the great mass of people whose dissatisfaction is vaguely felt rather than clearly formulated. If put into words their feelings would sometimes run thus: Here am I after ten or twelve years in the Theosophical Society; I've read all the books, attended lectures regularly, been a strict vegetarian (perhaps), led a good and moral life, done all I can to help others, and still I have no powers, no astral perception, not even an occasional clear memory of an astral experience at night. And yet there is X, who joined long after I did, who has reached the Buddhic plane in full consciousness; Y, who has only been at the thing for three or four years, and has the full use of his astral faculties when awake; Z, who is quite unbrotherly and says hard things about people, but constantly has recollections of nightly journeyings in the astral; surely it is not just or fair! And so on: only it is more often someone who has been in the Society a short three or four years, and whose knowledge even of the books is hardly more than rudimentary, who feels thus, than one who has really borne the burden and heat of the lean years. The fact is that we most of us possess an astounding fund of self-complacency and self-satisfaction; we have not begun to realize our own imperfections, not even enough to enable us to appreciate the good points in others; we have not begun to take ourselves really in hand and strive to mould ourselves after a noble ideal. But we all think we could make good use of astral powers and faculties, that we are quite fit to be entrusted with them, and we are discontented—not as we should be, with ourselves and our own lack of all the qualities we ought to have developed—but vaguely with the Society and its teachers, because they do not give us what we think our due. And such a state of feeling is by no means uncommon; indeed, its partial absence is a rarity, its complete absence—— (?). All I know is that, to speak personally, the last fourteen years have been one long continued finding out of the most purblind self-complacency in my own case, and I see no reason whatever to flatter myself that I am anywhere near the end. But this at least experience has taught me—that this self-satisfied egotism is *there* all the time, ever lurking unseen and unsuspected somewhere or other, most usually astoundingly visible to everyone else, but perfectly imperceptible to myself. And having learnt this much, it has at least taught me to be discontented with myself and to realize that, very far from having any deserts or merits or rights, nine people at least out of every ten are probably ever so much better in most respects than I can hope to be in many a year. And, if I may say it without offence, I venture to think that the sooner all the members of the Theosophical Society make the same discovery and *realize* what it means, the sooner are they likely to be of some use in the world.

BERTRAM KEIGHTLEY.

ECKHARTSHAUSEN'S CATECHISM.

Translated from the German by MADAME DE STEIGER.

(*Concluded from p.* 426.)

FOURTH PRINCIPLE.

Q. What is the fourth principle of the inner Light-Community, the true Understanders of nature?

A. It is the knowledge of the analogy of the Communion and link with our holy Father, and the holy Angelic Salutation, the Ave, with the purest nature-force and natural form.

Q. What analogy is this?

A. Highest Light-power, which Thou, the God-like in nature, art, and who dwellest in the inmost part of the same, as in Heaven, hallowed be Thy qualities and Thy laws.

2. Where Thou art all is perfect; may the kingdom of Thy knowledge come into Thine own.

3. May our will in all our work be Thou, the only self-working Life-force; and Thou performest all things in all nature, so likewise work with us.

4. Give us of the dew of heaven and of the fat of the earth, the fruit of the sun and moon from the Tree of Life.

5. And forgive us all our errors, which we, without Thy knowledge, have committed in our work, as we would persuade those from error, who have, from error, offended against our rules; leave us not to our self-conceit, and to our own knowledge, but deliver us from all evil through the accomplishment of Thy work. Amen.

ANALOGY OF THE AVE.

Welcome, Thou pure Source of Self Movement, pure Form, capable of the reception of Light-force! with Thee alone the Light-force of all things is united.

Thou art the most blessed of all susceptible Forms, and holy is the Fruit which Thou conceivedst, the essence of the united Light and warmth-matter.

Pure Form, Thou, mother of the most perfect being, rise to the Light-force for us, now, while we work, and in the hour when we accomplish the work!

Q. What is the main tenor of the Lord's Prayer of the Light children, and its analogy in nature?

A. They pray for the sum of all spiritual and temporal benefits, for the well-being of the soul and of life—through that, which is the highest Light-force—the Godlike in nature, to receive the great work of nature; they pray that God shall lead them to wisdom, protect them from errors in their works, and teach them to be charitable to men, their brothers, so that what God promised to the descendants of Abraham, Isaac and Jacob, be attained, and God's alliance with men be fulfilled.

Q. Why have the Light children also an analogy with the Angelic Greeting?

A. For this reason, that they admire the greatness of God not only in the all-causing force of nature (having analogy with the Christus), but also that they recognize the glory of the purest virginal form, of which Mary is the analogy, and with which the higher force has united itself for the production of the highest perfection. For as the Holy Ghost united with Mary to produce the most perfect spiritual man, so the pure nature-spirit unites with the purest matter to produce the most perfect physical form, the physical nature-Saviour, who brings all other physical things to perfection; which secret is the secret of the wise.

Therefore he only can understand this art, who follows Christ, and the analogies of religion alone lead us to the fullest perfection, as the operations, which the Light children perform, likewise lead them by analogy to the highest mysteries of Faith.

Q. Is it not enough, if a Light child knows and perceives all the rules?

A. No! It is not enough; he must also bring them into practice and show his knowledge by works; on this depends the art of analysis of the Light children, which stands in analogy with Christian righteousness.

Fifth Principle.

Q. What is the fifth principle of the children of Light?

A. It consists of two parts, namely, that a follower of Light everywhere purifies the impure, with good results through the grace from above, which is our Dew. It is also our ♀[*], because perception must accord with execution; that is to say, that theory must accord with practice; for it is not enough for a knower of Light to perceive the art, he must also put it into practice; knowledge alone effects nothing, practice also is required.

Q. What is the sin which, in our Light science, is most to be avoided?

A. That which can destroy in men this highest natural good, which is the highest perfection of nature.

Q. What are the chief faults or sins in working?

A. Those which during the course of the operation, as well as in the application of this treasure, are *after* the operation, against the design of God; they are the following:—

Too great elevation through fire.

Too intense concentration.

Profusion.

Excessive economy of matter.

Overloading.

Inflammation.

Chilling.

It is written of these chief and deadly sins which kill the spirit: He who does such things, will not attain the highest perfection in physical nature.

Q. How many faults, or chemical sins, are there against the nature spirit?

A. 1. Building anything presumptuously on this spirit without inspection and reason, sinning through its mercy.

2. Doubting immediately if one does not directly see its working.

3. Opposing the perception of chemical truths.

4. Grudging favours to a Brother.

5. Having a hardened heart to salutary exhortations.

[*] The Egyptian cross and the Hebrew letter Tau ת. (Translator's note.)

6. Persisting in ignorance.

These faults are unpardonable because they can never be restored to the work.

Q. What faults cause Heaven to weep?

A. 1. Wilfully destroying the Work.

2. Profaning the Work.

3. Misusing it for the oppression of the people.

4. Depriving a fellow-labourer of his reward.

Q. Which are the extra-chemical sins?

A. 1. Advising another in a chemical error.

2. Influencing another to sin.

3. Agreeing with the errors of others.

4. Praising the errors of others.

5. Being silent about the errors of others.

6. Overlooking them.

7. Participating in them.

8. Defending them.

Thus we become participators in errors, as if we had committed them ourselves.

Q. Is it enough, if one is in possession of the Work, to forsake wickedness and avoid sin?

A. No, we must do good, for God only bestows this grace, that the favoured mortal may bring forth the ripe fruit to perfection.

We should also live righteously and piously before God and men, adorning our high calling with good works.

Q. How many good works are there?

A. Three.

1. The wise man should have his mind always turned towards God and wisdom.

2. He should abstain from all which is not Godlike and wise.

3. He should always relieve the wants of men, his brethren.

Q. Of what use are good works?

A. Good works are for this reason, that individuals as well as the whole world may become happy.

Q. What bodily works of mercy can the wise man perform when he has attained the highest perfection of physical nature?

A. 1. He can feed the hungry.

2. Give drink to the thirsty.

3. Clothe the naked.
4. Shelter strangers.
5. Heal the sick.
6. Revivify dead matter.

Q. What spiritual works can the same wise man perform?

A. 1. He can punish sins.
2. Teach the ignorant.
3. Counsel the doubtful.
4. Comfort the afflicted.
5. Bear wrong patiently.

Q. What are the eight chemical Beatitudes?

A. They are those, which are received through the enjoyment and possession of the highest perfection as the highest Nature-good, and which John taught in the Apocalypse according to the Revelation of the Lord. .

1. "To him that overcometh will I give to eat of the tree of life, which is in the midst of the paradise of God." Rev. ii. 7.

2. "He that overcometh shall not be hurt of the second death." Rev. ii. 11.

3. "To him that overcometh will I give to eat of the hidden manna, and I will give him a white stone, and in the stone a new name written, which no man knoweth saving he that receiveth it." Rev. ii. 17.

4. "And he that overcometh, and keepeth my works unto the end, to him will I give power over the nations:

"And he shall rule them with a rod of iron; as the vessels of a potter shall they be broken to shivers: even as I received of my Father.

"And I will give him the morning star." Rev. ii. 26, 27, 28.

5. "He that overcometh, the same shall be clothed in white raiment; and I will not blot out his name out of the book of life, but I will confess his name before my Father, and before his angels." Rev. iii. 5.

6. "Him that overcometh will I make a pillar in the temple of my God, and he shall go no more out: and I will write upon him the name of my God, and the name of the city of my God, which is new Jerusalem, which cometh down out of heaven from my God: and I will write upon him my new name." Rev. iii. 12.

7. "To him that overcometh, will I grant to sit with me in my throne, even as I also overcame, and am set down with my Father in his throne." Rev. iii. 21.

8. He who overcometh will receive all that he desires and wishes from me, by the right of heritage. I will be his God, and he shall be my son.*

Q. Which are the evangelical or heavenly counsels in this art?

A. There are three.

1. To be poor amidst all riches.

2. Abstemious because we can enjoy all.

3. Obedient because we command.

Q. What are the four last things?

A. 1. Death, as the destruction of matter.

2. Judgment or separation of (3) the heavenly living, (4) from the earthly dead.

Meditate, O Man! in all thy work on the four last things, and thou wilt not fail in thy work.

Concluding Remarks.

The most subtle power is united with the grossest matter in the magnet.

Divisible force is united with the indivisible points.

Practice

Though the magnet may be divided into as many points as one likes, the pieces keep the same points and poles.

What is manifested in the magnet in the exterior parts, appears to lie unnoticed in all bodies. Doubtless all have their points and poles of force, by which they are attracted and repulsed. According to the principle, *principio infinitorum similium*, the structure of the whole world appears to hang together in the greatest and smallest things according to magnetic conditions, the most subtle with the most gross, and the most gross with the most subtle—all according to arrangement. Both, equality and inequality, arise from a single source, which is force.

* The reference cannot be found (Translator).

PROBLEMS.

1. How can a large thing be divided into innumerable others, so that the smallest always remains in a similar condition to the whole?

OR:

How do innumerable potencies and acts follow in proportionate continual dependence on each other, so that the innumerable remain in a similar condition?

OR:

How is the interior force to be united with the exterior, so that the hidden form may be revealed?

Since in parabolical mirrors, the focus lies between the tangent and the secant, ought not one to combine the tangent with the secant if one wishes to attain the interior point with the exterior form according to like angles?

Would it not be possible to unite the *puncta harmonica* in the air at a certain place?

What does it mean to "square the circle"?

Does it not appear to be against the nature of things if one believes that "to square" means to express a circle by a square?

Does not to "square the circle" mean much more; to make a cyclic space with rational numbers, so that there is a regularly ascending connection from the smallest to the largest?

How can one find the root and area of each irrational square?

How find the true proportion of the lateral and perpendicular lines?

How can one show with the rational contents of the equilateral triangle (without knowing its square lines beforehand), how many feet or fragments the square of the triangle contains?

What did the ancients understand generally about quadrature, and about the *arithmetica novenaria* and what discovery was made to the world when the *arithmetica novenaria* was united with quadrature?

Does not the *principium infinitorum similium* rule in physics as the *principium cognitionis*, and cannot the *principium unitatis* in metaphysics and theology be the *principium conscientiæ* (self-consciousness)? Could not the destructible and fleeting be made firm and abiding by these two principles?

Is it not an eternal law, that the spiritual has its subsistence in the bodily, and that the spiritual is enclosed in a bodily space? Is this bodiliness (or that in which nothing could be expressed by the word space) a bodily form, in which the spiritual works?

Are there not three foundation principles, and do not they work in seven forces?

Are not these three foundation principles three self-moving sources, which bring the seven forms into one concept, of which the first three forms decide the first principle, the fourth and fifth forms the second principle, and the sixth and seventh, the third? From the appearance of the world, which is held so immutably together, should reason conclude that there is an eternal, indissoluble bond of Divinity, by which all is held together?

For in the material world is seen the indestructible, and in the perishable, the imperishable.

Man can perceive this; but for this perception he requires Something, which makes the subjective perceptible to him. This Something is the inner Light, or that soul power bringing sight as the outer light entails visibility to the outer eye.

This soul power is unknown as Light to man, so long as he is not born of God, that is, so long as he regards things in his own mind and that of nature, and not in the Divine. If he begins to regard God in his spirit he perceives that God is outside all space and time, place and movement, and that nevertheless something must be in God, which moves and arranges space, time, place and all; this something is the Word, the Wisdom and Glory of God, and this Word is no ideal being, but something real, in which the Divine united with the human in the purest form, the transcendental united with the carnal, the spiritual united with the bodily, bringing about:

The receptibility of the Divine in the human;

The capability of the elevation of the carnal man to the transcendental;

The capability of the material to glorify itself in the spiritual.

A SINGULAR DREAM.

TRANSLATED FROM THE SWEDISH BY MRS. HAIG.

Taken from "Reminiscences of Wisby," by Professor Bergman.

ON a warm and lovely Sunday afternoon, of twenty years ago, I was invited to be present at a christening, which took place in the house of a highly respected family in the ancient town of Wisby. After the baptismal rites had with all due solemnity been performed, the guests wandered aimlessly through the capacious rooms, and endeavoured to while away the time in the usual manner with conversation and coffee-drinking. Many, however, found this kind of entertainment exceedingly uninteresting, and it certainly seemed almost too trying that the whole of such a beautiful summer afternoon should be passed within doors in warm and crowded rooms.

In one of the window recesses, where I had seated myself, I found Madame X., a pleasant, elderly lady. We tried to keep up a conversation, but somehow or other it seemed to flag, and for the greater part of the time we sat silent, looking out of the window, envying the passers-by, who, free and untroubled, were enjoying the balmy air and the sunshine.

"Yes, it certainly seems a pity," said Madame X., "to sit indoors on a day like this."

I agreed with her. There was another pause. Presently my neighbour began as if she had just remembered something.

"By the way, Professor, I know that you have a wonderful amount of knowledge concerning these old ruined churches in which our town abounds, and you can no doubt tell me the name of that particular church which is situated close to the yard of Vendt the dyer, and also if there is more than one entrance into it?"

"It is St. Lars," I replied, "and according to an ancient saga it is also called the Southern Sister Church. You can enter it from Vendt's yard through the choir-door, as the big west doors are at present barred by gratings. But why do you ask?"

"Well, I am almost ashamed to confess that I have never been there; I have no time to examine these old ruins which visitors find so interesting."

"But why in the world do you enquire so especially about St. Lars?"

"It came accidentally into my thoughts," she said hesitatingly and with some embarrassment, which she sought to hide by hastily thrusting into her hand-bag a saffron cake and a couple of small biscuits which she had not eaten with her coffee.

"Have you heard, Professor, that Herr A. and Mademoiselle B. are engaged?" she enquired, evidently with the purpose of completely changing the subject.

"Be so good as to tell me," I persistently continued, "why you so recently questioned me concerning St. Lars? In some way it must have particularly interested you, I imagine. I am well acquainted with all its nooks and corners, and any information I can give on the subject is completely at your service. Be candid and tell me what has happened to direct your thoughts so particularly to that ruin."

I observed instantly that she was most reluctant to continue the subject, but I became all the more curious, and urgently repeated my question. At last she said: "If you will promise to be silent, Professor, I will relate to you something very strange concerning that church."

"I will be as silent as a stone, I promise you, since you desire it."

Then Madame X. drew her chair nearer to mine, and in a low voice she began: "Last night it happened that I dreamed of that church, which, as I have told you, I have never entered. From Vendt's yard I came into it, through a curious little door. Everything around me seemed gloomy and awful. I stood for awhile and looked about, when suddenly a monk attired in a black gown came towards me and took me by the hand. I was not in the least afraid. He led me forward between two pillars, and then turning to the right we went through a doorway, and mounted some steps in the wall. In the corner of the stairway the monk stopped, and with a glance which I can never forget, he laid his hand upon a stone in the wall. And this stone was cut differently from the others. Just as I was about to ask him the meaning of this, he vanished up the stairway which curved to the left—and I awoke. Now, was it not a curious dream? Professor, do you think it can mean anything? Could there possibly be some treasure lying concealed in the wall?"

"I have very little belief in either visions or dreams," I answered, "but I cannot deny that what you have just related seems peculiarly strange. Madame, you observed previously that it was a pity to sit indoors during such a lovely evening. Now, I suggest that we instantly go to St. Lars; it is close at hand—we can be back again in a quarter of an hour. The tea is just being served, so no one will remark that we are away."

Madame X. seemed altogether charmed with my suggestion, so we wandered off to St. Lars' Church.

This church, which is erected in the Romanesque style, is in the form of a cross, and is now considered one of the most venerable ruins the town possesses. The very unusual arrangement with broad and spacious passages in nearly all the side walls, which have wide openings into the church itself, invests this ruined temple with a particular adaptability which has caused it upon several solemn and festive occasions to become the scene of beautiful and interesting dramatic and musical representations. From Vendt's yard, or garden, we entered the church through the formerly exquisite little choir-door, and I then began to observe closely and with great attention the countenance and the actions of my companion.

"Yes, yes," she cried, with unfeigned astonishment. "It looked precisely like this. The same small windows, and open arches, and the same mysterious duskiness, and here—*here* it was that the monk came towards me, and then we went forward. I recognize these pillars, then to the right—see here! The entrance to the stairway up which we went—precisely as it was in my dream!"

She hurried eagerly up the flight of steps in the eastern side wall of the right arm of the cross and I followed closely behind her. In the corner where the stairway curved to the left she stopped, and exclaimed with unconcealed delight: "Here, here is the stone upon which the monk laid his hand. Yes! it is the same stone—

and there, further up the steps, he vanished. Oh! what am I to think of all this?"

What she really did think in the matter was only too apparent, for her eyes were glistening like fire in the darkness of that narrow stairway. She seemed already to see in anticipation the wall open and disclose to view the shining and costly hidden treasure of the ancient sanctuary. The stone to which she pointed was completely unlike the other roughly-cut blocks of freestone of which the wall was built, by its regular rectangular form, and its obliquely cut corners.

"Yes, in truth," I observed,. "this begins to look serious and requires investigation. As I said before, I have but little faith in dreams, but neither is it possible totally to disregard them and their probable prophetic meaning. Listen to me, Madame X.," I continued when we were again in the church, "something ought to be done. This is my advice. You and I must get hold of a reliable mason, who must come here with us at a fitting time, bringing with him the tools necessary to move out that stone. Anything that may possibly lie hidden beneath or behind it, will belong to you—to you—and to no one else. If you find anything valuable, you shall pay the mason; if you do not find anything, then I will defray the expense. But one positive condition I must insist upon, that the possible treasure, in case it should possess any rare value, and of whatever metal or stuff it may be composed, must by you be handed over to the crown, so that it may be purchased for the State collection. It will certainly in this way be better paid for than if you take it to a goldsmith. You will receive the whole of the prize-money, and I shall most probably have the pleasure of seeing rare and curious antiques, and be privileged to rescue them from being destroyed in crucibles and melting-pans."

Madame X. received my advice with much gratitude. She could not sufficiently value my good-will and sympathy. She would soon send me a message fixing the time when together we should undertake the mysterious task of searching for the possible treasure.

"But the whole of the prize-money will be mine?" she repeated questioningly, as if further to be perfectly certain of my meaning, and her voice at the same time was trembling with hope and joy.

"The whole, the whole of it will naturally be yours," I sincerely and solemnly assured her. After this we silently shook hands, thus sealing our compact.

We quickly made our way back again to the house where we were guests. The tea was still going on, and no one had remarked our absence. When the company dispersed after supper, and bade one another farewell, Madame X. came over to me, and curtseying said meaningly, "Thanks, Professor, for good companionship."

"Remember your promise," I whispered in answer, "and send me word when it is convenient, but on that occasion you must take with you something rather more capacious than that little hand-bag, for indeed you may have something much more weighty to take home with you than saffron cake and sweet biscuits."

Without being annoyed at my nonsense, she nodded with a pleased familiarity, heartily squeezed my hand, and we both went our way.

. . . .

Owing to the many pleasant diversions which occupied the summer visitors to our town of Wisby, and in which I had often the pleasure of sharing, I altogether forgot during the following days all about Madame X. and her dream.

But very shortly afterwards I had occasion one day to take some visitors to see St. Lars, and when making the usual tour through its extraordinary passages, on coming to the before-mentioned corner on the stairway—what did I see?—the mysterious stone had vanished, and in the wall appeared an opening so large that a considerable amount of substantial treasure might very well have been concealed there. I must confess that I felt tremendously staggered as I stood and peeped into the opening, around all the sides of which I could easily pass my arm.

In my indignation I sought to ascertain if by any possibility some trace might have been left behind of the dreamed-of treasure. But nothing remained—it was quite empty.

The same afternoon I took the opportunity of calling upon Madame X., and prepared myself to take her soundly to task about her broken promise. When I entered she appeared much embarrassed; she guessed my errand.

"So," I began, "Madame has nicely kept her word! You have been to St. Lars, and you have had that stone removed without in any way informing me. Perhaps you will be so good as to tell me what you have found, and permit me to see it."

"You must not be offended with me, Professor," she began in an almost beseeching tone, "but I could not possibly keep myself from relating the dream to my husband, who returned home from a journey in the country the day after you and I had met at the christening. He thought in this way—that my dream concerned no one else but ourselves. We went together, and a workman accompanied us; he had a great deal of trouble in moving the stone, but before Heaven I assure you," and then she continued in a rather faltering voice, "that as true as I am a sinful creature, there was not anything to be found there, except some old rags and ropes. May I die on the spot if every word is not as true as the day. You must believe me, Professor, there was hardly as much as—*that*," and she swept her long thin hands past each other with such force, that a gold ring from her left hand fell with an ominous clatter on the floor.

"And that means," I hastily replied, "that there was gold in the treasure trove—if I am to take you at your word, and understand aright the significance of that gold ring. But why cannot you place confidence in me? I will not deprive you of any part of your treasure."

But she only continued her protestations of denial, in still stronger terms. Her extreme vehemence appeared to me, however, to be somewhat strained and unreal, and my suspicions were awakened thereby, but there was no possible evidence or proof. Before I left I gave her to understand that as she had broken her promise to me, I no longer considered myself bound to keep silence on the subject. If, in consequence of this remarkable dream, she really found any treasure or not, I am not able to state, but it is to be observed that a short time after this Monsieur and Madame X. commenced a great alteration and restoration of their house, and a certain amount of affluence began to reveal itself more and more in their way of living. But the money for all this might certainly have come from some other source. The only facts, therefore, which are absolutely certain and true in this little story are—its leading characteristics, the description of the dream, and the unquestionable confirmation of its meaning proved by our visit to this romantic and mysterious ruin.

REALITY IN THEOSOPHY.

It has often been observed that this is an age of shams. Through all the sections into which life is subdivided there appears an element of unreality, a trace of pervading tendency to gloss or plate or conceal. Society seems artificial, not in the sense merely that it is far removed from natural promptings and ways, but in the sense that it is constructed on fictitious lines and sounds hollow when sharply tapped by the statesman or the philosopher. We note this everywhere.

Business rests on a credit system which is insecure and which crumbles rapidly when even a small part gives way; and business methods are supposed impracticable unless made plausible with some outlay of allurement or misrepresentation. All through the operations of commerce runs a practice of adulteration, inaccuracy, trickery, even fraud. That a merchant should be successful only from honesty and thrift seems to a large part of the community an antiquated idea, quite impossible of realization in existing times.

Journalism reeks with humbug. Anything is held legitimate which will increase circulation and income. Facts are believed valueless unless flavoured to whet the palate of the populace, and, when facts are wanting, inventions fill their place. To apologize for an error committed is to a journalist a weakness, one which would impair his reputation for consistency and any future confidence in his assertions. Papers are made to sell, and must be pleasing to those who buy; and so, the popular taste being for the striking and the minute, vigorous imaginations dispense with conscience, and the interviewer who has intruded into family affairs is aided by the engraver who draws solely upon his fancy.

Politics are almost avowedly insincere. Platforms are framed to catch votes, not to express policies, and he who is most adroit in popularizing himself has most chance for the office he desires. A contest of principles has degenerated into a game of skill,

The professions, too, follow steadily the prevailing mode. Medicine has long caused suspicion by its professed knowledge and its actual empiricism, for even the gullible public have seen that there is much more of experiment and guess-work than of wisdom in its professors.

Law has become a by-word for uncertainty. Not only do judges rival each other in frivolous distinctions which discard all right and justice, but counsel undertake cases which they know to be wrong, and consider only the professional *éclat* which will follow the rescue of a scoundrel from his deserts or the acquisition of a property from its owners.

In the general decadence of the moral sense so deplored by the loftier spirits of the age, a decadence which so greatly exhibits itself in habituation to unreality and sham as if normal instead of aberrant, it is inevitable that the clerical order should share. Priests, like laymen, are the product of their time, born, trained, surrounded by the same social atmosphere and thought, hearing the same ideas, influenced by the same environment, stimulated by the same forces. From childhood accustomed to certain universally-held axioms, these sway them alike with their parishioners, for the views of life which pervade the schoolroom and the parlour and the college, pervade also the theological seminary, and ordination does not dislodge or change them.

Of course the influence of books and professors impresses a certain conventional tone, and the unquestionable sincerity of most men who enter the ministry ensures a generally higher grade of conscience and a more earnest purpose to adhere to it; but these facts are to some extent offset by two others, the artificial relation held to laymen by the members of the clerical caste, and the temptation to duplicity arising from the growth of new thought conflicting either with an inflexible creed or with the prejudices of the flock who maintain the shepherd. Thus finer aspirations become dulled under the pressure of society and the pews, and current maxims assert themselves in the parsonage as in the counting-house.

It is no utterance of a cynic or an infidel to assert that the convictions of the average clergyman are in striking antithesis to those recorded of the Founder of his religion. The latter were incisive if they were anything. They went straight down to the root of all thought and all life, waived glosses and surface indications aside as of absolutely no worth, made reality the final test in every case, upheld genuineness as the *sine quâ non* to any identification with true religion.

No matter how orthodox the views or how full the purse, no matter how copious the benefactions or how public the prayers, if the life did not comport with the professions, and if claim and fact did not correspond, all was valueless. Men might call him Lord, Lord, with effusive homage; it was of no consequence so long as they did not do what He said.

But surely this is not the attitude of the pulpit as we know it. Sinners who contribute largely to missions or generously maintain the denominational apparatus have ever the kindly eye of their pastor; sermons are toned down if sure to hit some conspicuous parishioner; friends are readily made with the mammon of unrighteousness. If the Sermon on the Mount was preached instead of read, how many incumbents would retain their cures!

And so it has come to pass that the flavour of unreality which is so noticeable in the markets and counting-rooms and the professional offices pervades the churches no less, and that everywhere in society reform must come if men are to awake to truth and give it efficacy in their lives. Transformation is needed in each department of the social system, a transformation which shall turn sham into genuineness, pretence into actuality, which shall give solidity and soundness and endurance where has been a weak imitation or a beguiling fraud.

There are two respects in which Theosophy, as the avowed regenerator of individuals and society, manifests the requisites exacted for such a mission. The first is in the truths it enforces. Nothing of reform can possibly be effected in any region unless all the facts contained in it are known, the principles and laws thoroughly perceived, the actual problems precisely grasped. Mere theorizing will almost certainly divert into fantasy, and so ensure loss of strength, as also an increase of the very difficulties already so vast. To attain a workable prescription the real nature of the undertaking must be ascertained, and every fact given its value in the whole.

Theosophy looks over the entire field of human activity, and then propounds the treatment which alone can be effectual because it alone recognizes all the items in the case. First of all it seizes the great truth that the whole universe is one vast organism, no one part isolated or managed on different principles from the rest, but all connected and inter-related, all under common law and responding equally to like impressions.

It never for a moment supposes that this earth is a domain walled-off from the remainder of the cosmos, or that man is a unique being who has a distinct set of rules and experiences imposed as an arbitrary whim, or that human life and character are to be handled without reference to the universal scheme; but unifies the whole cosmic order, relegates earth to its place therein, treats humanity as an inherent and necessary factor in the entire equation. All regions and spheres and forces and laws contribute to man's make-up and maintain his connection, and there is no content of the universe with which he is not in touch and influence.

Of course this different handling makes short work of the theologies and philosophies which separate the world and its inhabitants from the rest of space, and which concoct strange theories and stranger destinies for both. Fictitious, arbitrary inventions drop away when once is seen the essential unity of all that is, for then becomes apparent a harmony of design and purpose and operation, humanity fitting into its place and Divinity manifesting throughout. Order supplants caprice, union succeeds to dislocation, fancy gives way to fact.

When Theosophy has thus restored universal connection to all the planes of being, it proceeds to exhibit the common laws which everywhere prevail. Evolution, not in the restricted sense accepted by the science of the day, is displayed as the grand process of the whole cosmos. The idea germinal in the Divine mind works itself out by the Divine power, beginnings of manifestation being crude and elementary, their onward development slow to inconceivability, yet steadily advancing through centuries and ages and æons.

Very gradually thought-forms take visible shape, primeval matter becomes more dense and plastic, worlds and beings come slowly into existence. Each is adapted to the other, for a common impulse pushes forward their advance. All, too, proceed under laws which rule steadily, inflexibly throughout. There is not one regulation for the solar system and another for a system beyond, not one rule for this earth and a different one for Venus or Saturn, not one administration for us men and a second for planetary beings. The method of evolution is all-pervading, and stages in the process both exhibit and demonstrate its unity.

Two of those laws are that no stage can be passed until its possibilities are thoroughly worked up, and that no force disappears till it has exhausted its energy. These two laws explain why the evolutionary process is so exceedingly prolonged in its operations, and also why the complications are so intricate and far-reaching. Focussing them upon human life, Theosophy shows them as epitomizing its philosophy. For the fact that no stage can be left till the working-up of its contents is completed necessitates the appearance over and over again in earth-life of everyone who has once begun a career in matter; and the fact that force continues till it is spent necessitates all the physical and moral experiences which such a pilgrim undergoes while he is creating force and returning here to receive its consequences.

Thus two of the laws most conspicuous in the cosmic order take visible shape in human affairs as reincarnation and karma. Reincarnation expresses the truth that we cannot advance to a mode of existence apart from flesh till we have used up all the multiform lessons which a fleshly embodiment ensures, but must continue on and on in a succession of incarnations upon earth until the soul has extracted therefrom every element of value.

Karma expresses the truth that the forces we have aroused by thought, word and deed cannot die without result, but of necessity give birth to their effects, which effects fall upon us through incarnations until their vitality is expended and ends. Thus Theosophy applies to our career the principles which inhere in the universe at large, and shows our essential identification with all being by our absolute identification with the process everywhere else so clear.

But there are further truths which this great philosophy elucidates. We men are not mere machines, puppets through which the forces of Nature resistlessly work. We are endowed with free-will, the prerogative of choice, and the character of the evolution each makes is determined by himself alone. True, the operation of all these forces is towards establishment of good, for they ceaselessly tend to moral results, their pressure upon each individual being to incline him to the true way.

The one great lesson blazoned on every experience of happiness through right, and sorrow through wrong, is that it is to one's interest not less than one's duty to adhere to right, and this lesson, iterated and reiterated countless times in incarnation after incarnation, naturally may impress itself on that permanent part of our being which reincarnates.

It is ingrained in the constitution of things that the evolutionary trend should be upwards. Yet by no means does this trend override individual preference, and force to a spirituality which is not desired. That would indeed be a strange moral system which constrained people to be good whether they wished to be or not, and with iron hand twisted tastes and preferences into conformity with one type. Nothing of the kind exists, as we know full well.

We ourselves are conscious that it is possible either to harmonize with the sweet influences inciting us to elevating purpose, or to waive them aside that we may indulge the fancies which at the moment are more congenial. In fact, the very existence around us of characters with every shade of colour and degree of strength proves that each has unfolded as it chose.

Now the truth upheld by Theosophy is this double one of entire freedom of action coupled with a pressure from experiences of life to make that action right. And so Theosophy comes to men with a very clear utterance on the most vital question of existence. It says that the thousand incidents of every day are not accidental, nor are they meaningless. They have not come about without causes, as if they were mere fortuitous events which had no antecedents and may have no results, but are the consequents of forces we ourselves set in motion. And they are not meaningless, for each contains the spur to a higher quality of action which shall impel both the character and its experience to a loftier plane.

Thus Theosophy says to us, "You are and you shall be what you make yourselves. But it is better for your well-being and your happiness that you make of yourselves the finest possible future, and this you can do if you honestly take to heart the lesson of each event befalling you in life, conforming your thought and motive thereto. Moreover, the constitution of things being as it is, and the purport of all these events being towards right, you are sure that your conformity brings you more and more into harmony with the universe of which you are part, ensures safety, confidence, joy, dispels misgivings and annuls risks. Incline your free-will to prefer what all reason and all experience commend, and then you will surmount not only doubt, but disaster and suffering as well."

And still further. Theosophy is not a juiceless array of ethical texts. It does not provide a dry moral code or an unillustrated chart of progress. Such would be all very well, but would lack the vivid interest of distinct illustration. In fact, however, Theosophy shows just what a code of ethics can produce when fully carried out, just what is the result of a true system of manly development perfectly effectuated.

For it displays to us the Masters, those highly evolved men who have harmonized themselves with the whole Divine plan, and have steadily emerged, incarnation after incarnation, from the weaknesses and evils of ordinary humanity. In a long, orderly process, each stage expressing some advance in self-control or added power, every incident of life receiving its just interpretation and bearing its proper fruit, the Master was formed. The very essence of him was utter identification with nature and her designs.

In no respect did he resemble those strangely distorted beings, the canonized saints of later Christendom. These saints are unpleasant to contemplate. Their pose is artificial, there is a cadaverous odour, even their virtues repel, the whole of human instinct rises in protest against imitation. Even if their powers can be verified, they seem to have been unaccompanied by wisdom, for the devotional and emotional side of human constitution had absorbed all care, and none was left for study of fact or evolution of judgment. There was no wisdom in throwing away all one's property indiscriminately among the poor, for that use of it only stimulated idleness and pauperism; none in the multiplication of self-torments and tedious prayers, for they neither sweetened the spirit nor strengthened it for service; none in an asceticism, solitude, discipline which was altogether arbitrary, had no scientific reason or method, and was undergone merely because it was disagreeable. Knowledge came through none of the practices which covered the life—not even self-knowledge, for true knowledge of self must include the possibilities within, not merely a partial cognizance of its actualities.

And so the mediæval saint is neither a loveable being nor a wise one. He may have a zeal for Divine and spiritual things but only on one line. All the universe exhibits God, displays His nature in its many aspects; and he who would have any rounded conception of the Divine, must understand the material world and the social world and the psychic world and the spiritual world. This is not done by starving the body and repeating prayers, nor can it be accomplished save through earnest study and a nature pervious at every point to truth.

With these cramped and artificial saints, so unwholesome in mind and body, the Masters of Theosophy have little more in common than earnestness and devotion. For they have expended energy not only on aspiration, but on direct study of every section of the accessible universe. To knowledge of facts they added wisdom in their use.

The subjugation of the body was, indeed, a necessity, and so a certain well-directed asceticism was undergone; yet this was not as a self-torment pleasing to God, but as a freeing from carnalities binding down the soul. Nor were self and its achievements ever the stimulus to the course, for the whole purport of the disciple's struggle was emancipation from that separate interest which is the curse of humanity and the bar to its advance. At every stage that was to be wrestled with and put beneath, and only as larger thought emerged did the ideal become distinct.

To copious study of the seven-planed cosmos whereof man is the epitome they added as copious study of man himself, thus learning all the relations and interactions of the two. Germinal faculties were slowly developed, a systematic unfoldment of all latent power went on, constant work for others broadened both the sympathies and the means to utilize them. Thus in every section of his nature the incipient Master brought about a realization of the Divine plan, and when the issue was far enough advanced he took his place among the Elder Brothers of humanity, those who are its leaders and friends and aids. The chart is not unillustrated, for Masters are the living evidence of how to progress and what the outcome is.

I said that there are two respects in which Theosophy, as the avowed regenerator of individuals and society, manifests the requisites exacted for such a mission; and that the first is in the truths it enforces. Now the second is in the spirit it enjoins. This spirit is one eminently of reality. Theosophy probes down to the very centre of the being, and insists that any unsoundness there shall be utterly corrected, for only as the motive is pure can right consequences follow.

This central motive, that which is to determine all the quality of the career, has a two-fold aspect. Behind it lies an assured conviction that the evolutionary scheme decreed by the Supreme is wise and should be conformed to. From this conviction, accepted alike by the intellect and the moral sense, springs the double motive. One is that the man himself shall earnestly strive that his whole nature, in each of its departments, may adjust itself to the law and in accordance therewith be developed onward to perfection. The other is that the end of such development is not personal gratification, or even the attainment of personal success, but ability to co-operate the better in the great purpose of enlightening and saving humanity. In short, the spirit which Theosophy dictates is an intense desire to become precisely what Divine Wisdom has decreed, and to become it that the race too may be upborne.

This may seem in part a little unreal. It is quite conceivable that anyone may wish conformity to a sanctioned ideal, for certainly no better outcome can be surmised than that which expresses the thought of the Divine Mind. No one would have the folly, not to say temerity, to suppose that he has a finer conception of evolutionary possibilities than had Almighty God. So there is no great strain upon anyone in admitting that the progressive course of a human being up to Divinity itself is entirely worthy; and when that fact is clearly perceived, the further step of honestly desiring it for oneself may well be near. But to desire it less for oneself than as a means to aid the race sounds as an exaggeration of unselfishness, rather an altruistic affectation than a sober choice.

Yet is it? We know, of course, that ordinary human activities are spurred by the principle of emulation. Men strive for money or conspicuity, because of the wish to surpass others, and behind all the commercial and social and political machinery is the hope of each participant that he may succeed because it is nice to succeed. Indeed, economical science holds that without this impulsion of the individual to struggle for his own advantage there would be no advance of the community, no increase of commerce and wealth and general good.

Doubtless this is true, for in nations destitute of tense, wide-awake energy in each citizen, there is a common torpor upon business and society, generation succeeds generation without progress being made, national life and public spirit sleep. The competitive principle has its evils, but it certainly arouses all powers to their fullest vitality, makes possible the enormous growth of business enterprises distinguishing the era, and indirectly sends comfort and conveniences to the dwellings of the poorest. We often read undiscriminating tirades against this principle, and yet but for it how could individual genius blossom, capacity and industry receive their due reward, communities rise in mental and social quality, human power over nature be extended? Surely it is not upon a wise and indispensable impulse that we should frown, but upon that misuse of it which destroys sympathy and co-operation, sacrifices all else to itself, and multiplies sorrow everywhere around its seat.

Then there is the restless search for pleasure. It has all forms and all varieties, physical and mental, and is of every grade of delicacy and refinement. Yet the instinct for happiness is natural, and the wish to be happy is not unworthy. Happiness is a beautiful thing, salutary, uplifting; and to be in harmony with the sunlight of nature rather than with its clouds and gloom is truly human. Men have erred, not in desire for happiness, but in the sources where they sought it. The Ego within, the real individuality where peace abides, cannot be satisfied with pleasures proffered by the senses or the emotions, but demands food consonant with its own nature, that which shall be healthful and fine and permanent. And as it is a spark from the central fire, an emanation from the great centre of all life, it is a part of the universal organism, no isolated entity to be sustained and kept aloof by separate joys, but only in true harmony and health when in union with all else that lives. Hence search for its sole benefit must ever fail; the soul which aims and struggles and competes simply that it may have its fill, loses of necessity its hold on the common good which alone can meet the wants of each integer of the whole. Selfishness is self-destructive; happiness sought simply for oneself ever eludes the grasp.

Moreover, there is another fact. Aside from the solidarity of humanity which forbids separation from it to result in joy, there is that beautiful ordinance of nature that the finest satisfactions come from altruistic effort. We all know, for perhaps there is no one who has not in his best moments experienced it, that there is a sweet serenity, a broad and generous glow, when we have handed over to another something we well prized ourselves, and have seen the pleasure it has brought. That was a fuller sensation, a deeper thrill, than the joy of self-indulgence. But if a single experience illustrated the fact, it also demonstrated it. That one case in the history of any life made certain the truth of richer pleasure from altruism than from selfishness, and established the broad generalization that men attain the highest happiuess as they confer happiness on others.

What, then, would seem to be the ideal of a rational, scientific, devotional ambition? In other words, what is that motive which is in accord with all the facts of human nature and ot philosophy, and which is therefore the commended of Theosophy? Simply this: that the individual shall make of himself all that can be made, that he shall struggle to attain the highest evolutionary possibilities, that he shall do this in order that he may co-operate fully in the grand general scheme, and thus, through the generosity of a widened sympathy, find the perfection of a thorough happiness. "He that loseth his life shall save it": how true is the philosophy of this axiom!

ALEXANDER FULLERTON.

THE CONFESSION OF TRITHEMIUS.

From "Traité des Causes Secondes."

TRANSLATED BY A. A. WELLS.

GOD is an essential and hidden fire, which dwells in all things and chiefly in Man. From this fire is everything engendered. It engenders them and will for ever engender them; and what is engendered is the true Divine Light which exists from all eternity. God is a Fire; but no Fire can burn, no Light can manifest itself in Nature without the presence of Air to maintain the combustion; thus the Holy Spirit should act within us as a Divine Air or Breath, causing a breath to spring from the Divine Fire upon the interior Fire of the heart so that the Light may appear, for the Light must be fed by the fire, and this Light is love, bliss and joy in the eternal Divinity. This Light is JESUS, who emanates for all eternity from JEHOVAH. Whoever does not possess this Light within him is plunged into a fire without light; but if this Light is within him, then the CHRIST is in him, is incarnate within him, and he will know the Light as it exists in Nature.

All things we behold are interiorly fire and light, in which is hidden the essence of the Spirit. All things are a Trinity of fire, light and air. In other words the Spirit (the Father) is a superessential light; the Son is the Light manifested; the Holy Spirit is a moving Breath, divine and superessential. This Fire dwells in the heart and sends out its rays all through the body, and thus maintains its life. But no Light arises from the Fire without the presence of the spirit of sanctity.

. . . . .

All things have been made by the power of the Divine Word, which is the Spirit or Divine Breath emanated from the beginning from the Divine fountain. This Breath is the Spirit or Soul of the World, and is called *Spiritus Mundi*. It was at first like air, then condensed into a nebulous substance or fog, and finally transmuted itself into water. (Fr. trans. "the Âkâsha of the Hindoos.") This water was at first spirit and life, because it was impregnated and vivified by the Spirit. Darkness filled the abyss, but by the emission of the Word the Light was engendered, the darkness was illuminated by the Light and the Soul of the World (Fr. trans. "The Astral Light") was born. This spiritual Light which we call Nature or Soul of the World is a spiritual body which may be rendered visible and tangible by alchemical processes; but as it is naturally invisible it is called Spirit.

It is a living universal fluid, diffused throughout Nature, and which penetrates everything. It is the most subtle of all substances; the most powerful, by reason of its inherent qualities; it penetrates every body, and determines the forms in which it displays its activity. By its action it frees the forms from all imperfection; it makes the impure pure, the imperfect perfect, the mortal immortal, by its indwelling.

This essence or Spirit emanated from the beginning from the Centre, and incorporated itself with the substance of which the Universe is formed. It is the "*Salt of the Earth*," and without its presence the plant would not grow, nor the field become green, and the more this essence is condensed, concentrated and coagulated in the forms the more stable they become. It is the most subtle of all substances; incorruptible and immoveable in its essence, it fills the infinities of space. The sun and planets are but coagulations of this universal principle; from their beating heart they distribute the abundance of their life, and send it forth into the forms of the inferior world, and into all creatures, acting about their own centre and raising the forms on the way of perfection. The forms in which this living principle establishes itself become perfect and durable, so that they no longer decay nor deteriorate nor change in contact with the air; water can no longer dissolve them, nor fire destroy them, nor the terrestrial elements devour them.

This Spirit is obtained in the same way as it is communicated to the earth by the stars; and this is performed by means of the Water, which serves as vehicle to it. It is not the Philosopher's Stone, but this may be prepared from it by fixing the volatile.

I advise you to pay great attention to the boiling of the Water;

do not let your spirit be troubled about things of less importance. Make it boil slowly, then let it putrefy till it has attained the fitting colour, for the Water of Life contains the germ of wisdom. In boiling, the water will transform itself into earth. This earth will change into a pure crystalline fluid which will produce a fine red Fire; and this Water and this Fire, reduced to a single Essence, produce the great Panacea composed of sweetness and strength—the Lamb and the Lion united.

THEOSOPHICAL ACTIVITIES.

EUROPEAN SECTION.

The activities of this Section are usually not many at this period of the year, and several of the most prominent workers are absent, Mr. Mead in Holland and Miss Cooper in Sweden. Mr. Leadbeater is in the North of England visiting the Branches there and attending the Confederation.

Mrs. Cooper-Oakley will leave for Germany and Russia towards the end of August, after the return of Mr. Mead, and will visit a number of places, paying especial attention to the libraries, in which she will spend much of her time.

The Blavatsky Lodge is closed during August, and a large proportion of the other English Branches has adopted the same course.

AMERICAN SECTION: MRS. BESANT'S TOUR.

CHICAGO, July 14th.—A run of over twenty hours from Sheridan brought us early on Saturday morning, June 19th, to Grand Island, Nebraska. Mrs. Besant lectured that evening and the next day passed on to Lincoln, whilst the Countess went direct to Chicago. In spite of the want of air in the Lincoln Universalist Church it was packed both on Sunday and Monday, and the drawing-room meetings at Mrs. Holmes' were also crowded. Some people joined the Society, and a class was forming when we left on Tuesday for Omaha, where Dr. and Mrs. Jensen made their hospitable house our home, and in many ways proved their strong interest in the Theosophical Society. A reception was held for Mrs. Besant by a prominent Woman's Club in Omaha the same afternoon, and that evening and the evening following, lectures on "Man, the Master of his Destiny" and "Theosophy and its Teachings" were delivered in the Opera House to a fair audience, thinned by the heat, which had driven all who could go from the town to the country.

On Friday evening, after an afternoon parlour talk, Mrs. Besant crossed the Missouri river on the electric car line and lectured in Council Bluffs, returning with Dr. and Mrs. Jensen to Omaha for the night; the next afternoon we left for Chicago, feeling sure that before long the small Lodge she had formed in Omaha would attract to itself some of the more thoughtful people of the town, and become a strong and useful centre of work.

On Saturday, June 26th, we reached the goal of the first half of our journey—Chicago—and were conducted to the rooms of the Theosophical Society in Van Buren Street, where a reception was given in the evening to Mrs. Besant and the Countess. The next morning, Sunday, June 27th, the American Section held its annual Convention. Many delegates and members were present, and the other Sections were represented either by delegates, or letters and telegrams of greeting. Mr. Fullerton called the Convention to order shortly after ten o'clock and Mr. George Wright was elected its chairman.

Mr. Chidester extended a warm welcome to the foreign delegates, and Mrs. Besant, after a sketch of the work in India and Europe, spoke of the new literature, which is of such value to the usefulness of the Society, and laid stress upon the duty of members to perfect themselves in a knowledge of the fundamental teachings of Theosophy, that they may be ready to give help to those who enquire. "No movement that is ignorant *can* live," she said, "and no movement that is ignorant *ought* to live. The Masters are the Masters of Compassion, but they are Masters of Wisdom as well."

The General Secretary's report showed great increase in the Society, and in the discussion which followed it was remarked that much of the new membership was due to the long travels of the Countess Wachtmeister and to the present tour of Mrs. Besant. The Countess pointed out that this propaganda work was of great importance, and ways and means were discussed whereby lecturers could be found to go round to help the young Lodges in their studies, and to interest the public at large. One hundred dollars were voted from the treasury, the nucleus of a fund to be devoted to this purpose, and committees of propaganda will be formed in the various districts.

A committee likely to be productive of much good was one formed to draw up plans of study for the use of lodges, and to advise upon methods of work. Mrs. Besant was asked to give her aid in drawing up the plan, which considers the needs of young Lodges and also of more advanced students.

The necessity for a list of the names of people interested in Theosophy in the various towns of America was recognized, and volunteers were deputed to make it. Much time will be saved by such an arrangement, and all members are requested to help by sending in names.

Various other schemes to forward the movement were mooted, and some adopted, and others referred to committees for consideration. The support required to keep up *Mercury* was stated by the Count Axel Wachtmeister, who had acted for some time as editor, and could speak from personal knowledge of the financial strain upon Mr. Walters involved in the printing of the helpful little journal. It was pointed out by one member that a magazine which receives the support of the Section should be of first-rate ability and contain articles by the leading writers in the movement, so that the members would naturally subscribe to it to keep themselves in touch with the life of the Section.

After a busy day the Convention adjourned until the evening, when a public meeting was held in Steinway Hall, and addresses were given by Mr. George Wright, Mr. Fullerton, the Countess Wachtmeister, Mrs. Besant and others. The hall was tightly packed with people, who listened to the speakers with the greatest attention. When all was over the members congratulated each other on the great success of the Convention, and parted with the brightest hopes for the future of the American Section—hopes justified by the interest of the public, and by the presence in the chief cities throughout the land of earnest and devoted people whose one object is to help forward the great movement.

The following fortnight was one of incessant work, and it speaks well for the interest of the people that all classes, receptions, etc., were crowded, in spite of the fact that Chicago was suffering from a heat wave and the thermometer between 90° and 100° in the shade did not render close rooms attractive.

Mrs. Besant held morning classes for the instruction of members, and afternoon and evening receptions and lectures for the public, besides very many private interviews. The lectures were given in different parts of the town that all might have an opportunity to hear.

The attention shown was most encouraging and a great many new members joined one or other of the four Lodges already existing there; the Chicago Lodge, the Englewood White Lodge, the Shila, and the Eastern Psychology. There is much to be hoped for in the work of the next few years in Chicago. A. J. W.

Dutch Section.

The first Annual Convention of the Dutch Section was held at Amsterdam on Sunday, July 18th. On the Saturday evening a reception was held at the Headquarters, the rooms at 76, Amsteldijk being crowded. Mr. Mead, who had gone over to inaugurate the proceedings and represent the European Section, answered a number of questions on various subjects during the evening.

On Sunday the Convention was called to order in the Hall of the Werkenden Stand at 10 a.m. Mr. Mead, after conveying the greetings and congratulations of the European Section to the new Section, referred to the past history of the Society and its present strength and prosperity; he insisted that the real bond of the Society was one of mutual help in theosophical life and study, and not of legislature, and wound up by referring to the grand pioneer work of H. P. Blavatsky, its nature and character, on the lines of the remarks in our last "On the Watch-Tower." Mynheer W. B. Fricke was then chosen chairman of the Convention and Mynheer Wierts van Coehoorn read a report embodying a history of the Society in Holland. The officers of the new Section were all unanimously elected and were as follows:

General Secretary--W. B. Fricke; Treasurer—H. Wierts van Coehoorn; Executive Committee—the General Secretary and Treasurer, and Messrs. J. L. M. Lauweriks, F. J. B. van der Beek, S. Gazan, and Mevrouw Meuleman van Ginkel; Auditors—Messrs. A. Noteboom and Grundtke.

The main work of the Convention was the adoption of a constitution and rules; this occupied the major part of the morning and afternoon sessions, the recently revised rules of the European Section being finally adopted with hardly any alterations. The rest of the afternoon session was occupied with reports and suggestions. The two business meetings were very well attended and the proceedings followed with intelligence and interest. The evening meeting was packed; it was entirely devoted to speeches, the lecturers being Mr. Mead, Mrs. Windust, Mevrouw Meuleman and Mynheer Fricke. Monday afternoon and evening were also devoted to receptions and there was much conversation and answering of questions. The whole Convention was a decided success.

REVIEWS.

Sayings of Our Lord.

Discovered and Edited by Bernard P. Grenfell, M.A., and Arthur S. Hunt, M.A. [London: Henry Frowde; 1887. Price, boards, 2*s*. net.; paper, 6*d*. net.]

One single battered leaf of papyrus, and that is all. Yet how precious to the Western world, and how important for the history of the Gospel tradition! Some 120 miles south of Cairo is a small hamlet called Behnesa; there a series of low mounds marks the site of what was once the capital of the Oxyrhynchite nome, a flourishing city once when Rome held sway over the ancient land of Khem, and one of the chief centres of early Christianity in Egypt. Under the auspices of the Egyptian Exploration Fund, Messrs. Grenfell and Hunt have unearthed in the rubbish heaps of the town large quantities of papyrus, mostly Greek, embracing every variety of subject, and extending in date from the first to the eighth centuries. We hear of papyri of Homer, Æschylus, Thucydides, of some stanzas of Sappho, and much else of interest to the classical student, all of which will require much labour to edit, and the earliest specimens of uncial texts thus discovered will be of the first importance to palæography, and may perhaps decide several important points in the dating of the MSS. fragments of the first three centuries. But the most precious treasure in what is perhaps the richest deposit of papyri ever discovered, is a torn, tattered and defaced leaf, barely six inches by four. The importance of this, the earliest relic of Christian scripture, is so great that the discoverers have at once hastened to place it before the public. It is no less than a leaf of the Logia, or Sayings of the Lord, a copy of the Gospel-deposit of early Christendom, unadulterated with the later pseudo-historical settings.

All New Testament students are aware that the "starting-point in any discussion of the synoptic problem" is a single phrase in the Church History of Eusebius, quoted from the ancient worthy Papias (c. 150), namely, "Matthew wrote down the Logia in Hebrew, and everyone interpreted them as he was able." Most scholars have taken the word Logia to mean Sayings or Oracles, but a number of apologists of the canonical Gospels have denied this.

Our precious leaf of papyrus sets the question at rest for ever. The Logia are the Sayings of Jesus, and were so called quite naturally from the introductory formula before each Logion, "Jesus says." As we pore over the new treasure and scan every letter that can be deciphered, how simple and pure, how virgin of offensive exaggeration and symbolic mythology, seems this straightforward collection of Sayings; how easy is it to believe that such words were spoken by the Christ through the mouth of Jesus! And yet we have not the words themselves; they were spoken in Hebrew. Who translated them into Greek; or rather, when were they translated? We may with some certainty believe that this was not attempted until the time of Paul's fiery propaganda among the Gentiles. Prior to that the sacred deposit of Christianity was in the hands of the Hebrew nation alone. But for how long? As to this, history has as yet no word to offer. The present mythical dates are far from the truth.

The Sayings, then, which Jesus spake to the people during the short months of his public ministry, were collected first of all in Hebrew, apparently without order, and certainly with no admixture of narrative. Later they were translated into Greek; far later still, they were edited and re-edited by many hands with various and contradictory settings of legends; and finally, out of these numerous versions, the four canonical Gospels were chosen.

The fragment of the Greek Logia which has so strangely been preserved to us is of course a copy; but even so, it is, compared to the existing texts of the various books of the New Testament, of a very early date. The editors have of course to be exceedingly cautious for fear of bringing the whole swarm of orthodox critics about their ears. It cannot be later than 300 A.D., in fact it belongs to one of the earliest types of uncials used before this date. The editors are inclined to place it about 200 A.D., but there is nothing to show that it is not a century earlier. The papyri found near it belonged to the second and third centuries.

Our fragment originally contained eight Logia, four on the verso and four on the recto side, but the fourth and eighth are so damaged as to be entirely illegible.

Logion 1: ". . . and then shalt thou see clearly to cast out the mote that is in thy brother's eye."

This is exactly the same wording as in Luke vi. 42. The variant in

Matthew vii. 5, is easily accounted for by translation from the Hebrew.

Logion 2: "Jesus saith, Except ye fast to the world, ye shall in no wise find the Kingdom of God; and except ye keep the sabbath, ye shall not see the Father."

This is entirely new to the present Christian world. More important still, it is filled with the spirit of the great teacher who would have his hearers wean themselves from the letter of the Law which taught men to abstain from physical food and observe a certain day of the week, and turn them to the Wisdom of God.

"Moses taught you to fast and keep the sabbath, but *I* say unto you, Except ye fast *to the world*. . . . ." The Christ gives the higher Law of Wisdom. Here is one of those "dark sayings" which the "people" could not understand, but which the "disciples" could comprehend. Needless to say that such "fasting" formed the burden of all the best Gnostic teaching, and the same terminology is found in the letters of Paul and in the fourth Gospel. The "eternal sabbath" is also an idea easy enough for the theosophical student to grasp.

Logion 3: "Jesus saith, I stood in the midst of the world, and in the flesh was I seen of them, and I found all men drunkards, and none found I athirst among them, and my soul grieveth over the souls of men, because they are blind in heart."

This is also entirely new. Yet another "dark saying," but how luxurious with inner light! The men of the world are those who are plunged in the life of the senses, drunken with the intoxication of the delights of the world; none were athirst for the living God, not even when Jesus was there in person, "Jesus, the living one," he in whom the "Living Æon," the Logos, tabernacled for a space. Thus at any rate would a Gnostic have interpreted the saying.

Logion 5: "Jesus saith, wherever there are . . . and there is one . . . alone, I am with him. Raise the stone and there thou shalt find me, cleave the wood and there am I!"

This is also entirely new. The first part is mostly illegible; though it recalls the familiar text in Matt. xviii. 20, "For where two or three are gathered together," etc.; it is a further statement of the truth, namely, that the Christ is present even with the solitary believer. But the gem of the whole six Logia is indubitably the concluding paragraph, "Raise the stone and there thou shalt find me, cleave the wood and there am I." How simple and yet how graphic a way to instruct the simple minded in the marvellous truth that the Logos is everywhere, in all things, at all times! We wonder what the Shepherds of the Little Bethels of Christendom will have to say to this grand truth of universal religion. But what care they for the Logia! Even the scholarly editors have shied at the obvious meaning; the fear of the Lord of theology is evidently upon them.

Logion 6: "Jesus saith, a prophet is not acceptable in his own country, neither doth a physician work cures upon them that know him."

It is to be remarked that in Logion 1 and Logion 6, the readings confirm Luke and not the other synoptics. This is a not unimportant fact, and should be borne in mind by those who remember that the text of Luke was very like that of the Gospel which Marcion said he had received from Paul, who, he declared, alone understood Jesus. The second half of the Logion is new, and seems to imply that the physician of those days used other means than drugs for the cure of his patients, in which means the faculty of belief entered largely.

Logion 7: "Jesus saith, a city built upon the top of a high hill, and stablished, can neither fall nor be hid."

This is an expanded form of one of the verses in the collection of Sayings in the first synoptic, called "The Sermon on the Mount."

So many and of such a nature then are the few sayings preserved on our scrap of papyrus, the most precious document of Christendom.

The unearthing of this fragment permits us to hope that, even at this late date, some real historical light may be shed on the origins of the great religion of the Western world. It proves once more that the nearer we get to those origins, the easier we find the burden placed upon our reason and intuition, and the more we find the truths enunciated to pertain to universal religion.

G. R. S. M.

Traité des Causes Secondes.

Bibliotheque Rosicrucienne, No I., by Jean Trithéme. [Paris: Chamuel; 1897.]

Wurzburg—Trithemius! It is not possible for any one who has known and loved Robert Browning's "Paracelsus" to hear these words without a pleasant recollection of Wurzburg,

> Which the Mayne
> Forsakes her course to fold as with an arm;

and of the class to which "Trithemius deigned to teach a portion of his lore." We are grateful to the editor of this little book for bringing them before us somewhat more clearly out of the mist of time, and hardly need the assurance of Éliphas Lévi, that Trithemius was the greatest dogmatic magician of the Middle Ages to add interest to it.

The biography prefixed presents him in the character so dear to mediæval times—the marvellous genius under the rule of the wicked relation (in this case the stepfather), breaking forth in spite of neglect and cruelty from childhood up; and when he has attained his ideal life—the headship of a monastery where he can surround himself with his beloved books—a reminiscence of Abelard and *his* monks intrudes itself. We do not hint a doubt of the *fact*—it must have happened many times over; but we cannot help a smile when we read that the German peasants whom he ruled found his efforts to civilize them very trying to *their* flesh and blood, and at last took the opportunity of his temporary absence to send him formal notice that their gates would not be opened for his return. After remonstrating in vain, the gentle scholar submitted to the inevitable, and thus we find him transferred to Wurzburg, where the last ten years of his life were spent.

Still more interesting than the biography is the fragment given by the editor on p. 24, and characterized by him as a kind of profession of faith. It commences thus:

"God is an essential and hidden fire which dwells in all things, and specially in man. From this fire everything is engendered. . . . That which is engendered is the true divine Light which exists from all eternity. God is a fire; but no fire can burn, no light can manifest itself in nature without air . . . and thus the Holy Spirit must act in us as a . . . Divine breath which breathes from the Divine fire upon the inner fire of the soul, so that the Light may appear. . . . This light is Jesus, who emanates from all eternity from Jehovah. . . ."

The whole passage is worthy of very careful study, and seems to form a commentary upon the curious catechism which Mme. de Steiger has just published in these pages.

After an elaborate bibliography we come to the work itself. The "Secondary Causes" are the seven Rulers of the Planets. Trithemius takes them as the Rulers of successive world-periods, each of 354 years and four months, and gives us a summary History of the World from this point of view, adapting each period to the special character of its Ruler. Even to the vulgar reader, whose hardened soul gives no responsive thrill to the editor's assurance that "the book contains great mysteries, carefully enveloped by the author in a Latin altogether hieroglyphic and Qabbalistic, impenetrable to the eye of the profane," the book is not unreadable. There are every here and there touches which, under the hand of the French translator, are distinctly delightful. Thus under the reign of the Angel of Venus we are told that numberless heresies arose, which were only stifled, after much time and trouble, "in the blood of virtuous men!" Again, under Zachariel, "Dagobert, King of France, vanquished and exterminated the English, at that time called Saxons." And here is a hint our Socialists would do well to ponder. Under Samael, the Angel of Mars, "a troop of shepherds, coming from Spain, approached Paris, appropriating the possessions of the clergy, to the great joy of the common people; but when they began to lay hands on those of the laity, they were massacred!"

In conclusion, our author makes a prophecy which seems to have been fairly well fulfilled, that in the year 1525 the moon will take up the government of the world until the year 1879; and it somewhat adds to our respect for his powers that he does not in so many words assert that her rule will cease even then. But, as he still more wisely adds, "I do not guarantee all that I write, most respected Cæsar, to be correct; but one may reasonably believe it without prejudice to the orthodox Faith—everything contrary to which I reject as vain and superstitious fiction."

The chief importance, however, of this translation lies of course in the introduction and notes; in which the Editor undertakes "to raise a little corner of the veil, as far as is permissible." On this we can only speak as one of the profane, and give a brief summary, without presuming to judge. The author's school is shown by his reference to the "centres initiatiques" of the G. D. "which claims descent from the Rosicrucians," and of the Martinists, "continued to our own day by Dr. Papus." His French extraction and his private sentiments come out in his identification of the reign of Louis XI. as that of Saturn, of Louis XIV. as Jupiter, and Napoleon as Mars ("Even to-day," says he, "our soldiers are the only ones in Europe whose red trousers reveal their fiery and Martian nature") and his old prophecy that "under the influence of the strong Michael, a young man with golden hair shall come from Brittany and bring back peace to France."

The "secrets displayed by the raising the corner of the veil" are fairly summed up in the note on p. 89.

"This little treatise is divided into twenty-one periods, of which Trithemius only describes twenty, corresponding to the first twenty cards of the Tarot and to the twenty letters of the Hebrew alphabet. It is constructed like various analogous works, as the Gospel and

Apocalypse of St. John, the *Tableau Naturel* of Saint Martin, *Light on the Path*, etc. . . . The triple septenary of the Treatise of Second Causes describes the evolution of consciousness through the three worlds."

The requisite delicate "suspicion" of the flesh without which no work of art could gain attention in Paris is supplied by a set of notes of which the first runs:

"In the physiological life, this period is the act of love which unites the Father and the Mother—the third side of the triangle which joins the two others."

But this is simply the rubbing the dish with garlic which is similarly obligatory and natural in Parisian cookery, and means no harm.

The book is an interesting, and as far as we can judge, a valuable one. If our notice has conveyed the impression that, notwithstanding our respect for the editor's learning, we feel a certain shrinking (we might use a stronger word) from the perpetual boasting of the "secrets" possessed which is characteristic of many other writers on the subject, we think that the feeling will be shared by many of our readers, who have been taught (like ourselves) that the true Adept in mixing with the world will conceal his *possession* of secrets as anxiously as the secrets themselves. This much at least we outsiders may claim; that when secrets are thus brought to market and a "corner of the veil" lifted for us to peep, we have a certain right to express an opinion upon what is shown; and for our own part we doubt exceedingly whether any deliverance is likely to come for the world from any kind of shuffling of the cards of the Tarot or the letters of the Hebrew alphabet. Our friends will doubtless assure us that the bulk is far better than the sample. Be it so; but why give us such a sample at all?

A. A. W.

The Works of Dionysius the Areopagite.

Translated by the Rev. John Parker, M.A. [Oxford: James Parker and Co.]

We presume that by entitling his volume *The Works of Dionysius* the translator intends to promise another volume, as the present contains only the treatise on the Divine Names, the little tract on Mystic Theology, and the letters.

The belief that these writings actually came from the pen of St. Paul's convert and pupil was of vast importance during the Middle

Ages. They thus formed a sort of Magna Charta for those whose love of the mystical might otherwise have brought them into collision with established authority, then, as now, inclined to be suspicious of everything metaphysical. The palmary quotation, familiar to every spiritual-minded man and woman for many centuries, contained in the first chapter of the "Mystic Theology," is thus given by Mr. Parker:

"But thou, O dear Timothy, by thy persistent commerce with the mystic visions, leave behind both sensible perceptions and intellectual efforts, and all objects of sense and intelligence, and all things not being and being, and be raised aloft unknowingly to the union as far as attainable, with Him who is above every essence and knowledge. For by the resistless and absolute ecstasy in all purity, from thyself and all, thou wilt be carried on high, to the super-essential ray of the Divine darkness, when thou hast cast away all, and become free from all."

We were not, however, prepared to find any one who would seriously defend this thesis at this time of day. It needs only a glance at what is translated in this volume to recognize in the endless flow of words and the luxuriance of superlatives the unmistakable style of a far later period. Nor can we take the Rev. John Parker *quite* gravely when he assures us that "John has followed Dionysius step by step, for the purpose of exploding the puerile supposition that such complex writings as these could have been evolved from the elementary treatises of Proclus and Plotinus"! And again when he asks, looking up mildly through his spectacles, Can we reasonably doubt that Pantænus took the writings of Dionysius and the more abstract works of Hierotheus to India? Have we not here an explanation, says he, of the remarkable similarity between the Hindu philosophy as expressed by Shankara in the eighth and Ramanuja in the thirteenth century, and the "Divine Names"? I cannot but believe, he adds, that many of the beautiful expressions about Vishnu the Redeemer, in the Râmâyana of Tulsi-das, are Christian truths under a Hindu dress!

All this is very delicious to read, in the year 1897; but, my dear Mr. John Parker, we *can* reasonably doubt it; nay, such things belong to the class which (according to Sidney Smith's profane joke) nobody *can* believe, unless it were the Examining Chaplain to an Anglican Bishop. But the similarity *is* remarkable enough; and if some of us who are apt to think and speak somewhat slightingly of Christian Mysticism would carefully study the small volume which forms the foundation upon which the whole of that science is built, I think they could hardly fail to rise from its perusal with increased respect for the Masters of such a school. It has not been left for the nineteenth century to introduce the Indian philosophy to the West; we are but renewing in our time what Dionysius and his fellows did in their long-past centuries, and the spiritual life of the West up to our own day is the fruit of their labours.

A. A. W.

Ye Book of Ye Cards.

By Zuresta. [London: The Roxburghe Press, 1897.]

The book before us contains absolutely nothing new or original concerning the Tarot cards or their degenerate descendants the modern pack. Zuresta seems to be ignorant even of the well-known fact that the cards so long in use with us were adapted and altered from the ancient Tarot by a Court astrologer as an amusement for the imbecile Charles VI. of France, and her book, while possibly it may prove useful as a guide to the efforts of the embryo professional fortune-teller, is from any other point of view entirely worthless. It is a collection of various methods of card "divination" copied, in one or two instances, from forgotten chap-books, but chiefly from Raphael's well-known *Book of Fate*, and as they all more or less contradict each other, the aspiring sibyl who seeks guidance from them will find herself greatly exercised as to which of the many confusing "modes" is "the only genuine or reliable."

Indeed the only feature of the book worthy of remark is the concluding chapter on the Tarot. This is a literal though unacknowledged copy from a small and learned book on the subject, written by S. L. Macgregor Mathers, and published in 1886 by Mr. G. Redway. Such literary "conveying" is of course a great economy of time and trouble, but the copyist might have made her transcription with a little more intelligence.

In describing the 22 Keys Mr. Mathers in one instance makes use of the Latin term *Vesica Piscis*. This is copied by Zuresta as "*Pescia Pescis*." Further on "six Hebrew jods" reappear as "six Hebrew *gods*."

As a specimen of the Roxburghe "Occult" series Zuresta's *Book of Ye Cards* is neither of occult nor literary value; it might have been otherwise if she had cared to make some original research concerning her subject. The Tarot symbols in their origin are as old as Egypt. Tradition says that they were engraven on tablets of stone or plates of metal, and used in the temples as means of divination; also that a knowledge of the 22 Atouts was one of the first secrets made known to the neophyte in the mysteries. Be this as it may, the words Tarot and

Atout are known to be ancient Egyptian, and according to Count de Gebelin the Tarot should be regarded as an Egyptian book based on the sequence of "sevens."

Whether the origin of the mediæval Tarochi can be traced to the Pyramids or no, undoubtedly they contain traces of Egyptian symbolism, sadly marred and debased through the ages by the successive generations of card makers ignorant of their hidden meanings. Note something of this in the Seventh Key, the Conqueror, so splendidly restored by Éliphaz Lévi in his *Dogme et Rituel.* In another of his works Levi says concerning Tarot divination: "It (the Tarot) is in its various combinations a revelation of the harmonies pre-existing among its signs, letter and numbers, and is therefore capable of truly marvellous application. But we cannot with impunity thus wrest, solely for ourselves, the secrets of our intimate communication with the astral light. The consultation of cards or of Tarots is a veritable conjuration which cannot be prosecuted without danger. In all evocation we compel our astral body to appear before us and hold converse in the divination which results." This, however, is Lévi's own opinion. Other writers on the subject ascribe such results as may be obtained by diviners to the influence of the nature spirits. We recommend this view of the subject to the compiler of *Ye Book of Ye Cards.*

T. O.

The Mind of the Master.

By John Watson, D.D. [London: Hodder and Stoughton, 1896.]

In looking back over the history of the Christian Church, we perceive every now and then a sense arising that religion was falling too much into mere dry Theology, and an attempt, more or less successful, to put life and warmth upon the dry bones. The formation of the Society of Jesus was one of these efforts; and the rise of the Evangelical School in England nearly a century ago—the Protestant Jesuits, as they may be very fairly entitled, was another. Not that there was conscious imitation; similar circumstances produced marvellously similar results. Not only the exclusiveness, as of the sole possessors of "the Gospel," was common and unpopular in both; both were characterized by a certain unscrupulous use of means for a good end, in which the Evangelicals have come noways short of their prototypes; and even the painfully edifying children and the "good young man who died" were exploited by the Jesuits centuries before Newton and Romaine.

But by throwing aside Theology altogether, the Evangelical party gained a temporary success at the expense of rendering their future impossible. The memorial lately presented to Parliament, showing pitifully how they have been neglected in the distribution of Church patronage, might have been answered, and probably will be, by the simple question, "Where are the Evangelical clergy fit to be promoted?" Now that the vulgar notion of the Atonement which formed their whole religious outfit has been hopelessly discredited by modern research, it is growing yearly more and more impossible for a young man educated at our universities to speak their Shibboleth. But the need remains the same; men's hearts are crying out for a light and warmth which popular religion does not furnish; and the fact that such men as Dr. Pulsford and Dr. Watson have arisen in Scotland, and that even there, in the last stronghold of Protestant obscurantism, the recent attempt to silence the latter has failed, is one of vast interest to the student of religious thought.

What then is this new Evangelicalism which in the hands of such men as Dr. Watson seems likely to supersede the old? In Scotland more decidedly than in England, the Reformation was the rehabilitation of the Old Testament. Of the New Testament certain portions of St. Paul's Epistles were all which in practice survived. To the ordinary Scotchman of less than fifty years ago, St. Paul's Epistle to the Romans contained the whole system of the Gospel; and it is a bold thing even now when Dr. Watson comes forward, as Count Tolstoi in Russia, to remind men that it is Jesus, not Paul, to whom men should look as their Master. In his first lecture, "Jesus our Supreme Teacher," he says:

"If Jesus' delicate poetry be reduced to prose, and the fair carved work of His parables be used for the building of prisons, and His lovely portrait of God be 'restored' with grotesque colouring, and His lucid principles of life be twisted into harassing regulations, then Jesus has been much wronged, and the world has suffered irreparable loss. This is the disaster Jesus dreaded, and no one will deny that it has, in some degree at least, come to pass. . . . The pragmatical seventeenth century forged a yoke of doctrines so minute, tedious and unreasonable that it became too irksome even for our more patient fathers. Every side of truth and every rite of Jesus was turned into a test by which honest-minded and simple-hearted disciples of Jesus were tried, condemned, cast out, burnt. . . . The Scottish Church seems to suppose that Christianity was only once thoroughly understood when an assembly of English divines met at Westminster. . . It comes as a shock on one to attend some heresy trial, and hear the prosecution quoting a foreign divine of almost miraculous woodenness, and the defendant taking refuge in a second-rate commentator. . . . But is not the only vital question, What saith the Master?"

No wonder that the orthodox were alarmed at such teaching, and that Dr. Watson was soon the defendant in a heresy trial of his own. But that the prosecution should be allowed, by general consent apparently, to fail *is* a wonder: and a most encouraging sign that the World Religion is making progress in unexpected places. Take a few lines more of what is *not* condemned by Scotch Presbyterianism of this day:

"We are living in a second Reformation, and it were an immense blunder for us to go back on the principle of all Reformation, and insist directly or indirectly that Protestant councils should come in between Christians and Christ . . . . What must strike every person about the Sermon on the Mount is that it is not metaphysical but ethical. . . . Upon the man who desired to be His disciple and a member of God's Kingdom were laid the conditions of a pure heart, of a forgiving spirit, of a helpful hand, of a heavenly purpose, of an unworldly mind. Christ did not ground his Christianity in thinking, or in doing, but first of all in being. It consisted in a certain type of soul—a spiritual shape of the inner self. Was a man satisfied with this type, and would he aim at it in his own life? Would he put his name to the Sermon on the Mount, and place himself under Jesus' charge for its accomplishment? Then he was a Christian, according to the conditions laid down by Jesus in the fresh daybreak of His religion."

Shades of Calvin and John Knox! Works—mere *legality*, instead of Faith! That all Jesus wanted was to make Theosophists of his people—for this is what it comes to! Take once more his treatment of the Atonement.

"The Cross . . . . has been lifted out of the ethical setting of the Gospels, and planted in an environment of doctrine. The Cross has been too laboriously traced back to decrees and inserted into covenants; it has been too exclusively stated in terms of Justification and Propitiation. This is a misappropriation of the Cross; it is a violation of its purpose. . . . Jesus did not describe His Cross as a satisfaction to God, else He had hardly asked His disciples to share it. He always spoke of it as a Regeneration of man. . . . The Cross may be made into a doctrine; it was prepared by Jesus as a discipline."

Of course there are many things in Dr. Watson's eloquent paper to which we should demur, or which we ourselves should express differently, but the whole atmosphere of the book is fresh, open, and unprejudiced to a degree which we can hardly match in our English religious literature. One might, indeed, be encouraged to think that the second Reformation of which he speaks so boldly, without quite understanding its full scope, may actually first take shape amongst a people warm-hearted and open-minded enough to relish such teaching as *The Mind of the Master*. There could not be a better book to bring a Christian friend to the level of our own wider and higher doctrine; and the large number of our own people who prefer to retain the Christian form as the mould into which to cast their devotion to the Higher Self will find in it a Christianity which has very little indeed to jar upon their Theosophical principles. When Christianity has completely "reformed" itself upon the lines laid down by Dr. Watson, it will not be hard to add our own doctrine to it.

A. A. W.

THEOSOPHICAL AND MYSTIC PUBLICATIONS.

The Theosophist opens as usual with its editor's history, in which is an account of a visit from the Master K. H. who came, apparently in the physical body, to see both Damodar and the Colonel. Following this the Colonel describes in a vivid manner the visit to a Mahârâjah, and gives us an admirable picture of Eastern life in his story. "Theosophy in the Sixteenth Century," treats of various mystics of that period, among them Sebastian Franck, Paracelsus, and Cornelius Agrippa. C. G. K. contributes some notes on the first fragment of *The Voice of the Silence*, and Mr. Marques concludes his paper on "The Days of the Week, and their occult Correspondences." "Hawaiian Folk Lore" is a most interesting contribution, containing a number of quaint tales which have an individuality of their own. Captain Banon writes on modern prophecies, translating a portion of Eugene Bareste's *Nostradamus*. The predictions and their fulfilment are of much greater interest than most of such things, but it would be well to have the evidence critically examined. "Madame Blavatsky among the Spiritualists," and "Manifestations of Shiva and His Spouse," with Activities and Reviews conclude a more than usually interesting number.

The Prashnottara contains a short but excellent answer on the caste system, in which its present condition is criticized strongly. It is pointed out that the necessary reform must come from the natural growth of inner feeling or public opinion and not from any outside interference. The *Ârya Bâla Bodhini* contains an account of one of the innumerable Hindu saints, set forth for the benefit of the youthful reader. This is followed by a story of an Anglo-Indian girl and a dialogue on the subject of food. In *The Thinker* "A Student" propounds a large number of technical questions dealing with astronomy and comparing the Hindu calculations and those given in *The Secret Doctrine*, with the modern scientific ones. No answers have as yet appeared. "Prayâschittendu Sekharam" contains a formidable list of acts which are ceremonial sins, a list which would put to shame the makers of the old Judaic statutes; as however, most of the penalties lie in the direction of fasting and of greater cleanliness, some utility may be claimed for them, but it seems a pity to bind up such excellent things with such trivial offences as are some of those given. Some of the other papers in these issues are of considerable merit.

The Journal of the Mahâ Bodhi Society for July and August forms more entertaining reading than is usually the case. The account of the travels of Hiuen Tsiang makes an interesting story, and this is followed by the tale of the building of a monastery by Asoka, the famous Buddhist monarch. The first part of the report by P. C. Mookerjee, on the finding of Buddha's place of death, is given. Mr. Mookerjee was officially instructed to search for the place, and after an extensive survey found what he considered to be the spot, on which there is an old monument erected by Asoka about 260 B.C. *Chromopathy* is a small pamphlet by an Indian writer, dealing with the cure of diseases by colours. The cause of disease according to this science is the want of a certain colour in the system. The lacking colour is decided by that of the eye-balls, nails, etc. The treatment consists of doses of pure water, the water having been charged with some alleged power by exposing it to sunlight in coloured bottles. Coloured glasses or windows are also used, behind which the patient sits in order to absorb the necessary colour. Practically there seems to be some evidence for the curative effect of light, but on the theory it is not easy to see why the man should not be cured by eating the contents of a box of colours or applying the same to his person! *The Theosophical Gleaner* contains its usual Zoroastrian contribution, the subject this time being "The Sun as a Symbol of Ahura-Mazda." This little magazine will prove a useful reference for any who wish to study one of the least known of the great religions. The other articles are mainly reprints, but the notes at the end contain an amusing criticism of the members of the Bombay Branch, which publishes the journal. *The Dawn* and *Rays of Light* are acknowledged from India and Ceylon.

The first number of Vol. VII. of *The Vâhan* contains a formidable list of German works which have lately been given to the library of the European Section by an anonymous donor. C. W. L. opens the "Enquirer" with some further information on lunar influence on vegetation, confining himself, however, to the purely scientific investigations pursued by the Trinidad Committee, which seems to have succeeded in avoiding the discovery of any remarkable facts. Four answers are given on a question dealing with the "auric shell," and suggesting that it might tend towards selfish isolation. S. M. S. and A. A. W. are particularly good. B. K. discusses the astral bodies of embodied and disembodied persons and the so-called "occult sciences," giving very sensible answers, and A. P. S. replies to a question based on *The Growth of the Soul*, the remaining answers dealing with mediumship and its effect on health.

In *Mercury* for July Mrs. Besant writes on "The Law of Sacrifice." The paper is to form a chapter in the promised work, *The Ancient Wisdom*. Mrs. Besant has, of course, written on this subject before, but now takes more pains to avoid giving rise to some misconceptions which she had previously noted, such as the idea that the self-sacrifice of the Logos is essentially painful. Mr. Marques gives some "Scientific Corroborations of Theosophy," and the subject of killing out desire is ably treated by A. F. in "The Forum Department."

Le Lotus Bleu publishes a remarkably interesting account of psychic experiments by Col. de Rochas. The experiments were made with a mesmerized subject, but unfortunately a great deal of the information has to be based on the observations of the subject herself. Articles appeared some time ago in *Le Lotus Bleu* dealing with the same kind of experiments, and the present paper gives us some further investigations. The peculiar feature is that the double of the subject appeared to be divided, coming from the body in two layers, one double emerging at the side and the other at the front. Only one of these, however, was sensitive. Both merged together when the experimenter desired. The first and sensitive double was of a brilliant blue and transparent, and the other red and thick. How much of all this may be verified by future observers we cannot yet say, but the notes form a valuable record.

L'Hyperchimie for July contains an illustrated biographical sketch of M. Poisson, and several alchemical papers.

Theosophy in Australasia keeps up its greatly improved form and matter, the "Outlook" supplying quite a quantity of information on subjects appealing to the Theosophical reader. An astonishing sketch of a boy who remembers four of his past incarnations is taken from an American paper, but it wants a good deal of corroborative evidence. P. writes on dreams and their value when properly studied and appreciated. If the writer refers to the ordinary dream his assumption that the man when dreaming is awake to the scenery of the astral plane, is somewhat unfounded.

In *Theosophia* the opening paper is on the Druses, by Afra, and besides the continued translations, a new article is begun on "Theosophy and Occultism." The same writer, Afra, has also just issued a useful elementary book on Theosophy, *Eenvondige schets van de Theosophie*. *The Teosofisk Tidkrift* is filled by business matter, and reports in connection with the recent Convention of the Scandinavian Section.

From Sweden we have received the first number of a new publication, *Questions of the Day* which is to consist of a collection of essays, edited by Mr. Sydney Alrutz, with the collaboration of several Professors and Lecturers of the Universities of Upsala in Sweden, and of Helsingfors in Finland. The purpose of this series of papers is to throw light upon the religious and ethical questions of the day. The reasoning and results arrived at by the psychologist and the idealistic philosopher with regard to certain of these questions, will be brought forward as far as may be possible, in a popular scientific form. The first number contains a lecture on the promises made at Confirmation.

Sophia for July is noticeable for an article by Señor Soria y Mata, of whom the readers of LUCIFER have recently heard. A series of these articles will appear, entitled "Génesis" and the list of matters at the beginning shows that a very wide range will be covered. The basis of the whole will be of course the investigations of the author into geometry, and the first section is devoted to the "Secret Doctrine of the Pythagoreans." Señor Soria believes that he has discovered or rediscovered the old mathematical teachings of Pythagoras and some of the secret wisdom that we are told Pythagoras gave to his disciples. Be that as it may, whether new or old, the writer has something of interest to tell us. *Sophia* will be no loser in devoting some of its pages to the subject. "Filadelfo" writes a historical sketch of the times of Jesus.

German Theosophical literature has had some valuable additions made to it by the translations of Mr. Leadbeater's "Invisible Helpers" and Mrs. Besant's *The Future that awaits us*. A lecture on Böhme also has just been published. The author is Dr. C. Kawerau. The *Metaphysische Rundschau* is filled with somewhat heavy material, including articles on electrohomeopathy, phrenology and the freedom of the will.

The new *Borderland* is as interesting as ever, and contains as usual the largest quantity of information relating to matters psychic and mystic, of any magazine which comes before our notice. Julia's sermonette is on the finding of the soul. There can be no doubt but that of all the communicating spirits which revisit this earth of ours and publish their ideas through another's body, Julia is one of the most interesting. She has always something really good to say, and although it may be nothing new, it is vigorously expressed and in a distinctly individual style. "On the Trail of a Ghost" enlivens the pages by a series of personalities and generally quarrelsome matter referring to the now famous, or notorious, case of the Society of Psychical Research made public by *The Times*. The correspondence on the subject introduces a little human interest into the usually rather dreary enquiries of more or less scientific occult investigators. Theosophy as usual is well represented, Colonel Olcott and Mr. Leadbeater supplying the substance.

Nova Lux continues Signor Calvari's article on "The Ego and its Vehicles," the astral body forming the subject of the chapter. The whole of the remainder of the number is occupied by a letter to Signor Calvari, the author of which is Fulgenzio Bruni. The letter is entitled "The Two Traditions: Martinism and Theosophy," and appears to be aroused by some disputes as to the Congress of Humanity proposed to be held in Paris in 1900.

Modern Astrology prints a portrait of its editor, Mr. Alan Leo, as a frontispiece to its new volume, and also appears in an enlarged form. The horoscope of Mr. Barnato is given. *Star Lore*, a small magazine, also devoted to the culture of astrology, appears to have fallen foul of its larger companion, and makes unkind remarks about its name and its methods.

We have also to acknowledge the receipt of *The Rationale of Reincarnation*, a small pamphlet published in Canada, intended to present Theosophical ideas in an elementary form; *Light; The Agnostic Journal; Ourselves; The Literary Digest; Notes and Queries*, with more mathematical curiosities; *Intelligence*, containing papers on "The Unseen World," astrology and mysticism; *The Vegetarian; The Irish Theosophist; The Temple*, the first issue of a new mystical journal, admirably printed, but of the familiar type, the chief article being by Rosicriæ, "By Order of Her who is Nameless," which is quite sufficient to stamp the mark of charlatanry upon the undertaking; *The Vegetarian Review; Food, Home and Garden; La Paix Universelle; Theosophia; The Pacific Theosophist; Reformador; The Sanmarga Bodhini.*

A.

NOTICE.

The Editors beg to give Notice that with the next Issue of this Magazine (the first Number of Volume XXI.), the Title will be changed to THE THEOSOPHICAL REVIEW. The Price will remain unaltered; the Form, Type and Paper will be improved, and the Size of the Magazine enlarged to 96 Pages.